INDUSTRIAL
ECONOMICS
AND ORGANIZATION

A EUROPEAN PERSPECTIVE

SECOND EDITION

INDUSTRIAL
ECONOMICS
AND ORGANIZATION

A EUROPEAN PERSPECTIVE
SECOND EDITION

BERNADETTE ANDREOSSO
& DAVID JACOBSON

The **McGraw·Hill** Companies

London Boston Burr Ridge, IL Dubuque, IA Madison, WI New York San Francisco
St. Louis Bangkok Bogotá Caracas Kuala Lumpur Lisbon Madrid Mexico City
Milan Montreal New Delhi Santiago Seoul Singapore Sydney Taipei Toronto

Industrial Economics and Organization: A European Perspective
Second Edition
Bernadette Andreosso and David Jacobson
ISBN-13 978-007710-422-1
ISBN-10 0-07-710422-6

Education

Published by McGraw-Hill Education
Shoppenhangers Road
Maidenhead
Berkshire
SL6 2QL
Telephone: 44 (0) 1628 502 500
Fax: 44 (0) 1628 770 224
Website: www.mcgraw-hill.co.uk

British Library Cataloguing in Publication Data
A catalogue record for this book is available from the British Library

Library of Congress Cataloguing in Publication Data
The Library of Congress data for this book has been applied for from the Library of Congress

Acquisitions Editor: Kirsty Reade
Development Editors: Emily Jefferson and Catriona Watson
Marketing Director: Petra Skytte
Production Editor: Jennifer Harvey

Text Design by Jonathan Coleclough
Cover design by Ego Creative
Typeset by Fakenham Photosetting Limited, Fakenham, Norfolk
Printed and bound in the United Kingdom by The Bath Press, Glasgow

ISBN-13 978-007710-422-1
ISBN-10 0-07-710422-6

Dedication

A papa, à qui je dois la passion pour la construction européenne, *in memoriam*.
(Bernadette Andreosso-O'Callaghan)

To the memory of my parents, Hy and Sonia Jacobson, who taught me to question.
(David Jacobson)

Brief table of contents

Detailed table of contents

Preface

In some respects this book is a new book rather than the second edition of an old book. The first broad aim in the re-write of the first edition was to reduce the size and increase the number of the chapters; there are now many more chapters (16, compared with 7 in the first edition). This is in response to the experiences of lecturers (including us) who have adopted the book as their course text. Large chapters with many sections of uneven size proved difficult to break down into lecture-sized bites. We have in this edition given much thought to chapters as topics. The book is, of course, an integrated whole and there is a significant amount of cross-referencing between chapters; there is nevertheless a choice in relation to what topics to include in, for example, a twelve-week module.

For lecturers following traditional course outlines, Chapters 1 to 7, 9, 10, 12 and 15 will provide topics for eleven weeks, leaving a final week for revision. If more material can be covered within this period, or if a semester is more than twelve weeks, there are additional empirical chapters, in particular Chapters 13 (on the performance of firms in Europe) and 16 (on industrial policy in Europe).

As an alternative, and especially for students who have had good introductory courses in microeconomics, Chapters 3 and 5 could be omitted. With the extra two weeks, lecturers or students could choose two topics from location (Chapter 8), technology (Chapter 11) and globalization (Chapter 14). While the subject of technology is frequently included in textbooks in this area, the treatment in Chapter 11 draws on the type of material that is of most relevance to policy, and is in this sense non-traditional in industrial economics. In relation to the other two topics, both their presence and the way they are covered are also atypical for textbooks in this area.

The second broad aim of the revision was to add new content and update the old content. The main new section is Chapter 14 on multinational enterprises and globalization. Even here, some of the material is drawn from sections of the previous edition but it is largely a completely new element of the book.

In updating, we examined both theoretical and empirical developments; much has changed in relation to both since we completed our work on the first edition nearly ten years ago. Game theory has continued to pervade the discipline, existing theories of the firm have continued to develop and new ones have emerged, and new hypotheses continue to be posited in many of the almost infinite variety of relationships that can exist between elements of firms, their performance and aspects of their environment. New trends have emerged in some of the key focuses of our discipline, for example mergers and acquisitions. There are also ten new members of the European Union. Between March 1979 and 31 December 2001, the common currency in the making in the EU was the ECU, whereas since January 2002, the euro has been in operation. ECUs or euros are used in the text, depending on whether we refer to a period prior to or after the beginning of the third stage of economic and monetary union (EMU), which started on 1 January 2002.

We have attempted in all chapters to incorporate the most important of these developments, not by showing the technicalities and details of the increasingly sophisticated research methodologies, but by summarizing their results. In this we have attempted to minimize the use of mathematics. Where we use mathematics it is either in an appendix (as in Chapter 2) or it can be skipped without losing continuity (as in Chapter 6).

While we shared all the work between us, we had different primary responsibilities. Bernadette's were Chapters 1, 3, 5, 7, 9, 13, 15 and 16; David's were Chapters 2, 4, 6, 8, 10, 11 and 14. We shared Chapter 12 equally.

Bernadette Andreosso
David Jacobson

Guided tour

Learning objectives

Each chapter opens with a set of learning objectives, summarizing key topics from each chapter.

Summary

The summary briefly reviews and reinforces the main topics covered in each chapter to ensure a solid understanding of key topics.

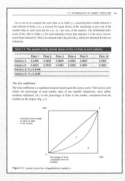

Figures and tables

Each chapter provides a number of figures and tables to illustrate and summarize the various economic models and important concepts.

Boxed features

Boxed features appear within the text to provide the reader with illustrative insight to the topic.

Case studies

Case studies can be found in some chapters to illustrate industrial economic theory in practice.

Websites

A comprehensive list of websites to a wealth of economics sources available online.

Questions

Questions appear in each chapter to check the reader's understanding and knowledge of key topics.

Notes

These notes provide you with useful additional information relating to topics and issues discussed within the chapter.

Chapter appendices

Chapter appendices can be found at the end of some chapters offering increased flexibility and introducing additional mathematical concepts.

Resources for lecturers

Online Learning Centre (OLC)

Lecturers can find a range of resources and tools to support their teaching at the OLC website.

- Case study guide
- PowerPoints
- Solutions to questions in the book
- Additional examination questions

To access all of the OLC lecturer resources, and to contact your McGraw-Hill representative, simply visit the website at **www.mcgraw-hill.co.uk/textbooks/aj** and follow the instructions to register for a password.

Primis Content Centre

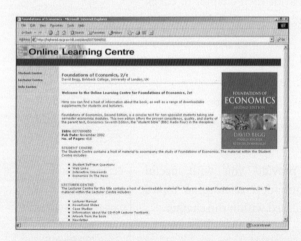

Can't find the perfect book for your course? If you need to supplement your course with additional cases or content, create a personalized e-Book for your students. Visit **www.primiscontentcenter.com** or e-mail **primis_euro@mcgraw-hill.com** for more information.

Resources for students
Online Learning Centre (OLC)

After completing each chapter, log on to the supporting OLC website. Take advantage of the free study tools offered to reinforce the material you have read in the text and to develop your knowledge of marketing in a fun and effective way. A range of resources are offered providing revision tools and handy exam practice.

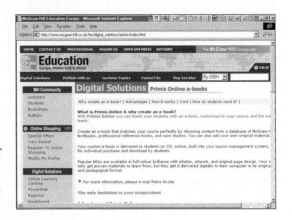

The new edition provides the complete package of materials for students of economics:

* **Additional case studies** – new cases in economics with questions enable students to apply and analyse concepts from the book.

* **Interactive self-assessment questions** – to check understanding of key topics and ideas with progress tests online.

* **Web links** to a wealth of economics sources available online.

Visit the OLC at **www.mcgraw-hill.co.uk/textbooks/aj** for access to all these materials free with every student purchase of the textbook.

Study skills

Need help with exams, essays, assignments or research projects? Open University Press publishes guides to study, research and exam skills, to help undergraduate and postgraduate students through their university studies.

Visit **www.openup.co.uk/ss/** to see the full selection.

Computing skills

If you'd like to brush up on your computing skills, we have a range of titles covering Microsoft® Office applications such as Word, Excel, PowerPoint, Access and more.

Get a £2 discount off these titles by entering the promotional code 'app' when ordering online at **www.mcgraw-hill.co.uk/app**

Acknowledgements

We would like first to thank all the students who went through courses in which the first edition of this book was the prescribed text. Their comments and complaints made us think about how to make the material more accessible without oversimplifying. Second, much of what we have learned from our research students appears in this book, either directly or indirectly. In forcing us to explain ourselves, they have pushed us to answer questions where we could. Where we couldn't, messy reality has had to remain inscrutable but not without juxtaposing the contradictory theories or contrasting pieces of evidence. In particular, Chris van Egeraat and Rachel Hilliard made suggestions; long after completing their PhDs, they remain important factors in David's academic life. The useful comments of Helena Lenihan on the policy aspects of the book are also greatly appreciated. Special thanks are owed to Anne Coulon and Marie Dineen for their help in collecting some of the statistical information, as well as to Grainne O'Connell for her assistance in the editing process at the final stage of the manuscript. Liam Gallagher, Kevin Heanue, Sarah Ingle, Yvonne Jacobson, Claire McBride, Siobhain McGovern, Helen McGrath, Des McLaughlin and Fiona Whitney all also helped in various ways. Much of this second edition was produced during David's sabbatical, mostly spent at Frederick Institute of Technology in Nicosia, Cyprus. He would like to thank them for hosting him so hospitably. Finally, we would like to express our gratitude to our families for their perennial support.

Our thanks also go to the following reviewers for their comments at various stages in the text's development:

Mark Bailey, *University of Ulster*
Maria Brouwer, *University of Amsterdam*
Samuel Cameron, *University of Bradford*
Adrian Gourlay, *University of Loughborough*
Jeffrey Harrop, *University of Sheffield*
Uma Kambhampati, *University of Reading*
Claudio Piga, *University of Nottingham*
Michael Ryan, *University of Hull*
Kevin Tinsdale, *Manchester Metropolitan University*
Phil Tomlinson, *University of Bath*
Jian Tong, *University of Southampton*
Lambert van der Laan, *University of Erasmus*

CHAPTER 1

Introduction

1.1 Scope and method of industrial economics in the European context

It is our purpose in this book to describe and analyse the theory and practice of what normally goes under the general heading of *industrial economics* (in Europe) or *industrial organization* (in the United States). This is a distinctive field of economics that deals with the functioning of markets and industries in a specific business, institutional and legal environment. We present both the traditional approaches and recent and alternative developments in the field. Many of these developments emanate from criticisms of the deterministic nature of the structure–conduct–performance (SCP) paradigm.

Many of the issues in this area of economics date back to Adam Smith in the eighteenth century, with his writings on the subtle way to organize industrial production more efficiently, through the division of labour. More recently, Cournot in the first half, and Marshall in the second half of the nineteenth century, from different parts of Europe, in different ways, laid foundations that, as we shall see, remain appropriate concerns in industrial economics today. In particular, in his *Economics of Industry*, Marshall (1899) describes the conditions for an efficient organization of industry. In the twentieth century, Chamberlin and Robinson, on either side of the Atlantic, influenced developments which led, among other things, to Bain's work on SCP. Thus, although in the United States, for example, industrial organization did not appear as a distinctive branch of economics until the 1930s, main concepts such as pricing strategies, and collusive and non-collusive behaviour, had already been formulated.[1]

There have been two major traditional concerns of industrial economics. First, there has been a focus on the functioning of firms within various market structures. This includes the conduct or behaviour of firms, and their performance; the determinants and consequences of different market structures; and the relationship between behaviour and performance of firms, and the market structure within which firms operate. Second, both in separate chapters, and with frequent references throughout the texts, attention has been paid to the role that governments play in influencing the organization of industry. These two areas remain central, and our discussion of work on these and related issues forms a large part of this book.

In relation to *method*, the work of industrial economists was for many years subject to the predominant influence of the SCP paradigm. This was expressed in numerous econometric exercises testing relationships between aspects of structure, conduct and performance. Methodologically this approach was in essence *positive* rather than *normative*. Starting with the observation of the real world, it aimed to identify a number of economic laws that could eventually be generalized (and become theories), by, for example, studying the extent to which various factors affected the conduct of firms. As a result, industrial economics has been dominated by hypothesis-testing experiments. The conclusions of these tests were, however, often normative. In relation to structural determinants of firms' behaviour, for example, a positive finding that certain market structures are related to higher than average profits, led to the normative conclusion that where these structural characteristics prevailed, the state should intervene to prevent excessive profits. Such normative conclusions may not be appropriate, depending on one's political preferences. We do not avoid normative conclusions. However, we show as clearly as possible the reasons for these conclusions. More broadly, we are aware of and, where appropriate, draw out the relationships between theory and policy (see the discussion on contestable markets in Chapter 2).

The SCP paradigm has itself changed and developed. The unidirectional causality sought in the early work has given way to acceptance of the possibility that structure, conduct and performance are interrelated in various ways. Even with these changes, however, much of the work in this tradition is less than satisfactory. The empirical work has had to become more complicated, but even the most sophisticated econometric tests have assisted little in explaining key features of how the industrial world operates and changes.

A major methodological response to these problems has been to focus on individual firms and their strategic behaviour as factors requiring explanation. At the same time, richer *theoretical depth* to industrial economics was demanded. *Game theory*, facilitating both a focus on firms' strategies and a means of regenerating theoretical thinking, has become a cornerstone of modern industrial economics, and central to what has been called 'new industrial economics'. This book, without going into the mathematical complexities of game theory, provides an introduction, particularly to the use of the *payoff matrix* as a means of organizing thinking about strategic behaviour.

A recurrent theme in the book is the experience of European industry. What we mean by European industry is the industry of the members of the European Union (EU). Taking into account the May 2004 enlargement, the EU now has 25 member states. Our data will in general include all of the 15 pre-enlargement countries within the Union and, wherever possible, will refer to all 25. We will also refer to, and where appropriate provide comparisons with, other countries within Europe,[2] Asia and the United States.

1.2 Major concepts defined: firms, industries, industrial structure, industrial system

We provide here a brief definition of some of the key concepts. Of necessity, brief definitions involve simplification. In most cases the complexities of the concepts are drawn out later in the book.

The *firm* (enterprise, company or organization) is the basic decision-making entity. It converts inputs (capital, labour, raw materials, entrepreneurship) generally into marketable outputs. It may comprise many establishments and divisions.

An *industry* is the aggregation of units of production selling goods that are in some sense similar. The notion of industry is also often referred to as a branch of production. The *market* is the realm of interaction among all buyers and sellers.

Under *industrial structure* we study 'the relative importance of individual industries or groups of related industries within an economy and . . . the pattern of transactions between these industries' (Devine *et al.*, 1985, p. 27). One way of describing this pattern of transactions between industries is by using an *input–output table*. This is a table that shows all the value and volume transactions as between industries, during a period of one year. Table 1.1 is a hypothetical and simplified input–output table for a given economy. It represents only the inter-industry matrices (or matrix of intermediate consumptions). To complete the picture, the matrices of final demand and other transactions such as imports, taxes, wages, depreciation and profits would have to be included.

Table 1.1 Hypothetical input-output table, year *t* (€m)

	Industry 1	...	Industry *j*	...	Total
Product 1	30	...	50	...	600
Product 2	20	...	40	...	500
...	...	...	...	...	...
Product *i*	40	...	70	...	900
...	...	...	...	...	...
Total domestic flows	400	...	800	...	8000

The inter-industry matrix facilitates a detailed examination of industrial structure. It shows the sales of domestically produced goods and services by domestic industries to those same industries. For example, the first row of Table 1.1 shows all the sales of Industry 1 (i.e. Product 1) to the other domestic industries. The first column represents all inputs bought by Industry 1. This column informs us that Industry 1 has bought a total of €400 million worth of inputs, of which €20 million came from Industry 2, €40 million from Industry i, and €30 million from itself (retained). A similar matrix, showing the pattern of transactions as between industries at the EU level is computed by the Commission of the EU.

The notion of industrial structure needs to be distinguished from that of *market structure*. The traditional, neoclassical theory of market structures presents a range of types, from perfect competition to monopoly. The main elements of market structure are the number and size distribution (concentration) of firms, and the barriers to entry into the market. The method used in examining market structures has been primarily *comparative statics*. This is used to answer such questions as what difference it would make to increase the number of firms, or introduce taxes, or reduce costs. The difference is introduced as a difference between two time periods. Having been introduced into the model, the implications – in terms, for example, of price and profit – are identified. That firms will make more or less profit, or that consumers will have to pay higher or lower prices, are examples of the concerns of this type of analysis, rather than the process that firms, industries and markets will go through in adjusting to the change. While we present in some detail, and in various parts of the book, diagrams showing the comparative static methods in the neoclassical approach, elsewhere we focus on processes and emphasize *dynamic* perspectives. In relation to theories of the firm, for example, dynamic approaches such as the evolutionary theory are introduced.

Using the idea of an *industrial* – or production – *system*, allows the industrial economist to adopt 'holistic' perspectives. What holistic refers to generally is the notion that the whole is greater than the sum of its parts. Here, what we are referring to is the view of the firm or a group of firms as a set of interconnected components; as an industrial system there is a pattern of interactions that is reproduced. At the level of the firm, the industrial system refers to the set of different stages of the transformation process as well as to the nature of the connections between these stages. In the case of a perfectly vertically integrated firm, the transformation process includes everything from the extraction of raw materials to the distribution of the final product on a market. However, very few firms are perfectly vertically integrated; it is referred to here to illustrate the notion of the firm as an industrial system. All firms are composed of a specific number of stages, and have forged specific connections between these stages. Some firms develop well-known, seminal production systems. Outsourcing, subcontracting and relying on sub-suppliers are all equivalent notions found in the modern literature, that mirror the business trends of the past decades. The Ford system, for example, has traditionally been characterized by standardization, large scale, extreme specialization of the productive functions, and large amounts of stocks and inventories; the Toyota production system is centred around the notion of 'just in time', with its connected stock minimization, information maximization, very high quality, and close integration between the productive functions.

At a wider – meso – level (meso = medium), industrial systems involve a number of firms. The various ways in which firms relate to one another – whether sharing technologies, supplying or buying goods or services, at arm's length or in alliances – and their various geographical removes, constitute different industrial systems. Among the types of industrial systems at this wider level discussed in this book are *industrial districts, filières and clusters.*

Industrial structures, market structures and industrial systems are all discussed in Chapter 5. The discussion is both theoretical and empirical. The empirical focus is the EU, in which the standard industrial classification system is NACE (Nomenclature des Activités de la Communauté Européenne), the General Industrial Classification of Economic Activities. The NACE system classifies industries on the basis of the nature of goods and services produced and/or the nature of the production process employed.[3] Appendix 1.1 shows a taxonomy of industries based on the two-digit classification.

1.3 Approach of this book

In a number of respects, this book is different from other industrial economics texts. Our approach is to incorporate, as much as possible, the EU as a focus or theme. In order to achieve this aim, it is necessary to include explanations of the specifically EU-related complexities of many of the aspects of industry in Europe. To understand changes in *barriers to entry* in the EU, for example, one must have a clear idea of the nature and results of the developments towards the single European market. More generally, the use of a major group of highly integrated trading partners like the EU as a focus in an industrial economics textbook has necessitated the inclusion of a number of issues not usually found in books of this kind. Among these, the geographical, trade and legal dimensions of industrial economics stand out.

Another important difference between this and other texts is this book's attention to a wide range of different theoretical approaches. A number of theories of the firm are described, for example. In general, where work elucidates a discussion, it is brought in, irrespective of its theoretical origins.

1.3.1 Geographical dimension: locational and regional aspects

As noted in the seminal work of Alfred Marshall (1899), the location of a firm is crucial to the organization of production. Yet, little attention has been paid to the geographical dimension in conventional texts on industrial economics or industrial organization. Locational aspects are essential to an understanding of firms' activities in the EU.

To explain – or even define – industries or markets in an area in which, although significantly diminished, international borders still exist, can be significantly different from a similar exercise in a homogeneous economy (such as Japan) or even a federal state (such as the United States). With the process of international economic integration, which started among the six founding members of the EU in the late 1950s, the national boundaries between member states have been lowered. The 1992 programme on the completion of the internal market, however, is proof that thirty years after the Treaty of Rome these national barriers had not completely disappeared. In relation to some industries and markets, integration within the EU is still not total. The implications of this for both the location of firms and the relevant product market are important to economists studying firms or industries in the EU. In addition, there is the question of whether the lowering of barriers between member states encourages firms to locate in particular regions or sub-regions of the EU, or whether it results in a more even distribution of industrial activity throughout the Union. If the former, then firms' location decisions jeopardize the objective of convergence, namely the reduction of inequality and uneven development; if the latter, then firms' decisions promote this objective.

Our aim of incorporating the spatial dimension is expressed in various parts of the book. For example, we have included concepts such as location quotients, agglomeration effects, industrial districts, clusters and *filières*; in discussion of EU action to prevent illegal pricing practices, the importance of regional issues is brought out; and throughout the text, an effort is made to make the spatial aspects of firms' activities clear.

1.3.2 International trade, foreign investment and industrial organization

International trade theory has, since the 1980s, begun to acknowledge the importance of developments in industrial economic theory. Trade theory had for many years been based on assumptions of perfect competition; imperfect competition, product differentiation and increasing returns to scale, although central concerns of industrial economics, had been ignored, at least by neoclassical trade theorists. We have included a discussion of this development and of its significance to the understanding of developments in the EU, in Chapters 13 and 14.

Localization, where a firm or group of firms concentrates their activities in a particular place, may appear to conflict with the phenomenon of globalization, which is related to the increasing significance of multinational enterprises (MNEs). However, they can and do co-exist. For example, MNEs, through their international trade, foreign investment and licensing activities can, while seeing their markets as global entities, still cause spatial concentration. Both the way MNEs perceive markets on the one hand, and their production and distribution activities on the other, impinge on economies in various ways. All these have spatial implications. We attempt, by our attention to such implications in this book, to construct a bridge across orthodox, spaceless industrial economics, modern approaches to firms and industries, and European economic integration.

1.3.3 Legal framework

The concept of the EU firm did not convey a precise legal meaning until 2004. As part of our focus on the implications for firms of operating in the EU, we discuss this problem in Chapter 7. That this legal issue is worthy of discussion in a text on industrial economics is easy to show. The fact that the law in relation to the rights and obligations of different forms of enterprise is not identical across all member states means that additional information is required for firms wishing to operate in more than one member state. This extra information is costly and constitutes a barrier to entry. Barriers to entry are a fundamental concern of industrial economics, and are the target of much of the effort in Europe to complete the Single Market. Attempts to harmonize the legal frameworks in which European firms operate, and to define a *Societas Europaea*, are discussed in Chapter 7.

1.3.4 Wide range of theoretical approaches

Like most industrial economics texts, this book describes the origins and development of the structure–conduct–performance (SCP) paradigm. It also, like most texts, provides critiques of this paradigm. Unlike most other texts, this book also includes a discussion of how debates around similar issues have taken place in a number of other, radically different traditions, including the Marxian, Austrian and Schumpeterian traditions.

Neoclassical approaches are discussed throughout the text. We accept the usefulness of many of the applications of neoclassical economics, at least for pedagogical purposes. Most such applications in this text are diagrammatic. Where they are appropriate, we provide critiques of the neoclassical perspective.

Emerging into great prominence within industrial economics since the 1980s is game theory. Rather than a theory, this is a tool used by economists from a number of different traditions. We use game theory throughout the text as a means of representing problems in strategy.

Different theories of the firm are introduced in Chapters 3 and 4. The discussion includes their sources, origins, applications and differences. A concept such as transaction costs, which we show is the basis for a theory of the firm, is also useful in explaining government intervention. We use the concept for this purpose in Chapter 15.

There are other links between the discussion of theories of the firm and different parts of the book. For example, we show in Chapter 4 that economists working on the evolutionary theory of the firm are close to, and in some cases overlap with, those working on new approaches to technological change and innovation. This is drawn out further in the discussion of national and regional *systems of innovation* in Chapter 8. Here, *institutional*, including cultural, aspects of the context within which firms operate are shown to be important.

1.4 Structure of the book

Chapter 2 reviews the standard SCP paradigm, highlights its limits and goes on to describe the arguments of the critics of SCP. Chapter 3 provides a discussion of the neoclassical theory of the firm and problems with the assumption of profit maximization. Chapter 4 proceeds with outlines of other significant theories of the firm. It concludes with a discussion on the similarities and differences among these theories. The following three chapters as well as Chapters 9 to 13 cover, in turn, aspects of the structure, conduct and performance of firms and industries in theory, and in the EU in practice. After an examination of market structure (in Chapter 5), Chapter 6 provides an extensive discussion of oligopoly theory. This includes a presentation of Cournot's original model as basic, and of the main developments since then as variations. The industrial structure of the EU is described and discussed in Chapter 7, followed by the theory and types of location of industry in the EU (in Chapter 8). Chapters 9 and 10 cover various types of behaviour of firms in theory and in the EU, including pricing, advertising and corporate integration. Chapter 11 is devoted to technological change and innovation, while Chapters 12 and 13 deal with the performance of firms, countries and the EU, in a comparative perspective. Chapter 14 presents a discussion and analysis of multinational enterprises and globalization, and Chapters 15 and 16 conclude with elements of industrial policy in general (Chapter 15) and in the specific case of the EU (Chapter 16). Chapter 15 also provides an insight into the industrial policies of other countries in the world.

1.5 How to use the book - a route map

Compared with the previous edition, this book presents a larger number of shorter chapters so as to make it more compatible with the teaching structure of modules on industrial economics. The 16 chapters correspond roughly to a semester cycle of 12 to 16 weeks. The chapters have been organized in a logical way (that is, from a number of definitional issues and presentation of key concepts, to aspects of industrial policy). However, the chapters on location (Chapter 8) and on multinational enterprises (Chapter 14) can be left until the end, leaving the instructor free to decide upon his or her own course structure.

For the student, the revised and updated content includes also a number of new pedagogical features such as a clear statement of learning objectives at the beginning of each chapter and a list of websites at the end.

Websites

The EU websites dealing with industrial affairs are broken down into:

Enterprise: **http://europa.eu.int/comm/enterprise/index_en.htm**
Research and technology: **http://europa.eu.int/comm/research/index_en.cfm**
Competition: **http://europa.eu.int/comm/competition/index_en.html**

Questions

1.1   What is industrial economics and how would you differentiate it from micro-economics?

1.2   What is the difference between an industry and a market? Discuss in detail, giving examples.

1.3   Provide examples of three questions that might be answered using input–output tables.

1.4   Why might regional and spatial issues be important in industrial economics?

Notes

1   Edward Chamberlin and Edward Mason taught the first graduate courses in industrial organization in Harvard in 1936 (Grether, 1970).

2   Such as the EFTA (European Free Trade Area) countries. The members of the EFTA are: Iceland, Liechtenstein, Norway and Switzerland.

3   This is subdivided into divisions (one-digit code), classes (two-digit codes), groups (three-digit codes), sub-groups (four-digit codes) and items (five-digit codes).

Appendix 1.1

European Statistical Classification of Industrial Activities (NACE system)

A   Agriculture, hunting and forestry

B   Fishing

C   Mining and quarrying

D   Manufacturing

DA   Manufacture of food products, beverages and tobacco
- 15   Food and beverages
- 16   Tobacco products

DB   Manufacture of textiles and textile products
- 17   Textiles
- 18   Wearing apparel, dressing and dyeing of fur

DC   Manufacture of leather and leather products
- 19   Tanning and dressing of leather; manufacture of luggage, handbags, saddlery, harness and footwear

DD   Manufacture of wood and wood products
- 20   Manufacture of wood and of products of wood and cork, except furniture; manufacture of articles of straw and plaiting materials

DE   Manufacture of pulp, paper and paper products; printing and publishing
- 21   Pulp, paper and paper products
- 22   Printing, publishing and reproduction of recorded media

DF   Manufacture of coke, refined petroleum products and nuclear fuels
- 23   Manufacture of coke, refined petroleum products and nuclear fuels

DG   Manufacture of chemicals, chemical products and man-made fibres
- 24   Manufacture of chemicals and chemical products

DH   Manufacture of rubber and plastic products
- 25   Manufacture of rubber and plastic products

DI   Manufacture of other non-metallic mineral products
- 26   Manufacture of other non-metallic mineral products

DJ   Manufacture of basic metals and fabricated metal products
- 27   Basic metals
- 28   Fabricated metal products except machinery and equipment

DK   Manufacture of machinery and equipment n.e.c*
- 29   Manufacture of machinery and equipment n.e.c.

DL   Manufacture of electrical and optical equipment
- 30   Office machinery and computers

31   Electrical machinery and apparatus n.e.c

32   Radio, TV and communication equipment

33   Medical, precision and optical instruments; watches and clocks

DM   Manufacture of transport equipment

34   Motor vehicles, trailers and semi trailers

35   Other transport equipment

DN   Manufacturing n.e.c

36   Furniture, manufacturing n.e.c

37   Recycling

E   Electricity, gas and water supply

F   Construction

G   Wholesale and retail trade; repair of motor vehicles, motorcycles and personal and household goods

H   Hotels and restaurants

I   Transport, storage and communication

J   Financial Intermediation

K   Real estate, renting and business activities

L   Public administration and defence; compulsory social security

M   Education

N   Health and social work

O   Other community, social and personal service activities

P   Activities of households

Q   Extra-territorial organizations and bodies

* Not elsewhere classified.

CHAPTER 2

Industrial organization

2.1 Learning objectives

The main objectives of this chapter are:

◆ To describe how industrial economics and organization began and developed

◆ To understand why the original frameworks are still contributing to this development

◆ To describe how alternatives to the original frameworks have added analytical tools

◆ To appreciate how and why disagreements among scholars are part of the evolution of the discipline, and

◆ To consider what game theory contributes to the analysis of oligopoly

2.2 Approaches and methods in industrial organization

In this chapter we discuss the evolution of industrial economic theory, identifying the weaknesses that have given rise to change. The main changes will be emphasized, in terms both of the underlying theories and of the methodologies.

The chapter provides descriptions of both historical background to and main frameworks in industrial economics. Central to this is the story of how Bain developed a framework that seemed to contradict some of the main tenets of the economics of markets. That framework has been revised, and new, more mathematically sophisticated tools have been introduced to address some of the same questions. Other changes have involved more awareness of the importance of place, and more generally, spatial aspects of industrial development. Some, including the economic geographers, have eschewed the mathematical sophistication and have adopted alternative methodologies.

Until recently, most analyses of industries were conducted according to the linear relationship prevailing in the well-known paradigm of structure–conduct–performance (SCP). In the paradigm, the market structure of the industry determines the conduct of the firm which, in turn, determines the firm's performance. The conflicting results of the numerous tests carried out on the causal relationship underlying this paradigm, as well as the need to deepen the theoretical base of industrial economics, paved the way to what became known in the 1980s and 1990s as the *new industrial economics* (see Schmalensee, 1982; Norman and La Manna, 1992). (Note that in this book we use the terms 'industrial economics' and 'industrial organization' interchangeably.) While new industrial economics continues to pervade the journals and textbooks, SCP remains 'the dominant empirical tradition' in industrial economics (Kay, 2002). Most SCP work is now, however, much more open to different directions of causality.

2.2.1 The SCP paradigm and its limits

Industrial organization emerged during the 1950s and 1960s essentially as an empirical study, centred on the SCP paradigm. According to the simple form of this framework, exogenous types of market structure (such as oligopoly) determine endogenous types of market behaviour (such as collusion) which in turn determine performance (such as high profitability). More specifically, a number of factors, including the numbers and sizes of buyers and sellers, degree of product differentiation, and barriers to entry, together form the elements of market structure (see Chapter 5). Market structure determines conduct which is, broadly speaking, the policies and strategies of firms, including pricing behaviour, investment, research and development, and various types of strategic alliances with other firms. (Conduct of firms is treated in its various aspects in Chapters 6, 8, 9 and 10.) Conduct, in turn, determines performance, measured, for example, by profitability or efficiency (see Chapter 12).

This analytical framework was popularized by Bain (1958), who himself claimed his roots to be in the work of Mason (1939, 1949) and Clark (1940). Others (for example, Hay and Morris, 1991) suggest that the theoretical basis for the work on structure, conduct and performance was laid by Chamberlin (1933). Chamberlin's (and, simultaneously, Robinson's (1933)) development of a model of monopolistic competition involved an examination of the theoretical relationship between industrial structures on the one hand, and prices and profits on the other, and it was just this type of relationship that Bain and his followers attempted to test empirically. Monopolistic competition (as well as the other neoclassical models of market structure) are discussed in some detail in Chapter 5. For the purposes of the present discussion it is sufficient to explain that what Chamberlin did was to define a market in which there was at first a fixed number of similar firms producing goods that were to some extent differentiated. There were two main assumptions: first, that the firms were all profit maximizers, and second, that firms could freely enter or leave this industry. The result was that, in the long run (that is, relaxing the condition that the number of firms is fixed and allowing the second assumption to take effect), the price would settle at a point at which price was equal to the average cost of production. Average cost includes 'normal' profit, that is, a return on capital just sufficient to keep the firms in the industry. If price is equal to average cost then each firm makes only normal profit, so this would be a long-run equilibrium in the sense that there would be no incentive for additional firms to enter or existing firms to leave the industry.

The advantage of the approach was that, if the direction of causality was, as assumed, from S to C to P, then for policy purposes all that had to be shown was the relationship between S and P. In Chamberlin's model, for example, all that had to be done about conduct was to impose the reasonable assumption that the firms would behave as profit maximizers. The result was that if there was monopolistic competition (S), long-run equilibrium would be where price was equal to average cost (P). In general, if it could be shown that certain industrial structures were associated with some firms earning excess (above-normal) profits, then the government should intervene to prevent that type of industrial structure. This obviated the need for 'direct inquiry into the inherently more intractable, and largely unobservable, process of market conduct' (Cable, 1994).

A famous debate ensued between what came to be known as the *Harvard School* and the *Chicago School*. The Harvard School generally saw value in the Chamberlin, monopolistic competition model. An interest in market structure, monopoly power and in the effect of policy was common in the Harvard School. This therefore included Bain and the other industrial economists who saw a need to identify circumstances requiring government intervention. The Chicago School opposed the Chamberlin model in favour of the original perfect competition model, generally opposed government intervention and indeed saw no need for industrial economics as a specialism separate from applied microeconomics.

Since the first wave of industrial economists accorded structure an influential or even deterministic role, their view came to be known as a *structuralist* conception of industrial organization.

The causal relationships posited by the structuralists have been widely tested. Many of the results of this empirical work were contradictory; for example, even so basic an issue as the relationship between firm size and profit rates was apparently contentious. Relying upon the simple correlation between firm size (as a measure of market structure) and profit rates (as a measure of performance), Haines (1970) found that 'the firms that appear most frequently among the 10, 50, or 100 most profitable are small or medium-sized rather than large'. This went against the results of studies by Baumol (1967) and Hall and Weiss (1967), among others, which suggested that profitability is directly related to firm size. Somewhere between these two extremes, Marcus (1969) found that 'size of firm influences profitability in *some*, but not in all, industries'.

SCP critics

These controversies contributed to the dismantling of the simplified form of the SCP paradigm as the core of industrial economics, though at least in the 1960s, they generated a great deal of research and constituted a rich vein within which to develop and sharpen econometric techniques. The SCP model came under attack on a number of different fronts. We attempt here to identify four such critiques of SCP. They are not mutually exclusive, some having writers and ideas in common, others methods. Each is associated to some extent with the traditional, neoclassical perspective.

1 The Chicago School criticized the model for being non-theoretical and for having diverged too far from the basic neoclassical price theory (Stigler, 1968; Davies and Lyons, 1988).[1] Even if their empirical work was based on more realistic assumptions, the Chicago School argued, Bain *et al.* came up with nothing more powerful in predictive ability than the traditional *perfect competition model*.[2] In another important difference, within the SCP paradigm high concentration (a small number of firms accounting for a large part of the market – see Chapter 5) was believed to lead to collusion, and hence to higher profits. Demsetz (1974) of the Chicago School, on the other hand, argued that where concentration was high, firms tended to be large; larger firms tended to be more efficient and it was this greater efficiency that led to higher profits. Clearly, if improved profitability was a result of collusion, intervention may be desirable, whereas if the reason for higher profits was greater efficiency, intervention would be counter-productive.

2 Even among those working within the SCP paradigm (for example, Scherer, 1970), the linearity of the structuralist view came into question. The possibility was identified, for example, of behaviour and performance affecting market structure. In this partial reversal of the direction of causality, conduct such as product differentiation may exclude some firms and may thus alter market structure; advertising, for example, may be used to raise entry barriers (Comanor and Wilson, 1967). This 'anti-structuralist' view considered the paradigm as an iterative process. Scherer (1970), summarizing the work of others, introduced the notion of a simultaneous interdependence of the three elements of the triad. (For an excellent critique of the structuralist view, see Auerbach (1989, especially pp. 44–6). Auerbach's contention is that 'the behaviour of participants in a market (whether oligopolistic or otherwise) can never be determined exclusively by a set of market parameters which are exogenous to this behaviour' (p. 46).) According to Cable (1994), these problems of causality were damaging to the SCP framework, leading to disagreement over the interpretation of results of statistical research. The theoretical and empirical weaknesses reinforced one another. Nevertheless, the idea of examining industries, and, to some extent, of organizing theory, under the three

headings continues to have a role. Without implication as to the direction of causality among them, structure, conduct and performance remain important elements in the present text, as they do in most other well-known texts on industrial organization (IO).

3 With roots going back to Cournot in the nineteenth century, more recent contributions in the field of IO have accorded behaviour or conduct the dominant role. Implications in terms of both market structure and performance are then derived (see, for example, Stiglitz and Mathewson (1986), and for a summary of work in this area, Davies and Lyons (1988, pp. 7–10)). Even more important than this, the methodologies used to posit the conduct and derive the implications, have changed. Economists such as Spence (1977) and Dixit (1979) began to apply game theory to the analysis of the conduct of firms, and this induced a transformation in the nature of the subject of industrial economics: it has become more theoretical. A great number of the articles on IO now published in British, American and European journals contain game theoretic models or methods (game theory is discussed in more detail in Section 2.2.3 of this chapter).

4 Also emerging from an older tradition, a number of economists have focused on firms and markets as alternative means of organizing production. Williamson (1985) has called this range of theories the *new institutional economics*. Coase's *transaction cost* theory expounded in 1937 and greatly extended by Williamson (1985), and *principal–agent* theory associated with, among others, Ross (1973), Stiglitz (1974) and Mirrlees (1976), are examples of this intensified interest in the 'nature of the firm' (this is the title of Coase's 1937 article). These theories are discussed in some detail in Chapters 3 and 4. (See also, on the economics of organization and management, Milgrom and Roberts, 1992.) In an early example of this attention to the implications of the structure of the firm, Williamson (1967) incorporated aspects of organization theory into an examination of management as a limitation on the growth of the firm. Arguing that the behaviour of government bureaucracies is in many respects similar to that of hierarchical firms, Williamson presented a model in which loss of control in such firms constituted a limitation on their size. The question of diminishing returns to management, as we shall see in our discussion of theories of the firm in Chapter 4, continues to be a subject of debate in this literature.

While there are differences among them, the above four streams in industrial economics can in many respects be considered to be mainstream. The training, concerns and broad methodologies of the economists discussed under each of them, are all similar to those of the neoclassical tradition.[3] For example, they all use marginal analysis (explained in Chapter 3), they all attempt in various ways to model the behaviour of firms mathematically, and they all rely to a greater extent on deductive than inductive theorizing. While there have been debates and disagreements in the IO literature in these streams, there is a certain commonality of language among them.

In addition to the debates within the mainstream of IO, there have also been a number of critics writing from what Davies and Lyons (1988, pp. 10–19) call 'radical' perspectives. They emphasize three such approaches: Hayekian, Schumpeterian and Marxian. Aspects of the work of each of them continue to reverberate in IO.

Hayek and his followers (all part of the *Austrian School*) based an intensely anti-interventionist policy prescription on the belief that important economic information is held by individuals in an extremely disaggregated way (Hayek, 1949). The centralization of information which is necessary for governments to decide on whether and how to intervene, is thus impossible. Competition, for the Austrian School, is a process of continual interaction between the entrepreneur and the environment; the distinction between perfect and imperfect competition as static structures determining the behaviour of firms is therefore inappropriate. Indeed, for Hayek, 'the economic problem of society is mainly one of rapid adaptation to changes in particular circumstances of time and place' (quoted in Williamson, 1985, p. 8). To remain in business, firms must, in this view, constantly obtain information about market conditions and how they change. But knowledge and learning are, in Hayek's theory, held and gained only by individuals. This has led O'Sullivan (2000, p. 36) to argue that the 'Austrians have thus far failed to integrate a theory of the firm into their conceptual framework'. They have, she continues, 'failed to come to terms with the possibility that resource allocation can be organizational as well as individual . . .'.

Auerbach (1989, pp. 22–7) agrees with the necessity for viewing competition as a dynamic process, but points out that Hayek's 'categories are deeply rooted in the static utilitarian calculus of choice inherited from the earlier Austrian school of Menger and others'. There is, Auerbach argues (1989, p. 26), a contradiction between the dynamic conception of competition and the static theory of utility upon which Hayek bases his individualist philosophy of economics. Davies and Lyons (1988), too, while finding some validity in the Austrian notions of 'entrepreneurial alertness' (to replace the neoclassical 'optimization') and 'order in the competitive process' (to replace 'equilibrium'), nevertheless conclude that 'the Austrian creed [is] at odds with a more dispassionate and balanced view of government policy'.

Schumpeter[4] was a contemporary of Hayek's, and a fellow Austrian, though not of the Austrian School. Schumpeter disagreed with the dominant economic perspective, according to which the economy was generally in equilibrium, with minor fluctuations. For him, the fluctuations were more important, and among the most powerful causes of these fluctuations were technological and organizational innovations and entrepreneurial activity. The economy was usually not in equilibrium, according to Schumpeter, because of the massive shifts brought about by 'the new commodity, the new technology, the new source of supply, the new type of organization (the largest scale unit of control for instance)' (Schumpeter, 1943, pp. 83–5). His view was that incessant innovations by firms destroyed existing economic structures and created new ones. This is Schumpeter's famous notion of 'creative destruction' (ibid.). If the investment required to create these shifts involved elements of collusion, monopoly and even government intervention, then, for Schumpeter, such elements were acceptable. The determination of these shifts was, moreover, at least for the later Schumpeter, a collective, co-operative process (O'Sullivan, 2000, p. 15). The Schumpeterian view is thus different from both the neoclassical insistence on the import- ance of perfect competition and the Austrian antipathy to government intervention; it also differs from both in that they emphasize the individual.

The importance of large-scale and monopoly power for innovation in Schumpeter's later work is at odds with his earlier view, in *The Theory of Economic Development* (1983),[5] that inno- vations were more likely to emanate from small, new firms. (This was first published in German in 1912. See Scherer (1992) for this comparison, for a review of Schumpeter's work and for the reaction to it over the past 50 years.) This distinction among the types of structures most conducive of innovation has continued to be debated, and although much of the literature 'supports a conclusion that Schumpeter overstated the advantages of large, monopolistic corporations as engines of technological change' (Scherer, 1992), a great deal of research on this and other aspects of Schumpeter's work continues to be done (see also Chapter 3). Irrespective of the size of the firm introducing the innovation, the innovative activity remains crucial for Schumpeter. Schumpeterian competition – as dis- tinct from the price competition of standard neoclassical models – is the 'competition from the new commodity, the new technology, the new source of supply, the new type of organization' (Schumpeter, 1943, p. 84). These notions of change in the products, pro- cesses and organizations of production and distribution have deeply informed a rather heterogeneous group of post-SCP industrial economists, including Auerbach (1989), Porter (1990), Best (1990), Lazonick (1991) and Scherer (1996) and, among those particu- larly interested in technological change, Dosi *et al.* (1988), Lundvall (1992), Nelson (1993) and O'Sullivan (2000). (The work of many of these writers is associated with the evolu- tionary theory of the firm, discussed in Chapter 4. On technological change and innovation, see Chapter 11.)

Schumpeter, though politically conservative,[6] had a 'professional sympathy for socialism' (Stolper, 1994). He was greatly influenced by *Marx*, the third of the radical theorists. Much of Marx's work has relevance to IO, but we concentrate here on his view of the determinants of the growth of the firm. For Marx, the accumulation of capital was crucial both to the existence of capitalism and to the growth of firms (individual capitals). Accumulation began historically with such developments as the enclosure movements, the great trading monop- olies and the colonies. From then on, competition forced capitalists to continue to accumulate: 'Competitors were constantly developing new and better methods of produc- tion. Only by accumulating new and better capital equipment could this challenge be met' (Hunt and Sherman, 1990, pp. 91–2).

Accumulation, according to Marx, would lead to a tendency for larger and larger firms to be concentrated in the hands of fewer and fewer capitalists, for three reasons. First, compe- tition forces firms to adopt more and more capital-intensive means of production. As capital intensity ('organic composition of capital') increases, so does the minimum efficient scale. 'Large capitals, therefore, get the better of small ones' (Marx, 1972, p. 691). Second, small firms will concentrate in industries not yet dominated by larger firms. Here, 'competition rages in direct proportion to the number and in inverse proportion to the magnitude of the competing capitals. It always ends in the overthrow of a number of the lesser capitalists, whose capitals to some extent pass into the hands of the conquerors ...' (Marx, 1972, p. 691).

Third, the credit system, developing concomitantly with capitalist production is, with competition, one of the two 'mightiest levels of concentration' (Marx, 1972, p. 691). Large, growing firms are a better credit risk than small ones, and therefore more likely to succeed in obtaining loans and other forms of credit.

Clearly, there is much of interest in Marx for IO, and modern industrial economists have indeed paid attention to Marx.[7] Davies and Lyons (1988), referring to Marx's claim that natural monopolies 'do not prevent the equalisation of profits between industries', argue that this suggests that he 'deserves credit as an early contestability theorist!' (Contestability theory is discussed in Section 2.2.4 below. It argues that in the absence of barriers to entry, firms in imperfectly competitive market structures will behave as if there is perfect competition.)

Apart from these radical critics of, and alternatives to, SCP, there have been a number of other recent frameworks for analysing industries that have in some senses displaced SCP. Among these we mention two. First, and probably the most frequently used such framework, is that of Porter (1990, 1998a). Second, a recent alternative to Porter is Best's (2001) *productivity triad*. The work of both of these writers to some extent addresses locational issues, which we discuss in the next section of this chapter and in Chapter 8. Here it is important to note that these approaches only in some ways constitute alternatives to SCP; they provide new ways of examining competitiveness. For some specific purposes, such as examining relationships between size of firms and innovation, SCP-type hypotheses remain important, and continue to generate new work. But for general questions about which of an economy's industries are most internationally competitive, and why, Porter's work in particular has become very popular among policy-oriented analysts.

Central to Porter's (1990) analysis is his 'diamond', the four elements of a firm's environment that explain the firm's competitiveness. These are: factor conditions; demand conditions; related and supporting industries; and firm strategy, structure and rivalry. The more intensely these factors together favour a particular industry, the more likely that industry is to be successful. Moreover, these four elements are all to varying extents place specific. Thus firms in that successful industry and associated industries are likely to cluster in that place. *Clusters* of firms and related institutions have emerged as the focus of Porter's work on competitiveness. As Best (2001) points out, '[in] the 1990s, Porter's diamond and cluster analysis was widely adopted as a conceptual framework for shaping regional and national industrial strategies'.

Best (2001, p. 8) praises Porter's work for bringing into view 'a richer understanding of the sources of industrial development and a menu of industrial policy options that are obscured, or denied, by the market failure framework'. However, he sees weaknesses in Porter's approach, in particular that it ignores the internal organization of the firm. Best (2001, p. 9) offers the 'capability and innovation perspective' as an improvement. From this perspective there emerges a 'productivity triad': 'three interactive domains that shape a region's capability development processes'. These are: business model, production system and skill formation. The first domain, business model, addresses the different models that firms or economies develop to facilitate firms in differentiating themselves from other firms so as to gain competitive advantage. Examples include the Japanese firm, 'kaisha', and the networked groups of firms in the industrial districts of 'the third Italy' (discussed in Chapter 8). Production system, the second domain, is the way in which products are designed and manufactured. Mass production of high-volume consumer products, and low-volume, complex product systems of production, are two examples. Finally, skill formation addresses the demand for, education in, and development in the workplace of, technological skills. The idea of the productivity triad 'captures the systemic character of change at enterprise and regional levels'. The three domains in the productivity triad are 'interconnected sub-systems' (Best, 2001, p. 14). There is perhaps some evidence of the usefulness of Best's approach in the fact that he has been a consultant on industrial development to a number of governments and international agencies.

SCP survives

Notwithstanding all the radical critiques of, and recent alternatives to, SCP, new work – and in particular empirical work testing SCP ideas – continues to be generated. Neuberger (1998), for example, adapts the recent versions of SCP for analysis of the banking industry. She takes the revised SCP paradigm – 'where all variables are endogenous because of interdependencies between variables of market structure, conduct and performance and feed-back effects on basic conditions and public policy' – and adds to it a number of variables which are specific to banking. The most important of these is 'asymmetric information between borrowers and lenders and the costs of gathering information' because they 'have an impact on the activity of banks, their structure and performance'. Using this framework, she reviews the literature on banking. She concludes, among other things, that for 'the largest banks ... there is no significant relationship between size and profitability, which indicates [most plausibly] ... a compensation of market power gains by decreasing returns to scale. ... Also the merging to financial conglomerates does not seem to be efficiency enhancing, because there is no evidence for global economies of scope' (Neuberger, 1998).

In another recent example of work utilizing SCP, Whittam and Danson (2001) combine a 'radical Coasian framework' (see Chapter 4) with SCP to analyse the issue of power relationships within the Scotch whisky industry. The power they are analysing is the power 'broadly to determine a firm's geographical orientation, its relationship with rivals, with governments and with its labour force' (Cowling and Sugden, 1998). Whittam and Danson (2001) argue that looking at S, C and P, and how each influences and is influenced by the other two, 'allows the power relations in the industry to be made more transparent, with a link from the structure (potential for domination) to be related through conduct (use of power) to performance (impacts on firms, workers, communities, and the wider economy)'. In their empirical analysis they identify the increasing dominance of the Scotch whisky industry by two global companies. Their conclusion is that the possibility of gains from the development of related industries will not be realized – 'to the detriment of indigenous players' – if the strategic decision making remains in the hands of these two companies.

There are many other examples of research in which the revised SCP framework is applied to particular industries (Tu and Chen (2000) on Taiwanese banking) and further stretched to facilitate application to other industries (Ramstad (1997) on the media market). In the case of the work of Imai (2000), SCP is used as the basis for the development of a new theory. A new theory is necessary, he argues, to analyse the dynamics of industrial organization in the context of what he calls the 'explosion of information technology'. He proposes the concept of 'platform' as a part of structure, 'real options' to analyse uncertainty, and suggests that there is a new form of competition that takes place among different platforms (for example between Microsoft® Windows and Linux). We can conclude that SCP is alive and well and continuing to evolve, adjusting to and merging with new theories, and being revised and re-revised to analyse new empirical realities.

It is clear from the way that SCP has evolved that there is, in theoretical development, cross-fertilization of ideas. This is even common ground between radical and mainstream economists, as well as among those in different groups within the mainstream of industrial economics. In some cases the same or a similar conclusion seems to be arrived at independently. In an example of two groups arriving at the same conclusion from very different perspectives, the Chicago School and Hayek's Austrian School both profoundly oppose government intervention. Also showing links, albeit in a different way, some institutional economists draw explicitly on the radical economists. North (1990), for example, in his attempt to develop a new theory of institutional change, adopts much of Coase, and builds not only on Williamson but also on Schumpeter and Marx. Common attention to the same ideas even occurs across disciplines; the forces behind localization of industry, identified by Marshall in the nineteenth century, have been researched and analysed in recent decades by geographers, sociologists and economists. These forces are a key aspect of economic geography, to which we now turn.

2.2.2 Economic geography

Despite its importance to an understanding of how firms and industries behave, geography is rarely addressed in industrial economics textbooks. Among the questions addressed by economic geography are those relating to firms, such as how and why firms in some cases do, and in others do not, tend to locate themselves close to:

- other firms in the same industry, and/or
- other firms that are suppliers to the same industry, and/or
- other firms that are buyers of their products or services, and/or
- other firms that use the same technologies.

There are also related questions about regions, such as how and why some regions develop more rapidly than other regions, and how and why this can change over time.

All these are questions that seem to us to be of relevance to the behaviour of firms and industries. After all, if firms cluster together spatially in various ways in order to enhance their performance, then surely spatial concentration becomes an element in structure, conduct and performance. Without specifying a particular direction of causality, it is clear that there are relationships between the spatial distribution of activity in a particular industry, where a firm in that industry is located relative to the spatial distribution, and the performance of that firm and, indeed, of that industry. The application of economic geography to firms and industries is described in more detail in Chapter 8.

Among the authors most significant in bringing the attention of economists to geography in recent years is Krugman (1993, 1998). Krugman sees in methodological issues the explanation of why mainstream[8] economics in general ignored spatial distribution. He argues that because spatial concentration is caused by increasing returns to scale (where average costs of production decline as output grows), and because this made it difficult to model mathematically, mainstream economics ignored it (Krugman, 1998). This is not to suggest that Krugman is here criticizing mainstream economics for being too dependent on modelling. On the contrary, he is praising the virtues of new modelling 'tricks', as he calls them, which have enabled economics to use general equilibrium theory[9] among other things to theorize about spatial distribution of economic activity. This, he suggests, is the main contribution of the 'new economic geography'. Interrelated possibilities such as path dependence, circular causation and discontinuous change – all of which are associated with spatial distribution – emerge naturally, he asserts, from the new models.

The present text is not exclusively in the 'mainstream'. While we address some of Krugman's ideas and examine in more detail the relevance of his contributions to industrial economics, we also focus on other economists' work on economic geography. Long before Krugman, Marshall (1898)[10] had addressed localization of industry. He was both an originator of neoclassical economics (especially in the appendices of his *Principles of Economics*) and an important influence on industrial sociology (for example in his work on *industrial districts*). He also addressed increasing returns and imperfect competition, but, from the point of view of localization, he emphasized external economies. Increasing returns are the economies (or reductions in costs) arising internally from the increase in the size of a firm. The external economies identified by Marshall arise from relationships between firms and among people who work for different firms. As Whitaker (2002) points out, this notion 'remains seminal, if elusive'.[11]

Through deductive, mainly general equilibrium methodology à la Krugman, questions like those at the beginning of this section have begun to be addressed in the past decade in the mainstream economics journals. Among hundreds of examples, we can mention here articles on trade and industrial location in the EU (Amiti, 1998), on regional production structures (Davis and Weinstein, 1999), and on spatial concentration (Ricci, 1999; Ciccone, 2002). However, through a discursive methodology closer to the Marshall of the text (as opposed to Marshall of the appendices), one that generally avoids mathematical modelling, the questions at the beginning of this section have long been addressed, and continue to be addressed, in literally thousands of articles in the regional economics and economic geography journals such as *Economic Geography*, *Regional Studies*, *European Urban and Regional Studies* and *European Planning Studies*, and heterodox economics journals such as *Cambridge Journal of Economics* and *Economy and Society*. One of the main differences between the articles in the mainstream journals and those in the regional studies journals is that the former are mainly deductive in methodology, in the neoclassical tradition, whereas the latter are more empirically driven, more inductive, frequently critical of the neoclassical tradition and often written by people in geography departments and business schools. Among well-known non-traditional economists in this latter tradition are Porter (1990, 1998a) and Best (1990, 2001).

It is instructive to compare and contrast an article by a proponent of new economic geography with that of a critic. Let us select Krugman (1998) and Martin (1999). Krugman reviews the work in the area, identifying its origins in his own article (1991) 'Increasing returns and economic geography'. He goes on to describe the differences between the new approach of economists to geography and what he calls the 'long if somewhat thin history' of work by economists on the location of production. He offers a brief list of the main contributors to this history, from von Thunen (1826) (who was regarded by Marshall as a founding father of marginalism) to Henderson (1974) (on urban systems theory) and points out that they all adopted a partial equilibrium approach, with many significant factors taken as givens. Second, he posits that many of them described 'planning solutions rather than market outcomes'. In other words, it was not inherent in their models as to how the outcome would result from individuals acting to maximize their welfare, and firms acting to maximize their profits. His third criticism is that they all accepted, and built into their models, increasing returns. However, the way they built it into their models was more or less as a static constraint. Thus, for example, in many cases increasing returns resulted in a limit on the number of locations in which a firm could undertake production.

This description of the 'old' models by Krugman sets the scene for his identification of what is new about the new models. First, they are full, general equilibrium models. The constraints are in finances and resources, and the distribution in space of population, supply and demand are endogenous. This means that it is their interaction that is being modelled. As Krugman puts it, it is the 'two-way feedback between location decisions by individual agents and these distributions that is the main source of interesting stories'. Second, in contrast to the 'planning solutions' approach, the new models derive equilibrium location solutions from the ways that markets behave in the models. And third, the way in which increasing returns are incorporated into the new models is very different. In the old models, the impact of increasing returns is in a sense already complete – for example, limiting the locations of production. This was because 'unexhausted economies of scale at the level of the firm necessarily undermine perfect competition' and there was no way of modelling imperfect competition. In the new models, the impact of increasing returns can be observed and markets are characterized by imperfect competition. In most of the rest of the article, Krugman explains some of the new modelling tricks, and some of the difficulties in testing the new models empirically. What emerges very clearly is how important the notions of equilibrium, and, in some cases multiple equilibria, are to the modelling economists. Krugman concludes that what the new modelling tricks have done is to make 'geography a field that is safe for mainstream economists'. The new economic geography has so far been more successful at 'creating a language with which to discuss issues than at creating solutions to those discussions'; its future depends on research which will either prove its empirical relevance, or, failing this, lead to it being discarded.

Martin (1999) also begins his article with some discussion of the historical precedents. To a greater extent than Krugman, Martin identifies Losch (1954) as seminal. Losch's work, he argues, had little influence on economics, but it provided the foundation for two other disciplines: regional science and economic geography. The former had become, by the 1970s, 'a highly mathematical and esoteric theory of abstract, equilibrium economic landscapes …'. The latter, in contrast, was already very different: 'more eclectic and empirically orientated', less neoclassical, drawing rather from business cycle models, cumulative causation and 'Marxian theories of uneven accumulation'. More recently, these diverse influences have been added to by, among others, 'Schumpeterian models of technological evolution, and institutional economics'. The new economic geography, which he identifies primarily with Krugman, 'represents a reworking of regional science and urban economics, precisely the sort of approaches that geographers discarded years ago.'

Martin (1999) next turns to a description of the new models of increasing returns and spatial agglomeration, in much the same terms as Krugman, and drawing in some detail from Krugman's – and other similar – work. Having done so he points out, as does Krugman, that there is a paucity of empirical work. While Krugman seems neutral on the possibility of the empirical relevance of the theory being shown, Martin is negative; the models are 'too abstract, oversimplified and too idealised'. Acknowledging that some empirical work has shown the relevance of increasing returns and externalities in spatial agglomeration, Martin goes on to point out, first, that there are many other important factors, and second, that increasing returns, externalities and cumulative causation have been key issues in the work of economic geographers for decades. He cites a large number of studies as evidence, suggesting that much of the argument about what is new in the new economic geography is really only new to formal mathematical modelling of the spatial distribution of economic activity. (This, to be fair, is what Krugman himself asserts.) Martin's most effective criticism is in arguing that the work in economic geography provides 'greater insight into the roles of labour and technology in regional development than do the new spatial agglomeration models'.

In the next section of his article, Martin describes the application of the new types of models to regional growth and convergence. Here again he provides a reasonable survey of the work, and concludes, as most of the authors in this genre would agree, that 'the regional convergence models raise as many questions as they answer'. And again he argues that economic geographers (as opposed to 'new economic geographers') have asked similar questions – about differences between rates of development in different regions – and have provided more convincing answers, for many years. As an example, he shows that new economic geographers acknowledge the inability of their models to account for reversals, where convergence between particular regions occurs in one period and divergence in the next period. 'Economic geographers, in contrast, see these oscillations as inextricably bound up with the periodic systemic shifts in the structure and organisation of capitalism (such as the transition from Fordism to post-Fordism.'

To show that he is not just against the modelling of the new economic geography, Martin follows this with a critique of mathematical modelling in general. He points out that, of necessity, what he calls 'messy' factors in spatial economic development are neglected in the models. What he means by this is the imprecision, or unquantifiability, of factors such as culture and institutions. He asserts that because these factors cannot be expressed in mathematical form, they are assumed by mainstream economists to be of secondary importance. He quotes Krugman as stating that they are 'best left to sociologists'. As in the previous sections, Martin goes on to argue that economic geographers have incorporated, and continue to incorporate, such factors into their analyses.

In the final sections of his article Martin argues that the new economic geography is not really geography because it does not focus on 'real places'. A particularly interesting criticism, from the point of view of a book on industrial economics, is his comment on the regional convergence models: 'Even industrial-structure differences between regions are assumed to be unimportant (or simply reduced to dummy variables).' He then reviews recent work in economic geography and concludes that there are fundamental methodological differences between the two disciplines.

While we have described the methodology of neoclassical economics as 'deductive', Martin calls it 'logical positivism'. He shows that economic geographers have largely abandoned this methodology 'in favour of realist approaches, in which explanations are built "from below", often relying on close dialogue with individual agents and organisations, and linking this "local" knowledge with wider, larger stylised facts and theoretical frameworks . . .'. These fundamental differences make the two approaches irreconcilable.

This account of the articles by Krugman (1998) and Martin (1999) should encourage students to read the two articles, and other work by these and similar authors. In this chapter on approaches and methods in industrial organization it is instructive to note that virtually the same questions can be addressed in very different ways. Moreover, each of the different ways rejects the other; writers in each tradition are convinced that they are correct and that other traditions are wrong. The economic policies that emanate from different approaches are also usually different and, it can be argued, are often associated with the ideologies that underlie the different approaches. In this book our intention is to provide as eclectic an introduction to the discipline as possible. While, by and large, we do not provide instruction in mathematical modelling, nor do we reject it. This book can stand as an introduction not only for students who go on to approach questions of industrial location through mathematical modelling, but also for those who wish to adopt more realist, or other heterodox approaches to industrial economics.

2.2.3 Game theory

Since the late 1970s, a wide range of mathematically sophisticated, mainly game theoretic, models have been introduced into the mainstream of industrial economics. Contributing to the revision of the traditional SCP approach, many of these models continue to examine the types of issues underlying the SCP paradigm. For example, the debate over size of firm and profitability, and the related issues of concentration, market power and efficiency, still concern both theoreticians and empirical researchers. This debate, among other theoretical concerns, at first dominated the work in game theory. It is only in recent years that the wide number, range and complexity of the hypotheses generated by the game theoretic models have begun to be tested empirically.

According to Martin (1994, p. 221), most economists now accept Demsetz's (1974) compromise explanation for the conflicting empirical results of structure–performance relationships. This compromise is that where high profits for large firms, but low profits for small firms in highly concentrated industries, are observed, the explanation could be both greater efficiency and greater market power of the large firms. Efficiency could arise from the lower unit costs of large-scale production (returns to scale), and market power could be expressed through collusion by the large firms to keep prices high, but not so high as to facilitate high profits for the small firms. The extent to which each of these – efficiency and market power – is present, varies from industry to industry. They also vary within industries. As a result, empirical work on size and performance was, as we have seen, inconsistent. Recent studies attempting to avoid this problem have focused on single industries, or even single firms. The papers discussed above by Neuberger (1998), Whittam and Danson (2001), Tu and Chen (2000), Ramstad (1997) and Imai (2000),[12] all to varying extents provide evidence of this more sector- or sub-sector-specific focus.

This narrowing of the focus of industrial economics, together with an increasing recognition of the importance of the *strategic behaviour*[13] of firms, has both encouraged and facilitated the application of game theory. Strategic behaviour is a fundamental element of conduct, and as such is a natural concern of those who have in recent times accorded conduct the key role in the SCP triad. We introduced this type of work above as a critique of SCP with roots going back to Cournot in the nineteenth century.

Correctly speaking, game theory is not itself a theory of IO but a method that can be used to describe and test other theories. Basically, game theory is a mathematical modelling technique in which the players' moves (or decisions) are influenced by their expectations of the responses of the other player(s). (Gardner (1995, p. 4) defines a game as 'any rule-governed situation with a well-defined outcome, characterized by strategic interdependence'.) This is so close to the definition of oligopoly, that the application of game theory to IO, and particularly to strategies within oligopolies, was inevitable.

There is some disagreement over the roots of game theory as applied in IO. Some (for example, Hyman, 1992, p. 373) credit von Neumann and Morgenstern (1944) with the original formulation, whereas others (for example, Forges and Thisse, 1992) argue that 'game theory and industrial economics . . . have been very much intertwined from the outset', an outset that goes back to Cournot (1838). Recent work suggests that the models like those of Cournot were later incorporated into game theory, but that von Neumann and Morgenstern were the crucial progenitors: 'Had von Neumann and Morgenstern never met, it seems unlikely that game theory would have been developed' (Leonard, 1995). Whoever was originally responsible, it is clear that the modern use of game theory in IO builds on the work of a number of mathematicians and economists, including Cournot (1838), Bertrand (1883), Hotelling (1929), von Stackelberg (1934), Nash (1951) (Nash was among three Nobel prizewinners for economics in 1994) and Schelling (1960), as well as von Neumann and Morgenstern.

In game theory,[14] as in neoclassical economics in general, there is usually an equilibrium concept. In the neoclassical approach the equilibrium relates to the structure of a market, but in game theory it relates to the conduct of the firms. In the Cournot equilibrium, for example, the firms each choose a level of output which together constitute an equilibrium if, given the outputs chosen by its rivals, no firm can increase its profit by changing its output. In this case, output is the strategic decision variable. The Bertrand equilibrium is one in which price is the decision variable. (The original Cournot and Bertrand models are presented mathematically under the discussion of oligopoly in Chapter 6.) More generally, where a firm optimizes in this way, given the strategic choices of its rivals, the result is known as a Nash equilibrium. Thus a Nash equilibrium where output is the decision variable is a Cournot (or a Nash–Cournot) equilibrium, and where price is the decision variable it is a Bertrand (or Nash–Bertrand) equilibrium.

The basic tool of game theory is the *payoff matrix*. (The presentation of game theory in terms of equations and reaction – or best response – curves is illustrated in the discussion of oligopoly in Chapter 6. See also the mathematical appendix to Chapter 2.) This shows the strategies available to the players, and the outcomes for each player, depending on the strategy chosen by rivals. Most common, both for analytical and heuristic purposes, are two-player games. The analogy in economics is the duopoly, that is an industry in which there are only two firms. Figure 2.1 illustrates. In this industry there are two, and only two firms, and they are identical. Each has a choice of output, either 3 or 6 units. The cells of the matrix indicate the payoff in euro of profit. The choice of 3 units by Player A and 6 units by Player B will give Player A the payoff which is the first figure in brackets (-3, or a loss of €3) and Player B the payoff which is the second figure (a profit of €33).

		Player B	
		3 units	6 units
Player A	3 units	(27, 27)	(-3, 33)
	6 units	(33, -3)	(12, 12)

Figure 2.1 The payoff matrix

The aim in game theory is to identify each player's best strategy, that is, the strategy that will maximize the player's payoff, taking the other player's strategy into account. If, for example, Player B chooses 3 units, Player A's best strategy would be 6 units (a profit of €33 for an output of 6 units is preferable to a profit of €27 for an output of 3 units). If Player B chooses 6 units, again Player A would choose 6 units. So, from Player A's point of view the two possible outcomes are the two bottom cells of the matrix (33, -3) or (12, 12). By analogy, from Player B's point of view the two possible outcomes are the two cells on the right-hand side of the matrix (-3, 33) if Player A chooses to produce 3 units and (12, 12) if Player A chooses to produce 6 units. The cell (12, 12) is one at which, if either player has chosen to produce 6 units, there is no incentive for the other to choose any other strategy. This is the Nash–Cournot equilibrium position in this game.

The same result would be arrived at by assuming, as is most commonly done in such situations, that the *maxi-min* strategy will be adopted. Here Player A will compare the worst possible payoffs in each of the choices facing it, and choose the best of these – thus maximizing the minimum payoff. In our example, if Player A chooses 3 units, the worst possible outcome is where Player B chooses 6 units, a payoff for Player A of $-€3$. If Player A chooses 6 units, €12 is the worst possible payoff. Because €12 is preferable to $-€3$, Player A will choose to produce 6 units. By analogy, Player B will also choose to produce 6 units, and although each firm, and the industry as a whole, could make greater profits if the 3-unit option had been chosen, by acting independently the firms will choose to produce 6 units. Acting independently is indeed the essence of non-cooperative games: the players cannot collude.

Where the results are such that, if collusion were possible then both firms could improve their payoffs (as in the example in Fig. 2.1), then this is known as the *prisoner's dilemma*. More formally, the prisoner's dilemma is 'where the pursuit of self-interest leads to a Pareto-inefficient solution for the players' (Forges and Thisse, 1992). (Pareto efficiency in this context is where there is no way of reallocating decisions to improve one player's situation without worsening another player's situation.) There is a dominant strategy, the payoff of which is less than the best possible outcome. This situation is called prisoner's dilemma because its original application was to an example in which two people are charged with an offence (Fig. 2.2). If both confess, then each will be sentenced to say, three years in jail. If both hold out, they both go to jail for one year. If either confesses (and implicates the other), the confessor goes free and the other is sentenced to ten years. Both will confess because each will fear that holding out may result in a much longer sentence. It is also appropriate to call this situation prisoner's dilemma because, as Gardner (1995, p. 52) writes, 'the players are prisoners of their own strategies'.

| | Defendant B | |
	Confess	Hold out
Confess	(3, 3)	(0, 10)
Hold out	(10, 0)	(1, 1)

Figure 2.2 The prisoner's dilemma

Depending on the payoffs, and the assumptions about the behaviour of the firms, different results can be obtained. If, for example, the choice of 6 units by both players had given a payoff of (27, 27), the choice of 3 units by both players a payoff of (12, 12), with all other things the same, then the two players would still both choose 6 units, but this time it would have given them both the best possible payoffs. Where a player chooses a strategy (6 units), irrespective of what the other firm does, then this is called a dominant strategy, and where, as in this case, both players have *dominant strategies*, it is an equilibrium of dominant strategies.[15]

The above are examples of variable sum games. Where the payoff to Player A is derived entirely from B, and vice versa, then it is called a *zero sum game*. An example of a zero sum game is where there is a duopoly with a fixed market size. An increase in the market share of either firm is at the cost of market share of its competitor, and the size of the increase of the share of Firm A is equal (and opposite) to the loss of the share of Firm B. This is illustrated in Fig. 2.3, in which the amounts in the cells are the share of the market that will go to Firm A. (A minus figure is the share that will go to Firm B.)

If this is the market for a transducer used in the electrical engineering industry and the total demand is known to be 2000 units a week, then Firm A adopting strategy a_1 and Firm B adopting strategy b_1 will result in A supplying an additional 200 units (10 per cent), and B 200 fewer units, per week. The adoption of a maxi-min approach to choice of strategy will direct A to a_3, where the worst that can happen is no change, and it will direct B to b_2, where again the worst that can happen is no change. With A having chosen a_3, B has no incentive to change; b_1 will result in a decline in demand for its transducers of 40 units per week, and

b_3 will mean a decline of 100 units per week. Similarly, B having chosen b_2, A has no incentive to change. This position, a_3 and b_2, is thus a Nash equilibrium.

	Firm B		
	b_1	b_2	b_3
Firm A a_1	10%	−8%	−12%
a_2	18%	−15%	−4%
a_3	2%	0%	5%

Figure 2.3 Zero sum game

We have so far dealt with variable and zero sum, two-player games, in which the two players are either identical or similar and in which each player only makes one move. Let us now relax some of these conditions, beginning with the assumption that there is only one move. Returning to Fig. 2.1, we can ask whether the same result would occur if the game were to be repeated many times. Firm A and Firm B both know that each producing 3 units would be a better outcome for both, and both know how much the other is producing. If there is only one move, the fear that the other firm will choose 6 units drives both to choose 6 units. If the output in the payoff matrix is, say, monthly output, then, assuming demand is constant, the decision has to be made every month. The best strategy to adopt in such cases is the *tit-for-tat strategy* (Axelrod, 1984). This states that a player should co-operate on the first move, and thereafter do whatever the other player did on the previous move. If both choose 3 units the first month, then both achieve higher profits than if they had both chosen 6 units. The next month Firm A might again choose 3 units but, hoping to make extra short-term profits, Firm B might choose 6 units. Firm A, if it adopts tit-for-tat, will, in the third month, choose 6 units. This will reduce B's third month profits, whether it chooses 3 or 6. Eventually, both will realize that their long-term profit interests are best served by producing 3 units continually. A dynamic approach, allowing for learning effects, brings about a different (Pareto-efficient) result from the static, one-move approach.

Where games involve a sequence of decisions (and not just one decision, simultaneously taken by both players) then they are usually represented by *game trees*, also known as the *extensive form*. The presentation of a game in a payoff matrix is known as the *normal*, or *strategic form*. In Fig. 2.4 we show the extensive form of the prisoner's dilemma game of Fig. 2.1. The ovals represent *decision nodes*. If they use the tit-for-tat strategy and start off by co-operating, then A chooses 3 and, at decision node B_{A_3}, B also chooses 3. In this case the outcome is Pareto efficient and they both end up with payoffs of 27. If B decides to choose 6 and receives a payoff of 33, leaving A with a payoff of −3, then in the next play A will choose 6. Ultimately, the losses from playing 6 will lead back to the choice of 3.

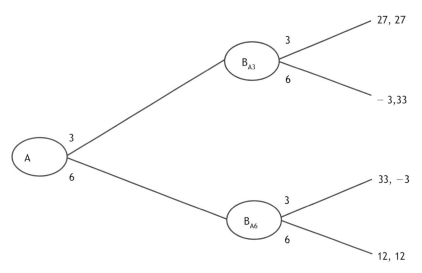

Figure 2.4 Extensive form of prisoner's dilemma

Where a firm's behaviour is based on its expectations of the behaviour of its rival(s), then the rules governing the way it makes its decisions together constitute its *reaction function* (see *reaction curve* in Chapter 6). Modelling the situation in which one firm learns another firm's reaction function, is an example of a game where the firms are not, as in previous examples, similar. Here, one firm has a clear advantage over the other(s); there is *asymmetric rivalry*. This example, developed by Heinrich von Stackelberg and known as the Stackelberg model, results in the firm with the information about the likely reactions of the other firm(s) becoming the leader; it takes the lead in setting output. The Stackelberg leader incorporates the reaction function of the followers into its maximization behaviour. The follower(s) take the leader's output as given, and responds accordingly. The result is a Stackelberg equilibrium.

The mathematical presentation of basic game theory is not difficult,[16] but as variations are introduced, so the models become more complex. The dynamic, multi-player games are beyond the appropriate confines of this book. In general, and as argued by Radner (1992), in particular in relation to the economics of management, 'game-theoretic treatments typically leave us with a serious multiplicity of equilibria, and hence with indeterminate predictions of behaviour'. Game theoretic models 'have helped us understand better the logical consequences of choices over some important strategy variables', according to Michael Porter, but, he continues, 'they fail to capture the simultaneous choices over many variables that characterize most industries' (Porter, 1991). Game theoretic models are best used metaphorically, rather than literally (as argued by Saloner, 1991); they are useful in the illustration, in particular, of the theory of oligopoly, and will be used to do so in Chapter 6. The optimal use of game theory is in many cases the simple, stylized representation of industrial economic (and other) problems.

Among the most quoted recent such uses of game theory, is that of Krugman (1987a). In this example, Krugman illustrates the incorporation of industrial economics into international trade theory. He shows that there is a possible role for strategic trade policy where 'government policy can tilt the terms of oligopolistic competition to shift excess returns from foreign to domestic firms'. He assumes two regions, Europe and America, in each of which there is one firm that can produce a 150-seat passenger aircraft, the market for which is such that if either of the firms produces it, that firm will make a profit, but if both produce it, both will make a loss. With Airbus and Boeing as the two firms, Fig. 2.5 is a possible payoff matrix (slightly different from that used by Krugman). There is no obvious equilibrium in this case. A maxi-min strategy will result in neither firm producing, (0, 0), but if one firm can provide a clear, early indication of a commitment to produce, then this may deter the other firm from entering. This is known as a *pre-emptive strategy* (see Mansfield, 1993, pp. 449–50). The point of strategic trade policy is that if Europe's government can commit itself to paying Airbus a subsidy of, say, 15, prior to any commitment by Boeing to produce, then this will create a different payoff matrix, shown in Fig. 2.6. In this altered situation, if both firms adopt the maxi-min strategy, the outcome will be (0, 115). A subsidy of 15 results in an increase in Airbus's profits from 0 to 115.

		Airbus	
		Produce	Not produce
Boeing	Produce	(−10, −10)	(100, 0)
	Not produce	(0, 100)	(0, 0)

Figure 2.5 Possible payoff matrix for Airbus and Boeing

		Airbus	
		Produce	Not produce
Boeing	Produce	(−10, 5)	(100, 0)
	Not produce	(0, 115)	(0, 0)

Figure 2.6 Pre-emptive strategy

The example raises many questions, and does not necessarily prove the efficacy of strategic trade policy, but it does show the power of game theory to illustrate an argument. Krugman, in fact, seems to insist that his example does no more than this when he states, first, that in reality the government of Europe could not know what the response of Boeing (or, for that matter, the government of America) would be to its subsidy; second, that there is uncertainty in relation to the response of any economic policy; and third, that there is even greater uncertainty in relation to the effect of policy on oligopolistic competition. Krugman would clearly agree with Radner. Economists, he writes, 'do not have reliable models of how oligopolists behave' (Krugman, 1987a).

Even the most recent work on game theory suggests limitations in its applications. As we pointed out earlier, Imai (2000) shows how game theory can be used to analyse how a public good might be developed and supplied. The setting up of the game is straightforward. The number of contributors before the public good (for example, Linux) will be supplied is, say, m. If the actual number, k, is less than m, then none of the contributors gets any return and the good is not supplied. If, on the other hand, $k \geqslant m$, then the public good is supplied and each of the contributors receives a return equivalent to the opportunity cost of the time contributed. Imai (2000) adapts an 'assurance game with weak links' and shows that 'these are useful constructs for understanding the essence of the problem'. However, he concludes that 'it is difficult to gain insights for further discussions solely from such numerical experiments'. More generally, Imai (2000) seems to praise game theoretic analyses for being innovative in what he calls 'micro-micro analyses of actual market competition'. However, the limitations pointed out by Radner (1992) still seem to hold, in that 'results depend on many delicate parameters of a game …' (Imai, 2000, fn 2). Imai (2000) suggests that game theory has not contributed to a better understanding of 'drastic and qualitative changes' in market structure. Like others, though, he has not given up on game theory and seems to think that it is possible that future developments of the game theoretic tools will contribute insights to some of the important issues in industrial economics.

2.2.4 Contestable market theory

Like game theory, the contestability school associated with the names Baumol, Panzar and Willig (1982) attempts to inject theory into IO. The notion of contestable markets is, in some respects, an example of (or an application of) the type of reasoning that is done in game theory. It is based on the argument that firms (call them Group A) will refrain from behaving in certain ways because of their expectation that behaving in those ways will bring about responses on the part of other firms (Group B) that are undesirable to Group A.

The originators of the theory, focusing on perfectly free entry and exit, claimed that it was a new 'unifying framework', and it did, to some extent, provide a bridge between the criticisms brought to the linear SCP paradigm by the anti-structuralists and the emerging views of the new wave of industrial economists. Baumol *et al.*, suggesting an alternative to the unrealistic notion of perfect competition, show that, under the condition of perfectly free entry, the threat of entry will drive prices down and guarantee efficiency, even in the limit case of one monopoly firm in the market. What is meant by perfectly free entry is that if a firm must purchase assets (for example, plant and equipment) in order to enter the industry, then, if the firm subsequently wishes to leave the industry, those assets can be resold with no loss on the transaction. Another way of expressing this is to say that there are zero sunk costs. Thus if there are zero *sunk costs*, firms in the industry will refrain from raising prices above what the price would be if the industry were perfectly competitive. This result is independent of the structure of the industry. *Economies of scale and scope*[17] may limit the number of firms in the industry, but if there is perfect contestability the price will still be set in the market to be equal to the average cost of production. Contestability theory thus incorporated both the interest in structure of the SCP paradigm and the notion of strategic behaviour in pricing – pricing in ways determined by expectations of the responses of competitors (or, in this case, potential competitors) – that is a fundamental element of game theory.

Martin (1993, pp. 297–325; 1994, p. 76), among others, is sceptical of the claims of the contestability theorists, and has pointed out, first, that other than the mathematical presentation, there is nothing new about the theory, and second that the theory has very limited application.[18] Nevertheless it has the merit of exploring the adjustment in the behaviour of firms to the threat represented by potential entrants into that market. An application to the airline industry, for example, while rejecting perfect contestability, identifies circumstances in which the threat of entry can have an impact on the performance of firms (Hurdle *et al.*, 1989).

The contestability theorists, in fact, used the airline industry as the prime example of a contestable market throughout the development of the theory during the early 1980s (see, for example, Bailey and Panzar, 1981; Baumol *et al.*, 1982; Baumol and Willig, 1986). At first they treated the airline industry as perfectly contestable, based on the fact that, if it was deregulated, then airline companies could simply fly planes into airports to compete with existing companies flying the routes from that airport. The capital assets, it was argued, are perfectly mobile. There are no sunk costs because a decision to leave a particular route simply means flying the plane out and into another route. Investments in aircraft, Baumol *et al.* (1982, p. 7) asserted, did not involve sunk costs because they constituted 'capital on wings'. By 1986, they had accepted that the airline industry was not perfectly contestable. In particular, Baumol and Willig (1986, p. 24) identified three departures from perfect contestability that became clear in the aftermath of deregulation in America: the heavy sunk costs in the construction of airports, shortages in the availability of aircraft arising from technological change, and the lower costs facing newcomers because of the absence of the labour contracts prevalent among established carriers.

The argument that the American airline industry was perfectly contestable was at least part of the justification for its deregulation in that country. As early as 1978, for example, a proposed merger of two airline companies was passed by the Civil Aeronautics Board (CAB), despite the fact that it involved an increase in concentration which in previous merger cases had been declared unlawful by the American Supreme Court. The CAB justified this on the grounds that the Airline Deregulation Act 1978 made possible the entry into the airline industry of even small carriers (this case is reported by Martin (1993, p. 320), quoting Bailey (1981, p. 181)). Contestability theory suggested that there may have been an increase in concentration, and therefore of the market power of the fewer, larger firms, but this would be offset by increased efficiency arising from the threat of entry of new competitors. In a careful study of the impact of mergers in the wake of deregulation, Kim and Singal (1993) show that while mergers between airlines resulted in both efficiency gains and increases in market power, 'on the whole, market power dominated efficiency gains, making the consumer worse off'. According to Martin (1993, pp. 324–5), despite the evidence, and the admission on the part of the contestability theorists themselves, that the theoretical basis for deregulation was unfounded, the contestability doctrine remains influential in Washington.

There is an echo of contestability theory in the attempts of the EU to define markets for the purposes of competition policy. As recently as 1988, for example, in the *Eurofix-Bauco v. Hilti* case, the notion of *supply substitution* began to be introduced (see Chapter 5, Section 5.4). Supply substitution refers to the potential provision of additional supplies on the part of both incumbent firms and potential entrants, and was introduced in an attempt to assist in determining the likely level of concentration in an industry following a merger. On the basis of the American evidence, this consideration of potential entrants may not be appropriate, unless there are very low barriers to entry.

This is not to say that the EU should not make efforts to keep barriers to entry low. Notteboom (2002) identifies a number of ways in which, in the European container handling industry, efforts could be made to keep barriers to entry and exit low. He quotes the European Commission (2001) as proposing that the managing bodies of ports, for example, should 'not discriminate between service providers'. Clearly, favouritism towards one cargo handler constitutes a barrier to entry for others.

Rather than determining a strategy on the basis of what market structures actually are (structuralists' view), the contestability school assumes that firms adjust their strategy to what market structures could become. Firms, in this view, follow a sort of pre-emptive, or entry-deterring strategy. The primary weakness of the theory lies in its extreme assumption of perfectly free entry and exit. Hurdle *et al.* (1989), for example, in their examination of the circumstances in which the pricing of firms is influenced by potential entrants, show that this influence is only significant where potential entrants are not deterred by economies of scale or scope. While this discussion is pitched in terms of contestability, its real focus is the relation between structure and conduct. As such, it can be argued to add little to what could have been done under the SCP paradigm. To the extent that it is not the threat of entry, but the actual entry of competitors that influences the prices set by incumbent firms, the discussion could as well be set in terms of a Bertrand, price-setting game.

While contestability has had theoretical interest, it seems not to have fulfilled its promise. What the theory has added to industrial economics is an intensification of interest in the effects of economies of both scale and scope. These are discussed in more detail in Chapter 5. Contestability continues to be of concern to policy makers and the courts, however, particularly in the context of increasing concentration, consolidation and globalization. Given this context, contestability encourages research on barriers to entry and exit in specific industries. Examples of such research include that of Notteboom (2002) on the European cargo handling industry and that of Ryan (2000), with application to public utilities. Ryan (2000) shows that regulation can itself influence contestability. He also adds an interesting distinction between industrial and market contestability, 'referring respectively to conditions of entry and exit for the marginal potential producer and the marginal potential supplier in a region'.

2.3 Summary

We have discussed in this chapter the origins and development of industrial economics in terms of broad theoretical approaches. The SCP paradigm, in its simple, linear-determinist form, was considered defective and has been revised by some and replaced by others. Nevertheless, in terms of interest in the three elements – structure, conduct and performance – the SCP paradigm continues to have an influence throughout the discipline, this book included. Indeed, aspects of each of the theories discussed will appear again in the following chapters, but none has influenced the overall shape of the book more than SCP.

Other theories, or other aspects of theories, introduced here, and finding a place in later chapters, include game theory, whose roots in Cournot and Bertrand will be shown in detail in Chapter 6 under the discussion on oligopoly, and neoclassical theory, whose models of market structure are discussed in Chapter 5.

The theories of the firm, to be discussed in Chapters 3 and 4, in many ways reflect a narrowing of focus of the broad theoretical approaches discussed in this chapter. Thus, for example, Schumpeterian perspectives on the nature of economic change become focused, in the evolutionary theory of the firm, on the important elements in the strategic behaviour of individual firms, in particular successful, innovative firms. The new institutional economists have already been shown to be interested in firms as well as markets, and the theories of the firm – transaction cost and principal–agent – emerging from this tradition are explained in Chapters 4 and 3 respectively. The oldest, neoclassical, theory, and a recent, co-operative game theory, are discussed Chapter 3.

Websites

On many aspects of industrial economics and organization, including most of those mentioned in this chapter, the IDEAS site at **http://ideas.repec.org/** is extremely useful. It provides access to many thousands of downloadable articles, working papers and so on. This site is part of Research Papers in Economics (**http://repec.org**) a 'large volunteer effort to enhance the free dissemination of research in economics'. As the IDEAS database is so large (for example, typing in 'structure conduct performance' will find 121 matches), it is necessary to use quite narrow search criteria, such as the names of specific authors, and/or to include some closely related concepts.

On game theory there are many web sources; we mention here just four. First, much of Roger A. McCain's recently published book *Game Theory: A Nontechnical Introduction to the Analysis of Strategy* (South-Western, Mason, OH, 2003) is publicly accessible at **http://william-king.www.drexel.edu/top/eco/game/game.html**

Second, introductory parts of Martin J. Osborne's slightly more technical book *An Introduction to Game Theory* (Oxford University Press, Oxford, 2003), are available online at **http://www.chass.utoronto.ca//~osborne/igt/**

Third, the online *Stanford Encyclopedia of Philosophy* (**http://plato.stanford.edu/**) provides an excellent, detailed introduction to game theory, including an extensive annotated bibliography and additional links to other websites.

Finally, there is also an entire website, maintained by Mike Shor of Vanderbilt University, at **www.gametheory.net**. There are many links from this site to other game theory websites, organized by level and discipline.

Questions

2.1   What were/are the Chicago and Harvard Schools and what are the differences between them?

2.2   Compare and contrast any two criticisms of the SCP paradigm.

2.3   Are there alternatives to SCP?

2.4   Why is there disagreement among industrial economists?

2.5   What is game theory? Why is it not a theory?

2.6   Use a game theoretic model to address the following question: should I look for a job after I graduate, or should I try to start my own business?

2.7   Explain why contestable market theory has been so vociferously criticized.

Notes

1   The neoclassical approaches are discussed in more detail in Chapter 3. Suffice to say here that what is referred to is the set of assumptions including rational individual behaviour, profit maximization by firms and the relative efficiency of markets, leading to an equilibrium market price and quantity. The methodology is deductive, involving assumptions that give rise to principles or hypotheses that may then be tested. The analysis is through differential calculus, leading to the use of the term 'marginalism' to describe neoclassical methods. At least some of the work in SCP has been inductive, involving the examination of data in order to draw out patterns or hypotheses.

2   Among the key assumptions of perfect competition are: a large number of firms, that consumers are each too small to affect equilibrium price or quantity; products are homogeneous; there is free entry and exit from the industry.

3   Not all would agree with this. Williamson (1985, p. 18), for example, clearly differentiates his own transaction cost perspective from neoclassical theory, on the basis, among others, that 'transaction cost economics ... regards the business firm as a governance structure rather than a production function'.

4   It is interesting to note a contrast between the view of Schumpeter as a radical with the view, as expressed in Auerbach (1989, p. 266), that his approach is 'paradoxically, congruent with the traditional practice in orthodox economics of pushing the question of technological change to one side'. Most economists consider one of Schumpeter's main contributions to be the argument that 'technological changes were the principal sources of economic growth' (e.g. Scherer, 1996).

5   First published in English in 1934.

6   He was briefly finance minister in the socialist cabinet of the Austrian Republic in 1919, but left due to the contrast between the conservative policies he wished to implement and the radical socialist agenda of his cabinet colleagues (Wood, 2002).

7   See, among those who pay attention to Marx and modern Marxian economists, Williamson (1985, pp. 231–38), Davies and Lyons (1988, pp. 16–19) and Auerbach (1989). Williamson, for example, devotes a chapter of his book (chapter 9) to an examination and critique of the Marxian notion that hierarchy is the organizational device by which bosses exploit workers.

8   In the context of this book, 'mainstream' and 'neoclassical' are synonymous.

9   The general equilibrium approach is more theoretically sound than the partial equilibrium approach introduced by neoclassical economists in the late nineteenth century. Partial equilibrium focuses on the interactions in a single market, assuming away the impacts that this market might have on others (as in the familiar supply and demand diagram). It is still widely used in applied economics, primarily because it is easier to model. In general equilibrium, impacts of different markets are incorporated.

10   First published in 1890.

11   The notion is addressed in more detail in Chapter 8.

12   Imai's (2000) work in particular provides an excellent link between SCP and game theory. He shows how a game theoretic approach might be used to show why software developers contributed (with no financial return) to the development of Linux.

13   Strategic behaviour is where a firm acts in ways influenced by its expectation of how its competitors will respond to its actions. One type of strategic pricing behaviour, for example, is where a firm deliberately keeps the prices of its products below the profit maximization level in order to prevent the entry of competitors into the market. On the economics of strategic behaviour, see the special issue of *Strategic Management Journal*, vol. 12, Winter 1991.

14   This paragraph draws on the explanation of Davies and Lyons (1988, p. 7). For a more complete description of game theory at a level equivalent to the present text, see Gardner (1995). See also suggested websites at the end of this chapter.

15   Note that the Fig. 2.1 example of a prisoner's dilemma game is also an equilibrium of dominant strategies because if Player B chooses 3 units, Player A will choose 6 units, and if Player B chooses 6 units, Player A will choose 6 units. Note, too, that an equilibrium in dominant strategies is also a Nash equilibrium, i.e. given the choices of its rivals the choice of each firm is such that no other choice would give it higher profits. However, the opposite is not true: not all Nash equilibrium situations are necessarily situations of equilibrium in dominant strategies.

16   See the appendix to this chapter. See also Chapter 6.

17 There are economies of scale when the average cost of producing the good declines the greater the number of units of the good produced; there are economies of scope when two or more goods, when produced together, cost less than when produced separately.

18 For further critical appraisal of the assumption of ultra-free entry, see Shepherd (1990, pp. 282–5). For the first large, international comparison of entry and exit of firms and market contestability, see Geroski and Schwalbach (1991).

In this appendix we provide an algebraic example of a game. The example anticipates much of the discussion in Chapter 6 on Cournot models; it is introduced at this stage to illustrate the point that, in addition to payoff matrices and game trees, algebra is also frequently used in both heuristic and analytical applications of game theory.

We are given the information that the market demand for the specialist blades for programmable wood-cutting machines that are used in the furniture industry is:

$$Q = 250 - \frac{1}{2} p \qquad (2.1)$$

where Q and p are, respectively, the quantity and the price.

We know that these machines are in most of the many furniture firms in the industry, but that there are only two manufacturers of the specialist blades. These two manufacturers have similar technologies. They both face unit costs of €50. They compete on the basis of quantity and the nature of the supply chain for their raw materials is such that they must make their decisions about how much to produce simultaneously. They both have the same information that we do.

We are asked to speculate on the outcome of the competition between these two firms, in terms of the equilibrium output and profit.

As explained in Chapter 3, firms maximize their profits where marginal revenue (MR) is equal to marginal cost (MC), where:

$$MR = \frac{dTR}{dQ}$$

that is, marginal revenue is the change in total revenue arising from a small-unit change in quantity, and

$$MC = \frac{dTC}{dQ}$$

that is, marginal cost is the change in total cost arising from a small-unit change in quantity.

To arrive at the quantity that will give each firm maximum profit, we must therefore solve for $MR = MC$. The easiest way to do this is using the *inverse demand function*. Here, we set the price as the dependent variable.

From Eq. (2.1), $2Q = 500 - p$, and, therefore,

$$p = 500 - 2Q \qquad (2.2)$$

Firm 1's total revenue, R_1, is the product of price and quantity. The total quantity, Q, is the sum of the quantity produced by Firm 1 and Firm 2, q_1 and q_2. Firm 1's total costs, C_1, are the product of the cost per unit and the number of units produced.

$$R_1 = q_1 \left[500 - 2(q_1 + q_2) \right] = 500q_1 - 2q_1^2 - 2q_1q_2$$

$$C_1 = 50q_1$$

Differentiating,

$$MR_1 = \frac{dR_1}{dq_1} = 500 - 4q_1 - 2q_2 \tag{2.3}$$

$$MC_1 = \frac{dC_1}{dq_1} = 50 \tag{2.4}$$

For Firm 1's profit maximization, Eq. (2.3) must equal Eq. (2.4):

$$500 - 4q_1 - 2q_2 = 50 \tag{2.5}$$

Solving for Firm 1's quantity, we get:

$$q_1 = 112.5 - \frac{q_2}{2} \tag{2.6}$$

This shows Firm 1's best choice of quantity to produce, q_1, for every q_2 chosen by Firm 2. It is Firm 1's reaction, or best response, function. This is the key strategic, game theoretic element of the argument, namely that Firm 1 is making a decision based on expectations about what the decision of Firm 2 might be.

By analogous reasoning, Firm 2 will arrive at:

$$q_2 = 112.5 - \frac{q_1}{2} \tag{2.7}$$

which is Firm 2's reaction, or best response, function.

With Eqs (2.6) and (2.7) we have two equations with two unknowns. We can, therefore, solve for q_1 and q_2. From (2.6),

$$2q_1 = 225 - q_2$$

Therefore,

$$q_2 = 225 - 2q_1 \tag{2.8}$$

Subtracting Eq. (2.7) from Eq. (2.8) we get:

$$0 = 112.5 - \frac{3}{2}q_1$$

$$q_1 = 75$$

And, therefore,

$$q_2 = 75$$

This is the Nash–Cournot equilibrium, the intersection point of the two firms' best response functions. The total quantity, Q, will be 150.

The profit that each firm makes is obtained from the difference between total revenue and total cost. From Eq. (2.2),

$$p = 500 - 300 = \text{\euro}200 \tag{2.9}$$

Firm 1's profit, π_1 is, therefore,

$$\pi_1 = R_1 - C_1 = 200 \times 75 - 50 \times 75$$

$$= 11,250$$

Each of the two firms will thus make profits of €11,250.

As will be shown in Chapter 6, if the firms co-operate they make higher profits than if they compete. However, because there is an incentive for each of the firms to cheat, co-operation would not give rise to a stable equilibrium. The market will therefore tend towards the competitive outcome shown here.

CHAPTER 3

The neoclassical theory of the firm

3.1 Learning objectives

The main objectives of this chapter are:

- To review the neoclassical theory of the firm, and its criticisms, with a specific focus on profit maximization

- To provide early neoclassical responses to these criticisms (by discussing the managerial theories as well as the principal–agent theory), and

- To consider some recent developments – such as the firm in the 'new economy' – and the inability of neoclassical thinking to explain innovation

3.2 A review of the neoclassical theory of the firm

Parallel with the developments in IO, the theory of the firm has evolved from representing the firm as a purely profit maximizing automaton or 'black box', operating in a spaceless and timeless environment (neoclassical theory). While to some extent this view continues to prevail in introductory courses in microeconomics, a number of other perspectives are widely held.[1] The firm is now seen either as a more complex organization where control and ownership are distinct, and/or as a nexus of different activities, composed of diverse constituents. The roles of transactions, of technologies and of contracts have all been focused upon, with varying degrees of intensity by the different schools of thought.

In several articles, Chandler (1992a, b) referred to four 'established theories involving the firm'. These he named as the *neoclassical, principal–agent, transactions cost* and *evolutionary theories*. In addition, particularly important in the context of the development of modern theories of the firm, there is the *managerial theory*. Finally, not 'established', but interesting as an example of the application of the new IO, is the *co-operative game theory* of the firm. After a brief review of the neoclassical theory of the firm, this chapter discusses the managerial and principal–agent theories, as two early responses to the neoclassical paradigm. Chapter 4 will deal with the other theories of the firm, such as the transaction cost and co-operative game theories.

3.2.1 Profit maximization as the objective of firms

The competitive equilibrium paradigm has been the dominant representation of the economic system since the writings of Adam Smith. According to this paradigm:

- On all markets, supply and demand are equated.
- This equilibrium is achieved by price adjustments.
- Individuals react primarily to price signals. The firm (or its owner-manager) takes the input prices as given.

With the work of economists such as Walras, Marshall and Jevons, this developed during the second half of the nineteenth century into what became known as the neoclassical theory. They introduced the concept of *marginal analysis* and the mathematics with which to execute this analysis. Among the first such presentations was that of Walras, who, in 1874, published a highly formalized version of the competitive equilibrium paradigm. Modern mathematical economists, for example Arrow and Debreu (1954), have built on this Walrasian vision.

Central to the neoclassical view of the firm is that the objective determining the behaviour of the firm is *maximization of profits*. Here we briefly discuss the meaning, limits and alternatives to the profit maximization objective.

According to the neoclassical vision, the firm is an abstraction, an idealized form of business,[2] whose existence is explained solely by the purely economic motive of generating a profit. Generally, profit is generated through satisfying wants by producing a good or a service on a given market and at a given price. The firm's legal or organizational characteristics are insignificant. The only objective guiding its operations is the desire to maximize profit (or minimize costs).

The neoclassical firm is thus a profit-maximizing (or cost-minimizing) entity operating in an exogenously given environment which lies beyond its control. It is described by a simple and static *production function* which shows the relationship between inputs and outputs. *Costs* can be derived from the production function, as long as the prices of the inputs on the input (or factor) markets are known. *Revenues* can be derived from the demand schedule. The demand schedule shows the number of units of the good that the consumers are willing to buy at each different price per unit; the price actually paid multiplied by the number of units bought is the firm's revenue. The quantity the firm will produce is the profit-maximizing level of output. Profit is the difference between total revenue and total cost (i.e. $\pi = \text{TR} - \text{TC}$). The firm will continue to increase output as long as the last (*marginal*) unit produced adds to total profit. If the revenue obtained from selling the last unit produced (*marginal revenue*) is greater than the cost of producing the last unit (marginal cost), then output will continue to be increased. When the last unit no longer adds to profit – when marginal revenue (MR) equals marginal cost (MC) – then profit is maximized. This can be written as:

$$\frac{\Delta\pi}{\Delta Q} = \frac{\Delta\text{TR}}{\Delta Q} - \frac{\Delta\text{TC}}{\Delta Q} = 0 \qquad (3.1)$$

where $\Delta\pi/\Delta Q$ denotes the change in profit resulting from a one-unit increase in output, and where $\Delta\text{TR}/\Delta Q$ and $\Delta\text{TC}/\Delta Q$ are marginal revenue (MR) and marginal cost (MC) respectively. When an additional unit of output produced no longer adds to profit (that is, when $\Delta\pi/\Delta Q = 0$), we can see that $\text{MR} - \text{MC} = 0$.

This formulaic approach to the behaviour of firms does not provide for much leeway in the decision-making process within the firm. As long as the assumptions hold – in terms, in particular, of the information that the firm is assumed to have – then, as a profit maximizer, it will behave in such a way as to set $\text{MR} = \text{MC}$.

3.2.2 Impediments to profit maximization[3]

Since the early 1930s, research both within and critical of neoclassical theory has cast doubts on the profit maximization principle. We discuss in this section objections to the profit maximization principle under three main headings: that $\text{MR} = \text{MC}$ is not a conscious goal of decision makers in firms; that information, particularly about the future, is imperfect and this undermines a basic assumption of the theory; and that the organizational complexity of firms may impede the application of the profit maximization principle. The discussions under these headings are not mutually exclusive. For example, the lack of, or distortion in the transmission of, information is an aspect of the objections to profit maximization under both other headings, as well as constituting an objection in itself.

Decision makers do not aim for $MR = MC$

One of the first challenges to the neoclassical theory of the firm as a profit-maximizing centre was presented by Hall and Hitch (1939).[4] In their famous article, which rests to a large extent on earlier research, in particular on Chamberlin (1933) and Robinson (1933), the authors criticize the 'obscurity' surrounding the precise content of the terms 'marginal and average revenue', and raise questions about the nature of the demand curve assumed to be facing the firm. Their major criticism, however, focuses on that tenet of neoclassical theory according to which entrepreneurial behaviour will result in the equating of marginal cost with marginal revenue. Hall and Hitch's objection to this principle stems from the results of a questionnaire submitted to a small sample of manufacturing firms on how they decide the price to charge and the output to produce. The most striking finding of their research is that the firms interviewed appeared not to aim at profit maximization by equating MC and MR; instead, they applied what Hall and Hitch called a 'full-cost' principle. According to the results of their survey, this is normally computed as follows: a 'direct' cost per unit is taken as a base; this is augmented with overheads (or 'indirect' costs), as well as with a conventional addition for profit (generally 10 per cent). This 'full-cost' principle enables the firm to charge the 'right' price, or the price that 'ought' to be charged, according to the interviewees (Hall and Hitch, 1939, p. 19). If maximum profits were reached as a result of the application of this 'full-cost' principle, it was only 'accidental'.

There are a number of orthodox defences against this objection to the MR = MC principle. First, the conventional allowance for profit may itself be variable. Thus, as demand shifts downwards, lower profits will be accepted and price will be reduced. While not behaving precisely in accordance with profit maximization, the direction of response will be the same. Second, profit maximization may be accidental in the absence of perfect knowledge and data, but those decision makers with the best intuitive understanding, or who make the best guesses – that is, the managers of the successful firms in an industry – will get closest to MR = MC. Those that do not get near this level of profits will probably leave the industry. Even if the neoclassical profit maximization principle is not something that is consciously acted upon by decision makers in firms, the defence of orthodoxy suggests that it is still *ex ante* the best way of explaining the behaviour of surviving firms. (For a similar argument in defence of orthodoxy, see, for example, Machlup, 1946.)

More recent empirical research has, however, further substantiated the argument that firms do not profit- or value-maximize. 'The most marked examples entailed firm behavior with respect to taxes and takeovers' (Stiglitz, 1991). Many firms, 'perhaps most', do not minimize tax payments, and 'many studies have found that firms undertaking hostile takeovers experience no increase in share value' (Stiglitz, 1991).[5] Moreover, among such firms are major, long-surviving firms in key industries. This suggests that, even *ex ante*, profit maximization does not seem to be the best way of explaining at least some important aspects of firms' behaviour.

Information is imperfect

In the neoclassical paradigm, profit maximization is performed in the light of perfectly known cost and demand conditions. Imperfect information, and thus uncertainty, are irrelevant in this theory since markets are characterized by transparency, and since the equilibrium reached by the firm is the result of the interactions between variables defined in the present period of time. The firm operates in a timeless environment; the future is ignored.

When time is incorporated into the analysis of the firm, uncertainty as to the outcome of a given strategy arises. Decision makers cannot know precisely how interest rates and exchange rates will evolve in the next period, whether or to what extent demand will change, or how stable prices of raw materials will be. However, firms can improve on the static notion of profit maximization (and can reduce uncertainty) by systematically looking at the determinants of future streams of profits. Statistical and computer techniques in business and finance have become more sophisticated, particularly in relation to comparisons between different projects. As such techniques have improved, so they have been increasingly utilized in large companies, though there are still arguments in favour of 'satisficing and rule-of-thumb strategies'.[6] The following example illustrates how the common technique of net present value (NPV) may be applied in an attempt to estimate profit beyond the present. Long-run profit maximization implies maximizing the discounted present value (*pv*) of the firm's future stream of profits:

$$PV = \sum_{i=0}^{n} \frac{\Pi_i}{(1 + r)^i} \tag{3.2}$$

where:

n = time horizon (the highest value of i)
i = number of interest compounding periods (for example, number of years, from year 0 to year n)
r = discount rate (in the long run)
$\Pi_i = R_i - C_i$ = profit in the ith year
R_i = revenue
C_i = costs.

In the future, revenue and costs may depend, among other things, on the following:

◆ *The actions of competitors.* They may, for example, introduce substitute products that reduce the demand for the firm's product.

◆ *Changes in technology.* Costs may be reduced by an improvement in technology, and/or increased by the need to introduce new machinery to achieve higher quality.

◆ *Changes in consumer tastes.* Fashion may shift away from the firm's product, reducing demand.

◆ *Changes in the markets for inputs.* Most typically, wage costs may rise.

◆ *Government policies.* A change in monetary policy, for example, could change interest rates, and, consequently, the appropriate discount rate at which to calculate NPV.

Each possible project or strategy must be assessed on the basis of such combinations of future occurrences. The profits from each may have different NPVs because of different time horizons and discount rates, as well as different costs and revenues. To complicate matters further, the forecasts as to the future values of any of these variables may be made with different degrees of uncertainty. There are thus different possible combinations of factors influencing profit, and any particular choice of action or strategy may have different possible outcomes, with different degrees of likelihood.

Assume, for example, that a firm has three possible strategies, A, B and C. The best possible profit level of any of them is considered to be €100,000. Strategy A is assessed as having a 30 per cent chance, Strategy B a 20 per cent chance and Strategy C a 15 per cent chance of achieving this top profit level. Such assessment, though often subjective and imprecise, may actually be a factor in a firm's decision making and, with no other information, this firm will probably choose Strategy A. However, it is not just the probability of a high profit that determines the firm's choice of strategy. The probability distribution (and in particular its variance) may also be important. Thus, Strategy A, as well as having a 30 per cent chance of high profits, may also have a 30 per cent chance of bankrupting the firm, and a 40 per cent chance of average profit. This is shown, together with the probabilities of different outcomes of Strategies B and C, in Table 3.1.

Table 3.1 Probability distributions of different profit levels for Strategies A, B and C			
Outcome	High profit	Average profit	Bankruptcy
Strategy A	0.3	0.4	0.3
Strategy B	0.2	0.6	0.2
Strategy C	0.15	0.7	0.15

While, on the basis of the high profit column alone, Strategy A is the best choice, when the average profit and bankruptcy probabilities are also known, there is no longer an obvious best choice of strategy. It depends on the attitudes of the firm's decision makers. Risk-averse decision makers are more likely to go for Strategy C, while those more willing to take risks would choose Strategy A or B.

Attitudes to risk are variable, and may, like the length of time horizon, differ from firm to firm, from industry to industry, country to country, and period to period. In the UK during the 1980s, for example, many firms responded to the increase in competitive pressures by cutting research and development (R&D) expenditures. These firms have either gone out of business or found alternative sources of new technology in the 1990s. For some of these firms, the reduction in R&D may have been necessary to safeguard short-term profit levels, but it jeopardized their long-term survival. In another example combining risk aversion, time horizon and R&D, Abegglen and Stalk (1985) compare the firms in the Japanese and American semiconductor industries during the 1980s. Debt-financed Japanese firms, they argue, in comparison with their American counterparts, would have had closer relations with their bankers, taken more financial risks by borrowing more, distributed lower proportions and reinvested higher proportions of profits, and spent more on R&D and market development. As a result of these strategies, the Japanese semiconductor industry and other sectors such as machinery and transport equipment were able to establish themselves on international markets, and their firms grew faster than their American counterparts, at least up until the early 1990s (Lawrence and Weinstein, 1999). It should be noted that the 1985 Plaza Accord (leading to a substantial appreciation of the Japanese yen against the American dollar) and the ensuing burst of the financial bubble in Japan have tended to jeopardize these trends during the 1990s. As documented by Guelle (2001) employment in the Japanese electronics industry in Japan reached a peak in 1991. The decrease in general manufacturing employment in Japan (a phenomenon known as *kudoka*), coupled with a loss of competitiveness of Japanese industry and with an accumulation of bad debts in the Japanese financial sector, have somewhat changed the Japanese attitude to risk.

However, in spite of the changes in both the American and Japanese economies since the early 1980s, that differences did exist during the period corresponding to the surge of the Japanese economy is substantiated by a well-known survey of Japanese and American managers. The survey showed, among other things, that while American managers ranked return on investment as their primary goal, Japanese managers ranked improving products and introducing new products as theirs; the American managers ranked higher stock prices as second out of eight goals, the Japanese ranked it eighth (Scherer and Ross, 1990, p. 40). These differences reflect the managers' different time horizons. The introduction of new products, for example, may reduce current profits, but the aim is to have a positive impact on future profits. The Japanese have taken more financial risks but, with their longer time horizon, have reduced competitive risks by investing in the future of their companies (Abegglen and Stalk, 1985, p. 14). Among the traditional reasons for the longer time horizon of the Japanese are: lower cost of capital arising from a higher Japanese propensity to save;[7] close relations between firms and banks, and between buyers and suppliers; and culture.

A similar contrast to that between American and Japanese business behaviour could be drawn between British and German business behaviour. The British financial system is, like that of the United States, based more on capital market funding than on bank credit, and Germany, like Japan, is more credit-based than capital-market-based. As a result, the problem of 'diverse shareholders who take little interest in the development of the firm, except for the short term prices of their shares' (Christensen, 1992, p. 161), is likely to be more prevalent in the UK (and the United States) than in Germany (or Japan). The financial system is just one factor in the differences between the time horizons of firms and countries. Whatever the reason, it is clear that firms – even in the same industry – can and do attach different values to n in Eq. (3.1).

The choice of r (discount rate) is also important. The higher r, the lower the NPV. The higher n, the less certainty there can be about r. Arguably, firms will tend to choose as a discount rate the rates of interest they would have to pay on borrowed money, or the rates of interest they could obtain from a bank if they deposited the money instead of investing in projects (the *opportunity cost* of the investment). The greater the discount rate, the greater the opportunity cost of the investment and, in particular, the greater the opportunity cost of forgoing current income for the sake of some future return on the investment. Where interest rates are high, therefore, the immediate future will be more important to firms, and where they are low, the projection of calculations will be further into the future. If, as suggested above, there is a higher propensity to save in Japan and, therefore, lower rates of interest, time horizons will indeed be longer in Japan than in economies with higher rates of interest.

The differences between firms, industries or countries may not prevent – and may indeed encourage – attempts by firms to obtain more accurate and complete information. An important factor here is the cost of and expected returns from information. Arguably, if particular information is seen as potentially contributing to the profitability of the firms in an industry, the market for that information will be competitive. The more competitive this market is, the lower the net return from purchasing the information. The information *market structure*, like that of all other inputs into the production process, will be a factor in determining the value of information to the buyer.

This discussion may lead to the conclusion that attempts to increase the sophistication of analysis are misplaced. After all, no matter how sophisticated or precise the formulae, the information will be inaccurate. However, the increase in the sophistication of means of assessing potential profitability may itself have an impact on competition between firms, even if rules of thumb are as good as mathematically complicated formulae in terms of their accuracy in forecasting profit. One channel through which this influence on competition may occur is through business schools, where ability to handle mathematics and statistics has become increasingly important. The analytically inclined graduates of these schools may in general be better suited to the demands of managerial decision making in large firms (Auerbach, 1989, p. 112). On the basis of this argument, even without actually applying the techniques, the people who have successfully mastered them make better managers. The future may not be 'knowable' and profit maximization may therefore be impossible, but the development of techniques can, in this way, contribute to the success of large, complex firms.

Firms are organizationally complex

The complex structure and size of organizations form the basis of another objection to the focus on modern corporations as profit-maximizing entities. The production of most goods and services takes place in business organizations that are multi-plant operations structured into multiple divisions, such as the research and development, production, advertising, sales, and accounting/finance departments. As firms become larger, activities become increasingly separated, and so it becomes more difficult to ensure that information is communicated rapidly and accurately between them. Decisions that might be consistent with profit maximization are more difficult to enforce. Bureaucracy may set in. In addition, the separation of activities may breed diverse and conflicting objectives. There are at least two broad reasons for these conflicts of interest. The first is technological, the second cultural or psychological.

The *technological* reason arises from differences in the number of products that the various parts of the firm produce efficiently. Let us take, for example, a large software firm which also produces its own software manuals. The technology of software manual printing may require that in any one print run, 10,000 manuals have to be printed if the average cost of printing manuals is to be minimized. The distribution department may require no more than 1000 manuals in any one delivery from the printing department. There are techniques available to the firm to help decision makers to decide how to solve this problem, such as including storage costs for manuals in the costs of production. However, there is a conflict of interest that arises from the nature of the technology in printing, a conflict that requires resolution.

The *cultural/psychological* reason arises from the established customs and practices of different disciplines' training, education and experience.[8] For example, in a given pharmaceutical company, the scientists of the research division may be convinced that they are about to make a breakthrough in relation to a new medicine they are developing. The accounting department may have already extended all the finances allocated for that particular project. The research division requests that additional finance be made available, and the accounting division refuses. The scientists in the research division optimistically perceive the possibility of a breakthrough; the accountants perceive their role as cost-containment and the confining of expenditure to that which was planned.

Where there are such conflicts, efforts may be made to resolve them by passing decision making up the line to more senior management. But senior management may get messages distorted by the interests of the parties in conflict. Each will want management to be convinced of the immutability of its position, and will attempt to present it in such a way as to achieve that end. In addition, management itself may be more closely associated with one side than another. Managers with an accounting background may lean towards cost-constraining decisions, while those from an engineering, production or scientific background may prefer process- or product-improving decisions.

There is a partial counter-argument to that which posits increasing organizational complexity as an impediment to profit maximization. Increasing complexity leads to an awareness of the need for more precise cost accounting. Auerbach (1989, p. 109) writes that 'interest in the problems of costing increased with the growing scale and complexity of business, the ever greater importance of overheads in total costs, and the need for a method for setting prices in heavy goods sectors such as engineering'. This is related to the discussion above of the impact of improved techniques on the training of managers. Both developments – in costing and in techniques for assisting in decision making – may improve information, but information remains imperfect.

Another partial counter-argument is that if we consider the value of the firm to be the NPV of the differences between all its future revenues and all its future costs then this can be used to assess the impact of decisions in different functional areas. In the example of the software firm, a decision as to whether to improve the efficiency of manual printing by buying in larger machines, would be analysed for its impact on the value of the firm as a whole. While the printing department may reduce its printing costs, the distribution department would increase its storage costs.

Thus, various decisions in different departments of the firm can be appraised in terms of their effects on the value of the firm as expressed in the NPV equation (Eq. 3.2). Therefore, the value maximization model is useful in describing the integrated nature of managerial decision making across the functional areas of business (Hirschey and Pappas, 1993, p. 2).

While it is true that growth in size and complexity of firms drives them to find better ways of measuring their costs and of assessing and integrating the different functional decisions, this does not obviate the possibility of intra-firm conflict of interests (due in particular to the divorce between ownership and control, which is discussed in Section 3.3, below). As long as these exist, there will be incentives for misinformation to be generated.

Differences within firms, and between firms, industries and societies, thus all raise difficulties for the profit maximization theory: those within firms because they engender separate interests from those of the firm; those between firms because they suggest that there might be different types of profit-maximizing behaviour.

The decision about the appropriateness of assuming profit maximization to be the objective of firms is inconclusive. Under each of the three headings, arguments both for and against have been put. For example, under the first heading, it was argued that firms may not consciously aim for MR = MC. However, some evidence suggests that *ex ante* those firms that succeed/survive may be those that have actually achieved this result. Other evidence suggests that, even *ex ante*, some aspects of the behaviour of long-surviving, successful firms are not profit maximizing. Generally, neoclassical theory continues to assume profit maximization as the objective of firms whereas other theories focus either on other objectives or on factors other than the goals or objectives of firms in their long-term survival and success. However, there are neoclassical elements in other theories of the firm, and many economists working on the nature and behaviour of firms use more than one approach to enhance their attempts to understand and explain firms. We now turn to some of these alternative theories.

3.3 Neoclassical responses

Among teachers of management theory, the dissatisfaction in the 1930s with the simple conception of a firm as a mechanism which transforms atomistic inputs into marketable outputs resulted in alternative perspectives. A legal–economic view of the firm emerged, aimed at revealing key aspects of the internal structure of the corporate firm. One development of this view formed the basis of the managerial theory of the firm (Section 3.3.1). Other developments will be introduced in the following section (3.3.2), with a focus on the principal–agent theory.

3.3.1 Managerial theory

Throwing some light into the neoclassical black box, the managerial theory emphasized the complex nature of the modern corporate firm. In their pioneering work, Berle and Means

(1932) described the diminishing influence of shareholders in the decision-making process of large corporations in the United States from the turn of the century. This left much of the decision making to the manager, whose objectives, it was suggested, could be different from those of the owners of the firm. If, in terms of its influence on managers' salaries, size of firm, for example, was more important than a firm's profitability, then growth could be a more important objective of firms than profit.

Reasons why hired managers may be more preoccupied by sales or revenue maximization than by profit maximization include, according to Baumol (1967), the following:

◆ If sales fail to rise, this is often equated with reduced market share and market power, and consequently, with increased vulnerability to the actions of competitors.

◆ When asked about the way his or her company performs, an executive would typically reply in terms of what the firm's level of sales are.

◆ The financial market and retail distributors are more responsive to a firm with rising sales.

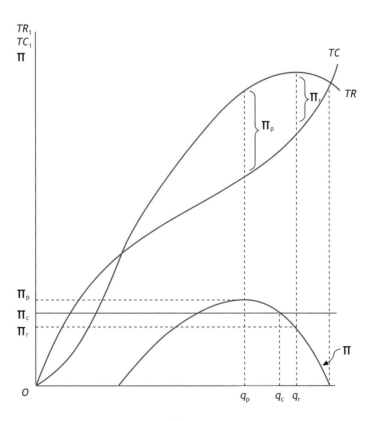

Figure 3.1 Revenue maximization: q_p, profit-maximizing output; q_r, revenue-maximizing output; q_c, revenue-maximizing output, subject to a minimum profit constraint, π_c

The model developed by Baumol attempts to reconcile the behavioural conflict between profit maximization and the maximization of the firm's sales (i.e. its total revenue). It assumes that the firm maximizes sales revenue subject to a minimum profit constraint. Figure 3.1 depicts the firm's total sales revenue (TR), total cost (TC) and total profits (π). The quantity q_p represents the output produced by a profit-maximizing firm, and q_r the output produced by a revenue-maximizing firm.

The revenue-maximizing level of output is the level at which the marginal revenue is zero (and the elasticity of demand is unity).[9] The output q_c is that which is produced by the revenue-maximizing firm *when constrained by a minimum profit* π_c. The difference between the maximum possible level of profit and minimum constrained profit (that is, between π_p and π_c) is called 'sacrificeable' by Baumol. In his view, these profits will be voluntarily given up by the firm in order to increase sales revenues. If the sacrificed profits are too apparent, they would tend to attract other firms acting in the same market, and would tend to create the ultimate threat of takeovers. This is why the sacrifice 'will be done quietly and only in ways which don't look like sacrificing' (Shepherd, 1990, p. 251). In any event, the profit-

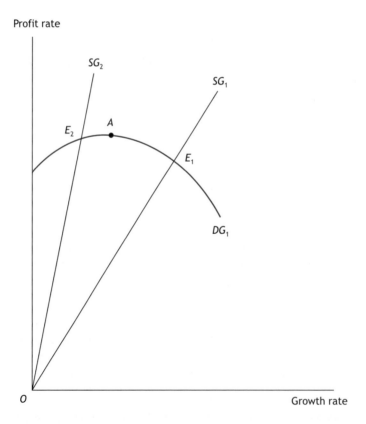

Figure 3.2 Growth maximization

maximizing output will generally be less than the revenue-maximizing output. The profit-constrained revenue-maximizing output may be greater than or less than the revenue maximizing output. If $q_c < q_r$, then the firm will produce q_c. If $q_c > q_r$, then the firm will produce q_r. Baumol argues that the unconstrained equilibrium position never occurs in practice.

The managerial theory of the firm was further developed by a number of writers, and in particular by Marris (1963, 1966), whose 1966 formulation has become 'the standard one for analysis of [the growth of] the managerially controlled firm' (Hay and Morris, 1991, p. 328). In this model, Marris formalized the hypothesis that managerial control would lead to growth as an objective, showing that shareholders were a less important constraint on such firms than financial markets. Marris's model is dynamic in the sense that it incorporates growth. Like Baumol's model, it assumes that managers will act to maximize their utilities rather than profits, but in contrast to Baumol, it assumes that this will be achieved through growth rather than sales (Fig. 3.2).

At its simplest, the model has two curves, one of supply growth (SG_1), and one of demand growth (DG_1). The axes are profit rate and growth rate, with growth arising through diversification into new products, rather than expansion of output. The supply growth is the maximum growth of supply that can be generated from each profit rate, given management's attitudes to growth and job security. Supply growth is directly and constantly related to profit, because a higher profit facilitates both more investment from retained earnings, and more funds to be raised in the capital market. Unlike in relation to demand growth, the positive relationship between supply growth and profit is possible at both low and high levels of profit (and growth).

The demand-growth curve DG_1 shows the maximum profit rate consistent with each growth of demand. With demand growth, growth is seen as determining profits, rather than – as in supply growth – profit determining growth. Growth, which is diversification into new products, leads to an increase in profit at low levels of growth because the first new products that the firm introduces will be the most profitable. As more and more new products are introduced (that is, as the growth rate increases) so more has to be spent on R&D for the next lot of products and on advertising for the sale of the current new products. In addition, other costs will increase as a result of the need for more complex management of increasing numbers of products. So, at some point (A in Fig. 3.2), further growth will lead to a decline in the rate of profit.

In the Marris model, where the supply-growth and demand-growth relationships are satisfied, there will be a unique state of growth and profit equilibrium. The rate of growth of demand will match the rate at which investment in the firm provides the volume and range of products required to meet this demand. This occurs at the point of intersection between the two curves, at point E_1 in Fig. 3.2. Rather than at point A, where the profit rate would be maximized, management chooses to situate the firm at point E_1, where, under certain constraints, the growth rate is maximized.

To elaborate on the nature of these constraints, the model introduces the possibility of alternative supply-growth curves. Assume, for example, that rather than the rate of retention inherent in SG_1, management had chosen to retain a much lower proportion of profits for reinvestment. This would lead to a much steeper supply-growth curve, say SG_2. Along SG_2 each profit rate will result in a much lower level of growth than was the case along SG_1, and the equilibrium will be at E_2, at a lower growth rate than E_1.

In this model, what determines which retention rate is actually chosen? Management would prefer to be at point E_1, shareholders would prefer the firm to be at point A (though in the short term they presumably would not mind a high proportion of profits being redistributed in dividends). Ultimately, managers' desire to keep their jobs, interacting with the financial markets, will determine where the equilibrium will be situated. If managers pursue growth in such a way as to borrow too much, fail to maintain appropriate levels of liquidity and/or retain too high a proportion of profits, then shareholders will begin to sell shares, share prices will decline and the company will become subject to takeover. Alternatively, the company will become bankrupt. Either way the managers are likely to lose their jobs. So the relative weights of job security and desire for growth in the utility of management on the one hand, and the sensitivity of the financial market to the company's performance on the other hand, will determine the position of the supply-growth curve and, by implication, the equilibrium point. For example, the more expansionist the management, and the less sensitive the markets, the further to the right, beyond point A, will be the equilibrium.

There are other managerial theories of the firm and, as will be shown in Section 3.3.2, more recent theoretical developments arising from some of the basic principles of managerial theory. The three major principles around which general managerial theory came to be articulated during the 1960s are as follows:

- In a firm, the ownership (by shareholders) is distinct from control (exercised by managers).

- Because of this separation, it is possible to conceive of a divergence of interests between owners and controlling managers.

- Firms operate in an environment that affords them an area of discretion in their behaviour. Attempts to verify empirically the difference in motivation between owner-controlled (OC) and management-controlled (MC) firms have been inconclusive, primarily because of the variety of exogenous (outside-the-firm) factors facilitating the growth of the firm. Comparing two groups of firms (OCs and MCs) in order to identify the differences in motivation is possible only if these exogenous factors (such as growth-of-demand and growth-of-supply conditions) are identical (Hay and Morris, 1991, pp. 356–62).

Douma and Schreuder (1992, p. 80) suggest that the inconclusive results of empirical attempts to verify the difference in profitability between OC and MC firms may be because there are in fact no such differences. There are three mechanisms, they explain, that may act to prevent managers from enriching themselves at the expense of the shareholders: the market for corporate control, the market for managerial labour and the market for the company's products.

Market for corporate control

Where there is a market for corporate control, a decline in the performance of a management team can result in its displacement by another management team. For example, if the company is quoted on the stock market, incompetence or other underperformance on the part of the managers will result in a decline in the company's share price. If this decline is perceived to have resulted from poor management, and therefore rectifiable by its replacement, the shares can be subject to purchase by individuals or institutions aiming to gain control of the firm. Having gained such control, they can then replace the management. Alternatively, existing shareholders, to prevent takeover, may themselves replace the management. The point is that where, as in this example, there is a market for corporate control, there is pressure on top managers who wish to hold their jobs, to keep the firm's performance near to what is perceived to be its potential by the market.

Market for managerial labour

The market for managerial labour is one in which shareholders are the buyers, and managers the sellers of their managerial expertise. The better this market works, the less likely is a top manager to enrich him or herself at the expense of shareholders. To do so – and be caught – would damage the manager's reputation, and prevent him or her from getting a better job elsewhere. If there are few top managerial jobs in comparison to the number of people seeking these jobs, arguably these people will attempt to get the best-paying, most prestigious of these jobs. Their desire for higher income will be expressed in their attempts to manage the firm as best they can, in the shareholders' interests.

Market for the company's products

Even if there is no market for corporate control, a competitive market for the company's products can ensure that managers act in the interests of the owners. Self-enrichment on the part of the manager will increase the company's costs, it will have to charge higher prices or reduce the quality of its products and this will result in a loss of market share. At the extreme, the company will be forced out of business, and the manager will lose his job. In this way a competitive product market can generate disincentives to inefficient management. It is possible that all three of these mechanisms either do not operate, or do not operate efficiently in a particular industry. Even in their absence, there are ways of ensuring that the interests of managers (agents) are brought into line with those of the owners (principals) of a firm. We discuss this issue in Section 3.3.2.

3.3.2 Principal-agent theory[10]

At its simplest, principal–agent theory examines situations in which there are two main actors: a principal who is usually the owner of an asset, and the agent who makes decisions which affect the value of that asset, on behalf of the principal. As applied to the firm, the theory often identifies the owner of the firm as principal, and the manager as agent, but the principal could also be a manager, and an employee nominated by the manager to represent him in some aspect of the business could be the agent. In this case the asset, which the agent's decisions could enhance or diminish, is the manager's reputation.

To explain the relationship between principal–agent (or agency) theory, and other theories of the firm, we turn to Williamson's (1985, pp. 23–9) categorization of approaches in terms of their views on contracts. There are two main such approaches or branches: monopoly, which views contracts as a means of obtaining or increasing monopoly power; and efficiency, which views contracts as a means of economizing. The early work on SCP and particularly on barriers to entry, for example, belongs on the monopoly branch of contracts. Both transaction cost and principal–agent theories belong on the efficiency branch (together with most of what Williamson calls 'the new institutional economics'). Thus, in Williamson's perspective, agency theory is the theory that focuses on the design and improvement of contracts between principals and agents.

Among the major concerns of principal–agent theory is the relationship between ownership and control, and in this respect it can be seen to have emerged from the managerial theory tradition. Early important articles on principal–agent theory include Mirrlees (1976), Fama (1980) and Fama and Jensen (1983). Later work in this area tended to become highly theoretical.[11] More recent contributions include the article by Bolton and Scharfstein (1998), who apply this argument to the case of a vertical integration, and of Cantillo Simon (1998) for the US banking industry at the turn of the twentieth century. In that it focuses on the contractual aspects of that relationship, and often adopts game-theoretic methods, principal–agent theory can be seen as a new IO version of a subset of managerial theory.

Principal–agent theory sees the firm – as does neoclassical theory – as a legal entity with a production function, contracting with outsiders (including suppliers and customers) and insiders (including owners and managers). There is information asymmetry between principals and agents but, unlike in transaction cost theory (which usually assumes *bounded rationality*), there is often assumed to be *unbounded rationality*. We discuss this in more detail below; in the context of the design of contracts between principals and agents, unbounded rationality refers to the ability of those designing the contract to take all possible, relevant, future events into consideration. The principal may know various things not known to the agent (in relation, for example, to the prospects of the firm), and vice versa (the agent may have a lower commitment to the firm than he leads the principal to believe), but if the obligations of both under the contract can be specified, taking into consideration the possibilities arising from private information, then there is unbounded rationality despite the information asymmetry.

The agency theorists' concerns – and in this they are different from neoclassical theorists – are with 'owners' and managers' problems of coping with asymmetric information, measurement of performance, and incentives' (Chandler, 1992b). The major difference between principal–agent and transaction cost theories is that the former focuses on the contract, the latter on the transaction. The problem for principal–agent theory is how to formulate a contract such that the *shareholders* (the *principal*) will have their interests advanced by the *manager* (the *agent*), despite the fact that the manager's interests may diverge from those of the shareholders. Or, to express it in terms closer to those of the theorists in this area, the problem is 'whether there exists any class of reward schedule for the agent (the manager) such as to yield a Pareto efficient solution for any pair of utility functions both for the agent and the principal' (Aoki, 1984, p. 49).

Where objectives of the agent are different from those of the principal, and the principal cannot easily tell to what extent the agent is acting self-interestedly in ways diverging from the principal's interests, then the problem of *moral hazard* arises. The problem originated in the insurance industry, referring to the possibility that people with insurance will change their behaviour, resulting in larger claims on the insurance company than would have been made if they had continued to behave as they did before they had insurance. This change in behaviour may, moreover, be known to the insurer, but may not be fraudulent. In the context of relations between principals and agents, moral hazard refers to the possibility that, once there is a contract, the agent may behave differently from how they would have behaved had they not had the contract. It must, in addition, be difficult to determine whether this behaviour has conformed to the terms of the contract.[12] This arises particularly where the agent is a member of a team.

Principal–agent theorists have attempted, by specifying conditions such as that the manager's salary be equal to the expected value of his or her marginal product, to design contracts on the basis of which there will be an incentive for the manager to act in the shareholders' interests. However, the importance of the *team element* in managerial jobs discredits the notion of a manager's marginal product (Aoki, 1984, ch. 2 and p. 50). This team element (raised by Alchian and Demsetz, 1972) is also present at the production level. Doeringer and Piore (1971, p. 27; quoted in Aoki, 1984, p. 26) emphasized the importance of 'social cohesion and group pressure' in the establishment of work customs. The process whereby such routines are created, and their importance in the success or otherwise of firms, are central concerns of the evolutionary theory of the firm (Section 4.6 in Chapter 4). Principal–agent theory is more concerned with implications for *shirking*, that is, a reduction in effort by an agent who is part of a team. There may be a slight decline in total output as a result, but the cause will usually be unidentifiable. The shirking manager knows that his or her diminished effort is unobservable. Shirking is the moral hazard arising from the employment contract. What the principal can do, in the formulation of contracts, to offset shirking (and other types of management misbehaviour), is a key problem of principal–agent theory.

There are a number of ways of controlling moral hazard. Rather than attempting to calculate the value of each manager's marginal product, managers could each be paid a salary plus a bonus based on the performance of the company. The problem here is that if the utility of leisure is different for different managers, then again some may work more and others less at maximizing the long-run value of the firm. (On the other hand, where there is a great deal of cultural homogeneity, as can be argued to be the case in Japan, this salary plus bonus system seems to be effective.) Other examples of suggestions by principal–agent theorists for solving employment contract problems include the development of efficient ways of *monitoring* the performance of individual managers (or management teams), providing *incentive contracts* which reward agents only on the basis of results, bonding (where the agent makes a promise to pay the principal a sum of money if inappropriate behaviour by the agent is detected) and mandatory retirement payments. This last acts like a bond in that there is a disincentive for the employee to misbehave for fear of being fired, with the resultant loss of retirement payment.

It should be emphasized that, to the extent that managers want to keep their jobs, the three markets (for corporate control, managerial labour and the firm's products) can control moral hazard. In relation to the market for corporate control, for example, 'many observers have interpreted the hostile takeovers [of the 1980s] as a corrective response to managerial moral hazard: the takeovers, it is claimed, were intended to displace entrenched managers who were pursuing their own interests at the expense of the stockholders' (Milgrom and Roberts, 1992, p. 182).

The fact that the acquisition share prices were higher than they had been in the market prior to takeover, may be evidence of management misbehaviour or moral hazard. This would be so if the original market value of the shares had been the equivalent of the company's value (net present value of the future stream of profit that could reasonably be expected) under the original management, and the acquisition price was the company's value under the new management. It may, on the other hand, indicate an overestimation by the acquiring firm of its capacity to improve the performance of the company. Milgrom and Roberts (1992, pp. 182–3) seem to conclude that the takeover premium was indicative of moral hazard when arguing that there is other evidence of management misbehaviour in the adoption during the 1980s by management of the poison pill defence against takeovers. The poison pill is a special security, which gives the holder the right to acquire shares at very low prices in the event of a hostile takeover. Poison pills were created by management, in some cases without shareholder approval.

If, as Stiglitz (1991) suggests, the acquiring firm in takeovers generally experiences no increase in its own share values, then it is more likely that there has in fact been an overestimation by the acquiring firm of its ability to improve the performance of the target company. This is indicative, in other words, of an overestimation of the moral hazard of the managerial employment contract in the acquired firm.

The most obvious solution to the problem of conflict of interest between the principal and agent is for the principal to become his or her own agent. Where there is team production, and the existence of a monitor can reduce shirking by enough to pay his or her own salary, then it may be appropriate for that monitor also to be the owner of the firm. If he or she is not the owner, then there could be a need to monitor the monitor, to ensure that he or she does not shirk. This leads to the conclusion that the existence of firms in which there is an owner and a group of people working as a team for that owner, is a consequence of the need to monitor team production, and the need for the monitor to be the owner – with, for example, the power to fire shirkers, to pay each of the members of the team in accordance with his or her view of their productivity, to keep the residual and to sell the firm.[13] We return to the question of the basis for the existence of firms in the next chapter, where transaction cost theory, among other things, takes exception to principal–agent theory's conclusion about the significance of the need for monitoring.

3.4 Recent developments: neoclassical theory of the firm, technology and the 'new economy'

Micro- and macroeconomic success during the 1990s and early 2000s has quasi systematically been coined with such terms as 'new economy', 'knowledge economy' and 'information society'. This has in part been the result of a shift of theoretical economic thinking towards the so-called endogenous growth models, which acquired prominence between the mid-1980s until the dotcom crash of 2001 (see Section 11.4 in Chapter 11). In short, whereas neoclassical theory represents technological change as being an exogenous trend, the endogenous growth models see technological change as a variable with a fundamental explanatory power of output (and growth) increases. Consequently these models endogenize technology, that is, they integrate a proxy for technical change or technological innovation into a growth or production function.

The endogenous growth models have developed along two major streams: (i) along the neo-Schumpeterian stream, consolidating thus the field of evolutionary economics, which represents a radical departure from neoclassical thinking, and (ii) by suggesting a less radical departure from the neoclassical framework (by keeping, for example, some neoclassical elements such as marginal behaviour, and by relaxing others such as pure and perfect competition). The next chapter provides an account of the evolutionary theory, whereas Section 11.4 of Chapter 11 will explore neoclassical-based endogenous growth models. The purpose of this final section is to highlight the inability of the neoclassical theory, as developed by Walras and as presented in many microeconomics textbooks, to tackle satisfactorily the issue of technological change.

In Walras's *Élements d'Économie Politique Pure*, every economic activity is conceived as being reduced to an exchange on a specific market. Walras views indeed any (closed) economy as being a myriad of exchange activities on the different markets for goods, services, factors of production, as well as money and credit.[14] As we will see, technology per se is subsumed into several types of capital goods such as machines, instruments and tools. Technological know-how or knowledge is consequently nothing more than a mathematical relationship existing between the factors of production (including the capital goods mentioned above) and the various commodities sold on the markets. In particular, Walras's production theory is extremely simplified in that production activities are seen simply as interactions between buyers and sellers on two major distinct markets:

- The market for services where landlords, workers and 'capitalists' sell their productive services to the entrepreneurs. The entrepreneurs are a socio-economic category distinct from that of capitalists.[15] These services are captured by rent, profit (emanating from the ownership of land and capital respectively), as well as by labour.

- The market for products where the entrepreneurs sell their products to the other three categories of economic agents (Walras, 1874, 18th–20th Lessons).

His production theory is therefore represented by several systems of equations, of the following type:

$$S_i = F_i(p_{il}, p_{ip}, p_{ik}, \ldots, p_{ia}, p_{ib}, p_{ic}, p_{id}, \ldots)$$

for the system of n equations relating to the total supply of service i, where: p_{il}, p_{ip}, p_{ik} refer to the prices of productive services, namely of land, labour and capital, and $p_{ia}, p_{ib}, p_{ic}, p_{id}$ refer to the prices of products A, B, C, D, etc. These are introduced into the system of supply equations, because each owner of services will equate his marginal utility of a given service to its price; in turn, each marginal utility will depend on what the owner of services can consume, that is, on the prices of commodities, A, B, C, D, etc.

Furthermore, the system of m equations relating to the demand for product j is:

$$D_j = F_j(p_{jl}, p_{jp}, p_{jk}, \ldots, p_{ja}, p_{jb}, p_{jc}, p_{jd}, \ldots)$$

The way in which Walras links these two apparently disconnected systems of equations, and the way in which he therefore treats the problem of technology, is quite subtle. He assumes that the quantity of productive services necessary for the production of each product j is a determined parameter, which he calls a 'fabrication coefficient'. He defines a fabrication coefficient, which is denoted $a_l, a_p, a_k, \ldots, b_l, b_p, b_k, \ldots, c_l, c_p, c_k$, etc. as being the respective quantity of each service, L, P, K, used in the production of one unit of commodity A, B, C, respectively. We can write therefore:

$$a_l D_a + b_l D_b + c_l D_c + d_l D_d + \ldots = S_l$$
$$a_p D_a + b_p D_b + c_p D_c + d_p D_d + \ldots = S_p$$
$$a_k D_a + b_k D_b + c_k D_c + d_k D_d + \ldots = S_k$$

This system of equations stipulates that the quantity of services used (or demanded) in the production process is equal to their supply (another market equilibrium reached through the exchange process). Walras goes on to write that the market price of each product A, B, C, ..., is equal to its cost in terms of productive services. That is, the market price of commodity A (denoted as p_a) is equal to $a_l p_l + a_p p_p + a_k p_k + ...$ Marginalist reasoning is used again at this stage to help determine the optimum quantity and price of services employed in the production process.

It is clear from such a representation of an economic system, that each economic agent is a provider of services – everyone has something to trade on some specific market – while being a consumer of commodities (or of services in the case of entrepreneurs). Quantities and prices of goods and services, and specific methods of production, are all explained by a number of relationships, culminating with the demand supply relationship existing between the fabrication coefficients and the prices of services.

As a result, technological change, expressed by the fabrication coefficients, is reduced to being a mathematical relationship existing between factors of production (or productive services) and the various commodities sold on the markets. Walras's production theory, and consequently his treatment of technology, is enshrined in a general model of pure exchange. Indeed, every economic activity, including technological change, is reduced to being an exchange activity. The reason why Walras placed the concept of exchange at the core of his theory is rather simple and unambiguous. Eager to reconcile the ideal of social justice with the virtues of perfect competition, he was keen to refute the rather compromising labour theory of value by showing how, mathematically, the scarcity theory of value combined with the concepts of exchange and utility provided a satisfactory explanation to economic activity.[16]

The most unsatisfactory element in Walras's theory, and consequently in any formalized neoclassical model since that time, is its inability to deal with and explain technological change or innovation. In spite of its many refinements since the work of Walras, the neoclassical theory of the firm is inadequate to explain innovation, a central feature in modern corporations. O'Sullivan (2000) provides a rich diatribe against the inability of neoclassical theory to deal with the innovation process. The author notes that innovation is characterized by three main features: (i) it is a cumulative process (since it is concerned with the accumulation of the stock of knowledge); (ii) it is a collective learning process; and (iii) it is a process surrounded by uncertainty. This entails that the future possible states of the world are unknown. In contrast, she notes that the neoclassical theory treats the resource allocation process as being: (i) reversible (meaning that today's resource allocation has no effect on tomorrow's allocation); (ii) based on individuality (there is no co-ordination between economic actors, and each one acts in their own best interest according to the utility maximization principle); and (iii) optimal. The optimality principle suggests a choice among alternative economic outcomes, which are a known set of possibilities. These are essential conflicting characteristics that make innovation unfit to be fully integrated into the neoclassical framework

3.5 Summary

This chapter has proposed a review of the neoclassical theory of the firm, and of its major criticisms. These criticisms have been discussed along the dimensions of profit maximization, uncertainty and organizational complexity of firms. We have also suggested several early reformulations of neoclassical thinking through various attempts such as the responses proffered by the managerial school, and by the principal–agent theory. The managerial theory was the first to focus on the importance of the structure of the firm, leading to hypotheses on the determinants of the growth of firms. Principal–agent theory, on the basis of a similar view of the structure of firms, focuses on contracts and how they might encompass conflicts of interest to enhance the efficiency of firms. For each of these theories, it has been found to be very difficult to undertake empirical work to test or validate their hypotheses. Table 3.2 summarizes these conclusions.

One early weakness was the absence of a time dimension. The contract view of the firm, as in the principal–agent theory with its emphasis on eventualities over different time frames, has gone some way towards incorporating this dimension. Again, rigorous empirical research is rare.

Table 3.2 Major theories of the firm (neoclassical and neoclassically inspired)

Theory of the firm	Point of focus
Neoclassical	Firm (black box)
Managerial	Firm (owners v. managers)
Principal-agent	Contract (employer v. employees)

The last section of the chapter emphasized the inability of the neoclassical theory of the firm to explain modern economic business, even more so since the advent of the so-called new economy in the 1990s. A major weakness of the neoclassical theory is indeed its inability to deal with technology and innovation. As has been shown, Walras's general equilibrium paradigm treats technological change, and production, under the broad realm of his exchange theory.

The next chapter shows how this technology view has been incorporated in subsequent and more modern theories of the firm, with, for example, a review of the evolutionary theory.

Websites

For an historical insight into the developments of the theory of the firm, visit **http:// homepage.newschool.edu/het/**

Questions

3.1   What are the most important impediments to profit maximization: (i) for firms; and (ii) as an assumption on which to build theory?

3.2   If profit maximization has so many impediments, why do so many economists continue to assume it?

3.3   In Table 3.1, which strategy would you choose, and why?

3.4   Exchanging goods and services is the central and critical activity of economic actors according to the neoclassical theory. Discuss.

3.5   Why is the neo-classical theory of the firm unfit to explain innovation in modern and dynamic economies?

Notes

1   According to one reviewer of work in industrial organization, 'Neoclassical decision-theoretic analysis and competitive general equilibrium theory have been supplanted almost completely by non-cooperative game theory' (Porter, 1991).

2   The firm is often said to be a 'black box' in the neoclassical view, suggesting that the internal structure of the firm is irrelevant.

3   This section draws on George *et al.* (1992, pp. 29–38).

4   According to the authors, a 'real' demand curve shows what actually happens when prices are altered. A hypothetical demand curve 'is based on some particular assumption regarding the behavior of other firms'. An 'imaginary' demand curve 'shows what the entrepreneur believes will happen when price is altered' (Hall and Hitch, 1939, p. 14).

5   See discussions on the Marris model (Section 3.3.1 below) and on principal–agent theory (Section 3.3.2 below), where it is suggested that one of the goals of takeovers is the replacement of the existing management.

6   Referring to March and Simon (1958), Stiglitz (1991) writes of the finding that because of imperfect information, managers would, in general, not act in such ways as to maximize shareholder value, and, in particular, the cost of obtaining and processing information encouraged the adoption of 'satisficing and rule-of-thumb strategies'.

7   'The corporate management decisions of Japanese firms are subject to the dual control (influence) of financial interests (ownership) and employees' interests rather than to unilateral control in the interests of ownership' (Aoki, 1990).

8   Hofstede (1983) writes, in a different context, of culture as 'that part of our conditioning that we share with other members of our nation, region, or group but not with members of other nations, regions or groups'. The example that follows does not mean to suggest that optimism is necessarily an aspect of the culture of scientists, nor that dogmatic 'sticking to the plans' is necessarily an aspect of the culture of accountants. It aims merely to suggest that there are differences in such cultures and that they may cause conflicts of interest.

9   The revenue-maximizing level of output implies that $MR = dTR/dQ = 0$, i.e.:

$$MR = \frac{dPQ}{dQ} = 0 \Rightarrow MR = Q\,\frac{dP}{dQ} + P = 0 \Rightarrow MR = Q\,\frac{dP}{dQ}\,\frac{P}{P} + P = 0 \Rightarrow$$

$$MR = P \left[1 + \frac{Q}{P} \frac{dP}{dQ} \right] = 0$$

Since $\varepsilon = (dQ/dP)(P/Q)$, it follows that: $MR = P \left[1 + \frac{1}{\varepsilon} \right]$ for all points where dQ/dP is defined. This is the general relationship between marginal revenue and the elasticity coefficient ε. It can be seen that MR is zero when $\varepsilon = -1$.

10 This section draws in part on Milgrom and Roberts (1992, ch. 6). The reader is encouraged to read that chapter for more details, particularly on the relationship between moral hazard and performance incentives. For game theoretic perspectives on the relationship between principals and agents, see Gardner (1995, ch. 10).

11 See, for example, Maskin and Tirole (1992), who analyse as a three-stage game the relationship between the principal and agent in which the principal has private information that directly affects the agent's payoff.

12 An example of moral hazard in employment contracts arises in universities, where there are two different groups of employees, those on short-term contracts and those with tenure. Tenure is supported by many as a feature of the independence of the academic, and the need to protect the academic against political pressure. Tenure may perform this function to some extent but it also enables those who have it, to change their behaviour and shirk various duties. The academic on short-term contract, it can be argued, works hard, prepares excellent lectures, volunteers for administrative duties, does above-average research and publishing. Then he or she obtains tenure, relaxes more, gives last year's lectures, avoids administration, and does less research and publishing. In practice there is, no doubt, moral hazard in tenure, but given that the best teachers, administrators and researchers in academia have tenure, academics certainly do not always, or even usually, change their behaviour in the way predicted by moral hazard.

13 For a more detailed discussion on the issue of team production and the monitor as owner, see Holmstrom and Tirole (1989), or at a more introductory level, Douma and Schreuder (1992, ch. 6).

14 Note indeed that Walras treats money as a specific commodity, which 'simplifies the determination of general equilibrium current prices' (Walras, 1952 edition, p. 157).

15 The 'capitalist' is defined by Walras as being the owner of capital goods such as industrial buildings, machines as well as raw materials. These capital goods (or simply, capital) are seen by Walras as being factors of production that give rise to services at the disposal of entrepreneurs. On the other hand, the worker is the owner of 'personal faculties or attributes'. Note that this latter category includes liberal professions.

16 Note that the labour theory of value, made popular through the writings of Adam Smith and David Ricardo, was the cornerstone of the Marxist theory. It is important to understand that Walras was so preoccupied with the exchange mechanism that he failed to acknowledge the importance of technological change in the economic development of the industrializing nations at the time. The quote by Ellis (1826) in Chapter 11 (Section 11.2.1) shows how the Industrial Revolution of the late-eighteenth and nineteenth centuries was in fact the equivalent of the first major knowledge revolution of humankind. Technological change at the time could not go unnoticed.

CHAPTER 4

Other theories of the firm

4.1 Learning objectives

The main objectives of this chapter are:

- To introduce theories of the firm that have emerged from the criticisms of the neoclassical theory

- To suggest strengths and weaknesses in these theories, and

- To provide examples of the application of these theories

4.2 Behavioural theory of the firm

The ideas of Herbert Simon were important in the emergence of behaviourism.[1] Central to these ideas was a critique of the assumption of rationality that underlay – and still underlies – neoclassical economics (March and Simon, 1958; Simon, 1960). Simon introduced the notion of *bounded rationality*. Under limited, or bounded, rationality it is accepted that decision makers in firms – and, more generally, in organizations – cannot have perfect knowledge about all the possible options and their outcomes. In neoclassical theory, such perfect knowledge is essential in order to choose the best option, that which is optimal – for firms, the one that maximises profits. A decision taken with bounded rationality arrives at an option that satisfies knowable, identifiable, criteria. These might be, for example, cost or time based. Other options may also satisfy these criteria, but because there is no way of knowing which of these options is best, the first such option is chosen. This is closely related to Simon's notion of *satisficing* – of making decisions that are satisfactory rather than spending large amounts of time and money to obtain information on more and more options and their outcomes. What makes the decision satisfactory is that it is consistent with some or other rule or norm; in practice managers use 'rules of thumb', rough rules of behaviour that have been seen to work in the past.

Following – and building on – his work with Simon, March collaborated with Cyert on what became a classic and much-quoted text, *A Behavioural Theory of the Firm* (Cyert and March, 1963). This work is close both in time and in treatment of key issues, to the managerial theories discussed in the previous chapter. The similarity between behavioural theory and the managerial theories is in the idea that the firm has multiple objectives, driven by different constituencies, constrained in various ways by external factors. As we saw in Chapter 3, the multiple objectives in the case of managerial theories are those of owners and managers, and the external constraints are mainly those of the various markets. The managerial theories are thus in a sense special cases of the behavioural theory.

The behavioural theory views the firm as a coalition. Among the members of this coalition are managers, workers, shareholders, customers, suppliers, bankers and any others with an interest in the firm. They may have different or even conflicting interests in the firm. Increased wages for workers are, at least in the short run, at the expense of profits for shareholders, for example. For the coalition to survive, there have to be compromises. And for compromises to be arrived at, there has to be some kind of bargaining process in which the demands of each of the members of the coalition are defined. This process is at the heart of decision making in the firm.

It is here that bounded rationality enters the picture. All the members of the coalition have some, perhaps different, notion of what would be a satisfactory outcome. Each is only a satisficing objective because the members are boundedly rational and because of the cost of obtaining the information necessary to identify a more optimal outcome. The choice of options, for the survival of the coalition, must be based as much as possible on achieving the range of satisfactory outcomes defined by the different constituencies. This choice of option is, thus, not a maximization of anything. It is, rather, the result of aiming to achieve multiple objectives in the face of multiple constraints. The example above of wages and profits is appropriate here. There are many other objectives; managers and workers in different sections of the firm, would aim to achieve improved performance in their own sections. For managers and sales staff, for example, sales and revenue growth would be the objective, for production workers, output growth. Each of these objectives might be achievable only at the expense of one of the other objectives. The theory suggests that *organizational slack* is necessary to solve the conflicts that arise as a consequence of conflicting objectives.

Organizational slack refers to what at first might seem to be inefficiency. A firm might be able to cut costs to significantly below current levels. However, the difference between the current levels and the 'efficient' levels may be necessary to enable the firm to maintain its coalition of interests. In the example of wages and profits, it may be necessary to pay skilled workers out of this difference between current and 'efficient' levels, in order to keep them 'on board', without reducing profits. Organizational slack can thus be used to achieve a particular objective without preventing the firm from achieving its other objectives.

That organizational slack exists in many organizations is clear, though the basis of this slack is not always seen as consistent with that suggested in behavioural theory. Principal–agent theory, as we saw in the previous chapter, interprets underperformance of a company as moral hazard. Managers shirk their responsibilities under their contracts and this results in suboptimal performance. Organizational slack in this view of the firm will result, if there is an efficient market for corporate control, in the firm being taken over by different major shareholders with a more effective management team. In the behavioural view, organizational slack has a positive function of ameliorating problems arising from conflicting objectives.

Given the cogency of its critique of neoclassical theory, and the success of many of its proponents (Simon was awarded the Nobel Prize for Economics in 1978), it is interesting to ask about the extent to which behavioural theory has impinged on the mainstream theory of the firm. Stigler's (1961) seminal contribution to the 'economics of information' introduces into the neoclassical framework, bounded rationality and the search behaviour that leads to decision making in the firm. The marginalist solution, as he shows, is for search to continue up to the point where the cost of additional search (marginal cost) is just equal to the returns – in terms of improved performance – from the additional search (marginal revenue). Simon refuted this, stating that it requires that management have some idea of the returns from additional search, and, given bounded rationality, they in practice could not know this. As with other applications of neoclassical theory, a reply to Simon could be that the decision makers need not know MC and MR; it is a *post hoc* explanation for what must have happened for the firm to be profit maximizing. This reply, however, emphasizes the limits of neoclassical theory, suggesting that it has no value as a prescriptive aid to management.

Other neoclassical economists rejected the idea of bounded rationality on the grounds that 'the assumption of economic man gave a sufficiently accurate account of human behaviour to allow predictions to be made in the aggregate' (Butler, 2002). This criticism from the neoclassical mainstream is one reason why behaviourism has had a limited impact in economics. Another is clearly expressed by Kay, writing about theories that 'described facets of business behaviour that were ignored by conventional models. If their impact on mainstream business economics was modest, this was because they failed to generate the clear-cut predictions and prescriptions associated with the assumptions of profit maximization and perfect competition' (Kay, 2002). There is an interesting contrast here, in that, as we have just argued, despite its precision neoclassical theory's weakness may be in its inability to provide prescriptive aid to management. At the same time, theories and arguments, like many of those in behavioural theory, that are not amenable to mathematical precision are unlikely to be incorporated into neoclassical economics, the main tools of which are mathematical.

4.3 Stakeholder theory

In some ways similar to behavioural theory, stakeholder theory also focuses on the interests of all the participants in the firm, and on how those interests can best be met. It is different from behavioural theory in that it does not explicitly adopt concepts such as bounded rationality and satisficing. Many versions of stakeholder theory are more about politics, polemics and ethics than they are about economics (Jones, 1995; O'Sullivan, 2000, p. 52).

The stakeholder view argues that the firm will perform better by being concerned with the interests of all the stakeholders than by being concerned exclusively with the interests of the shareholders. Stakeholders include all those working in the firm (insiders), and those others such as suppliers, customers, creditors, shareholders, government and the local community (outsiders), who are affected in some way by the actions of the firm.

There are a number of reasons why the stakeholder firm is expected to perform better than a firm run by a management more directly focused on shareholder value and profit maximization. Among these are the following:

- The stakeholders see themselves as part of the team that makes up the firm. Their closer association with the firm results in more personal benefit from the performance of the firm than in more conventional situations. They will therefore put in more effort to achieve better performance.

- As part of a team, stakeholders also have a reluctance to let down other members of the team. Because of their loyalty to the firm they will not shirk any of their responsibilities.

- Co-operative behaviour will improve performance. To borrow from behavioural theory, there is no need for organizational slack as there will be more agreement and less need to compensate one group in return for allowing another group's objective to be achieved.

- The stakeholder firm is more likely to engender trust among the participants. As will be shown in Section 4.5 below, where there are high levels of trust, there is less opportunistic behaviour – less exploitation of weaknesses in contracts. Opportunistic behaviour is costly, and its exclusion or reduction is another possible advantage of stakeholder firms.

- Aiming to achieve objectives other than those of the shareholders leads to less short-termism. A narrow concern for the share price of a firm can result in a long-term decline in performance (see above, Section 3.2.2).

One of the difficulties in testing whether the stakeholder firm does in fact perform better than the shareholder firm is definitional. What exactly is a stakeholder firm? Moschandreas (2000, p. 197) makes clear that all firms 'consider the interests of all stakeholders'. However, the shareholder firm does so as a means to an end, that end being the maximization of profit and shareholder value. The objective is profit maximisation subject to constraints, those constraints including the interests of the other stakeholders. The objective of the stakeholder firm, on the other hand, is to advance the interests of all the stake-holders. Moschandreas shows that there is no consensus as to precisely how this is to be achieved, however. For Aoki (1988), stakeholder firms have an overall objective of value added maximization. This is similar to Blair's (1995, cited in O'Sullivan, 2000) contention that stakeholder firms should be assessed in the context of the objective of corporations, namely to create wealth for society.

Rather than adding value or creating wealth, Moschandreas (2000, p. 97) emphasizes that 'stakeholding behaviour is expected to lead to enhanced competitive advantage through behaviour which is "inclusive" and socially efficient. . . . Stakeholding objectives must . . . be expressed in terms of both the creation of surplus and its distribution among the stake-holders'. This leads to the short-term objective of maximization of surplus and its fair distribution among stakeholders, and the long-term objective of stability and corporate viability.

O'Sullivan's (2000, pp. 52–8) critique of stakeholder theory rests on what is meant by fair distribution of the surplus. In Blair's (1995) analysis, institutional reforms are necessary to ensure that there are adequate incentives for stakeholders to invest in firm-specific assets (for example, for workers to invest time and effort in obtaining firm-specific skills). Blair's focus remains – similar to that of neoclassical theory – returns on investment. For O'Sullivan (2000, p. 56), Blair

> *fails to go beyond the neoclassical preoccupation with static resource allocation. The returns to all participants (productive factors) in the enterprise – in such forms as wages, rent, and interest – remain strictly determined, as they are in the neoclassical model, by technological and market forces that are external to the operation of the enterprise and human control more generally.*

What is missing from stakeholder theory, in O'Sullivan's view, is the relationship between firm specificity and innovation.

Accepting that there are differences in what is meant by the stakeholder firm, and that there are critiques of stakeholding both from neoclassical and anti-neoclassical perspectives, is there any evidence about whether stakeholding enhances performance? There is at least evidence of lack of co-operation leading to corporate failure. Dertouzas et al. (1989) found 'a lack of cooperation between individuals, between groups of individuals within firms, between firms and their suppliers or their customers, between firms in the same industry and between firms and government' to be key factors in the failure of firms (Moschandreas, 2000, p. 198). The opposite was the case – high levels of co-operation – in best practice firms. Further indirect evidence is provided by Appleyard (2001). She shows both theoretically and through case-based example that a close relationship between buyer and supplier firms is important in the successful implementation in the buyer's processes of a tool provided by the supplier.

Finally, the question arises as to whether, assuming co-operation and stakeholding are advantageous, their introduction can be left to the market. We refer here to three different arguments. First, Freeman and Phillips (1999) have a libertarian perspective on stake-holding which, though favouring stakeholding, broadly opposes government regulation to support stakeholding. Second, providing evidence against stakeholding and related transparency, Almazan et al. (2003) seem to provide the basis for an argument in favour of regulation. Using a theoretical model, backed by anecdotal evidence, they show that the transparency associated with stakeholding can reduce the value of the firm. Moreover, as a result of this negative implication of transparency, the incentive for 'firms and stake-holders to undertake relationship specific investments' is reduced. More conservative capital structures are preferred. What is particularly interesting in this paper is that in opting for this conservative capital structure the firm forgoes advantageous investments ('positive NPV investments'). Arguably, regulation is necessary to offset the transparency effects and encourage firms to adopt the advantageous investments. Third, in the context of increasing globalization, and the consequential distancing and fragmenting of stake-holder groups, it is unlikely that a stakeholder approach will be adopted on a voluntary basis. As Moschandreas (2000) concludes, referring to Maltby and Wilkinson (1998), 'governments should create mechanisms to promote socially responsible behaviour'.

4.4 Co-operative game theory

Not among established theories, but clearly related to stakeholder theory in content and to principal–agent theory in methodology, Aoki has developed the co-operative game theory of the firm which sees the firm as a coalition of various parties (Aoki, 1984).

As argued by Aoki, the firm can serve 'as a nexus for co-operative relationships between the employees and the shareholders which makes possible the optimal redistribution of risk as well as the efficient collective use of skills, knowledge, and funds' (Aoki, 1984, p. 56).[2] Strongly opposed to the managerial conception where the objective of the firm is identified with the objective of one of its separate constituents, the idea of a 'nexus of co-operative relationships' provides a link between the various units forming the firm. The behaviour of the firm on the market emerges from this nexus; this behaviour is a co-operative game solution called the 'organizational equilibrium' (ibid., p. 69).

This 'coalitional view' disregards, reluctantly, other potential players. Financial institutions, supplying capital to the firm, customers and suppliers, interacting closely with it, and other firms, in competition with it, are all potentially influential players. Although they all lie outside the boundaries of the firm itself – except in the case where some of the employees are also shareholders and customers of the firm – their actions do matter for the determination of the co-operative game solution. Aoki acknowledges in particular among these outsiders, his omission of the role of the customers of the firm. More importantly, from the point of view of his analysis, he also acknowledges the omission of the 'Schumpeterian entrepreneurial role' of the manager (Aoki, 1984, p. 196).

Recent developments of aspects of co-operative game theory have focused on consultancy and direct advice on business strategy. Nalebuff and Brandenburger (1997), for example, have written about 'co-opetition'. The book's two subtitles provide apt descriptions of its content: '*A revolutionary mindset that combines competition and cooperation*' and '*The game theory strategy that's changing the game of business*'. They are explicit about the extent to which, rather than competing in a zero sum world, in many instances firms stand to gain from co-operating with others. The gains of other firms are not necessarily at a cost to the firm in question. In another such example, Groot Bruinderink *et al.* (2003) write of the consultancy firm Arthur D. Little's 'development of stable coalitions' (DOSC) approach. This, they write, is 'based upon the principles of "Cooperative Game Theory" '. It is 'particularly useful for analysing potential partners prior to entering negotiations, and for obtaining a stable and reasonable share of the gains from the intended partnership.'

Non-cooperative game theory (see Chapter 2) is much more common in IO. It is, indeed, regarded as a 'characteristic feature' of what came to be known in the 1980s as the 'new IO' (see Davies and Lyons, 1988, p. 7). Focusing on the strategies of rival firms, it is concerned primarily with the external environment of the firm and less with its internal coalitional nature.

4.5 Transaction cost theory

In stakeholder theory it could be argued that firms exist to enhance the interests of the stakeholders. In transaction cost theory, firms exist to minimize transaction costs. To explain transaction cost we introduce the notion of *property rights*. Rights of ownership (or property rights) to a good or service must be able to be established before a market for that good or service can exist. In an as yet relatively clean-air world, for example, property rights over breathable air cannot be established and no market in this good exists. Transaction costs 'are those incurred in enforcing property rights, locating trading partners, and actually carrying out the transaction' (Hyman, 1992, p. 134). If property rights over a good cannot be established, then transaction cost theory is inappropriate. This definition is particularly apt for contracts in which a good is changing hands. In other contracts, for example where a firm subcontracts another to carry out some operation or provide a service, there may be an ongoing need to ensure that the terms of the contract are being fulfilled. A more complete list of transaction costs would include not just the search and information costs, bargaining and negotiation costs, and measurement and implementation costs, but also monitoring and enforcement costs (Pitelis, 2002).

Work incorporating transaction cost theory has been applied to such issues as the absorption of risk in subcontracting by the Japanese car industry (Asanuma and Kikutani, 1992), problems in the transformation of institutions in the post-Communist period in eastern Europe (Iwanek, 1992; Williamson, 1992) and the design of policies to encourage research and development (R&D) given the problems related to the low appropriability of the results of R&D (Itoh *et al.*, 1991). Transaction cost theory also has considerable potential to influence the formation and application of competition law (Pitelis, 2002).

Originally a rather narrow, minority-interest specialism within IO, the work of Coase and his followers has thus clearly become a major concern of the discipline. In the title of his speech on receipt of the 1991 Nobel Prize for Economics, Coase called this work 'the institutional structure of production' (see Coase, 1992). In this speech, Coase was critical of the continuing tendency among some theorists of the firm to ignore the fact that 'the efficiency of the economic system depends to a very considerable extent on how these firms conduct their affairs'. He was even more surprised at the 'neglect of the market or more specifically the institutional arrangements which govern the process of exchange'. He was pleased to acknowledge, however, that institutional factors were beginning to be introduced into mainstream economics (1992, p. 714).

What have Coase's contributions been, and how have they been developed in recent years? His seminal article 'The nature of the firm' (1937) argued that it is due to the existence of transaction costs that firms exist. If it is through the market mechanism that prices determine how factors of production are to be combined to produce what goods, for what markets, then why are organizations necessary? Coase's answer is that where transactions between individuals would be too difficult, inefficient or expensive, such that an organization could co-ordinate them at a lower cost than if they were market transactions, then firms emerge to do this co-ordination and thereby, in a sense, obviate these transactions by *internalizing* them. In general, 'if the costs of making an exchange are greater than the gains which that exchange would bring, that exchange would not take place and the greater production that would flow from specialization would not be realized' (Coase, 1992, p. 716).

The internalization of transactions enables the exploitation of economies of scale or of scope.[3] The extent to which economies of scale can be exploited determines the size of a firm. Under what circumstances will transaction costs be lower when internalized than when left to be negotiated in an external market? This is among the questions asked by Williamson (1985), whose 'many significant insights' have given 'substance to Coase's suggestion that firms reduce transaction costs' (Alchian and Woodward, 1988, p. 65).

Williamson focuses on *bounded rationality* and *opportunism*, and *asset specificity*, in his study of economic organization. Bounded rationality refers to the imperfect ability to solve complex problems. In a game like chess, for example, each player has the same amount of information as the other (there is symmetry of information), but there are so many possibilities that even a brilliant player may not be able to make a fully rational decision. There is bounded rationality when there is imperfect ability to process the available information, and/or when the information itself is imperfect (that is, there is uncertainty) in relation to both present and future events. Opportunism relates to how people will respond to conflicts, given the existence of bounded rationality. They will behave opportunistically if they act in their self-interests by, for example, finding loopholes in contracts. If there was unbounded rationality, the potential opportunistic behaviour would be known, and avoided.

Asset specificity refers to assets, involving non-trivial investment, that are specific (or idiosyncratic) to particular transactions (for example, skills in an employer–employee contract). There are two types of assets in this context: physical and human. Physical asset specificity relates to site specificity – plant or equipment located close to supplier or customer; and to process specificity – plant or equipment that can be used only for a particular customer. These latter Williamson calls 'dedicated assets'. Human asset specificity is where there are individual ('learning by doing') or collective ('team configuration') skills that are useful only (or mainly) for the particular transaction.

Bounded rationality is a cognitive condition, opportunism a behavioural condition and asset specificity a technological condition. Williamson shows that different combinations of these three conditions give rise to different contractual models (Williamson, 1985, p. 31).[4] (This attention to contracts, in terms of the relations both within and between firms, has been a central feature of Williamson's work on transaction cost analysis.)

To illustrate, if there was no opportunism, there would be no need for internalization. Without opportunism, Williamson (1985, p. 51) argues, 'there is no occasion to supplant market exchange by other modes of economic organization if promises to behave in a joint profit-maximizing way are self-enforcing and if sharing rules are agreed to at the outset'.

Without opportunism, the transaction would take place within the market, rather than within a hierarchy. But bounded rationality is a precondition for opportunism. So, opportunism and bounded rationality are likely to give rise to internalization. This, however, is still only part of Williamson's explanation for why and when internal governance will be preferable to market governance. The third element is asset specificity: 'Market contracting gives way to bilateral contracting, which in turn is supplanted by unified contracting (internal governance) as asset specificity deepens' (Williamson, 1985, p. 78). So, as Lazonick (2002) points out, asset specificity is the 'critical condition that, according to Williamson, favours hierarchies over markets'. For asset specificity, assets involved in the transaction are, by definition, not freely available for other uses. There are costs involved in applying them in any other than this particular transaction. This results in a need for continuity, so that those who have invested in the assets can derive revenues from them. In terms of an individual adapting skills for a particular firm, for example, once that has been done, this is no longer the kind of 'faceless contracting' characteristic of market transactions – the 'pairwise identity of the parties' now matters (Williamson, 1985, p. 62). The more specific the asset, the greater the need for continuity, the more likely it will be that internal governance will replace market governance.

There are importance differences between Coase and Williamson. Williamson himself (1985, p. 78) differentiates his theory from that of Coase as follows:

	Coase	Williamson
Factors favouring organization of production in the firm rather than in the market	Bounded rationality	Bounded rationality, opportunism and asset specificity

While they understand the determinants of transaction costs differently, both Coase and Williamson are agreed that minimization of transaction cost is the basis for the existence of firms. Nevertheless, there is not unanimity on this issue. Alchian and Demsetz (1972) argued that *technological non-separability* is the main factor responsible for the existence of firms. This refers, for example, to essential co-operation among workers in order to load freight. The firm exists to monitor, measure and allocate the benefits of team performance. While this concept has been useful in emphasizing the network of relationships underlying – and created by – firms, it has not, in general, been as successful as transaction cost in the analysis of more complex organizations (Alchian, 1984; Williamson, 1985, p. 88). It should be added, however, that Demsetz (1988) has more recently argued that much of the work on transaction cost does not adequately take into account the role of the firm in the acquisition and use of knowledge. Loasby (1990) points out that 'Demsetz recognizes the need for patterns of organization which foster the development and use of knowledge, and of the embodiment of knowledge in people, in a way which suggests an unrecognized link with the evolutionary theory of the firm'.

This particular inadequacy of Williamson's transaction cost approach is elaborated by Lazonick (1991, ch. 6). Lazonick argues at length, and convincingly, that 'Williamson has viewed the organization as an economic institution that can *only adapt* to a given economic environment' (1991, p. 214). Williamson's is a theory of the *adaptive* firm, and not the *innovative* firm. Lazonick draws on the work of Schumpeter and, in particular, Chandler, to develop an alternative theory, that of the innovative organization. He shows that, although dismissed by Williamson, strategic behaviour of firms is extremely important. Strategic behaviour includes, for example, the development of an organization's resources, making them organization-specific assets, 'with unique productive capabilities' (Lazonick, 1991, p. 217). Lazonick (2002) shows that, in effect, Williamson takes the three sets of conditions – cognitive, behavioural and technological – as given and examines the optimal decision (market or hierarchy) under these constraints. What Williamson ignores, and what is crucial for a proper understanding of the modern, innovative firm, is an understanding of 'innovative strategy' – the ways in which the firm actually transforms the constraining conditions, particularly the technological conditions. So, whereas for Williamson asset specificity is an expression of market failure, for Lazonick it is an outcome of organizational success. And although Williamson accepts asset specificity as critical in the explanation of why firms exist and grow, he does not examine how firms change their physical and human assets.

In summary, Lazonick's (1991, p. 224) view is that:

> At best, Williamson's transaction cost perspective explains what some established business organizations do to survive in a capitalist economy. With his focus exclusively on the adaptive organization, his ... framework cannot explain how innovative organizations attain and sustain competitive advantage.

Related to the transaction cost theory's difficulty in explaining the innovative organization, is the problem of the innovation itself. We will discuss the theory of technological change and innovation in detail in Chapter 11. Among other recent concerns in that theory is the notion of incremental change, that is, change not arising from any revolutionary, patentable invention or innovation. Such changes can often not be patented, that is to say ownership rights cannot be established over them. By definition, therefore, they are not amenable to explanation by transaction cost analysis.

There are other criticisms of transaction cost theory. Hodgson (2004), for example, focuses on opportunism. He points out that, for Williamson, all transactions are affected by opportunism: 'self-interest seeking with guile'. This is, for Williamson, a crucial factor in the existence of hierarchies rather than markets. Hodsgson (2004) shows that 'Williamson ignores several other reasons for the existence of hierarchical management structures. The undue emphasis criticised here is not on the *existence* of opportunism but on the identification of opportunism as the *principal cause* of management hierarchy'. Hodgson (2004) goes further, arguing that this overemphasis on opportunism in Williamson has implications for both analysis and practice of management. He shows that, in addition to opportunism, the problems of miscommunication and misinterpretation also influence governance structure. He concludes that 'management practice should be informed by actual and likely empirical realities, not by a false universal and *a priori* assumption that without opportunism, no governance structures would have any advantage over another'.

At an even more fundamental level, there is criticism even of Coase's basic conception of transaction cost minimization as the fundamental reason for the existence of the firm. Best (1990, p. 112) shows that Coase relies on diminishing returns to management to explain the size of the firm. The firm will grow, according to Coase, until the point is reached where 'the costs of organizing an extra transaction within the firm are equal to the costs involved in carrying out the transaction in the open market' (quoted in Best, 1990, p. 112). This dependence on substitution at the margin is a failing of neoclassical theory, too, Best argues, and it is a failing because it does not take into consideration that the firm may continue to grow until the industry is monopolized, before the point of diminishing returns to management is reached. If this were possible, it would lead to the indeterminacy of both price and firm size. Best applauds Coase for 'dropping the assumption of perfect information about the future', and for showing that market co-ordination is not synonymous with efficiency, that 'under certain conditions planned co-ordination within a firm could be more efficient'. But 'Coase, like Marshall, was constrained from developing promising concepts for analysing business organization by ... the specter of inconsistency with the equilibrium theory of price' (Best, 1990, p. 112).

In similar vein and in the context of a discussion about the boundaries of firms, Penrose (1995, p. xvi) supports the notion that the dichotomy between firm and market is an inadequate foundation for the analysis of economic organization. Referring approvingly to Richardson (1972), she writes that 'the firm in reality is not an island in a sea of market transactions, but itself part of a network consisting of rivals in direct competition, of suppliers of goods and services in special relationship as well as of consumers, be they individuals, organizations, other firms or even governments also in special relationship . . .'.

Another criticism of Coase is provided by Auerbach (1989, ch. 6), who argues that Coase, among others, is wrong to assume that markets exist, and that then, as a response to market imperfections, firms are created. This assumption results in a 'failure to see the role of firms in the *making* of markets'. A market, according to Auerbach, is a behavioural relation. Without the participants (for example, firms), there would not be a market (Auerbach, 1989, pp. 121–2).

Penrose, Lazonick, Best, Auerbach and Hodgson, while criticizing other theories of the firm, have also developed their own theories, each of which is in some respects similar to the other, and all related closely to the evolutionary theory of the firm, to which we now turn.

4.6 Evolutionary and related theories of the firm

Evolutionary theorists, while acknowledging Williamson's contribution and particularly his concern with firm-specific assets and skills, differ from him in relation to their basic unit of analysis. (See Chandler, 1992a, for a discussion of Williamson's contribution to Chandler's thinking.) For Williamson the basic unit of analysis is the transaction; for Chandler and other evolutionary theorists it is the firm itself 'and its specific physical and human assets' (Chandler, 1992b).[5] The features of the firm on which they focus are strategy, structure and core *organizational capabilities*. Broadly defined, organizational capabilities refer to a firm's spare managerial capacity arising from indivisibilities or different rates of growth of the various aspects of the firm, as well as the knowledge, skills and experience within the firm. The spare capacity can be in virtually any area of operation of the firm, including marketing, production, raw material procurement and finance (see Robertson and Langlois, 1995). Best (1990, p. 128) – drawing on Penrose (1959) – explains one aspect of the generation of spare capacity by arguing that 'each time a new system is in place and procedures become routinized, idle managerial resources appear'. *Organizational routines* – different at different levels in the organization – are thus the building blocks of organizational capabilities. There are learned routines in each of the various functional areas of the organization – including buying, production, distribution, marketing and R&D – and, even more importantly, in the co-ordination of these functions (Chandler, 1992b).[6] As Clark and Juma (1987, p. 59) put it: 'Routine is the genetic code of the firm; it carries the adaptive information required for competition and survival.'[7] Routines are the organizational memory of the firm (Nelson and Winter, 1982, p. 99).

Robertson and Langlois (1994) clarify the relationship between capabilities and routines by pointing out that 'routines refer to what an organization actually does, while capabilities also include what it may do if its resources are reallocated. Thus a firm's routines are a subset of its capabilities that influence but do not fully determine what the firm is compe-tent to achieve'.

It is important to note that the recently developed evolutionary theory of the firm is critical of that expounded by Alchian (1950), which was in essence a social Darwinist theory. According to this theory, the internal workings of the firm are irrelevant, because the 'pressure to survive will in the long-term dictate the behaviour of firms' (Auerbach, 1989, p. 46). Those that do not follow what turns out to have been the correct course of action (pursuit of profit) will not survive. Alchian's theory ignores the patterns of behav-iour, attitudes and motivations of firms or, to be more precise, he reduces all these to 'adaptive, imitative, and trial-and-error behaviour in search for profits' (Alchian, quoted in Clark and Juma, 1987, p. 52). The criticisms of Alchian's evolutionary theory are that it was concerned with outcomes rather than processes, it was static, ignoring the time dimension (Auerbach, 1989, p. 48), and that it made technical change 'exogenous to economic evolution', a response to but not affecting market conditions (Clark and Juma, 1987, p. 53). Alchian's was an extreme form of the structuralist view (Auerbach, 1989, p. 46).

Chandler (1992a, b) applies the evolutionary theory of the firm to the empirical infor-mation in his book *Scale and Scope* (1990). The theory, emphasizing 'the continuous learning that makes a firm's assets dynamic', provides an understanding of how and why certain firms have succeeded (Chandler, 1992b, p. 98). In the late nineteenth century, for example, Britain had all the comparative advantages necessary for domination of the world dye markets, including the scientific knowledge, the raw materials and large markets, yet, by the turn of the century, German firms such as Bayer, BASF and Hoechst had become the world leaders. The explanation is the investment in production, distribution and management undertaken by the German firms. This investment was designed for – and succeeded in – the exploitation of economies of scale and scope. The German firms thereby achieved com-petitive advantage which offset the British comparative advantage.[8] Moreover, like other successful firms in other industries, they continued to lead by expanding into foreign markets and related industries, 'driven much less by the desire to reduce transaction, agency and other information costs and much more by a wish to utilize the competitive advantages created by the coordinated learned routines in production, distribution, marketing and improving existing products and processes' (Chandler, 1992b, p. 93).

'Economists,' Chandler (1990, p. 593) writes, 'particularly those of the more traditional mainstream school, have not developed a theory of the evolution of the firm as a dynamic organization'. His work contributes to, and encourages others in the development of, such a theory. Best (1990), for example, like Lazonick, draws on Schumpeter and, although critical of Chandler, formulates a theory of the firm which is consistent with the type of theoretical development that Chandler calls for. 'Schumpeterian competition' on which Best bases his theory, is very different from price competition. It focuses on competition from new commodities (which includes both new products and new versions of old products), new sources of supply, new technologies and new types of organization. The firms most likely to face such competition successfully, Best argues, are not the hierarchically organized firms on which Chandler concentrates, but what he calls 'entrepreneurial' firms (Best, 1990, p. 11). There are three main characteristics of such firms. First, they act strategically, 'choosing the terrain on which to compete'. Second, they seek strategic advantage not through continuity and long production runs aimed at achieving cost minimization, but through continuous product, process and organizational innovation. Third, they organize production not by repeating the same operation but by maintaining organizational flexibility at all levels, including the micro-production level. 'They depend upon learning to maintain competitive advantage' (Best, 1990, p. 13).

Unlike Best, but also contributing to the evolutionary theory, Lazonick (1991, ch. 3) writes of the 'innovative' firm as one which adopts a high fixed cost strategy of developmental investments. The formation of a new cost structure is an 'evolutionary process' which, if successful, gives the firm competitive advantage. The process involves innovation because it 'creates quality–cost outcomes that previously did not exist' (1991, p. 97).

One implication of the difference between the perspectives of Best and Lazonick is that the former – with an emphasis on organizational flexibility – underlines the advantages of small firms, whereas the latter – emphasizing the advantages of a high fixed cost strategy – suggests that large firms are more likely to succeed. This difference shows that among writers broadly within the evolutionary tradition there is not necessarily unanimity, even on basic questions about firms. Robertson and Langlois (1994), in focusing on inertia, uncover another difference among evolutionary theorists of the firm. They show that Nelson and Winter (1982) are aware of both the positive and negative aspects of routine: 'To the extent that these routines are efficient and difficult to come by, they are a most important asset, but they also induce inertia because they are difficult for the firm to change once in place.' Teece (1982), on the other hand, though he discusses the positive aspects of routines, 'neglects the negative side . . . and fails to note that the inflexibility, or inertia, induced by routines and the capabilities that they generate can raise to prohibitive levels the cost of adopting a new technology or entering new fields' (Robertson and Langlois, 1994).

It could be argued that these differences among evolutionary theorists are increasing. In his recent work, Best (2001), for example, develops the idea of a *productivity triad* of business model, production system and skill formation to explain why some firms are successful. Examples of business models include the Japanese firm (*kaisha*) and industrial districts (see Chapter 8); examples of production systems include mass production of high-volume consumer products, and low-volume, complex product systems of production; and skill formation refers to the formal and informal training and education systems, both within and external to the firm, that contribute to the development of technological skills. The idea rests on what Best calls a 'capabilities and innovation perspective'. It involves a complex dynamic between the firm, its networked relations with other firms and its response to and strategic reconstituting of the market. That it departs from Nelson and Winter's conception of an evolutionary theory of the firm is clear from the fact that Best (2001) makes no reference at all to 'routines'.

Even more clearly at odds with some of the fundamental tenets of evolutionary theory is the recent work of Lazonick (2002) and O'Sullivan (2000). O'Sullivan's critique of neoclassical theory of the firm, as we saw in Chapter 3, is based on the argument that neoclassical theory assumes that decisions are reversible, are taken by individuals, and are optimal. Innovation, on the other hand, is the result of processes that have three main characteristics. They are developmental or cumulative; organizational, involving co-ordinated action by a number of people, sometimes in different firms; and strategic, actually changing market conditions. While evolutionary theory of the firm comes close to answering her critique of neoclassical theory, she argues that it fails to provide for strategic decision making. It is developmental and organizational, but not strategic (O'Sullivan, 2000, pp. 30 and 36–8). She goes further, arguing that the very notion of routines as the basis for understanding organizational learning makes it difficult to integrate strategic decision making into evolutionary theory. Even the recent development from 'capabilities' to 'dynamic capabilities' (see below) does not solve the problem; evolutionary theory still 'ignores the influence that purposeful decisions have on' learning in the organization. As in neoclassical theory, she argues, there is 'automaticity' of decision making in evolutionary theory. In Lazonick's (2002) words, 'the dynamic capabilities approach has thus far ignored critical issues of strategic control within the innovative enterprise and the relation of strategic control to the organizational learning processes that are central to the development of an enterprise's core competences'. Lazonick (2002) refers to his and O'Sullivan's 'social conditions of innovative enterprise' (or SCIE) perspective, drawn from comparative-historical analysis of advanced economic development, as the theory of the innovative enterprise that can answer their criticisms of evolutionary and other theories. The SCIE perspective identifies 'three social conditions of innovative enterprise: *financial commitment, organizational integration,* and *strategic control*'. The first refers to commitment of finances to innovation, whether from the firm's own resources or those of other institutions. The second requires a commitment on the part of people throughout the organization to 'apply their skills and efforts to engage in interactive learning in pursuit of organizational goals'. The third condition enables decision makers 'to allocate resources in ways that can transform technologies and markets to generate innovations'.

There are two issues to take up at this point. The first is the question of whether there are responses from evolutionary theory to the above critiques. The second is the sense, if any, in which Best, Lazonick, O'Sullivan and others should be included in a discussion of evolutionary theories of the firm.

In relation to the first, let us focus on whether the accusation of 'automaticity' of decision making in evolutionary theory is appropriate.[9] Does purposeful decision making have a place in evolutionary economics? Even before the idea of 'dynamic capabilities' was introduced, evolutionary economics had explicitly not excluded strategic decisions.

> Undoubtedly, there is a great deal of business behavior that is not, within the ordinary meaning
> of the term, 'routine.' Equally clearly, much of the business decision making that is of the highest
> importance, both from the point of view of the individual firm and from that of society, is non-
> routine. High-level business executives do not, in the modern world, spend humdrum days at the
> office applying the same solutions to the same problems that they were dealing with five years
> before. We do not intend to imply any denial of these propositions in building our theory of busi-
> ness behavior on the notion of routine (Nelson and Winter, 1982, p. 15).

It could be argued, nevertheless, that this non-routine decision making is peripheral to
evolutionary theory. Recent work on dynamic capabilities has explicitly aimed at integrating
such decision making into evolutionary theory. Zollo and Winter (2001) distinguish
dynamic capabilities, which they define as 'systematic change efforts', from organizational
routines which are 'geared towards the operational functioning of the firm' and consider
that dynamic capabilities derive from learning mechanisms that 'go beyond semi-automatic
stimulus–response processes and tacit accumulation of experience'. Dynamic capabilities
include an element of experiential learning, but are also the outcome of more deliberative
cognitive processes aimed at developing explicit knowledge: 'dynamic capabilities emerge
from the co-evolution of tacit experience accumulation processes with explicit knowledge
articulation and codification activities'. This type of learning can result 'in adaptive adjustments to the existing sets of routines or in enhanced recognition of the need for more
fundamental change'. Zollo and Winter's developed conception of dynamic capabilities
captures the strategic actions of deliberate reflection on firm learning and capability.

It is clear, at least, that the criticism of 'automaticity' – that strategic decision making is
excluded from evolutionary theory – is being addressed by evolutionary theorists. It is also
clear, however, that there are important differences between some of the writers discussed
in this section. Are there also common elements in the work of these theorists?

Among the unifying themes, they are all interested in change over the long term – years
and decades rather than weeks and months. They are all convinced of the importance of
change within firms, not just in terms of products, but also in terms of processes of production and of decision making. They all focus to some extent on industries as well as firms,
their concern for what goes on within firms being related to their interest in the determinants of success of one firm or group of firms over another. Finally, they all adapt and use
elements of other theories – in particular, managerial and transaction cost – in the development of their own views on the nature of firms and industries.

Hodgson (2002),[10] calling them 'evolutionary, resource-based or competence-based perspectives', finds a more fundamental commonality. In these perspectives, he writes, 'the
existence, structure and boundaries of the firm are explained by the associated existence of
individual or team competences – such as skills and tacit knowledge – which are in some
way fostered and maintained by that organization'. This is in contrast to the 'contracterian'
theories, in particular Williamson's transaction cost theory, principal–agent theory and
other 'nexus of contract' theories. What the contracterian theories have in common is that

in all of them 'the informational and other difficulties in formulating, monitoring and policing contracts are the crucial explanatory elements' (Hodgson, 2002).

The ideas of the evolutionary and related theorists will be among those that inform our discussions of the conduct and behaviour of firms. It should be pointed out that, as a far more empirically based and inductive approach than many of the others discussed above, evolutionary theory is also more difficult to rigorously operationalize. As a result of this, research losses may be incurred, but there are also gains to be derived from the extent to which this approach is empirically and historically rooted. Schmalensee (1987) has written of the continued necessity for empirical studies as 'an important source of the general stylized facts needed to guide the construction of useful theoretical tools'. Chandler's work, and that of other evolutionary theorists, can be seen in this light.

4.7 Applications

We briefly address in this section applications of some of the theories described in this and the previous chapter. We begin with neoclassical theory. With its assumptions of rational, optimizing behaviour, market-based solutions and equilibrium outcomes, neoclassical theory of the firm is analytically useful in situations where there are strong markets and high levels of competition. The 'neoclassical' firm, smoothly shifting between capital and labour inputs, for example, will use automated equipment rather than skilled labour if wages rise. The rapid rise of wages of computer software experts in the late 1990s can be seen, from a neoclassical perspective, as a key factor in the increasing tendency for firms to outsource software development during that period. They increased their internal capital–labour ratios in response to the rise in the price of labour.

From a principal–agent perspective, the same issue of whether to directly employ software engineers or to outsource the service, would be addressed differently. The question would be one of the nature of monitoring, moral hazard and shirking. Let us assume that there is a software task to be undertaken that is clearly specifiable. Managers in the firm have no expertise in software development and therefore have no way of monitoring employees. This, they believe, increases the likelihood of the moral hazard of shirking. Given the shortage of software engineers, managers also have a problem selecting appropriate candidates for internal employment. They therefore turn to the market and hire the best software house – in terms of reputation, price and time – to undertake the task.

Transaction cost theory directly addresses, in the same circumstances, the make or buy decision. If the costs of outsourcing (that is, those costs other than the costs of the software service itself) are too high, then the firm will employ software engineers directly. It is generally assumed in transaction cost theory that, given the existence of bounded rationality and opportunism in inter-firm contracts – the risks/costs of outsourcing – the firm will internalize. The exception would be where there is a high level of asset specificity. In the above case this would be a software project that really is one-off, for example a software product that requires no ongoing maintenance. The less likely this is, the more likely is the firm to employ software engineers directly, even at a high wage cost. (High wages would have to be paid in the contracted firm, too, raising the price of the out-sourced service.)

In behavioural and stakeholder theories, it could be argued that it makes little difference as to whether software is produced by additional direct employees or by an outside firm. Both become members of the coalition – or stakeholders. However, behavioural theory, for example, can help answer the question by focusing on how each of the two options threatens or enhances the interests of existing constituents. Employing additional, highly paid workers could be opposed by existing workers if they feel that this reduces the likeli-hood of increases in their own wages. On the other hand, outsourcing could be seen as transferring profit to an outside company that could be earned by the firm itself. It is in the bargaining process among the constituencies, possibly with the taking up of some of the organizational slack to offer compromises, that the 'correct' decision is taken. It will be correct in the sense that it is satisficing – that it provides sufficient profit to keep the firm in existence without threatening the coalition.

Evolutionary theory is best applied to changes in firms that take place over relatively long periods of time. However, there are examples of the application of the theory to more immediate changes in the firm's environment (Hilliard and Jacobson, 2003). Here we focus on the firm's capabilities and routines. If there are existing routines for responding to a situ-ation, then, all else being equal, these routines could again be used. However, if the firm has dynamic capability then it can depart from past routines (overcome path dependency). The suggestion in our discussion of the application of principal–agent theory, that managers have no skills in software development, would not apply here. Firms with dynamic capa-bility are firms that have the ability to 'identify and implement new learning, new kinds of knowledge and new organisational processes'.[11] While this may not help us to determine whether the firm will internalize or outsource the software project, it does help us to identify those firms that will face the question with a strategic rather than simply a reactive focus. In a changing environment, the most important factor for successful adaptation is the ability to identify and implement new learning, new kinds of knowledge and new organizational processes, but this will only happen where the firm's perceptions of future opportunity support such a strategy.

4.8 Summary

This and the previous chapters have briefly reviewed the major theories of the firm. Each theory has merits, and each has limitations. They are not necessarily mutually exclusive, in that some economists will use one theory for one application, and another for a different application. It is also true, however, that in relation to some questions – for example, in relation to the nature and survival of the firm – different theories will provide different answers. Among the key differences between theories is the extent to which mathematics is used in their application. Although we aim to minimize the use of mathematics in this book, most of the theories in Chapter 3 are amenable to mathematical application, whereas most of those in this chapter are not.[12] Table 4.1 is a continuation of Table 3.2, showing the points of focus of the theories of the firm covered in this chapter.

Table 4.1 Major theories of the firm

Theory of the firm	Point of focus
Behavioural theory	Firm as coalition (satisficing decision)
Stakeholder theory	Returns to stakeholders (fair or market-based)
Co-operative game	Firm (organizational equilibrium)
Transaction cost	Transaction (firm v. market)
Evolutionary	Firm (organizational capability)

As mentioned earlier, rigorous empirical research is rare. Chandler (1992a), as a business historian working within (and developing) the framework of evolutionary theory, is unusual among theorists of the firm in having an empirical basis for his views. Indeed, in his book on *Scale and Scope* (1990), he compares 'the fortunes of more than 600 enterprises – the 200 largest industrial firms at three points in time (First World War, 1929, and Second World War) in each of the three major industrial economies' (Chandler, 1992b). On a much more limited basis, Hilliard and Jacobson (2003) show the importance of dynamic capability among a group of 16 pharmaceutical firms in Ireland.

The significance of technological change (including organizational innovation) as a factor in the conduct (and structure) of firms and in the structure of markets, is accepted in much of the literature. The technological non-separability and transaction cost views both to some extent incorporate this, but it is more fully accounted for by the evolutionary and related theories.

Within the historical, empirical and inductive approaches adopted by the evolutionary and related theorists, the roles of technology and innovation are included. Chandler, for example, compares the role in the growth of firms of specific technologies and market situations with that of existing competitive advantages arising from learned routines in 'production, distribution and marketing, and improving existing products and processes'. Specific technologies and market situations were, he concludes, more important in the vertical integration of firms. The desire to exploit competitive advantages arising from the learned routines was more important in the growth into new markets (Chandler, 1992b). This includes expansion into markets in regions new to the operations of the firm, which brings in the geographical dimension of industrial structure to which we turn in Chapter 8.

Best, Lazonick and O'Sullivan also explicitly incorporate technology and innovation, and this perspective leads them also to address locational issues. In Lazonick's words, firms' strategies and structures 'take on a national character because the relevant business organizations do not develop and utilize resources in a political and cultural vacuum' (Lazonick, 1991, p. 109). Best accepts even sub-national regional differences, as evidenced in his focus on small-firm industrial districts in Italy. These, too, are addressed in the context of the locational aspects of industrial structure in Chapter 8. Regional and national systems of innovation are also considered in Chapter 8, but first we turn to industrial structure in general.

Websites

As for most of the other chapters in this book, the IDEAS website at **http://ideas.repec.org/** provides many online resources on the topics covered, and authors mentioned, in Chapter 2.

There is a vast amount of information, articles and references available on the web on Coase and transaction cost economics. Just one example, which also contains many links to other sites, is **http://faculty.washington.edu/krumme/readings/transaction_cost.html**

A number of individual economists' websites are of particular interest for this chapter. A great deal of information on, and papers by, Herbert A. Simon are available at **http://cepa.newschool.edu/het/profiles/simon.htm**. Geoffrey Hodgson's site is **http://www.herts.ac.uk/business/esst/Staff/g-hodgson/hodgson.html**, where many of his papers can be viewed. Nicolai Foss, although he is not referred to in this chapter, has produced many books and articles that are of direct relevance to many of the questions raised here. His site, **http://web.cbs.dk/staff/nicolai-foss/njf.html**, provides online access to some of his work. Richard Langlois, whose work is in some respects similar to that of Foss, has a site at **http://web.uconn.edu/langlois/**

Interesting material on and by early economists who were influential in the development of evolutionary theory, including Thorstein Veblen and Joseph Schumpeter, is available at **http://cepa.newschool.edu/het/**. A great deal of other material on evolutionary economics, including many downloadable papers and links to other sites, is available at **http://www.business.aau.dk/evolution/**, which is a site maintained by Esben Sloth Andersen, at Copenhagen Business School.

Questions

4.1 What is the behavioural theory's critique of neoclassical theory?

4.2 Do you agree that stakeholder theory is not really a theory, but rather a prescription for an ethical business world?

4.3 According to Coase, what is the essence of the firm?

4.4 Why is the evolutionary theory of the firm so called?

4.5 Apply the theories of the firm to the question of how firms will respond to more rigorous environmental protection regulation.

Notes

1 For a brief account of Simon and his contributions, see Butler (2002).

2 See also Aoki (1988) and Aoki *et al.* (1990).

3 Economies of scale arise when the production cost per unit of a good decreases as the number of units produced increases. Economies of scope exist when the cost of producing good x and good y together is less than that of producing either of them separately. For a detailed study of the significance of scale and scope in the evolution of firms, see Chandler (1990).

4 Different contractual models in this context refers primarily to internal governance and market governance or, in other words, hierarchy and market.

5 The most important evolutionary economists are Nelson and Winter (1982). See also Nelson (1995) and Teece (1987). Among the more important and prolific of recent evolutionary economists is Hodgson (1998a, b, 2002). It should be noted that at least some writers using 'an evolutionary approach to economic change' focus as much on the process of innovation as on firms. Thus Clark and Juma (1987, p. 64) attempt 'to examine the co-evolution between technology and institutions'. Auerbach (1989), although he is clearly concerned with the evolution of 'giant firms' (p. 149) and the changing pattern of firm organization (ch. 8), focuses primarily on the competitive process (chs 4 and 9).

6 This article also shows how evolutionary theory, drawing on transaction cost analysis but emphasizing the 'continuous learning that makes a firm's assets dynamic', clarifies the basis for the emergence and development of firms in some of the major industries of the world (Chandler, 1992b).

7 Demsetz (1988) is interested in the preservation of commitments, which may be either efficiency enhancing or stultifying. As Loasby (1990) points out, this reinforces Demsetz's unrecognized link with the evolutionary theorists. For a brief discussion of the biological analogy in evolutionary theory of the firm, see Hodgson (2002).

8 The comparison between comparative and competitive advantages is also made by a number of other authors, including Teece (1987) and Porter (1990).

9 This and the following two paragraphs draw directly on Hilliard and Jacobson (2003).

10 Drawing on Foss (1993)

11   Hilliard and Jacobson (2003) conclude that, 'in a changing environment, the most important factor for successful adaptation is the ability to identify and implement new learning, new kinds of knowledge and new organisational processes, but that this will only happen where the firm's perceptions of future opportunity support such a strategy.'

12   It should be noted, however, that with simplifying assumptions, mathematics can be used in any theory.

CHAPTER 5

Market structure

5.1 Learning objectives

The main objectives of this chapter are:

- To clarify the concepts of market, industry, and market structure
- To discuss the notion of 'the relevant EU market', in theory and practice
- To provide a clarification of the determinants of market structure, and
- To review briefly perfect competition, monopolistic competition and monopoly as the primary examples of market structure

5.2 Evolving views on market structure

Analysing the structure of a market implies determining the intensity of competition therein. For many years, the analysis of market structure has been confined to measuring the degree of seller concentration only, but the new theoretical inputs synthesized in the contestable school's notion of 'potential entry and exit' (see Chapter 2), have weakened somewhat the predominance of concentration measures. As will be seen in this chapter, EU policy makers have gradually extended the notion of market structure and that of market by including novel elements in their definitions. The logic enshrined in the early structure–conduct–performance (SCP) paradigm fits well with the neoclassical theory of the firm, where the firm's conduct is almost irrelevant, as it is confined to adjusting to the given market price. By contrast, other theories, such as the evolutionary theory of the firm, countenance greater independence in the strategies of individual firms.

As a result, the contrast between the definition of market structure by those operating within the early SCP paradigm, and the more modern, strategically based definition of market structure, is indicative of the evolution of the SCP paradigm itself. The two following definitions will clarify this evolution. According to Bain (1958), market structures are 'the characteristics of the organization of a market that seem to exercise an influence on the nature of competition and pricing within the market'. On the other hand, Koch (1980) sees market structures as 'the relatively permanent strategic elements of the environment of a firm that influence, *and are influenced by*, the conduct and performance of the firm in the market in which it operates' (Koch, 1980, p. 90). Whereas Bain's definition identifies only a one-way causality, from the organization of the market to competition and pricing, Koch's definition envisages the structure influencing and being influenced by conduct and performance. Both definitions of market structure call for the clarification of the concept of a market.

5.3 Defining the market and the industry

Although the terms *industry* and *market* are often used interchangeably in economics, they actually refer to different types of economic institutions and activities. An industry is a firm or group of firms, and a market is a nexus of interaction between buyers and sellers. (These terms are defined more comprehensively in the paragraphs below.) In general, in order to discuss either industries or markets, we need to find ways of distinguishing between them. Two obvious ways of doing so are, first, in terms of the output or product of the industry (or market), and second, in terms of the spatial or geographical extent of the industry (or market).

5.3.1 The nature of the product

A market is normally defined as the locus of purchase by buyers and sale by suppliers of similar goods. More broadly, it is the institution within which the interaction between economic agents performing these two functions – buying and selling – establishes the price of the good. For the buyer, two goods x and y are 'similar' if the purchase of x brings the same level of utility as the purchase of y, and if x and y are deemed to satisfy the same need. In other words, x and y belong to the same market if they are highly *substitutable*. The degree of substitutability is computed with the help of the *cross-elasticity of demand* (CED) between products. The CED between two products measures the responsiveness of quantity sold of one product to a change in the price of the other product. In other words, it is the degree to which the price change of product y will affect the quantity sold of product x, or:

$$CED = \frac{\Delta Q_x / Q_x}{\Delta P_y / P_y}$$

If, for example, a 30 per cent rise in the price of butter causes a 50 per cent increase in the quantity sold of a soya-based butter substitute, the cross-elasticity of demand will be equal to 1.66, a relatively high value. The two goods will be close substitutes and will be classified in the same market, say the market for spreads. The more narrowly defined the product market, the higher the CED would have to be for the two products to be in the same market. Two goods for which a change in the price of one has little or no effect on the quantity demanded of the other can clearly not be considered as part of the same market.

On the producer side, the market becomes the industry. In her *Economics of Imperfect Competition*, Robinson (1933) attempted to provide a definition of the industry. She defined it in terms of a commodity, where a 'commodity is a consumable good, arbitrarily demarcated from other kinds of goods but which may be regarded for practical purposes as homogeneous within itself'. She continued:

> An industry is any group of firms producing a single commodity. In some cases where a commodity in the real world is bounded on all sides by a market gap between itself and its closest substitutes, the real-world firms producing this real-world commodity will conform to the definition of an industry sufficiently closely to make the discussion of industries in this technical sense of some interest. (Robinson, 1933, p. 17)

In some respects, the 'market gap' identified by Robinson is more difficult to detect today. Indeed, technical change, increased product differentiation and consumers' sophistication render industries' edges more blurred (particularly true for products incorporating new technologies).[1] Nevertheless, we continue to examine industries in terms of relatively homogeneous products, such as the car industry, the computer industry or the clothing industry.

5.3.2 The geographical extent of the market

If the technical boundaries of an industry and of a market are difficult to draw, the geographical limits of a market for a manufactured good are just as difficult to identify. One possible way to solve the problem is to make a convention (rule of thumb) on how much is actually shipped in and out of a particular region at a particular time (Shepherd, 1990). For example, region r_i will be a geographically distinct market for soft drinks, if less than, say, 10 per cent of its local production is shipped out, and less than 10 per cent of its local consumption is shipped in. Other criteria have been suggested for the delimitation of regional and local markets: a low sales value per unit of weight, a high ratio of transportation cost per unit of sales over a standardized distance, or a short average shipment radius (Scherer and Ross, 1990). Although the intuitive meaning of the EU market for cars, as opposed to the Japanese one, is straightforward, the specification of intra-EU geographical limits of the market is a more arduous task. (A comprehensive analysis of the difficulties arising from the definition of the EU market may be found in Fishwick, 1986.)

5.4 Definition of the relevant EU market

The Commission of the EU and the European Court of Justice have on many occasions attempted to draw the boundaries of the market within the EU. They have done so because of the necessity to deal with the problems of market domination, of concentration and mergers, and in general, of practices seen as endangering the smooth functioning of competition.[2] These are all dealt with in the Competition Policy of the Treaty (mainly Articles 81 and 82, formerly Articles 85 and 86 of the Treaty of Rome) and by the Merger Regulation (see Chapter 16). Articles 81 and 82 did not specify what a market was. The first quantitative measurement was to be found later in the preamble of the Merger Control Regulation, where it was specified that concentration is unlikely to impede competition where 'the market share of the undertakings concerned does not exceed 25 per cent either in the Common Market or in a substantial part of it'. Under the Guidelines of the newly revised Merger Regulation, which have applied from 1st May 2004, benchmarks of 25 per cent and 50 per cent are selected as corresponding to concentration levels for which the Commission is likely to have competition concerns, depending on the case.[3] Based on case law, a market share of 50 per cent or more is considered as evidence of a dominant market position, whereas in some instances, mergers resulting in concentration levels below 40 per cent can also lead to the creation or strengthening of a dominant position. However, these market concentration levels are only indicative, for market domination depends also on other indicators.

Already the 1965 Memorandum of the Commission (CEC, 1965), had indicated that market domination could not be solely defined on the basis of quantitative elements of a given market structure, such as the market share held by the firm. Market domination is regarded first and foremost as *putative economic power*. A firm with a small market share, but with the ability to evict other competitors from a market, can be said to hold such economic power. An analysis of all cases where the Commission established dominance as a result of mergers, and of other cases pertaining to the year 2002, shows that some 'special circumstances' made the estimates for the market share not very informative. In many instances, these crude measures of concentration would have actually underestimated the potential competition effect of mergers. The 'special circumstances' refer, for example, to a case where one of the merging parties was a recent entrant on to the market.

Throughout the period since the establishment of the European Community, the Commission and the European Court of Justice have tried to avoid defining the relevant geographical and product market. In many of the cases dealt with under Competition Policy such definitions were unnecessary. As documented by Fishwick (1993), in one-third of all proposed concentrations (mergers and takeovers) examined under the Merger Control Regulation in the first few years of its implementation, precise definitions of the market were unnecessary. This is because even with the narrowest definitions of the product and geographical market, the 25 per cent threshold limit was not reached. Only when it was considered essential, have the Commission and the Court of Justice attempted to define the market. This has led to a myriad of definitions of the relevant market, varying from case to case. 'The definition of the market and the degree of power necessary for a dominant position vary with the offense' (Fox, 1983, p. 368).[4] A case by case approach is inevitable since a firm's strategy can be regional, national or EU-wide.

Arguably, precise benchmarks are required so that a generic definition of the market can be provided. Progress towards this end has been made with the advent of the single European market in the early 1990s (see Fishwick, 1993).[5] The application of Articles 81, 82 and of the Merger Regulation requires different frameworks, but these variations have been built around the same theme. Under the three policy instruments, the relevant market is defined in terms of (i) product range and (ii) geographical area on the basis of the concept of demand substitution in the short term and supply substitution in the short term. *Supply substitution* refers to the potential provision of additional supplies on the part of both incumbent firms and potential entrants.

The inclusion of the notion of supply-side substitution is relatively new as it was introduced for the first time in 1988, in the *Eurofix-Bauco v. Hilti* and *Tetra Pak II* cases which fell under Article 82.[6] The potential expansion of supply helps in determining the likely concentration level in the market.

Issues surrounding both product and geographical extents of markets and industries have been clarified by Kay's (1990a) concept of the *strategic market*, 'the smallest area within which it is possible to be a viable competitor'; the strategic *product* market is 'the minimum feasible product range'. The geographical dimension of the industry is different from that of the market when 'the location of production can be determined independently of the location of consumption'. For example, a hairdressing salon must be within its market, and production and consumption must occur at the same time and place, whereas the production of watches can take place where it is cheapest, even though the market is global. Beer is somewhere between, not usually brewed on the premises where it is consumed but for consumption in Europe usually brewed in Europe. In terms of product or process, the 'scope of the industry is influenced by cross elasticities of supply'; we can think of the product/process boundaries of the industry in terms of 'the degree to which manufacturers can choose to substitute one line of production for another'.

It follows from Kay's analysis that although the method used is the same in each case, the market and industry can only be defined on a case by case basis. Applying this to the Single European Market, Kay points out that the strategic market for a good or service may or may not coincide with the aggregate market of the members of the EU.

5.4.1 The relevant product market in practice

In the *Aérospatiale-Alenia/De Havilland* case (CEC, 1991), the Commission repeated the definition of the product market based effectively on cross-elasticity of demand: 'A relevant product market comprises in particular all those products which are regarded as interchangeable or substitutable by the consumer, by reason of the product characteristics, their prices and their intended use' (Commission Regulation No. 2367/90).

In its *XXIst Report on Competition Policy* (1991), the Commission adds the time dimension, specifying the short-term nature of the definition of the product market: 'In order to belong to the same market, two products must compete to a sufficient degree. . . . This competition must exist or be brought about in the near future and not only be based on a medium or long-term change in demand or supply' (CEC, 1991, p. 357).

In the *Lucas/Eaton* case examining the braking systems industry, the Commission took into account a period of one year when considering the supply substitution between different systems.

In the *Astra Zeneca/Novartis* case, the determination of the relevant product markets proved rather difficult. Again, in this case, the Commission did not rely exclusively on the existing market position of the different firms, but it took primarily into account the 'projected future developments of their product portfolios' (CEC, 2001a, p. 75).

5.4.2 Determination of the relevant geographical market

The Commission has endeavoured to define local, national, regional, Union and world markets in the various product markets considered. The relevant geographical market was defined as the EU-wide market for bleach sulphate pulp in the 1985 *Woodpulp* case. The allegation was that the Canadian, US, Finnish and Swedish firms were colluders fixing prices at above competition levels. The fact that there was price parity across the EC market constituted evidence that there was an EC-wide market for this particular product (Fishwick, 1993). In the *Mannesmann/Boge* case,[7] the Commission similarly defined the relevant market (for shock absorbers) as the Union market.

In the *Nestlé–Perrier* case, the market was defined as France, among other factors because of the insignificance of imports – less than 2 per cent of the market. In Belgium, the fact that 51 per cent of consumption is met by imports and the 42 per cent of domestic production is exported, was evidence that Belgium is not a separate market. The relevant geographical market was similarly defined as national in the *Alcatel/Telettra* case (transmission equipment) and in the *Varta/Bosch* case (starter motors). In other instances, the market was, for various reasons, defined as local (retailing), and as international (*Aérospatiale-Alenia/De Havilland* and *Mannesmann/VDO* cases).

In the 2002 *Aventis Pharma SA and Rhône-Poulenc Biochemie SA* case, the market for methylglucamine – a chemical used for the synthesis of pharmaceuticals and colouring – was defined as having a worldwide dimension (CEC, 2003a).

The increasing incidence of the supply of goods and services by digital means since the 1990s contributes to a substantial reconfiguration of markets. In theory, online transactions have the potential to increase competition by contributing to the further integration of separate geographical markets. Through the increase in market transparency and through the reduction of transaction costs, e-commerce can lead to substantial efficiency gains. These positive effects can, however, be offset by a number of problems such as 'network dominance' or the exchange of sensitive and strategic information between buyers or sellers (see

CEC, 2001a, p. 65). Given the global nature of these transactions, the competition assessment of e-commerce – through the definition of the relevant geographical market – is still evolving, and this is done in close collaboration with other competition authorities worldwide.

5.4.3 Statistics on regions and industries in the EU

Information exists that facilitates rough definitions of industries in terms both of their product and their spatial range. Eurostat, the statistical office of the European Union in Luxembourg, gathers and publishes data on a wide range of economic and social indicators in the EU by region and by industry. The regional data are provided on the basis of the Nomenclature of Statistical Territorial Units (NUTS). There are three NUTS levels: NUTS 1, at which there are 87 regions in the EU-15 (including the 'extra-regio' territories, that is, those parts of the economic territory that cannot be attached to a certain region, such as territorial waters); NUTS 2, at which there are 228 basic administrative units; and NUTS 3, at which there are more than 1000 subdivisions of basic administrative units. To illustrate, Spain has seven regions at the NUTS 1 level. Most of these (the exceptions are the smaller regions) break down into a number of basic administrative units at the NUTS 2 level; the NUTS 1 region Noroeste, for example, contains Galicia, Asturias and Cantabria at the NUTS 2 level. Each of the NUTS 2 units in turn is made up of different numbers of NUTS 3 units, depending on size. As they were preparing for the fifth enlargement, the ten new members of the EU adopted a coding of statistical regions, in line with Eurostat guidelines. For example, Poland has 16 NUTS 2 regions, whereas Latvia, a much smaller country, has only 5 NUTS 3 regions.

The General Industrial Classification of Economic Activities, NACE, provides a system for classifying such economic variables as earnings and numbers employed. Like NUTS, these data are provided at different levels of disaggregation. For example, at the two-digit level, the code 29 refers to the manufacture of machinery and equipment. This breaks down at three-digit level into seven different categories of machinery and equipment (such as machine tools – NACE 29.4). The code 33 refers to medical, precision and optical instruments, 34 to transport equipment, etc. Each of these two-digit classes in turn subdivides into a number of four-digit groups; under 29, the code 29.11 refers to the manufacture of engines and turbines, except aircrafts, vehicle and cycle engines. The NACE classification has evolved over the years, to comply with the UN international classification, and also to mirror industrial change. For example, the code 37 refers to recycling activities, an increasing manufacturing activity in recent years.

Combining the NUTS and NACE data can facilitate researchers in answering questions about the relative importance of certain industries in certain countries, regions or units. Jacobson and Mack (1994), for example, use a location quotient methodology to compare Ireland with Denmark as peripheral regions in the EU.

A location quotient (LQ) is a simple measure of spatial concentration based upon either employment or income. Using the notation of Table 5.1:

Table 5.1 Location quotient notation	
Employment in industry *i*	**Total employment**
e_{ip} = a peripheral place	e_{op} = a peripheral place
E_{io} = total base	E_{oo} = total base

$$LQ_p = \frac{e_{ip} / e_{op}}{E_{io} / E_{oo}}$$

In the example referred to, location quotients were calculated for employment in Ireland and in Denmark as peripheral regions, with the EU as the total base. Each set of LQs (that is, one set for Ireland and one set for Denmark) contains as many LQs as there are NACE two-digit classes. The two sets were then compared. The main finding of the research is that business services are more concentrated in Denmark than in Ireland.

Such research does not, however, answer questions about the relative importance of firms within industries. It is to a closer examination of market structures that we must turn for the focus on the relationships between firms and markets or industries.

5.5 Determinants of market structure

Market structure refers to the way markets are organized. In general, this structure is the result of actions and interactions of individuals and institutions including firms, other business organizations and public bodies. The structure of the market is defined in terms of the number and size distribution of the competing firms. In the traditional model, there are three main elements of market structure:[8]

◆ The degree of seller (and buyer) concentration

◆ The degree of product differentiation within individual markets

◆ The conditions of entry and exit.

In simple competition models, large numbers of firms sell a standardized product on a determined market. However, a high level of price competition gives firms an incentive to differentiate their products. Product differentiation exists when products sold on the same market are no longer considered as perfect substitutes by buyers. Moreover, the greater the extent to which a firm has succeeded in differentiating its product, the greater the extent to which it has raised a barrier to entry into its market. Product differentiation can thus be regarded as an element of market structure but in many empirical studies it is also included as a barrier to entry.

Measurements of product differentiation have been attempted, based on the following assumption: in a given market, the degree of product differentiation is reflected in the advertising intensity. Since product differentiation can be a means of softening price competition, and since it is included as such in the list of strategies available to firms, it will be developed in Chapter 10. Our analysis of determinants will focus solely on the two other elements of market structure, concentration and entry conditions. A slight reference to product differentiation will however be made in this chapter in the context of the discussion on monopolistic competition (in Section 5.6.2).

5.5.1 Measures and definition of concentration

Concentration is a measure of the intensity of competition or of control. It provides information about the relative size of firms in a specific market. The relative size of firms can be measured through their market shares. The market share (MS_{ij}) of firm i (F_i) in a particular industry (I_j) is normally defined as the share of firm i's sales revenue in the total sales revenue of industry j, or:

$$MS_{ij} = \frac{\text{Sales revenue of } F_i}{\text{Sales revenue of } I_j}$$

Among other possible variables for the measurement of market shares are the output, turnover, value added, numbers employed and assets. There are various ways of summarizing the distribution of market shares of the firms in an industry using a single figure known as a concentration index. The most commonly used indices are:

+ The n firm concentration
+ The Herfindahl index (H)
+ The Gini coefficient
+ The entropy index
+ The Lerner index.

The CRn or n-firm concentration ratio

CRn refers to the cumulated market shares of the n leading firms in the industry. Normally, n is between 4 and 8, but the four-firm concentration ratio (CR4) is most widely used. CR4 measures the share of the market (or industry) held by the four largest firms. CRn is computed as:

$$CR n = \sum_{i=1}^{n} S_i$$

where the ith firm has rank i in descending order (that is, where the largest firm has rank i = 1, the second largest i = 2 and so on); S_i is the share of firm i in the market. This share can be defined on the basis of output, turnover, sales, numbers employed, shipments, and so forth.

A value close to zero would indicate that the largest n firms supply a small share of the market. Conversely, a value close to 1 denotes a high level of concentration. The concentration ratio is popular because of its limited data requirements. Information on size of markets and on shares of the largest firms is available from several sources in the EU. In spite of its popularity, this ratio is flawed by its inability to inform us of the relative importance of firms within a particular industry. For example, let the four-firm concentration ratio be equal to 0.9 in two hypothetical industries A and B. The relative market shares of the four largest firms is given in Table 5.2. The same ratio represents two radically different distributions of firms.

Table 5.2 Market shares of the four largest firms in two industries

	Firm 1	Firm 2	Firm 3	Firm 4
Industry A	0.80	0.05	0.03	0.02
Industry B	0.25	0.23	0.22	0.20
Industry A: CR4 = 0.90				
Industry B: CR4 = 0.90				

The fact that CR4 for industry A is equal to CR4 for industry B suggests that concentration is the same in the two industries and yet, in Industry A, a dominant firm covers 80 per cent of the market, whereas Industry B is characterized by equal-sized firms. The four-firm concentration ratio does not reveal the extent to which one or more firms *within* the top four dominate a particular market. This criticism can be answered by providing other CRn ratios, such as CR1, CR2. However, this solution is only partial in that, ideally, the index should be a single figure.

The Herfindahl index (*H*)

The Herfindahl index, which is the second most widely used concentration index, is defined as the sum of the squares of the market shares of the n firms in the industry, that is:

$$H = \sum_{i=1}^{n} (S_i)^2$$

where the ith firm and S_i are as defined for CRi. S_i, can, for example, be measured in terms of firm i's sales on the market (Q_i) as a fraction of total sales (Q_t).

Defined in this way the H index would be:

$$H = \sum_{i=1}^{n} \left(\frac{Q_i}{Q_t} \right)^2$$

The H index combines information about the size of all firms in a market. It is a measure of dispersion and can vary between 0 and 1. The higher H, the higher the dispersion. If H is 0, this suggests that there is a large number of equal-sized firms in the particular industry, and that concentration is low. If H is close to 1, the market is dominated by one large firm.

Let us use as an example the same data as in Table 5.2, assuming that in both Industry A and Industry B firms 5 to 14 account for equal shares of the remaining 10 per cent of the market (that is, each accounts for 0.01, or 1 per cent, of the market). The Herfindahl index (sum of the cells in Table 5.3 for each industry) shows that Industry A is far more concentrated than Industry B. This is in contrast with CR4 and CR14, which are identical for the two industries.

Table 5.3 The squares of the market shares of the 14 firms in each industry							
	Firm 1	**Firm 2**	**Firm 3**	**Firm 4**	**Firm 5**	**...**	**Firm 14**
Industry A	0.6400	0.0025	0.0009	0.0004	0.0001	...	0.0001
Industry B	0.0625	0.0529	0.0484	0.0400	0.0001	...	0.0001
Industry A: $H = 0.6448$							
Industry B: $H = 0.2048$							

The Gini coefficient

The Gini coefficient is a statistical measure based upon the Lorenz curve.[9] The Lorenz curve relates the percentage of total market value of any variable (shipments, value added, numbers employed, etc.) to the percentage of firms in the market, cumulated from the smallest to the largest (Fig. 5.1).

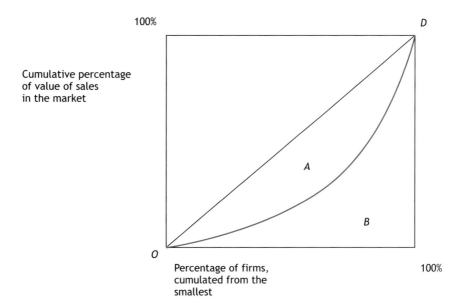

Figure 5.1 Lorenz curve for a hypothetical market x

The diagonal line OD represents the limit case of perfect equality in the distribution. It suggests that there is an even distribution of the market's value of sales among the firms in the market. The greater the deviation of the curve from the diagonal OD, the greater the inequality in firms' sizes. The Gini coefficient (GC) enables us to calculate the concentration area, which is situated between the diagonal and the Lorenz curve. It can be defined as the area A over the area $A + B$.

$$GC = \frac{S_A}{(S_A + S_B)}$$

If the Lorenz curve is the diagonal OD, then, in a sense, $S_A = 0$ and $GC = 0$. It can be shown that, at the other extreme, where there is complete inequality in the sizes of the firms (and $S_B = 0$), the Gini coefficient will tend towards 1.

A limitation of the Gini coefficient is that the same coefficient can correspond to different distributions of firm sizes in the market.

The entropy index

The entropy index (E) is equal to the sum of the shares weighted by their logarithm:

$$E = \sum_{i=1}^{n} S_i \cdot \log \frac{1}{S_i}$$

Borrowed from the information theory, the entropy index measures the degree of uncertainty associated with a particular market structure. If there is only one firm in the market, the index is 0, and the uncertainty for the monopolist in relation to whether it can keep a random customer is at a minimum. Conversely, when all market shares are equal, the uncertainty is maximum, and $S_i = 1/n$. In this case

$$E = n \cdot \frac{1}{n} \cdot \log n = \log n$$

In an industry comprising n equal-sized firms, the entropy index is equal to $\log n$. The advantage of the entropy index over other measures of concentration is that, in the case where a distribution relates to groups of firms belonging to different size classes, to different industries and/or to different countries, the index can be decomposed into several components; this facilitates the measurement of the entropy within different groups as well as between groups (see Jacquemin, 1979, p. 40).

The Lerner index

The Lerner index (Lerner, 1934) is in fact a measure of monopoly power. It is defined as follows:

$$L = \frac{(P - MC)}{P}$$

where P = price and MC = marginal cost.

As is shown in Section 5.6.1 below, in markets defined as perfectly competitive, no single firm can influence price; the demand curve is perfectly elastic. As a result, the price the firm will obtain for each unit sold will be the same as the price obtained for all other units. In other words, price is equal to marginal revenue (MR). If, in accordance with neo-classical assumptions, the firms are profit maximizers, production will occur where MR = MC. In a perfectly competitive market, where MR = P, the Lerner index will be zero. The higher the index, the more concentration (or at least power to extract above-normal profits) there is.[10]

5.5.2 Difficulties arising from indices of concentration

The various measures of market concentration incorporate, usually implicitly, the assumption that there is a clear correspondence between a firm and a market, and that firms operate within their national boundaries. In practice, neither condition is fulfilled.

Multi-plant and multi-product firms, for example, do not belong to precisely definable, single markets. It follows that an industry is not necessarily congruent with a market. In which industries should one classify groups such as Ferruzzi, and LVMH (Louis Vuitton Moët Hennessy)? Published accounts do not report in detail the results of the different divisions of a firm, which may be specialized in the production of different products. Concentration indices are thus not able to reveal the dominant positions hidden within conglomerates.

The second problem relates to the association between concentration and competition. The greater the level of concentration, the less competitive the market is considered to be. To illustrate the problem, let us assume two industries with identical concentration ratios, say Industry A and Industry B, in each of which the top three firms account for 75 per cent of the market. The three firms are, respectively, A_1, A_2 and A_3, and B_1, B_2 and B_3. From whatever measure of concentration we choose, with no other information we would conclude that the two industries have the same level of competition. However, if we further assume that Table 5.4 indicates changes in the positions of the three top firms over time, then, even though the concentration ratios remain the same, the level of competition can be seen to be different.

Table 5.4 Market shares of the top three firms in two industries

Year	Firm					
	A_1	A_2	A_3	B_1	B_2	B_3
1999	40	20	15	40	20	15
2000	30	15	30	40	20	15
2001	20	20	35	40	20	15
2002	25	25	25	40	20	15

Such large changes in firms' share as those indicated for the leading firms of Industry A are very unlikely over a small number of years. In fact, there is empirical evidence of an inverse relationship between changes in firms' market shares and levels of concentration (Caves and Porter, 1978). Nevertheless, the table does indicate the possibility of high rank mobility, where the rank of top firms changes frequently, together with constant concentration ratios. Whether through price or non-price competition, the table suggests that the firms in Industry A are vying far more intensely for market leadership than those in Industry B.

The third problem refers to the omission of international trade from the data computed according to these methodologies, based on output, turnover, sales or employment figures. This omission is particularly disturbing in the case of highly open economies such as the Benelux countries, Ireland, and the Czech Republic, and also in the case of specific industries where import penetration is high (such as the office machinery and data processing equipment industries) in the EU as a whole. In the case of an open economy, a domestically based concentration index may exaggerate the actual degree of concentration. We can use an example to demonstrate this.

Assume that in country A, one firm represents 90 per cent of the total domestic turnover, and $n - 1$ other firms make up the remaining 10 per cent of domestic output. The computation of the concentration ratio through any of the methods described above would suggest a high level of concentration; the four-firm concentration ratio, for example, would be close to 1. If, however, we introduce international trade considerations, and assume that the n firms export a high percentage of their total turnover, and that a high percentage of domestic sales are accounted for by imports, then the real concentration ratio drops sharply. The dominant firm may account for far less than 90 per cent of domestic sales (depending on the relative proportions of the domestic firms' turnovers that are exported), and foreign firms may actually be dominant in country A's market.

In order to take into account the greater openness of international markets such as that of the EU market, and the increased phenomenon of intra-EU trade, an adjusted-for-trade concentration ratio can be used. It is defined as:

$$C_{ati} = [(Q_i - X_i)/Q_t - (X_t - M_t)] \cdot 100$$

where:
C_{ati} is the concentration, for the top i firms, adjusted for trade
Q_i = the turnover of the top i firms
X_i = the exports of i firms
Q_t = total domestic turnover
X_t = total domestic exports
M_t = total imports.

Using adjusted-for-trade concentration ratios is also necessary in the case of large and more diversified economies such as the UK. Including imports in the UK market's sales will have the effect of reducing UK concentration ratios (unless an importer is among the larger suppliers). However, allowing for imports in general increases the degree of competition for the domestic market because, as Caves (1971) found, the intensity of collusion between domestic producers and importers is less than that among domestic producers alone. More imports/importers thus means less collusion and more competition among domestic suppliers. If imports represent an increasingly large share of the total supply in a given market, we eventually reach a point where we must redefine the market as greater than the national market.

5.5.3 Conditions of entry

Entry in a particular market or industry may be difficult or impossible, depending on the height of barriers. Barriers are all types of obstacles erected at the market edge by incumbent firms, by the nature of the product or process and/or by the government, which make entry difficult for potential entrants. The idea of barriers is an old one, the erection of barriers first having been observed in the 1894–1901 trust wave in the United States (see Bullock, 1901). Bain's (1956) taxonomy of entry barriers included technology, economies of scale and product differentiation. Much work has been done in this area since then. For example, Shepherd (1990) identifies two broad categories of sources of entry barriers.[11]

First, he argues, there are exogenous conditions which are 'fundamental causes that cannot be altered'. They lie outside the leading firms' control and are related to the nature of the product. They comprise: capital requirements, economies of scale, product differentiation, absolute cost advantages, diversification, R&D intensity, high durability of the firm's specific capital which includes sunk costs, and vertical integration (Shepherd, 1990, p. 274). These are all of an economic nature. To this list we could add institutional barriers more or less outside firms' control, such as government regulation,[12] though some writers (for example, Sapir, 1993) include regulatory barriers as a third type of barrier (in addition to exogenous and endogenous).

Second, there are endogenous conditions which emanate from the dominant firms. These are the results of the strategic actions of the dominant firms. They include: retaliation and pre-emptive actions, the building up of excess capacity to bar entry, advertising and other selling expenses, patents, control over strategic resources, and other strategies such as 'packing the product space' that leave no room for other potential branded products. These barriers reflect the degree of imperfection in the market. They can be used by the incumbent firms against both potential entrants and existing rivals.

While at first the classification into exogenous sources (given to the firm) and endogenous sources (created by the firm) of barriers seems neat, it can in practice be difficult to determine whether a barrier has an endogenous or exogenous source. For example, product differentiation (included in the exogenous category) is in fact intimately related to advertising which is directly determined by the firm's decisions (that is, it is endogenous). R&D intensity (defined by Shepherd as exogenous) is a direct result of the strategy of acquiring a leading edge in technology developments and/or application (that is, it is endogenous). Patents are also closely associated with R&D intensity.

A second criticism of this categorization of barriers relates to how fundamental and unalterable the exogenous conditions actually are. This depends on one's view of the firm. A dynamic perspective, such as that of the evolutionary theorists, would suggest that even the fundamental underlying technology (capital requirements, economies of scale, and so on) of the firm is variable.[13] To this criticism can be added the 'capture theory of regulation', according to which, regulation is influenced by the firms in the industry being regulated, such that the design and operation of that regulation is primarily in the interests of that industry, rather than in the interests of the consumers of the industry's product or of the public at large.

Many strategies implemented by firms are aimed either at deterring entrance or at neutralizing the actions of existing competitors. A more detailed examination of these strategies is undertaken in Chapter 6, and barriers to entry in Europe are described in Chapter 7. In the next section, we concentrate on several types of market structures, with the exception of oligopoly.

5.6 Market structures

In introductory neoclassical theory, concentration, product differentiation and barriers to entry are considered to be the main factors differentiating among four models of market structure. The two extremes are perfect competition and monopoly, where competition and the number of firms are greatest in perfect competition, and least in monopoly. The other two are monopolistic competition and oligopoly. In line with the theoretical developments in the field of industrial organization over the past decades, oligopoly is devoted a special attention in this book (see Chapter 6). Duopoly is a special form of oligopoly in which there are only two firms (see Fig. 5.2).

Real markets rarely conform to any one of these market structures, which are abstract models derived from sets of assumptions. The assumptions vary from large numbers of small firms producing a homogeneous product and no barriers to entry under perfect competition, to a single firm under monopoly. The models enable us to examine how firms would behave (in terms of a limited range of options) if operated within one of these abstract models. The 'firms' examined here are, in general, neoclassical firms.

Figure 5.2 Models of market structure

5.6.1 Perfect competition

The perfect competition model is familiar from all introductory textbooks. Diagrammatically the model is based on the notion that the demand curve faced by the individual firm is perfectly elastic (that is, horizontal). This follows from the assumption that there are many firms, each too small to influence price or quantity; the price is given for the individual firm. The level (price) at which this horizontal line is drawn is determined by the intersection of market demand and supply. The horizontal price/demand line facing the firm is also the marginal revenue. This is because the price received by the firm for each unit is the same, and that is also the price that will be received by the firm for each additional unit.

Like all profit-maximizing firms, the firm will produce a quantity determined by the intersection of the marginal revenue (MR) and marginal cost (MC) curves. Where the demand curve is horizontal, MR = MC also implies price = MC. If that price is such that profits are made above the normal amount already incorporated in the average cost (AC) curve,[14] then additional firms will enter the market. This follows from the assumption that there are no barriers to entry. (If the initial price was too low, there would be losses, and some firms would leave the industry. There are no barriers to exit.) The diagram for the firm is representative of that of any firm in the industry because, in view of the assumption of perfect flows of information, each firm will adopt the best methods of production and obtain inputs and

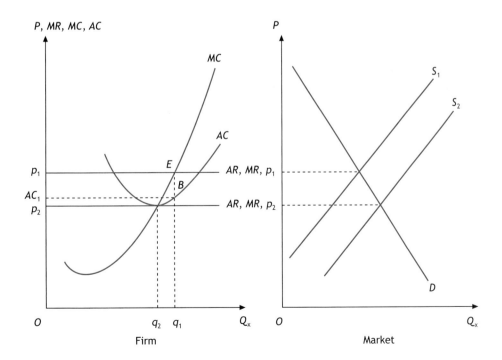

Figure 5.3 Perfect competition

factors of production at the best prices; they will all have the same cost curves. Referring to Fig. 5.3, if $p_1 > AC_1$, then the rectangle p_1AC_1BE represents above-normal (or supernormal) profits, and new firms will enter the industry. The market supply curve[15] will shift to the right from S_1, and will continue shifting in the short run until the intersection of market supply and demand (at the equilibrium price and quantity) is at a price equal to the minimum average cost (p_2). This is the long-run equilibrium position.

It can be argued that there are inherent contradictions in this model. On the one hand it follows from the two assumptions that information flows perfectly among all suppliers, that there is no product differentiation and that all firms are identical. However, in deriving the long-run equilibrium position, the model states that, if there are losses, then some firms ('leader' firms?) will leave. If, on the other hand, there are supernormal profits being made, then some firms not in the industry (leader firms) will enter. In the first case the market supply curve will shift to the left, and in the latter case the market supply curve will shift to the right. If there were no means of differentiating leader firms from other firms, then all firms would leave the industry if losses were being made and the industry would cease to exist, and all non-industry firms would enter if supernormal profits were being made. So, all firms are not identical.

In addition, once it is accepted that there are leader firms, then, if short-run supernormal profits are being made, they are more likely to be made by leader firms than others. These firms will then accumulate supernormal profits and have capital to differentiate themselves from other firms. If they are quicker-acting than other firms, they will stay ahead, differentiate their product, change their process or organization structure, and/or expand either internally or by taking over some of their competitors.[16] Some firms will, as a result, become larger than others and, perhaps, dominant firms in this industry.[17] The conditions underlying perfect competition are thus in some sense contradictory.

In practice, no firm would prefer a perfectly competitive market structure to one in which supernormal profits could be made. It follows that firms will constantly be trying to find ways of impeding the operation of perfect competition: differentiating their products, preventing information about their operations and products from leaking out, imposing barriers to the entry of new competitors, and so on. As soon as one or more of the firms in the industry achieves any of these objectives, perfect competition breaks down.

That the perfect competition model is theoretically defective did not undermine its power and influence. After all, if the conditions were achieved, the price would be as low as possible and optimize the interests of the consumers; the greatest possible number of firms would be sustained by the market and the interests of the suppliers would be optimized;[18] even efficiency is optimized because production takes place at the lowest possible average cost per unit. It is this general optimality[19] that is the attraction of perfect competition. It provides a basis for ideological arguments against government intervention, against concentration (for example through mergers and acquisitions), and in favour of small firms. From the model there follow generalizations such as: the more firms in a market, the lower the profits of each firm; the lower the barriers to entry, the more competition; the more competition, the lower the price; and the lower the barriers to information flows, the more rapidly innovations will be diffused among the firms in the industry. Each of these has been empirically tested, with mixed results. It is out of the theoretical critiques and empirical tests of perfect competition that other market structure models and, ultimately, much of industrial economics in general, has evolved.

5.6.2 Monopolistic competition

The perfect competition model was the main model in neoclassical theory all the way into the fourth decade of the twentieth century. Then, mainly because the behaviour of firms and markets was at odds with the model, efforts were made to develop models that were more consistent with this imperfectly competitive behaviour. Koutsoyiannis (1979, p. 202) mentions three main empirical deviations from perfect competition: products were differentiated; firms advertised; and firms experienced declining average costs, and expanded output to exploit these returns to scale, but only up to a point – they apparently stopped growing even though an increase in output would result in lower average costs. The attempt during this period to bring neoclassical economic theory into closer touch with reality culminated in the monopolistic competition model.

The monopolistic competition model, developed independently by Chamberlin (1933) and Robinson (1933), centres on the idea that, under certain circumstances, even relatively small firms in markets with large numbers of firms can exercise a degree of monopoly power. The assumptions of the model of monopolistic competition are close to those of the perfect competition model, the main difference being that the product is not homogeneous (there is a degree of product differentiation). Another way of expressing this is to say that, while in perfect competition the products of the different firms in the industry are *perfect* substitutes, in monopolistic competition they are close substitutes. Thus, in monopolistic competition there are a large number of buyers and sellers and there is freedom for firms to enter or exit the industry.

In the monopolistic competition model there is a single market, but differentiated products.[20] We may consider the market to be *segmented*, with each firm (or product) fitting into a different market segment. Firms differentiate the products they sell in a number of ways: quality, technical performance, durability, design, prompt service, and so on (see Chapter 6, Section 6.4). Product differentiation is perceived and enhanced through brand names and trademarks.

Chamberlin (1933) incorporated for the first time the notion of selling costs into the theory of the firm. The rationale for this inclusion is to account for the costs of advertising and other selling activities. The seller, Chamberlin wrote, 'may influence the volume of his sales by making expenditures, of which advertising may be taken as typical, which are directed specifically to that purpose. Such expenditures increase both the demand for his product, and his costs'. He went on to argue that this was one of the distinguishing characteristics of monopolistic competition because there can be no reason for a perfectly competitive firm to advertise; perfectly competitive firms can, after all, sell as much as they like without advertising (Chamberlin, 1962, p. 72).

We could not now agree with the view that advertising is, to use Chamberlin's words, 'peculiar' to monopolistic competition, as firms in both oligopoly and monopoly market structures can derive benefits from advertising. However, Chamberlin's main point in this context was to differentiate between his new monopolistic competition model and the perfect competition which was the main theoretical model at the time.

Selling costs were defined by Chamberlin 'as costs incurred in order to alter the position and shape of the demand curve for a product. ... Advertising of all varieties, salesmen's salaries and the expenses of sales departments, margins granted to dealers, ... window displays, demonstrations of new goods, etc., are all costs of this type' (Chamberlin, 1962, p. 117).

Chamberlin assumed that the selling-costs curve is U-shaped, exhibiting economies and diseconomies of, for example, advertising. Beyond a certain level of output, the firm will have to spend more on advertising and other promotional strategies to keep and/or attract customers. Because of product uniqueness, a firm can raise price without losing all of its sales. If it reduces its price, it will attract customers from other competitors. The demand curve facing the firm is thus downward sloping, as in the case of all other than the perfect competition model.[21] The uniqueness of the product may be a consequence of its style, the services offered by the firm, and/or the firm's particular selling strategy.

The model as presented in most modern textbooks is still more or less as first presented by Chamberlin and Robinson in 1933. Monopolistic competition is defined as a market structure characterized by a large number of sellers of differentiated products. They are assumed to compete on the bases of price, quality, advertising and other non-price characteristics of the product. There is assumed to be free entry into and exit from the market.

Figure 5.4 shows the cost curves for an individual firm in a monopolistically competitive market structure. The firm faces a demand curve, D_1, which represents the part (or segment) of the market primarily interested in its product.[22] It will maximize its profits where MR = MC, that is where the marginal revenue curve (MR_1) and the margin cost curve (MC) intersect. This indicates that the firm should produce the quantity q_1, and, if it produces that quantity the demand curve D_1 indicates that it will be able to sell the product at a price of p_1 per unit. The cost per unit of producing (and selling)[23] q_1 of the product is AC_1. The price (which is also average revenue) is greater than the average cost, so the firm is making supernormal profits. The total supernormal profits is the profit per unit ($p_1 AC_1$) multiplied by the quantity (q_1) represented by the rectangle $p_1 AC_1 BE$.

Because there are no barriers to entry, new firms, responding to the possibility of making supernormal profits in this market, will enter. The increase in the number of firms will reduce the demand facing each firm, and the demand curve for our individual firm will shift to the left. Eventually (in the long run), this model suggests, all supernormal profits will be

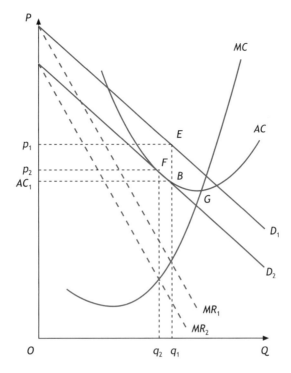

Figure 5.4 Monopolistic competition

eliminated. This occurs when the demand curve shifts to D_2, which is tangential to the average cost curve at a point F such that the line q_2F is also the profit-maximizing price. In the long run, the price (p_2) is equal to the average cost, so the firm will earn zero super-normal profits.

   The point F must clearly be to the left and above the minimum point of the average cost curve, G. (Minimum average cost is also known as the minimum efficient scale, MES.) Thus, the monopolistically competitive firm operates at less than efficient output. The difference between the price and the minimum average cost is interpreted in welfare economics as the cost, accepted by consumers, of having a choice of product among a variety of similar products rather than, as in perfect competition, a single, homogeneous product.

   It is the combination of price reduction and the entry of new firms that brings about equilibrium in this model. But the incorporation of selling costs, as distinct from production costs, makes the model interesting from a strategic point of view. These selling costs are in some sense discretionary: firms may increase or reduce them. Their function is to change the demand curve facing the firm, in the firm's favour. This means that there is a choice of strategy for the firm, as between reducing price and increasing, say, advertising. In Fig. 5.4, the firm has a choice between shifting its AC curve down and having the demand curve shift down and to the left (and, perhaps, becoming flatter), or shifting its AC curve upwards and having the demand curve shift up and to the right (and, perhaps, becoming steeper).

The monopolistic competition model allows for the three empirical contradictions of perfect competition mentioned above; it incorporates both product differentiation and advertising, and it shows the possibility of an equilibrium position on a downward-sloping part of an average cost curve.

Hotels, laundry services, business services (for example, legal and consultancy services), repair services, barber and beauty shops, all have product differentiation and operate to some extent like monopolistically competitive firms. In particular, there may be many sellers in the market, the product is differentiated and the firms advertise. However, entry is never free. The more differentiated the products are, and, for example, the stronger the brand loyalty that has been established by each firm for its product, the more difficult it will be for new firms to enter the market. This suggests that, as with perfect competition, there is a theoretical inconsistency in the model. Barriers to entry – particularly through collusion – are characteristic of oligopoly.

Another important difference between the monopolistic competition model and the oligopoly model in this context is that, in the former, firms act independently whereas in the latter, firms are continuously aware of, and act in ways influenced by, the behaviour of their competitors. While strategic choices for the firm can be incorporated into the monopolistic competition model, these choices are not influenced by the possible responses of competitors. However, in the presence of differentiation among products that are close substitutes, firms are highly unlikely to ignore their competitors' possible responses to their actions. Once product differentiation is allowed for, therefore, the market structure is likely to become oligopolistic.

In terms of the empirical definition of monopolistic competition, a major difficulty is how high the cross elasticity of demand must be for the products in the industry to be close substitutes. This is an inevitably subjective issue, for two products considered by one person (or group of people) to be close substitutes may not be considered such at all by others.

From the perspective of our critiques of both the perfect competition and the monopolistic competition models, even structures at first consistent with the assumptions of the models are likely to evolve into oligopolies. For this reason, among others, oligopoly has become the most important focus of modern industrial organization.[24] This is why, therefore, oligopoly will be examined in detail in Chapter 6. This chapter will conclude with the monopoly market structure.

5.6.3 Monopoly

In monopoly, the industry consists of a single firm that produces and sells a product with no close substitutes. For the firm to remain a single firm in the industry, there must be either barriers to entry, or no supernormal profits. By definition, the demand curve facing the monopolist is the industry demand curve, and therefore, as for a firm in monopolistic competition, downward sloping.

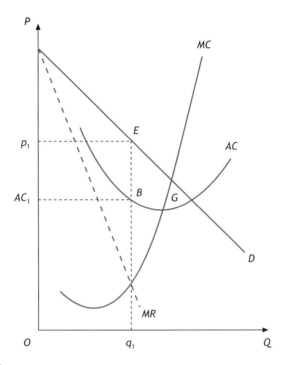

Figure 5.5 Monopoly

Referring to Fig. 5.5, the monopoly firm will maximize profits where $MR = MC$, that is, at quantity q_1. At this quantity it can charge the price p_1. (Once the firm has chosen the quantity to produce, the price will be determined by the market demand.) The cost per unit, if it produces q_1, is AC_1. The supernormal profits are $(p_1 - AC_1) \times q_1$, represented by the rectangle $p_1 AC_1 BE$. Supernormal profits in perfect competition are eliminated by a reduction in price resulting from the entry of new firms into the industry. If new firms are prevented from entering, then the monopoly firm can continue to earn supernormal profits. It may reduce costs in the long run by using different plant and equipment (shifting its AC curve downwards), but it is unlikely, except by coincidence, to produce at the bottom of its AC curve. Monopolies result in *allocative inefficiency*; social welfare would be enhanced if output was expanded up to the point where price (indicative of the marginal benefit to society), and marginal cost (the cost to society of the last unit produced) are equal.[25] The only beneficiary of the monopoly market structure is the monopoly firm itself.[26]

Allocative inefficiency explains the hostility to monopoly in virtually all European countries. Monopolies have been tolerated in the limit case where the minimum efficient scale is so large, in relation to demand, that only one firm can realize economies of scale. These are *natural monopolies*, monopolies that produce on the downward-sloping parts of their average cost curves. (The diagram in Fig. 5.5 is that of a natural monopoly.) Many utilities, such as electricity, gas and water distribution, and local telephone services are natural monopolies.

Only natural monopolies can make losses. Monopolies other than natural monopolies (where MR cuts MC to the right of minimum AC, that is, to the right of point G in Fig. 5.5) by definition must be making supernormal profits.

Elsewhere in this book (Section 7.5) we discuss the ways in which monopolies have been regulated and deregulated in the EU. Among ways of reducing the supernormal profits of monopolies in theory, are (i) taxes, (ii) price control and (iii) removal of barriers of entry.

◆ Taxes on profits simply reduce the after-tax profits, and do not affect the profit-maximizing price or quantity. A sales tax will shift the MC curve upwards, quantity produced will go down and price will go up. The incidence of the tax will fall more on the monopoly than on the consumers. If it is a natural monopoly, production will take place even further from minimum average cost; if it is not a natural monopoly, the sales tax may bring production closer to minimum average cost.

◆ The government (or monopoly regulating authority) can also reduce a monopoly's profits by imposing a maximum price. To be effective, this must be between the profit-maximizing price and the average cost at the profit-maximizing quantity; referring to Fig. 5.6, the maximum price must be between p_1 and AC_1. Let us assume the maximum price is set at p_m. The horizontal line from p_m to the demand curve D represents the price that the monopoly will charge for those quantities; it is the equivalent of a perfectly

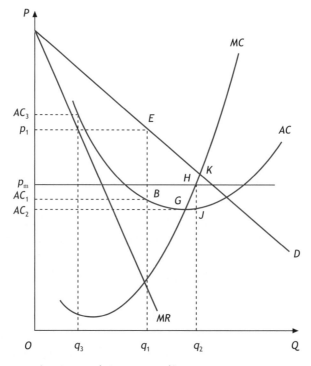

Figure 5.6 Maximum price to regulate monopolies

elastic demand curve, and, therefore, also a marginal revenue curve. The profit-maximizing quantity (where $MR = MC$, that is, point H) is q_2. Supernormal profits will have been reduced from $p_1 AC_1 BE$ to $p_m AC_2 JH$. If the aim of the intervention is to move the monopoly towards allocative efficiency, then it will impose a maximum price such that $MC = P$, that is a maximum price through point K. This is known as marginal cost pricing. It is possible that where the MC curve cuts the demand, the monopoly is making losses. In this case the government can impose a maximum price where average cost cuts the demand curve (known as *average cost pricing*). This will leave the firm with just enough (normal) profits to keep it in the industry.

♦ Where it is in the government's power to do so, it can remove barriers to entry. If new firms enter the industry, the entire market structure will change, either towards monopolistic competition or towards oligopoly. Note that this is not likely to be an effective way of dealing with natural monopolies because, as can be seen from Fig. 5.6, if one or two additional firms entered the industry, each producing, say, q_3, their average costs would be AC_3 and even if they made no supernormal profits the price would still have to be higher than the natural monopoly price to keep them in the industry. The average cost, even if below p_1, would still be far above the AC_1 of the natural monopoly, and therefore even further from the MES.

Public ownership is also sometimes suggested as a means of controlling monopolies (see Chang, 1994, p. 9). However, it is arguably not the ownership of a firm but the competition it faces – and, in general, the incentive structure facing its decision makers – that determines its pricing and other strategies.

The analysis of monopoly can be extended to the cases of the multi-plant monopoly, the price discriminating monopolist and the bilateral monopolist. These are demonstrated in most microeconomics and managerial economics textbooks. They all provide examples of marginalist analysis. For a multi-plant monopolist in a single market, it can be shown that if MR is the marginal revenue derived from the market demand curve, and $MC_1, MC_2, \ldots, MC_n$ are the marginal costs of producing the good in each of the n plants, then $MR = MC_1 = MC_2 = \ldots = MC_n$ is the condition for profit maximization.[27] For a (single-plant) monopolist able to sell into distinct markets, if $MR_1, MR_2, \ldots, MR_n$ are the marginal revenues in each of the n markets, then the profit will be maximized where $MC = MR_1 = MR_2 = \ldots = MR_n$.[28]

In view of the fact that the bilateral monopoly model takes us towards the bargaining models underlying much of modern oligopoly theory, we will demonstrate this in more detail. In the bilateral monopoly model there is a single seller (monopoly) and a single buyer (monopsony). Let us assume that the buyer is a firm that is the only firm requiring workers with a particular skill and the seller is a trade union that organizes all the workers with that skill. The firm could, for example, be the sole beer manufacturer in the economy (the monopsony buyer of brewing skills), and the trade union organizer of all brewers (the monopoly seller of brewing skills).

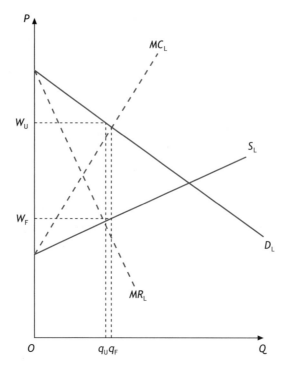

Figure 5.7 Bilateral monopoly

Referring to Fig. 5.7, the firm's demand for labour, which is also the marginal revenue product of labour (MRP_L), is D_L. MRP_L is the extra revenue generated by employing an extra unit of labour (or marginal revenue times the marginal product of labour). S_L is the supply of labour and, from the firm's point of view, has a related marginal cost, MC_L. This is because to increase employment by an additional unit, the firm must raise the wage for all units (workers).[29] So, the firm will wish to employ workers up to q_F, where D_L and MC_L intersect. It can obtain this quantity at a price of w_F per unit and this is, therefore, the wage that the firm will offer.

From the union's point of view, the demand curve facing it, D_L, is the average wage. Moving down the demand curve, the union sees that the extra revenue arising from an increase in employment (MR_L) is less than the payment per unit of employment; extra workers must be offered much less if the wages offered to them brings the average of all wages down. The union will wish to offer for employment q_U of labour, where its supply curve (and marginal cost from its point of view) intersects the marginal revenue curve. For this quantity it will expect to receive w_U per unit.

This model has the advantage of a result which, like much that occurs in the competition among firms, is indeterminate. The union wishes to charge w_U per unit for q_U units of labour; the firm wishes to pay w_F per unit for q_F units of labour. They will have to bargain with one another. The end result is likely to be a wage between w_U and w_F, its precise level being dependent upon many other factors. This type of indeterminacy, of results contingent upon such elements as relative power and strategic skill, is common in modern approaches to oligopoly, on which we focus in Chapter 6.

5.7 Summary

Market structure, or the intensity of competition on a market, is of crucial importance to both individual firms (who are eager to obtain information pertaining to their macro-economic environment) and to EU policy makers (who are keen to guarantee the smooth functioning of the EU domestic market). By clarifying what is meant by market, industry and market structure, this chapter has shown the evolving nature of the definition of the relevant market as it applies to the case of the EU. The increasing importance of notions such as supply substitution and putative economic power (of a firm) have introduced a dynamic stance to the analysis (making the static measurement of concentration ratios, in time period t, sometimes redundant). This evolution should be seen in parallel with the increasing focus of modern industrial organization theory on oligopoly as one of the key market structures. By focusing on perfect competition, monopolistic competition and monopoly as primary market structures, the discussion on market structures which opened in this chapter will find an extension in the next chapter which deals with oligopoly.

Websites

Eurostat does not provide figures on concentration data. Information on concentration levels in the EU can be obtained from the different national statistical bodies, such as the INSEE in France: **http://www.alisse.insee.fr/SelectionMesureT1.jsp?item=CONDIS**

In the United States, the Bureau of Economic Analysis (US Department of Commerce) is a good source of figures on industrial activity in the country: **www.bea.doc.gov**

Questions

5.1 What is cross-elasticity of demand and how can it help to define a market?

5.2 Use Kay's concept of the strategic market to explain why the extent of both market and industry can be defined only on a case by case basis.

5.3 The definition of the relevant EU market does not depend solely on crude measures of concentration. Explain why this is the case.

5.4 Use the data in Table 5.3 to calculate the CR_1, CR_3, CR_5 and CR_7 ratios. What can you say about the results?

Notes

1 For a discussion on the problems arising from the difficulty in drawing the boundaries of the market clearly, see Shepherd (1990, pp. 55–60).

2 The issues of dominant firms, concentration and mergers refer to non-competitive markets, such as oligopolies. Oligopolies are developed at the theoretical level in Chapter 6.

3 Council Regulation No. 139/2004, 20 January 2004 (*Official Journal* OJ L 24, 29 January 2004).

4 For a critical appraisal of the variable definitions of the relevant market, see Fishwick (1986), Focsaneanu (1975), and the Commission's annual reports on competition policy.

5 The single European market is discussed in Chapter 7.

6 See OJ L 72, 18 March 1992, p. 1.

7 This and the cases in the next paragraph are referred to in CEC, 1991, annex III, unless otherwise specified.

8 There is, arguably, a fourth, the level of information. This is discussed in Chapter 3, Section 3.2.2.

9 The Gini coefficient and the Lorenz curve are familiar devices for studying the distribution of income and wealth in a nation, and less frequently used to measure concentration in industry.

10 Above-normal profits are also eliminated (and the Lerner index is zero) under contestable market conditions. See Chapter 2, Section 2.2.4.

11 In Chapter 7, we describe another (though possibly complementary) way of categorizing barriers, in terms of first-order and second-order barriers, the former referring to impediments to entry facing firms within the same economy, the latter to impediments facing firms from outside the economy.

12 There is a substantial literature on the extent to which particular American firms have influenced regulation. Tomlinson (1993) provides a review and critique of this 'regulatory capture' literature.

13 Despite these criticisms, aspects of the exogenous/endogenous classification are widely accepted.

14 This normal amount of profit is defined as just enough to keep existing firms in the industry but not enough to attract additional firms into the industry.

15 Note that while the price axis for firm and market are identical, the scale of the firm's quantity axis represents a much smaller quantity than that for the market.

16 Arguably, under conditions of free entry and exit, there is nothing for the leader firm to take over, but once differentiation becomes possible, the condition of completely free entry and exit must also be relaxed. (This, as we show below, is also a criticism of the monopolistic competition market structure.)

17 Against this and in favour of the perfect competition model, it can be argued that if there are constant returns to scale in perfect competition, then there are no incentives for firms to grow. However, constant returns to scale apply only at the long-run equilibrium and what we are arguing is that it is in moving towards this equilibrium that the model breaks down.

18 It should be emphasized that the interests of the suppliers in general are optimized by perfect competition; any individual supplier would prefer to be a monopoly.

19 An example of the welfare economic concept is Pareto optimality, where no change is possible without reducing the welfare of at least some player in the situation.

20 Chamberlin used the concept product group to refer to products that are close *technical and economic substitutes*, technical in that they fulfil the same basic function, and economic in that they have similar price ranges. Two houses might be technical substitutes in that they both supply shelter, but if the price of one is €1 million, and the price of the other one-tenth of that, then they are unlikely to be economic substitutes. It should be noted that Chamberlin later abandoned the concept of the product group,

though it did at least contribute to the development of ideas on the relationship between firms, industries and markets.

21 Product differentiation as a basis for establishing a downward-sloping demand curve was first introduced by Sraffa (1926).

22 Note that if the demand curve is downward sloping, the marginal revenue curve is also downward sloping, and below, the demand curve. It can be proved that $MR = p(1 + 1/\varepsilon)$, where ε = price elasticity of demand. Where $MR = 0$, $\varepsilon = -1$; where $MR = p$, $\varepsilon \to -\infty$

23 Note that if the average selling costs curve is U-shaped, and the average production costs curve is U-shaped, then the sum of the two is also U-shaped.

24 Note that Augustin Cournot had already developed an algebraic model of monopoly in 1838.

25 This definition implies the absence of externalities. See Chapter 15 for a discussion on externalities.

26 At least in neoclassical economics. There is, as we shall see in Chapter 11, a Schumpeterian view according to which technological change and innovation are best generated by monopolies, in which case there are also social benefits to monopolies.

27 For diagrammatic and algebraic proofs, see Koutsoyiannis (1979, pp. 186–9).

28 For diagrammatic and algebraic proofs, see Koutsoyiannis (1979, ch. 7). The separation of markets is usually considered in geographical terms. For an example based on differentiable characteristics of consumers, see Hirschey and Pappas (1993, pp. 629–37). In this example Hirschey and Pappas show how a university football club could maximize its profits by charging students one price and the general public another (higher) price.

29 The relationship between S_L and MC_L is analogous to the relationship between demand and marginal revenue.

CHAPTER 6

Structure and strategy: oligopoly

6.1 Learning objectives

The main objectives of this chapter are:

- To define and explain oligopoly, in theory and in practice
- To show the origins of oligopoly theory in the duopolies of Cournot and Bertrand
- To present the various theories of oligopoly as variations to or departures from the basic assumptions of Cournot and Bertrand, and
- To show that the ideas continue to be developed in recent literature

6.2 The market structure and the firm

As is already clear from comparisons in Chapter 5 between monopolistic competition and oligopoly, the main factor that differentiates oligopoly from other market structures is that, in oligopoly, firms operate in ways influenced by their expectations of the reactions of other firms. There is an explicit acceptance in oligopoly theory that decision makers in firms are aware of other firms and take them into consideration when choosing strategies and, indeed, when making decisions of all kinds. In addition, unlike other market structure definitions, that of oligopoly does not refer explicitly to numbers of firms, product differentiation or barriers to entry.[1] This is because as oligopoly theory has developed, so it has incorporated a range of possibilities, of various combinations of these traditional determinants of market structure. Indeed, oligopoly has arguably become the main focus of modern industrial economics, its definition being based on behavioural, strategic factors rather than structural ones.

Firms in an oligopolistic structure have more decision-making leeway than firms in other market structures. The theoretical firm in perfect competition is not just a price-taker. Such a firm also uses the best technology available, even though it is unlikely that that particular firm developed that technology. There are no decisions to be taken about the product, either, because the product is identical to those of all the other firms in the market. The firm in this market structure thus uses the process, produces the product and charges the price of the market.

In monopolistic competition there is a small amount of decision-making leeway. In particular, the homogeneity constraint is relaxed and firms can differentiate the product. There is a limit to how much they can differentiate; if the cross-elasticity of demand is too low then the firm's product ceases to be in the market. If the quantity demanded of a product is clearly responsive to changes in the price of other products then the products can all be considered to be in the same market. So, the decisions taken by those running a firm in a market characterized as monopolistically competitive are limited to how to differentiate the product. To the extent that strategic thinking is relevant for such firms, it is limited to whether and how to differentiate their products (see below, Section 6.5). All other decisions are determined by the neoclassical condition of profit maximization, $MR = MC$. A firm that makes a decision to change – for example to change production entirely by introducing a new range of products not currently on the market – is a firm that acts independently, that acts strategically, not just reacting to the market but also changing and indeed making markets.

Such a strategically oriented firm can become a monopoly, at least for a short time, while other firms find ways of entering its market. In the monopoly market structure as described in the previous chapter, however, the firm has only one decision: how to set either price or quantity in such a way as to maximize profits by getting MR equal to MC. The question of how that firm became a monopoly is not considered; the theory and the model focus on profit maximization once the monopoly already exists. The monopoly firm may have a strategy of preventing entry of competitors but this is usually illegal. Moreover, if there is a degree of contestability, that is, if the firm acts (for example, setting low prices) on the basis of the expectation that other firms will react in certain ways (for example, refraining from entering the market) then the firm can be argued to be operating in an oligopolistic market.

Thus, only the firm in oligopoly is capable – within the confines of the theory – of developing proper strategies. It should be pointed out that, traditionally in economics, strategy and oligopoly are tautologically linked. Oligopoly is defined as the only market structure in which firms, in their decision making, take into consideration the possible reactions of their competitors. There is, in other words, uniquely in oligopoly 'mutual interdependence of producers' (Petrochilos, 2004, p. 255). Strategy, in turn, is usually defined as decision making in which a plan of action is chosen on the basis of the expected reactions of competitors. If, as in game theory, a player can look at all her own possible actions, and the actions in each case of her competitor(s), then she can choose the strategy that maximizes her minimum outcomes (maxi-min strategy). So, because only in oligopoly are the reactions of competitors taken into consideration, only in oligopoly are strategies relevant.

The sense in which we have used the term 'strategy' above – for example in the case of the firm changing existing markets or creating new ones – does not contradict the traditional definition. The firm that develops a new range of products does so, at least in part, to avoid competition in existing product markets. That is, the reactions of competitors are considered in the strategy development process. However, our usage goes beyond the traditional definition. Similar to Best (1990, p. 11), we consider strategic action to involve choice of terrain on which to compete – product, process, market, quality, price, service and so on. A strategy goes beyond deciding what price to charge; it involves also the decision as to whether to compete on the basis of price at all.

It should be clear from our description of the various theories of the firm in Chapters 3 and 4, that certain strategies are more amenable to inclusion in some theories than in others. For example, the strategic choice between buy and make is one most obviously incorporated into transaction cost theory. The question of what a firm's main strengths are – its core competences – and, therefore, of what it should emphasize in its strategic development, is best considered in the context of evolutionary theory. At the same time, theories such as principal–agent, behavioural and evolutionary, in which much of the focus is on aspects of the internal organization and operation of the firm, are suggestive of a degree of independence from market forces. The firms described in these theories therefore have some leeway within which to make strategic choices; such theories are thus most suitable for firms in oligopolistic markets.[2]

Characteristics of oligopoly can be found in a wide range of industries, including the mining industry, banking sector, car industry, air transport, inter-city bus lines, much wholesale trade and retail trade in so far as it is dominated by chains of supermarkets. Even small grocery stores could be part of an oligopoly, where, for example, there are three of them vying for market share in a small town. In general, firms within oligopolies have a greater degree of control over price than firms in perfect competition. How much control depends on the number and size distribution of firms, the intensity of competition and product differentiation.

The models of oligopoly discussed in this chapter follow closely the discussion of game theory introduced in Chapter 2. The difference is that, in relation to Cournot and Stackelberg in particular, in this chapter an algebraic approach is followed. It will be clear to students who followed the example in the appendix to Chapter 2, that that was a specific example of Cournot's general duopoly model. For those students who do not need to understand the mathematical models, the maths of Sections 6.3, 6.7 and 6.9 can easily be skipped without losing continuity.

6.3 Cournot's duopoly

Among the roots of the modern theory of oligopoly is the work, first published in 1838, of the French philosopher and mathematician Augustin Cournot. At that time, Cournot was overshadowed in France by the *laissez-faire* principles presented most prominently by Jean Baptiste Say – which became accepted almost as dogma.[3] It was not until the 1860s that economists, such as Walras, recognized the value of Cournot's work, and in particular his development of a mathematical approach to political economy.[4] It is both for this general contribution and for his specific work on duopoly that Cournot is remembered today.

Cournot's duopoly (two-firm) model is a quantity-setting oligopoly in which each firm selects a quantity of output to maximize its own profit. Cournot builds his model around the strategies of two firms, each of which owns a natural mineral water spring, of identical quality, and equidistant from the same market. Assuming that the two producers have the same cost structures, the price will be the same for each. Each firm does not have any influence on the quantity produced by its rival. Cournot's behavioural assumption is that each firm knows what its rival produces, takes the rival's output as given, and selects its own output so as to maximize its own profit. This assumption is a simplification in that it means that, should Firm 1 alter its output, its rival will not react. The *conjectural variation* – Firm 1's view of the extent to which its rival will change its output in response to Firm 1's output decisions – is thus zero.

In fact, since Firm 1 treats Firm 2's output as fixed, Firm 1 believes that it faces a residual demand curve; Firm 1's residual demand curve is obtained from the market demand curve by subtracting the output of Firm 2, that is,

$$q_1 = Q - q_2 \tag{6.1}$$

where Q denotes the total output in the market.

Using the notation $p = f(Q)$ or $p = f(q_1 + q_2)$ to denote that price is a function of quantity, Firm 1's total revenue, R_1, will be:

$$R_1 = q_1 \cdot f(q_1 + q_2) \tag{6.2}$$

and Firm 2's total revenue will be:

$$R_2 = q_2 \cdot f(q_1 + q_2) \tag{6.3}$$

Equations (6.2) and (6.3) show that the rival's output is a variable taken into account in each firm's strategy, though this variable is fixed by the rival. In Cournot's own words: 'Firm 1 cannot directly exert an influence on the fixing of output [q_2]; the only thing the firm can do after [q_2] has been fixed by Firm 2, is to choose for [q_1] the value that suits him best, something he can achieve by modifying the price appropriately.'[5] Firm 1's revenue-maximizing (and profit-maximizing, if we ignore production costs) output will be determined as a function of q_2 under the condition:

$$\frac{d[q_1 f(q_1 + q_2)]}{dq_1} \tag{6.4}$$

Similarly, q_2 will be determined by:

$$\frac{d[q_2 f(q_1 + q_2)]}{dq_2} \tag{6.5}$$

The values of q_1, q_2 and p will be determined by the following system of equations, derived by differentiating Eqs (6.4) and (6.5):

$$f(q_1 + q_2) + q_1 \frac{df(q_1 + q_2)}{dq_1} = 0 \tag{6.6}$$

$$f(q_1 + q_2) + q_2 \frac{df(q_1 + q_2)}{dq_2} = 0 \tag{6.7}$$

Assuming, with Cournot, that Firm 1 believes that Firm 2 does not respond to Firm 1's actions, Eq. (6.6) can be written as:

$$f(q_1 + q_2) + q_1 \frac{df(q_1 + q_2)}{d(q_1 + q_2)} = 0 \tag{6.6a}$$

Similarly, if Firm 2 believes that Firm 1 does not respond to Firm 2's actions, Eq. (6.7) can be written as:

$$f(q_1 + q_2) + q_2 \frac{df(q_1 + q_2)}{d(q_1 + q_2)} = 0 \tag{6.7a}$$

It follows that, if both firms optimize under these conditions, $q_1 = q_2$, which indicates that both firms supply the same quantity (measured in Fig. 6.1 by the segments q_1 and q_2 respectively).[6] Adding Eq. (6.6a) to Eq. (6.7a), and substituting p for $f(Q)$, we get:

$$2p + Q \frac{dp}{dQ} = 0$$

or:

$$2p - \frac{dQ}{dp} + Q = 0 \tag{6.8}$$

that is:

$$p = \frac{(-Q)}{2\frac{dQ}{dp}} \tag{6.9}$$

Cournot goes on to say that if the two springs had been part of the same firm, or if the two producers had co-operated, p would have been determined by the equation:

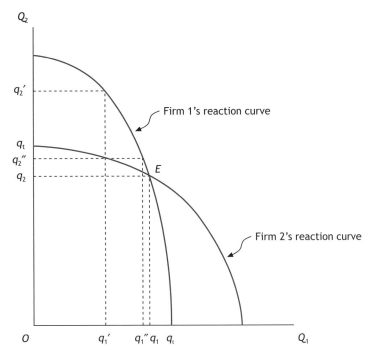

Figure 6.1 Reaction curves and Cournot duopoly equilibrium

$$p - \frac{dQ}{dp} + Q = 0 \qquad\qquad (6.10)^7$$

that is :

$$p = \frac{-Q}{(dQ/dp)} \qquad\qquad (6.11)$$

Clearly, p in Eq. (6.11) – that for which total revenue in the industry is maximized – is greater than p in Eq. (6.9). *Through co-operation, price would be greater, and each firm would obtain a total revenue greater, than that derived from Eq. (6.8).* This illustrates the costs of non-cooperative (competitive) behaviour, and shows that, under these assumptions, it would be in the interests of the two firms to co-operate.

Cournot rules out co-operation or collusive behaviour in practice, because:

> Firm 1, *having fixed its production level according to equation [6.10] and to the condition* [q₁ = q₂], *the other [firm] will, with a temporary benefit, be in a position to bring its own production to a higher or lower level; however, Firm 2 will soon be punished for his wrongdoing, in that he will force the first firm to select a new production level that will have an unfavourable impact on Firm 2. These successive reactions, far from bringing the two producers closer to the original state [of equilibrium], will make them increasingly diverge from it. In other words, this*

state [Eq. (6.10)] will not be a situation of stable equilibrium; and, although it is the most favourable to the two producers, it cannot last unless there is a formal link (Cournot, 1980, p. 62, authors' translation).[8]

Cournot generalizes his model to n producers. He shows that, under the same circumstances as before, Eq. (6.8) would be replaced by:

$$3p - \frac{dQ}{dp} + Q = 0 \qquad (6.12)$$

in the case of triopoly, and:

$$np - \frac{dQ}{dp} + Q = 0 \qquad (6.13)$$

in the case of perfect competition (that is, where n is a large number).

His conclusion is that 'the resulting value of p would diminish indefinitely through the indefinite increase in the number n' (Cournot, 1980, p. 63, authors' translation). Since the value of p reached by the monopolist (or by a co-operative duopoly) is always greater than the value of p derived from a non-cooperative duopoly, which in turn is always greater than the value of p obtained in a competitive framework, this implies that the total revenue of the monopolist is greater than the total revenue of the duopolist, which in turn is greater than that of the competitive firm.

Cournot shows that the introduction of cost functions does not change the conclusions as to the situations in which producers maximize profits. For the same value of p, or for the same total quantity produced, the costs of production will always be greater for rival firms than for the monopolist (see Cournot, 1980, p. 65).

Cournot's diagrammatic representation of duopoly is shown in Fig. 6.1. Each curve is a *reaction curve*[9] showing a firm's profit-maximizing output, given the output of the other firm. If Firm 2 produces nothing, Firm 1 is a monopolist and maximizes profit (which is in this case equal to total revenue) by producing the monopoly output q_1. Point E represents for Cournot a point of stable equilibrium, at which q_1 and q_2 are produced by Firms 1 and 2 respectively. If either firm deviates from this position of stable equilibrium, a series of 'reactions' will bring it back to the equilibrium. The point of intersection of the two reaction curves is referred to as a Cournot non-cooperative equilibrium point.[10]

Cournot's major aim was to show (algebraically and graphically) the existence of a stable duopoly equilibrium. His explanation of the diagram was as follows. If Firm 1 decides to produce an output $q_1' < q_1$, its profit can be maximized only for a value of $Q_2 = q_2'$. In other words, Firm 1 produces q_1' in the expectation that Firm 2 will produce q_2'. However, Firm 1's production of q_1' leads Firm 2 to react by planning to produce q_2'' such that $q_2 < q_2'' < q_2'$. Firm 1 will react to Firm 2's production of q_2'' in turn by increasing his output to q_1'' Each reaction is of a smaller and smaller magnitude, up to the point where the stable equilibrium is reached.

Walras was later to call this repeated adjustment towards a convergent equilibrium the *tâtonnement* process. With all its limitations, Cournot's was the first attempt to describe dynamically the process whereby a static equilibrium is arrived at.

Criticism of Cournot has focused on three main issues: the nature of the relationship between the two variables q_1 and q_2; the ruling out of co-operative behaviour; and the fact that Cournot treats the duopolists as quantity setters rather than as price setters.

- *Relationship between q_1 and q_2.* In his famous short article published in 1883 in *Journal des Savants*, Joseph Bertrand criticized Cournot for treating the outputs q_1 and q_2 as two independent variables. According to Cournot, when q_1 changes as a result of the strategy of Firm 1, q_2 remains constant. In Bertrand's view, it is 'obvious' that under these circumstances q_2 will change. In that it led to the question of how responsive Firm 1 expects Firm 2 to be to Firm 1's actions, it was this criticism of Cournot by Bertrand that gave rise to the *conjectural variation* approach.

  Pareto (1911, p. 606) later showed, in a critique of both Cournot and Bertrand, that the fact that q_1 and q_2 are treated as independent of one another does not imply Cournot's behavioural assumption according to which Firm 1 can act only on q_1 and Firm 2 only on q_2.[11] This undermines part of Bertrand's objection to Cournot, but leaves intact his criticism of Cournot's assumption that each duopolist acts in the belief that the other's output is fixed.[12]

- *Co-operative behaviour.* The second criticism relates to whether the firms will continue to compete in all respects. The question is whether it is possible that each duopolist will, rather than maximize its own profit only, co-operate in some way with the other to maximize joint revenue. The fact that Cournot ruled out co-operative or collusive behaviour was strongly criticized by Bertrand (1883), who argued that it would be in the interests of the two firms 'to come together, or at least to fix a common price, so that they can derive a maximum possible revenue from the buyers; but this solution is rejected [by Cournot]'.[13]

- *Price-setting oligopoly.* Finally, probably the most fruitful criticism has been that Cournot neglected the price variable in the strategies of firms. The Cournot model is a quantity-setting model as opposed to a price-setting model. The price variable is treated as a result of duopoly behaviour, rather than as a strategy available to the firm. Bertrand's main contribution was his development of a price-setting alternative to the Cournot model.

6.4 Bertrand and price-setting oligopoly

Bertrand (1883) regarded price-setting oligopoly as a more acceptable alternative in practice. A firm exhibiting Bertrand behaviour selects a profit-maximizing price under the assumption that its rivals will maintain their prices at the current levels. His assumption is that, if Firm 2 does not react, the entire market can switch to Firm 1 in response to a slight reduction in price.

Note that if consumers respond to price changes only, then Bertrand's model does not allow for any product differentiation. Hence, if we assume that the products sold are standardized and that there is no inertia in behaviour, the Bertrand duopoly model leads to a competitive equilibrium, even if as few as two firms supply the entire market. To show that each firm will charge the same price – and that that price will allow only for normal profit – assume that the two duopolists are charging a price above marginal cost. If Firm 1 keeps its price at that level, Firm 2 can attract all the buyers if it charges a slightly lower price. Firm 1 will then react by cutting its price even further. The process will stop only when any further reduction in price would result in one of the firms leaving the industry.

Diagrammatically, *price reaction curves* can be drawn, showing the price that Firm 1 will set in order to maximize its profits, given the price set by Firm 2. This is shown in Fig. 6.2.

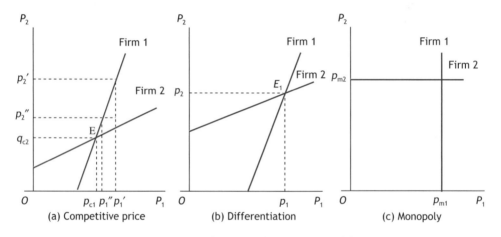

Figure 6.2 Price reaction curves and Bertrand duopoly equilibrium

Price reaction curves are positively sloped because the higher the price one firm charges for the good, the higher will be the price set by the other firm. Similarly, the lower the price set by one firm, the lower the price that will have to be set by the other firm if it wants to compete. When the good is homogeneous, the price reaction curves will intersect at E, at which point the price p_{c1} set by Firm 1 will be equal to the price p_{c2} set by Firm 2. This price, as explained above, will also be the competitive price (no supernormal profits). The process of adjustment is analogous to the Cournot case, except that each firm changes price, rather than quantity, in the convergence towards equilibrium. Thus if Firm 1 charges a price p_1' above p_{c1} (in the expectation that Firm 2 will charge p_2') Firm 2 will actually respond by charging p_2''; Firm 1 will then change its price to p_1'' and so on, until the equilibrium is reached at E. This is the result of the basic Bertrand model.

There are a large number of possible variations to Bertrand and Cournot. Here we concentrate first on relaxing Bertrand's assumption of product homogeneity, and second on different reactions by firms in different circumstances. In a variation on both Cournot and Bertrand, we examine, thirdly, the implications of relaxing the implicit assumption of symmetric information by allowing one firm to obtain information on the other's reaction function. In a fourth variation we will consider the possibility of a collusive oligopoly. Conjectural variation is the fifth and final variation in oligopoly theory that we discuss. It involves – as do the second, third and fourth – departure from the implausible assumption that the oligopolist believes that rivals do not respond to his changes.

6.5 Product differentiation[14]

If there is a degree of differentiation between the products of Firms 1 and 2, then the second firm to enter the market will be able to set a price for its product above that of the first firm. This is the basis for differentiation strategies, such as advertising to establish brand loyalty. Each firm's price reaction curve will shift (Firm 2's upwards and Firm 1's to the right) because, for each price that one firm charges, the other will be able to set a price above the price that would have been possible if the two firms' products had been identical. With a degree of differentiation, if each firm is less reactive to a change in price by the other firm then the price reaction curve of Firm 1 may also be flatter, and that of Firm 2 steeper than if the good were homogeneous. The equilibrium, at E_1, will be at a price higher than the competitive price (see Fig. 6.2b).

If there is complete differentiation, so that each of the firms becomes a monopolist, the price will be still higher. Each firm can now ignore the price charged by the other. Firm 1's price reaction curve becomes vertical, and Firm 2's horizontal; Firm 1 sets the price at its profit-maximizing monopoly price (p_{m1}) irrespective of the price Firm 2 charges for its product, and Firm 2 similarly sets the price at p_{m2} irrespective of the price Firm 1 charges for its product (see Fig. 6.2c).

Product differentiation in oligopolies has been the subject of a great deal of attention both in theoretical model-building and in empirical tests of the impact of product differentiation. Theoretical papers include, among many others, Cellini *et al.* (2004) on product differentiation and how quantity competition might be more welfare improving than price competition, Hoernig (2003) on horizontal differentiation and strategic complementarity, and Belleflamme and Toulemonde (2003) on product differentiation in vertical oligopolies. There is rather less empirical work in this area. In an elaborate example that provides the expected result, Mazzeo (2002) uses a variety of mathematical and statistical techniques to examine the behaviour of firms in the motel sector. He provides evidence that 'price competition, product differentiation, and the entry and product-type decisions of firms . . . operate simultaneously to determine market structure and outcomes in product-differentiated oligopolies'. Using such factors as affiliation and quality to reflect differentiation, what he shows in essence is that product differentiation is used as a means of reducing the intensity of competition in the motel sector. In his words, 'firms choose to be different from their competitors because when products are differentiated, the resulting competition is less tough and profits are higher'.

In another application of a differentiated product oligopoly model to an empirical case, Goldberg and Verboven (2001) examine the European car industry. They demonstrate first that there are price differences between members of the EU – allowing for quality differences – and that there is price volatility over time. They show that the reasons for high prices are different in different countries. In Italy, the main reason is a strong preference for the local brand (Fiat) that enables that firm to set high mark-ups. In the UK, the two main explanations for high prices are that the cars sold on the UK market are on average better equipped than those in other European markets and that there are aspects of dealer discount practices in the UK that apparently increase prices.

6.6 Differentiated reactions

Published in an article in 1939, Sweezy's model formally introduced the idea that under reasonable assumptions the demand curve may not be a smooth, differentiable function.[15] Sweezy's major assumption is that a firm expects its competitor(s) to behave differently in their responses to price increases and decreases: a firm believes that its rival(s) will respond immediately to a price cut, but will be reluctant to match a price increase. Sweezy's behavioural assumption generates a kink (point A in Fig. 6.3) in the firm's perceived demand curve at a given price. This provides a theoretical explanation for why prices may be stable, or 'sticky' under conditions of oligopoly.

Let us assume the firm faces a demand curve, DD_1. At point A, the oligopolist considers the possible responses to an increase or decrease in price. His competitors, he believes, will not respond to an increase. If he increases price above p_A, by keeping their price at p_A his competitors will undercut his price and force him out of business. If he decreases his price they will have to respond by decreasing their price too, or else they will be undercut and forced out of business. Now, if DD_1 is the firm's demand curve under the assumption that all other things remain the same, and if those other things include the prices set by competitors, then above A the relevant demand curve is DA, but below A it is a steeper demand curve, Ad_1. If his reduction in price was not followed by a reduction in the price of competitors' products, DD_1 would be relevant throughout its length. When competitors' response is also to cut price, then the quantity left for our firm is less than it would be if the response was to stay at p_A. So, instead of the greater quantities available along AD_1, he faces the lower quantities along Ad_1. The relevant demand curve is DAd_1. Raising his price leads to a much greater response on the part of his customers than a price reduction (DA is more price elastic than Ad_1).

Because of the kink in the oligopolist's demand curve, his MR curve will be discontinuous at the level of output corresponding to point A. The relevant marginal revenue curve for DA is DA_1 and the relevant marginal curve for Ad_1 is A_2MR_d. The marginal revenue of the demand curve DAd_1 is $DA_1A_2MR_d$. Any marginal cost curve that intersects the vertical section of the

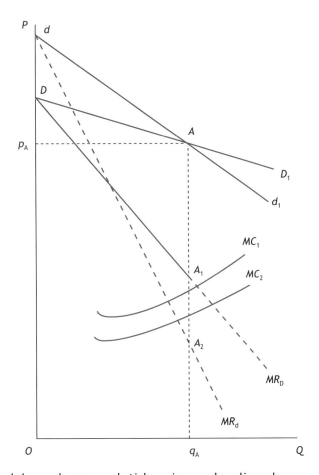

Figure 6.3 Kinked demand curve and sticky prices under oligopoly

marginal revenue curve will result in the profit-maximizing price and quantity combination of p_A and q_A. Changes in cost conditions that shift the marginal cost up or down will not result in a price change, as long as the shift is between A_1 and A_2. This is the main result of the kinked demand curve model, namely that under these conditions the price under oligopoly will tend to be sticky.

The equilibrium point in the model is the original point on the demand curve. There is no explanation of how equilibrium in oligopoly comes about. Notice that, in drawing the diagram, we identified A as any point at which the oligopolist was located, and from which he was considering a move. All the model provides is a theoretical basis for the notion that price might be sticky in oligopolies.[16]

The idea of differentiated reactions can also be applied to different firms in a particular industry responding to the same event. Gatignon et al. (1989), in a well-cited paper, offer an explanation for the different reaction of firms to the entry of a new competitor. What they show is that firms work to their strengths. In an application to the airline industry, for example, they show that the more positively a firm's revenues increase in response to the introduction of new flights (the more flight elastic revenue is), the more likely is that firm to react to a new competitor by adding new flights. The lower the flight elasiticity of revenue, the more likely is the firm to react to a new competitor by reducing flights.

There continues to be a great deal of interest in the kinked demand curve. Stiving (2000), for example, uses it to show that firms 'that are using high prices to signal quality are more likely to set those prices at round numbers'. And in an interesting, non-technical application to the regional markets for health care in the United States, Malone (1998) argues that these markets are oligopolistic with classic kinked demand curves, in which 'the only chance of pricing above the kink without losing market share is to initiate strong consumer loyalty by creating significant product differentiation'.

6.7 Stackelberg leadership[17]

In 1934, the German economist Heinrich von Stackelberg brought some refinement to oligopoly theory by developing the idea that the industry might contain a dominant firm that acts as the leader in setting quantities.

In the Stackelberg duopoly model, it is assumed that Firm 2 follows the Cournot behavioural assumption, whereas the other firm is a first mover. For the follower, the problem is simple: it observes Firm 1's output and tries to determine a profit-maximizing level of output. The leader takes Firm 2's behaviour into account; knowing Firm 2's reaction curve, the leader will pick the point on Firm 2's reaction curve where it (Firm 1) has the largest possible profit.

The price leadership model is the logical extension of the Stackelberg model. Suppose that Firm 1 is the price leader, and that Firm 2 follows and reacts to signals given by Firm 1. Suppose also that Firm 1 is aware of Firm 2's behaviour.

The market demand curve assumes, for the sake of simplicity, the linear form:

$$p = f(Q) = a - bQ$$

where $Q = q_1 + q_2$. Firm 2's reaction function is thus:

$$q_2 = \frac{a - c_2}{2b} - \frac{1}{2}q_1 \tag{6.14)[18]}$$

Either firm will see price as:

$$p = a - b(q_1 + q_2) \tag{6.15}$$

Because Firm 1 knows Firm 2's reaction curve, it can substitute it into Eq. (6.15), so that, from Firm 1's point of view:

$$p = a - b\left[q_1 + \frac{a - c_2}{2b}\right] - \frac{1}{2}q_1 \tag{6.16}$$

$$p = \frac{1}{2} (a - bq_1 + c_2)$$

The dominant firm's profit is:

$$\pi_1 = pq_1 - c_1q_1$$

where c_1 is the average cost of producing q_1 (and marginal cost if average cost is constant). Substituting from Eq. (6.16):

$$\pi_1 = q_1(\tfrac{1}{2}a - \tfrac{1}{2}bq_1 + \tfrac{1}{2}c_2) - c_1q_1$$

Firm 1 will maximize its profit where:

$$\frac{d\pi_1}{dq_1} = \frac{1}{2} a - bq_1 = c_2 - c_1 = 0$$

which gives:[19]

$$q_1 = \frac{(a + c_2 - 2c_1)}{2b}$$

Substituting this result into Firm 2's reaction function Eq. (6.14), we get:[20]

$$q_2 = \frac{a - c_2}{2b} - \frac{1}{2} \frac{(a + c_2 - 2c_1)}{2b}$$

The greater the leader's cost advantage (the smaller is c_1 in comparison to c_2), the greater will be q_1 and the smaller will be q_2; in other words, the greater will be Firm 1's share of the market.

If we assume that neither firm has a cost advantage over the other, then $c_1 = c_2$, and:

$$q_1 = \frac{(a - c)}{2b}$$

$$q_2 = \frac{1}{2} \frac{(a - c)}{2b}$$

Even without a cost advantage, Firm 1 will supply twice as much as Firm 2. The total supply of the industry, in terms of number of units of output, is:

$$q_1 + q_2 = \frac{3(a - c)}{4b} \tag{6.17}$$

and the price, in terms of monetary units, is:

$$p = a - b(q_1 + q_2) = \frac{(a + 3c)}{4} \tag{6.18}$$

The leader's profit will also be twice that of the follower.[21]

These results can be compared with the Cournot solution. With linear demand,[22] the two reaction functions derived from each firm's profit-maximizing quantity (see Eq. (6.14)) are:

$$q_1 = \frac{a-c}{2b} - \frac{1}{2}q_2 \qquad (6.19)$$

$$q_2 = \frac{a-c}{2b} - \frac{1}{2}q_1 \qquad (6.20)$$

Solving, we get equilibrium output:

$$q_1 = q_2 = \frac{(a-c)}{3b} \qquad (6.21)$$

Total output is:

$$q_1 + q_2 = \frac{2(a-c)}{3b} \qquad (6.22)$$

and price is:

$$p = a - b(q_1 + q_2) \qquad (6.23)$$

$$= \frac{(a+2c)}{3}$$

We see that in the Stackelberg model of asymmetric rivalry, the quantity supplied by the industry, Eq. (6.17), is greater than in the Cournot symmetric duopoly, Eq. (6.22). Because the market demand is linear and downward sloping, it follows also that the Stackelberg price, Eq. (6.18), is less than the Cournot price, Eq. (6.23).

This result leads to the suggestion that the Stackelberg model is associated with higher levels of welfare (or less welfare loss) than the Cournot model. This suggestion is borne out in a study by Cable *et al.* (1994). They find that differences in conduct (as reflected in the different variations on the basic oligopoly model) have a major impact on welfare loss. In particular, in this context, they rank models of duopoly, from greatest to least welfare loss, as follows: collusive duopoly, Cournot, Stackelberg and Bertrand models. Of those discussed here, only the Bertrand model gives rise to less welfare loss than the Stackelberg model. A model with a dominant firm and a competitive fringe has even less welfare loss than the Bertrand model, but this finding, unlike the others in their study, is sensitive to product differentiation.[23]

Work on these types of models has from the first, and remains, predominantly theoretical. Recent contributions include examination of what happens if one firm in a Stackelberg duopoly is foreign (Matsumuro, 2003), what strategy should be adopted if there is a public Stackelberg leader with both domestic and foreign competitors (Fjell and Heywood, 2002) and the extension of the Stackelberg model to any number of non-identical firms (Pal and Sarkar, 2001). This last has some particularly interesting, counter-intuitive results, such as that 'entry of an additional firm may increase the quantities and/or profits of some existing firms; it may also increase the total industry profit.'

6.8 Collusive duopoly

The behavioural assumptions that the oligopolist will make changes in output (Cournot) and price (Bertrand) in the belief that competitors will not react to those changes, is implausible. It was Chamberlin's (1933) view that when the number of firms became so small that they all recognized their interdependence, the monopoly quantity would be produced and sold at the monopoly price.[24]

Where two or more firms come to an agreement on the price at which their product is to be sold, and/or on the quantities to be produced, and/or on the spatial division of the market, then this is called *collusion*. Collusion can be overt – when it is usually called a *cartel* – or covert. Collusion of any kind among firms is illegal in most countries (see Chapter 16).

There is a simple, diagrammatic way of explaining the gains from and potential instability of collusion. We concentrate on the case of two firms with different cost structures. We assume that the firms produce a homogeneous product. In Fig. 6.4, the horizontal summation of the two MC curves gives the industry MC curve denoted by ΣMC. Given the market demand DD, the cartel maximizes its joint profit by producing the output at which $\Sigma MC = MR$ (point L) in Fig. 6.4c. From point L, a horizontal line to the left identifies, at the intersection point with MC_2, the quantity to be produced by Firm 2 (q_2) and at the intersection point with MC_1, the quantity to be produced by Firm 1 (q_1). By construction (ΣMC is the horizontal summation of MC_1 and MC_2), the quantity at L will equal $q_1 + q_2$. The price to be

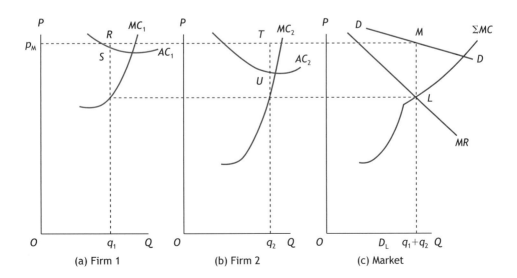

(a) Firm 1   (b) Firm 2   (c) Market

Figure 6.4 Collusive oligopoly

charged is the price that $q_1 + q_2$ can be sold at, identified at point M as p_M (monopoly price). Firm 1's profit will be RS $\times$ q_1, Firm 2's profit TU $\times$ q_2.

The neoclassical profit maximization condition, $MC_1 = MC_2 = MR$, is satisfied. The total profit of the two firms together will be greater through collusion than if they had competed. The profit of one of the firms may have declined through collusion, but if so, then the other's profits must have increased by more. In such a situation, collusion will still be beneficial to the two firms, but one will have to make a *side payment* to the other to keep it in the cartel.

Depending on circumstances, there may be an incentive for one or both of the firms to attempt to cheat. From Fig. 6.4a, if Firm 1 cheated and produced more than q_1 – and was still able to sell at p_M per unit – both its quantity and its profit per unit would increase, so its profit would also increase. However, even if in the short term it manages to achieve a higher profit, in the longer term it will become clear to Firm 2 that Firm 1 is cheating, because the quantity left for Firm 2 at price p_M will be less than its allotted q_2.

In a market in which there are unstable demand conditions, heterogeneous products, low entry barriers, widely differing firms in terms of size or cost conditions, tight legal restriction on non-competitive behaviour, or any other factors that make it difficult for firms to monitor each other's activities, collusion is unlikely.

Huck *et al.* (2004) find evidence from Cournot experiments to support the idea that the number of firms is a key factor in the likelihood of collusion. Only with two firms do they find collusion; with as few as four or five firms they find that there is never collusion, and in some cases there are outputs 'close to the Walrasian outcome'. In another recent theoretical paper Østerdal (2003) combines collusion with product differentiation. He considers whether 'stick and carrot punishment schemes' will increase the stability of the collusive agreement. He finds that the greater the product differentiation, the greater the stability of the joint profit-maximizing output.

6.9 Conjectural variations

The conjectural variations (CV) approach provides for a range of possible beliefs on the part of the oligopolist as to how his rivals will respond to his actions. The kinked demand curve results from expectations of different reactions to an increase and reduction in price; the CV approach builds on similar, but more general assumptions. Here we show the CV approach in relation to quantities.

Let $\lambda_{1,2}$ be the conjecture about how Firm 2 would respond to a choice of output by Firm 1. In the Cournot model, Firm 1 assumes that Firm 2 does not respond to Firm 1's actions, in other words the $\lambda_{1,2} = 0$ (the conjectural variation is zero). If $\lambda_{1,2} = 1$, this means that Firm 1 expects Firm 2 to respond to, say, a reduction in Firm 1's output, by an equivalent reduction in its output; $\lambda_{1,2} = -1$ means that Firm 1 believes that a reduction in its own output will be responded to by an equivalent increase in its rival's output.

From Firm 1's point of view, where Q_{-i} is the total output of all firms excluding the ith firm:

$$\lambda_{i,-i} \cong \frac{dQ_{-i}}{dq_i}$$

CVs are easily introduced into the Cournot duopoly model. In Cournot's original model (Eqs (6.6) and (6.7)) and in the linear version (Eqs (6.19) and (6.20)), each firm assumes that the other does not respond to its actions. If we now allow Firm 1 to expect some response to its actions on the part of Firm 2, then the change in total quantity arising from a change in Firm 1's quantity is no longer the same as the change in Firm 1's quantity alone. Instead of as in Eq. (6.19), Firm 1 will now maximize its profit for a quantity:[25]

$$q_1 = \frac{(a - bq_2 - c)}{(2b + b\lambda_{1,2})} \tag{6.24}$$

Similarly,

$$q_2 = \frac{(a - bq_1 - c)}{(2b + b\lambda_{2,1})} \tag{6.25}$$

If each firm has an identical conjectural variation then, as before, $q_1 = q_2$. Solving, we find the equilibrium output for each firm:

$$q_1 = \frac{(a - c)}{(3b + b\lambda_{1,2})} \tag{6.26}$$

Substituting and solving for p, we get:

$$p = \frac{a - (2a - 2c)}{3 + \lambda_{1,2}} \tag{6.27}$$

Note that if we set $\lambda_{1,2} = 0$, then q_1 in Eq. (6.26) becomes the same as q_1 in Eq. (6.21) and similarly p in Eq. (6.27) becomes the same as p in Eq. (6.23).

The conjectural variation approach has been valuable in the theoretical specification of the SCP relationship in oligopolistic industries. Cowling and Waterson's (1976) work on CV and industry structure has been at the forefront of these developments.

Structure is brought in through the following relationship:[26]

$$\frac{p - MC_i}{p} = i - \frac{S_i}{\varepsilon} \tag{6.28}$$

That is, the larger a firm's market shares S_i, the more market power it has, and the more price elastic (denoted by ε) the market demand, the less market power it has. As will be recalled from Section 5.5.1 on concentration ratios, $(p - MC)/p$ is a measure of monopoly (or market) power known as the Lerner index.

By multiplying all the terms in Eq. (6.28) by S_i and summing for all n firms, we get:

$$\frac{(p \sum_{i=1}^{n} S_i - \sum_{i=1}^{n} MC_i S_i)}{p} = -\frac{\sum_{i=1}^{n} (S_i)^2}{\varepsilon}$$

or

$$\frac{(p - \overline{MC})}{p} = -\frac{H}{\varepsilon} \tag{6.29}$$

which shows the relationship between the weighted average industry price–cost margin and the Herfindahl index of industry concentration.

Now, introducing non-zero conjectural variation, it can be shown that:[27]

$$\frac{(p - MC_i)}{p} = -\frac{S_i}{\varepsilon} (1 + \lambda_{i,-i}) \tag{6.30}$$

This can be aggregated as in Eq. (6.29) to give the following result at market equilibrium:

$$\frac{(p \sum_{i=1}^{n} S_i - \sum_{i=1}^{n} MC_i S_i)}{p} = -\frac{\sum_{i=1}^{n} S_i^2}{\varepsilon} - \frac{\sum_{i=1}^{n} S_i^2 \lambda_i}{\varepsilon}$$

or

$$\frac{(p - \overline{MC})}{p} = -\frac{H}{\varepsilon} (1 + \overline{\lambda}) \tag{6.31}$$

where $\overline{\lambda}$ is a market shares–weighted average conjectural variation.

Cowling and Waterson's (1976) form of Eq. (6.31) has been influential in empirical studies. They show that:

$$\frac{(\Pi + F)}{R} = -\frac{H}{\varepsilon} (1 + \lambda) \tag{6.32}$$

where Π, F and R are, respectively, industry aggregate profit, fixed costs and revenue.[28]

Equation (6.32) indicates thus that 'the profit–revenue ratio is related directly to the Herfindahl index of concentration in the industry and inversely to the industry price elasticity of demand' (Cowling and Waterson, 1976, p. 269). In other words, the firm's profit to revenue ratio is determined by the number and size distribution of firms in the market and by the price elasticity of demand for the product.

There has been a large amount of empirical work using CVs to examine the relationships suggested above.[29] Among the few writers focusing on European data, Haskel and Martin (1994) examine 81 manufacturing industries in the UK. Using a model based on the relationship between λ and capacity constraint, they show that the greater the capacity constraint, the higher the profits. The greater the capacity constraint, the more will competition be quantity based (Cournot-like), and the less the capacity constraint, the more will competition be price based (Bertrand-like). These results are intensified by concentration; the higher the levels of concentration in an industry, the more positive the relationship between capacity constraint and profits.[30]

The major criticism of the CV approach, as Fraser (1994) puts it, 'derives from the fact that it is a static equilibrium approach, while oligopolistic interactions are inherently dynamic'. It is for this reason that many industrial economists prefer multi-period game theory as a method for modelling oligopoly. However, as Fraser argues (agreeing with our conclusion in Chapter 2), game theory does not eliminate the problem of a serious multiplicity of equilibria. Another criticism relates to the assumption inherent in the theory of profit-maximizing behaviour on the part of oligopolists, an assumption which is at best hard to test and at worst inappropriate.

There have been responses to these criticisms. Slade (1987), for example, provided a dynamic analysis by incorporating CVs into a repeated game-based examination of the retail petrol market in Vancouver. The findings were that price responses during a period of price war were greater than would have been the case for a one-play game. The author interpreted this as indicative of 'punishment strategies' to enforce collusion. Shaffer (1991) considers alternatives to profit maximization as the objective of oligopolists in a paper on 'Consistent conjectures in a value-maximizing duopoly'.

Most of the recent literature on CVs incorporates game theoretic approaches to dynamic modelling. Erickson (1997), for example, 'develops a differential-game model of advertising competition that incorporates dynamic conjectural variations in an oligopoly with Lanchester dynamics'.[31] In an empirical application, Erickson goes on to show that his model explains aspects of the advertising behaviour of firms in the ready-to-eat cereal industry. Friedman and Mezetti (2002) also seem to be responding to earlier criticism. They develop a dynamic model of an n-firm oligopoly providing what they call a 'logically consistent reinterpretation of conjectural variations'.

We can conclude that the CV approach continues to be one that provides a great deal of work for both theoretical and empirical economists who continue to be interested in fundamental relationships between structure, conduct and performance. As to whether oligopolists actually act in accordance with CVs, it is interesting to note 'that management journals now advocate the use of conjectures by businessmen as one way of improving the business planning process and their competitive position' (Fraser, 1994).[32]

6.10 Summary

This chapter on oligopoly has shown the theoretical relationships between structure and strategy. Where structure is such that a firm can choose from a range of possible strategies, then these strategies and choices become the focus of attention. Unlike perfect competition, for example, where the structural assumptions mean that firms have little or no choice about what to do, in oligopoly a firm may adopt different quantity, price, differentiation and other strategies. It is this notion of choosing among alternatives, in the context of competition among a small number of firms, that has made oligopoly the main field within which game theory is now being applied and developed.

The first model described was that of Cournot; we presented the model almost exactly as he did in 1838. Cournot focuses on quantity as the strategic variable, Bertrand on price. Most of the rest of the chapter was presented as variations on the main Cournot and Bertrand models. We covered five such variations: product differentiation, differentiated reactions, asymmetric information, collusion and conjectural variation. The general aim in these variations is to incorporate more realistic assumptions.

In relation to each part of the chapter, we have introduced the basic arguments and conclusions, and then indicated the recent research interests. Although there are many more small firms than large ones, for obvious reasons large firms attract more attention. The major industries in the world are dominated by relatively small numbers of large firms, and, as a consequence, are oligopolies. This chapter is, therefore in some sense a theoretical backdrop to Chapter 14 on multinational enterprises. That oligopolies are empirically important is obvious; this chapter has shown the theoretical interest in oligopoly. Oligopoly in general has become the most important market structure in industrial economic research.

Websites

As for most other chapters, the IDEAS website at **http://ideas.repec.org** is a source for many working papers and articles of relevance for this chapter.

For additional examples of applications of game theory to Cournot and Stackelberg oligopoly, see **http://www2.owen.vanderbilt.edu/mike.shor/courses/GTheory/docs/oligopoly. html**. This is part of Mike Shor's website, already mentioned in the list of sites in Chapter 2.

Questions

6.1 Why is there a need for so many variations on Cournot's basic oligopoly model?

6.2 Why are firm strategy, game theory and oligopoly so closely related?

6.3   Discuss the relationship between product differentiation and oligopoly.

6.4   Would you expect collusion to be more or less stable in an oligopoly with product differentiation?

6.5   What is conjectural variation? Discuss whether CV has a practical application in the development of firms' strategies.

Notes

1   It should be noted, though, that the word comes from *oligeo*, the Greek word for 'a few' and *poleo*, Greek for 'to sell'.

2   It should be emphasized that, empirically, the more intense the competition and the fewer the imperfections in the market, the more likely is the outcome to approximate that suggested by neoclassical theory.

3   Since Cournot's work provided a basis (explicitly in places) for arguing that monopoly was better than competition, it would have been seen as contrary to the strongly held accepted wisdom of time.

4   It was 40 years after publication in French before Cournot's *Recherches* appeared in Italian, and it was nearly two decades more before the first English version was published.

5   This is the authors' translation of 'Le propriétaire (1) ne peut pas influer directement sur la fixation de D_2: tout ce qu'il peut faire, c'est, lorsque D_2 est fixé par le propriétaire (2), de choisir pour D_1 la valeur qui lui convient le mieux, cet à quoi il parviendra en modifiant convenablement le prix' (Cournot, 1980, p. 60).

6   This is logical, as Cournot writes, 'since the two springs/wells are assumed to be identical and identically located' (translation of 'ce qui devrait être puisque les deux sources sont supposées semblables et semblablement placées') (Cournot, 1980, p. 61). Cournot's firms each had possession of a natural water source.

7   The co-operative total revenue is $Q \cdot f(Q)$. Profit is maximized under the condition $dTR/dQ = 0$, that is,

$$Q \cdot f'(Q) + f(Q) = 0$$

$$Q \cdot dp/dQ + p = 0$$

$$Q + p \cdot dQ/dp = 0$$

8   This is the prisoner's dilemma situation familiar from Chapter 2.

9   Because there is a sense that 'reaction' implies a different period to the action that caused the reaction, most modern economists use the terms 'best response curve' and 'best response function' rather than 'reaction curve' and 'reaction function'.

10   As has been frequently pointed out, Cournot's equilibrium laid the foundation for the Nash equilibrium.

11   Being independent of one another, Pareto argued, meant that their relationship to price would be $p = f(Q_1, Q_2)$ rather than Cournot's $p = f(Q_1 + Q_2)$.

12   Note, however, that Bertrand was guilty of a similar simplifying assumption, namely that each duopolist acts in the belief that the other's price is fixed.

13   Leur intérêt serait de s'associer ou tout au moins de fixer le prix commun, de manière à prélever sur l'ensemble des acheteurs la plus grande recette possible; mais cette solution est écartée' (Bertrand, 1883, p. 503).

14 See also, in Chapter 10 on non-price strategies, the sections on product differentiation and advertising.

15 The intuitive notion of a kinked demand curve as an operational tool in economics originated in the early 1930s with the work of Chamberlin, although Chamberlin himself did not use the words 'kinked' or 'kinky' in his analysis. It is only later, in 1939, that Sweezy introduced the kinked demand curve as a workable concept.

16 According to Freedman (1995), this focus on sticky prices and equilibrium arises from a misinterpretation by Stigler, intent on propagating a Chicago approach. Sweezy's real point, Craig argues, is that 'you cannot simply use a smooth continuous demand curve as an appropriate model to explain oligopolistic markets unless you are willing to assume that decisions by one firm have no, or little, effect on a competitor's decisions. The consequence of abandoning the dominance of the simple continuous curve is far from trivial. Sweezy's alternative formulation leads to a dismissal of simple theories of income distribution based on marginal productivity'. The effect of Stigler's misinterpretation was to shift attention away from what might have contributed to a fundamental critique of neoclassical economics, and the possibly radical distributional implications of Sweezy's model.

17 For a relatively recent account of the emergence and contributions of Stackelberg's ideas, see Heertje (1996).

18 Equation (6.14) is obtained as follows:

For Firm 2 (as for Firm 1),

$$p = a - b(q_1 + q_2)$$

Firm 2's profit π:

$$\pi_2 = [a - b(q_1 + q_2)]q_2 - c_2 q_2$$

where c_2 is Firm 2's average cost (and marginal cost if average cost is constant). Firm 2's profit will be maximized where:

$$\frac{d\pi_2}{dq_2} = 0 \Rightarrow a - bq_1 - 2bq_2 - c_2 = 0 \Rightarrow 2bq_2 = a - bq_1 - c_2$$

Equation (6.14) follows.

19 It can be shown that this result can be generalized for a Stackelberg leader with n followers each with identical cost functions:

$$q_L = \frac{(a - c_L) + n(c_f - c_L)}{2b}$$

where q_L is the quantity and c_L the average (and marginal) cost of the dominant, or leader firm, and of the quantity and c_f the average (and marginal) cost of each of the follower firms.

20 Again, this can be generalized for n followers:

$$q_f = \frac{(a - c_f) - (n - 1)(c_f - c_L)}{2b(n + 1)}$$

21 For Firm 1, $\pi_1 = (a/4 + 3c/4)q_1 - cq_1$ from which,

$$\pi_1 = \frac{(aq_1 - cq_1)}{4}$$

For Firm 2, $q_2 = \frac{1}{2}q_1$, so:

$$\pi_2 = \left(\frac{a}{4} + \frac{3c}{4} \right) \frac{1}{2} q_1 - \frac{c}{2} q_1$$

From which:

$$\pi_2 = \frac{(aq_1 - cq_1)}{8}$$

22 Note that in the 1838 original, which we have more or less reproduced in our discussion of Cournot and Fig. 6.1 above, reaction curves were not linear.

23 According to Cable *et al.* (1994), 'the constraining influence of competition from the fringe is much weakened where products are heterogeneous'. This suggests the need for close attention by antitrust agencies to cross elasticities of demand. 'However, this recommendation may need to be balanced by dynamic considerations, insofar as it may be argued that new and different products are the lifeblood of dynamic market economies.'

24 In modern, game theoretic terms, the equivalent of what Chamberlain argued is that a prisoner's dilemma game, where there are repeated plays, will result in a Pareto-efficient solution.

25 Equation (6.24) is derived as follows:

$$\pi_1 = pq_1 - cq_1$$
$$= [a - b(q_1 + q_2)]q_1 - cq_1$$
$$= aq_1 - bq_1{}^2 - bq_1q_2 - cq_1$$

For profit maximization:

$$\frac{d\pi_1}{dq_1} = a - 2bq_1 - bq_2 - bq_1 \frac{dq_2}{dq_1} - c = 0$$

that is:

$$q_1(2b + b \, dq_2/dq_1) = a - bq_2 - c$$

Substituting $\lambda_{1,2}$ for dq_2/dq_1 and simplifying gives Eq. (6.24).

26 This is derived as follows:

$$p = a - bQ, \text{ where } Q - q_1 + Q_{2i}$$
$$\pi_i = pq_i - c_i q_i$$

For π_i max, $d\pi_i/dq_i = p + q_i (dp/dQ)(dQ/dq_i) - c_i = 0$. Now if the only change in Q arising from a change in q_i is q_i itself (i.e. $\lambda_{i,-i} = 0$), then $dQ/dq_i = 1$ and:

$$p + q_i \, dp/dQ - c_i = 0 \Rightarrow p + p(q_i/Q) \, (dp/dQ)(Q/p) - c_i = 0 \Rightarrow p + pS_i/\varepsilon - c_i = 0$$

where S_i is Firm i's market share, and ε is the market price elasticity of demand. With the usual assumption of constant average cost, Eq. (6.28) follows.

27 As in n. 26, without the assumption that $dQ/dq_i = 1$.

28 Note that some economists include the minus sign, and some do not. The market price elasticity of demand is inevitably negative, so the end result will be positive.

29 Most of this work examines American or Japanese industries. See Fraser (1994) for a brief examination

of some of this literature.

30 Note that the association between higher profits and Cournot competition is consistent with the findings of Cable *et al.* (1994) on welfare loss, discussed above, according to which Cournot duopoly is associated with greater welfare loss, and Bertrand with less.

31 See Kimball (1957) for the development of the Lanchester model.

32 Note, however, that in the special issue of *Strategic Management Journal* on fundamental research issues in strategy and economics (vol. 12, Winter 1991), there is not one mention of 'conjectural variation'.

CHAPTER 7

Industry in the European Union

7.1 Learning objectives

The main objectives of this chapter are:

- To provide an insight into concentration and entry barriers in the EU
- To discuss public enterprise, procurement markets, deregulation and regulation in the EU, and
- To analyse briefly the structure of EU industry

7.2 Concentration in the EU

An early source of EU-based information that used to provide measures of market concentration was the Annual *Report on Competition Policy* published by the European Commission since 1972. Unfortunately, there has been no continuity over time in the methodologies and definitions of market concentration used in these reports, and the comparison of concentration in different periods has therefore been difficult. For example, the sixth Report (1977) presents a table of all product markets where the leading firm holds more than 25 per cent of the total national market for that product. All the markets in this table were considered by the Commission to be characterized by a high level of concentration. A sample of this distribution is given in Table 7.1.

Table 7.1 Market leaders in the EC (sample)

CRI	Market	Industry	Country	Year	Company
86%	Sugar	Food, drink	DK	1975	De Danske Sukkerfabrikker
85%	Beverages	Food, drink	B	1976	Coca-Cola
85%	Thread	Textiles	F	1973	Dollfus Mieg
85%	Electric coffee machine	Electrical machinery	F	1975	Moulinex
25%	Car tyres	Transport equipment	F	1974	Michelin

Source: CEC, 1977

The table shows the importance of certain firms in individual EU markets at the time. As can be seen, the market is narrowly defined (at the four or five digits level). In the full table, 39 per cent of the leaders at the time were to be found in the food and drink industry, 21 per cent in the chemicals industry, and 6.6 per cent in the paper industry. This suggests that in some industries there are more likely to be large, dominant firms than in others. The methodology used in subsequent Reports on Competition Policy (numbers 12, 13 and 14 for example) relies on the information gathered by the French business magazine, *Le Nouvel Economiste*. The CR4 ratios are calculated on the basis of the ranking, by the magazine, of the 1000 largest companies. The variables used are turnover and numbers employed. Publication of market concentration measures in the Reports was, however, discontinued during the 1990s. As a result, recent figures on market concentration in the EU have to be extracted from different sources.

In spite of the discontinuity of methodologies, data and sources, a time series analysis of seller concentration is attempted here. Figure 7.1 shows the trend in overall seller concentration in the EU from 1972 to 1981 based on turnover, and from 1975 to 1981 based on employment. Figure 7.1 is based on shares in turnover and employment. An alternative approach is to calculate the contribution of the largest industrial firms to gross domestic product. This is done by de Jong (1993) for the period 1962 to 1990. Figure 7.2 is based on his data. There is an upward trend in the level of concentration in EU industry during the 1970s. In that period, many large European firms caught up with their British counterparts. From Fig. 7.1 it appears that, in terms of the CR10 ratio for European industry as a whole, the increase in concentration was sharper during the early part of the decade, levelling off in the latter half. This could be related to the rise in energy prices in 1973 and the subsequent increase in concentration in the oil and coal-mining sectors. In the second half of the 1970s, the growth of concentration either stabilized or reversed (in sectors such as mechanical engineering, and food, drink and tobacco). According to the Commission:

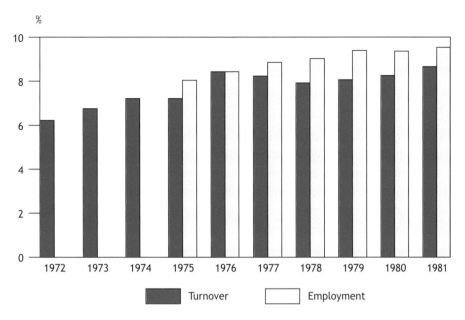

Figure 7.1 Concentration in European industry CR10
Source: CEC, 1984

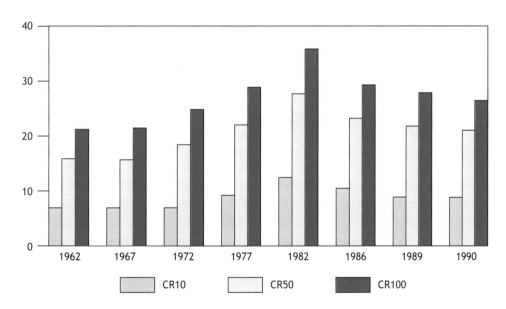

Figure 7.2 Concentration in European industry CR10, CR50 and CR100
Source: de Jong, 1993, table 1

Since 1972 the process of industrial concentration has been moving clearly towards stability and in some cases even slowing down in those industries which are already highly concentrated. According to modern economic theory, when the level of concentration passes a certain point in a given industry, a trend towards reequilibrium emerges in the form of declining concentration; it has also been found that maturity in an industry generally entails a degree of stability. (CEC, 1977, p. 206)

From Fig. 7.1 it would appear that this slowing down/reversal did not occur until 1976 and from Fig. 7.2, not until 1982. Whether these differences are because of different methodologies or different data sources, what follows from all studies is that there is a general upward trend in concentration for European industry as a whole in the 1970s. But, if different industries reach maturity at different times, it is not surprising that concentration in different industrial sectors moved in opposite directions during the period.[1]

Table 7.2 Concentration (CR4) in selected sectors, 1973, 1981 and 1989

	1973 %	1981 %	1989 %
Food, drink and tobacco	33	25	29
Chemicals	25	31	30
Elec. Eng., office machinery and data processing	38	43	36
Mechanical and instrument engineering	33	33	36
Production and processing of metals	24	26	44
Motor vehicles and other transport	34	44	44
Wood, furniture and paper	47	45	39
Textiles, clothing, leather and footwear	53	42	38

Sources: CEC, 1983; for 1989, authors' calculations derived from *Le Nouvel Economiste* (Nov. 1990)

Table 7.2 shows three sectors in which the CR4 ratio declined during the 1970s, and five sectors in which it either rose or remained stable. During the 1980s the CR4 declined in four sectors and either rose or remained stable in four. The trend seems to have been down in the 1970s and up in the 1980s in food, drink and tobacco,[2] up in the 1970s and down in the 1980s in chemicals and in electrical/electronic engineering, stable or continuously up in mechanical engineering, metals and motor vehicles, and continuously down in wood, furniture and paper and in textiles and clothing.[3]

In the year following the publication of the White Paper *Completing the Internal Market* (CEC, 1985a), concentration in some industries increased through mergers and acquisitions (see Chapter 10, Section 10.5). However, Fig. 7.2 convincingly demonstrates that *overall* concentration, having peaked in the early 1980s, declined thereafter towards levels similar to those of the mid-1970s.

Decreasing seller concentration trends continued in some traditionally concentrated sectors throughout the 1990s. Table 7.3 depicts evolving concentration ratios for industries characterized by a CR5 greater than or close to 30 per cent in 1987, that is, at a time when the process of completing the internal market had just been set in motion. These data are based on a sample of 225 leading firms in the EU manufacturing sector and refer to the three-digit level of the NACE classification.

Table 7.3 Concentration (CR5) in selected industries, 1987, 1993 and 1997

	1987 %	1993 %	1997 %
First processing of steel	36	38	39
Steel tubes	48	38	39
Glass	39	37	37
Soap, detergents, toiletries	31	40	32
Man-made fibres	65	64	37
Tractors and agricultural machinery	27	30	44
Office machinery and computers	57	58	61
Insulated wire and cable	36	39	71
Telecommunications and electrical equipment	42	45	32
Domestic electrical appliances	38	35	37
Lighting equipment and lamps	64	45	52
Motor vehicles	55	52	49
Motor vehicles – parts	37	32	25
Railway locomotives and rolling stocks	39	55	54
Cycles and motor cycles	43	43	41
Aerospace	60	66	44
Optical instruments	54	45	41
Sugar	42	46	38
Confectionery and ice cream	45	42	49
Tobacco	50	72	23
Rubber products and tyres	53	45	47

Source: European Commission, 2002

Out of the 21 industries with CR5 above or close enough to 30 per cent in 1987, 14 have experienced decreasing concentration ratios over the period. For the other industries shown in the table, seller concentration has risen. Particular increases are noticeable for insulated wire and cable, tractors and agricultural machinery, railway equipment and, to a lesser extent, confectionery and ice cream. Another nine relatively non-concentrated industries (not shown in the table), have experienced increasing concentration over the period. This is the case for a number of medium- to high-technology industries such as musical instruments (with a CR5 of 0.48 in 1997), clocks and watches (0.35), as well as medical instruments (0.33). This is also the case for a number of products belonging to the food industry: oils and fats (0.53); pasta (0.38); beer (0.32); and soft drinks (0.31). Concentration in traditionally weak EU industries, such as computer and office equipment has increased slightly over the period, suggesting a phenomenon of catching up with large global competitors (see Chapter 16). The figures released in the European Commission's study (European Commission, 2002) suggest that seller concentration has been overall fairly stable in the EU-15 over the 1990s.

Turning to the services sector, Gini coefficients of concentration show either a small decline or a stability in concentration over time, with the exception of transport, which remains nevertheless the least concentrated of all service industries in the EU (Fig. 7.3). As can be seen from Fig. 7.3, concentration is highest in the financial services industry, although it declined since the early 1990s. It should be noted, however, that concentration in these five service industries is lower than in manufacturing in general.

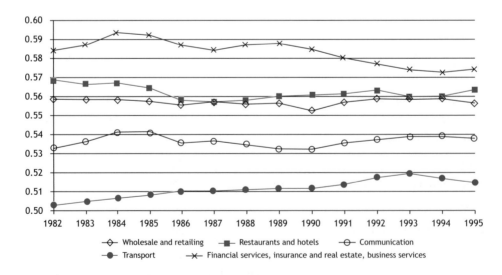

Figure 7.3 Evolution of concentration in the services sector, 1982-95
Source: European Commission, 2002, p. 250

It should be noted that a narrow definition of an industry, in terms either of product or of region, can give rise to higher concentration than a more general frame of reference. In the European pharmaceutical industry, for example, concentration ratios in each country are higher than in the EU as a whole; and concentration ratios in each therapeutic market are higher than in the pharmaceutical industry as a whole (de Wolf, 1993; Earl-Slater, 1993). As a result, the EU Commission is more tolerant of high concentration ratios in small EU countries than in large ones.

Concentration can be higher (or lower) in individual member states than in the EU as a whole. For the manufacturing industry as a whole, the UK, for example, has had a higher level of concentration than other EU economies, at least until recent years. Data from different sources collated by Ferguson and Ferguson (1994, p. 54) suggest that the 1982 manufacturing CR_{100} in the United States was 33 per cent, in the UK 41 per cent and in the EC 26 per cent. It had reached a peak of 42 per cent in the UK in 1975, and continued to decline to 38 per cent in 1989. It stabilized in the United States much earlier, and in the EC much later.

At a disaggregated level, the concentration ratio varies from industry to industry and from country to country. For example, in the software services industry (part of NACE 839), the CR_{10} ratio in 1992 was only 16.8 per cent in the UK, higher at 23.5 per cent in France, and lower at 13 per cent in Germany. In the EU telecommunications equipment industry (NACE 32), French and German firms are the market leaders; in 1991, the French manufacturer Alcatel had 29 per cent of the European market for transmission equipment against 27 per cent for the top German firm in the industry, Siemens.

As argued in Chapter 5, in the context of increasing internationalization, concentration ratios should be adjusted for trade. Marfels (1988) shows that in the automobile industry, for example, adjusting for trade sharply reduces concentration ratios in the United States, Britain and West Germany. The exception, not surprisingly, was Japan. The greater a country's trade surplus, the smaller is the adjusted ratio's denominator and, as a result, the greater the adjusted concentration.

The concentration ratio varies in a number of ways, including over time at different rates, and even in opposite directions in different industries and countries; it evolves in response to European and global market and specific industrial factors. To explain concentration in the EU, we turn now to these factors.

We deal here with two EU-specific explanatory variables:

◆ The change in the dimension of the integrated area

◆ The change in the intensity of integration in this area.[4]

A number of other factors also influence concentration ratios. There are broad, global developments such as the changes in enabling technologies that have facilitated internationalization of production, international division of labour, and regional concentrations of rising and declining industries. A narrower focus, on industry-specific technological change, understood to include both production and organizational technology, is also necessary if the interest is in the concentration ratios within that industry. At an even more disaggregated level, differences between firms, and the success or otherwise of the corporate strategies of leading firms can also contribute to changes in concentration in those firms' industries. These factors – not specific to the EU – are discussed elsewhere in this book (see Chapter 14 for example).

7.2.1 The dimension of the integrated area

Since the degree of concentration is a diminishing function of market size, enlargements should, *ceteris paribus*, reduce market concentration.[5] However, Figs 7.1 and 7.2 suggest that the first enlargement in 1973 was immediately followed by a sharp rise in the level of overall concentration; this trend slowed (at least in terms of turnover) after 1975. Subsequent enlargements, in 1981, 1986 and 1995 involved economies too small to influence overall concentration in the integrated area to a great extent, but it is clear from Fig. 7.2 that, whatever the reason, concentration over most of the 1980s declined. The *ceteris paribus* assumption is clearly not valid.

Table 7.4 Concentration ratios - EU-15 and central and east European countries compared, 1990, 1995 and 2000						
	CEEC-8			EU-15		
	1990	1995	2000	1990	1995	2000
CR5	62.5	60.2	60.8	59.3	59.3	60.5
CR3	47.2	45.4	42.7	39.5	39.0	39.3

Note: The industries are classified into 14 broad sectors at the two-digit NACE level. These sectors are: Food, Textile, Leather, Wood, Paper and pulp, Coke, Chemicals, Rubber, Mineral products, Metals, Machinery, Electrical and optical equipment (including computers and telecom equipment), Transport equipment and Others.

Source: CEC, 2003b

An interesting question at this juncture is to assess whether the fifth enlargement in May 2004 is likely to change dramatically these trends. Table 7.4 provides a comparison of concentration ratios between the EU-15 and eight new members from central and eastern Europe, the CEEC-8, namely Czech Republic, Estonia, Hungary, Latvia, Lithuania, Poland, Slovakia and Slovenia. As shown in the table, the share of total manufacturing output supplied in the CEEC-8 by the five (conversely three) largest industries is rather similar to the corresponding shares in the EU-15. In other words, overall manufacturing concentration ratios are comparable east and west. Since the fall of the Berlin Wall in 1989, the CEECs have experienced a great deal of restructuring, in line with the so-called Copenhagen Criteria that determined their political and economic suitability to enter the EU. In particular, the requirement that these countries 'put in place a market economy and [that they] cope with competitive pressures and market forces within the Union' (CEC, 1993f) meant that their state-owned enterprises had to be dismantled. The breaking-down of these large conglom-erates into smaller productive units, and the inflows of foreign capital, explain obviously the decrease in the concentration ratios over the 1990s. Whether concentration as a whole will decrease as a result of the fifth enlargement depends on the vigour of the small and medium-sized enterprises (SMEs) in the CEECs. Thanks to a relatively favourable environ-ment for private ownership in the past, which was consolidated in the countries of the former Yugoslavia by the 1988 New Enterprise Law, Slovenia is a first mover in this instance; the country has indeed experienced a wave of entrepreneurial activity and SME development in the 1990s. Its SME sector has been moving beyond the stage reached by all other CEECs, with small firms maturing, developing, growing and exporting over the 1990s, as docu-mented by Glas and Drnovsek (1999).

Arguably, spatial dimension and internal economic growth are similar in terms of their expected effect on concentration. This depends, however, on the cause of growth: if it is a consequence of new firms, concentration is diminished; if it is a result of an increase in the turnovers of all firms, then there may be no change in concentration; and if the growth is accounted for by expansion of the larger firms, then concentration will increase.

There is certainly some, albeit sketchy, evidence of an inverse relationship between growth and concentration. During the 1950s the rapidly expanding economies of the then European Community – Italy, Germany and France – experienced no or only slight increases in concentration. During the mid-1970s, with the post-oil crisis downturn, the CR100 in Germany rose significantly, but in the UK only very slightly. The German increase was, however, accounted for entirely by the six largest firms, possibly increasing their market shares in preparation for the anticipated competition of firms from the recently entered, more highly concentrated, British economy. Within industries (globally) over the period 1962 to 1990 'strong growth [was] accompanied by declining concentration, while slow growth, and *a fortiori* decline [were associated with] a rising degree in concentration' (de Jong, 1993, p. 10). Sluggish growth in the 1990s was not accompanied with increasing con-centration. It can be therefore concluded that overall, as can be seen from Figs 7.1, 7.2, as well as from Table 7.3, there is no indication of concentration increasing during recessions or declining during periods of growth.

7.2.2 Corporate activity and economic integration

By economic integration in this context, we mean the removal of barriers to the flows of goods, services and factors of production between countries in the region. Some barriers are more amenable to government and corporate action than others. Language and cultural dif-ference, for example, are far more difficult to remove than tariffs.

There was, until the 1980s, little work on the impact of the Common Market on the struc-ture of European industry. This is in sharp contrast to a wide literature, since the formation of the European Economic Community, on the trade effects[6] of economic integration. One explanation for this difference, given by Pelkmans (1984), is that economists have long been dominated by the static, neoclassical welfare theory of customs unions which ignores intra-union direct investment. Another reason has been the lack of reliable statistics; there seems to be a substantial 'statistical gap' between the EU and the United States.

Economists would expect increasing integration to have an impact on market structure. According to Scherer and Ross (1990, p. 89), during the first two decades of the EU 'the overall impact of integration was almost surely to create market structures more competitive than they otherwise would have been'. While the relationship between how competitive and how concentrated an industry is, is not always clear,[7] what Scherer and Ross appear to be arguing[8] is the following: because the concentration ratios for the EU as a whole were much lower than in each of the five main founding member states, and because the increase in the overall EU ratios from 1963 to 1978 was much lower than the increases in the national ratios in any of the five, so integration kept concentration down, that is it increased competition.

The behavioural aspect of this conclusion is that in the early stages of integration in Europe, characterized by the removal of tariff barriers, the extent to which leading firms dominated in national markets was greater than the extent to which leading firms dominated in the economy of the EU as a whole. Mergers, acquisitions and alliances (MAAs) during this period – in the MAA wave in the early 1970s, for example – were dominated by agreements between firms of the same nation (Hamill, 1992, p. 137; Thomsen and Woolcock, 1993, p. 22). National concentration ratios increased, but because this was happening in most member states the overall Community concentration increased less than in individual states.

A subsequent stage of economic integration (the so-called 1992 Programme) deals with the removal of all NTBs (non-tariff barriers), such as legal, technical and financial barriers so as to complete the single European market (SEM – see below). Eager to exploit economies of scale in the face of globalized competition, European firms started to implement intensive cross-border strategies. Thus, according to Thomsen and Woolcock (1993, p. 22), 'in 1989–90, for the first time, the largest EC manufacturing firms were more acquisitive abroad than at home.' Hamill (1992, p. 137) more generally concludes that the distinguishing feature of the [1985–90] boom in MAA activity . . . is the high proportion of cross-border deals'. This suggests expansion of leading firms at the European level, with more of an impact on concentration at that level than the earlier, national mergers. Referring to the merger wave of the 1980s, Shepherd (1990, p. 199) writes that 'the 1980s mergers have probably raised concentration ratios (and equivalent HHI [Herfindahl] values) by 2 or 3 percentage points'. However, the figures presented above show that the overall concentration ratios for either manufacturing as a whole or services as a whole have been stable over the 1990s (although these ratios would have tended to rise in some industries and over several years).

To summarize the above discussion on economic integration and concentration in the first decades of the EU, integration probably reduced concentration to less than it would have been without integration; more intense integration in the period since 1985 has increased concentration to above what it would otherwise have been. This increase was, however, short-lived, as concentration ratios decreased and stabilized over the 1990s. We examine MAAs in more detail in Chapter 10 (Section 10.5.1).

7.3 Barriers to entry in the EU

Barriers to entry (in a particular market) are all types of obstacles at the market edge that make entry for new firms difficult. They consist of all the factors that give incumbent firms advantages over those considering entry into the market. The study of barriers has tradition-ally been conducted at the level of the single economy.[9] These are the barriers faced by a firm in an economy wishing to gain entry into an industry and, by extension, a product market, in that economy. These barriers, which include economies of scale and product differentia-tion, can be referred to as *barriers of the first order*.[10] In the case of an open economy, we have to take into account the geographical dimension of the market, and cross-border transac-tions render the situation more complex.

A firm originating from country A and wishing to expand its activity beyond country A's borders has three broad means at its disposal: foreign direct investment (FDI) (whether through greenfield investments or mergers, acquisitions or joint ventures); other strategic alliances involving, for example, licensing agreements; and trade. In the case of FDI, the firm must overcome the barriers of the first order in the relevant industry in the host country. To some extent these will be similar to the first-order barriers in its home country, and to that extent the firm choosing FDI will already have overcome these barriers. Like firms undertaking FDI, firms attempting to enter a foreign market through exporting have usually already gained a foothold (that is, overcome first order barriers) in their home market. In addition, however, firms choosing exporting as their market entry strategy face barriers through which agents in the target country resist imports. These are *barriers of the second order*.

7.3.1 Barriers of the second order

Barriers of the second order are all restrictions (essentially of an institutional nature) faced by potential entrants into a given geographical market. They prohibit entry of a foreign com-petitor. They include tariffs,[11] quantitative restrictions and other measures of equivalent effect, and non-tariff barriers (NTBs). The NTBs encompass border checks, administrative procedures such as insurance regimes, differing legal and fiscal regimes, technical stan-dards, public procurement bias, exchange controls and other monetary controls. Cultural and language barriers are also included in this group.

In some cases, the barriers to entry by international trade into a given geographical market are so numerous and so high that the firm would choose FDI as an alternative strategy. This is particularly true for, but not confined to, non-EU firms attempting to penetrate the EU market. In order to bypass the Common External Tariff constraint, many US and Japanese multinationals have preferred to establish a presence in the EU market.[12]

The Treaty of Rome, Article 3, Part 1, called for the abolition of tariffs, quantitative restrictions and other measures having equivalent effect, on trade between member states. In the years following its signature, all tariff barriers among the six founding members were removed.[13] In the early years of the EU, it was assumed that NTBs were of limited importance compared with customs duties but, because of the recession in the 1970s, these NTBs multiplied as member states increasingly sought to protect their home markets and industries. Regional integration in the EU could only be strengthened by the abolition of the remaining NTBs. In 1985, the EC Commission produced a detailed legislative programme[14] aimed at the full integration of the economies of the member states by, among other things, the eradication of all barriers of the second order. This was known at the time as 'the 1992 Programme', for all remaining barriers were to be removed by December 1992. The Commission identified among remaining obstacles, impediments not just to the free flow of goods and services, but also to capital and labour. These obstacles have been classified as physical, technical and fiscal barriers.

Physical barriers at customs posts

These are barriers both because they cause delays and because there are formalities such as forms and documents that involve administrative costs. The delays include such problems as queues of trucks awaiting inspection at borders, which are costly in terms of drivers' wages and in terms of the opportunity costs of having vehicles unavailable for other uses. Most important in this context is the disadvantage that customs posts impose on suppliers or (consumer and producer) goods from other countries. As a first step towards the removal of these barriers, member states adopted in January 1988 the single administrative document (SAD) for importing and exporting goods among all members of the EU. All directives agreed at the EU level required action on the part of member states to incorporate them into national law and to implement them in practice. The transposition of EU directives into national law, and their implementation, has not been done without many delays (see Box 7.1).

Box 7.1 The long road to the SEM: eradicating barriers in the EU

EU directives with regard to the SEM come into force once the national parliaments pass equivalent legislation. In 1993, most of the measures needed to complete the SEM were adopted by the various parliaments. However, in early 2002, approximately 10 per cent of EU legislation still needed to be transposed at the various national levels. Two major problems remain: first, there are a number of areas in which there has been very little progress in the past ten years; second, in spite of the directives becoming part of national legislation, what has been found is an increase in the incidence of infringements.

Box 7.1 (continued)

Little or extremely slow progress has been achieved in the following areas: standards in the construction sector and in the machine tools industry; company law, intellectual property and VAT on electronic commerce.

The progress towards the completion of the SEM has been monitored all along, with the EU Commissioner for the SEM producing a regular evaluation of the member states in relation to their progress in that area. The evaluation is based on two major indices:

- The SEM *index* which comprises 20 variables, including price dispersion, intra-EU trade, the intensity of energy use, pollution, and

- The *Transposition Deficit index* which measures the transposition of new EC/EU directives into national law, as well as transposition of modified directives into national law.

The SEM index has evolved positively since 1996 due to the decrease of state aids and of telecommunications costs. However, these positive effects have been mitigated by increasing inefficiencies in the banking system, as well as increasing polution levels, all elements hampering the good functioning of the SEM. The Transposition Deficit index, measuring the average percentage of SEM dirctives that have not been transposed into national law was still as high as 6.3 per cent in 1997; it came down to 2 per cent a few months before the Barcelona Summit of March 2002. At that stage, the best performing countries were Finland, Denmark, Sweden and the Netherlands, whereas the worst scores were attained by Greece, France, Austria and the UK.

Finally, a low transposition deficit does not necessarily equate with good behaviour, in other words with enforcement. There are some 1500 infringement procedures relating to the SEM under way in 2004. Although France, Italy and Germany (three large countries) are involved in a large proportion of the cases, countries such as Ireland, Belgium and Greece cumulate a number of infringements which is more than pro-portional to their size.

Technical barriers

These are of two broad kinds: technical regulations and procurement markets.[15] Technical regulations in EU countries used to be enacted by national legislators in the interest of health, safety and environment, and would often have taken the form of technical standards. Standards have traditionally been defined by national standards bodies (such as the *Deutsche Industrie Normen*, the AFNOR in France and the British Institute of Standards). These national bodies used to test and certify that a product complies with national standards and regulations. National standards were NTBs because when issued at country level, they were not recognized by other member states. The best-known example of stringency embodied in national stan-dards resulting in an NTB was the purity decree of beer in Germany (*Reinheitsgebot*) that almost prohibited imports of foreign beers into the German market.[16] European standardization has enhanced the positions of European bodies such as the CEN (*Centre Européen des Normes*) and the Cenelec.[17] Different national standards have been predominant in the food industry, pharmaceuticals, telecommunications equipment, car and building products. Also included in technical barriers are regulations regarding workers' qualifications.

In the view of the Commission, technical barriers not only added extra costs but also distorted production patterns, increased unit costs, increased stockholding costs, discouraged business co-operation, and fundamentally frustrated the creation of a Single Market for industrial products. Until such barriers were removed, Union manufacturers were forced to focus on national rather than continental markets and were unable to benefit from the economies of scale which a truly unified market offers (CEC, 1985a, p. 17).

The 1992 Programme was motivated by the following theoretical expected gains: the removal of the technical barriers would improve market access; they would remove sheltered dominant positions and lead to a higher degree of competition. Also, a larger market and the restructuring of the EU's productive system would enable firms to undertake costly (and risky) R&D projects. As a result of the full exploitation of economies of scale, prices would be forced down and would be expected to converge in the medium to long term.

An estimation of possible gains was attempted by Cecchini (1988).[18] The welfare gains for EC producers and consumers were estimated at around ECU 200 billion,[19] representing between 4.3 and 6.4 per cent of the EC's GDP in 1988. Roughly one-third of the gains would have arisen as a result of scale economies and a quarter would have stemmed from increased competition. It should be noted that these estimates were done before and without obviously taking into account the dismantling of the Berlin Wall (as well as the costly reunification of the two Germanies), and the first Gulf War of the early 1990s. These two unforeseen political events had major implications for the EU economy at the time, dragging many of its countries into a prolonged economic recession.

A key element in the adoption of directives on the removal of technical barriers has been the new approach introduced in the programme for the completion of the single market. Up to the mid-1980s, the removal of technical barriers within the EU had been based on attempts to harmonize the technical standards of the member states. This proved to be an extremely complicated and therefore lengthy process. The new approach was based on mutual recognition, where intra-Union trade in products is unrestricted as long as those products meet the technical standards of any member state.

The origin of the mutual recognition principle is the *Cassis de Dijon* case, ruled on by the European Court of Justice in 1978. The ruling was that a product lawfully sold in any one member state must be admitted – and permitted to be sold – in other member states. This principle has increasingly guided international regulation within the EU since 1985.

Again, in spite of the '1992 deadline', some important measures were not agreed by the end of 1992, and some industries (such as the pharmaceutical industry) were not truly European and would not be until well after 2000. We have already mentioned the problem of delays in the transposition of EU directives into national laws. The Commission has identified protection of intellectual property as one of the main areas in which these delays have occurred. Another is double taxation of firms, which is discussed under fiscal barriers, to which we now turn.

Fiscal barriers

There have been, and continue to be, differences in the tax systems of the member states. For example, in 1987, excise duties on wine were zero in Spain, Portugal and Greece. In

Table 7.5 Evolution of corporate tax rates in the EU-15, 1991-2002

	1991 %	1994 %	1999 %	2002 %
Austria	39	Na	34	34
Belgium[a]	39	39	39	30[f]
Denmark	38	34	32	30
Finland	-	-	29	29
France	34	33.3	33.3	33.3
Germany[b]	57.5 (42)	45 (30)	40 (30)	25
Greece[c]	46	na	35	35
Ireland[d]	40 (10)	40 (10)	38 (10)	38 (10)
Italy	47.83	53.2	37	34
Luxembourg	39.39	na	30	22
Netherlands	35	35	35	34.5
Portugal	39.6	36	32	30
Spain	35.34	35	35	35
Sweden	30	28	28	28
UK[e]	33	33	30 (10)	30 (10)

Notes:

[a] A 43 per cent rate is applied to branches of non-resident companies (unless reduced by treaty provisions).

[b] Lower rates in brackets apply to distributed profits.

[c] Varies with activity, status and nature of investment (productive or not).

[d] The lower rate applies to export-oriented manufacturing and service activities (in the International Financial Services Centre in Dublin). A standard 12.5 per cent rate applies since 1 January 2003.

[e] Lower rate for corporations with profits below a certain threshold. For profits over £1.5m, the rate is 30 per cent.

[f] The September 2001 Corporate Tax Reform brought rates down gradually.

Sources: Supplement to *European Report*, no. 1754, 21 March 1992 (data for 1991); *Dictionnaire Permanent Fiscal*, Editions Legislatives, Paris, 2000; European Parliament, 2003 (for most recent data)

Ireland, the excise duty was ECUs 2.79 per litre of wine, and ECUs 0.13 in Luxemburg (Emerson et al., 1988). A final agreement on VAT and excise duty harmonization was reached by the twelve finance ministers in October 1992. This has involved substantial changes for some member states.

Another important example of fiscal barriers is the differences between the member states' corporate profit tax rates.[20] In 1991, overall (that is, central government plus regional government plus local government) corporate profit tax rates ranged from 10 per cent (for export-oriented firms) in Ireland to 57.5 per cent in Germany (see Table 7.5).

The Committee of Independent Experts on Company Taxation, headed by the former Dutch finance minister Onno Ruding, was set up in order to advise on the harmonization of company taxation. The Ruding Report's recommendations, submitted to the European Commission in March 1992, fell into three categories: elimination of the double taxation of cross-border income flows; harmonization of corporate taxes; and greater transparency between member states on other tax issues.

The Committee proposed a three-stage approach to harmonization of company taxation: first, that a uniform withholding tax of 30 per cent on all member states' companies be put into effect by January 1994 (whether the profits were distributed in the form of dividends or not); second, that from January 1994, a single type of tax on companies, varying from 30 to 40 per cent, be established; and third, that from the beginning of 1997 (and until economic and monetary union come into effect), the scope of the 'parent–subsidiary' directive adopted in July 1990 be extended. The aim here was to eliminate double taxation by giving individual companies the right to claim against such taxation. When double taxation arises, the firm concerned refers its case to the fiscal authorities in the member state where the firm is taxed. If no satisfactory decision is made, the firm refers its case to the authorities in the member state where the associated firm is taxed. As a last resort, the case is referred to an Advisory Commission (comprising a chairman, two representatives of the tax authorities concerned, and an equal number of independent members.

Some progress has been made on the transparency front. Since January 1992, a common taxation system on parent companies and their subsidiaries has been agreed.[21] On 1 January 1993, the withholding of tax on interest and royalty payments made between parent companies and their subsidiaries in different member states was abolished.[22] As Table 7.5 shows, there has been an important degree of harmonization with regard to corporate tax rates over the 1990s, with most (main) rates falling in the range 28 to 35 per cent (with the notable exception of Ireland).

In the new member states, corporate tax rates spanned, in 2002, from 15 per cent in Lithuania to more than 25 per cent in countries such as the Czech Republic and Poland, with most rates gravitating around 25 per cent. Obviously, the sophisticated industrial and regional policies implemented by these countries have encompassed an arsenal of schemes providing tax breaks and tax relief, such as: total tax exemption for ten years in Hungarian priority zones, (those with employment rates exceeding 15 per cent); reduced rates in

Slovenian free economic zones; and tax relief for foreign investors subject to a minimum investment and for ten years in the Czech Republic (Andreosso-O'Callaghan, 2004).

It should be noted that the removal of second-order barriers can, paradoxically, increase differences between economies in terms of industrial development. The implementation of the directive relating to the mutual recognition of higher education degrees, for example, would enable firms to recruit their most highly skilled employees from anywhere in the Union. The most profitable and prestigious firms would attract the best European graduates, contributing to the polarization of high value added economic activity in rich areas. However, evidence seems to suggest that the net (spatial) effects of the SEM have been positive by allowing geographical concentration to decrease over the 1990s (Aiginger and Pfaffermayr, 2004). Adverse effects in disadvantaged areas have been offset by, for example, structural funds aimed at improving the infrastructures of such areas.

Even with the completion of the SEM, barriers to entry persist in the EU. Little or extremely slow progress has been achieved, for example, in the following areas: standards in the construction sector and machine tools industry; company law, intellectual property, VAT on electronic commerce. Other types of barriers will remain for many years: cultural and language barriers will indeed still be a feature of the EU market for the foreseeable future. Cultural and language barriers were important in the *ABC/Générale des Eaux and Canal/W.H. Smith TV* case (CEC, 1991). In the 2001 *CVC/Lenzing* case, the Commission found high entry barriers in the European Economic Area (that is, within the EU and EFTA countries), due to perceived quality and cultural barriers (CEC, 2002a). Resistance to the removal of other barriers continues. Examples of other barriers include national buying preferences, different distribution channels, supply logistics and marketing methods in the member states, as evidenced in the *CVC/Lenzing* and *DaimlerChrysler* cases (CEC, 2002a). In the *DaimlerChrysler* case, the company was fined by the Commission for requiring foreign customers to pay a deposit of 15 per cent when ordering a car in Germany. This barrier was not faced by German consumers presenting the same 'risk', unknown to the seller or living far away (CEC, 2002a).

7.3.2 Barriers of the first order

The creation of a large European domestic market entails, by definition, the removal of most of the remaining NTBs, the barriers of the second order. It is, however, interesting to study the significance in the SEM of the barriers of the first order, as identified in Chapter 5.

With the elimination of most of the remaining NTBs, particularly in the new member countries, the EU-25 is supposedly a quasi homogeneous geographical market of 450 million people. Nonetheless, intensified competition is expected to change the intensity of other barriers, namely scale economies and product differentiation, the barriers of the first order.

Economies of scale in the EU

Under the assumptions of perfect competition, every firm produces where long-run average cost is at minimum; any increase in output will raise the average cost of the product (diseconomies of scale). In most situations, competition is less than perfect and, as we saw in earlier chapters, this can result in firms producing under conditions of increasing returns (or economies of scale), that is, above the minimum average cost level (to the left of point M on Fig. 7.4). Unexploited economies of scale would then materialize. Since the completion of the European market increases the level of competition, it can be argued that it also drives firms down their average cost curves. Ultimately, even if the result is fewer leading firms in any particular industry in Europe, each will produce greater output at lower average costs. Competition from outside Europe will keep prices close to average cost (that is, it will keep supernormal profits down).[23]

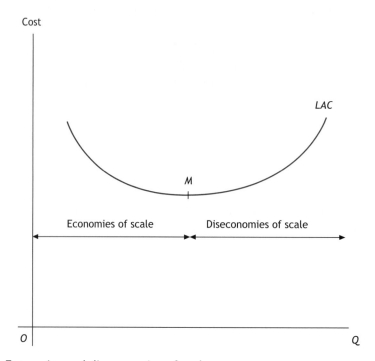

Figure 7.4 Economies and diseconomies of scale

Before the completion of the SEM, a number of manufacturing industries were seen as having potential for further exploitation of technical economies of scale in the EU.[24] Pratten (1987) estimated ranges of potential cost savings from increasing output. Even within industries, these ranges were wide, reflecting the heterogeneous nature of industries in terms of economies of scale.[25]

Broadly, unexploited economies of scale were large in motor vehicles, transport equipment, chemicals, mechanical engineering, electrical engineering, instrument engineering, and paper, printing and publishing. These industries accounted for approximately two-thirds of total manufacturing employment in the EU-10 and 55 per cent of industrial production in the EU-12 in the early 1990s. Production economies of scale were smaller in the more traditional industries: food, drink and tobacco, clothing and leather, timber and wood, and textiles. Note that economies of marketing and/or of distribution are different from those of production, and are particularly significant in the food industry.

Pratten's (1987) data rest on a strong assumption that the removal of NTBs within the EU has the effect of increasing plant size, enabling plants to realize all significant economies of scale. This hypothesis has been tested by various authors: Schwalbach (1988) for the UK and West Germany; Ranci and Helg (1987) for Italy. Drawing from experience, their studies confirm the role played by external trade in the expansion of the size of production units.

The larger size of the market, the benefits of which can be reaped by increased exports, and the challenge represented by imports, are the two major explanatory variables. Firms become more efficient and non-viable plants are removed from the respective domestic markets. In France, the average size computed on the basis of sales of the 250 largest domestic companies was US$1.3 million at the end of the 1980s; the figures for West Germany and the UK were US$2.2 million and US$2 million respectively. The 1992 deadline made these differences clear to the French business community. Mergers and acquisitions, as a means of achieving economies of scale, ranked first on the list of French firms' strategies for the early 1990s. The few hundred biggest firms in France acknowledged the fact that 'growth is imperative to achieve dominant positions in [the French] market' (Bain and Company, 1989, p. 98). The necessity to exploit economies of scale increases the average size of production units; this, in turn, tends to raise concentration ratios.

From the completion of the SEM arises a potential paradox. Driving costs down makes it even more difficult for new firms to enter the market, because it implies that the volume of output on first entering the industry has to be large. The completion of the SEM leads to the exploitation of economies of scale, which may inhibit competition.[26] Expressed another way, the removal of the barriers of the second order may intensify barriers of the first order.

Product differentiation in the EU

European integration has resulted in an increasing proportion of the total trade of the EU being accounted for by intra-EU trade. How does this relate to product differentiation? If the increasing tendency for member states to trade with one another is expressed in flows of very different goods out of one member compared with those that flow out of another, then integration has had no impact on product differentiation. On the other hand, if different members' exports are similar, then increasing integration may have increased product differentiation.

The traditional customs union theory (as developed simultaneously by Maurice Byé, Herbert Giersch and Jacob Viner in the early 1950s) focused on homogeneous products. In particular, the question Viner (1950) asked was whether welfare gains arising from joining a customs union were greater or less than the losses arising from no longer importing from a cheaper source. This question was to be asked for each product affected by joining. Some products would be exported by the new entrant to the customs union, others imported from the customs union. There was no room in the theory for a product to be both exported and imported.[27] In this sense the theory was basically Ricardian; trade would be in accordance with comparative advantage within the customs union.

In one respect, developments have been predicted by theory; intra-EU trade has increased since the 1957 Treaty of Rome and now represents almost two-thirds of total EU trade.[28] On the other hand, contrary to the predictions of the customs union theory, the increase in intra-EU trade has been more a result of intra-industry than inter-industry trade.[29]

The expectation was that Germany, say, would become a major European producer of cars and Italy, say, the major European producer of refrigerators. Germany would then be the main source of cars, and most of the imports of cars by member states would be from Germany, and similarly for refrigerators, most of the imports by members would be from Italy. Instead, all of the large member states (and some of the smaller ones) have continued to produce and export both cars and refrigerators. They have also continued to import both these products. 'Indeed, the trade figures for all West European countries show that each country has significant exports and imports in most product categories, and this intra-industry trade accounts for a high proportion of total trade' (O'Donnell, 1994).[30] Why should this be so?

From a supply perspective, the theory was based on a set of assumptions that were unrealistic. Among these was perfect competition and production at constant returns to scale. Many national markets were closer to monopolistic competition and oligopoly, with economies of scale (EOS) in production (and distribution), and these evolved into similarly structured markets at the European level. With production in different countries, information that firms had about the process, product and distribution strategies of competitors was far less than perfect. This inevitably led to differences between the products (in the same industry) made in different member states. Firms have acted to maintain these differences, physically differentiating their products from others in the industry, advertising to generate brand loyalty, and investing in R&D in attempts to stay ahead technologically. Finally, one industrial system in Europe may be better oriented towards the achievement of one characteristic of a product (for example, high quality), whereas another may be better oriented towards the achievement of a different characteristic (for example, low price).

Among consumers with increasing incomes, there has been an increase in technical knowledge and ability to isolate the many features of the same product; there is, for example, an increased awareness of quality. While some people focus on dependability and price, others focus on novelty and fashion. Over time, consumer demand interacts with the advertising of the sellers to create brand loyalty.[31]

Intra-industry trade is a consequence of these supply and demand factors, that is, the availability of a variety of EOS products in the same industry in different countries,[32] together with the increasing ability among consumers in different countries to differentiate among products in the same industry.

In his discussion of intra-industry trade, Root (1990, p. 115) emphasizes 'factors that are specific to the firm (product differentiation and internal economies of scale)'. Writing of the

United States, he points out that the 'firm-specific nature of intra-industry trade is highlighted when we recognize that about one-third of that trade occurs between multinational enterprises and their foreign subsidiaries. Any theory of intra-industry trade, therefore, needs to be linked with a theory of foreign investment that explains the behaviour of multinational enterprise.'[33]

The most popular index used to measure the intensity of a country's intra-industry trade (IIT) is the Grubel–Lloyd index. For a single industry, the index is given by:

$$IIT_{GL} = 1 - \frac{|X - M|}{X + M}$$

where X and M are, respectively, the country's exports and imports of the products of that industry.[34]

The index takes values between zero and one: zero when there are exports but no imports or imports but no exports, and one when exports equal imports. The closer it is to one the higher the level of intra-industry trade. Because of its numerous imperfections, such as in the case where a country experiences a large trade imbalance (see Mikic, 1998), this index has gradually been supplanted by dynamic indices (see, for example, Menon, 1996; Brülhart and Hine, 1998).

Whatever the index used, intra-industry trade is in general higher in manufacturing industries than in the primary sector because the production of a particular manufactured good can often be located in any of a large number of different places, whereas primary products must be exported from locations which have a natural comparative advantage for producing them. Arguably, manufactured goods are also subject to a greater degree of product differentiation than primary products. During the first decades of the EU, integration and enlargements were accompanied by a general intensification of intra-industry trade and, by implication, product differentiation.[35] This has kept increasing or has been sustained at high levels for the individual countries over the 1990s (Table 7.6). Whether increased intra-industry trade and product differentiation systematically imply catching-up, convergence or increased structural similarities between EU countries is debatable. As has been demonstrated elsewhere, in the 1990s the increase in intra-industry trade and product differentiation tended to involve structurally dissimilar countries or regions of the world (Andreosso-O'Callaghan and Bassino, 2001).

The degree of product differentiation is likely to be higher in less concentrated, or more competitive, industries. In oligopolistic industries (such as microprocessor production), the full exploitation of economies of scale involves product standardization and long production runs. As a result, product differentiation will be much less important than in less concentrated industries, such as office machinery. This raises a problem for EU competition policy: aiming to reduce costs can result in barriers to entry from economies of scale in concentrated industries, but encouraging competition in less concentrated industries can result in product differentiation which can also be a barrier to entry.

Table 7.6 Evolution of intra-industry trade within EU countries, GL index, 1970-97			
	1970	1987	1997
Belgium/Luxembourg	0.69	0.77	0.81
Denmark	0.41	0.57	0.67
Germany	0.73	0.76	0.80
Greece	0.22	0.31	0.27
Spain	0.35	0.64	0.72
France	0.76	0.83	0.87
Ireland	0.36	0.62	0.53
Italy	0.63	0.57	0.60
Netherlands	0.67	0.76	0.61
Austria	na	na	0.75
Portugal	0.23	0.37	0.55
Finland	na	na	0.50
Sweden	na	na	0.70
UK	0.74	0.77	0.80

Source: European Commission, 2003c

The classic example of product differentiation as a barrier to entry is the breakfast cereals market in the United States. The burgeoning number of new brands produced by incumbent firms between 1950 and 1970 was such that entry was deterred. Potential entrants could not find a niche in which to operate profitably, despite the persistently high profits earned by incumbent firms (Schmalensee, 1978a). Shaw (1982) has noticed the same effects in the UK fertilizer industry. In general, as a means of differentiating products, advertising which generates brand loyalty will make it difficult for new brands to compete.[36] In the Commission's examination of the *Sanofi/Sterling Drug* case (CEC, 1991), national branding was perceived as an entry barrier.

How high were barriers to entry in Europe, and did they differ between member countries? Geroski and Schwalbach (1991) measured the height of barriers in the UK and West Germany for the two periods 1974–79 and 1983–85. They used a model that compared the expected post-entry profits (of the entrant) with the long-run profits that are protected by entry barriers. For the UK, the sample consisted of three-digit manufacturing industries; for West Germany, more disaggregated four-digit data were available. The results were that in both the UK and West Germany entry barriers were 'fairly high', though which entry barriers were significant was different in the two countries. In the UK, for example, whereas capital requirement did not raise barriers to either domestic or foreign firms attracted by large markets with high demand growth, 'advertising outlays, on the other hand, are strongly positively correlated with the overall height of barriers. ... By far the most powerful entry barrier in West Germany [is] scale economies. In addition, R&D investments clearly raise entry barriers which is also true for capital intensity, contrary to the UK results' (Geroski and Schwalbach, 1991, p. 73).

Barriers of the second order, differentiating between the economies of Europe, have been lowered by the 1992 Programme, but the impact has been different in different sectors. The brief analysis of a few cases will shed some light on the issue. In the pharmaceutical industry, for example, both technical and fiscal differences continue to prevent a completely European (as opposed to national) perspective on the part of firms. In some service subsectors, such as telecommunications, changes in interpretation of regulations[37] has facilitated the entry of competitors into markets previously reserved for public monopolies. The domestic electrical appliances is a typical industry where national standards were restricting cross-border trade. The SEM has enabled major players in the industry (such as Electrolux) to acquire firms in Europe (such as Zanussi). As a result, the concentration ratio (CR5) has increased from 41.6 per cent in 1987 to 43.4 per cent ten years later (European Commission, 2002). In the area of alcohol and spirits, NTBs were extremely important (see the German purity law mentioned above). This is another industry where intra-EU cross-border deals (such as the merger between Guinness and Grand Met in 1998) have raised concentration ratios. Consequently, the CR5 had already attained the value of 52 per cent in 1997 (European Commission 2002). Conversely, in the wine industry, the persistence of national tastes and of cultural preference for local products still acts as an important barrier to cross-border firm activity, leaving the concentration ratio at a low 17.4 per cent in 1997 (and decreasing since the late 1980s).

7.4 Public enterprise and procurement markets

Public sector purchasing embraces all purchases of goods and services by governments and by public enterprise (nationalized industries). Government purchasing may be undertaken centrally, locally or by special agencies. For some products, such as defence equipment, the government is the only buyer (monopsony). It has to select a product, a contractor, and must negotiate a contract. Public procurement represents approximately 16 per cent of the EU's GDP and is therefore an important sector for the European economy. Public purchasing is concentrated in some industries such as construction and public works. Purchases by governments are also to be found in the defence sector, energy sector, transport equipment and other manufacturing industries (such as electrical goods and chemicals), and services (business services, distribution and telecommunications).

With the exception of important public utilities such as telecommunications, water, energy and transport, open tendering was in theory the rule for public procurement. In practice, however, public procurement has always tended to favour domestic (and often non-efficient) suppliers over foreign suppliers. In 1986, for example, public procurement represented 15 per cent of Community GDP, but intra-Community trade in the same area amounted to no more than 0.14 per cent of Community GDP (CEC, 1993a). The White Paper *Completing the Internal Market* proposed the enforcement of the rules on open competition for public contracts and the removal of the exemptions (such as in the telecommunication and energy sectors). In the early 1990s, the Commission estimated that the volume of public procurement that could be opened up to EU-wide competition was between 7 and 10 per cent of Community GDP (CEC, 1993a, p. 2). Three types of positive effects are expected from an increased degree of competition in the EU procurement markets:

- The static trade effect whereby public agencies can purchase from the cheapest source, or the lowest cost producer in the EU.

- The competition effect in which increased competitive pressures felt by the domestic firms force them to reduce prices in order to survive in a non-sheltered European market.

- The restructuring effect that enables firms to rationalize their production structure in the long term, thereby achieving economies of scale.

Total savings arising from the three effects have been estimated at around ECU 18 billion (at 1984 prices), of which more than one-quarter would be represented by savings in the defence sector alone (CEC, 1988). In addition, the dynamic effects of enhanced competition on innovation are other benefits that are difficult to quantify.

The first directives covering the purchase of goods in the construction sector date back to the 1970s but contained many gaps. It is only in the early 1990s that directives were adopted in the utilities sector (water, energy, telecommunications and transport) and services. In short, these directives request the public authorities – as well as some private utilities – to publish invitations to tender, for those that exceed a certain value (for example, €5 million for construction projects). As a result, the value of cross-border procurement as a proportion of total public procurement has been estimated to have risen from 6 per cent in 1987 to 10 per cent in 1998 (European Commission, 2003a). Some industries have been particularly affected: for example, railway transport companies have benefited from a 40 per cent decrease in the price of rolling stock (European Commission, 2003a).

7.5 Regulation and deregulation in the EU

Regulation narrowly defined refers to control by the state or state agency of prices and the imposition by the state of restrictions on entry into certain industries (Shughart, 1990, pp. 175–83). Price controls have been used in many countries, justified by the argument that they help reduce the allocative inefficiency of monopoly. Entry restrictions take the form of occupational licensing requirements, certification and franchising. In the case of monopolies, entry regulation has been justified by the fact that it prevents 'wasteful' duplication of capital investment. Regulation-based entry barriers were typically found in public utilities (firms supplying electricity, water, natural gas and telephone services), financial services, air and road transport, broadcasting, and business services (lawyers, accountants, pharmacists). The withdrawal of the state from the ownership of certain industries, by breaking down the natural monopolies into several entities through deregulation, has been a feature of the latter part of the twentieth century in the EU and elsewhere.

The most commonly argued basis for regulation is market failure. This was, for example, the basis for much of the EU's competition policy as enshrined in particular in Articles 81 and 82 of the Treaty (formerly Articles 85 and 86, see Chapter 16). These articles aimed to give the Community the power to prevent collusion between firms and to prevent any firm from abusing a dominant position in a market. However, in particular since the mid-1980s and the move towards the single market, a great deal of support has *de facto* been given by the EU to the development of large firms, in the belief that only such firms can compete on world markets with American and Japanese firms. We discuss these issues in more detail in Chapters 12 and 14. They are introduced here to show that there has been, and remains, an explicit acceptance at the European level of the need for a certain type of 'harmonized' regulation, in the sense of defining clearly for everyone the rules of a free market economy.

The belief in the need for regulating specific markets has, however, varied over time, and is also subject to debate over the nature and extent of regulation at any one time. In addition, some European countries have been consistently more interventionist than others, and more so in some sectors than others. According to Nugent (1994), north European countries have tended to regulate more than their southern (and less industrialized) counterparts, although this has tended to change since the 1980s.

Even among more industrialized European economies, there have been significant differences in the nature and extent of state regulation, though these also are diminishing. In the UK, regulation has evolved from policies, such as in regional policy, aimed at influencing allocation of resources, to state ownership of major industries such as the automotive and shipbuilding industries. There have also been corporatist bodies, such as the National Economic Development Office (NEDO), but its 'activities have generally been limited to a series of *ad hoc* initiatives' (Farrands and Totterdill, 1993). Potentially more significant was the establishment of the National Enterprise Board, which was supposed to achieve high-level economic co-ordination, but it was given inadequate powers and was abolished by the Thatcher government. There has been no consistent theme in regulation in the UK, not even since the advent of deregulation in the early 1980s. Together with the privatizations and general withdrawal from public provision has gone the development of such institutions as the Urban Development Corporations which 'have been highly interventionist in attempting to restructure local land and property markets' (Farrands and Totterdill, 1993).

In France, regulation over the same period has been far more direct (or *dirigiste*), through a series of national economic plans, state ownership of a large number of major firms,[38] state influence on the allocation and cost of credit, and significant amounts of state aid to both declining and expanding industries. Since 1986, as in many other countries, there has been a great deal of deregulation. For example, privatizations in the vast majority of state-owned firms have been carried out or announced.

Regulation in Germany has been far less intensive than in France. In the postwar period the German economy was among the least influenced by the state until the 1970s when, as in France, tax incentives and subsidies were given to both declining (for example, steel) and expanding (for example, electronics) sectors. There has also traditionally been a great deal of encouragement of vocational training and, both directly and indirectly, the state has been involved in technological innovation (see also Chapter 11).

The convergence among the members of the EU in terms of the nature and extent of regulation is due both to global economic forces and to developments in the EU itself. At the global level, deregulation is an attraction to mobile capital and when it occurs in some countries, this forces other countries to consider it. This is true at the EU level as well, and in addition, the EU's moves towards the single market involve the removal of national differences in policies towards business.

7.5.1 Deregulation in European countries and at EU level

The road freight industry provides an example of the international nature of deregulation. It began in the 1960s, among the earliest countries in the OECD to be involved being Switzerland, Sweden and the UK. Subsequently, Belgium (in 1987), Denmark (in 1988), Ireland (in 1988), Norway (in 1987) and Portugal (in 1986), all abolished or reduced quantity or capacity controls or rate-fixing requirements in this sector. In Denmark, the Road Freight Transport Act 1973, which regulated the issuing of licences, determined freight routes and established a system of approval of freight rates, was invalidated in 1988. In France, less deregulation took place: in 1986, the national quota system for licensing long distance freight transport was reformed to allow more entry (OECD, 1990). Passenger road transport services have been deregulated in the UK; 85 per cent of bus routes were found to be commercially viable after deregulation, and only 15 per cent required a subsidy through a system of public tendering (Balcombe, Hopkins and Penet, 1988).

With the directives of the 1990s, a road haulier from any member state can today transport goods between any destinations in the EU, as long as he or she holds a Community authorization. In particular, under the Council Regulation (EEC) No. 881/92 of 26 March 1992 on access to the market in the carriage of goods by road within the community to or from the territory of a Member State or passing across the territory of one or more Member States, quota restrictions for international traffic between member states and transit traffic to and from non-member states were abolished with effect from 1 January 1993 for EU operators.

However, the rise in competition in road transport and in the volume of goods transported by road across Europe, has also led to an increase in road congestion and in the volume of air pollution in the EU. The issue of pollution has been given some consideration by the European institutions (Commission, Council and Parliament), but, as seen above, progress to tackle the problem is extremely slow. This prompts the need for additional investment in infrastructure and in road safety, but also for more incentives given to alternative, less polluting, means of transport (such as rail transport).

It should be noted that, in this industry as elsewhere, common rules with regard to the conditions for admission to the occupation of road haulage operator have been strengthened, a point that we develop in the next subsection.

7.5.2 Harmonized regulation in the EU

There has been deregulation in the financial services sector too, and this is a sector which provides an excellent illustration of the combination of deregulation and the development – not always successful – of regulation at the EU level.[39] Banking and finance is a sector which has been highly regulated in most countries until recently. Some countries, including Germany, the Netherlands and the UK, had removed controls on capital movements in the 1970s and 1980s. Because of this, and because of deregulation in other key international financial markets for funds, deregulation of this sector in Europe became inevitable in the late 1980s.[40] The 1988 Capital Movement Directive was fundamental, stating that 'member states shall abolish restrictions on movements of capital taking place between persons resident in member states' (Vipond, 1994). A year later the Second Banking Directive was adopted.[41]

This directive is based on the principles of *single banking licence* and *country of origin regulation*. The single banking licence allows any credit institution to offer services in any member state (host country) so long as it is registered, and permitted to provide those services, in the country of origin (home country). This leaves a great deal of freedom as to the type of regulatory framework the bank can choose. For example, a German bank can set up an Italian subsidiary and operate under Italian rules in Italy; it can, alternatively, operate under German rules in Italy. Under this system, any financial institution is given the opportunity to shop around and choose among the less constraining regulatory frameworks. This is why the 'country of origin regulation will act as a powerful incentive to the Member States of the EC to adopt unified, harmonized regulations' (Gowland, 1991, p. 51). These developments have led to the *Third Banking Directive* which imposes uniform capital adequacy ratios on banks.[42] The 42 measures of the Financial Services Action Plan (FSAP), which was agreed by 15 EU member states in 1999 aim to create a single wholesale financial market (and complete the EU retail market) by 2005.

It can be argued that the diminution during the 1980s of national powers to regulate financial markets was responsible for the financial and currency crises in the early 1990s. According to Farrands and Totterdill (1993), national regulation proved 'feebly inadequate' in the succession of crises in the City of London in 1990–91. Only regulation at the EU level is appropriate, first because it 'has the information networks and has developed the skilled staff, as well as the legal competences in economic and monetary policy regulation, to take an overall supervisory role', and second, because it is 'at least potentially democratically accountable, whereas the main alternative, the Basle-based committee of European central bankers, is not'.

In some respects, Community regulation has shifted towards the use of fiscal instruments, including charges and levies to prevent pollution at source, penalties for polluters and other fiscal incentives to change firms' behaviour. In the area of noise pollution, there has been, for example, progress in the area of landing fees for aircraft proportional to noise levels. The March 2002 Directive of the Council on the establishment of rules and procedures with regard to the introduction of noise-related operating restrictions at Community airports prohibits the noisiest aircrafts at European airports.[43] In the area of air pollution, the Commission has been debating proposals to reduce the carbon dioxide emissions through a carbon and energy tax since 1991. This pan-EU carbon tax was supposed to be introduced in 1993,[44] but agreement at EU level was meeting enormous resistance. This is unfortunate as this carbon tax would be in line with the recommendations of the Kyoto Protocol. Nevertheless, some progress was made at the level of a few member states, and countries such as Sweden, Denmark, the Netherlands, Finland, Austria, Germany, and also (outside the EU) Norway have implemented taxes based on carbon or energy. At EU level, one should note the political agreement reached in November 2002 within the EU Council of Environment Ministers on a proposed directive for greenhouse gas emission capping and trading.[45] Starting in 2005, this imposes binding targets for carbon dioxide emissions from large industrial emitters such as: pulp and paper manufacturers; electricity and heat generators; cement, glass, ceramics and ferrous metals manufacturers. This cap-and-trade scheme should nevertheless be seen as a transition towards a pan-European carbon tax.

In the energy sector, 2002 marked the opening of the European gas and electricity markets (see the 'acceleration directive', Council Documents 14867/02 and 14869/02). It also provided for the regulation (that is, clear rules in more open national markets) on cross-border electricity trade. Deregulation entails, in particular, market opening for all non-domestic gas and electricity customers as of 1 July 2004, whereas harmonized regulation in this case implies the obligation to guarantee the supply of electricity at 'reasonable prices' (the latter not being defined). It also aims at 'setting fair rules for cross-border exchange in electricity, thus enhancing competition within the internal electricity market' (CEC, 2003a, p. 37). Another rule is represented by penalties for regulation infringements.

7.5.3 The legal status of companies – towards a European company?

In modern European economies, the firm may assume any one of several legal forms. Different national legal systems, in particular with reference to company law, have been singled out as representing important barriers to business in the EU. As a result, effort has been deployed in the area of company law, particularly since 1992, culminating with the creation of a European company. This stems from a bewildering variety of types of companies in the EU, which fit the following broad and general pattern:[46]

◆ *Sole proprietorship or sole trader*, in which the owner provides all the capital, has sole rights to all profits and is responsible for all losses.

◆ *Partnership*, whereby two or more people carry on business in common. A 'general partnership' implies that the partners are personally liable for the debts of the partnership; in a 'limited partnership' the partners are limited in their liability for debts incurred by the firm to the extent of the capital invested. The French *Société en commandite simple* and the German *Kommanditgesellschaft* are examples of limited partnerships.

◆ *Limited liability company*, which is distinct from its members. It combines three characteristics (Zaphirious, 1970):

– limited number of members (except in the GmbH)

– the transfer of its shares is subject to some restrictions

– the public does not participate in its shares.

In the UK, its nearest equivalent is the private limited company; in France, it corresponds to the *Société à Responsabilité Limitée* (SARL), in Germany, to the *Gesellschaft mit beschränkte Haftung* (GmbH), in Belgium, to the *Société de Personnes à Reponsabilité Limitée* (SPRL) and in Denmark to the *Anpartsselskab* (ApS).

◆ *Sole member company* is an EU corporate structure created by the Twelfth Company Law Directive. It is an amalgam of a sole proprietorship and a limited liability company, enabling one person to incorporate a business into a limited liability company. Prior to the Twelfth Directive, single member companies existed in Germany and France, among others, but not the UK. The aim is to allow individuals the protection of limited liability 'without the complications of using nominee shareholders' (Andersen, 1993, p. 86). The person setting up a single member company may not set up another single member company, and it therefore cannot be used to set up a chain of companies.

◆ *Joint stock company* (either private or public) with or without limited liability. These are companies with a large capital, and a more elaborate management and administration. The public is normally invited to participate in the stock company, whose shares are easily transferable.[47] In France, the stock company includes the *Société en Commandite par Actions* (SCA) and the *Société Anonyme* (SA), in Germany the *Kommanditgesellschaft auf Atkien* (KGaA) and the *Aktiengesellschaft* (AG), and in Italy, the *Società per Azioni* (SpA). For comparative purposes, the German AG is the equivalent of the French SA and of the British public and private company (plc and Ltd).

Some legal forms for firms are possible in some countries but not in others. For example, limited partnerships do not exist in the UK, in Ireland or in the Netherlands, and their existence is only theoretical in Greece. (Individual partners can limit their liability, but at least one partner must assume unlimited liability). The equivalent in Germany of a limited partnership is the *Kommanditgesellschaft auf Aktien* (KGaA), in France the *Société en Commandite par*

Actions (SCA), and in Portugal the *Sociedade em Comandita*. In the UK, Ireland, the Netherlands, Denmark and Belgium, the capital of private limited companies is divided into shares. In the other seven countries, the capital is made up of 'quotas' or parts.

Legal aspects of the management structure of firms also differ widely across the EU countries. For example, the French SARL is managed by one or more managers (*gérants*) appointed either by the company's general meeting or through the *status* of the company; it does not have a board of directors unlike equivalent companies in other EU countries. Whereas the Dutch *Anpartsselskab* provides for one management board of directors and for employee representation, the German GmbH is characterized by a two-tier board structure: a management board comprising one or more inside managers; and a second board, the *Aufsichtsrat*, combining supervisory and advisory functions. Members of the latter are outsiders and delegates elected by the company's workers.

The general complexities of, and differences between, the legal aspects of firms in different EU member states have prompted attempts to regulate at the EU level through the creation of the single legal framework.[48] One aim of such a framework is to remove distortions which give some locations within the EU artificial advantages over others. For example, a firm may avoid locating in a country because of the greater protection allowed to minority shareholders or creditors in that country. A second aim is to facilitate the EU-wide operation of firms by removing the difficulties – and costs – arising from different legal rules in different member states.

Among important steps in the process of harmonizing company law in Europe, is the Second Company Directive, passed in 1976 (in effect since 1983), and stipulating the capital and procedures for the formation of public limited companies. Another, more recent step, was the adoption in 1985 by the Council of Ministers of the EU regulation laying down the concept of a European Economic Interest Grouping (EEIG).[49] Effective since July 1989,[50] the EEIG is aimed at facilitating the economic activities of its members, and is intended to encourage links between small and medium-sized enterprises (SMEs) on matters of common interest such as scientific research, purchasing, production, sales, and mutual administration of specialized services and data processing. Before the EEIG, the two main forms of intra-EC cross-border co-operation between firms were joint venture companies and contractual agreements of co-operation. The EEIG combines the best of these, having the legal form of the company and the flexibility of the contractual agreement.

The most controversial aspect of the harmonization programme has been the Commission's Fifth Company Directive, the so-called 'structure directive', the first draft of which goes back to 1972.[51] This directive endeavours to harmonize the board structure and administration of public limited companies (plcs) in the EU. The initial proposal was subsequently amended in depth in 1989, by a directive which would give firms of more than 1000 employees the ability to choose between two types of board structure: a unitary board comprising management members and non-executive members (the Anglo-Saxon type of structure); and a dualistic system composed of a management board and a supervisory board with employee participation (close to the German and Dutch structures). To allow for employee participation, companies that opt for the dualistic structure will be able to choose among three different types of structure. Although the unitary system would be allowed for a certain number of years (after the implementation of the directive), it is envisaged that the dualistic system would predominate in the long term (Werlauff, 1992). The controversial nature of the directive is evident in its continued amendment and deferral: 'by 1993 the Directive itself had gone into seemingly indefinite abeyance' (Manser, 1994, p. 100).

Another harmonization proposal leading to lengthy discussions and inconclusive results for several decades has been the proposal for the creation of a European Company Statute. The first Commission proposal on a European Company Statute (*Societas Europaea*, SE) was issued in 1975.[52] Going beyond the approximation of the legal statutes of European companies, the proposal specifies the statutes, structure and workings of a genuinely European company. Its legal form would be that of a company limited by shares, with a minimum paid-up capital such that it ensures adequate resources at its disposal. It could follow a single-tier system (with an administrative board), or a two-tier structure that would comprise a board of management administering the company's affairs, and a supervisory board. The supervisory board would supervise the board of management and would appoint its members.[53] The statutory European company would have its own independent legal structure, separate from the national legal frameworks. It could be formed by such means as the merger of establishments in two or more member states and the formation of a joint venture by two or more companies or establishments.

Twenty years after the first draft, the SE had still not proceeded much further than the draft stage. The Council of Ministers stopped the examination of the Commission's proposal on the creation of a European Company Statute in 1982, and returned to it in 1988 (Hitiris, 1994). The Commission's early proposal was redrafted in 1989 and revised in 1991 (Werlauff, 1992). Each revision has involved removal of articles, leaving the text with 137 articles in 1987, 82 in 1989 and 65 in 1993. Among the sharpest opposition to the SE has been the objection to employee participation. A separate draft directive to which the SE is linked, and which forms part of the process of establishing the SE, states, that 'member states shall take the necessary measures to enable employees of the SE to participate in the supervision and strategic development of the SE'. This met with outright opposition by Germany and the UK, and varying degrees of opposition to the ways in which worker participation would be imposed by most other member states (Manser, 1994, p. 70).

Finally, pressure to complete the internal market led to the Council Regulation on the Statute for a European Company[54] and to the Council Directive on the Statute for a European Company with regard to the involvement of employees in the European company.[55] These two documents were released in October 2001, making the SE a reality. Under the Regulation, member states were given a time limit of three years within which to translate the Directive into national law, and to enact it in compliance with the new legislation. As a result, the first SEs are expected to be registered during 2004.

Combinations of such factors as the extent and nature of regulation, barriers to entry, nature and performance of firms, and market forces in general, have an impact on industrial structure. While some of these have been discussed above, individual firms' strategies and performance are covered in later chapters. We therefore briefly introduce the topic of industrial structure in the EU here.

7.6 Industrial structure in the EU

Industrial structure refers to 'the relative importance of individual industries or groups of related industries within an economy and to the pattern of transactions between these industries' (Devine *et al.*, 1985, p. 27). The industrial structure of an economy includes the service sector, both in its own right and because of its significant contribution (for example, through business services) to the operation of manufacturing firms. In this section we discuss only the relative importance of individual industries in the EU. Manufacturing, mining, and building and construction in the EU employed over 46 million people in 2001 (29 per cent of total employment), compared with 108 million people in the service sector (71 per cent of the total). The share of total employment in services increased in every country of the EU during the period 1995–2001, with the exception of Portugal where employment in services was 60 per cent of the total. This share reached 77 per cent in Luxembourg, mirroring the importance of the financial services sector in the country. The new member states are less service oriented than the EU-15, although the share of services is above 50 per cent in each case. Of particular relevance has been the increase of knowledge-intensive services (KIS) and of high-technology services (HTS). Knowledge-intensive services regroup all firms classified under NACE 61, 62, 64, 65, 66, 67, 70, 71, 72, 73, 74, 80, 85 and 92, whereas knowledge-intensive high-technology services correspond to NACE codes 64, 72 and 73.

Table 7.7 shows the evolution of employment in KIS and HTS over the period 1997–2002 and for a selected number of countries. The 'old' member states in the table, (Germany, Spain, France, Italy, Holland, Austria, Sweden and the UK) represented more than 88 per cent of total EU-15 employment in KIS in 2002. Employment growth in KIS and HTS has been more important than in overall services. The highest growth in KIS and HTS employment over the period was, according to the table, in Spain, although a full picture would show that Ireland has surpassed every other country in that respect. KIS and HTS employment in Ireland increased by 7.8 and 18.2 respectively over the period. The impressive performance of Spain and Ireland is explained partly by their lower level of economic development at the beginning of the period and by their ability to catch up with other advanced countries in the EU.

Table 7.7 Average annual growth rate of employment in knowledge-intensive services and high-technology services in selected European countries, 1997-2002

	Knowledge-intensive services %	High-technology services %
EU-15	3.1	5.6
Germany	2.7	3.9
Spain	5.7	12.3
France	2.6	4.4
Italy	3.5	4.6
The Netherlands	3.6	6.8
Austria	2.5	8.9
Sweden	3.4	7.5
UK	2.7	5.8
Czech Republic	0.3	−2.4
Hungary	2.3	3.1
Slovakia	−0.5	0.7

Source: European Commission, 2004, p. 119

In contrast to services, the number of persons employed in the manufacturing sector alone contracted from 26.3 million to 23.7 million between 1990 and 2001 (Eurostat, 2003a). A breakdown of manufacturing industries by employment and production performance is given in Table 7.8.

In terms of value added and production, the most important manufacturing industries in the EU are chemicals, electrical machinery, and transport equipment. Food, and metals and metal products are also in the top five most important industries, notably in terms of persons employed, whereas machinery and equipment, and wood are other relatively large industries. As can be seen from the table, textile, clothing, non-metallic mineral products and petroleum products belong to industries that have generally downsized enormously since the second world war. Because of different technologies of production[56] (and therefore different productivity levels), the ranking in terms of numbers employed in each industry is different. Metals and metal products is the largest employer. Note that rankings may change from year to year, first because industries may be at different positions in their business cycles at different times, and second because some industries may be in long-run decline whereas others are growing.

Table 7.9 shows a list of the three largest manufacturing industries (in terms of value added) in each of the EU countries, at the two-digit level of NACE. The relative importance

Table 7.8 Ranking of EU manufacturing industries by value added, production value and employment, 2001[a]

	Value added €bn	Production value €bn	Persons employed '000
Total manufacturing	**1,327**	**4,484**	**23,735**
of which:	%	%	%
Chemicals, rubber, plastics	16.5	14.5	12.3
Electrical machinery, optical equipment	13.3	12.0	12.2
Transport equipment	12.5	15.1	10.9
Food, beverages, tobacco[b]	11.3	13.2	11.5
Metals and metal products	11.7	10.2	13.1
Machinery and equipment	10.6	8.7	11.3
Wood, paper, publishing, printing	10.4	8.6	10.3
Textiles, clothing, leather	4.5	4.3	8.4
Non-metallic mineral products	4.4	3.3	4.5
Other manufacturing[b], recycling	2.7	0.2	0.2
Petroleum products	2.1	6.4	0.6

[a] Data covering enterprises with 20 persons employed or more.

[b] 'Tobacco' and 'manufacture of furniture and other manufacturing' not available except for value added but they have been integrated in the calculation of the aggregate 'total manufacturing'. They represent together between 3.4% and 4.7% of total manufacturing depending on the variable.

Source: Eurostat, 2003a

of industries varies among countries. As can be seen, the less economically advanced countries of the EU tend to have large traditional and low value added industries. This is the case of Greece and Portugal where food, textiles, non-metallic minerals and primary products are dominant. However, the food industry is also an important industry in some relatively rich countries (such as Denmark, France and the Netherlands, three countries with a relatively large and efficient agricultural sector), and in the EU as a whole. In 2001, this industry represented 11 per cent of the total EU manufacturing value added. Other equally important industries are: chemicals; transport equipment; machinery; electrical and optical equipment (although not in the top three), and basic metals and fabricated metal products. It should be noted that small and open economies tend to be less diversified than larger ones. As discussed in Chapter 5, one way of answering questions about the relative importance of different industries in different economies is to use location quotients. There are other ways, and we return to this subject in Chapter 8.

Table 7.9 The top three manufacturing industries in EU countries, 2001

	Largest	Second largest	Third largest
Belgium	Chemicals and chemical products	Food, beverages	Basic metals
Denmark	Food, beverages	Machinery	Chemicals and chemical products
Germany	Machinery	Motor vehicles	Chemicals and chemical products
Greece	Food, beverages	Textiles	Coke, petroleum, nuclear fuels
Spain	Food, beverages	Fabricated metal products	Chemicals and chemical products
France	Food, beverages	Chemicals and chemical products	Fabricated metal products
Ireland	Chemicals and chemical products	Food, beverages	Publishing and Printing
Italy	Machinery	Fabricated metal products	Food, beverages
Luxembourg	Basic metals	Rubber and plastic	Fabricated metal products
Netherlands	Food, beverages	Chemicals and chemical products	Publishing and printing
Austria	Machinery	Coke, petroleum, nuclear fuels	Food, beverages
Portugal	Food, beverages	Other non-metallic minerals	Textiles
Finland	Radio, TV, communication	Pulp, paper	Machinery
Sweden	Motor vehicles	Machinery	Pulp, paper
UK	Food, beverages	Publishing, printing	Chemicals and chemical products
EU-15	Machinery	Food, beverages	Chemicals and chemical products

Source: European Commission, 2003b

Table 7.10 The three largest service industries in EU countries, 2001[a]

	Largest	Second largest	Third largest
Belgium	Wholesale trade	Other business activities	Retail trade
Denmark	Wholesale trade	Other business activities	Retail trade
Germany	Other business activities	Wholesale trade	Retail trade
Greece	Other business activities	Wholesale trade	Hotels and restaurants
Spain	Wholesale trade	Other business activities	Real estate activities
France	Other business activities	Wholesale trade	Retail trade
Ireland	Retail trade	Wholesale trade	Other business activities
Italy	Other business activities	Wholesale trade	Retail trade
Luxembourg	Other business activities	Wholesale trade	Post and telecommunications
The Netherlands	Wholesale trade	Other business activities	Retail trade
Austria	Wholesale trade	Other business activities	Retail trade
Portugal	Wholesale trade	Retail trade	Other business activities
Finland	Wholesale trade	Other business activities	Retail trade
Sweden	Wholesale trade	Other business activities	Real estate activities
UK	Wholesale trade	Other business activities	Retail trade
EU-15	Other business activities	Wholesale trade	Retail trade

[a] Based on value added for services (NACE Divisions 50 to 64 and 70 to 74); estimates.

Source: European Commission, 2003b

Table 7.10 ranks the three largest service industries in individual EU countries by order of importance, again at the two-digit level of NACE, and based on value added data. The table shows that retail and wholesale activities are dominant, a not too surprising result given that all manufactured finished products end up being sold on markets. 'Other business activities' (legal services, accounting, market research, consultancy, advertising, architectural activities, and so forth) are an important service industry for the EU as a whole, and for specific countries therein, such as Austria, Belgium, Denmark, the Netherlands, Sweden, the UK, and also Spain.

Finally, the data presented in Tables 7.9 and 7.10 are rather descriptive, and suffer therefore from three types of limitations. First, in both the EU manufacturing and services sector, the relative importance of industries in terms of value added differs from that based on employment figures. Second, the direct comparison between manufacturing industries and services is limited, for by their very nature, some service activities are labour intensive activities (such as hotels and restaurants). Third, the data do not give any indication on the *relative* importance of each manufacturing or service industry for each country. In Chapter 13, we provide more refined data on the relative weight of each industry for each country, through the analysis of production and trade specialization.

Case study   Oligopoly in car production and parts suppliers in the European periphery

The industry of motor vehicles, parts and accessories is characterized by two main activities: the production of motor vehicles, including passenger cars, light commercial vehicles, trucks and buses (NACE 34.10), and the manufacture of parts and accessories for motor vehicles and their engines (NACE 34.20, 34.30). This is an industry characterized by a producer-driven production chain; it involves a myriad of sub-suppliers of parts and accessories linked to (and dependent upon) a small number of large motor vehicles manufacturers.

In terms of value added, production and employment, this industry is still important (Table 7.8). In 2002, total EU employment in the industry was roughly 2 million people, representing 6.8 per cent of total manufacturing employment. This was divided between motor vehicles (3.7 per cent of total EU manufacturing) and parts and accessories (3.1 per cent) (ACEA, 2004). Because of its web of intricate linkages with other industries and sectors of the economy, the Brussels-based Association of EU Motor-Vehicles Manufactures (ACEA) estimates that another 10 million jobs are linked to the industry in the EU. These activities are, for example: sale, maintenance and repair of motor vehicles; land transport (land passenger transport, taxi operation, freight transport by road); car and other vehicles rental services; construction of highways, roads and other civil engineering works; and recycling.

Case Study (continued)

The two major sub-industries have a rather different production structure, with the motor vehicles activity being dominated by a small number of key industries (a typical oligopoly), whereas the parts and accessories production is shared among a large number of sub-suppliers. Based on the number of new motor vehicle registrations in one year (2001), market concentration was as follows: 19 per cent for Volkswagen, 14.4 per cent for Peugeot PSA, while four other manufacturers (Ford Europe, GM Europe, Renault and Fiat) each held between 11 and 9.6 per cent of the market shares. The remaining firms, such as the Japanese, Korean manufacturers, but also, DaimlerChrysler and BMW were left with roughly one-quarter of the market between them (figures from European Commission, 2003b). When analysed at the country level, Germany represents more than 44 per cent of the total value added generated in the motor vehicle industry, whereas the next largest supplier, France, accounts for less than 18 per cent of this total. However, when related to the size of the respective countries, and in particular to the size of their manufacturing sector as a whole, Sweden stands out as being the EU country most specialized in this industry, while Germany is only relatively specialized (as seen above in Table 7.9). As a result of this relatively high level of concentration in the industry, the degree of intra-industry trade at EU level in motor vehicles is rather high; this has been estimated to reach 77 per cent in France in the late 1990s (Becuwe and Mathieu, 1998). By contrast, the incidence of intra-industry trade is much lower in the parts and accessories sub-industry, reflecting the higher level of specialization.

Restructuring and downsizing is what characterized most the industry during the 1990s. Falling employment numbers have been registered in all countries; the overall share of the industry in total manufacturing employment decreased from 7.5 per cent in 1999 to 6.8 per cent in 2002 (ACEA, 2004). The industry is still characterized by overcapacity, at both the EU level and world levels. The phenomenon of plant closure in EU countries must be analysed in parallel with foreign direct investment (by EU firms) not only in emergent markets (such as China) but also in the new members of the EU. We return to the issue of FDI in Chapter 14, but suffice it to add here that, because of a combination of tax, low cost, and high skills advantages, the Czech Republic, Poland and Hungary have become important platforms for the production of motor vehicles and parts in the past decade or so. The shares of the Czech Republic, Poland and Hungary in the EU-15 total imports of parts and accessories rose substantially between 1991 and 2001, reaching 11.6, 7.5 and 6.8 per cent, respectively, in 2001 (European Commission, 2003b).

Case Study (continued)

Given its assembly-type nature, the industry lends itself to a geographical separation of individual production and assembly processes. The intensity with which the spatial organization of production is carried out depends nevertheless on the nature of the firm. In particular, Japanese motor vehicle producers have traditionally concentrated geographically their motor vehicle and parts and accessories manufacturing activities, through their *keiretsu* networks. In general, technological improvements in transport and telecommunications have changed the organization of production in the industry, lessening the importance of proximity between suppliers of motor vehicles, their sub-suppliers (of components) and their customers. For the EU firms, the prospect of a new enlargement to east European countries (and the removal of all obstacles to trade and investment in an enlarging Union) has clearly led to a spatial reorganization of EU motor vehicles and parts production. The motor vehicles and parts industries have indeed accounted for a high proportion of foreign direct investment in the new member states during the 1990s (with Fiat establishing a plant in Poland, VW in the Czech Republic, and Audi in Hungary). As a result of these large investment outlays, many west European suppliers have located in these countries.

7.7 Summary

In this chapter we have discussed the empirical – especially European – aspects of structure. Our analysis of market concentration in the manufacturing sector shows that concentration tended to increase during the first half of the 1970s, and peaked again in the 1980s, declining thereafter to levels similar to those of the mid-1970s. In the subsequent decade (the 1990s), seller concentration was fairly stable. Different causes explain rises or decreases of concentration ratios during different epochs. The entry of relatively large and efficient British manufacturers in the early 1970s, as well as the completion of the internal market in the mid-1980s explain increasing concentration levels. In the service sector, concentration has either declined or been stable over the 1980s and 1990s. These are general trends in seller concentration, which nevertheless mask intra-industry differences. For example, restructuring in the EU food industry went in parallel with increasing concentration ratios over the 1990s (in particular in the confectionery and ice-cream, oils and fats, pasta, beer, and soft drinks segments of the industry). Also, concentration in the computer and office equipment industry has slightly risen during the 1990s, reflecting a phenomenon of catching-up.

The conventional study of barriers to entry (for example, economies of scale and product differentiation) has been enriched with the analysis of *barriers of the second order*. These are all inherent to a set of countries (such as the EU countries) that aspire to ever greater integration. We have looked at the progress made in the area of the single European market since the late 1980s. The brief study of public enterprises, procurement markets, regulation and deregulation in the EU has shown that the EU authorities have made progress in breaking down national barriers and allowing EU firms to avail themselves of a large market. This has led to a higher degree of harmonized regulation in the EU. In particular, the legal impediments to doing business on a European scale are now lessened by the entry into force of the *Societas Europaea*, or a genuine European company.

The brief overview of industrial structure in the EU has shown the increasing importance of service activities in most EU economies. Although representing a declining share of manufacturing and of economic activities in the EU as a whole, the motor car and parts and accessories industry is still one of the industrial strengths of the EU. The fifth enlargement has provided EU firms with new opportunities in terms of spatial reorganization of their production. The next chapter expands on these locational issues, as it deals with location and industrial development.

Websites

For more on NTBs, procurement markets, deregulation as well as on recent developments in the car industry, see **http://europa.eu.int/comm/competition/index_en.html**

Questions

7.1   Why would you expect there to be a difference between concentration at the EU level and concentration at the national level?

7.2   What are the implications for distribution of investment in the EU of different national corporate profit tax rates?

7.3   How does regulation at the EU level (rather than at the national level) facilitate the conducting of economic production activities by EU firms?

7.4   In which sense does the creation of a *Societas Europaea* decrease barriers to entry in the EU?

7.5   What are the main features of the European industrial structure?

7.6   Is the spatial organization of motor car and parts production made more attractive by further economic integration in the EU?

Notes

1   For a brief discussion on product life cycles, industry cycles and concentration, see de Jong (1993, pp. 16–19).

2   For more on concentration in the food industry during those years, see Linda (1991).

3   According to de Jong (1993, table 5), the curves of the global CR3 ratios (top three firms as a proportion of the output of the top 9, 15, 19 or 20) for the period 1962 to 1990 are, in most major industries, roughly U-shaped, i.e. concentration has gone down for some years and then up again towards the end of the period.

4   Integration refers here to spatial (or regional) as opposed to industrial integration. It entails the bringing together of different parts into a whole. The minimalist definition of integration (or the first degree of integration) at the EU level refers to the elimination of tariffs, quantitative restrictions and other measures of equivalent effect, and of non-tariff barriers (NTBs) impeding trade among the 25 European members. A maximalist approach (or a superior degree) entails the setting up of the European Central Bank (issuing a single European currency); a further degree would entail the definition of a common fiscal policy, etc.

5   The six signatories of the Treaty of Rome in 1957 have subsequently been joined by Denmark, Ireland and the UK in 1973, Greece in 1980, Portugal and Spain in 1986, Austria, Finland and Sweden in 1995, and the Czech Republic, Estonia, Hungary, Latvia, Lithuania, Poland, Slovakia, Slovenia, Cyprus and Malta in May 2004.

6   They are termed 'static effects' in economic integration theory.

7   See the discussion by Auerbach (1989, p. 263), in which he raises and subsequently discusses in detail, the co-existence in the twentieth century of increasing competitive pressure and the emergence of giant enterprises.

8   Their argument is based in part on Sleuwaegen and Yamawaki (1988).

9   An exception to this general rule is the approach followed by Jacquemin (1979).

10   Barriers of the first order would also include regulation (where this does not distinguish between firms from different countries; if it does so distinguish, it becomes a barrier of the second order), and such strategies of firms as alliances with other firms. Regulation is discussed in Section 7.5, and firms' strategies in Chapters 9, 10 and 11.

11   In the case of agriculture, deficiency payments and import levies played a substantial role in restricting trade in Europe in the interwar period.

12   On this issue, and in particular on the different responses of US, European and Japanese multinational companies with subsidiaries in Ireland to the completion of the single European market, see Jacobson and Andreosso (1990).

13   Paradoxically, quantitative restrictions such as production quotas were reintroduced in the 1970s in the EU steel industry and in the 1980s in the agricultural sector.

14   The White Paper *Completing the Internal Market* (see CEC, 1985).

15   Procurement markets are dealt with below, in Section 7.4. Note also that technical regulations are part of regulation in general, a topic discussed in Section 7.5.

16   Guinness was one of the few foreign beer products admitted on German soil. In 1986, the European Court of Justice found that the *Reinheitsgebot* violated Article 30 of the Treaty of Rome, and the decree had thus to be removed from German legislation. However, the change in German legislation did not lead to the expected entry of foreign beers into the German market. It seems that a successful marketing campaign highlighting the fact that the German beers sold in Germany were, unlike many other foreign

beers, brewed according to the defunct law, strengthened the attachment of the German consumers to their domestic product.

17 EFTA countries are also members of these two bodies.

18 See, in particular, Cecchini's table 9.2, p. 84.

19 At 1988 prices.

20 Note that high corporate profit tax rates can constitute both first- and second-order barriers.

21 Council Directive 90/435/EEC. Temporary derogations were granted to Germany, Greece and Portugal.

22 COM (90) 571 final.

23 If the second order barriers are significant enough, however, competition is limited and the dominant firms within Europe, though having lower average costs, may be able, in the absence of regulation, to charge higher prices. This will mean continued supernormal profits.

24 Most of the discussion on EOS in the context of the European market has focused on technical or production EOS in the manufacturing sector. However, EOS may also be important in relation to R&D, marketing, finance and distribution. For a concise appraisal of price reduction effects in the service sector, see Emerson *et al.* (1988, pp. 98–122).

25 For a less aggregated approach, see Pratten (1987).

26 To the authors' knowledge, Catinat was the only economist at the time who had written about this 'logical incoherence' contained in the White Paper (see Catinat, 1989, p. 104).

27 Among the vast literature on this subject, see Hitiris (1994).

28 Note, however, that intra-EU exports and imports have followed a downward trend during the 1990s (e.g. from 67.4 per cent in 1991 to 61.8 per cent in 2001 for intra-EU exports). Here again, it seems that the cold shower effect represented by the completion of the SEM was confined to a short period of time (late 1980s and early 1990s).

29 Intra-industry trade means trade between two countries within the same industry (e.g. cars exported by country A to country B, and by country B to country A); inter-industry trade refers to trade between two member countries and between different industries, more or less narrowly defined (e.g. cars exported by country A to country B, and trucks exported by country B to country A).

30 Again, while much trade in Europe was intra-industry up to the 1980s, there was some evidence of a reversal in the growth of intra-industry trade in a number of OECD countries in the late 1980s (Globerman and Dean, 1990). For a detailed study of a reversal of this kind in the case of Ireland, see Brülhart and McAleese (1993).

31 If two goods produced by different firms are in other respects identical, brand loyalty can be defined as that which prevents the cross-elasticity of demand between the two goods from being infinite.

32 In the incorporation of industrial organization into international trade theory the EOS element is emphasized. 'It is economies of scale that keep each country from producing the full range of products [within an industry] for itself, thus economies of scale can be an independent source of international trade' (Krugman and Obstfeld, 1991, p. 138).

33 Explanations of the behaviour of multinational enterprises are the subject of Chapter 14.

34 A single index of intra-industry trade in a number of (or all) industries can also be calculated:

$$IIT_{GL} = \frac{\sum_{i=1}^{n} (X_i + M_i) - |X_i - M_i|}{\sum_{i=1}^{n} (X_i + M_i)}$$

where X_i and M_i represent the value of the country's exports and imports of the products of industry i.

34 Grubel and Lloyd (1975) found that the IIT index for all industries in ten industrialized countries in 1967 was 0.48. The index for the EC was 0.67. Thus nearly half the trade among the ten was in goods belonging to the same industry, whereas among the then six of the EC the figure was two-thirds.

35 Advertising as strategy of firms is discussed in Chapter 10, Section 10.2.

36 See also below, on deregulation in Europe.

38 At the peak of state control in the mid-1980s, 'the state owned thirteen of the twenty largest firms in France and had a controlling share in many others' (Nugent, 1994).

39 Regulation at the EU level in the banking sector began in the 1970s with the First Council Directive of 1977 which co-ordinated the laws and regulatory frameworks of credit institutions.

40 Note that Italy was an exception. In relation to banking, 'Italy had the most restrictive regulation in the early 1980s and has undertaken only limited structural deregulation in the course of the last decade . . . and the Italian market is, if anything rather less integrated with Europe than in the early 1980s' (Gual and Neven, 1992).

41 It was adopted in December 1989 and had to be implemented by all member states by 1 January 1993. Council Directive 89/646/EEC; see OJCE, 30 December 1989.

42 A bank has three sources of funds: deposits, equity capital, and non-deposit loan capital (such as bonds). The capital adequacy ratio ensures that equity does not fall below a certain percentage of total assets.

43 International noise standards were first introduced by the International Civil Aviation Organization (ICAO) in 1971. They have been modified periodically since. In 1980, a Council directive introduced a noise emission limit at source based on ICAO standards. A noise landing fee was introduced in Paris-Orly in 1973 but had to be removed as it was against French law. (Airbus Industrie: Environmental Protection, France, March 1993.) Note, nevertheless, that the March 2002 directive led to, yet another, dispute between the EU and the United States.

44 Council Directive 93/76/EEC, 13 September 1993.

45 This tax is still not implemented in the EU. Note that when the pan-EU carbon tax was discussed, it was agreed that because of their lower carbon emission levels, Portugal, Greece, Spain and Ireland would be authorized to defer the application of the tax.

46 For more details on the following, see for example Zaphirious (1970), O'Malley (1982) and Campbell (1983).

47 In the UK, however, a stock company can be either private or public.

48 Some kind of homogeneous protection ('safeguards') can be traced as far back as the Treaty of Rome, signed in 1957 (see Article 54-3-g). This gave rise to the First Company Law Directive, agreed upon in 1968 and in effect since 1973.

49 See Council Regulation No. 2137/85, 31 July 1985, in OJ L 199, pp. 1–9. The EEIG is based on a French legal concept called *Groupement des intérêts économiques*, the most renowned applications of which have been by the Airbus consortium and Ariane Espace where it provided a corporate structure for international co-operation (Andersen, 1993, p. 79).

50 The delay between 1985 and 1989 was provided for within the regulation itself, to give member states time so that domestic law could be adjusted to allow for EEIGs.

51 See *EC Bulletin*, Supplement 10/72.

52 See COM (75) 150 final, Proposal for a Council Regulation on the Statute for European Companies.

53 The supervisory board would have one-third of its members representatives of the shareholders, one-third representatives of employees and one-third persons representing the general interest (Article 74a).

54 No. 2157/2001.

55 No. 2001/86/EC.

56 Different traditions and organization and production, trade unionization and skill development.

CHAPTER 8

Location and industrial development

8.1 Learning objectives

The main objectives of this chapter are:

- To introduce the theories upon which the study of spatial groupings of firms has developed

- To identify the main concepts that have been used in recent years to study the different forms of concentrations of economic activity in different places

- To provide examples of the application of these concepts, and

- To explain the differences between the various forms of spatial concentration

8.2 Localization

We introduced economic geography and the significance of location for industrial organization in Chapter 2 (Section 2.2.2). Few of the writers on theories of the firm – Porter (1990, 1998a) and Best (1990, 2001) included – view geography as a fundamental element. The region in which firms might operate is generally considered to be secondary. In fact, economics as a discipline has paid surprisingly little attention to the location issue. Krugman (1993) has discussed, and attempted to correct, this omission in the context of international economics. (The way he does so, as we show in Chapter 2, is disputed.) It is even more surprising that the industrial economics specialism too has left to others the locational concerns of firms; few industrial economics and industrial organization textbooks have chapters or even sections of chapters on location.[1]

That location is crucial to the organization of production is clear from as far back as Marshall (1898).[2] Marshall identified six main factors in the localization of industries, the first three of which he called causes of, and the second three advantages of localization: physical conditions, demand conditions, political/cultural influences, hereditary skill, the growth of subsidiary trades and the emergence of a local market for the special skills required by the industry.[3]

Physical conditions

An industry requiring raw materials that are expensive to transport is likely to locate near to the source of those raw materials. Similarly, other physical conditions, including the climate, the soil and the topography of an area will influence what industries locate in that area. Marshall gave a number of examples, including Sheffield cutlery, which, he wrote, is 'due chiefly to the excellent grit of which its grindstones are made'.

Demand conditions

Under some circumstances, products will tend to be produced close to their market. A high income market for example, Marshall argued, will generate 'a demand for goods of specially high quality, and this attracts skilled workmen from a distance, and educates those on the spot'.[4]

Political/cultural influences

Marshall referred to 'the character of the people, and their social and political institutions', and to individuals' 'ideals of life' as determining how they exploit natural advantages. These factors generate 'industry and enterprise' which, in turn, have 'localized the industrial leadership of the world now in this country and now in that'. Modern developments of these notions include those on culture and institutions by institutionalists such as North (1990), and on industry and enterprise by industrial economists/management theorists such as Porter (1990).[5]

Once an industry has located, from whatever combination of natural, political, social, cultural and accidental factors, in a particular place, there are cumulative advantages to its continued location in that place.[6]

Hereditary skill

What Marshall was referring to in this context, was the situation in which a large number of people lived and worked – using similar, specialized skills – in close proximity. The skills in production of the particular product become so well known in the area that 'children learn many of them unconsciously'. Inventions 'and improvements in machinery, in processes and the general organization of the business' become quickly known and copied. This is what Krugman (1993) refers to as technological spillovers, 'the more or less pure externality that results from knowledge spillovers between nearby firms'.

The growth of subsidiary trades

The localization of an industry attracts firms that supply intermediate goods, including manufacturing equipment, to that industry. As Marshall put it, 'subsidiary industries devoting themselves each to one small branch of the process of production' can employ specialized machinery, and keep it constantly busy if they are supplying a large number of local firms in the main industry. Localization thus also facilitates specialization.

Krugman (1993) argues that the concentration of suppliers of intermediate goods in the same location as their customers, 'depends crucially on at least some degree of economies of scale. . . . It is only the presence of increasing returns that makes a large center of production able to have more efficient and more diverse suppliers than a small one.' We would add to this the possibility of economies of scope but would emphasize the need to distinguish, as Marshall famously did, between internal and external economies. When Krugman writes of a large centre of production, he appears to be referring to a single firm, in which case it is appropriate to invoke economies of scale as prerequisite. However, if we include the possibility of a large number of small producers clustering spatially, and then consider the extent to which this attracts suppliers of intermediate goods, economies of scale, which would normally be understood to be internal, no longer apply. Instead we must rely on externalities: 'economies . . . dependent on the general development of the industry', as Marshall defined them. He defined internal economies as those 'dependent on the resources of the individual houses of business . . . . on their organization and the efficiency of their management'. This distinction and its relevance in terms of size of firm in localized industries is particularly clear in the case of industrial districts, discussed below in Section 8.3.

In a second addendum to Marshall's discussion about intermediate inputs, Krugman criticizes the generally accepted view that 'localized industrial complexes will emerge only if it is more costly to transport intermediate inputs than final goods'.[7] He provides both theoretical and historical evidence for the argument that lower transport costs in general (that is, for both intermediate and final goods), make the localization of industry more likely. Only if the costs of transporting intermediates are particularly low relative to final goods will localization not occur.

Local market for special skills required by the industry

A localized industry, Marshall wrote, 'gains a greater advantage from the fact that it offers a constant market for skill'. The interests of workers with these skills and their employers are mutually reinforced by localization. Employers will tend to locate where the skill is available, and those with the skill will tend to live where employers of the skill are concentrated: 'social forces here cooperate with economic'. Furthermore, where the skill is very specialized, then other industries, employing other skills, will be attracted by the availability of people in the locality who do not have the specialized skill required by the first industry.

Krugman (1993) describes this as labour market pooling, and provides a more formal explanation of the gains from pooling both to workers and firms. He assumes two firms, each producing a different product, but each with an average requirement of labour with the same specific skill of, say, 100 workers, but a peak requirement of 125 and a trough requirement of 75. He shows that all workers and firms will gain from both firms locating in a town with 200 workers with the required skill. This results from an additional assumption that the peaks and troughs of the two firms at least occasionally do not coincide. It follows from this assumption that workers laid off by one firm will at times find employment in the other, so they derive an advantage from pooling. Assume the alternative to the two firms and 200 workers in one town is that each firm locates in a different town, each town having 100 workers with the required skill. Then at the peak of its cycle, neither firm will be able to obtain the required number of workers, so the firms also derive a benefit from pooling.

As with intermediate inputs, Krugman argues that in relation to labour pooling, localization requires increasing returns to scale (IRS). Without IRS, he argues, there would be no reason for each firm to locate all its production in one location. A firm could, in the above example, have a plant employing 50 workers (on average) in each of the towns. We would add the proviso that, if the *external* economies are important, then both firms would have to locate a 50-person plant in each of the towns. IRS may well be significant, but in the context of localization (or spatial concentration), it must be considered in conjunction with external economies.

Krugman raises two further possible objections to Marshall's labour pooling: flexible wages and exploitation of monopsony power by firms. If wages were flexible in the example, rather than unemployment or excess demand, there would be falls and rises in wages in, respectively, trough and peak demand times. Does this rule out the gains from pooling? No, Krugman argues, because even though the pooling will mean each firms' having to pay a higher wage during the trough than it would if it was isolated and did not have to compete with the other firm for labour, it will also pay a lower wage at the peak. The gain at the peak, from pooling, is greater than the loss at the trough. In general, the 'gains from labour pooling do not rest in any essential way on a failure of labor markets to clear'.

In relation to monopsony, the question is why firms would locate adjacent to other firms that compete for the same labour. Surely, it could be argued, a firm would prefer the monopsony power (and extra profit from paying wages below the value of workers' marginal product) it would derive from being the sole employer of these workers in the town? Where there is labour mobility,[8] workers with the required skills will avoid such a town. Firms will locate in the same town as other firms requiring the same skills, in part to avoid such a flight of human capital.

According to Krugman, a town might be dominated by a single firm (as in the case of Dagenham in Essex and Ford Motor Company) because either there is an important natural resource in that location accessible to only one firm, or IRS are such that the scale of production is so large that the market may be dominated by a single firm that 'agglomerates its plants in order to achieve pooling'. Again, however, Krugman's conclusion requires amendment. Gains from pooling may not rest on the failure of labour markets to clear, but the argument against monopsony and 'company towns' is at least partially offset by unemployment. If there is high unemployment, and firms and workers expect this to persist, then the argument against company towns, namely that multiple firms avoid flight of human capital, does not apply. There will be no such flight if there are no jobs elsewhere.[9]

What follows from Marshall's six localization factors, is that under certain circumstances firms within an industry or in related industries will agglomerate, that is they will locate close to one another. The *agglomeration economies* will be greater than the benefits that firms derive from a more diffuse distribution. 'When a locality or region constitutes the site for an expansion of the common pools of labour, capital and infrastructure, or when pecuniary externalities can be traced to the new investments made by a firm in some particular place, then the lower unit costs of production facing firms in that place are called *agglomeration economies*' (Harrison, 1992).[10]

We can use agglomeration economies to distinguish between a 'mere' spatial concentration and a 'proper' industrial agglomeration (Jacobson *et al.* 2001). Agglomeration economies are benefits that a firm derives from the fact that there are other firms located in the same place. They are a subset of Marshall's external economies described above. An industrial agglomeration is thus a spatial concentration of firms where the motivations for, and results of, being spatially concentrated are that the individual firms are in some economic sense better off than they would have been if they were located in an industrially more isolated setting.

Even if agglomeration economies were not the initial driver of the spatial concentration, that concentration may still lead to what Weber (1909) called 'accidental agglomeration economies'. On the other hand, such spatial concentration may not lead to agglomeration economies, in which case it should not be called an agglomeration. For example, where a number of firms concentrate in a particular place because of a government incentive to do so but there is no gain from the fact that there are other firms in that place, such spatial grouping constitutes a concentration but not an agglomeration.

Can localization be observed in European industries? In Sections 8.3, 8.4 and 8.5 we describe three types of industrial agglomeration, all of which exist to varying extents within and between different European countries. These, in particular where they are cross-border, are elements in European economic integration. The broader consequences of European integration, such as the emergence of a core that is relatively developed, industrial and wealthy, and a periphery that is less advanced, are discussed in Chapter 14.[11]

8.3 Industrial districts

The term 'industrial district' was first used by Marshall. It was revived by a number of Italian economists (in particular Brusco, 1982) in the 1980s to describe the small-firm production systems of the Third Italy.[12] Piore and Sabel (1984) were most prominent in reintroducing the concept to an English-speaking readership. Their book, *The Second Industrial Divide*, suggested that these new, Italian production systems could contain the kernel of a new departure in the evolution of industrial capitalism.

Where a relatively large number of independent firms are located close to one another and are involved in the same or associated industries, then that location can often be identified as an *industrial district*. An industrial district is defined as a production system characterized by a myriad of firms specialized in various stages of the production of a homogeneous product, often using flexible production technology and connected by extensive local inter-firm linkages (Pyke *et al.*, 1990; Harrison, 1992). As small, owner-managed firms, often employing other members of the family, the communication lines within these firms are short. In addition, flexible production requires most people working in the firm to be able to do most of the jobs. Organizationally, this implies an absence of long top-down chains of authority: firms in industrial districts have relatively flat organizational structures. Between firms, while there is competition at some levels, at others the activities of these independent firms are strongly co-ordinated; they contribute to the production of the same good within the same geographical area (for example, toys in Canneto sull'Oglio in Lombardy). These geographically defined districts are said to form a 'social and economic whole' and have been partly responsible for the rejuvenation of the dormant economy of the Third Italy (Best, 1990, ch. 7).

The social, cultural and political aspects of the industrial district are important. Among the special characteristics of the industrial districts in the Third Italy (or what Brusco (1982) called 'the Emilian model') is a local set of rules, originating in civil society, that on one hand reduces transaction costs and on the other prevents inappropriate opportunism. Being ostracized for contravening local rules, customs or norms of economic behaviour would have serious social and economic consequences, and such contravention is therefore rare. The roots of these rules go back in some cases hundreds of years, evolving into an economy of agglomeration that has been an important element in the success of the industrial districts of that part of Italy (Brusco 1982).

The owners of the small firms are usually artisans (craftspeople), and members of the same artisanal association. The association is one means of distributing information. This sharing of information may also be encouraged by local (municipal or regional) authorities. For all this to exist, there must be a high level of trust: a shared socio-cultural identity 'facilitates trust relations between firms and between employers and skilled workers' (Schmitz and Musyck, 1994). Cooke and Morgan (1990, p. 40), in their analysis of Baden Wurtemberg, describe *networking* as: 'inter-firm linkages, technology transfer mechanisms, management–labour relations and public–private concertation'. Industrial districts are clearly highly networked systems.

Industrial districts are evidence of the potential for small firms to break into export markets, independent of large firms. More generally, according to those who have examined these regions closely (for example Best, 1990, pp. 204–26), they demonstrate the possibility of a high standard of living without corporate giants. The Emilia-Romagna region has received much attention because of its furniture, ceramic tile, textiles and clothing, metal-working and machine making, and other industrial districts.

There is some debate over the significance of the industrial districts, both theoretically and empirically. Questions relating to how successful industrial districts are, whether the same processes have given rise to different industrial districts, and whether conceptually or empirically there is anything new in industrial districts, have all been examined with differing conclusions. Piore and Sabel (1984) were the main proponents of the argument that industrial districts were special and should be studied closely. Amin and Robins (1990) argue critically that an account that 'acknowledges the complex and contradictory nature of the restructuring process – and particularly of its spatial dimensions – must . . . raise considerable problems about the industrial district paradigm'.[13]

While accepting as valid the description of the industrial agglomerations in the Third Italy as new 'Marshallian industrial districts',[14] Amin and Robins (1990) reject the generalization of this to different types of successful regions in different parts of the world. Product-pioneering industrial agglomerations, for example, such as Silicon Valley in California, are different from Marshallian industrial districts, they argue, and are more appropriately compared with other areas that have pioneered major products, such as Detroit as the centre of the automotive industry in the 1930s. Such inter-temporal comparison calls into question the argument that local agglomerations of this type are evidence of a change of an 'epochal' nature in the 1980s and 1990s. After all, if something similar happened in Detroit in the 1930s, then what is different about Silicon Valley is the product, not the fact of a localized origin of a new industry.

Amin and Robins (1990) are also critical of the view, attributed to Piore and Sabel (1984), that industrial districts are the way forward, that they are an inevitable consequence of a deepening break-up of large-scale, mass production (Fordism). This argument, based on a variant of transaction cost analysis, identifies a 'progressive externalisation' arising from flexible manufacturing which will lead to industrial districts (Scott, 1988, p. 175). Reality, Amin and Robins believe, 'is more equivocal, more ambiguous, more obscure'.

Many writers working on industrial districts do not hold the views that Amin and Robins ascribe to the 'industrial district paradigm'. Benton (1992), for example, emphasizes the 'openendedness of the widespread process of industrial restructuring' and the 'strikingly different outcomes of industrial restructuring'. Amin and Robins, she argues, focus in their criticism on extreme versions of the industrial district perspective.

Although not engaging in the industrial district debate, Camagni's (1991) analysis supports the views of Amin and Robins. Writing of Tuscany and Emilia-Romagna, two of the Third Italy regions, Camagni argues that a new organizational model has emerged in some light industries such as clothing and textiles. This is the large, vertically integrated firm, using advanced information and communication technologies to provide remote production control, linking sales with production management, and establishing 'tight relationships with fashion creation and international marketing' (Camagni, 1991, p. 156).

At the same time, a study of the knitwear/clothing district of Carpi found that, while there was a crisis in the industry in Europe in general, in Carpi it improved, expanded, increased employment and diversified its product line, despite higher labour costs than elsewhere in Italy. A major advantage of industrial districts in comparison with large firms 'is the presence of numerous centres of strategic decisions. ... In a large firm there is only a single strategic centre; in Carpi, these number several hundred. Thanks to this high number of active entrepreneurs, the district can find the best strategies by proceeding through trial and error.' In addition, there is constant experimentation, and information circulates rapidly – because 'in such a district everybody knows everybody' – producing 'an environment favouring imitation of the right strategies and innovative change' (Bigarelli and Crestanello, 1994).

Large firms with international links continue to be important, and in some cases are of increasing importance. This is not to argue that industrial districts and other forms of local agglomeration are not important, but that they must be seen as part of the global: 'the product of local, nation-wide and transnational influences' (Amin and Thrift, 1992).

Recent research shows that industrial districts continue to evolve in a variety of ways. They vary in terms of technology and product; from furniture, ceramic tiles, clothing and textiles, to sophisticated machine tools; in terms of size, from 60 firms to hundreds of firms; and in terms of the importance of large firms in the district. They have in common that they have high levels of both competition and co-operation, and that they are predominantly small-firm production systems with high external economies. However, some of them are undergoing significant change. In some cases, for example, larger firms are becoming increasingly important. There is evidence that 'the larger firms of the districts – albeit small by most standards – often orchestrate subcontracting relations, explore commercial avenues, and invest in R&D' (Lazerson and Lorenzoni 1999). This is supported by Carbonara's (2002) findings, that strategies of leader firms increasingly dictate the type, level and extent of inter-firm relationships within and outside at least some districts. The increasing significance of large, leader firms may reduce the effect of multiplicity of entrepreneurs noted earlier by Bigarelli and Crestanello (1994). However, such broad conclusions are difficult to draw because, as Lazerson and Lorenzoni (1999) argue, there is a greater organizational heterogeneity in industrial districts than is generally accepted.

Another problem for the academic work on industrial districts is that some researchers use the term more generically to include both Marshallian and neo-Marshallian industrial districts on the one hand, and various other forms of spatial concentration of firms on the other. Markusen (1996), for example, identifies, in addition to 'Marshallian and Italianate industrial districts', 'hub-and-spoke', 'satellite platform' and 'state-anchored' industrial districts. In the hub-and-spoke district there is at least one dominant, externally oriented, vertically integrated firm surrounded by a number of smaller suppliers. In the satellite platform district there are a number of unconnected branch plants of foreign-owned firms. In the state-anchored district the key tenant (or tenants) in the district is government owned or sponsored, surrounded by customers and suppliers. Such key state tenants include military bases, plants for manufacturing (or researching) military equipment, universities and state administration centres. Different types of district generate different levels of economies of agglomeration. To illustrate, because the firms in the satellite platform are unrelated to one another, there are greater economies of agglomeration in the hub-and-spoke district than in the satellite platform. The only agglomeration effects in the satellite platform are through a shared, generally unskilled, labour market. There are examples of all the different types of district in many parts of the world, in both industrialized and less developed countries. It should be noted, however, that Markusen is unusual in that most writers on industrial districts still focus on what she calls the Marshallian and Italianate forms.

Case study The wooden furniture industry in County Monaghan, Ireland: an example of an industrial district[15]

County Monaghan is a small county in the north east of Ireland on the border with Northern Ireland. It boasts a considerable number of industrial successes and among them a high concentration of wooden furniture firms. Monaghan accounts for the largest concentration of timber and wooden furniture firms after the two largest cities, Dublin and Cork. The largest wooden furniture firms in Ireland are located within six miles of one another in Monaghan and dominate the national industry's exports to Northern Ireland and Great Britain.

The focus is on the wooden furniture sector in Monaghan but it is of relevance that this is just one part of a whole range of wooden products manufactured in Monaghan. In addition to household furniture, these include audio speakers, builders' joinery products and wooden bars and other furniture for Irish pubs (see Table 8.1). What is most surprising is that there is no local supply of wood; even though there was a limited supply historically, it is long since depleted.

- *Primary*. This includes those firms that are involved in the preparation of wood. This is primarily undertaken outside of Monaghan as most of the wood is imported or brought from other regions in the country. Locally only one 'timber engineering' company has a timber impregnating and creosote treating service. In addition, a fire-retardant chemical for treating wood is manufactured locally by a small chemicals company.

- *Components*. These firms manufacture components that are assembled, combined or modified by the manufacturer who then sells the finished good to the retailer or public. Examples are cabinet and cupboard doors, chair frames, and turned or carved items. There are also a number of firms that manufacture wooden fittings

Case Study (continued)

Table 8.1 The stages of production in the manufacture of wooden products located in Monaghan

Stage of production	Description
Primary	Treatment of wood
	Fire retardents for wood
Components	Glass manufacturer
	Turning
	Carving
	Cabinet and cupboard doors
	Chair frames
	Chairs
Services	Wholesale distribution of timber
	Accountants and insurance
	Woodworking machinery reconditioning services
Final	Domestic furniture
	Pub and restaurant furniture
	Timber houses
	Picture and mirror frames
	Audio speakers
	Shopfronts
	Doors
	Chairs
	Staircases and landings
	Handrails
	Architrave's and trim
	Builders joinery products

for houses. These include one that produces wooden staircases and doors, one that manufactures wooden handrails, a third that specializes in wooden doors, staircases and landings, and a fourth that produces doors and wooden architraves and trim. Most of these goods can be sold directly to the consumer but it is more common for them to be purchased by builders and construction companies. The wooden bars of many of the Irish pubs around Europe are manufactured in County Monaghan.

Case Study (continued)

- ◆ *Services*. There are a number of service functions that are required by the firms in the industry. They include repair workshops, materials suppliers and wholesale distributors and accountancy services. One engineering firm in Newbliss, near Monaghan, services and repairs woodworking machinery. There are three local firms that undertake wholesale distribution of timber.

- ◆ *Final*. These firms produce goods which are sold directly to retailers or the public as finished goods. The final wooden goods produced in Monaghan are: domestic furniture, furniture for hotels and restaurants, fitted Irish pubs and shopfronts, speakers, picture and mirror frames, timber frame houses and builders' joinery products.

The wooden furniture industry in Monaghan can be traced back at least to 1801 when there were some 100 carpenters located in Glennon. This prevalence of carpentry skills as well as sawmills continued into the twentieth century. By the end of the 1990s the industry comprised some 32 firms and employed 879 people, producing medium quality but relatively cheap mahogany or cherry veneered furniture. It is relatively cheap because, rather than hard wood, MDF (medium density fibreboard) is used to make the items which are then veneered. The quality and finish of the products combined with a relatively low price enhances sales. The products range from large dining room suites and fitted kitchens to video units or occasional tables. Retail prices range from €50 up to €15,000 per item.

The oldest factory still in existence is James O'Reilly & Sons Ltd, which was established in 1923. It has always been very small, and employs only four people. The four largest firms in the industry were established pre-1970. Coyles was established in 1936, when its founder, originally an upholsterer from Armagh, decided to move to the area. Neeson Brothers chair makers began operations in 1950. McNally and Finlay opened their firm in 1962. Gola began business in the early 1940s, producing chicken coops and pig troughs before subsequently entering the wooden furniture business.

As Table 8.2 shows, there is a wide variety of sizes of firms, according to the number of employees. Aside from size there is also a clear distinction between the relatively large firms which compete with each other in the production of mid- to high-quality products, mainly for export to Northern Ireland and Great Britain, and the smaller ones which are located in outhouses and workshops, run most often by up to three people (most of whom are related) and making smaller items with less advanced machinery.

The proximity of hardwood forests was an important early factor in the concentration of wood-crafting skills in Monaghan. These had been depleted by the early part of the twentieth century, but the furniture and other wood-based industries remained. According to Dunford and Hudson (1996, p. 61), referring to Jutland in Denmark, 'one

Case Study (continued)

Table 8.2 Size of furniture firms in Monaghan

No. employees	No. firms	No. employees	Percentage of firms	Percentage of employees
1-5	13	35.5	46.0	5.3
6-25	6	100.0	21.4	15.1
26-35	5	142.0	17.9	21.4
36-70	0	0.0	0.0	0.0
70-150	4	387.0	14.3	58.3
Total	**28**	**664.5**	**100.0**	**100.0**

implication of this combination of a meagre natural resource base and a peripheral location was that people in Jutland were forced to rely heavily upon their own enterprise, ingenuity and skill in order to make a living there'. Similarly, entrepreneurship has developed in Monaghan and has had an important influence in both the emergence and the development of the wooden furniture industry.

An important source of growth in industrial districts is the emergence of spin-off firms. These are firms established by former employees or family and are usually involved in subsidiary or related trades. In some cases this can be done with the assistance of employers or family in the form of finance, guaranteed orders or assistance with machinery. In Monaghan, while only in a few cases was such clear and active support offered, nonetheless there is evidence of many spin-off firms.

The roots of most of the furniture firms in County Monaghan can be traced to Coyles. Young men (the few women who work in these firms work only in the office) who did their apprenticeship with Coyles later set up their own firms. Subsequently, many of the employees of these firms have done likewise. The reasons they did so are many and a common feature must be entrepreneurship. In addition, the recession in the 1970s left many who were put on short time or temporarily laid off, with few options; they chose to establish their own firms, in the area in which they lived, often in their garages or sheds. Some of these firms are little more than family enterprises with a total employment of less than five, but others are considerably bigger, employing up to 95 people.

The research shows that 75 per cent of the furniture firms in Monaghan are either directly or indirectly related to Coyles. The owners of nine firms did their apprenticeship in Coyles before establishing their own firms, and a further nine firms are indirectly related in that their founders worked in firms owned by those who had originally done their apprenticeship in Coyles. This mirrors other industrial districts,

Case Study (continued)

such as in Santiago in Mexico where 'it was generally accepted that owners would give assistance at some future date when the worker wished to separate and start his own business. ... For example, the pioneering owner in Santiago estimated that he had taught well over 100 men the arts of loom work and machine repair' (Wilson, 1992, p. 61). 'In Emilia-Romagna the new firms will be headed by a family member or trusted previous employee who wishes to estabish an independent firm' (Best, 1990, p. 207). There is no evidence of any assistance being offered to employees to establish their own firms in Monaghan, although the many new owners learned and developed their skills in Coyles.

It is this continual emergence of new firms that perpetuated the industry in Monaghan and assured its continued growth. The pattern of size related to age also indicates the internal growth of firms over time. Central to the emergence of spin-off firms, and a common factor identified by industry experts and owners of firms alike, is the business ethos that is evident throughout the county. This ethos encourages individuals to set up their own firms and encourages owners and managers to continually improve and develop their businesses. A study on new firm formations found that Monaghan is the county with the highest rate of successful business start-ups with a formation rate of 20.6 during the period 1980–90. This rate is almost double the national average of 11.5, and the findings correlate quite closely with a similar study of the period 1973–81 (*Business and Finance*, 11 August 1994).

Another important characteristic of the wooden furniture industry in Monaghan is the co-operation, even among direct competitors. They discuss customers, and will help each other to avoid giving credit to high-risk customers. At a more substantial level, two of the larger firms, McNally and Finlay, and Sherry Bros, share a brand name, Rossmore, under which their products are marketed in Britain.

8.3.1 Comparison of Monaghan with Emilian industrial districts

Two caveats must be expressed in relation to the Irish industrial district of the case study. First, the description is based on research undertaken in the late 1990s. Among changes since then is that at least one of the major firms in the region has introduced radically new technology and now manufactures flat-pack furniture for home assembly. This move has changed its relationships within the local production system; it has, for example, removed any linkages the firm had to local component manufacturers. Depending on the medium term success of these technological changes, other firms may also adopt them, with similar effects, namely the reduction of local inter-firm interactions. Changes in aspects of the wooden furniture production system in Monaghan do not necessarily distinguish it from

Italian examples, however. As Piore (2001) points out, writing of industrial districts in general: 'the relationship among the different firms is continually being reconfigured as the precise specification of the product changes in response to shifts in market tastes and new technological developments'.

The second caveat relates to the strong 'social capital'[16] element of the Emilian model. This has been explained in terms of a deep social and cultural homogeneity that generates a set of tacit rules. As stated above, these reduce transaction costs and make opportunistic behaviour more or less impossible. There is little evidence of this kind of civil society effect in the Irish example. There is a 'professional milieu' that has some of the same impact but is less embedded. Its advantage is that, like the deep social and cultural homogeneity of the Italian industrial districts, it facilitates communication. This is more than market-based, 'arms'-length' communication, as the example of competitors sharing information shows. However, it is more likely to break down in the face of competitive – or other – pressures than the deep, historically rooted, social and cultural homogeneity of the Italian districts.

The work on industrial districts of economists, geographers, sociologists and political scientists, has contributed to an analysis traversing the theoretical concerns of industrial organization, regional development and corporate and local governance. The next three sections outline industrial/regional concepts that have been considered to be particularly relevant for the development of industrial and innovation policy.

8.4 *Filières*

French economists such as Montfort (1983) have used the term *filière* to refer to a system in which a good or service 'is supplied to its final consumer through a succession of operations performed by independent units having different activities' (Montfort, 1983).[17] These units of production may belong to different industries linked together by buyer–supplier relationships. A *filière* thus consists of a chain of economic activities, ranging from the extraction of natural resources to the distribution of the end product.

While Montfort (1983) and de Bandt (1987) do not, other authors (for example Truel, 1983) incorporate a technological interrelationship as a part of the definition of the *filière*. Thus, referring to Truel (1983), Storper and Walker (1989, p. 133) state that the 'French term "filière" captures the idea of a connecting filament among technologically related activities'. Antonelli et al. (1992, p. 13) seem to accept the broader definition; the concept is, they argue, an attempt to select from and substantiate what is usually meant by the English term 'industry'. In their study of the economics of industrial modernization, however, Antonelli et al. (1992, p. 149) use as their unit of focus the *filière* 'taken as a set of interrelated production activities all affected by any sizeable technological change occurring in any of them'.

An important characteristic of the concept is its application to policy. Its origins lie in the study of agriculture, and particularly in the policy idea of adding value to agricultural products through manufacturing, that is, food processing. This agricultural focus related to its application in economic development policy in the French colonies. In the late 1970s, French economists found the concept to be relevant in the context of the declining competitiveness of French industry. They saw a need to recapture the domestic market,[18] and defined an 'optimal *filière*', among other things as one that is composed of strong and competitive French (as opposed to foreign) firms. The concept was suggestive of nationalistic and interventionist ideas because of its application. The different segments of *filières* were examined, for example, in terms of import penetration. A high import penetration, particularly in the upstream or core poles (see below), would have repercussions for the whole *filière*, and might imply a diminished national industrial independence. The implications for industrial policy were clear: to select important *filières* within which to build up a strong industrial complex of competitive firms able not only to recapture the domestic market but also to gain increasing shares of the world market.

A clear example of the policy focus in *filière* research is the work of Groeneweyen and Beije (1989) on the French communications industry. Incorporating all the aspects mentioned by others in this field, they define the *filière* as 'the network of relations actors create in their market and socio-political environment'. This network comprises the 'supply and demand relations of physical units (including subcontracting and co-makership), [and] the exchange of technical information (for instance in the national or supranational technology programs) between organizations ...'. Also important are relations 'of a more personal kind', for example among people who have graduated from the same college. In France, these latter were known as '*corps d'etat*', especially powerful in the Ministry of Industry in the 1970s and 1980s. Thus the *filière* includes both the firms and their interactions, and relations with and among policy makers.

A more recent example of a study of a *filière* that also clearly incorporates policy towards the industry is that of Jones and Clark (2003). They examine viticulture in the Languedoc region of France. Their focus is the conflict between the old, *filière*-based policies and the new French agricultural policy introduced in 1999, the *contrat territorial d'exploitation* (CTE), 'which is intended to generate links between agricultural production, environmental protection, and rural development in specific localities'. Until the introduction of the CTE, agricultural policy was more directly focused on production, and hence, in France, on the *filière*. The CTE has a more territorial focus 'in which farmers are encouraged to link environmentally-sound agricultural production with broader rural development objectives'. The *filière* is, nevertheless, still central to the implementation of the new policy. To bring about the desired changes, Jones and Clark (2003) argue on the basis of their viticulture case study, the *filière* must be involved directly. The *filière*, they show, 'operates on the basis of established rules, procedures, information channels and highly networked social relations'. It is, therefore, a key means for disseminating the CTE message in the region.

The focus of *filière* researchers has been institutional rather than neoclassical, 'concerned less about "getting the prices right" than about "getting the institutions right". Much research has focused on how public institutions create a smooth flow of commodities, and on how they affect local production systems' (Raikes *et al.*, 2000). The most recent work in this area, like Jones and Clark's (2003) study of French agriculture, continues to reflect these policy and institutional aspects of *filière* research.

Despite an interventionist industrial policy, French industry in major *filières* like that of the car and its components, lost shares in international markets during the 1980s. Was this because the wrong policies were adopted, because they were applied incorrectly, or because they were based on misconceptions? A more detailed examination of national and EU industrial policies will be undertaken in Chapter 15. Suffice to say at this point that it is at least possible that a successful *filière* requires an economic space greater than that provided by the French economy (Andréosso, 1986). As Raikes *et al.* (2000) state, 'the *filière* tradition mostly focuses on local or national levels of the [commodity] chain'.

8.4.1 An example of a *filière*

A *filière* may be composed of three poles: upstream, centre and downstream. The upstream pole is a set of supplier industries – they supply to, rather than buy from, the core industries of the *filière* (though they may buy from or sell to other upstream industries). The downstream pole consists of the industries that buy from, rather than sell to, the core industries of the *filière* (though they may buy from or sell to other downstream industries).[19] This leaves the central, or core pole, in which are situated the industries that are involved in the transformation of inputs such as raw materials or primary products into finished goods.

As an example, the agri-food *filière* comprises the following poles:

◆ The upstream pole, including farming and fisheries activities, agricultural machinery, and animal feed producers.

◆ The downstream pole, including specialized food haulage, catering services, and distribution.

◆ The core, consisting of the food processing industry itself.

The *filière* includes all the networks and institutions involved in this production and distribution, including links with policy makers and with representative associations. Formal and informal associations, alliances and subcontracting are also part of the *filière*.

The economy does not necessarily divide cleanly into a number of different *filières*. Using input–output tables we can identify how subsectors are interrelated; a close relationship among a number of subsectors suggests they belong together in a *filière*, but other subsectors may display similar linkages with all others across the range of industries, as was found for France. Such subsectors, not obviously part of any one *filière*, 'play a special role of intermediation' upstream of production (as in the case of electronics, which feeds into a number of different industries) or downstream of production (as in the case of distribution) (Antonelli *et al.*, 1992, p. 14). Some industries may be in both upstream and downstream poles. Transport is particularly pervasive, and in the agri-food *filière*, for example, the food-haulage industry may be involved both in upstream delivery of raw materials and in the delivery of end products to distributors. Antonelli *et al.* use communication, banking and finance as examples of intermediating downstream subsectors, but as prerequisites of production they are arguably more important upstream.

8.5 Clusters

We introduced the idea of clusters in Chapter 2 in the context of a discussion about developments in, and alternatives to, the structure–conduct–performance paradigm. Here we explain the concept in more detail and provide empirical examples.

Clusters, according to Porter (1990), who developed the notion, are related to *filières*.[20] The *filière* as a concept 'was a valuable precursor' to clusters (Porter, 1990, p. 789). Vague though the concept of a *filière* is, the cluster is even less well-defined, referring broadly to 'industries connected through vertical and horizontal relationships' (Porter, 1990, p. 73). As we shall see, even within Porter's work, what is meant by a cluster has changed;[21] and among different scholars and policy makers, differences in what is meant by industrial cluster are even more significant. Brown (2000) suggests that this is because there is no unifying cluster theory but 'rather a broad range of theories which constitute the logic of clusters'.

A nation's successful industries, Porter argues, 'are usually linked through vertical (buyer/supplier) or horizontal (common customers, technology, channels, etc.) relationships' (1990, p. 149). These links connect the different elements of the cluster. Moreover, because of agglomeration economies, the 'process of clustering, and the interchange among industries in the cluster, . . . works best when the industries involved are geographically concentrated' (ibid., p. 157). This interchange involves 'the exchange and flow of information about the needs, techniques, and technology among buyers, suppliers and related industries' (ibid., p. 152), and is a key process underlining the formation of clusters.

The geographical nature of clusters and the importance of information flows in their formation suggest a relationship with industrial districts, too, though Porter seems to have been only vaguely aware of this.[22] One of Porter's examples, the Italian ceramic tile industry (1990, pp. 210–25), is, in fact, an industrial district, though he does not say this. It is clear, nevertheless, that industrial districts are clusters or at least parts of clusters.

The cluster is also broader than the *filière*, including as it does horizontal as well as vertical relationships. In this respect the cluster is similar to another French concept, *meso-système*, which is defined by de Bandt (1987, pp. 51–2) in terms of all the vertical and horizontal relationships, direct and indirect – 'the agents which are supplying various kinds of inputs: services to enterprises, finance, R&D, training, etc., or which are moulding the market and/or consumer behaviours: distribution, advertising etc.' – competitive and co-operative, in an industry involved in a specific product category. The difference is that the cluster is again a broader concept, including firms in different product categories though this may depend on how the term 'product category' is defined.

Industrial districts are considered to be primarily an Italian phenomenon; *filières* have been examined more in the French than in other economies; clusters are the work, Porter (1990) suggests, of an important characteristic of all successful economies. Porter and his team examined a number of economies in an effort to identify and explain the existence of clusters, and to underline the implications for policy, both at the level of the firm and that of the government. Hundreds, perhaps even thousands, of cluster studies have been undertaken since then.[23] Porter (1998b) discusses the research on clusters and the impact of the idea on companies and policy makers in the introduction to the second edition of *Competitive Advantage*. In our book, strategies of firms are discussed in Chapters 3 and 4, and policies of governments in Chapter 15. In what follows we briefly discuss the identification of and explanation for clusters, and provide examples from the recent literature.

Porter's primary tool for illustrating 'patterns of national advantage' is the *cluster chart*.[24] This chart includes the successful (competitive) industries of a country, identified as such either by having 'a world export share greater than the nation's average share of world exports or an international position based on foreign investment that was estimated to be as significant'. Because demand conditions and vertical relationships among industries (*filières?*) have important roles in his theory, the competitive cluster chart groups industries by end-use application. At the top of the chart are 'upstream sectors', similar to the upstream pole of the *filière*. In the middle are 'broad end-use sectors involving *industrial or supporting functions*'. This, as is the bottom row of Porter's chart, is different from any of the *filière* poles. At the bottom are the 'end-use sectors most associated with *final consumption goods*'.

Using this method, Porter (1990) identifies the clusters of ten different economies, including large ones such as the United States, Japan and Germany, and smaller ones such as Denmark, Sweden and Switzerland. In Sweden, for example, he identifies (ibid., pp. 333–42) five major clusters of internationally competitive industries which are, in order of importance: transportation and logistics (including cars, trucks, engines, distribution services); forest-related industries (including timber, pulp and paper, paper-making machinery, and furniture); ferrous metals and fabricated metal products (including mining equipment and metalworking tools); health-related products (including electromedical equipment and pharmaceuticals); and telecommunications (including telecommunications equipment and mobile telephone networks).

The explanation for a country's success in particular clusters is based, in Porter's model, on what he calls the 'diamond'. The diamond is the combination of four factors.[25] These factors are: *factor conditions* (including all factors of production, as well as such means as training and education for improving those factors of production); *demand conditions* (for example, the bigger the home demand for an industry's product, the better, and the more sophisticated the demand, the better for innovative products); *related and supporting industries* (the presence in a country of internationally competitive supplier industries, for example, will enhance the competitiveness of the buyer industries); and *firm strategy, structure and rivalry* (including domestic rivalry, and rules and institutions governing that rivalry – the more intense the domestic rivalry, the greater the potential for the firms to be internationally competitive). If these four elements are strong, they can combine to produce a 'dynamic, stimulating and intensely competitive business environment. A cluster is the manifestation of the diamond at work' (Porter, 1998a, fn 1).

The key elements of Porter's explanation for competitiveness and its national and regional specificity are the diamond and clustering. Whereas it is possible for governments to generate clusters, they are 'far more likely to succeed in reinforcing an existing or nascent industry cluster' (1990, p. 655). This, for countries without clusters or at an early stage in industrialization, limits the model's relevance to that of *ex ante* explanation. However, he seems to be arguing for broad policies that, rather than targeting individual industries or clusters, provide an environment that is more likely to generate clusters. In his recent work, for example, Porter emphasizes productivity as the key to competitiveness. He sees general policy prescriptions for governments as emerging from this: to ensure that education systems provide a skilled and educated labour force; to ensure that the physical infrastructure is of high quality; to provide a regulatory framework for competition that protects intellectual property and prevents anti-competitive behaviour; and to promote the formation and upgrading of clusters 'and the buildup of public or quasi-public goods that have a significant impact on many linked businesses' (Porter, 1998a).

There has been both interest in, and criticism of, Porter's approach. Brittan (1990) and Jacobs and de Jong (1991) have found fault with the criteria for including industries in the chart. Brittan's (1990) view is that 'Porter's measures are too influenced by the sheer size of industries, and countries' changing share in world trade'. Jacobs and de Jong (1991) would agree, pointing out that in Porter's approach an industry may be more competitive in Country A than in Country B, yet appear in B's cluster chart and not A's, 'because of the average performance of the other industries in both countries'.

Jacobs and de Jong (1991) also have two, more fundamental, criticisms of Porter's approach. They argue, first, that there is an overemphasis on end use. In their application of the model to the Netherlands, for example, they find that a cluster may be in an intermediate stage (upstream pole of the *filière*) and not at the end-use stage, which makes it difficult to identify accurately the cluster in Porter's chart. Second, the approach is one-sided in that international diversity is stressed. While Jacobs and de Jong accept that both international divergence and convergence are evident, Porter's approach, in their view, does not capture the dialectic between the two tendencies.[26]

Scassellati (1991) goes even further, criticizing Porter's focus on national entities. Porter fails to incorporate adequately the implications of the new type of corporation, corporations that in 'their inherent drive toward ever expanding accumulation . . . simply cannot afford to tie themselves to any territory'. His applause for the revival of the Swiss watch industry, for example, neglects the fact that several of the most famous Swiss brands are now owned by a US company, North American Watch (Scassellati, 1991).

In his review of Porter's book, Dunning (1992) agrees with the criticism that Porter's focus does not adequately incorporate MNEs. In an apt example, he points out that Nestlé, though a Swiss company, has 95 per cent of sales accounted for by its foreign subsidiaries. The diamonds of competitive advantage of the host countries in which those subsidiaries operate may therefore have more to do with Nestlé's contribution to Switzerland's GNP than Switzerland's own diamond of competitive advantage. Dunning constructively suggests the addition of a transnational business variable as a separate factor in the diamond of competitive advantages.

Another criticism relates to the limited extent to which Porter's model applies to very small, open economies (O'Donnellan, 1994). In such economies there may be too small a domestic market to generate national clusters, and larger economic spaces (for example, the EU) may have to be analysed to identify the extent to which industries in, say Ireland, are elements in a cluster.

Porter's (1990) definition of clusters as based primarily on domestic competition among firms also came under heavy criticism. Lazonick (1993), for example, uses extensive quotes from Porter's own work, particularly on the ceramic tile industrial district in Emilia-Romagna, to show that what Porter sees as 'domestic rivalry' is actually co-operation. Perhaps in response, in a revision of some of his ideas on clusters, Porter (1998a) describes them in terms that make it more difficult to distinguish them from industrial districts. He accords substantial weight to co-operation and trust, for example. Nevertheless, he still emphasizes the non-networked nature of the relationships in clusters. The firms in industrial districts are networked. Also, whereas there is both vertical and horizontal co-operation in industrial districts, the co-operation in Porter's clusters is primarily vertical.

Criticisms of Porter's model of cluster analysis continue to appear; to some extent both the criticisms and the responses result in the development and improvement of cluster research. As we discussed in Chapter 2, among the most recent of the critics is Best (2001). Best praises Porter for engendering the widespread use in policy discourse of such concepts as 'business strategy, value chain, home base, and cluster' (Best, 2001, p. 8); but he identifies what he sees as a number of weaknesses in Porter's approach.

According to Best (2001, p. 8), 'for Porter, firms are not the source of competitiveness. Instead, firms derive their competitive advantage from their home base environment'. While this is broadly true of the way the first cluster studies were done, Porter's (1998a) own more recent words seem to contradict Best: 'What happens inside companies is important but clusters reveal that the immediate business environment outside companies plays a vital role as well'.[27] While both are important, Porter seems to be saying, the latter is more important, or 'vital'. Best's statement may not be precisely correct, but it is clear that there are differences between their approaches, in that Best accords much greater significance to factors internal to the firm, such as its production system. As we showed in Chapter 2, Best offers a new framework for analysing clusters, the productivity triad. Each element of the triad – the business model, the production system and skill formation – reflects both the firm itself and its environment. Porter's continuing emphasis on the cluster and the diamond show that in his model factors outside the firm have greater weight.

The way in which Porter seems to respond to criticism by broadening his approach leads to another of Best's criticisms. 'Relaxing the conditions required to describe a cluster results in a proliferation of clusters and the concept loses meaning' (Best, 2001, p. 9). The fact that Porter (1998a) identifies 22 different clusters in Portugal is, for Best, an example of this loss of meaning.

On the other hand, some situations continue to be excluded from cluster analysis, according to Best (2001, p. 8), because competitiveness is sometimes not the result of the factors outlined by Porter. The success of countries such as Singapore and Ireland, with exporting industries based on multinational enterprises and inward investment, Best argues, contradicts 'Porter's home base theory'.[28]

The tension between overly narrow and overly broad definitions is also raised by Isaksen and Hauge (2002). They show problems with Porter's definition arising from the fact that, for him, clusters may or may not include governmental and other institutions. They prefer to impose stricter criteria and use the term 'regional cluster' to refer to a concentration of what they call 'interdependent' firms 'within the same or adjacent industrial sectors in a small geographical area'.

What is meant by 'industrial sector', however, can also cause problems. We can use Porter's work to turn the tables with a criticism of Isaksen and Hauge. New clusters (such as medical devices) may go unrecognized if concentrations of firms are sought under traditional sectors (such as plastics products and electronics equipment) (Porter, 1998a). Examining concentrations of firms in the 'same or adjacent industrial sectors' may not reveal some new industrial or regional clusters.

Returning to Isaksen and Hauge's (2002) search for definitional precision, rather than the term 'cluster' they prefer to use 'regional innovation system' (see below) in cases where organizations such as government agencies, research centres and so on are included with the concentration of firms. Where there is 'more organised co-operation (agreement) between firms, stimulated by trust, norms and conventions, which encourages firms' innovation activity', they identify this as a 'regional innovation network'. For Porter each of these – regional clusters, regional innovation networks, and regional innovation systems – would fall into his definition of industrial cluster.

The last in this long list of criticisms finds fault not with Porter in particular, but with research on clusters in general. (The article by Whittam and Danson (2001) may in fact be unique in that clusters are discussed without a single reference to the work of Porter!) What Whittam and Danson argue is missing from the cluster literature is the concept of power. An examination of the power relationships in a cluster is essential, in their view, for an appreciation of the likely future of that cluster in its current location.[29]

Despite all these criticisms, Porter has been extremely important as a contributor both to academic and consultancy work on clusters and competitiveness. As we have shown, even among his critics he is widely acknowledged as seminal. He is praised, for example by Jacobs and de Jong (1991), for introducing 'the idea to an audience of economists that globalization somewhat paradoxically leads to more emphasis on local conditions, and moreover, provides a global firm [with] opportunities to take advantage of these' (Jacobs and de Jong, 1991).

8.5.1 An example of a cluster

Porter (1998a) provides, among the illustrations of what he means by 'cluster', the example of the 'Italian leather fashion cluster'. This contains companies with world-famous brand names such as Ferragamo and Gucci. In addition, there are other firms that specialize in inputs into the production of shoes, such as leather, lasts and moulds, as well as those providing specialist services such as design. Closely related upstream firms include those producing footwear machinery. All these firms are involved in the production not only of fashion shoes but also of footwear for athletics, hiking and skiing. As Porter points out, the cluster 'consists of several chains of related industries'. Thus in addition to the footwear firms, 'linked by overlapping channels and technologies', there are various other leather goods manufacturers – gloves, belts, bags and clothing – that are 'linked by common inputs and technologies'. The Italian cluster in textile fashion is also related, producing complementary products and often employing common channels. 'The extraordinary strength of the Italian leather fashion cluster can be attributed, at least in part, the multiple linkages and synergies that participating Italian businesses enjoy.'

There are elements of both industrial districts and *filiéres* in this example. It is, however, clear that the cluster is wider than the industrial district, covering a greater area and including firms that are less directly related to each other than those in industrial districts. Firms in two or more industrial districts are part of Porter's Italian leather fashion cluster. The cluster is also different from *filiéres*, including as it does various horizontal relationships. Examining the same context as a *filiére*, we would focus more directly on companies manufacturing machinery for leather preparation, those undertaking the leather preparation, the footwear machinery firms, all as part of the upstream pole, the footwear firms themselves as the core pole, and distribution and marketing channels as the downstream pole. The various other firms less directly related to this particular value chain would be excluded.

8.6 Regional systems of innovation

Work on regional systems of innovation (RSIs) developed out of ideas on national systems of innovation (NSIs) first put forward by Freeman (1987), Lundvall (1992) and Nelson (1993). NSIs are discussed in detail in Chapter 11 with further application in Chapter 13. Here we focus on regional systems of innovation, on their relationship with the NSI, and on differences between the RSI and the other locational concepts discussed in this chapter – industrial districts, *filiéres* and clusters.

To discuss RSIs we must first introduce the general idea of a system of innovation. There have been a number of recent extensive reviews of the literature on systems of innovation, for example Fischer (2001) and Edquist (2001). In his introduction, Fischer (2001) emphasizes the contrast between traditional approaches to innovation, such as that of the OECD in which there is a narrower focus on research and development (R&D). This focus results, for example, in the categorization of economies (as high-tech, medium high-tech, and so on) in terms of the percentage of turnover that is spent on R&D (Hirsch-Kreinsen *et al.*, 2003). As Fischer (2001) points out, 'a too narrow focus on R&D overlooks the importance of other types of innovative effort in the business sectors and, thus, the innovative performance of low-tech sectors in the economy'. The systems of innovation approach aims to incorporate all the influences on the nature and level of innovation, not just R&D.

Following Fischer (2001) and Edquist (2001), we can define a system of innovation as a set of actors involved in the development, diffusion and use of knowledge in the production process, including firms and other organizations, and the social, political, economic and institutional factors that influence them in this context. Edquist (2001) calls for a clear distinction between 'organization' and 'institution'.

Organizations are formal structures, usually with an explicit purpose. They are the actors and include firms, universities, state innovation agencies and financial services companies. *Institutions* are 'the rules of the game', that is, 'the sets of common habits, routines, established practices, rules, or laws that regulate the relations and interactions between individuals, groups and organisations' (Edquist, 2001). An important institution in systems of innovation is the patent laws and the way they are policed. Another is the customs, norms and habits governing the interactions between firms and universities.

The question of the boundaries of systems of innovation leads to the possibility of different spatial (local, regional, national, global) and technological (sectoral) definitions. We return to sectoral systems of innovation in Chapter 11 and concentrate here on regional systems of innovation. The first serious examination of the idea of a regional innovation system was by Cooke (1992). Soon after, Malerba (1993) argued that there was a subnational, regional system of innovation in Italy – a small firm network – that was different from, and more successful than, the NSI. This argument could be generalized: 'there are ... in most EU countries, important subnational, regional systems of innovation' (Jacobson, 1994, p. 220). Cooke (2001) returns to regional innovation systems at some length, arguing that there is an apparent reluctance on the part of some economists to see systems of innovation other than in national terms, and shows that to the limited extent that RSIs have been studied, this has been by regional scientists and economic geographers, rather than economists. Among the most important economists defending the emphasis on national systems is Lundvall (1998). It is important to note, however, that – in Lundvall's own words – his argument is not

> *against alternative analyses of innovation systems at the level of intra- or transnational regions or at the level of technologies, sectors or firms. On the contrary, it is only by breaking down*

national systems into the sub-systems that constitute them that we can understand how they develop. Neither is it an argument for treating national systems as closed or even as especially coherent. The specific way that a national system gets integrated into the international economy is a key to understand its internal dynamics. My point is just that it is legitimate and important to make progress in the analysis of national systems. (Lundvall, 1998)

Lundvall is one writer in an ongoing debate about a continuing tension between regions and states (and between states and other, supranational levels of governance).[30] We would accept that because of a continuing spatial 'lumpiness' in economic development as evidenced by, for example, clusters (Jacobson and McDonough, 1999), regions are important for an understanding both of economic change and development in general, and specifically of the current process of globalization. That regions exist and that they are important is for us not in doubt. But the significance of the system of innovation in different regions, and the nature of the relationship between the system in the region and that in the national economy, remain difficult to research. Cooke (2001) has used five linked concepts to study RSIs:

♦ *Region* – a meso-level political unit between national and local, with at least some formal governance power to influence economic development, particularly innovation.

♦ *Innovation* – based on the broad definition of the neo-Schumpetarian school.

♦ *Network* – a set of linkages among actors, based on trust and co-operation, that result in the members being able to pursue common interests (in this context in relation to innovation). Once the common interest is achieved, the network can change or disappear.

♦ *Learning* – in particular 'institutional learning', where routines of firms and innovation support agencies change as new knowledge, skills and capabilities become embedded in them, displacing or supplementing old ones.

♦ *Interaction* – communications or meetings, formal and informal, focused on innovation, such that all the relevant actors can '*associate* to learn, critique or pursue specific project ideas or practices of collective and individual economic, commercial or communal relevance' (Cooke, 2001).

Applying these concepts as 'dimensions' of the 'systemness' of a region, the strength of the RSI in a particular place can be assessed. In this way, Cooke and his colleagues were able to show that there was a highly developed, heterarchical RSI in Baden Wurtemburg and a less developed, more hierarchical RSI in Wales. Similar and other differences have emerged in further studies that Cooke and his colleagues have undertaken in a number of other regions. What emerges from the research is a framework that provides a means of assessing the significance of the RSI in different regions.

The RSI in each case also has a relationship to the NSI. The latter, Cooke (2001) suggests, has a 'powerful, persisting role . . . to set scientific priorities, and fund basic research and university-level training'. The RSI is subordinate, having the power only to influence or in some cases disburse allocations from the centre. As long as the centre continues to have sole tax-raising and tax-retaining powers, there will be 'an NSI monopoly'. However, given the increasing significance of clustering, Cooke (2001) argues, specialized RSIs will have to develop relationships with the central, NSI, centres of scientific policy and funding of the kind up to recently maintained by corporate and sectoral lobbies. In this way, RSI governance 'becomes a litmus-test of industry capability'. Cooke (2001), in a manner similar to that of Scott (1998), thus identifies elements of RSIs and suggests ways in which the significance of RSIs may increase over time.

Among the critics of the RSI approach, most significant are those invovled in the development of the concept. Most of the following criticisms are drawn from Edquist (2001), for example, who is a key recent contributor to systems of innovation theory. First, as with many new theories or theoretical frameworks, some of the writers in the area assign different meanings to the same concepts, and similar meanings to different concepts. Most obvious in this respect is the concept of 'institution', in that some consider it to include both organizations and the various types of rules of the game. (For Edquist it refers only to the latter.) A second criticism is that the systems of innovation approach is not a theory, merely a framework. Edquist (2001) suggests that the consistency – required by theory – in the relationships among different elements of the framework will be achieved through empirical work functioning as a 'disciplining' device. Third, the approach can be argued to ignore learning processes that do not lead directly to innovations. Edquist (2001) provides the example of 'certain kinds of organizational learning, such as the building up of firm routines and databases'. The recent work, both in systems of innovation in general, and on RSIs in particular, have to various extents responded to these criticisms. The articles already mentioned in this section, especially those by Edquist (2001) himself, Cooke (2001) and Fischer (2001), are examples of the ongoing theory-building process.

In this section we do not devote space to providing examples of RSIs first because the Baden Wurtemburg and Wales examples already illustrate the idea, and second, as suggested by Isaksen and Hauge (2002), RSIs are very similar to clusters, with a particular emphasis on relations among firms and between firms and research organizations, influenced by those institutions – including education – that influence innovation. Indeed, it could be argued that RSI is a policy-oriented approach to the building of clusters.

8.7 Summary

Table 8.3 Types of industrial system

	Industrial districts	*Filières*	Clusters	RSIs
Horizontal relationships	X		X	X
Vertical relationships	X	X	X	X
Implications for internal organization of firm	X			
Marshallian localization	X			
Market or hierarchy	M/H	M	M	M/H?
Institutional learning	X			X
Significant local governance	X			
Significant regional governance				X

The theories and realities surrounding industrial districts, networks, *filières*, *meso-systèmes*, clusters and RSIs all underline the need for a sharp awareness of the regional or spatial aspects of industries. Industrial economics must incorporate the fact that different industries are concentrated to different extents, and in different organizational forms, in different locations, but also that these distributions change over time.

Key aspects of the four main types of industrial system are summarized in Table 8.3. Unlike the other types, industrial districts imply various things about the nature of the internal organization of the firms, such as flexible specialization and relatively flat organization structures. Geographical proximity (Marshallian localization) is also far more important for industrial districts than for any of the others. Like clusters, there are in industrial districts and RSIs both horizontal relationships (for example, shared technologies) and vertical relationships (for example, buying or supplying) between firms. In *filières* there are only vertical relationships between firms. In view of the greater closeness in the relationships among industrial district firms than is the case elsewhere, we can conclude that industrial districts constitute an industrial system somewhere between market and hierarchy. This may or may not be the case in RSIs. In both *filières* and clusters relationships are primarily market relationships, though it should be noted that anywhere where firms co-operate closely with other firms – for example, where a firm over many years obtains a particular component or input from the same supplier – the relationship can become one somewhere between market and hierarchy. Finally, some level of local governance is present in industrial districts and, as we have shown, some level of regional governance is present in RSIs.

In this chapter we have discussed the theoretical, empirical – especially European – and geographical aspects of structure. In the next chapter we turn to the behaviour or conduct of firms which is interdependent with the structure of industries.

Websites

A large number of papers on various aspects and approaches to systems of innovation are available from the DRUID – Danish Research Unit for Industrial Dynamics – website for the summer 2001 DRUID Nelson and Winter Conference: **http://www.druid.dk/conferences/nw/conf-papers.html**

DRUID is also a key source for many of the other issues discussed in this chapter. Searching the website for articles on industrial districts, for example, results in 33 matches, for articles on clusters, 62 matches, and for articles on regional systems of innovation, 47 matches. The site is at **http://www.druid.dk**

Other relevant sites of research organizations include:

Centre for Urban and Regional Development Studies: **http://www.ncl.ac.uk/~ncurds/index.html**

International Centre for Regional Regeneration and Development: **http://www.dur.ac.uk/icrrds/**

Science and Technology Policy Research: **http://www.sussex.ac.uk/spru/**

West Virginia University Regional Research Institute: **http://www.rri.wvu.edu/**

This last is particularly important as the location of *The Web Book of Regional Science*: **http://www.rri.wvu.edu/regscweb.htm**. For the purposes of this chapter, the section of *The Web Book* that is most relevant is that by Bergman and Feser, *Industrial and Regional Clusters: Concepts and Comparative Applications*: **http://www.rri.wvu.edu/WebBook/Bergman-Feser/contents.htm**

Many of the main writers referenced in this chapter have their own home pages, where their recent work is at least referenced and, in some cases, available for downloading. See, for example, on Charles Edquist, **www.innovation.lth.se/charles.edquist/**, and on Charles Sabel (for his work on industrial districts), **http://www2.law.columbia.edu/sabel/**

For detailed information on the work of Philip Cooke, past and present, go to the Centre for Advanced Studies in the Social Sciences at **http://www.cf.ac.uk/cass/**; on Michael Porter, go to **http://www.isc.hbs.edu/**, which is the homepage of the Institute of Strategy and Competitiveness that he set up at Harvard.

Questions

8.1 Marshall developed his approach to localization in the nineteenth century. Is it still relevant?

8.2 What are the relationships between agglomeration economies, networks, industrial districts and clusters?

8.3 Can a *filiére* also be a cluster?

8.4 Provide an example from any two European countries of each of the following: industrial district, cluster and RSI.

8.5 Discuss the argument that none of the forms of spatial concentration described in this chapter is useful for the study of very small countries.

Notes

1   Porter (1990) is among the exceptions; Porter, however, although with a training in formal economics, moved into the management discipline in the 1980s. Note, too, that while economists have, in general, ignored locational issues, economic geographers have not. See, among many examples, Estall and Buchanan (1973) and Dicken and Lloyd (1990).

2   See chapter X of Marshall's (1898) book, 'Industrial organization continued: the concentration of specialized industries in particular localities'.

3   Krugman (1993, ch. 2), basing his discussion on Marshall, identifies three sources of industry localization – labour market pooling, intermediate inputs and technological spillover – equivalent, respectively, to Marshall's local market for special skills, subsidiary trades and hereditary skill. Our description of the factors determining localization is based partly on Marshall (1898, pp. 347–52) and partly on Krugman (1993, pp. 36–63). Quotes from and references to Marshall and Krugman in this section are from these sources.

4   Porter's (1990, p. 71) discussion of the importance of demand conditions in a country to the success of that country's industries is similar to, though a modern elaboration of, Marshall's.

5   Aspects of two parts of Porter's 'diamond' – factor conditions and firm's strategy, structure and rivalry – can be seen as related to this element of Marshall's theory of localization. See Section 8.5.

6   Krugman, too, considers this factor to be of importance. In a discussion about core and periphery in Europe, he writes that 'northwestern Europe is relatively rich for reasons that have to do more with culture than with geography'.

7   Note that Marshall's point, under 'Physical conditions' above, that an industry that requires raw materials that are expensive to transport, will tend to locate near the source of those raw materials, is not necessarily contradicted by this.

8   Even where there is not labour mobility, the decision of workers as to whether to obtain the skills required by the industry (invest in industry-specific human capital) has the same effect.

9   It may not be coincidental that the process of establishing the Ford plant in Dagenham took place at the height of the Depression (or trough in the cycle), culminating in the opening of the plant in 1931.

10 More precisely, the reduction in unit costs of production arising from production in that place is the agglomeration economies.

11 Among attempts to measure and explain core–periphery patterns in Europe, see Jacobson and Mack (1994). Krugman (1993), too, accepts that the 'center–periphery pattern is there: that is, the poorer regions of Europe are in general also relatively distant from markets'.

12 Neither the large-firm, industrialized north of Italy, nor the relatively less industrialized, more rural Mezzogiorno of the south.

13 Note that there are replies to Amin and Robins's attack on industrial district theory by the main proponents thereof, Sabel, Piore and Storper, in the same publication – see 'Three responses to Ash Amin and Kevin Robins' in Pyke *et al.* (1990).

14 Not all agree that industrial districts are Marshallian. Harrison (1992) argues that modern industrial district theory implies more than Marshallian (neoclassical) industrial districts, in particular 'interde-

pendence of firms, flexible firm boundaries, co-operative competition and the importance of trust in reproducing sustained collaboration'. Robertson and Langlois (1994) also differentiate between Marshallian and Third Italian industrial districts: 'As applied to the Third Italy, the term indicates a higher degree of cooperative coordination than would be present in a Marshallian industrial district.' For a discussion of the differences between the Marshallian cotton textile industrial districts in Lancashire in the late nineteenth century and the Emilian industrial districts of post-1960s Italy, see Jacobson et al. (2002).

15   This example of an industrial district draws directly from Jacobson and Mottiar (1999).

16   'Social capital consists of the norms and networks that define groups and influence actions of people within groups. A degree of trust, an expectation of reciprocity, and exchange of information are expected to prevail in relations among members within a group if that group is to constitute social capital' (Castle, 2003).

17   This is our loose translation from Montfort's French.

18   See, for example, the article by de Bandt (1983), under the title 'Apropos de la reconquête du marché intérieur'.

19   For a related discussion on the double process of spatial and industrial integration, see Andréosso and Jacobson (1991).

20   Note that clustering is not new. It is, according to Storper and Walker (1989, p. 141), rediscovered once a generation.

21   A second edition of Porter's book was published in 1998 (Porter, 1998a), in which year he also published a new article on clusters (Porter, 1998b).

22   There is only one mention of industrial districts in the 855-page book, and that is in a footnote (p. 790, fn 20).

23   For a recent review of the literature, see Jacobson and McGrath (2004, appendix D).

24   This paragraph draws on Porter (1990, pp. 287–8) and any quotes are from that source.

25   This paragraph is based on Porter (1990, p. 71). These four factors are the headings under which the successful clusters of any economy can be explained.

26   This point is very similar to that made, and described by Amin and Robins (1990) and Amin and Thrift (1992), concerning the interrelationship between the local and the global.

27   Porter's own emphasis.

28   This is reminiscent of Dunning's criticisms, discussed above. Note, however, that some consider Porter to have reconsidered the question of whether foreign-owned firms can be part of a cluster (see, for example, Cooke, 2001).

29   See also our discussion of Whittam and Danson (2001) in Chapter 2.

30   See, for example, Scott (1998) who argues that the power of the state has declined relative to both subnational regions and supranational organizations, and compare with Gilpin (2000) who argues that nation states are still the dominant powers in the world economy.

CHAPTER 9

Pricing behaviour of firms

9.1 Learning objectives

The main objectives of this chapter are:

- To review the neoclassical price theory
- To explain the various pricing strategies such as price leadership, price discrimination, limit price, collusive pricing and predatory pricing
- To delve into pricing and competition law in Europe, and
- To provide examples of recent EU cases of pricing strategies in non-competitive markets

9.2 Introduction

Among the objectives of the establishment of the single European market (SEM), is to improve the performance of EU firms, such that they sustain, reinforce, gain or regain a competitive advantage on the international market. As was shown in Chapter 2, a satisfactory level of performance entails, in pure microeconomic terms, determining the most efficient production process, avoiding waste of resources, and responding appropriately and rapidly to new qualitative and quantitative needs of consumers. At the macroeconomic level, good performance of firms can be appraised through their contribution to the long-run growth of GDP per capita, and through their participation in the maintenance of high levels of employment. It should be emphasized that the objective of profit maximization under competitive equilibrium is not often achievable, and the various second bests, towards which competition policy strives, are not always compatible with such goals as the maintenance of high levels of employment.

To attain these levels of performance, a variety of conducts, behaviours or strategies can be selected by the firm. Conduct, narrowly defined, refers to *pricing* and/or the setting of *quantity* by the seller to *maximize profits* in a specific market. More broadly, conduct may include product differentiation and advertising strategies, inter-firm mergers, acquisitions and alliances (MAAs), research and development (R&D), legal tactics, and pricing strategies such as predatory pricing and price discrimination. These different conducts are not mutually exclusive. The promotion of newly created products through high advertising expenditures, for example, can go hand in hand with a strategy of price discrimination, and its success can at the same time be partly attributable to R&D.

The conduct of a firm in a perfectly competitive framework is restricted to a minimum. The only actions the firm can undertake are, in the short run, to respond to market price by producing a quantity that maximizes profit and, in the long run, if it is making losses, to leave the industry.[1] In such a market structure, advertising, action to discourage entry of new firms, and reacting to the activities of rivals, are all precluded by definition. In neoclassical theory, firms' conduct depends on the market structure in which they are defined as operating. This is the basis of the structuralist view, according to which market structure determines conduct. As was shown in Chapter 2, revisions of this view have indicated that a number of different directions of causation are possible in practice.

The specific strategies adopted by EU firms are also, at least in part, influenced by EU-specific institutions and developments. The level of international economic integration and expectations of changes in this level can, for example, constitute an incentive for firms to merge with other firms in order to operate more effectively in the larger market. In particular, among the factors in the late 1980s wave of MAAs in Europe – and between European and US, and European and Japanese firms – were the proposals for the completion of the single European market by 1992.

With these observations in mind, the present chapter will examine the various pricing strategies followed by the firms situated in an increasingly integrated region: the EU. Non-price strategies are dealt with in Chapter 10.

9.3 Pricing: a review of neoclassical price theory

Price is the amount that must be paid in exchange for a commodity. The exact amount paid depends on the structure of the market. We turn first to a brief reminder of the two limit cases in neoclassical theory: perfect competition and monopoly.

A *perfectly competitive market* is one characterized by the absence of rivalry between firms, of market barriers, and of product differentiation. Buyers and sellers are so numerous that each individual firm is a 'price taker' (hence the flat, or infinitely elastic, demand curve), and no monopsonic power can affect the working of the market. The individual firm adjusts its sales volume to the profit-maximizing level, where marginal cost (MC), marginal revenue (MR) and market price (p) are all equal, and because of freedom of entry and exit, this will also be at the minimum average cost (AC), ensuring that no firm earns above the level of profit just sufficient to keep it in the industry (see Fig. 5.3 in Chapter 5, page 105).

Monopoly is a market structure characterized by a unique seller, no close substitutes for the product, and high entry barriers. The firm (which is also the industry) demand curve is now downward sloping. By maximizing its profit, the monopolist will choose the price–output combination[2] such that MC is equal to MR (see Fig. 5.5 on page 111). At that point, p will exceed both MC and AC. In the long run, the monopoly firm will earn supernormal profits, represented by the area p_1AC_1BE.

With both perfect competition and monopoly, once we assume that the firms are profit maximizers, and that they have the required information on supply and demand, there is little remaining choice over price. Firms will produce the quantity at which MR = MC, and the price will follow from the market. Alternatively we could argue that firms set the price at which MR = MC and the quantity follows from the market. The point remains: it is MR = MC that dictates price, either directly or via the demand curve. These simple neoclassical models preclude strategic pricing.

9.4 Pricing as strategy

The existence of an oligopoly, or of a high level of concentration with the emergence of a *dominant firm*, gives rise to different pricing practices, such as price leadership, price discrimination, limit pricing, collusion and predatory pricing.[3] In the following sections we discuss first the theoretical aspects of pricing, then the legal aspects.

9.4.1 Price leadership

Price leadership refers to the process by which all price changes in a market emanate from a firm recognized by other firms as the leader. The other firms follow the leader's initiatives. The notion of price leadership normally refers to two different situations: price leadership through a dominant firm, and barometric price leadership.

Dominant firm price leadership

This occurs in an industry characterized by the co-existence of a single large firm and a number of fringe firms, each of which supplies only a minor share of total output. One model, also known as the *suicidal dominant firm* model, assumes first that, below a certain price, the fringe firms produce less than the total quantity demanded, and second, that the dominant firm accepts as the demand for its products what is left of the market after the fringe firms have supplied the quantity they are willing to supply at each price. The dominant firm sets price in response to quantity, the fringe firms set their quantity in response to price. This is shown in Fig. 9.1. The market demand is DD. At price p_1, the fringe firms would altogether produce the entire demand, so there is nothing left for the dominant firm. At price p_2, the fringe firms could not make a profit, so they would not produce at all; the entire demand would be supplied by the dominant firm. At p_1 the demand facing the dominant firm is zero, and at p_2 and below, the demand facing the dominant firm is the entire market. Assuming, as we have done, linear functions, the dominant firm's demand curve is p_1D_1D. At any price, the quantity indicated by p_1D_1 will be the quantity supplied by the dominant firm, and the quantity indicated by the horizontal distance between p_1D_1 and DD will be the quantity supplied by the fringe firms. The dominant firm will maximize its profits where MR_D, the marginal revenue curve derived from p_1D_1D, intersects MC_D, the dominant firm's marginal cost curve; this occurs at quantity q_1. For a quantity of q_1, the dominant firm can charge a price of p_3. At a price of p_3, the fringe firms will supply the quantity AB, or q_1q_2, and the dominant firm will supply its profit-maximizing quantity of p_3A, or q_1.

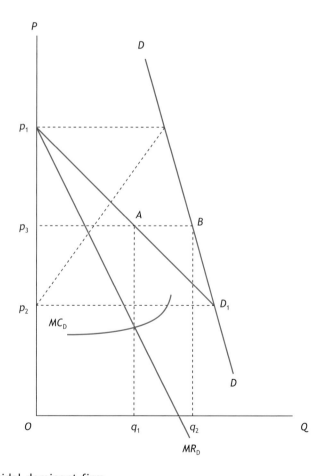

Figure 9.1 Suicidal dominant firm

Why is this called the suicidal dominant firm model? First, if the price fixed by the dominant firm is such that the fringe firms can earn supernormal profits, this will attract additional firms into the industry. Second, once the dominant firm has fixed the price at p_3, this changes the conditions under which the fringe firms operate. Any uncertainty that existed about price for the small firms in the industry has been removed. They are now willing to supply more at p_3 than they were if p_3 was just one of a series of possible prices. As the quantity supplied by fringe firms increases – to greater than $q_1 q_2$ – this reduces the remaining quantity to less than q_1. Acting as a 'quantity taker' and 'price fixer' reduces the dominant firm's market share.[4] It can reduce it – in effect shifting $p_1 D_1$ down and to the left – to such an extent that the dominant firm can no longer produce at a profit.

A dominant firm is unlikely to behave like this in practice. There are other ways in which dominant firms succeed (often illegally) in setting price, and ensuring that their competitors conform to that price or pricing system. This usually involves threats (explicit or implicit) to harm competitors in some way if they do not conform. Thus price leadership in practice often includes other types of anti-competitive behaviour. We discuss the subject below in our examination of the legal aspects of various types of pricing.

Barometric price leadership

In this case a particular firm is accepted by the other firms in the industry as the best judge of when to change prices. The firms themselves are assuming asymmetric information, in that they believe that the leader has knowledge or ability that they do not have. Which firm acts as leader can change over time, as different criteria for judging when to alter price come into play. Thus, during a period of stability in methods of production, a firm with particular expertise in marketing may be seen as price leader, whereas during a period of rapid technological change, a firm more highly regarded as a production innovator will be watched more closely for signals.

If the ultimate price – once the firms have responded to the leader – is close to what it would have been under competitive conditions, then there is generally considered to be nothing anti-competitive about this type of behaviour in an industry.[5] While the leader is likely to be one of the larger firms in the industry, it will not have the power to dominate; there will occasionally be resistance to price initiatives by the leader, possibly leading to a change in leadership; and there will generally be leadership in the raising of prices 'only when rising costs or demand warrant price hikes' (Scherer and Ross, 1990, p. 250). As we shall see, it can be difficult to distinguish between legal and illegal pricing behaviour.

9.4.2 Price discrimination

Price discrimination occurs where identical products are sold in different markets at different prices. Following the work of Pigou (1932), it is customary to distinguish three degrees of price discrimination. First-degree price discrimination occurs when each unit of output is sold at a different price. The firm captures all the consumer surplus in the market by selling each unit of output at its maximum demand price. It is difficult to imagine a situation in which this type of price discrimination could be implemented, and it is generally considered to be of theoretical interest only.

Second-degree price discrimination is simpler in practice since it requires less information about demand. The firm divides output into successive batches and sells each batch for the highest price consumers are willing to pay. Block pricing and quantity discounts represent two forms of second-degree discrimination.[6]

In third-degree discrimination the firm segregates customers into distinct groups characterized by different elasticities of demand, which are explained by exogenous criteria such as location (urban versus rural, residential versus industrial), age, sex or occupation. The diagrammatic representation of third-degree discrimination is based on the neoclassical profit-maximizing rule of $MR = MC$. With a different marginal revenue curve in each of the different markets, an appropriate point must be found at which the price-discriminating firm's marginal cost is equal to all of them ($MC = MR_1 = MR_2 = \ldots = MR_n$, for a market segregated into n parts).[7] This is shown in Fig. 9.2, in which we assume a market divided into two parts.

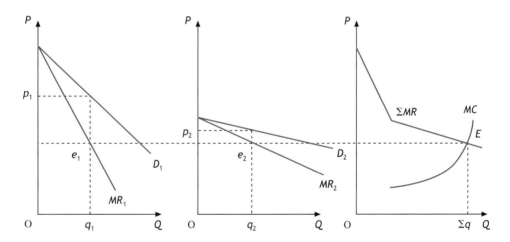

Figure 9.2 Third-degree price discrimination

The profit-maximizing quantity is Σq, which is the quantity at which $MC = \Sigma MR$, ΣMR being the horizontal summation of the two marginal revenue curves (MR_1 and MR_2). From E, the point of intersection of MC and ΣMR, a horizontal line is drawn to the left, intersecting with MR_2 at e_2 and with MR_1 at e_1. The quantity at e_1, q_1, is sold for p_1, and the quantity at e_2, q_2, is sold for p_2. The condition for profit maximization, $MC = MR_1 = MR_2$ is satisfied.

Pigou's categorization is not accepted by all economists, and there have been a number of definitions of price discrimination. An early definition was given by Robinson (1933), according to whom price discrimination is 'the act of selling the same article, produced under a single control, at different prices to different buyers'. This definition is restrictive in the sense that price discrimination can also exist where identical products are sold to the same buyer at varying prices over time, and, as Stigler (1966) points out, where non-identical, but similar, goods are sold at prices which are in different ratios to their marginal costs.

Let us take, for example, the case of a medical service. Robinson's definition applies in the sense that two buyers, one in desperate need of the service and the other considering it worth while but not essential, would be willing to pay different prices for the service. For each patient there is a different demand curve (and marginal revenue curve). The price-discriminating doctor would set her marginal cost equal to marginal revenue, for *each* patient, thus charging each a different price.

If the second patient becomes ill and also now sees the service, say a check of his blood pressure, as essential, he would also now be willing to pay a higher price. The price-discriminating doctor will charge him more now that he needs the service more (his demand for it is less elastic).

An alternative to the ordinary taking of blood pressure might be a full check of a patient's cardiovascular condition. If the demands for these two services are different enough, then the price-discriminating doctor will charge prices such that:

$$\frac{p_1}{MC_1} \neq \frac{p_2}{MC_2}$$

where p_1 and MC_1 are the price and marginal cost respectively of the blood pressure service, and p_2 and MC_2 are the price and marginal cost respectively of the full cardiovascular check-up. As Stigler (1966, p. 209) points out, this definition has the merit of separating the price-discriminator's behaviour into two parts: first, the restriction of output such that price is greater than marginal cost; and second, the misallocation of goods or services among buyers, 'which is zero if prices are *proportional* to marginal costs'.

It is worth noting that where prices for the same good differ, this does not necessarily imply price discrimination, and where the price is identical this does not necessarily imply an absence of price discrimination. An example of identical goods with different but non-discriminatory prices is a bulk buyer obtaining a large quantity of a good at a lower unit cost than a small-scale consumer. The pricing would not be discriminatory if there are lower administrative, transport and other handling costs in the case of the bulk buyer. An example of identical but discriminatory prices is where a college charges the same tuition fees for a large class taught by a junior lecturer, and a small class taught by an experienced (and expensive) professor.[8]

Before a firm can successfully practise price discrimination, three conditions must be satisfied. First, the discriminator must exercise some monopoly power. Without a significant degree of monopoly power in at least one of the markets into which the discriminator is selling, attempts to extract supernormal profits in any of the markets will result in competitors undercutting its prices. Second, it must be able to segregate the customers into different subgroups with different price elasticities of demand. With identical demands in two markets, profit-maximizing behaviour on the part of the firm will result in identical prices in the two markets. Third, the cost of segregating the markets must be less than the gains derived from price discrimination. If the firm can only effectively segregate the markets at very high cost it may not be worth while doing so. Note that the effective segregation of markets implies the elimination of the possibility of arbitrage (the resale of the product by low-price customers to high-price customers).[9]

9.4.3 The limit price

The limit price is the price set by a dominant firm at a level above costs, but not so high that it encourages new entrants (see Fig. 9.3). It is set, in other words, at a low enough level to block entry. The dominant firm is concerned with determining how far above costs price can be held without inducing entry.

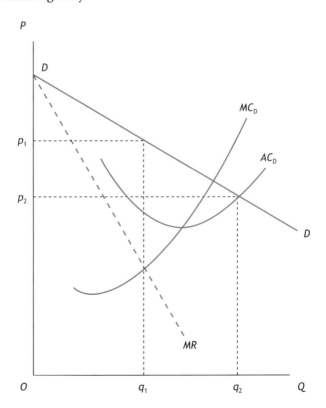

Figure 9.3 Limit pricing

Rather than setting the price at the profit-maximizing level, p_1, where MC_D, the dominant firm's marginal cost, is equal to MR, the dominant firm will set price at some point below p_1. A small, fringe firm would be a price taker, able to enter the market without influencing price. If part of its AC curve is below p_1, then it could profitably enter the market. Note that if fringe firms do enter, then DD is no longer the demand curve facing the dominant firm. Some of the market will have been taken by the fringe firms and the demand now facing the dominant firm will be to the left and below DD. If the dominant firm's strategy is simply to set price as above, and then produce whatever quantity is left over after the fringe firms have entered, then it might find itself unable to continue to operate profitably in this market.[10]

To prevent the entry of fringe competitors, the dominant firm must identify the minimum average cost of the typical fringe firm. This will be the limit price. As long as the limit price is between p_1 and p_2 then, by setting a price just below the limit price, the dominant firm will block the entry of the fringe competitors. It will pay fringe firms to produce any quantity for which their average costs are below price; there will be no such quantity if price is below their minimum average cost. If the limit price is below p_2, then the dominant firm cannot use the limit pricing strategy. Any price below p_2 will result, prior to a shift in demand arising from the entry of the fringe firms, in a loss to the dominant firm, because for any quantity greater than q_2 price is less than AC_D.[11]

If fringe firms do enter, and the dominant firm now faces a demand curve below and to the left of DD, then this new demand curve will cut AC_D to the left of q_2, and possibly below p_2. However, in terms of pricing strategy to prevent entry, the option of setting a price below p_2 is not available to the dominant firm. Either, as shown above, the dominant firm will make losses or, if it restricts quantity to less than q_2, there will be a surplus of demand over supply and market price will be forced up. The limit pricing strategy will thus involve estimating the typical potential entrant's minimum AC and, on condition that it is between p_1 and p_2, setting a price just below that minimum AC.

In practice, the dominant firm may not be able to find out the minimum AC of the potential competitive fringe firms without trial and error. At p_1, fringe firms may begin to enter; the dominant firm will reduce price. Fringe firms may still continue to enter. Once the dominant firm is no longer alone in the market, the strategy it adopts to drive competitors out is called *predation*.[12]

What is the appropriate strategy if a dominant firm wishes to deter the entry of large firms? According to the Sylos-Labini (1962) argument, dominant firms are more likely to use a quantity-based strategy to deter entry where that entry is of relatively large firms. If the potential entrants are small, then no single firm will have a significant impact on quantity, and a quantity-based strategy will therefore not be effective. The higher the minimum efficient scale relative to the total market, the more easily will the incumbent firm prevent the entry of newcomers. By continuing to produce the total market quantity (q_1 at p_1 in Fig. 9.3), the dominant firm will directly discourage entry, and if, as might reasonably be assumed, there are cost rigidities, the dominant firm will in any case wish to produce the full quantity because any less will result in underutilization of capacity.

9.4.4 Collusive pricing

Collusive pricing is illegal in most countries. It consists of agreement among a group of firms to charge the same or similar prices for the same or similar products. Agreements for which documentary evidence can be found – which can occur only if the agreement is explicit – are easier to prosecute than cases in which the collusion must be inferred.

We have already presented, in Chapter 6 (Fig. 6.4, page 133), a diagrammatic model of collusive pricing as an example of oligopolistic behaviour. This was an explicit agreement to set price as though the firms were a monopoly. Arguably, price leadership also involves collusion, either explicit or tacit, in that other firms in the industry allow the leader to set price, and then follow (or collude), rather than set different prices. It has long been known that price leadership can be 'in lieu of overt collusion'[13] and it is often adopted in order to avoid (or reduce the likelihood of) prosecution.

The main reason for colluding is to increase profits by avoiding competition but, at least in the short term, there may be even more profit for the individual firm if it cheats, either by charging a higher price and selling the same quantity, or charging the same price and selling a higher quantity than that agreed by the cartel. A collusive duopoly in which the likely outcome is that both firms cheat on the agreement to collude would have the payoff matrix shown in Fig. 9.4. This shows collusive duopoly as a (symmetric) prisoner's dilemma with the Nash equilibrium where both firms cheat, if:

$$N_c < C_c < N_n < C_n$$

		Firm B: Cheat	Firm B: Not cheat
Firm A	Cheat	(C_c, C_c)	(C_n, N_c)
	Not cheat	(N_c, C_n)	(N_n, N_n)

Figure 9.4 Payoff matrix of a collusive duopoly

where N_c is the payoff if the firm does not cheat and its competitor cheats, C_c is the payoff if the firm cheats and its competitor also cheats, and so on. The Pareto optimal position for the two firms is where they both do not cheat (N_n, N_n), but because N_c is the worst possible outcome for either firm, they will both avoid the strategy that contains that possibility and cheat (C_c, C_c).

A wide range of factors can increase or reduce the possibility of stable collusion. How stringently law against collusion is implemented is a major factor. Even before collusion is considered, however, the parties to the agreement must believe that it is capable of succeeding. Each firm must believe that the others can and will stick to the agreement, and that they will be able to be seen to be sticking to the agreement. Any factors that make it difficult for firms to adhere to the conditions of the agreement, or difficult to know whether others (or which of the others) have broken the agreement, will reduce the likelihood of collusion. A product subject to highly volatile demand, for example, will be unlikely to be produced by a collusive oligopoly; prices and quantities agreed in conditions of high demand are unlikely to be maintained in a slump.

9.4.5 Predation

This normally involves the use or the threat of use by the dominant firm – or the firm attempting to become dominant – of one of the following variables: price, quantity supplied, quality. In particular, predatory pricing is a strategy that calls for reductions of price to below the short-term profit-maximizing position, so that other firms are driven out of the market or weakened to the point of being taken over by the dominant firm. It is sometimes referred to as a 'pricing below-cost' strategy. Based on Areeda and Turner's (1975) influential contribution to the debate on predation, Fig. 9.5 defines predatory pricing as any price below average variable cost (AVC).[14] At any price between p_1 and p_2 the firm is covering its short-run variable costs. It can remain in business in the short run since although there will be a loss on each unit, the excess of price over average variable cost will partly offset average fixed cost.[15] At any price below p_2, the firm may be engaged in predatory pricing.

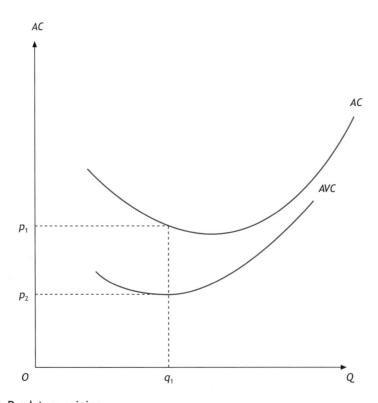

Figure 9.5 Predatory pricing

Two separate, though related, debates in relation to predation deserve attention. The first is theoretical, based around the Chicago School argument that, in the *absence of barriers to entry*, and under *conditions of perfect information*, predation cannot occur.[16] The second is practical, empirical and legal, and rests on the need for competition law to distinguish between illegal predation and legitimate business practice aimed at gaining competitive advantage. This second debate is discussed in Sections 9.4 and 9.5, under the law in relation to dominant position and predatory pricing in Europe.

In essence, the Chicago School argument is anti-interventionist: predation is unlikely, and therefore policy to prevent it is unnecessary. Let us assume that a firm incurs losses in the short run, with the expectation of driving out or taking over its competitors so that in the long run it can increase price and derive supernormal profits. To make this worth while, the long-run profits will have to more than make up for the short-term losses. However, in the absence of barriers to entry, there is nothing to stop new firms from continuing to enter, even after the first competitors have been eliminated. So the dominant, or would-be dominant, firm will have to incur losses in the long run, as well.

Perfect information has a similar effect to the absence of entry barriers, because if the dominant firm's decision makers know that the firm will be able to improve its long-run position by predation, then so will the other firms and/or consumers. For example, consumers, aware of the potential in the predatory activity of the dominant firm to monopolize the market, may support the competition and prevent monopolization.

The counter-arguments to the Chicago School's objection to predation in theory aim primarily at the improbability of the School's assumptions. The first is similar to that against contestable market theory (see Chapter 2), namely that entry is rarely completely free. If barriers exist, then the dominant firm will be able to raise prices after eliminating the competition. The extent to which supernormal profits can be extracted will be directly related to the height of the barriers. As long as the barriers are imperfect, however, it may be that predation is unprofitable. It will depend on the level and duration of short-term losses, the discount rate, and the subsequent level and duration of supernormal profits, as well as the height of the barriers to entry. The basic point is that if there are entry barriers, predation as a rational strategy cannot be ruled out.

If information is imperfect, then this, too, means that predation as a rational strategy cannot be ruled out. Information is, moreover, likely to be asymmetric between the firms in an industry and potential providers of capital. This is exacerbated when the firms in question are under threat to a dominant firm's predatory strategy. Their self-interest will make it difficult for the capital market to trust the information they provide, but there will be transaction costs in obtaining the information independently. As Martin (1994, p. 464) puts it: 'The result is that while a target might be able to acquire additional funds, it can do so only at a cost of capital greater than that available to the predator firm. This cost differential will make predation a feasible strategy.'

We have shown that, under certain circumstances, predation is rational. Even if it is not, an aggressive firm can drive out the opposition by behaving irrationally.[17] Aggressive price reductions might convince competitors that the aggressor will 'stop at nothing' to eliminate opposition. Rather than suffering the consequences of a struggle in which, although the aggressor will lose, so will the competitor, the competitor may simply leave the market. The aggressor becomes a monopoly supplier without the loss and its apparent irrationality turns out to have been rational.

This kind of argument about strategy suggests the usefulness of a game theoretic approach to the problem. Selten (1978) introduced what has become known as the 'chain store paradox' to examine in game theoretic terms a situation in which a firm in a number of markets faces possible entrants in each of them.[18] He assumed that the firm faced the entrants, one after the other, for example first in Market 1, next in Market 2, and so on up to Market N. So, there is a firm with N branches, facing other firm(s) considering entry into each of its N markets, in turn.

What we have is a game with up to N moves. The first move might have a payoff matrix as shown in Fig. 9.6. Prior to the entry of competition, the firm was making a profit of €50,000 in Market 1. Following entry it has a choice between price cutting to resist the entrant (in which case both will make losses of €5000), and co-operating (in which case both will make profits of €20,000). Faced with these payoffs, and ignoring for a moment the other N − 1 markets, the entrant will enter, and the incumbent will co-operate (and both will make profits of €20,000). This is the Nash equilibrium.

		Entrant	
		Stay out	Enter
	Resist	-- --	(−5, −5)
Incumbent	Co-operate	-- --	(20, 20)
	Stay in	(50, 0)	-- --

Figure 9.6 Chain store paradox

Adopting what is called a repeated game approach,[19] Selten (1978) showed that this result would hold for each of the N moves. Assuming the firms are in the last (or Nth) market, if the payoff matrix is similar to that in Fig. 9.6, then the competitor will enter and the incumbent will co-operate. The alternative, aggressive pricing strategy will result only in a loss to the incumbent, with no possibility of later gain. If, instead of the Nth market, we assume that the firms are in the $(N-1)$th market, the incumbent might consider the aggressive strategy as a means of frightening the entrant away from the Nth market. The incumbent and the entrant would both lose €5000 in the $(N-1)$th market and, if the entrant does in fact take the warning and refrain from entering the Nth market, then the incumbent will have a payoff of €50,000 in the Nth market. The incumbent's total payoff for the Nth and the $(N-1)$th markets will be €45,000. This is shown in Table 9.1.

Table 9.1 Incumbent's payoffs from the last two markets

Market	Strategy	Payoff	Total
Nth	Monopoly	50	
$(N-1)$th	Resist	−5	45
Nth	Resist	−5	
$(N-1)$th	Resist	−5	−10
Nth	Co-operate	20	
$(N-1)$th	Resist	−5	15
Nth	Co-operate	20	
$(N-1)$th	Co-operate	20	40

If the entrant does not take the warning (indeed, if the entrant realizes that he should not take the warning), then the incumbent will again be faced by the entrant in the Nth market. With no possibility of recouping losses (the Nth being the last market), the incumbent will co-operate.

Moreover, if he co-operates in the Nth market, then he will surely co-operate in the $(N-1)$th market. Choosing the aggressive strategy in the $(N-1)$th market and the co-operative strategy in the Nth market will give him a total payoff of only 15, instead of 40 by co-operating in both. Similarly, beginning in the $(N-2)$th (or any other, back to the first market), we can show that if it is likely that the entrant would not 'take the warning', then the rational incumbent will choose the co-operative strategy.

The rational (and Nash equilibrium) solution, argued in this way, is for the incumbent to co-operate in all N markets. Selten called this a paradox because, he argued, in reality the incumbent firm would be much more likely to adopt an aggressive strategy from the beginning, in Market 1.

One resolution of the paradox is that, as we argued above, a dominant firm might act apparently irrationally, adopting a 'stop at nothing' approach to eliminating competition. This, in effect, uses a different paradox to explain the behaviour of Selten's chain store. It was described by Schelling (1960, p. 22) as follows: 'that the power to constrain one's adversary depends on the power to constrain oneself irrevocably'. The more convinced the entrant is that the incumbent means to resist in all N markets if necessary, the more likely the entrant is to withdraw rather than face losses (unless the entrant, too, adopts a similarly aggressive and irrational approach, in which case they both turn out to have been behaving irrationally). If the incumbent manages to convince the entrant that no matter what the entrant does, the incumbent will not back off, then the entrant will withdraw, and they will both have behaved rationally. This resolution of the paradox also results from imperfect information where the entrant is uncertain about the incumbent's payoffs (Kreps and Wilson, 1982; see also Milgrom and Roberts, 1982). If the entrant believes that the incumbent's payoffs are such that the incumbent is more likely to resist repeatedly following resistance in an early game/market, then the entrant will withdraw. If the entrant believes that the incumbent is bluffing, but that the incumbent will behave rationally in the end, then the entrant will continue to compete. In general, where there are two firms competing in a single product market in a number of different locations, the fewer the locations that are left following earlier struggles between the firms, the less likely they are to adopt aggressive strategies.

9.5 Pricing and competition law in Europe

The law in Europe broadly aims to prevent firms from using strategies to reduce competition, except where these strategies improve the production or distribution of goods, or lead to technical progress. European competition law is closer to the German approach than to that of the UK (Pearson, 1994, p. 327), though in some respects, as we will show, American law is the precedent followed by Europe. All collusive agreements or practices are covered by Article 81 (formerly 85), and situations in which a firm or firms achieve a dominant position are covered by Article 82 of the Treaty (formerly 86). (Both these Articles are discussed further in Chapter 16.)

9.5.1 Collusion

In general, collusion is prohibited by competition law in Europe. There have been a large number of cases of collusive oligopoly, successfully pursued by the Commission under Article 81. Here we discuss two such cases.

The plastics cartel

'The plastics cartel was possibly one of the most spectacular illicit cartels to have been blown open by the Commission . . .' (Welford and Prescott, 1994, p. 92).[20] This case involved a group of 23 large companies accounting for a very high proportion of the total European supply of PVC. There had been a substantial expansion of the industry immediately prior to the oil crisis in 1973; then, costs had increased and there was a downturn in demand. The firms responded by secretly agreeing quotas for each firm, and by fixing prices across Europe which were sufficiently harmonized to discourage buyers from switching suppliers. Despite this, many firms in the industry continued to make losses, and the best of them (such as BASF of Germany) experienced stagnation in profits. Some firms contravened the quota and price agreements, but frequent meetings kept this to a minimum.

The Commission in turn responded by monitoring the industry closely, and imposing a series of fines, totalling ECU 120 million for the period 1984 to 1987. Finally, following raids in January 1987 by the Commission on the firms involved in the cartel, there has apparently been an end to collusion, overcapacity has been corrected by lay-offs, plant closures and general rationalization. There has also been an upturn in demand and an improvement in the industry's profitability. Arguably the collusion achieved stability for the industry during a period of slack demand, at the cost of the fines levied by the Commission.

Italian flat glass cartel

In 1989 the Commission concluded an investigation of the Italian flat glass industry, finding that the firms in the industry had practised parallel pricing. The firms had offered the defence that while their prices were identical, they had arrived at their decisions independently. It had earlier been established by the European Court of Justice (ECJ), in a number of cases, that circumstantial evidence of concerted practice – such as where firms adopt the same prices – is insufficient. A key principle is that 'each economic operator must determine independently the policy which he intends to adopt on the Common Market'.[21] Where this holds, there is no collusion. In the Italian flat glass industry case, firms admitted that because of their fear of loss of market share, when price rises were being considered 'each producer [took] the precaution of checking whether the others [were] prepared to increase prices as well'.[22]

9.5.2 Restrictive practices other than price collusion

In the words of Article 81, 'all agreements . . . and concerted practices which may affect trade between Member States and which have as their object or effect the prevention, restriction or distortion of competition within the Common Market are prohibited'. This includes more than just collusion. Note that a distinction should be drawn between per se cases and rule of reason cases. The former applies to straightforward instances such as price collusion (which represents by itself a violation of Article 81), whereas the latter refers to cases involving a thorough analysis of the situation. Perhaps among the most contentious agreements are sole agency – or 'exclusive distribution' – agreements, where a manufacturer gives to an agent the exclusive right to distribute the product in a particular country. In the *Consten and Grundig* (1966) case, Grundig provided Consten with the sole right to distribute Grundig products in France and, in addition, the two firms attempted to prevent parallel importing.[23] Pearson's (1994) discussion of this and related cases suggests that it is this last element, the attempt to provide 'absolute territorial protection', that contravenes European competition law. In a 1987 case, *Pronuptia de Paris v. Schillgalis*, where such territorial protection was not a part of the distribution agreement, the Court found that it was not restrictive.[24]

The basic economic point of Article 81 is that competition must be possible. As for collusion, so for other restrictive practices, where the actions of firms prevent fair competition by other firms, then such actions are prohibited.

9.5.3 Exemptions and exceptions

Exemptions and exceptions to the prohibition of restrictive practices are allowed in some cases. Pearson (1994, p. 333) outlines the two ways in which an agreement can obtain exemption from Article 81.[25] First, the firms involved can submit their agreement for individual exemption; second, an agreement can be automatically exempt if it conforms to the criteria issued by the Commission for block exemptions.

Individual exemptions can be permitted where four conditions are satisfied:

1 The benefit from agreement or concerted practice is greater than the losses arising from the restriction of competition. Examples include agreements that achieve standardization and simplification, improvements in distribution, and rapid diffusion of new technology.

2 The consumer receives a fair share of the benefit arising from the restrictive practice.

3 The agreement must contain only indispensable restrictions, that is, only those absolutely necessary to achieve the benefit.

4 Competition must not be eliminated by the agreement. It may restrict competition, if it also provides broad benefits, including consumers in the share of those benefits, and if only indispensable restrictions are included in the agreement. But even if the other criteria are satisfied, an agreement that also eliminates, or almost eliminates, competition, will not be exempt from prohibition under Article 81.

Block exemption has been granted for six types of agreements:

1 *Specialization agreements.* A specialization agreement exsits where, for example, two firms that produce a product that has two components, agree that one will produce all the requirements of the first component for both firms, and the other firm will similarly produce the other component. The exemption applies under the condition that the combined market share of the participating undertakings does not exceed 20 per cent of the relevant market, and that the total turnover of all participating firms does not exceed €1 billion.[26]

2 *Exclusive distribution agreements.* These are subject to a block exemption only where competition is not wholly eliminated,[27] the agreement is bilateral and the two parties are not competing manufacturers.

3 *Exclusive purchasing agreements.* Two firms agree that one (say, A) will buy a good – either for resale or as an input into its production process – only from the other firm (say B). B may sell the good to other firms in the same area. The benefits are that A has continuity

of supply and B is better able to plan production. Such agreements must be bilateral to be subject to block exemption.

4 *Research and development agreements.* A wide range of R&D agreements are subject to block exemption but they must satisfy a number of conditions, including precise ones, such as that all parties to the agreement must have access to the results, and more contentious ones, such as that the results 'must be decisive for the manufacture of the product or application of the process (Pearson, 1994, p. 336).

5 *Motor vehicle distribution and servicing agreements.* There are special regulations for the block exemption of these agreements.

6 *Licence agreements.* The holder of a patent may license another undertaking to make or use the patented invention, exclusively in the licensee's territory. The licensee may be prohibited by the agreement from exploiting the licensed product or process in other territories, though the licensee can, in general, respond to unsolicited orders from other territories.

The prohibition of restrictive practices and the accompanying exemptions constitute two sides to competition policy. On one hand, there is a set of principles according to which both consumers' and producers' interests are met by competition in which there are as many firms as possible, each independently making decisions about price and quantity. On the other hand, efficiency, competitiveness, and even in some cases the interests of consumers, are best achieved by restricting competition. The problems arising from this contrast are discussed in Chapter 16.

9.5.4 The law in relation to dominant position and predatory pricing

The legislatures and judiciaries of various countries have attempted to make laws and pass judgments as to where the activities of firms become illegal monopolization, exceeding legitimate competition. Among the earliest laws and policies of this type were those in the United States, and in particular the Sherman Antitrust Act 1890.[28] Much has been written about what the legislators intended and what the results of the Act were.[29] Much has also been written – by economists and others – about how the courts should interpret the law, and these normative injunctions now apply not only to American law but also, for example, to the laws promulgated in the process of economic integration in Europe.[30]

An important early application of the Sherman Act[31] led to what has become known as the rule of reason doctrine. According to the US Supreme Court, a company or group of companies contravened the law if it (i) acquired a monopoly position and (ii) did so with the intention of excluding rivals from the market. The question was how to tell whether there was such intent in the monopolization activities. This is where the rule of reason came in: 'if the acts unduly restrained competition, going beyond normal business practice, intent could be inferred' (Scherer and Ross, 1990, p. 450).

It is not always clear when a firm's activities go 'beyond normal business practice', however, and, as a result, prominent cases have been decided on split decisions by the judges, in some cases in favour and in some against the dominant firms.[32] According to Scherer and Ross (1990, p. 478), neither the Areeda–Turner marginal cost rule nor its average variable cost surrogate has 'demonstrably superior welfare effects' yet these are the rules 'adopted most often by U.S. courts'. Other rules have been proposed. We outline four such alternatives:

1 Williamson's (1977) quantity rule forbids dominant firms from increasing output for 12 to 18 months following the entry of competitors. This prevents the dominant firm from driving price down by flooding the market.

2 Baumol's (1979) price rule permits the dominant firm to reduce price following the entry of competitors, but if the competitors then leave the market, the rule forbids post-exit real price increases on the part of the dominant firm. This would prevent below-cost pricing in the short run by ensuring that the level to which price is reduced is maintained in the long run.

3 Joskow and Klevorick (1979) propose a two-stage rule. In the initial stage an analysis of market structure and the dominant firm's market power is undertaken to determine whether predatory pricing would be a reasonable strategy.[33] Only if it can be shown that it would be, should the court proceed to the next stage, where the rule is a combination of the Areeda–Turner average cost rule and Baumol's no post-exit price increase rule.

4 Dodgson, Katsoulacos and Pryke (1990) apply a framework similar to that of Joskow and Klevorick – which they call a Modified Rule of Reason – in which the first step is to determine whether, in the given industry, and in particular in the firm under consideration, there are specific factors that render predation a feasible and rational strategy. If there are such factors, an economic model of oligopolistic rivalry is constructed and used to verify that predation did in fact occur.

Ideally this model is based on information about the nature of demand and costs prevailing in the market and is used to estimate the incumbent firm's (or firms') and new entrant's (or entrants') profits in a situation of competitive equilibrium (the so-called *anti-monde* hypothesis). The estimated normal equilibrium profits of an additional firm $\hat{a}_e$ are compared with the actual profit level of the new entrant a_a. If $\hat{a}_e$ is greater than a_a, there is a strong suggestion of predation, assuming that all other possible variables explaining the difference between the two levels of profits (for example, price discrimination, mismanagement) have been discarded.

The first stage for Joskow and Klevorick on the one hand, and Dodgson *et al.* on the other, is very similar, but whereas the former focus on the pricing activity of the dominant firm, the latter focus on the entrant's profit level. Joskow and Klevorick also incorporate, as does Baumol, a temporal dimension, suggesting the need for a time series of prices before predation can be identified.

Of the many alternatives, no single rule has been shown to be economically best in all cases. Martin (1994, p. 484) concludes that each rule has costs and benefits, and that which 'rule one prefers depends on the importance one attaches to different costs and benefits and on one's political preferences concerning the role of antitrust policy'.

In the EU, predatory pricing is condemned under Article 82 of the Treaty of Rome because it is anti-competitive (see Chapter 16). As in the Sherman Act 1890, it is not the existence of a dominant position that contravenes competition law, but abuse of that position. In the *AKZO Chemie v. Commission* case (1985), AKZO appealed against the imposition by the Commission of a fine of ECU 10 million for predatory price cutting. AKZO Chemie BV, a Dutch-based multinational, is the biggest producer in the EU of benzoyl peroxide which is used both as a flour additive and in the production of plastics. ECS, a firm based in the UK, sold into the flour additives market and was attempting to break into the plastics market. The Commission found that, to deter ECS, AKZO implemented a campaign of price cuts – to 'uneconomic levels' – aimed at the smaller firm's main customers in the flour additives market in Britain and Ireland; this AKZO did in spite of injunctions obtained by ECS in the English Courts against such action. AKZO's appeal before the European Court of Justice against the Commission's decision was unsuccessful. The ECJ upheld the decision of the Commission, and clarified its position in stating that a pricing strategy of a dominant firm is predatory pricing:

- if pricing is below average variable cost, or
- if the price is above average variable cost, below average total cost, and is part of a plan of the dominant company to eliminate a competitor.[34]

This ruling is close to those in the United States under the Sherman Act, in particular in its focus on the intent of the dominant firm's strategy. It also follows more recent cases in the United States in the extent to which it relies on the Areeda–Turner rule.

Intent was again an important factor in the *Napier Brown v. British Sugar* case, in which the Commission focused on the intention of the dominant firm's strategy.[35] In this case, the Commission found against British Sugar (BS) with the argument that, 'should British Sugar have maintained this margin in the long term, Napier Brown, or any company equally efficient in repackaging as BS without a self-produced source of industrial sugar, would have been obliged to leave the United Kingdom retail sugar market'.[36] The point was that, as in the *Alcoa* case (1945) in the United States,[37] the verdict went against the dominant firm because of the firm's control over the industry's main ingredient (industrial sugar).[38]

Predation is just one type of abuse of a dominant position. Before such abuse can be considered, the existence of dominance must be shown. What is meant by dominance is market power so great that the firm possessing that power can, if it so wishes, eliminate or control competitors in its industry. This gives rise to problems of definition of market, already discussed in Chapter 5 (Sections 5.3 and 5.4).[39] Once the market has been defined, the Commission must decide whether the firm under consideration has a dominant position. A first indication is market share, dominance being indicated by a share in excess of 40 per cent. A large firm with as little as 20 per cent of the market can, however, have a dominant position if its competitors are highly fragmented. In some cases, dominance can be inferred from behaviour, as in the *Eurofix-Bauco v. Hilti* (1988) case, in which the Commission found that Hilti's behaviour – insisting that purchasers of Hilti nail cartridges use only Hilti nails – was evidence of its 'ability to act independently of, and without due regard to, either competitors or customers'; in other words, it was evidence of Hilti holding a dominant position.

Having defined the market and ascertained that the firm has a dominant position, the next question is whether the actions of the firm constitute abuse of that position. We have shown how predation has been identified in European competition law, but it is just one of many types of abuse of dominant position. In the next section we consider two more: price leadership and price discrimination.

9.5.5 Price leadership and price discrimination

There is a great deal of evidence of price leadership and price discrimination in Europe, both from empirical research published in the industrial economics literature and from cases pursued by the Commission. Among the sectors in which economists have identified price discrimination are retail banking, conveyancing and the automotive industry. Heffernan (1993), analysing competition in British retail banking, suggests that if savers could switch easily between products and, perhaps, banks, they would be better off. There are, however, high information and transaction costs, which contribute to consumer inertia. The result is different groups of consumers with different elasticities of demand for loans (and different elasticities of supply of deposits), enabling the banks to practise price discrimination. In conveyancing, Stephen *et al.* (1993) show that deregulation in England and Wales was responded to differently by different firms, increasing the extent of price discrimination.

The automotive industry has been the subject of particular attention. Kirman and Schueller (1990) show how the segregation of markets through price leadership in the European automotive industry tends to perpetuate itself. Specifying a theoretical model in which they assume, among other things, that all (but one) of the markets are characterized by a Stackelberg equilibrium, the authors reach the following conclusions:

- In markets where the dominant producer has high costs, the prices of all competing products will be higher.
- In markets where the tax rate is high, pre-tax prices will be lower.
- In the market where there is no dominant individual producer, prices will be lowest.

In a comparison of these theoretical results with the empirical evidence, Kirman and Schueller conclude that there is price leadership, usually with the domestic manufacturer the leader in its home market, and that there is price discrimination, there being significant differences in the pre-tax prices of cars in the different European markets.

In his description of pricing behaviour in the European automotive industry, Rhys (1993) suggests four factors that make price discrimination likely. First, there are different levels of sales tax on cars, from as low as 15 per cent in Germany to as high as 197 per cent in Denmark; second, there are price controls in some countries (Belgium); third, because of a combination of product differentiation and consumer preferences manufacturers sell cars with slightly different specifications into the different EU markets; and fourth, the manufacturers and distributors have different discount schemes in different markets. These factors make it difficult for consumers to know whether, and to what extent, the prices paid to the manufacturers vary between markets. It is this ignorance on the part of the consumers (or information asymmetry between sellers and buyers), together with the selective distribution system that the car firms are permitted to adopt, that enables these firms to separate markets. According to Rhys (1993), the selection of distributors in different countries enables 'the car-makers [to] determine who can sell their cars, thereby restricting entry to the new car retail sector. This prevents independent retailers buying cars in a cheap market and selling them in a dear one, undercutting the price in the official network'.[40]

There has been an increasing awareness of price discrimination in the automotive industry, and it has received the attention of the Commission. The Commission is particularly sensitive to geographical price discrimination because this type of price discrimination involves the partitioning by firms of the EU market along geographical boundaries, which contravenes the fundamental principles of European integration and the single market.

In relation to the automotive industry, the Commission has examined the actions of the manufacturers and official distributors (those appointed by the manufacturers) to prevent parallel imports. As between the Continent on the one hand, and Britain and Ireland on the other, discrimination was maintained by such devices as delivery of right-hand drive vehicles only in bulk, refusing warranty services unless the car was bought from the distributor or one of its official dealers, and withdrawing credit and discount facilities from dealers who imported directly. 'Such practices are now illegal, as a result of pressure from the Commission and the verdict of the Court' (de Jong, 1993, p. 408). Price discrimination will, however, probably continue to be practised to some extent in this industry as long as the selective distribution system remains.[41]

The *Chiquita* case (1976) is another example of geographical price discrimination. United Brands, a banana producer, was selling its produce under the brand name Chiquita to distributors/ripeners at different prices in various member states. The lowest prices were charged in Ireland, whereas the highest prices were charged on bananas destined for the West German market. The differences in price could not be explained by transport costs, since it costs more to transport goods to the Irish market than to any other member state. The Commission argued that differences in transport costs, taxes and duties or marketing conditions might justify different levels in price or resale at the retail level. These differences can, however, never justify objectively UBC's different prices to its distributors/ripeners for equivalent transactions at Bremerhaven and Rotterdam, and still less so given that the quantities of bananas sold to each such distributor/ripener are approximately the same.[42]

The judgment could be criticized in that it was inducing United Brands to charge a uniform price higher than that charged in its low-price markets, in order to avoid losses in Germany, leading to detrimental effects for the Irish consumer. The welfare effects of price discrimination are in fact ambiguous, and therefore so are the welfare effects of the removal of price discrimination. This has been shown by Armstrong and Vickers (1993), both for situations in which the dominant firm is a pure monopoly and where the incumbent firm faces competition as a result of regulation to remove the discrimination. If a result of the introduction of uniform pricing is that the previously lower-priced markets are no longer supplied, then it can be shown (see Layson, 1994) that price discrimination is preferable from a welfare point of view. In general, however, unless regulation to prevent price discrimination results in a substantial reduction in output, it will be preferable to price discrimination (Schmalensee, 1981).

Many cases of price discrimination involve other types of anti-competitive behaviour as well. One example of this was brought to light following the Commission's examination of the ice cream market in Ireland. Unilever's Irish ice cream subsidiary, HB, provides freezers to retailers but insists that these hold only HB products. The prices paid for HB products by retailers that accepted this arrangement were the same as the prices paid by retailers that did not agree to the condition (and therefore did not have HB freezers). Other ice cream companies issued a formal complaint to the Commission. The Commission upheld the objection on two grounds. First, 'exclusivity' – the preclusion of non-HB ice creams from HB freezers – and second, 'inclusive pricing' – in effect price discrimination in favour of those retailers who accept the freezers. If both sets of retailers nominally pay the same price for the ice creams but one set also gets free freezers, then those who have to pay for their own freezers are, in effect, paying more for ice creams.

In upholding the objection, the Commission left the door open to HB to respond to the criticisms. It was reported in March 1995 that HB had agreed to alter its distribution system as follows:

- By giving rebates to retailers who do not use HB freezers who sell a reasonable amount of HB products.

- Introducing similar non-discriminatory pricing schemes in all other EU countries during 1995.

- Selling freezers to the retailers who accepted them, at the wholesale price.

- In future, giving retailers the option of taking freezers under hire purchase terms, which would include the condition that exclusivity be limited to the five-year purchase period.

These changes were sufficient, in the view of the Commission, to justify exemption from 'EU rules barring anti-competitive practices'.

Case study Pricing strategies in non-competitive markets[43]

The market for fine arts auctions is a typical example of a non-competitive market, with two major auction houses leading the market: Christie's and Sotherby's. In 2000, the strategies of these two firms were found to be in breach of EU competition rules, for they had been colluding by fixing commission fees and other trading terms such as payment conditions. The two firms had in fact operated within the terms of an anti-competitive cartel agreement between 1993 and early 2000, with the aim of reducing the harsh competition that had developed between them during the previous decades. The Commission's investigation into the case started in 2000, and it collaborated with the US Department of Justice under the 1995 co-operation agreement.[44] This is an interesting case highlighting the global dimension taken by the fight against anti-competitive behaviour by the EU authorities.

Anti-competitive behaviour is found in a large number of markets, sometimes involving a large number of firms. These markets are often defined as narrowly as possible. For example, in the graphite electrodes market, the German SGL Carbon AG, the US firm UCAR International and six other companies were fined by the Commission in 2001 for price fixing and market sharing.[45] Price fixing and other restrictive practices such as allocating sales quotas were also found in the market for vitamins. These anti-competitive practices involved a relatively large group of manufacturers (13 firms). In the case of Yamaha Corporation Japan and of various of its subsidiaries in major EU countries, distinct product markets were proposed for acoustic pianos, home digital pianos, portable keyboards, and so forth. Yamaha's European subsidiaries were found in 2003 to have implemented various agreements and/or concerted practices (such as market partitioning and resale price maintenance) that aimed at restricting competition in different member states.

In 2001, Deutsche Post AG was found by the Commission to have engaged in predatory pricing in the market for business parcel services by granting fidelity rebates. In the same year, the Commission investigated the pricing behaviour of Wanadoo Interactive, a subsidiary of France Telecom in charge of internet access provisions. According to the Commission, this firm was pricing its high-speed internet access via the ADSL technology below cost (variable cost), a clear case of predatory pricing.

As can be seen, anti-competitive behaviour is quite commonplace; it happens in any market and in any country, and it can involve many players.

9.6 Summary

Pricing is, in practice, a complex aspect of an overall strategic approach to marketing products. The resultant price per unit of the product may well, as would be expected from neoclassical theory, involve less profit the more intensive the competition. Most of the chapter has dealt with situations of imperfect competition, reflecting a large proportion of markets in the modern world. In non-competitive markets, firms can use several pricing strategies to ameliorate their performance. We have looked at price leadership and price discrimination as typical pricing strategies in oligopolistic markets. In contrast to these tolerated practices, other pricing strategies such as collusive pricing and predatory pricing are totally condemned by law. Through the study of several EU cases, we have seen how the European Commission deals with these anti-competitive strategies. Price fixing, allocating sales quotas or predatory pricing affect all industries (including services). It is interesting to note how globalization has exerted an influence on European law during the 1990s by leading to the collaboration between the EU Commission and the US Department of Justice in the fight against anti-competitive behaviour in the EU. In the next chapter, we turn to non-price strategies such as advertising and product differentiation.

Websites

The EU Commission's website: **http://europa.eu.int/comm/competition/index_en.html** is an excellent source for further information on the issues discussed in this chapter.

Questions

9.1   What is the difference between dominant firm pricing and barometric pricing?

9.2   What are the different types of price discrimination?

9.3   Referring to specific EU cases, show how collusion distorts competition in Europe.

9.4   Why do firms engage in predatory pricing?

Notes

1   This is from a Cournot-type perspective; a Bertrand-type perspective would be that firms can adjust price until their optimal quantity is sold.

2   The monopoly firm can set either the price or the quantity, but not both, for whichever it sets, the other will depend on the market demand.

3   For a discussion of the behaviour of firms under the conditions of oligopoly, see Chapter 6.

4   Note that in planning to produce q_1 at price p_3, the dominant firm is assuming that there will be no

response on the part of the fringe firms to its action of setting price, i.e. it has a conjectural variation of zero.

5   Lanzillotti (1957) considers competitive price leadership to be most likely.

6   Block pricing entails a decreasing average price with increasing use. Public utilities often use this pricing practice. Note that there is an underlying assumption in this definition of price discrimination that the costs are the same irrespective of whether the sale is in batches or in units. We argue below that if different prices for batch than for single units are a result of different costs, then this is not discriminatory.

7   See the discussion on monopoly in Chapter 5, Section 5.6.3.

8   This example was originally suggested by Stigler (1966, pp. 209–10), but there continues to be a great deal of interest in US colleges as a monopolistic price discriminating cartel. See, for example, Brimelow (1994). Note that, as with many other examples of anti-competitive practices, this one includes more than one: collusion and price discrimination.

9   Services are consumed during the process of delivery and are, therefore, not susceptible to arbitrage. Price discrimination is thus easier to implement in relation to services than goods.

10   That is why this strategy of the dominant firm – to set price on the assumption that no other firms will enter (i.e. zero conjectural variation), and if they do, to respond by keeping price where it is and producing the remaining share of the market – is known as a suicidal dominant firm pricing model.

11   Thus the limit pricing strategy can only be used if the dominant firm can make a profit at prices at which potential entrants would make a loss.

12   Predatory pricing is discussed later in this chapter.

13   Markham (1951) as quoted in Scherer and Ross (1990, p. 249).

14   Actually Areeda and Turner argued that predatory pricing was being practised when price was below marginal cost. However, MC is more difficult to estimate, so they settled for AVC as the value below which predatory pricing could be said to exist.

15   In the short run there are fixed costs; in the long run all costs are variable. The average fixed cost (AFC) is the vertical distance between the AVC and the ATC.

16   See Martin (1994, ch. 16) for a detailed discussion of this debate.

17   See Schelling (1960), who uses the example of a driver at an intersection to illustrate such strategies. The driver makes it clear to oncoming traffic that he cannot see that traffic by turning his head the other way. As long as he either knows, or is willing to take the chance that, oncoming drivers (i) can see his head is turned, and (ii) can stop in time, then he can enter the intersection. Not looking at the oncoming traffic may seem to be irrational, but it can achieve the driver's aim of quickly entering the intersection.

18   Note that if the incumbent remains a monopoly in this example then it is, in fact, a case of deterrence, rather than predation.

19   There are two types of multi-period (or multi-move) versions of single-period (or single-move) games: repeated game, in which the players must choose a strategy for a single-period game, for each game in succession, up to the total number of games (in our example, N games); and super game, which is an infinitely repeated single-period game.

20   The rest of the discussion on this case is from the same source.

21   This quote, and the related discussion, is from Pearson (1994, pp. 328–36).

22   Quoted by Martin (1994, p. 178) from OJ L 33/47, 4 February 1989. The Italian flat glass industry's price fixing is also mentioned in Reekie and Crook (1995, p. 518).

23 This is where, though not being supplied by Grundig in France, another distributor imports Grundig products from another country into France for sale in France.

24 As is mentioned below, exclusive distribution agreements are subject to a block exemption.

25 This discussion draws heavily on this source.

26 See OJCE L 304/3, December 2000.

27 As discussed above, absolute territorial protection – or the prevention of parallel importing – is an example of total elimination of competition, which, if it is part of an exclusive distribution agreement, would render it ineligible for exemption.

28 Note, however, that in Britain and the United States, unlike in continental Europe, 'Under common law, combinations in restraint of trade were illegal' (Chandler, 1990, p. 72). This made it impossible for aggrieved members of cartels to use the courts to obtain retribution, but, until the Sherman Act, no government had the power to prosecute alleged offenders (restrainers of trade). There was, moreover, no comparable law anywhere until the 1940s (Chandler, 1990, p. 73).

29 See, for example, Telser (1987), especially Ch. 2. Chandler is convinced that the Act 'and the values it reflected' were extremely important in explaining the differences between the long-term evolution of firms in the United States on one hand, and Germany and Britain on the other (Chandler, 1990, p. 73).

30 See, for example, the debates in the *Harvard Law Review* and *Yale Law Journal* in the late 1970s, often between economists and lawyers; and, on Europe, Dodgson *et al.* (1990).

31 In which the US Supreme Court in 1911 held that the Standard Oil Company of New Jersey had contravened the law by monopolizing the petroleum refining industry.

32 Standard Oil (1911), against; American Tobacco Company (1911), against; Eastman Kodak (1915), against; US Steel (1915 and 1920), in favour; American Can Company (1916), in favour; Alcoa (1945), against; IBM (case began in 1975, prosecution case dropped in 1982); AT&T (1981), against; *Zenith v. Matsushita* (1986), in favour of Matsushita. For a summary of these cases, see Scherer and Ross (1990, ch. 12).

33 For example, if it is a contestable market (zero sunk costs), then predatory pricing is unlikely. A dominant firm under such circumstances may set a below-cost price to drive one competitor out, but will be unable to follow this with an increase in price to recoup the losses. Relatively free entry will prevent such price increases. However, on the critique of contestable market theory, see Chapter 2.

34 The fine on AKZO was, however, reduced because the law on predatory pricing was not clear at that time.

35 A fine of ECU 3 million was imposed on the vertically integrated firm British Sugar for reducing its margin between the raw material and the final product to an amount that could not cover its own transformation costs.

36 OJCE L 284/41, 1988, pp. 54–5.

37 The crucial issue leading the Court to decide against Alcoa was the firm's control over the main input (aluminium ingots) into the aluminium production process.

38 Note that in this case the UK was identified as the market, because of the high cost of transporting the product. British Sugar would not have been able to control the British market for industrial sugar if the transport costs (second-order barriers to entry) were not high.

39 See also, Pearson (1994, pp. 336–8). The following discussion of dominant position is drawn from Pearson (1994, pp. 338–41).

40 See also Besanko and Perry (1994) who analyse exclusive dealership in a model with product differentiation by manufacturers and geographical differentiation by retailers. There is shown to be an incentive for manufacturers to insist on exclusive dealing because this type of relationship with retailers gener-

ates higher profits for manufacturers. Exclusive dealing also increases prices to consumers, but this may be offset to some extent by the reduction in fixed costs of retailing.

41 Rhys (1993) discusses the conflict between competition policy and industrial policy in relation to the automotive industry, the former aiming to prevent anti-competitive behaviour within the EU on the part of the firms in the industry, and the latter encouraging the development of a European automotive industry competitive with those of Japan and the United States. This may account for the continuation of the selective distribution system which the Commission might otherwise have prohibited.

42 OJCE L 95/1, 1976, p. 15. United Brands was also accused of trying to prevent arbitrage among the distributors/ripeners by not allowing them to transport unripened bananas.

43 All cases reported in this section are taken from the EC *Reports on Competition Policy*, various years, unless otherwise specified.

44 OJ L 95, 27 April 1995, Agreement between the European Communities and the Government of the United States of America regarding the applications of their competition laws (p. 7). For more on this case, see CEC (2003a), and *Competition Policy Newsletter*, DG Competition, Spring.

45 Graphite electrodes are ceramic-moulded columns of graphite used in the production of steel. See CEC (2002c).

CHAPTER 10

Non-price strategies

10.1 Learning objectives

The main objectives of this chapter are:

- To consider the non-price strategies that firms adopt in order to gain competitive advantage
- To identify the main theories and research in relation to each of the non-price strategies
- To show how firms behave in practice by using each of these non-price strategies, and
- To discuss the implications for firms of the European context and in particular of European integration

10.2 Product differentiation and advertising

The way a firm's products are priced is often part of a broader strategy aimed at distinguishing that firm's products from those of its competitors. The non-price parts of the strategy are our concern in this chapter. A list of all such non-price factors would be extensive, including, for example, physical characteristics such as colour, size, quality and packaging, and aspects of the services provided with the product such as delivery time and after-sales service. One type of non-price strategy is to differentiate any of these for products that are in other respects identical. In addition, firms may make an effort to differentiate their product in some more fundamental way. For example, a breakfast cereal manufacturer could develop a new product, say oat flakes, as an alternative to corn flakes. We cover technological change and innovation in the next chapter, but in this context it could be argued that all R&D expenditure on product innovation is an attempt to differentiate products. Even R&D on process innovation can contribute to differentiation by, for example, improving the quality or reliability of the product.[1]

In the perfect competition model, the product is homogeneous; each firm sells a product identical to that sold by the other firms. This identity goes all the way through, from production to sale. There is no incentive for any individual firm to expend special effort in increasing sales, because inherent in the model is the assumption that each firm can sell as much as it wants without such extra effort. Only in imperfectly competitive models can firms rationally implement strategies to increase sales. In both monopolistic competition and oligopoly, for example, a firm often develops strategies to avoid competition, making its product special to more and more consumers, so that its sales increase. These strategies can involve both changes in the product, and advertising to change the public's perception of the product. Other firms then have a choice. They can either make their products as similar as possible to those of the first firm, so that they gain the advantage of the efforts of the first firm to increase sales, or they can implement their own strategies to make their product special to consumers. The former strategy is more likely to lead to price competition. Among the interesting questions in this area of IO theory is, under what circumstances will product differentiation (and advertising) strategies be adopted?

10.2.1 Product differentiation[2]

Product differentiation, according to Bain, 'refers to the extent to which buyers differentiate, distinguish, or have specific preferences among the competing outputs of the various sellers' (1968, p. 223). This is consistent with Chamberlin's (1933) view that much of product differentiation is perceived rather than real. Following a discussion of (i) the differences between real and perceived differentiation, this section examines (ii) horizontal and vertical differentiation, (iii) measures of differentiation, and (iv) product differentiation in the EU.

Real and perceived differentiation

Real differences include those in quality, as expressed in reliability or performance. An example of this is where one make of car is less likely to break down, or is faster than another, even if it is identical in other respects. An example from financial services is where different banks offer different rates of interest on savings accounts. In services associated with the product, real differences include those in delivery time, in after-sales service and in proximity or accessibility of the supplier or distributor to the end customer.[3] Note that if two products or services have real differences, this does not mean that one is better than the other. Dark and milk chocolate are different, but neither is objectively better than the other, for example. (This issue is discussed below under horizontal and vertical differentiation.)

Perceived product differentiation is less easy to specify.[4] Two products may perform in an identical way, and yet some consumers may perceive a difference between them because of the presence of other factors, such as colour, packaging and design. For example, certain characteristics of a product may establish a link in the mind of the consumer between the product itself and some other, well-known, prestigious brand. Marketing theorists have shown that even apparently 'meaningless' differentiation can be used as a brand strategy, producing under certain conditions a separate brand identity which consumers will see as being relevantly and valuably different from competing brands (Carpenter et al, 1994). As Aaker (2003) puts it: 'If a brand fails to develop or maintain differentiation, consumers have no basis for choosing it over others'. Distribution can also be used to generate perceived differences, such as where a manufacturer of a mediocre product attempts to impress the consumer by distributing the product through prestigious retail outlets. This last example emphasizes the analytical problem in distinguishing between real and perceived differences. A 'prestigious retail outlet' may, in fact, be a real difference, because it provides better advice and other services related to the sale of the product.[5] A similar problem arises where the perception of a difference actually changes the performance of the product. In medicine this is called the placebo effect, where, if a patient believes that a pill will remove pain, then in some cases even though there is no painkiller in the pill, it will still have the effect of removing pain.

Horizontal and vertical differentiation

For analytical purposes, product differentiation is usually divided into horizontal and vertical differentiation. Horizontal differentiation is where a product has a number of key characteristics in relation to which consumers' tastes and preferences vary.[6] In the case of dark and milk chocolate there are characteristics such as how bitter and how creamy the chocolate is. Some people prefer more of the former, others prefer more of the latter. The colour, style and design characteristics of men's shoes provide another example. Shoes by different manufacturers, at similar prices, with different mixes of these characteristics, are said to be horizontally differentiated. Within this product range, an increase in the number of products offered will increase the likelihood that any individual consumer will find the pair of shoes that exactly fits his preferences.

Vertical differentiation is based on quality differences in relation to which all consumers agree. In the chocolate example, people who prefer milk to dark chocolate would all agree that a chocolate that has extra cream is better than one that has neither milk or cream. For them, the amount of cream vertically differentiates milk chocolate products. Vertically differentiated shoes would be ranked, in order of quality, in the same way by all buyers of shoes. This might refer, for example, to comfort and durability. If the only differentiation was vertical, then lower-quality products would sell only if they were priced lower than higher-quality products. Some men would be willing to pay more for higher-quality shoes, others would not, but all would agree with the ranking, both of brands of shoes and their associated prices.

The origins of the *theoretical work on horizontal differentiation* lie in Hotelling's (1929) duopoly model in which the firms produced identical goods, and consumers were assumed to be uniformly distributed along a street.[7] The differentiation was, then, in relation to location, with the difference between the firms as a proxy for product differentiation. Hotelling argued that, at equilibrium, both firms would choose the mid point as the location of their sales outlet. This is called the principle of minimum product differentiation. D'Asprement *et al.* (1979), using a slightly different model and correcting a mathematical error in Hotelling's model, came to the opposite conclusion, namely that each firm would choose a location as far away from the other as possible: 'maximum product differentiation'. More recently, Böckem (1994), with a slight adjustment in turn to the d'Asprement *et al.* model, has arrived at an intermediate conclusion: that the two firms may adopt neither minimum nor maximum product differentiation. All three models assume simultaneous choice of locations and Bertrand competition. Böckem's (1994) addition is to generalize the earlier models by allowing consumers the option of not buying the goods of either of the two firms. The result is a trade-off for firms between avoiding price competition and 'bringing the product closer to consumers' locations'. In terms of product differentiation, the more that firms wish to avoid price competition the more they will differentiate their products. The degree of product differentiation, other things being equal, will depend on assumptions about how price is determined.

Addressing similar issues, but using a non-mathematical approach, Soberman (2003) shows why differentiation might be minimized. He suggests that for differentiation to be advantageous to firms, consumers must have 'automatic access to information on the best alternatives'. In reality, in some markets, they do not. If 'a significant fraction of consumers make decisions with limited information about the available alternatives [then] differentiation may not be a profitable strategy'. This is because the cost of differentiating is wasted on those who do not know about it. It follows that the more products there are and the less symmetrical information there is in a market, the less profitable a differentiation strategy will be; where there are few products, and/or high levels of knowledge about the products (as in capital-goods trade fairs), differentiation is likely to be a profitable strategy.

In an interesting elaboration in the context of specialized upstream supply into a product-differentiated downstream market, Pepall and Norman (2001) use both mathematical and intuitive analysis to show the importance of the degree of differentiation in determining profits. They show, for example, 'that the profits of downstream firms increase when their complementary upstream suppliers form a network of alliances, but such alliances increase the profits of the upstream suppliers only if the degree of product differentiation downstream is sufficiently large . . .'. The point is that the greater the differentiation downstream, the less intense is the competition downstream. The less intense is the competition downstream, the greater the profits of the upstream suppliers.

Pepall and Norman's (2001) focus is on different arrangements of market organization. At the extreme, a monopoly producer must also choose between single and multiple-product strategies. Henry Ford famously offered the Model T in any colour, as long as it was black. Increasing competition forced him to change this policy. Peng (2004) models a spatial monopoly with product differentiation. He shows that the quantity of each variety produced is dependent on the consumers' preference for variety, though influenced too by the monopolist's pricing strategy.

Theoretical work on vertical differentiation has focused on the economics of improving the quality of products, and of producing a variety of qualities. Shaked and Sutton (1987), for example, have shown that the nature of product differentiation and the way in which quality is improved are important factors in market structure. Where there is only horizontal differentiation, an increase in market size is likely to attract new entrants, as long as there are no significant barriers to entry. On the other hand, if the main costs of improving products are fixed costs,[8] and if consumer preferences are such that at least some buyers will be willing to pay more than the increase in variable costs for an improvement in the product, then an increase in the size of the market will not – as might otherwise be expected – mean more firms and lower levels of concentration. Firms will compete by incurring higher fixed costs and improving their products; overall there will be higher fixed costs in the industry and improved products, but no increase in the number of firms, and no decline in the level of concentration. The high fixed costs of improvement are not necessarily the cause of high levels of concentration. It is the nature of competition in the industry, and in particular the strategic choices of the firms – to compete via vertical differentiation – that are the main factors in determining both high fixed costs and high levels of concentration.

More generally, the models of vertical differentiation have led to the conclusion that there will be more rather than less differentiation at equilibrium, that is, 'maximum product differentiation'. According to Elliott (2004), this is derived in part from the two assumptions: that people prefer high-quality products to low-quality ones, and that consumers have complete information even in the absence of advertising. She points out a number of examples of clusters of firms producing only high-quality products, such as regions of France known for their gourmet restaurants. Whether same-quality clusters are high or low quality, they are examples of minimum differentiation.

In her model Elliott assumes that consumers are originally ignorant of quality differences and that firms must overcome this ignorance with advertising. This leads to a conclusion different from that of most other models, namely that, at equilibrium, firms will produce high-quality products. 'The best response to a competing firm's choice to produce a high quality brand', she writes, 'is to mirror that quality choice'. Also, if the assumption of a high premium placed on quality is changed, then again there is minimum product differentiation, but at low quality, 'if the premium consumers place on high quality is relatively low, a firm will prefer to copy a low quality product choice of a rival'. Thus, relaxing the 'complete information' assumption leads to minimum product differentiation with only a high-quality product produced; relaxing, in addition, the 'premium on high quality' assumption leads to minimum product differentiation with only a low-quality product produced.

Measures of differentiation

In practice, products are often both horizontally and vertically differentiated. Firms will adopt mixed strategies of quality and other differences, charging higher prices for both. *Measures* of product differentiation do not, therefore, distinguish between horizontal and vertical differentiation. One such measure, already defined in Chapter 5 (Section 5.3), *cross-elasticity of demand* (CED). This measures the responsiveness of the quantity demanded of a product to changes in the price of another product. The greater (smaller) the difference between the products the lower (higher) the value of CED.

Another second measure, introduced in Chapter 5 (Section 5.5) as a measure of concentration, is the *entropy index*. The entropy-based measure of the degree of product differentiation was proposed by Bernhardt and Mackenzie (1968). It is based on the randomness of consumers' choice of retail outlet. At maximum entropy (E = 1), customers always buy certain products from the same store. There is very high differentiation. At minimum entropy (E = 0), customers distribute their purchases of those products evenly among all stores. There is homogeneity.

Thirdly, because of the close link between advertising and product specification/differentiation, the advertising-to-sales ratio can also provide an indication of the degree of differentiation.[9] It is reasonable to expect that the more that is spent by a firm on advertising, the more its product will be differentiated – at least in terms of consumers' perceptions – from the products of the firm's competitors.

A fourth, but more indirect, way of measuring differentiation empirically is through *hedonic prices*. This approach dates back at least to Lancaster (1979). The idea is that consumers demand a product for the variety of characteristics that that product has. A car, for example, has speed, style, comfort, fuel economy, and so forth. The price of a car is related to its characteristics. With data on the prices of cars and the various characteristics that affect their prices, we can calculate the influence each individual characteristic has on price.[10] In theory this means that, when making decisions about new models, a producer can take into consideration the impact of different characteristics on price. On this basis, a desire for variety among consumers will be reflected in product differentiation by producers.

Product differentiation in the EU

What are the implications of product differentiation for European integration, and vice versa? Product differentiation has long been accepted by industrial economists as having a role in the strategies of firms to improve the competitiveness of their products. For many economists writing on international trade, this eventually translated into the fact that product differentiation itself, even in the absence of comparative advantage, could cause trade.[11] However, the theory of comparative advantage, in particular in its modern guise as the Heckscher–Ohlin–Samuelson theory, remained dominant until the 1980s. According to this theory, countries' factor endowments are the main determinants of what goods countries will export or import. The work of Krugman (1980, 1987a) has been important in developing international trade theory beyond these foundations. In his examination of the implications of this work for industrial economics (Krugman, 1989), he shows that economies of scale and product differentiation – and imperfect competition in general – must be added to comparative advantage as factors in determining what goods countries will trade.

Despite this auspicious beginning, it can be argued that we still know 'little about the usefulness of the new trade theories in explaining the patterns of intra-industry trade' (Bernhofen, 2001). On the other hand, at a simple level, empirical evidence for the new theories lay in the growth, among EU member states, of trade in similar products. Comparative advantage theory led economists to expect that international trade within a barrier-free Europe would be increasingly inter-industry, but there was a great deal of evidence of intra-industry trade. Among other factors, product differentiation led to exports and imports of similar goods. From the perspective of firms, there were declines in shares of local markets, and increases in shares of foreign markets; from the perspective of consumers, there was an increase in the variety of goods available.[12] In some cases, though, despite the availability of alternatives, consumers have maintained a preference for their national brands. This is the case, for example, in relation to Italians' home bias for Fiat cars (Goldberg and Verboven, 2001).

From the perspective of Europe as a whole, a strong historical tradition of product differentiation – particularly in high quality products – has constituted a comparative advantage with respect to other major trading blocs. This tradition led to European leadership in, for example, luxury goods industries where product differentiation is high. Closely associated with this, brand awareness became highly developed in Europe. High-quality products and high-income markets reinforce one another: for example, French luxury goods industries, including fashion clothing and footwear, leather wear, and food and drink, export nearly three-quarters of their output, mainly to high-income countries (Japan, the United States, and other European countries). Even in markets like Japan, in which indigenous products have very high market shares, European branded goods in general are considered to be sophisticated, chic and to express a good sense of design. This applies not only to such handcrafted luxury goods as clothing, but also to complicated industrial products such as Mercedes-Benz cars.[13]

The completion of the single European market and the later enlargement of the EU to 25 members raise a number of difficulties for firms adopting product differentiation strategies:

◆ Increasing homogenization of markets suggests the need for increasing scales of production to compete in these markets; but in the different member states – and even in some regions within member states – there are continuing cultural and linguistic differences that call for strategies to differentiate products to match the preferences of local consumers. Should firms develop Euro-brands or should they modify generic brands to suit local differences in tastes? The optimum strategy depends on what Kay

(1990a) calls the strategic market.[14] Comparing, say, a hairdresser with a microchip manufacturer, it is clear that the market for the former will be a local one, whereas that for the latter will be a much wider one. The size of the industry depends on economies of scale and scope; the size of the market on such factors as whether it is a consumer or producer good, and the degree of homogeneity of consumer tastes. A firm already producing more than enough for its share of a local market, and with significant economies of scale, will attempt to identify which among its existing products can be mass marketed under Euro-brands. If, instead, it has significant economies of scope, it may attempt to identify a range of differentiated products for local markets.

♦ Even where all other factors suggest the distribution of a product throughout Europe, the plurality of languages can cause problems. If companies have to print the majority of EU languages on the package, the wording related to the specifications of the product can become confusing, the amount of text can be excessive and the design of the package distorted. It has been suggested that to overcome the language barrier, firms operating on the European market should use strong visual design elements that do not rely on language, in order to present a single visual identity across Europe (Lynch, 1990).

♦ A successful product differentiation strategy in Europe can be hampered by the remaining non-tariff barriers (NTBs). For example, exchange rate movements and different VAT rates create price distortions in the EU, which can distort the 'value for money' element that would otherwise contribute to the differentiation of certain products. Another example can be found in the food industry. The EU provides, under certain circumstances, protection for foods with local and regional identities through legislation on protected designation of origin and protected geographical indication (PDO/PGI). These are indicative of local standards, qualities and traditions in the production of particular foods. There is a clear advantage to be derived from the protection that PDO/PGI provides. Greek producers, for example, were happy to register 'feta' as a type of Greek cheese. This would mean that only they could market products with this designation: a barrier to entry for any non-Greek producers. It was challenged in the European Court of Justice, which in 1999 revoked the registration of feta as Greek, ruling that it had 'been used as a generic description for a long time in some member states other than Greece' (Parrott *et al.*, 2002). Until this ruling, a cheese producer outside Greece was unable to adopt a product differentiation strategy in which feta was one of the varieties to be produced.[15]

♦ Pan-European product differentiation strategies involve greater physical distances in Europe, and hence higher costs. Since American firms have historically been accustomed to the long distances between different markets, they have had time to consolidate this comparative advantage over their EU counterparts. For this reason, the determination of the optimal distribution channel has been of particular concern to EU firms eager to benefit from the single market and European enlargement. A firm based, for example, in Hamburg has to determine the appropriate type of sales back-up that can be provided in the event of its entry into the Hungarian market. (Should it use an independent local agent? Can it rely on a large, well-established distributor, still under-represented in Hungary? Should it set up its own sales network?) In general, under what circumstances will a firm wish to distribute its product through its own retail outlet (downstream vertical integration)?[16]

The question of the relationship between differentiation and choice of distribution channel is an important one. It can be shown game theoretically that different degrees of differentiation will lead to different equilibrium choices of distribution channel (Moner-Colonques *et al.*, 2004). There are different views, however, on the precise relationship between differentiation and distribution. According to Welford and Prescott (1994, p. 178), in an industry in which, because of limited scope for product differentia-tion, there is mainly price competition, firms will produce (or license other firms to produce) their product in final markets rather than using wide distribution networks. This is because, under such circumstances, 'there is little scope to support transporta-tion costs across wide distances'. It follows that the less differentiated a product is, the more likely it is to be produced in final markets, rather than be exported to, and distrib-uted by agents in, those markets. This, however, contrasts with the view of Anderson and Coughlan (1987) that if non-differentiated products 'are sold through middlemen, ... the manufacturer's ability to respond to price changes (wage price wars) is inhibited, thereby protecting the manufacturer's product'. This is to say that the greater the extent to which competition is through product differentiation, the more likely it is that the product will be sold by the manufacturer itself,[17] rather than be exported to and sold by agents in, foreign markets.

So, is competition through product differentiation more likely (Anderson and Coughlan, 1987) or less likely (Welford and Prescott, 1994) to result in the cutting out of the mid-dleman? The historical evidence provides more support for Anderson and Coughlan than for Welford and Prescott. As Chandler (1990, p. 263) has shown, during the second half of the nineteenth century, when transport systems improved rapidly, firms such as the choco-late manufacturer Cadbury adopted improved, high-volume production processes to take advantage of the expanding markets. The firm began to brand its products and advertise nationally – its main competitors in the UK were Fry and Rowntree – and 'took over the mar-keting functions that, until then, had been handled by intermediaries'. Thus the increasing importance of differentiation was associated with greater control by the manufacturer over distribution.

In addition, there is anecdotal evidence from some highly product differentiated markets, such as those for fashion items. Here, retail specialization through the segmentation of markets into specific niches has been adopted by a number of European firms in recent years (Body Shop from the UK, Bally from Switzerland).

This conclusion is far from final, however. Let us take, as a counter-example, the case of the personal computer industry. Given that a computer is a relatively high expenditure item, it seems intuitively obvious that the greater the differences among the types and makes, the more the potential purchaser will want to see and try out different models before making a decision. In this case the products are more likely to be marketed through high street shops that carry a range of PCs. On the other hand, if computers are more standardized then people will be willing to buy them by mail order or over the internet. It is clear that direct marketing became more important in the 1990s as companies such as Dell and Gateway sold their products only directly to the customer. Dell remains the world's leading PC manufacturer. This has also been a period, it can be argued, of increasing standardization (declining differentiation) in the PC industry, as all producers rapidly introduced the same product types and characteristics. Dell's distribution channel, more than the Dell computer itself, is among the company's main ways of differentiating itself from other PC manufacturers (Frigo, 2004).[18]

The answer to the question of the relationship between product differentiation and how much control firms have over marketing, may relate to the relative strengths of economies of scale and scope in production and distribution. Particularly in relation to economies of scope, there is much research to be done. As Robert Porter (1991) has argued: 'it would be useful to learn whether economies of scope result from the production technology, or whether economies of scope in distribution and marketing are more important empirically'.

10.2.2 Advertising

It is important at the outset of the discussion on advertising to note that there is no necessary relationship between the promotion of a product and its social desirability or usefulness. Products are advertised because the owners of firms manufacturing those products wish to sell (more of) them. The normative question of the desirability of advertising is more complicated than the question of the desirability of the products themselves. Most people might agree that cigarettes are harmful, and that means should be found to reduce their consumption,[19] but there could still be an argument that among those continuing to smoke, competitive advertising by different cigarette manufacturers performs a useful function. Such advertising might inform smokers of innovative new products that reduce health risk. If advertising achieves these ends without inducing non-smokers to start smoking, then few would argue against such advertising. On the other hand, milk is generally accepted as healthy. This does not necessarily mean that people's welfare is enhanced by the advertising of milk. It is at least conceivable that advertising results in people buying (and consuming) more milk than is optimal given their incomes and nutritional needs.

Advertising, as already pointed out, may be closely related to product differentiation. In relation to a homogeneous product like milk, for example, different companies marketing milk will advertise to attempt to generate brand loyalty. If this is successful, generating consumer loyalty to different brands of what are otherwise identical products, then the advertising can be considered to have been a way of achieving 'image', or perceived, differentiation.

A simple neoclassical approach to advertising

Adopting neoclassical conventions, from the firm's point of view advertising might be considered as just another part of the costs of getting the product from raw material, via manufacturing, distribution and sale, to the consumer. Whether to advertise, and how much to advertise, can then be answered by the question: is the marginal cost of advertising covered by the marginal revenue from the additional sales generated by the advertising? From the consumer's point of view, advertising does not change significantly the neoclassical condition for optimization: that the marginal utility derived from the consumption of the good be equal to the price paid for the last unit. If advertising increases that marginal utility, then the producer will be able to charge a higher price, and the consumer will be willing to pay that higher price because of the additional satisfaction they get as a result of the advertising.[20] From this perspective a producer may increase profits, and consumers may or may not increase consumer surplus, depending on the impact of the advertising on the demand curve.

This is most simply represented in the case of monopoly. Figure 10.1 shows that if the firm advertises, the marginal cost curve will shift from MC_1 to MC_2; advertising also shifts the demand curve to the right, from D_1 to D_2. Both the firm's revenue and its costs will increase, but its revenue by more than its costs. If not, then the firm will not advertise. Consumer surplus – the area of the triangle below the demand curve, above price – is also increased.

The usual way of presenting the neoclassical perspective on advertising is with the Dorfman–Steiner condition (Dorfman and Steiner, 1954). According to this condition, the optimal level of advertising for a profit-maximizing firm is where the advertising to sales ratio is equal to the price cost margin multiplied by the advertising elasticity of demand:

$$\frac{p^A A}{PQ} = \frac{P - c}{P} E_A \qquad (10.1)$$

where E_A is the advertising elasticity of demand, p^A is the per unit price of advertising, A is the number of units of advertising purchased, P is the per unit price of the advertised product, Q the quantity sold, and c is its average cost.

The more sensitive the quantity demanded is to advertising, and/or the more firms can make on the sale of the marginal unit, the higher the level of advertising. There is an assumption in the equation as presented in Eq. (10.1) that costs are constant and that therefore $AC = MC$. If this is relaxed, then it becomes:

$$\frac{p^A A}{PQ} = \frac{P - MC}{P} E_A \qquad (10.2)$$

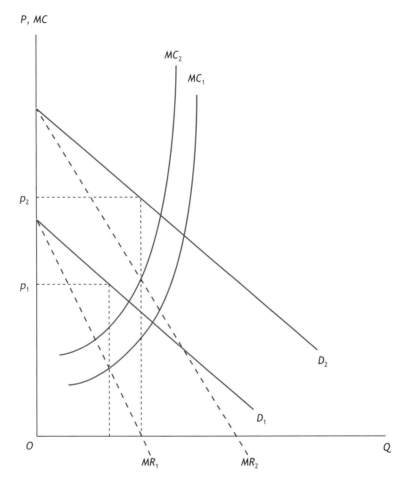

Figure 10.1 Advertising under monopoly

The term $\dfrac{(P - MC)}{P}$ on the right of the equation is the Lerner index. As shown in Chapter 5, Section 5.5, this is a measure of the degree of monopoly power of the firm. It follows from Eq. (10.2) that, for profit maximization, advertising expenditure will be greater, the greater is the firm's[21]

- sales revenue, PQ,

- monopoly power, and

- advertising elasticity of demand (the responsiveness of quantity demanded to a change in advertising expenditure).

It can be shown that $\dfrac{(P - MC)}{P} = \dfrac{1}{E_p}$ where E_p is price elasticity of demand.

It follows from Eq. (10.2) that, while advertising expenditure for profit maximization is positively related to advertising elasticity of demand, it is inversely related to price elasticity of demand. This makes sense intuitively. The greater the advertising elasticity of demand, the more effective expenditure on advertising is in increasing revenue, so the more will be spent on advertising. The greater is price elasticity of demand, the greater the extent to which a firm can increase its revenue simply by reducing price. It could alternatively be argued that the more advertising a firm does, the less elastic will be the demand for its product.

The Dorfman–Steiner relationship also suggests that any of the factors that affect the market structure, such as product differentiation and barriers to entry, will affect advertising if, and to the extent that, they have an impact on the advertising elasticity of demand. As is shown below, advertising intensity is not only a result but also a cause of market structure. The effects of advertising on market structure and welfare must also be appraised.

Recent work on advertising, often using game theoretic techniques, builds on two separate perspectives: one, originating from Stigler (1961), focuses on advertising as information; the second, at the root of which is the work of Bain (1958), sees advertising primarily as persuasion.

Advertising as information[22]

Stigler (1961) showed that if consumers lack information about the prices charged by different sellers of a product, then the sellers will, in general, be able to charge higher prices than if the consumers had perfect information. Moreover, the more a consumer intends to spend on the product, the more he or she will be willing to spend on the search for the lowest price. The more consumers in general spend on their search, the less will the prices vary. From this analysis, Stigler concluded that advertising of prices by competitors provides the information necessary for consumers to decide on which outlet to choose. Advertising thereby reduces search costs. By improving consumers' information, advertising will also reduce the range of prices. If we see search costs as part of the costs of the transaction, then advertising reduces transaction costs.

Nelson (1974) considered advertising as a signalling device rather than as a means of providing price information. He modelled advertising as signalling that the product exists and that the advertiser's confidence in the product is such that he is willing to spend money on it. If it is impossible to know in advance how good the product is (that is, if it is an *experience good*)[23] then consumers must buy it and try it. The more satisfied the consumers are, and the more they repeat their purchase, the higher the stream of profits the firm will make. The more confident the firm is that there will be repeat purchases, the more it will be willing to spend on advertising. From this, Nelson concluded that high expenditure on advertising is in fact a signal of high quality of the product. It should be noted that it follows from this that Nelson's model – and all the subsequent models built on a relationship between advertising expenditure and quality of product – implies that the market is a vertically differentiated one.

Building on Nelson's work, Bagwell and Ramey (1994) argue – for retail advertisers – that even where advertising is ostensibly uninformative, if it directs consumers towards the firms that offer the best deals it will achieve *co-ordination economies*. This is where increased expenditure on advertising reduces selling costs, results in an expansion of the product line and an expansion in sales per customer. The firms offering the best deals will gain, there will be higher levels of concentration, and consumers will also gain because of greater variety and lower prices.

It might reasonably be argued, in relation to both Nelson and Bagwell and Ramey's models, that once it becomes established that high expenditure on advertising is a signal of high quality, some firms will raise advertising to high levels despite the low quality of their products. They will expect thereby to attract a large number of buyers expecting high-quality products (or the best retail deals). Indeed, Hertzendorf (1993), also using a signalling model, concludes that when the 'advertising channel is noisy' the low-quality firm is able 'to take advantage of consumer ignorance by partially mimicking the strategy of the high-quality firm'. The economic condition for firms selling low-quality products to be able to adopt this approach profitably is that the extra returns from sales to first-time buyers be greater than the extra costs of advertising, which is close to the original neoclassical condition introduced above.

Both the establishment of a positive relationship between advertising expenditure and quality, and the idea that mimicry gives the low-quality firm a temporary advantage, are based on models in which advertising is a device to signal quality. This is known as *dissipative advertising*:[24] 'advertising that potentially signals quality to consumers within the context of a signaling game. Firms essentially burn money to make a point. This is in contrast to other roles that advertising might serve, such as directly conveying information' (Hertzendorf and Overgaard, 2001).

Zhao (2000) adds to the literature a model in which advertising is considered both as a signalling device, that is, dissipative advertising, and as an informational device. Though he does not reference Hertzendorf's 1993 paper, Zhao addresses the question of mimicry by the low-quality firm and arrives at similar conclusions. Focusing on the appropriate strategy for the high-quality firm introducing a new product, he shows that high advertising expenditure is likely to attract mimicry by the low-quality firm. 'A firm with a truly high-quality product', he concludes, 'is wise to let price send the signal and initially to conduct a modest advertising campaign'.

In another attempt to bring the model closer to reality, Hertzendorf and Overgaard (2001) introduce varying degrees of vertical differentiation. Their article, they write, is the 'first attempt to extend the literature by allowing actual price and advertising competition between [two] vertically differentiated oligopolists'. Among their most interesting results is that, up to a point, the less differentiated the products of the two companies, the more efficient the advertising signal relative to the price signal. However, 'advertising signals reach their zenith at intermediate levels of vertical differentiation'. Beyond the intermediate level, that is, as the two products become very similar, the advertising signal again becomes less efficient.[25]

Orzach *et al.* (2002) provide an argument that in some respects is similar to Zhao's, in others to that of Hertzendorf and Overgaard. Like Zhao, Orzach *et al.* include both signalling and direct information effects, that is, advertising is both dissipative and it informs people about the existence of the product. The former effect, as in all signalling games, is that high expenditure on advertising leads the consumer to believe that the product has high quality. The latter effect means that the more is spent on advertising, the greater the proportion of consumers that are aware of the product. Like both Zhao and Hertzendorf and Overgaard, they consider the impact of less than full information. Again as in both other papers, Orzach *et al.* (2002) find theoretical explanations for why 'modest advertising may signal high quality'.[26]

All three of these recent additions to the literature relate their game-theory-based ideas to empirical evidence. They show that the empirical evidence has failed to provide strong support for the standard theoretical argument that there is a positive relationship between advertising and vertical differentiation (and, in particular, between advertising by a firm and the quality of its product). They provide different theoretical explanations for this lack of clarity. The essence of Zhao's explanation is that where there is incomplete information, high advertising expenditure by the firm with the high-quality product will attract mimicry. Although it may lose some market share by doing so, it should therefore spend less on advertising. Its profit, his model suggests, will be greater as a result of lower advertising expenditure. The mixed empirical evidence, it follows, is a result of incomplete information in the real world.

Hertzendorf and Overgaard's (2001) explanation for the mixed empirical evidence seems to boil down to the 'intricate relationship between price and advertising as joint signals of quality'. In their model, as in Zhao's, the presence or absence of complete information is important. But other aspects of their model, and – what for our purposes is most important – the underlying intuition, are different. Where there are high levels of vertical differentiation, advertising by the high-quality firm will be low because, as for Zhao, price increases are a more efficient signal of quality. (High advertising expenditure attracts mimicry.) However, as the two products become more similar, price elasticity of demand for the high-quality good goes up. With higher elasticity, the impact on quantity of an increase in price is much greater and advertising becomes a more efficient signal of quality. As the two goods become even more similar, approaching perfect substitutability, advertising loses effect. This is why 'advertising by the high-quality firm peaks at an intermediate level of vertical differentiation, and then declines steadily towards zero as the high-quality and low-quality products become indistinguishable' (Hertzendorf and Overgaard, 2001). This is consistent with the mixed empirical evidence, because in some cases – depending on the degree of vertical differentiation – advertising and quality are positively related, and in others inversely related.

The logic in Orzach *et al.* (2002) for what they call 'signal reversal', is that for some goods – such as consumer durables – there are significant marginal costs, and these are directly related to quality. If among potential consumers of such goods (say, fridges) 'willingness-to-pay increases only moderately with quality, then we would expect to observe high-quality brands being advertised modestly during the introductory phase'. If the proportion of consumers who are indifferent to quality is high, in other words, then the return to advertising as a signal of quality is low.

It is interesting to consider the process of evolution of neoclassical research on advertising as discussed above. The first game-theoretic papers, like that of Nelson (1974), found a theoretical basis for the idea that advertising and quality were directly related. Empirical evidence – mostly in the 1990s – has not unambiguously supported this hypothesis.[27] Since then, variations on the models have been found which lead to conclusions more consistent with the empirical evidence. While the methodology of each of the papers is primarily deductive, the process driving change from one paper, or group of papers, to the next can be argued to be more inductive.[28]

Advertising as persuasion

This approach sees advertising as a means of establishing brand loyalty, as a result of which barriers to entry might be created. Assume, for example, that a contact lens manufacturer develops a new type of lens. It may be difficult to patent because it is so easily copied. The firm may therefore decide to advertise heavily, attempting to establish in the minds of consumers that its brand of the new contact lens, as the first one, is the best and most reliable. If this advertising campaign is successful, it will make entry by new firms into the market difficult. By persuading the consumers (that is, by altering what would otherwise be their preferences), the firm increases its market power. Again advertising leads to higher levels of concentration, but in this view it does not lead to gain for the consumer. In the tradition of Bain, the early work on advertising as a means of creating barriers to entry was reviewed by Comanor and Wilson (1979), who were themselves seminal contributors to the empirical literature in this field (Comanor and Wilson, 1967).

Among the main scholars laying down markers on the key questions in this area was Kaldor (1950). He was one of the first to see in advertising a means of increasing entry barriers through the building up of *consumer loyalty* or *inertia*[29] for a particular product. In his words:

> Advertising makes the public 'brand conscious'; it is not so much a question of making the consumer buy things he would not have bought otherwise; but of crystallizing his routine habits, or making him conscious that keeping to a certain routine in consumption means not only buying the same commodities in a vague sort of way, but sticking to the same brand.

Because of unconscious 'routine buying' or a deliberate fervour to stick to a product on the part of consumers, potential new firms are barred by the practice of 'packing the product space'; a proliferation of differentiated (branded) items makes no niches available for new firms who want to gain a foothold in that market.[30]

Using a variety of techniques, a number of economists have, since Kaldor, and Comanor and Wilson, provided arguments both in favour of and critical of advertising. Schmalensee (1974) set out to show that advertising that creates brand loyalty can thereby have the dynamic effect of setting up barriers to the entry of new firms. Modelling advertising under conditions of profit maximization, he apparently surprised himself by finding the opposite: 'Instead of supporting the standard view of advertising's effects, however, the work reported here demonstrates that under plausible assumptions brand loyalty created by advertising is not a source of entry barriers'.

Rather than barriers to entry, Dixit and Norman (1978) considered the question of socially optimal levels of advertising. They used conventional welfare-theoretic methods[31] to study advertising that leads to changes in consumer tastes. Their conclusion was that it pays firms to advertise to a socially excessive level, and that this is true for monopoly, oligopoly and monopolistic competition.

Shapiro (1980) criticized this result on the grounds that the analysis assumed that pre-advertising consumption is distributed efficiently according to post-advertising tastes. If this is not the case – and Shapiro argued that generally it was not – then there were additional gains to advertising not accounted for by Dixit and Norman's approach.

Using an approach not susceptible to Shapiro's criticisms (by assuming that the consumer has imperfect information), Kotowitz and Mathewson (1979) also conclude that advertising, at least in the short run, can be profitable for the seller, but misleading to the consumer. Taking the limitations of consumers even further, Nagler (1993) develops a model of advertising and consumer reactions in which consumers exhibit a form of bounded rationality. On the basis of a set of reasonable assumptions he shows that there will be firms that have an incentive to advertise deceptively, causing a net welfare loss to society in the absence of corrective policy. This is further substantiated by Ordonez de Haro (1993), who uses a horizontal differentiation model to consider the strategic effects of persuasive advertising, and concludes that 'even under "benevolent" interpretation of persuasive advertising, a threatened monopolist, in order to deter the entry of potential competitors, will undertake too much advertising relative to a social planner'.[32]

In recent work addressing persuasive advertising, 'consumer inertia or lock-in is a critical parameter that drives the market outcome in [Banerjee and Bandyopadhyay's] model' of competitive advertising (Banerjee and Bandyopadhyay, 2003). They admit that under their 'simultaneous move game' there is a multiplicity of equilibrium outcomes but there appears to be a strong first-mover advantage. 'In particular, if the firms' advertising decisions were sequential, then the firm moving first may advertise in such a way as to force an equilibrium, where advertising as a competitive tool is not viable for the follower firm'. Their model does not indicate whether or not this means that the first mover can generate barriers to entry. For firms of different sizes, their model suggests that only the large firm will advertise, but that the small firm will derive the benefit, and increased profits, from the increased prices in general that are generated by the large firm's advertising. So both large and small firms gain from advertising; consumer welfare is not addressed.

It would appear that advertising – whether as provision of information or means of persuasion – can, under certain conditions, reduce consumer welfare. It should also be emphasized that it is possible, under different conditions, that advertising, even if intended to persuade, does not reduce consumer welfare. It may, for example, fail to raise barriers to entry, as Schmalensee (1974) argued. Among the key factors in determining the results of advertising are how informed the consumers are – and assuming there are asymmetries, how rapidly they learn – and how easy it is to imitate the advertiser's product. Mizuno and Odagiri (1990) show that the more rapidly consumers learn, the less likely they are to be misled by advertising; and the greater the ease with which the product can be imitated, the less able will the seller be to mislead the consumer. These are certainly plausible results. However, as shown in Section 2.2.3 on game theory in Chapter 2, and as seems to be illustrated by the game theoretic approaches to advertising since the 1970s, the results are in general highly sensitive to small changes in parameters. There is in many cases also the problem of multiple equilibria. If the choice of equilibrium is a matter of logic and plausibility, then all that the research proves is that the likely outcome is also a possible equilibrium outcome.

The research, both empirical and theoretical, does have some clear outcomes nonetheless. Advertising, it is clear, informs and persuades; it may also change the structure of the industry if, for example, it enables one firm to obtain a dominant share of the market. How is advertising measured? How important is it in the EU? How might firms choose an advertising strategy? What are the effects of advertising? It is to such questions that we now turn.

Measures of advertising intensity

There are broadly two ways of measuring the advertising intensity of firms. The most common is the *advertising to sales ratio*. This ratio, A/S, varies with the type of industry. Luxury goods industries tend to spend more than others, for example. (The perfume industry spends as much as 15 per cent of turnover on advertising.) Some toiletries and food products are also heavily advertised. Table 10.1 shows the top ten companies in the world in terms of their advertising expenditure. Most of these companies are on the list because of their size rather than because of their A/S ratios. In other words, they have huge revenues (S) and huge advertising expenditures (A) as well. Thus the car companies appear among the top advertisers even though they have relatively low A/S ratios. On the other hand, some of the largest corporations in the world – such as Wal-Mart and Exxon Mobil – are not on the list of top advertisers. This is because the retailing and oil sectors tend to have lower advertising expenditures (a smaller A/S ratio). At the same time L'Oréal is not among the top 200 companies in the world and yet it is among the top advertisers. This is indicative of the fact that the cosmetics industry has a relatively high A/S ratio.

Table 10.1 Top ten companies in terms of global advertising expenditure, 2002

Rank	Company	Industry	Expenditure (in $bn)	A/S ratio (estimate)
1	Procter & Gamble	Personal care/cosmetics	4.5	0.12
2	Unilever	Personal care	3.3	0.08
3	General Motors	Automotive	3.2	0.02
4	Toyota	Automotive	2.4	0.02
5	Ford	Automotive	2.4	0.01
6	Time Warner	Media	2.3	0.09
7	DaimlerChrysler	Automotive	1.8	0.01
8	L'Oréal	Cosmetics	1.7	0.12
9	Nestlé	Food	1.5	0.03
10	Sony	Consumer electronics	1.5	0.03

Sources: Advertising Age Global Marketing, 2003; company websites

Because of the above, as Cowling (1976) has noted, national A/S ratios are less appropriate the more diverse is the cross-section of industries or firms covered. Industry- or firm-specific A/S ratios are therefore sometimes preferred.

Nevertheless, a second way of measuring advertising intensity is by comparing advertising spend in different countries, and over time. Globally, advertising expenditure peaked in 2000 and dipped sharply in the recession of 2001. Table 10.2 provides 2001 data on advertising expenditure in the 19 European countries for which the World Advertising Research Center (WARC) provides comparable data. For most countries, advertising expenditure was less in 2001 than in 2000. The exceptions are the transition countries: Poland, Hungary and the Czech Republic. These countries also had among the highest growth rates in expenditure in the period 1997–2001. As transition countries, their markets were developing most rapidly in this period. In terms of share of total, however, the advanced industrialized countries with the largest, most developed markets rank highest. It is clear from Table 10.2 that rank in terms of advertising expenditure is not the same as rank in terms of population; Germany is much larger than the UK, Greece is larger than Switzerland, and so on. Similarly, advertising expenditure is not directly related to GDP, (though it may be related to growth in GDP).

For comparative purposes it is interesting to note that, despite that fact that the 19 European countries in the table have a total population of over 450 million, substantially more than the United States' 290 million, advertising expenditure in the United States is in general 30 to 40 per cent above that in the 19 European countries. This is indicative of the relatively developed nature of markets and the media in the United States.

Table 10.2 Advertising expenditure in 19 European countries, 2001

	Value (€m)	% change, 1997-2001	Share of total (%)
UK	18,842	9	23
Germany	18,568	3	22
France	9,621	12	12
Italy	7,839	35	9
Spain	5,095	17	6
Netherlands	3,740	11	4
Switzerland	2,747	18	3
Poland	2,150	99	3
Austria	1,984	32	2
Belgium	1,964	24	2
Sweden	1,782	8	2
Portugal	1,484	78	2
Norway	1,334	8	2
Denmark	1,272	−9	2
Greece	1,238	33	1
Finland	1,145	11	1
Ireland	1,072	60	1
Hungary	790	68	1
Czech Republic	779	106	1
Total	**83,446**		**100**

Source: International Journal of Advertising, vol. 22, no. 1, 2003

Apart from the size and level of development of markets and media in different countries, different regulations also contribute to the explanation of ranking in terms of advertising expenditure. For example, the total ban on alcohol advertising on French television could partly explain the relatively low advertising expenditure. (France has a similar population and a higher GDP than the UK, but has a lower advertising expenditure.) Controls have been operated with different degrees of strictness according to the medium used. The control of advertisements on television is more stringent in the Scandinavian countries (Sweden, Norway, Denmark, Finland), in the Netherlands and in Switzerland than in Italy, the United States, Japan or the UK. The differences between regulations in EU member states are, however, diminishing over time.

Table 10.3 shows that television and, particularly, radio advertising account for a higher share of the total in the United States than in Europe.[33] Magazine and outdoor advertising account for a higher proportion of advertising expenditure in Europe than in the United States, and the share of newspaper advertising is similar in both regions. The structure of

Table 10.3 Percentage share in total advertising by medium, region and year

United States	1998	1999	2000	2001	2002
Newspapers	37	36	34	34	34
Magazines	12	12	12	12	11
Television	38	38	38	38	39
Radio	12	13	13	13	13
Cinema	–	–	–	–	–
Outdoor	1	1	3	3	3
Total	100	100	100	100	100

Europe	1998	1999	2000	2001	2002
Newspapers	38	38	37	36	36
Magazines	18	18	18	18	18
Television	33	33	34	34	35
Radio	5	5	5	5	5
Cinema	1	1	1	1	1
Outdoor	5	5	5	6	6
Total	100	100	100	100	100

Japan	1998	1999	2000	2001	2002
Newspapers	28	28	28	28	27
Magazines	10	10	10	10	10
Television	44	44	45	45	46
Radio	5	5	5	5	5
Cinema	–	–	–	–	–
Outdoor	13	13	12	12	13
Total	100	100	100	100	100

Source: Based on data in *International Journal of Advertising*, vol. 22, no. 2, 2003

media share differs sharply in Japan. In Japan, television and outdoor advertising are much higher than elsewhere, and all other media are lower than elsewhere. The high share of outdoor advertising is explained by the fact that Japan is a highly urbanized society with extensive public transport systems on which available space is used for advertising. In all countries the medium used depends on the type of product: fast-moving consumer goods would tend to be advertised on television and radio, whereas consumer durables (computers, cars) and to an even greater extent capital goods (industrial machinery, equipment) would mostly be advertised in specialist magazines and at trade fairs. In all countries, too, television accounts for an increasing share of advertising, and newspapers for a declining share. It should be noted that although it is still a very small proportion of advertising expenditure, internet advertising is growing rapidly.

In relation to advertising, as in relation to other strategies of pan-European differentiation pursued by EU firms, EU regulation imposes controls and limits. Among the main pieces of legislation affecting advertising is the 'Television Without Frontiers' directive, adopted on 3 October 1989. It was updated by a directive adopted on 30 June 1997. This introduced a regulatory framework that is appropriate for digital broadcasting. Among the main changes are the tightening up of certain legal concepts, clarification in relation to member states' jurisdiction over broadcasters, and introduction of rules governing teleshopping and coverage of major events. In addition, protection for children has been increased (Aubry, 2000). The 'Television Without Frontiers' directive explicitly restricts advertising in the following areas:

- It bans tobacco advertising. Cigarettes and other tobacco products may not be advertised on the screen.
- It bans prescription pharmaceutical advertising, and calls for the inclusion of detailed label information in advertising.
- It introduces guidelines on alcohol advertising.
- It introduces guidelines on advertising to children.
- It introduces rules for sponsorship.

This directive also specifies a maximum proportion of time devoted to advertising beyond which a broadcaster is not permitted to go. (The directive also introduces a minimum quota for programmes of European origin, although this relates more indirectly to advertising.)

The firms most affected by the restrictions imposed by the 'Television Without Frontiers' directive are those in the pharmaceutical, drink/tobacco and toy industries.

10.3 Corporate integration

The transformation of a combination of inputs into a marketable output involves several stages: a product moves along the transformation line from the conception and design stage, through the production stage to the distribution stage.

The production process itself comprises many different steps, that range in the case of a car, for example, from the cutting of metals, stamping of body parts (and the production of machine tools required for these tasks), to the various operations performed at the finishing stage (painting and polishing) (Fig. 10.2). These different functions can either be performed by a single firm, or by several separate specialist firms, each one at a different stage of the transformation process. If the former, then the firm can be viewed as a *vertically integrated* organization. Of particular interest is the dynamic process of integration; this is the actions that the firm undertakes, including changes in the organizational characteristics of production, in order to incorporate different parts of product transformation into the firm. It is appropriate to differentiate between *corporate integration* in which different stages are incorporated into a single firm, and *industrial integration* in which the different stages are undertaken by separate firms in a particular industry in a particular region or country.[34] It is also important to emphasise that some of the stages in the production process can take place simultaneously. R&D for example, in relation to both product and process, is continual and does not simply precede production.

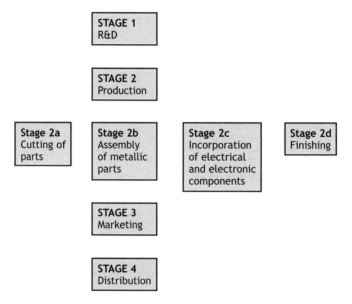

Figure 10.2 Stages in the product transformation process in the car industry

There are three types of corporate integration:

♦ Horizontal integration is the taking control, by expansion, acquisition or merger, of two or more distinct firms, plants or processes that lie at the same stage of the transformation process.

♦ Vertical integration is the taking control, by expansion, acquisition or merger, of two or more firms, plants or processes that are at separate stages of the same transformation process.

◆ Conglomerate integration is the taking control, by expansion, acquisition or merger, of two or more firms, plants or processes that are in different product areas.

Much of the discussion on corporate integration is similar, irrespective of whether the focus is horizontal, vertical or conglomerate integration. In all three, there is the possibility of two broad effects: an increase in market power and an increase in efficiency arising from economies of scale and/or scope. Much of the theoretical work on horizontal integration is closely related to the oligopoly models discussed in Chapter 6, and horizontal integration in practice is included in Section 10.5.1 of this chapter. Moreover, aspects of both horizontal and conglomerate integration are covered in the discussion on diversification, below. We therefore concentrate here on vertical integration.

Vertical integration can be upstream (backward) or downstream (forward). Fiat (motor car) merging with Comau (machine tools) provides an example of upstream vertical integration. Downstream vertical integration is where, for example, a car company acquires a distribution company. Two-way vertical integration is also possible. An example of this would be the merger of a petroleum refiner with a company owning oil reserves (upstream) and with retail petrol stations (downstream).

It may be required, under certain circumstances, to measure the degree of vertical integration. One way of doing so is to use a vertical integration ratio:

$$\text{VI ratio} = \frac{\text{Value added of a firm}}{\text{Final sales revenue}}$$

Computing the value added to a product by a single firm, as a proportion of the final cost to the consumer of that product, gives an indication of the significance of that firm (as a vertically integrated entity) in the production of that product. A similar ratio can be computed – as industrial, rather than corporate integration – for a group of firms, or a region, to identify their significance in the total industry.

Among the problems with such ratios is that value added is not necessarily synonymous with vertical integration; one firm that has resulted from a series of upstream and downstream mergers or acquisitions – and which is therefore the result of a great deal of vertical integration – could still be adding less value than another firm that works only on one part of the product transformation process. Design, for example, may add more value than assembly, distribution and retail sales together. Another problem is that it is not always easy to distinguish between corporate and industrial integration.

This problem is discussed by Robertson and Langlois (1994) who contrast the 'nexus of contracts' view of the firm with the 'property rights' view of the firm. The former is close to what we called the principal–agent theory in Chapter 3, and the latter is close to the transaction cost theory in Chapter 4. The point is that if the firm is seen in terms of contracts, then what goes on inside the firm differs from how the firm relates to other firms only in degree, not fundamentally. Both are governed by contracts; the only difference is that the contracts governing the firm's interactions with other firms usually have a greater degree of specificity than those governing the firm itself. On the other hand, the transaction cost view of the firm sees it in terms of ownership of assets; assets are either owned by the firm or they are not. In the transaction cost view, the firm does differ fundamentally from other firms. Vertical corporate integration is clear from a property rights perspective: 'two stages of production are held to be vertically integrated when the assets involved are under common ownership'. But the 'boundaries of the firm [are] rather fuzzy under the "nexus" view' (Robertson and Langlois, 1994).

Recalling the continuum between market and hierarchy introduced in Chapter 4, vertical corporate integration is apparently within a hierarchy. The process of upstream or downstream vertical integration is the process of removing transactions from the market and internalizing them into the firm. However, a firm could own one of its suppliers, but deal with it in the same way as it deals with other suppliers, in terms of market criteria. Moreover, there are many situations in which firms control other firms without owning them. Jacobson and O'Sullivan (1994), for example, describe the relationship between subsidiaries of software multinationals and small software manual printing firms in Ireland, as one in which the former to a great extent control the latter through demand for high quality and exclusive dealing. Robertson and Langlois (1994) conclude that there are two types, or dimensions, of integration: ownership and co-ordination integration. Let us call them OI and CI. A holding company, which merely owns a number of different, and perhaps unrelated businesses for investment reasons, has a high degree of OI but virtually no CI. A large, vertically integrated firm that is involved in all the stages of the transformation of a product will have a high degree of both OI and CI. An industrial district of the type we discussed in Chapter 8 is a group of firms that has a high degree of CI but no OI.

Notwithstanding the above discussion about how differently two theories of the firm treat vertical integration, most research in this area rests on transaction cost theory. For example, vertical integration is in general assumed to be a strategy driven by the interest in reducing transaction costs (Peyrefitte and Golden, 2004). Whether directly through ownership, or indirectly through control, there are three broad reasons why a firm will attempt to achieve greater vertical integration: to increase efficiency; to bypass government regulations; and to reduce uncertainty. They can all be related in some way to transaction costs.

10.3.1 Efficiency

We can understand efficiency in this context as relating to minimum efficient scale (MES), that is, the smallest size of firm for which average cost is minimized. In an enlightened discussion of this concept and its role in the evolution of large, modern industrial enterprises in the late nineteenth and early twentieth centuries, Chandler (1990, pp. 21–38) points out the following:

- Independent intermediary firms can have *scale* advantages through buying finished goods from, or selling inputs to a number of different manufacturers of the same product.

◆ Such intermediary firms can also have *scope* advantages through buying from or selling to manufacturers of different products.

◆ Where specialized knowledge about a particular product or about any part of that product's transformation process is required, or where some specialized system of buying inputs or selling the finished product is necessary, then this can offset intermediaries' scope advantages and lead to vertical integration by the manufacturer.

◆ To be successful, vertically integrating firms of this kind require highly skilled management.[35]

◆ There is a complex relationship between the MES of the plant and the MES of the firm.

A somewhat different, though not necessarily contradictory, view of vertical integration as a means of increasing efficiency is to see efficiency in terms of the minimizing of transaction costs.[36] If the transaction costs in using the price mechanism exceed the costs arising from the non-market co-ordination of exchanges within a firm, then ownership integration is likely. From our earlier discussion, note that this non-market co-ordination may in some cases be between firms, in which case it is CI and not OI.

Introducing *asset specificity* into the discussion shows a degree of overlap between Chandler's and the transaction cost perspectives on vertical integration. What Chandler shows is that vertical integration is more likely when some specialized knowledge or system, specific to the product manufactured by that firm, is required. A transaction cost approach can lead to the same conclusion: where there is asset specificity, such as where equipment or skills are required only for the production of a particular product, then where technology is such that only one firm uses that equipment or those skills, they are more likely to be internalized than become the property of a separate firm. In other words, if a transaction requires an investment in a specific asset, internalization of the asset by the firm is more likely than ownership of the asset by a second, separate firm and purchase of the product of the asset on the market by the first firm.

Jacobson and O'Sullivan's (1994) study of the software manual printing industry again illustrates. The highly specific nature of the machinery required for the high quality printing of manuals led to the close relationship (CI rather than OI in this case)[37] between the Irish printing firms and the subsidiaries of the software multinationals. If the printing firms could have used their printing equipment for other purposes, the tight, often exclusive subcontracting relationships between them and the software firms would not have developed.

That the nature of the technology is crucial is shown by reference to the neoclassical literature on *fixed* and *variable proportion technologies*[38] and their implications for vertical integration.

We assume, for simplicity, that the product transformation process has only two stages. In the case where production is subject to fixed proportion technology, it can be shown that an incentive to integrate vertically exists if there is a monopoly at each of the stages prior to integration. Integration would lead to the upstream output being transferred to the downstream division at its marginal cost of production,[39] the price of the final product would be reduced, and the final output would expand. As a result, the total profit of the vertically integrated monopoly would exceed the sum of the profits of the two monopolies prior to integration. Under these assumptions there is clearly an incentive to integrate vertically, though it is arguable that there will be efficiency/welfare costs associated with increasing monopolization.

Scherer and Ross (1990, p. 526) argue that where there is variable proportion technology, 'the efficiency gain from improved input proportion choices [as a result of vertical integration] at least partly offsets the efficiency loss from elevated end product prices'. Here there is more than one input, and the production of one of them is monopolized. Vertical integration between the upstream and downstream monopolies leads to control by the vertically integrated firm of both inputs. It can now, following vertical integration, determine the proportions in which to combine the two inputs undistorted by one of the input suppliers being a monopoly.

There are two factors at work: how variable the proportions are, and how competitive production at each of the stages is. If there are variable proportions, we have shown that vertical integration can improve efficiency. It depends, however, on what the market structures at the various stages of production were before vertical integration. For example, if the downstream market was competitive prior to integration, vertical integration can lead to efficiency losses – from the point of view of the industry and consumers – that more than offset the gains from improved choice of input proportions (Waterson, 1982). The cost reduction translates into increased profit for the firm (Vernon and Graham, 1971), but not necessarily to reduced prices for the consumer.

We can conclude that, from a neoclassical point of view, the impact of vertical integration on efficiency (and welfare) depends, among other things, on the variability of proportions (or the elasticity of input substitution) and on how competitive the various markets up and down the product transformation process are before and after integration.

That technology has an effect on the determinants and results of vertical integration also seems to follow from a recent study that, while statistically sophisticated, is not neoclassical. Sorenson (2003) examines vertical integration and organizational learning in the computer workstation industry. He finds that vertical integration seems to reduce learning where the environment – including technology – is stable. On the other hand, in 'volatile environments, non-integrated firms benefit less from production experience, presumably because much of the value of their experience erodes as new technologies replace old'. Interestingly, Sorenson rejects a transaction cost explanation for his results. Among his reasons are that 'models of the decision to integrate vertically show a decline in the propensity to integrate under technological uncertainty in direct contradiction to the expectation [under transaction cost theory] that such uncertainty should increase integration'.

10.3.2 Bypassing government regulations

The avoidance of government regulations is another incentive for vertical integration. This is best explained in terms of actions by firms to overcome or exploit differences in tax and price control regulations in different countries or regions, or in relation to different parts of the product transformation process. Where such differences exist, they can be overcome or exploited by vertically integrated firms in ways that would not be open to separate firms interacting on the basis of market criteria.

By vertically integrating across the boundaries between regions or countries (and/or between upstream and downstream) in which the different regulations exist, firms can remove the buying and selling of the product of the upstream part of the production process from open market transactions. That product is now transferred downstream *within* the firm for further processing. The firm can determine for itself – internally, administratively – at what price this transfer should take place. This internal transfer price can be used to switch profits from a high tax location or part of the production process to a low tax location or part of the production process.

According to Shepherd (1990, p. 366) this type of profit-switching transfer pricing (PSTP) has been a common practice in the United States, where oil extraction has been taxed at lower rates than refining. In the EU, where corporate profit tax rates are significantly higher in some member states than in others (see Table 7.3), firms can reduce their global tax payments by switching profits between high tax areas such as Germany, and low tax areas such as Ireland. There is, in fact, a great deal of evidence that Ireland is used as a location into which to switch profits using PSTP (Stewart, 1989). The formation of multinational corporations through the establishment of subsidiaries in Ireland (that is, corporate vertical integration into Ireland) is at least partly in order to exploit the differences in corporate profit tax rates.[40]

Where the government regulation is through price controls, similar arguments can be used to explain the advantages of vertical integration. Where, for example, an input is subject to price controls, vertical integration will enable the firm to use transfer pricing to insulate itself from these controls. More generally, to the extent that EU-wide competition leads to downward pressures on prices, this will further encourage 'firms to internalise their production or downstream functions and embark upon a period of manipulative transfer pricing to make up the short-falls in their profitability' (Welford and Prescott, 1994, p. 145).

Note that vertical integration to avoid government regulations, as discussed in this section, must be OI, and not just CI. It is the internalization into the single firm's information systems of what had been separate operations that makes possible the avoidance of the regulations.

10.3.3 Uncertainty

Uncertainty can also be a factor in vertical integration. Transactions between firms at different stages of the product transformation process are all subject to uncertainty. For example, the supply of some raw materials (uranium, bauxite, oil, coffee) is highly variable in nature. Political as well as climatic considerations explain this volatility. The demand for the final good is also often uncertain. As Chandler (1990, p. 24) points out, maintaining throughput at the level of the minimum efficient scale (MES) requires careful co-ordination not only of production, 'but also of the flow of inputs from suppliers and the flow of outputs to intermediaries and final users'. If, because of the independence of those suppliers, intermediaries or final users, the supply of inputs or demand for outputs is uncertain, then vertical integration is likely to reduce the uncertainty and improve co-ordination. Chandler goes on to show (1990, p. 25) that it was in order to improve this type of co-ordination that the Standard Oil Trust (the precursor of Exxon) was formed in the late nineteenth century.

Uncertainty can lead to vertical integration, but it can also explain why that vertical integration is CI and not OI. In the context, for example, of rapid technological change, a manufacturer can reduce uncertainty by buying inputs from a subcontractor rather than itself investing in the possibly short-lived technology required to produce those inputs. Once again the software manual printing industry illustrates the point. The major software firms, such as Microsoft and Lotus, avoided setting up their own printing divisions and instead bought in printing services from local firms, often established entirely for that purpose. The uncertainties in relation to the life expectancy of the technology – and of the product – were borne by the printers. In the event of the displacement of printed manuals by manuals and online help functions in various machine-readable formats, the manual printers' investments in specialized printing equipment become sunk costs. Under these circumstances, the software firms themselves, on the other hand, can simply shift their demand to the new type of input (Jacobson and O'Sullivan, 1994). Note that this is consistent with Sorenson's (2003) suggestion mentioned above of a decline in the propensity to integrate under conditions of technological uncertainty.

Another example of where CI rather than OI results from what would otherwise be vertical integration is where high levels of trust exist between independent firms. Heanue and Jacobson (2002), focusing on the furniture industry in Ireland, have shown that trust between independent firms – even where they are not spatially proximate – can result in a successful joint venture. In the absence of trust, and where each of the firms would be too small to compete by itself, vertical (or horizontal) integration would be essential.

Thus uncertainty can in some circumstances enhance the likelihood of vertical corporate integration, and in other circumstances make a strategy of outsourcing more likely. As we showed above, vertical integration can improve co-ordination in comparison with the situation where there are many firms with autonomous governance. On the other hand, uncertainty about technology change can result in outsourcing rather than backward integration.

Despite the almost ubiquitous presence of transaction cost arguments in the literature on vertical integration, we have shown that it cannot explain some of the facts surrounding vertical integration (and non-integration) in practice. Among the reasons for the limits of transaction cost economics in this context is that it is 'effectively a comparative static approach' (Pitelis, 2002). Vertical integration – especially of the 'innovative firm' in the context of technological change (Lazonick, 1991) – cannot be explained by transaction cost economics (TCE) because 'TCE assumes technology and innovation as constant' (Pitelis, 2002).[41]

The literature on corporate integration has traditionally focused on factors giving rise to increases in the size of firms. Large-scale production developed in the context of technologies that increased the MES. These technologies were usually based on assembly lines, and came to be known as Fordist production methods. In practice, as we saw in our discussion of industrial districts in Chapter 8, in some circumstances small firms can be more successful than large ones. Some writers, including Piore and Sabel (1984), have gone so far as to argue that new technologies in recent decades have provided the basis for disintegration, for a new industrial era in which small firms, using sophisticated production, distribution, marketing and co-ordination technologies, could in *general* be more successful than large firms.

These new, post-Fordist systems of organization are associated with what has come to be known as flexible specialization. They are based on small firms because, it is argued, small firms can respond more rapidly both to changes in consumer tastes and to process innovations. Moreover, the argument continues, new production technologies – and the application of computers to all stages in the product transformation process – are accessible to small firms, or at least to groups of small firms.[42]

As we have shown, there is some validity in the argument that new technologies can facilitate the development of smaller firms.[43] In addition, there is some evidence of a resurgence of smaller firms since the 1970s (Acs, 1996; Acs and Preston, 1997). However, large firms continue to dominate in global markets and in particular industries. It seems appropriate, therefore, to conclude (along with Best, 1990; Robertson and Langlois, 1994; and Rothwell and Dodgson, 1994) that different technological, cultural, institutional and market conditions can result in large firms predominating in some circumstances and small firms in others. 'There is no single degree of integration, or form of firm or industry organization, that suits all purposes' (Robertson and Langlois, 1994).[44]

10.4 Diversification

Diversification refers to the movement of a firm into new, related or unrelated product areas (product extension), and/or, less frequently, to the movement of a firm into a different geographical market (geographical extension). When the firm diversifies into an unrelated field of production, this is called pure or conglomerate diversification. In most cases, however, firms tend to diversify into adjacent product lines.

Diversification as an increase in the number of product lines may be through internal expansion into the production of different products, or through mergers or acquisitions. Diversification through mergers or acquisitions is also a form of corporate integration, more horizontal where the firms are in related areas, more conglomerate where they are in unrelated product areas. The theories of mergers and acquisitions are thus similar to those of corporate integration, discussed above.[45]

There have been a number of examples of this latter type of diversification (horizontal and conglomerate integration) in the merger and acquisition (M&A) boom of the late 1980s and 1990s. Examples of recent M&As in the drinks industry are provided in Box 10.1, but similar examples could be provided in many other industries, including the pharmaceutical industry,[46] the food industry and the automotive industry.

Box 10.1 Diversification through mergers and acquisitions in the drinks industry, 1987-2004

Guinness (stout beer producer) acquired the Bell Scotch whisky company; Louis Vuitton (up-market manufacturer of morocco leather articles) merged with the champagne producer Moët et Chandon which had earlier acquired the Hennessy brandy company; LVMH (Louis Vuitton Moët Hennessy) then acquired the up-market French couturier, Givenchy; Guinness merged some of its operations with LVMH; Guinness and GrandMet merged to form Diageo; Pernod-Ricard acquired Irish Distillers; Diageo and Pernod-Ricard jointly acquired Seagrams.

It should be noted that, while at first, some of the activities involved conglomerate diversification, by the end of the 1990s corporate activity seemed to have become more focused. Thus Diageo (see Box 10.1) sold off Burger King to concentrate on the drinks industry, and LVMH, while retaining its champagne interests, is not primarily in the alcoholic drinks industry, but rather an umbrella company for high-quality, high-priced products in the 'image' brand sector.

Diversifications that are into more or less closely related adjacent – or complementary – markets are examples of horizontal integration. An example of pure diversification (conglomerate integration) is acquisition by the Swedish car manufacturer Volvo of firms in the food and drinks sector in Sweden.[47]

Examples of diversification through internal expansion are given by Chandler (1990). Focusing on the emergence of modern, giant, industrial enterprises in the first half of this century, he writes that 'product diversification came from opportunities to use existing production, marketing and research facilities and personnel by developing products for new and more profitable markets' (Chandler, 1990, p. 39). This is closely related to economies of scope, for where a number of different products could be produced using at least some of the same production, marketing, etc., facilities, then this sharing of resources would reduce the average costs below what they would be if each product line were to have its own production, marketing, etc.

In the 25 years after the Second World War, most diversification in Europe was through internal expansion. Moreover, while in the 1970s in the United States a great deal of conglomerate diversification through acquisition took place, in Europe there was much less expansion through acquisition. There was, as in the United States, some over-diversification by European firms, but because they – and this applies particularly to

German firms – 'continued to rely on long-established relationships with banks and other financial institutions, they were able to pull back when such expansion did not prove profitable, and they appear to have done so in a more orderly fashion than their American counterparts' (Chandler, 1990, p. 626).

There is an interesting question arising from the discussion of diversification thus far: why in some cases – and during some periods – is diversification through merger or acquisition, and in others through internal expansion? In answer to this question, de Jong (1993) suggests that the choice is related to the industry life cycle.[48] When an industry is new, firms will be optimistic and expand capacity. Growth will occur, but for no product is there indefinite market growth. Eventually, demand will cease to expand. Arguably (though de Jong does not say so), at some point between the new and the mature phase of the industry, when there is still optimism about its future, if diversification takes place into related product lines, it will be through internal expansion. However, in the mature phase,

> large, financially strong firms with uncertain or unpromising prospects diversify into other industries by means of takeover. As the invention of basically new products cannot be achieved at will and the means of production of a new product cycle are not instantly available for such mature firms, despite extensive research facilities, external diversification is often considered to be a way out of the mature phase. (de Jong, 1993, p. 19)

According to Chandler (1990, p. 626), one reason for the predominance of mergers and acquisitions in the United States and of internal expansion in Europe during the 1960s and 1970s is the 'smaller size of the European capital markets, in terms of volume and turnover of transactions, and the continuing strength of the banks (particularly in Germany) and of the financial holding companies'. Unlike in the United States, as a result, in Europe there was little development of an active market for corporate control.

We have shown that, since the mid-1980s, a large number of firms have diversified through acquisition in Europe. Either the industries in which these firms operate are in mature phases (if de Jong is correct) or the size of the capital markets of Europe have grown since the 1970s (if Chandler is correct). Both the explanations are to some extent correct. First, in relation to the argument that diversification through M&As is more likely in the mature phase, while there has been a general increase in the number of M&As in most sectors in the second half of the 1980s and the 1990s, the increase has been most noticeable in mature, slow-growth sectors (Jacquemin and Wright, 1993). In particular, chemicals, a mature industry experiencing low growth since the 1970s, had a significantly higher number of M&As in the second half of the 1980s than any other industry (an annual average of 88, over 17 per cent of the total; de Jong, 1993, table 2). Second, with respect to the growth in the European financial market, a combination of the integration of the financial markets of Europe since the mid-1980s and increasingly free flows of capital internationally, both within and beyond Europe, have provided large firms, even national ones, with new options (Vipond, 1994).

In the context of the discussion on M&As versus internal expansion, it is appropriate to point out that the two strategies are not necessarily alternatives; both can be employed by the same firms. Moreover, while in the 1980s and early 1990s M&As, joint ventures and internal expansion were seen as the main means of diversifying, there is now a much greater focus on looser, networked forms of organization. Chandler, for example, has more recently co-edited a book on the 'dynamic firm' which does not address the issue of M&As versus internal expansion, but pays a great deal of attention to networks and clustering (Chandler *et al.*, 1998). And the key issue in a book entitled *The Twenty-first-century Firm* is whether the porous boundary, flattened hierarchy, networked organization of production identified by Powell (2001) is the dominant new form.

Thus it is clear that using the number of M&As is only a partial measure of diversification, excluding as it does all diversification through internal expansion and alliance networks. There are two other measures commonly used by industrial economists (see, for example, Scherer and Ross, 1990, pp. 91–2). The first is based on a system of classification of activity of firms. The European system, already discussed in Chapter 5, is called NACE. At the three-digit level there are 130 activities or product/service categories. The first measure simply asks in how many of these 130 categories each firm operates. The result of such a count clearly depends on the classification system. The more disaggregated the system, the higher will be the number. The International Standard Industries Classification (ISIC), for example, has 512 different categories.

The weakness of this measure is that it does not take into account the relative importance of the different activities of the firm. A firm realizing 90 per cent of its turnover in the sale of one product i, and one per cent in the sale of each of ten other products, will appear as diversified as another firm engaged equally in 11 product lines.

Because of this weakness, a second, weighted, measure of diversification is sometimes used. This diversification index, di, derived from the Herfindahl index of seller concentration, is found as follows:

$$di = \frac{1}{\sum\limits^{n} z_{ij}^2}$$

where z_{ij} is the fraction of firm i's sales in the jth activity or product. If the firm operates in only one activity, then $di = 1$. If the firm had 10 activities, each accounting for one-tenth of total turnover, then:

$$di = \frac{1}{\sum\limits_{j=1}^{10} \left(\frac{1}{10j}\right)^2} = 10$$

Similarly, whatever the number of activities in which the firm has equal shares, the di will equal that number. A high fraction of the firm's activities in one activity, and low fractions in others will bring the diversification index near to one.

Both this and the unweighted diversification index have the weakness that must be common to all such indices based on the traditional definition of the firm. It is clear that, even if Powell's (2001) prediction of the loose, networked form of production organization becoming the dominant form is not realized, it will still constitute a significant element of economic activity. If a firm participates indirectly – through its relationships with other firms – in a product area, then this will not be reflected in the indices. Developments in these new, less clearly demarcated forms of production organization are much more difficult to quantify. The many case studies of clusters (see Chapter 8) are among the responses to this problem.

The few empirical studies on diversification in Europe reveal that diversification has proceeded by spurts, and along different paths in different European countries, at different times and in different industries. In the UK, Kumps (1975) found that between 1958 and 1963, the degree of diversification increased. During this period, the number of lines of business in which firms were involved increased by 33 per cent. In the case of German firms, the increasing degree of concentration in the second part of the 1960s went in parallel with an increasing degree of diversification (Schwartz, 1973).

During the same period, diversification in France and in Germany was not a common strategy, with the exception of the luxury goods industry (Dior and Cartier diversifying into spectacles, Porsche into watches and spectacles), and the food industry. The aggressive strategy of BSN (world-wide leader of mineral water drinks) was unusual for the period in Europe. As a French firm, it was also unusual in diversifying through acquisitions abroad. Most acquisitions by French firms during that period were of other French firms, and it was not until the late 1980s that international mergers and acquisitions by French firms – for example, Sodima–Yoplait and Pernod–Ricard – became common.

As a strategy of firms, diversification opens up the possibility of a number of other strategies already discussed in this chapter. A factor often found in successful diversification is *cross-subsidization* (Edwards, 1955). Diversified firms can transfer resources across divisions situated in the various markets in which they operate. This gives them an incentive to carry out discriminatory strategies such as predatory pricing and price discrimination, and non-price strategies such as R&D and advertising.

The division engaged in predatory pricing can afford to do so because it can rely on funds coming from the other divisions of the firm. Once the other firms have been evicted from the market, the division can set monopoly prices – unless there are low entry costs, in which case the threat of entry will keep prices low; predatory pricing is unlikely in contestable markets.

The cross-subsidization argument, and the suggestion that it underlies a positive relationship between diversification and profitability, have been the subject of criticism.[49] First, as already suggested, while diversification can facilitate cross-subsidization, and cross-subsidization makes predatory pricing easier, predatory pricing is profitable only where there are significant entry barriers (see also Weston, 1973). Second, Cowling *et al.* (1980, p. 331) argue that diversification is intrinsically related to firm size, and that 'the effects of diversification can be analysed initially within the framework of traditional analysis in which relative size is a major determinant of a firm's monopoly power[;] ... this is implicit in the cross-subsidisation analysis but not fully recognised'. In other words, for small firms with little monopoly power, advantages to be gained from diversification and cross-subsidization are limited. In recent work that seems to some extent to contradict this, Phu *et al.* (2004) find that while size has a positive effect on performance, diversification has a negative effect. However, while their study is econometrically sophisticated, they focus on one subsector, German business-related services, and on one relatively short period, 1994–2000.

We have so far identified two main *reasons for diversifying*: to gain the benefits of economies of scope, and to facilitate other strategies such as cross-subsidization and predatory pricing. A third reason is to reduce risk.

The profitability of a diversified firm may be raised or the variability of profits may be diminished, because of a reduction in risk; with a presence in a number of markets, the likelihood of the firm as a whole failing, is diminished. The reduction of risk is greater the more disconnected are the markets in which the diversified firm operates. The three reasons for, or advantages of, diversification thus apply to three broadly different situations. The more complementary the diversification, the more the gains from economies of scope; the greater the barriers to entry, the more the potential gains to diversification from such strategies as cross-subsidization and predatory pricing; the more conglomerate the diversification, the more the gains from reduction of risk.

10.5 Strategic responses to regional integration

In the context of Europe, the 1980s were marked by the revival and intensification of the integration process. Among the immediate aims of the EC Commission's 1985 White Paper *Completing the Internal Market* was the removal of remaining non-tariff barriers. This would create a single European market and, as a result, would encourage European firms to see themselves increasingly as European, rather than as German, French or Dutch. This was based on a belief that the fragmented nature of European markets put European firms at a disadvantage with respect to American and Japanese firms; the more significant were increasing returns to scale in the major industries, the more would European firms in these industries gain from an expansion of their markets.[50]

The integration process does not seem to have been impeded by expansion, from a Community of nine at the beginning of the 1980s, to ten with Greece joining in 1981 and 12 with Spain and Portugal joining in 1986. The EU grew to 15 member states, with Austria, Finland and Sweden joining in 1995, and to 25 members when 8 CEEP[51] transition countries plus Cyprus and Malta joined on 1 May 2004. European integration and expansion, together with various global forces, have been a spur to a wave of mergers, acquisitions and strategic alliances among European firms, and between European and non-European firms since the mid-1980s.[52]

10.5.1 Mergers, acquisitions and joint ventures

Mergers, acquisitions and alliances (MAAs) have already been discussed in a number of places in this book. In Chapter 5, which was mainly about structure, mergers were mentioned in Section 5.4 in the context of a discussion about market definition. In Chapter 7, we mentioned mergers in Section 7.2 as a factor in the impact of European integration on concentration. In the present chapter, mainly about strategy, MAAs have again been discussed, first, as vertical integration in Section 10.3 and second, as horizontal and conglomerate integration in Section 10.4. Here we will examine the major trends in mergers, acquisitions and joint ventures (MAJVs)[53] before and since the upsurge in this type of corporate activity in the mid-1980s. In Section 10.5.2 we briefly examine other types of alliances.

An early example of empirical work on the strategy of European multinational enterprises (MNEs) after the first stage of integration was that of Franko (1976). Based on data covering the period 1958–71, his study concentrated on the conduct of over 80 European MNEs having their headquarters in the six founding members of the EC. He found that although there had been a substantial increase in European multinational operations in the EC, intra-EC operations were relatively limited and confined to a few sectors such as cars and electrical appliances. Given that most foreign direct investments are made through acquisitions, these findings are likely also to reflect mergers and acquisitions (see Thomsen and Woolcock, 1993, p. 22).

That the EC was not seen as an integrated entity within which to develop corporate strategy is confirmed by work specifically on M&As. There was a merger and acquisition wave in the 1960s in some ways analogous to that since the mid-1980s. They both followed significant steps in European economic integration. But the post-1958 wave was based decidedly on intra-national mergers, whereas the post-1985 wave has been much more evenly distributed among national, intra-EC and extra-EC M&As.[54] The national concentration of mergers, even in the UK, the most international of European economies, is shown by Hannah's (1983) data:[55] in the decade of the 1960s, 5635 firms disappeared in the UK as a result of mergers, more than the 5468 firms that disappeared as a result of mergers during the previous six decades.

Since the mid-1980s there has been an increase in cross-border MAJVs in Europe, both absolutely and as a proportion of the total. Data gathered by the EU and reported in the annual *Reports on Competition Policy* in the 1980s and early 1990s show that the percentage of MAJVs that were between firms within the same member state was lower from the mid-1980s on than the 65 per cent of 1983/84.

Cross-border M&As continued to increase in the late 1990s, driven both by the 'new economy' boom and by a combination of increasing integration and impending enlargement in the EU. Table 10.4 shows that the value of M&As continued to increase both in western Europe[56] and the United States. There is also some evidence that cross-border M&As were an increasing proportion of total M&As over the period (Bley and Madura, 2003, table 2A). This is, moreover, a global trend. As reported by Renner (2000), 'while cross-border mergers were typically below 20 percent of the value of all mergers in the early 1980s, today [1999] they represent 33 percent'.

Table 10.4 Value of M&As in western Europe and the United States, 1996-1999 ($m)								
	Origin				Target			
	1996	1997	1998	1999	1996	1997	1998	1999
Western Europe	109,591	152,921	323,768	517,269	87,996	117,305	194,346	350,282
United States	60,744	80,869	137,421	112,426	68,069	81,707	209,548	233,032

Source: Bley and Madura, 2003, table 1

Bley and Madura's (2003) analysis suggests that there is increasing industrial integration in Europe, accounted for by 'the use of a single European currency, to the recent removal of cross-border barriers within the Eurozone, or to a combination of these forces'.

If we differentiate between mergers and JVs, we find that the preference for one over the other is uneven across space and across sectors. Cox and Watson (1995) calculate the ratio of number of mergers to number of joint ventures, for the period 1986 to 1990, and show that in high-technology sectors (chemicals, electrical and electronic engineering, computers and data processing, and mechanical engineering) the ratio is much lower (3.8) than in the rest of industry (6.4). What this means is that while all firms prefer mergers and acquisitions to joint ventures, firms in high-technology sectors are more likely to opt for joint ventures than firms in other sectors.

Firms in industries with rapidly changing technologies will wish to 'hedge their bets' by co-operating in various ways with their competitors. They will, however, wish to select the projects in relation to which to co-operate. They may co-operate with one competitor in one project and another competitor in another. This way they will maintain independence but learn from their associations with other firms. This explains the choice of JVs over mergers.[57] As de Bandt (1987) has argued, success is achieved by high levels of both competition and co-operation.

In a study of the automotive industry, Kim and McElreath (2001) point out that in the context of foreign direct investment, JVs are often preferred over independent establishment of new factories.

> Joint ventures ... are less expensive, since the capital costs of starting foreign production are shared with the partner. They also can allow smaller companies larger economies of scale when buying supplies. But most importantly, companies can link with partners having in-depth knowledge of the foreign country, such as its language, consumer preferences and business culture. They also can share in technology or manufacturing know-how in which the partner has special expertise.

The merger/JV ratio also varies in terms of degree of internationalism. While the recent data in the annual *Reports on Competition Policy* do not include breakdown of mergers, acqui-sitions and joint ventures, reports up to the early 1990s did provide this data. The data showed that mergers, acquisitions and JVs tend to rise and fall together over time. However, as between national, EU and extra-EU transactions, there are differences in the preferences for each of the strategies. National refers to MAJVs between firms within the same EU member state; EU refers to cross-border MAJVs between firms within the EU; and extra-EU refers to cross-border MAJVs in which one of the firms is an EU firm and the other a non-EU firm. The difference between number of mergers and number of JVs is greatest for national, and least for international, deals; the more international the MAA, the more likely are firms to opt for JVs rather than mergers. Cox and Watson (1995) show similar results for aggregated 1986–90 data. In their terms, the more distant the firms from each other, the greater the aversion to mergers. Firms may begin with JVs to gain familiarity with a foreign market and/or foreign competitor. The greatest familiarity (and therefore greatest likeli-hood that the deal is a merger or takeover) is in relation to co-national firms, the next in relation to other EU firms, and least in relation to non-EU firms. This is consistent with the findings of Kim and McElreath's (2001) more recent case study of the automotive industry.

To summarize, MAJVs increased during the late 1980s and 1990s, peaking in 2000; mergers were more important than JVs; high-technology firms were more likely than other firms to use JVs; national deals are least likely to be JVs, EU deals more likely, and extra-EU most likely; cross-border mergers in the EU – as globally – have been increasingly important in recent decades.

In the context of the completion of the single European market, one objective was to facili-tate the emergence of European firms. 'There is increasing recognition within the European Commission . . . of the need for MAAs to allow EC firms to compete more effectively with non-EC firms' (Hamill, 1992, p. 155). The increase in cross-border, intra-EU M&As could therefore be seen as success. The study by Bley and Madura (2003) on European mergers in the late 1990s confirms that the increase in mergers during that period is indicative of greater economic integration.

Mergers and European regulations

Efforts at creating an integrated economy in Europe have been reflected at the level of regu-lation. (For detailed discussion of competition policy, see Chapter 15.) The merger regulation (Regulation No. 4064/89) that came into force in 1990 has undergone minor revi-sion but any merger or acquisition with a Community dimension must still be notified.[58] What 'Community dimension' meant was that the total worldwide turnover of all the under-takings concerned exceeded ECU 5 billion and that the total Community-wide turnover of at least two of the undertakings exceeded ECU 250 million. If each of the undertakings con-cerned accounted for more than two-thirds of its Community-wide turnover within one member state then this removed the Community dimension. A fundamental element of the system has been its provision of a European '"one stop shop" for the scrutiny of large cross-border mergers, dispensing with the need for companies to file notifications in several member States' (Monti, 2003).[59]

How the notifications varied annually over the period of operation of the 1990 merger regulations is shown in Fig. 10.3.

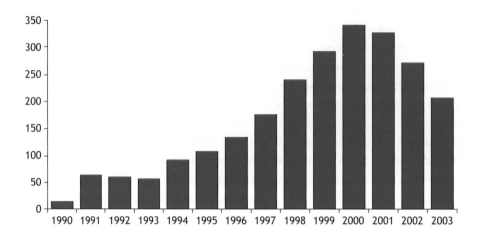

Figure 10.3 Number of M&As notified to the European Commission, 1990-2003
Source: CEC, 2003c

Although based on a measure of M&As very different from that of Table 10.4 (number rather than value), Fig. 10.3 shows a similar upward trend for the relevant years. The economic upswing of the second half of the 1990s is clearly reflected in the data. That M&As peaked in 2000 and fell back the following year is, according to the *Report on Competiton Policy 2002*, 'in line with the world decline in stock markets'. The factors underlying the rise in M&As during the late 1990s, the *Report on Competition Policy 1999* stated, were 'the globalisation of markets, the introduction of the euro, the completion of the single market and the forthcoming enlargement'.

Other important information provided in the various *Reports on Competition Policy* includes the breakdown by type of deal of the deals notified to the Commission. The 2003 Report provides aggregate data for the years 1994 to 2003, as follows: acquisition of majority, 59 per cent; joint venture/control, 33 per cent; takeover bid, 4 per cent; and others, 4 per cent. Takeovers or acquisitions are consistently the most important category over time.

Other aspects of MAJV trends

By analogy with the dominance by Japanese firms of the UK machine tool industry, there is a danger that, if non-EU firms in certain sectors come to dominate in the EU through MAJVs, then this will reduce R&D and other high value added parts of the production process in the EU. This will result if the non-EU firms shift these higher value added, more technologically sophisticated parts of the production process to their home bases and use their association with – or ownership of – EU firms to gain access to the EU market.

Cox and Watson (1995) show that among EU firms looking for cross-border MAJVs in major high-technology industries such as computers and electronics, there is a marked preference for association with non-EU firms. This is explained by the fact that the leading firms in these industries are non-EU firms. In chemicals, where European firms are the world leaders, the data suggest a preference for intra-EU deals. Cox and Watson also show that the industries in the EU that stood 'to gain the most from a round of merger activity – electronics, computers, chemicals, automotive, and aerospace – are clearly those industries which experienced the highest level of cross-border deals'. In other words, while in some industries non-EU firms may be gaining from the MAJVs, in the key sectors – at least up to 1990 – there was some Europeanization of industry.

The different levels of M&A activity and the extent to which it is cross-border in Europe are shown in Table 10.5.

Table 10.5 Intensity and cross-border nature of M&As in Europe, the United States and Japan, 1990s

	M&A activity[a]	Cross-border Ratio[b]
Austria	36.5	51.6
Belgium	36.5	45.0
Denmark	72.5	38.3
Finland	147.3	22.7
France	38.2	33.7
Germany	48.5	26.0
Greece	14.1	23.1
Ireland	45.7	52.4
Italy	19.9	36.3
Netherlands	48.2	43.1
Norway	93.4	36.7
Portugal	23.1	40.4
Spain	23.5	37.5
Sweden	84.7	35.4
UK	73.4	23.4
United States	59.3	8.7
Japan	6.0	13.2

[a] M&A activity = number of deals divided by average population (in millions)

[b] Cross-border ratio = percentage of completed deals where the acquirer and the target are from different countries

Source: Rossi and Volpin, 2003, table 2

The intensity of M&A activity varies widely across countries.[60] In terms of population it is particularly high in the Scandinavian countries – Denmark, Finland, Norway and Sweden – and the UK. Rossi and Volpin (2003) argue that, in general, M&A activity is greater in countries where there is better investor protection. It is certainly clear that the very different institutional context in Japan accounts for the low levels of both M&A and cross-border M&A activitiy in Japan.[61] Rossi and Volpin's analysis suggests that cross-border M&As are a consequence of differences in levels of investor protection; acquirers tend to be from countries with better investor protection than target companies. They conclude that M&As improve governance, constituting a driver for convergence in corporate governance regimes.

It is possible to extract from Rossi and Volpin's (2003) data[62] some interesting facts concerning the main sources of takeovers in European countries in the 1990s. This is shown in Table 10.6.

Table 10.6 Main sources of cross-border M&As in Europe, 1990s (percentage of deals)

	United States	UK	Other non-EU	Other EU	Main acquisitor	Total cross-border
Austria	3.9	2.5	6.9	36.7	Germany (27)	50.0
Belgium	6.1	8.3	2.0	28.2	France (8.6)	44.6
Denmark	6.1	4.8	2.5	24.3	Sweden (8.3)	37.7
Finland	2.8	1.9	1.3	15.5	Sweden (9.1)	21.5
France	7.8	6.6	3.6	13.8		31.8
Germany	6.6	3.7	4.2	11.1		25.6
Greece	2.1	2.8	1.4	13.3	France (3.5); Italy (3.5)	19.6
Ireland	11.9	28.9	4.3	5.0		50.1
Italy	5.8	5.1	5.0	17.3	France (6.6)	33.2
Netherlands	8.2	11.7	4.5	18.0		42.4
Norway	5.6	6.6	3.1	20.2	Sweden (9.1)	35.5
Portugal	3.1	3.6	3.5	28.1	Spain (12.1)	38.3
Spain	5.3	5.7	3.8	18.4	France (6.4)	33.2
Sweden	6.2	6.2	2.5	18.9		33.8
UK	10.3	na	4.2	6.8		21.3

Source: Derived from Rossi and Volpin, 2003, table 2A

Table 10.6 shows that, for most European countries, the main source of acquisitor companies is a contiguous country. In relation to Austria, for example, the final column shows that 50 per cent of all acquisitions in Austria were cross-border, made up of 3.9 per cent from the United States, 2.5 per cent from the UK, 6.9 per cent from other non-EU countries and 36.7 per cent from other EU countries (that is, all other EU countries in the table other than the UK). The second-last column shows the main source of companies taking over Austrian companies. Thus Germany accounted for 27 per cent of all acquisitions in Austria in the 1990s. Where the main acquisitor column is blank, then the main source of acquiring companies is either the United States or the UK. The findings in Table 10.6 do not necessarily contradict Rossi and Volpin's (2003) general argument about differences in investor protection. However, proximity – and, presumably, the greater knowledge about markets that comes with proximity – is clearly a key factor in determining the geography of M&A activities in Europe. Of the non-EU sources of acquiring companies, the United States was by far the most important. Other than contiguous countries, the United States and the UK are the most important sources of M&A deals for the countries in the table.

It also follows from Table 10.6 that M&As in most European countries in the 1990s were predominantly intra-national. That is, the parties to the deal were within the same country. The only country in the table that has a majority of cross-border acquisitors is Ireland. This may be explained by the fact that Ireland is an extremely open, international economy, with a high percentage of economic activity accounted for by subsidiaries of MNEs.

The reasons for M&As

Why do firms undertake M&As? From an economic point of view, M&As improve efficiency and/or increase market power. To the extent that they improve efficiency without increasing market power, welfare economics holds that they improve welfare; to the extent that they increase market power without improving efficiency, welfare economics holds that they reduce welfare. Moreover, the underlying factors in the merger boom included globalization, the euro and European enlargement. But these are not the immediate reasons or objectives of firms undertaking MAJVs.[63] Such objectives include the following:

1   To improve efficiency through economies of scale and scope

2   To facilitate technological development through exchange of information

3   To reduce risks ('hedge bets') by co-operating with one or more competitors

4   To increase control over the market through agreement (collusion) with competitors

5   To expand the range of markets accessible to the firm's products[64]

6   To improve access to (or terms for borrowing) capital

7   To avoid various types of government control, for example over trade.

It is highly likely that in most cases two or more of the above factors are relevant. While they may be the motivations of firms, implementing them may be illegal. Underlying any one of the above reasons may be the motivation of increasing the firm's power; expressed as dominance over competitors, suppliers or customers this may be illegal, for example if there is abuse of the dominant position.

Growth and expansion as a driver of firm's activities is common. This relates to both 1 and 6 above. In terms of economies of scale, it is particularly interesting that, given that most deals are intra-national, the appropriate scale of activity for most firms has been their national markets.

At the other end of the scale, in some industries the most successful firms are neither national nor European, but global. The dominant MAJVs in these industries have been between European on the one hand and American or Japanese firms on the other. In the pharmaceutical industry – in which American firms are the leading initiators of takeovers of European firms – many of the top firms are the result of Euro-American mergers and/or acquisitions, and all the top firms have alliances of various kinds across the Atlantic, and often with Japanese firms as well. For example, SmithKline Beecham and Glaxo Wellcome were both Anglo-American, and they merged to form GlaxoSmithKline; Rhône-Poulenc Rorer is Franco-American.

Between the national and global, the European scale is also relevant for many firms. McKelvey *et al.* (2004) point to Ciba-Geigy and Sandoz forming Novartis, Rhône-Poulenc and Hoechst forming Aventis, and Astra and Zeneca forming AstraZeneca, all M&As of European companies. In terms of motivation, they hypothesize that these are 'defensive' M&As of 'weakening' companies. 'In other cases', they continue, 'it is successful American corporations that acquire weaker European companies. It would appear, however, at first sight, that the stronger American companies (such as Merck and Pfizer) are less involved in this type of expansion than weaker US corporations or European firms.'

The assessment of trends in industrial M&As in Europe suggests a mixed reception: there has been a degree of Europeanization, but national M&As still predominate; and in some sectors M&As involving non-EU firms have been predominant.[65]

10.5.2 Other strategic alliances

In addition to MAJVs, firms can also adopt alliance strategies that involve less commitment, control or interdependence, for example, licensing and cross-licensing, subcontracting and other collaboration.

Licensing and cross-licensing

In a standard *licensing* agreement, a company having proprietary rights (the licensor) gives another company (the licensee) the right of use in return for a fee. Usually in industry[66] there is a product or process over which the licensor has a patent or trademark. This firm gives the information on how to produce the product or use the process to the licensee firm in return for a fee. Along with technical know-how, the licensor often provides support services. The fee can be a lump sum or a payment per unit sold (royalty). A firm would license rather than produce because transaction costs in licensing the particular product are lower

– using both direct and indirect costs – than internalizing the operation. There are a number of reasons why this might be the case:[67]

- ◆ While the licensor may have the knowledge, the licensee may have the experience in that type of production. A software firm, for example, may produce a new type of programme, but have no experience – or capacity – to manufacture and distribute multiple copies of the programme.

- ◆ The licensor may have the knowledge and experience, but not have a production presence in the location of the licensee. Because of lack of familiarity or other factors leading to high start-up costs, licensing rather than direct production takes place.

- ◆ The licensor may be fully utilizing its production capacity but not wish to expand because, for example, it believes that the need for extra capacity will be temporary. This type of licensing is also known as second-sourcing.

Licensing is in general more common where the product (or service) is clearly defined, and where the product or process is not technologically strategic, that is, where the firm holding the proprietary right sees no further development of the product or process that may be usurped by the licensee.

In the context of increasing integration and enlargement of the EU, licensing becomes a more attractive strategy to licensors only because it is a means of getting access to a larger market. However, the licensing strategy 'is particularly effective for smaller markets (niches) and in countries with which a firm is not sufficiently familiar to enter alone' (Jacobson, 1991). It is therefore particularly appropriate for small or medium-sized enterprises (SMEs) that have products with narrow markets. For example, SMEs in the Japanese pharmaceutical industry, of which there are a large number, are most likely to use licensing to gain access to the European market. Larger Japanese pharmaceutical companies have had their products manufactured and distributed by western companies in Europe for many years. They have, through this, gained familiarity with the European market. Following the completion of the single market in 1992, they saw a need for greater control and began to use other strategies to maintain or increase their presence in the EU, such as greenfield investments and MAJVs.

Cross-licensing is used, for example, as part of a technology exchange agreement. With cross-licensing, each company has something the other requires; they agree to exchange the information, usually as the start of an alliance the next step in which would be a joint venture (Hagedoorn and Schakenraad, 1990). In ordinary licensing, the licensor is usually more technologically advanced, or in some other respect ahead of the licensee; the former, after all, has something the latter wishes to acquire. Cross-licensing is usually an agreement between firms on a more equal footing. Cross-licensing is one of many types of agreement that firms in high-technology industries have used to ensure that they keep in touch with what their competitors are doing. Along with MAJVs, there has been an increase in cross-licensing both among European and between European and non-European firms since the mid-1980s.

Subcontracting

Like licensing, *subcontracting* is a form of co-operation whereby in-house production is rejected, reduced or restricted, in favour of production by independent firms. Also, as with licensing, the transaction cost analysis – compare all costs of 'make' with all costs of 'buy' to arrive at the 'make or buy' decision – is crucial. Often the job is tendered for, that is, the firm makes it known to a number of other firms that it will require a certain quantity of some product; the other firms respond by informing the first firm as to cost, quality and timing conditions under which they can produce the product. The first firm then chooses to whom to give the contract. If the contract is fulfilled satisfactorily, it can lead to exclusive supply agreements (see Jacobson and O'Sullivan, 1994).

According to Semlinger (1991), outsourcing (that is, 'the market procurement of formerly in-house produced goods and services') and subcontracting were on the increase in the 1980s. This is explained mostly by more intense competition on world markets, and the rise of Japanese firms as competitors in these markets. An important aspect of Japanese business organization is that firms often have extensive networks of affiliated subcontractors. American and European firms responded by developing similar networks. That these kinds of activities have continued to increase in the 1990s is clear from the work of Powell (2001), among others.

The nature and importance of subcontracting in the EC was analysed by Charbit *et al.* (1991). They found that, over the period 1980–86, intra-EC subcontracting increased sharply. (This is where both the principal and the subcontractor were EC firms.) The major principals were British, German and French firms.[68] The nature of the subcontracting networks differed:

- Those between Benelux, French and German firms involved a wide range of different industries, and were of a 'circular' type; there were principals and subcontractors in each of these member states.

- Subcontracting networks involving firms from Spain, Portugal and Greece were limited to a much smaller range of industries, and were 'centrifugal'; the firms in these countries were mainly subcontractors, with the principal firms predominantly in Germany, France and Benelux. Spain is particularly important as the home of subcontractor firms in parts of the automotive, metal and mechanical engineering industries.

- Because of strong links between the UK and Ireland on one hand and North America on the other, firms in these economies did not appear to have strong subcontracting links with the rest of Europe. This is consistent with our findings in relation to Table 10.6.

Recent research focuses more broadly on supply chain management rather than subcontracting. And it shows consistently that along with this change in discourse, there is also a change in behaviour. With intensification of competition arising from globalization and further integration in Europe, firms aim at increasing their cost effectiveness and at improving customer satisfaction. Among ways of achieving both these ends is to strategically emphasize their core capabilities and to develop supply chains and networks to do all the other aspects of the manufacturing and distribution of their products. There is a variety of ways in which this is done, including short-term coalitions and long-term partnerships. These coalitions and partnerships frequently, though not always, emerge in the context of regional clusters (Enright, 1998).

Other types of collaboration

Collaboration between firms can include vague discussions between managers at the simplest, most casual level, and formal exchange of information in preparation for a merger at the most intense level. The advantage of collaboration is that the firms maintain independence; the disadvantage is that success for all the collaborators depends on high levels of trust and integrity. It is relatively easy, for example in collaboration over R&D, for one party to obtain from the collaboration disproportionately more than it puts into it.

Collaboration is seen as particularly important in high-technology industries, and in R&D in general. Jacquemin (1987a) has pointed out, among other advantages of technological collaboration, the 'dynamic economies', whereby the collaboration accelerates invention and innovation through learning effects of working together. This can lead to increased market power.

Another advantage of collaboration is the support that it provides in the establishment and imposition of technical standards. Well-known standards such as VHS for video recorders and the MS DOS and Windows operating systems for computers, although resulting from the efforts of leading firms, also required collaboration from other firms. As Antonelli (1998) concludes, 'the emergence of standards is embedded in the circumstances of cooperation among rivals'. Using Antonelli's ideas, among others, Tan (2002) examines the establishment of standards in the mobile telecommunications sector. He shows that, in the establishment of the second generation (2G) GSM system, the role of the EU was crucial in the establishment of the standard. By more or less imposing the standard, the EU created certainty which 'resulted in rapid installation and expansion of 2G mobile systems in Europe, which built up a solid European base for rolling its GSM bandwagon to the global market. Being the first available digital standard in the world and having a significant installed base in Europe' resulted in the standard attracting new entrants into mobile telecoms. Thus, in addition to collaboration among firms in the establishment of standards, the EU had the advantage of collaboration among governments. Between 1997 and 2000, GSM subscribers went from 50 million to 350 million. Starting from roughly the same base, GSM went in three years to more than double the total number of subscribers to all other standards. Tan (2002) seems to conclude that this success suggests that the 3G European standard will also outstrip its American competitor.

Intra-EC collaboration, particularly in R&D, has been emphasized as an important, positive result of increasing economic integration in Europe (Hayward, 1995). The idea was to encourage the emergence of 'Euro-champions' in high-technology sectors. In sensitive sectors such as armaments, aerospace, machine tools, biotechnology and electronics, technological collaboration would enhance EC sovereignty. Once European firms had become the equals of their Japanese and American competitors they could then enter into various kinds of alliances with them. The fear was that if they did so too early, they would become merely subcontractors. In addition, collaboration would help in the achievement of the large and more integrated European domestic market by removing diverging technical standards.

Esprit and the various Framework Programmes discussed in Chapter 11 aim to encourage intra-EU collaboration in R&D, but such efforts have been limited. While there has been an increase in all types of strategic alliance, including research collaboration, among EU firms since the mid-1980s, there have also been increases in collaboration between EU and non-EU firms. Moreover, as Dienel *et al.* (2002) point out, there remain intensely nationalist biases in national research policies and institutions in the member states of the EU.

At this point, at the end of the chapter on non-price strategies, it should be emphasized that R&D and innovation are fundamentally important non-price strategies. They are, in fact, so important as to justify more attention than any one of the other non-price strategies. For this reason they are considered in much more detail in the next chapter, and, in terms of performance, in Chapter 13.

10.6 Summary

In this chapter we have addressed the various non-price strategies that have been adopted by firms. In relation to each of the strategies we have identified both theoretical and empirical issues. The empirical have usually included the European context. Among changes in recent years that seem to create difficulties for the way we measure strategies and their results, is that firms increasingly undertake activities in conjunction with other firms. This suggests an increasing significance of what we called CI (co-ordination integration), relative to OI (ownership integration), in firms' activities. Even giant corporations have a variety of strategic alliances with other, similar and smaller corporations. This makes it increasingly difficult to find ways of measuring in aggregate the way firms behave. This is not to suggest that aggregate measures of, say, diversification or mergers and acquisitions, is no longer necessary. On the contrary, such measures are still essential to show change over time. But it is important to be aware that they provide only a partial picture. Other, increasingly important, activities of firms in rapidly evolving networks are not indicated in these measures.

In relation to most of the strategies we have discussed, we have considered the implications of European integration. This has, however, been just one of a number of factors influencing firms. In relation to collaboration and strategic alliances in general, for example, EU policy may provide incentives for firms to work together, but they will participate in EU programmes only to the extent that it is in their interests. They will continue to hold options open, including among these options participation in all sorts of alliances with both European and non-European firms. It may in some subsectors be in the general European interest for greater industrial integration – including corporate integration – to take place. It may, however, not be in the interests of individual firms to follow this route. We discuss this issue in more detail in Chapter 15. First we turn to a more detailed discussion of technological change and innovation in Chapter 11.

Websites

For online descriptions of concepts relating to product differentiation, including formal models, see **www.economicswebinstitute.org**

The website of the Library of Economics and Liberty (**www.econlib.org**), which has a right-wing, American bias, provides access to an online *Concise Encyclopedia of Economics*. There are references to, and articles on, many of the concepts in this (and other) chapters in this encyclopedia.

Non-price strategies is a key interest of John Kay. Many of his regular articles in the *Financial Times* and elsewhere address issues raised in this chapter. They can be seen at his website, **www.johnkay.com**

There is a website maintained by the EU (**http://europa.eu.int**), a section of which relates to DG competition (**http://europa.eu.int/comm/competition/index_en.html**). Here can be found all the recent *Reports on Competition Policy* (**http://europa.eu.int/comm/competition/publications**), as well as descriptions of the application of EU policy and law in relation to specific sectors and companies. There are also links to all the member states' national competition authorities (**http://europa.eu.int/comm/competition/national_authorities**) and to other competition sites worldwide (**http://europa.eu.int/comm/competition/other_sites**).

The website **www.questia.com** is a vast online library, including many items of relevance to this chapter, and this book in general (though many of the most recent books listed are not available). There are occasional free items, but, unlike the other websites mentioned above, for full access Questia requires payment.

Questions

10.1 Define and explain product differentiation. As a decision maker in a firm, explain how you would decide whether or not to adopt a strategy of product differentiation.

10.2 Explain the differences between advertising as persuasion and advertising as information. Summarize the findings of research in each of these areas.

10.3 Use the Dorfman–Steiner condition to explain why some firms might adopt and others not adopt a strategy of advertising. Does your explanation fit the data on advertising in different industries?

10.4 Transaction cost theory is often used to explain vertical corporate integration. Provide arguments in favour and against this and explain why there appears to be no consensus.

10.5 What is diversification, how is it measured, and what are the weaknesses in these ways of measuring it?

10.6 What have been the main causes and patterns of M&As in Europe in the past decade?

Notes

1   Though note that if process innovation merely reduces the costs of production, then it does not contribute to the differentiation of the product.

2   See also, on product differentiation in oligopolies, Chapter 6, Section 6.5.

3   For a recent study of differentiation in relation to banks' service quality, see Zineldin (2002).

4   Note that the terms themselves can be confusing. By 'perceived' in this paragraph, we are implying 'perceived but not real'. (Another term for this is 'spurious difference'.) Real differences must, after all, be perceived to have any effect on the market.

5   For more on the role of the retailer in product differentiation, see Porter (1974). See also the section on differentiation in the EU.

6   An individual consumer's tastes and preferences may vary over time, but this is not the issue here. Here the variation is between consumers.

7   A summary of recent neoclassical work (mathematical models), among the aims of which is to find the equilibrium level of differentiation, along with some of the key papers, is provided by Cabral (2000, pp.105–144). See also Böckem (1994)

8   To illustrate, they contrast the high fixed costs in R&D required to speed up a computer, with the increase in variable costs involved in improving the quality of furniture by improving the quality of the raw materials.

9   Advertising is discussed in more detail below.

10 For an example showing the estimation of hedonic prices in the European automotive industry, see Goldberg and Verboven (2001).

11 This awareness of the role of factors such as product differentiation and increasing returns to scale was not incorporated into international trade theory until the 1980s. For discussions on product differentiation and international trade, see Krugman (1983) and McGovern (1994). McGovern points out that Lovasy (1941) had already, decades before the 'new international trade theorists', used product differentiation to explain aspects of international trade. Laussudrie-Duchêne (1971) had as well.

12 For a discussion on these and related issues on the economics of European integration, see Krugman (1987b).

13 This begs the question of why, in so many other high-quality products, Europe lost its leadership to Japan, for example in electronics and cameras. It nevertheless provides some indication of why European firms in some industries continue to be internationally competitive.

14 Kay's view of the 'strategic market' is set out in more detail in Chapter 5 (Section 5.4).

15 This is not an argument against PDO/PGIs which may in fact be a positive factor in the maintenance of food varieties. It is merely to point out that product differentiation strategies in the food industry may be circumscribed by existing PDO/PGIs.

16 This is where a firm sets up, takes over, or otherwise takes control of a part of the production/distribution process closer to the final consumer than itself.

17 Whether directly or by wholly owned distribution channels.

18 It can be argued that the compression of the product life cycle and time-based competition are as important as differentiation in leading computer companies to move closer to their markets. See Egeraat and Jacobson (2004).

19 Economists might wish to compare the gain in welfare from reduction of cigarette consumption – improvements in health, reduction in expenditure on public health and so on – with the reduction in welfare arising from unemployment in the tobacco industry.

20 Alternatively, the consumer will consume more of the good until the marginal utility for the last euro spent on the good is the same as the marginal utility for the last euro spent on all other goods.

21 In each case, all other things being constant and assuming $EA \neq 0$.

22 Note that while the previous subheading was 'A simple neoclassical approach to advertising' here we deal with more advanced neoclassical approaches to advertising. Unless otherwise mentioned, every author discussed here uses mathematical modelling under conditions of equilibrium to identify the nature of the relationships of various variables to advertising expenditure.

23 An experience good is one that has to be consumed before one can determine its quality.

24 The concept is used more generally as 'dissipative signalling' in game theory.

25 Mathematically what this means is that 'the relationships between price and quality and between advertising and quality are not monotonic' (Hertzendorf and Overgaard, 2001).

26 Their conclusions are very close to those of Zhao, though there is no reference to Zhao in Orzach et al.

27 See, for example, Caves and Greene (1996).

28 For an explanation of 'deductive' and 'inductive' see endnote 1 of Chapter 2.

29 'Loyalty' is defined as a rational (non-impulsive) preference, whereas 'inertia' involves routine buying.

30 Also, a proliferation of brands creates confusion among consumers.

31 Dixit in particular is better known now for using game theory in his work.

32 This is a quote from the English summary of the article, which is in Spanish.

33 The same 19 as in Table 10.2

34 In this latter sense we might say that a particular group of firms in a country or region is more industrially integrated if together they contribute all the stages of the product transformation process. There may not be vertical corporate integration, because there are many different firms, but there may be vertical industrial integration, because that region or country provides all the inputs, processing and marketing of the final product. A filière is an example of vertical industrial integration, and not necessarily vertical corporate integration.

35 'The combined capabilities of top and middle management can be considered the skills of the organization itself. These skills were the most valuable of all those that made up the organizational capabilities of the new modern industrial enterprise' (Chandler, 1990, p. 36).

36 Chandler's view of vertical integration is the *evolutionary* perspective. For explanations of both evolutionary and transaction cost theories of the firm, see above, Chapter 4.

37 As to whether the vertical integration induced by asset specificity is OI or CI, this may depend upon uncertainty.

38 A fixed proportion production function describes how one – and one only –combination of inputs is needed to produce a given level of output, for example, two wheels and a frame to produce one bicycle. A variable proportion production function describes how different combinations of inputs can produce a specific output. In this case, inputs can be substituted for one another, as for example where labour and machines can be mixed in different ways to produce the same quantity of a good. On the implications for vertical integration, see Blair and Kaserman (1985), and Shughart (1990).

39 If they were two separate firms, transfer would be something above marginal cost.

40 Attempts by the EU to monitor and control PSTP through harmonization of corporate taxation are discussed in Chapter 7.

41 See also the discussion on the transaction cost theory of the firm in Chapter 4.

42 See the discussion on industrial districts in Chapter 8 for references to the literature in which these arguments are common.

43 The question of size of firm and innovation is discussed in some detail in Chapter 11 under the heading 'Firm size, market structure and innovation'.

44 For a review of some of the more recent literature on size of firm and innovation, see Leavy and Jacobson (1999).

45 For a discussion and critique of the theories of mergers, see Collins (2003).

46 On M&As in the pharmaceutical industry in Europe, see below, Section 10.5.1.

47 For more on mergers and acquisitions, see below, Section 10.5.

48 'The growth cycle concept focuses attention on the various stages through which products, processes and sometimes whole industries pass from birth to death' (de Jong, 1993).

49 For contradictory empirical work in this area, see Cowling *et al.* (1980, p. 327).

50 The notion that there are large economies of scale waiting to be exploited has been questioned. See for example, Cox and Watson (1995), in particular their discussion on pp. 306ff under the heading 'European industrial concentration in the 1960s: the cult of scale'.

51 The eight central and east European countries that joined the EU on 1 May 2004 are Hungary, Poland, Czech Republic, Slovakia, Lithuania, Latvia, Estonia and Slovenia.

52 In addition to MAAs as a strategic response, there has also been a huge increase in foreign direct investment (FDI). Note that cross-border mergers and acquisitions are also FDI.

53 Mergers include majority acquisitions (or takeovers), and a joint venture between two or more firms involves the amalgamation of their business interests in a specific area, product or project, through the creation of a separate company. We will call mergers, acquisitions and JVs *types* of MAJVs.

54 For the earlier period, see Cox and Watson (1995), Geroski and Jacquemin (1985) and, on the UK, Hannah (1983).

55 As reported by Cox and Watson (1995).

56 Sixteen countries: EU 15 excluding Luxembourg, plus Switzerland and Norway.

57 Note that often firms will undertake JVs with other firms in which they hold minority shares. This may lead to acquisition or merger. The pharmaceutical giant, Glaxo Wellcome, for example, with a 17 per cent stake in the Canadian biotechnology company Biochem Pharma, also had, in the summer of 1995, two joint ventures with that company. In August 1995 newspaper reports suggested that Glaxo Wellcome was considering a complete takeover of Biochem Pharma (*Sunday Times*, 13 August 1995).

58 This is in contrast to antitrust cases where all agreements had to be notified but the notification system was discontinued as of May 2004.

59 Note that in this speech, given in Dublin in 2003, Mario Monti also described the Commission's proposals for revision of the merger regulations.

60 It varies less than it would if it was not weighted by population size. In terms of absolute number of deals, the UK with 4294 alone accounts for 26 per cent of the total number of deals in the European countries in Table 10.5. The UK, Germany, France and Italy together account for nearly 70 per cent of the total. It is likely that, in terms of value of deals rather than number of deals, the predominance of the big four in Europe would be even greater.

61 Note that this is consistent with the stylized view of Japan as having a less equity-based and more credit-based finance system – see Chapter 11.

62 The source of which is Thomson Financial Securities Data.

63 See also the discussion on reasons for diversification.

64 This is an application of economies of scope: where the distribution system of one firm facilitates access to markets of the products of its new partner, then the alliance is distributing two products (or ranges of products) cheaper per unit than if they were distributed separately.

65 Note that there is evidence that the broad conclusions arrived at in this section are true both for industrial and service sectors – see CEC, *Report on Competition Policy 1993*, annex iv, table 1.

66 In the service sector it is more common for the licensor to control a brand name. It franchises another firm or individual to use that brand name.

67 See also the various discussions on transaction costs especially in Chapter 4 and in the current chapter.

68 Italian firms were also important but the data for Italy were limited.

CHAPTER 11

Technological change and innovation

11.1 Learning objectives

The main objectives of this chapter are:

- To define and explain the context of the main concepts in the study of technological change and innovation

- To show the limitations of traditional perspectives on technological change and innovation

- To explain how economies are compared in terms of their performance in the areas of science, technology and innovation

- To introduce the concept of national systems of innovation, showing how it complements the traditional measures of national technology performance

- To discuss innovative behaviour of firms, in terms of size of firms and home country base of firms, and

- To consider the extent to which a European system of innovation is emerging

11.2 Technology gap?

Interest in technology and technological change and innovation as a strategy of firms is probably as old as firms themselves. But an intensification of interest in this issue in Europe in the 1970s and 1980s arose from concern that a *technology gap* may be opening up, with

European firms lagging behind those in Japan and the United States. What is meant by technology gap is a disparity in the levels and rates of change of technology. (A more detailed discussion can be found in Chapter 13.)

In this chapter we examine the level of technology and innovation within Europe, and compare Europe with other regions. To prepare the ground we begin with some basic definitions followed by an account of the development of ideas about technological change.

11.3 Basic definitions

Technology has been defined in a number of different ways. Dosi and Orsenigo (1988) define it in terms of information about input combinations, in Germany it is generally regarded as a body of knowledge and skill applicable in the production of goods (Warner, 1994), and Woods (1987) defines it as 'the systematic organisation of the production process'. Freeman and Soete (1997, p. 14) suggest that, at the most basic level, technology is 'that body of knowledge which relates to the production or acquisition of food, clothing, shelter and other human needs'. They go on to say that if that is what we mean by technology, then 'of course all human societies have used technology'. Nevertheless, they argue, the term 'technology' only came into general use in the nineteenth century, when the techniques of production reached a stage of complexity based more on science and less on the skills of hand and eye more common now in 'arts and crafts'. Freeman and Soete (1997, p.15) accept that there is still both science and craft in technology, but argue that 'the newer technologies are revolutionizing the relationships between science and society'.

We understand technology to mean something extremely broad, including production and distribution of goods and services, and the way we organize ourselves to do that production and distribution, although any specific technology is likely to be oriented towards either products or processes (Tunzelman, 2002). Freeman and Soete's emphasis on the importance of the newer technologies suggests the need to differentiate between 'technology' and 'high technology'.

High technology also has a number of different definitions. While it would be preferable to define this – as does the US Congress (1982) – in terms of new and/or innovative products or processes,[1] this is, in practice, very difficult to measure. No data are kept on new and/or innovative products or processes; it is not clear whether such data could be kept in any comprehensive way. As a result, it is more usual to define a high-technology industry as one with a high level of R&D (OECD, 1986). In its recent formulation, this taxonomy has the following categories (OECD, 1994):

High-tech industries:		R&D/Turnover	> 5%
Medium high-tech industries:	5% >	R&D/Turnover	> 3%
Medium low-tech industries:	3% >	R&D/Turnover	> 0.9%
Low-tech industries:	0.9% >	R&D/Turnover	> 0%

Industries that correspond to high-tech on the basis of this definition include aerospace, office machinery and computers, electronics, pharmaceuticals, and precision and measuring instruments. Among the many problems with this definition are that it ignores the fact that there are advanced technologies in traditional industries such as clothing, textiles and furniture, and that it excludes from 'high-tech' many important innovations[2] that are not the result of R&D (Hirsch-Kreinsen *et al.*, 2003).

A *key technology* is 'the specific knowledge that enables a firm to keep up with or ahead of its competitors' (Pavitt and Sharp, 1992). Similar to this is a *core technology* which is a technology the 'mastery of which is essential to the development of an industrial sector. Some may be specific to a given industry, while others may have more general application' (Woods, 1987, p. 17). The idea of a widespread application across many sectors leads to the notion of a *generic technology* or a *pervasive technology* (Pavitt and Sharp, 1992). Generic technologies are most evident in the mechanical engineering, chemicals, and office equipment sectors. A *strategic technology* is one that enables a nation (or an economically integrated area) to keep its economic independence. The concept was developed for use in conjunction with the notion of *filière* developed by French economists (see Chapter 8, Section 8.4).

11.4 Some contributions to the development of ideas about technology

That our interest in technological change and its causes is not new, is clear from the following sentence written in 1826: 'The rapidity with which during the last twenty years invention has followed upon invention may be taken as one of the signs of the increased quantity of knowledge and ingenuity which, by means of improved education, has been introduced into the community' (Ellis, 1826). However, economists have differed and ideas have changed about what technological change and innovation are and how they should be studied. Ellis was interested in the relationship between the quality of labour and capital on one hand and productivity and profitability on the other, and he focused on the consequences of the introduction of new machinery. This typically classical perspective related closely to the material conditions that prevailed at the time. Many classical economists asked whether industrialization could generate as much work as it was displacing through mechanization.

Following the marginalist revolution in economics in the late nineteenth and early twentieth centuries, the focus shifted to the theory and measurement of the relationship, at a point in time, between the inputs of factors of production and the resulting level of output. This relationship – the neoclassical production function – was based on the assumption of fixed technical knowledge. A change in technology would shift the production function. Technological change and innovation were exogenous to this static conception of how industrial economies evolve.

Working within the neoclassical tradition, Fabricant (1954), Abramovitz (1956) and Solow

(1957) produced ground-breaking conceptual as well as empirical studies, shedding some light on the famous 'residual'. Solow (1957), attempting to measure the contribution of technological change to productivity, showed that over a period of decades, the increase in output was far more than could be accounted for by the increases in the inputs. In particular, labour productivity could not be explained by increases in the capital/labour ratio alone. There had to be some 'residual' factor accounting for a large part – as much as 90 per cent – of the productivity change. From the early 1960s, Denison (1985) began extending Solow's work by decomposing the residual. 'This residual comprised all those awkward hard-to-measure elements other than labour and capital, such as technical and institutional change' (Freeman, 1994).

The studies on the residual opened the door to the dynamic models of growth, with publications from the 1960s by Arrow (1962), Uzawa (1965) and Phelps (1966), among others. Seeing human capital as a core variable, Arrow used the assumption of increasing returns to scale, whereas Uzawa used an optimizing growth model. A clear distinction between endogenous and exogenous technical change appears in the work of Heertje (1977), in his thorough review of contributions leading to the emergence of what was subsequently referred to as the 'new' growth theory. Heertje defines endogenous technical change with due reference to: '(i) long-term changes in the ratio between the prices of the factors of production; (ii) learning processes concerning production; and (iii) investment in education and research' (Heertje, 1977: 174).

Thus human capital accumulation, learning considerations and information and knowledge were already included as essential factors in the process of economic growth in some of the *modern* growth theories of the 1960s and 1970s. It is on these solid foundations that the so-called *new endogenous growth theories* emerged in the 1980s. Commonly associated with the names of Romer (1986) and Lucas (1988), the new endogenous growth theories provided some refinements of earlier models. By placing learning, human skills and human capital accumulation at their core, they lead to a consideration of the phenomena of externalities, of increasing returns to scale (technical progress), and of imperfect competition. In particular, education and knowledge produce positive externalities or increasing returns. The key concepts elaborated and emphasized by modern growth theorists have permeated all fields of economics, including agricultural economics, development economics, international trade theory, as well as Marxist theory.[3] A few examples can illustrate their impact on industrial economics.[4] Structural change (another key concept), or the way the mix of industries changes in an economy over time, is fuelled by innovation. Differences in technological capabilities cause differences in growth rates, implying that there is a natural divergence in growth. On a more optimistic note, technology diffusion either through trade or foreign direct investment can, in some circumstances, help laggard economies to 'catch-up', or to modernize their industries.

Working within a different, empirical/historical tradition, Kuznets (1930) had already identified a relationship between technology and economic growth. His view was that the output of a good tends to follow an S-shaped pattern over time, with eventual stagnation or decline (at the top of the S-curve) explained by the exhaustion of the inventive potential of that industry. These ideas were related to those of Schumpeter who, as we saw in Chapter 2, was interested in innovation and in the relationship between innovative industries and the economy in general.

What Kuznets and Schumpeter had in common was the view that this type of cyclical pattern underlies the growth of new industries and that technological change is a cause rather than a result of a whole range of other economic phenomena. This distinguished them from the mainstream, neoclassical approach to technology.[5]

At the intersection between the neoclassical and Schumpeterian traditions, economists like Rosenberg (1963) and Mansfield (1968) undertook both theoretical and empirical work in the 1960s and 1970s, paving the way for what Chris Freeman (1994) calls 'a wave of neo-Schumpeterian research [that] gathered force in the 1970s and 1980s'.

In recent years, at the forefront of this research have been economists like Freeman (1988a) himself, Nelson (1993) and Lundvall (1992). Among the earlier criticisms of the neoclassical production function approach was that it did not adequately account for the interdependence and complementarity of all the factors involved in technological change and innovation. The work of Freeman, Nelson and Lundvall avoids this problem by explicitly considering innovation and the general level of technology in a country to be systemically related to a whole series of institutional and cultural factors. Rather than focusing exclusively on narrow, quantifiable variables such as expenditure on R&D, patents, and so on, these writers have developed the idea of 'national systems of innovation'.[6] The *national system of innovation* (NSI) is the set of institutions, within an economy, 'whose interactions determine the innovative performance of national firms', where innovation is understood to refer to 'the processes by which firms master and get into practice product designs and manufacturing processes that are new to them, whether or not they are new to the universe, or even to the nation' (Nelson, 1992). This is the perspective we adopt in this section, using but identifying the weaknesses of quantitative measures and comparisons, and elaborating on them with descriptions of the nature and development of some of the major innovation systems in Europe.

A fundamental aspect of this approach is that the success or otherwise of firms' innovative activities is tied up in the system in which they operate. Firms' innovative strategies must therefore be based on awareness and understanding of systems of innovation.

11.5 Invention, innovation and diffusion

The procedure of developing new processes and products has traditionally been divided into three stages: invention, innovation, diffusion. In this view, *invention* is understood as the creation of a new idea, for example the devising or creating of new products, machines or methods; it may also be a new way of combining technical operations. *Innovation* is seen as the transformation of the idea into practical use; it is the application of the invention in new, improved or just different products or processes. *Diffusion* is 'the process by which the use of an innovation spreads and grows' (Mansfield *et al.*, 1977). In most modern writing on technological change and innovation there is less distinction between invention and innovation. Thus innovation is seen as including gradual or incremental change to existing products or processes. This is often conceptually the same as a series of inventions, though they are clearly not patentable.

As something new, innovation involves learning. 'If we think of technology as forms of knowledge related to productive transformations, then innovative learning is the process that expands the existing knowledge base' (Smith, 2002). If we think of this knowledge base as global, then a change is only an innovation if it is new to the world. In practice the knowledge base is different in different places because of different organizational and institutional contexts. Therefore we consider innovations to include changes that are new to a particular place, or even a particular firm, even though they may not be new to the world.

As Hall (2004) points out: 'without diffusion, innovation would have little social or economic impact.' She goes on to state that diffusion is not just the process whereby the innovation spreads, 'it is also an intrinsic part of the innovation process, as learning, imitation, and feedback effects which arise during the spread of a new technology enhance the original innovation.' The diffusion of an innovation can be inter-industry or spatial diffusion. Within a single nation, a new product or process, generated in a given industry, can spread across the industrial structure of that nation. Improvements in machine tools or in computers, for example, while the results of innovation in those (or supplier) industries, will lead not only to process improvements but also to product upgrading within the user industries. Innovation and diffusion of this type can occur almost simultaneously as, for example, where increased precision in production of a product arising from a particular innovation necessitates the introduction of the same or similar innovation in the firms supplying sub-components. Like innovation, diffusion depends on learning.

Spatially, and, specifically internationally, diffusion is enhanced by transfers through foreign direct investment (FDI), joint ventures (JVs), licensing and other strategic alliances. Diffusion can be both inter-industry and, simultaneously, international, as for example when it is a by-product of 'normal' market operations, such as the purchasing of capital equipment or of intermediate inputs into a production process. In addition to imitation, scientific exchanges, specialist publications and the inter-firm mobility of employees at various levels also enhance the diffusion process.

The perfect knowledge assumption of the neoclassical theory implies that imitation will be instantaneous. In practice, the diffusion of innovations across economies can be rapid or slow. According to the cross-industry study carried out by Mansfield (1961), the time required for the adoption of an innovation by imitators can vary from one year (packaging beer in tin cans), to twenty years (continuous annealing of tin-plated steel). The lag depends on the height of entry barriers and on the nature of the innovation. Among other early work on diffusion was that by Griliches (1957) on the agricultural sector. Studies of diffusion in manufacturing became more common in the 1960s and 1970s.

The early diffusion model used by economists was developed by Mansfield in 1961.[7] In this model, $x(t)$ is the fraction of firms that have adopted the innovation at time t. The rate of diffusion of the innovation is $dx(t)/dt$. This rate will be proportional to both the fraction of early adopters $x(t)$ and to the fraction of potential adopters remaining, $[1 - x(t)]$, so that:

$$\frac{dx(t)}{dt} = bx(t) \cdot [1 - x(t)]$$

where b is constant.

Now, as $x(t)$ rises, $[1 - x(t)]$ falls. As time passes, there are more and more adopters, and therefore greater likelihood that a non-adopter will come into contact with an adopter and itself become an adopter. On the other hand, there will be fewer and fewer non-adopters, so that beyond a certain point the likelihood of further adoptions diminishes. This relationship is represented in the S-shaped logistic curve shown in Fig. 11.1.

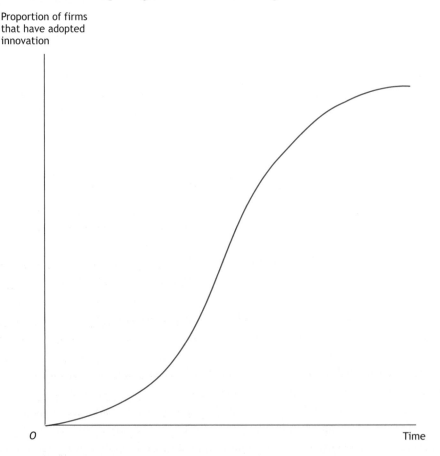

Figure 11.1 The S-shaped logistic curve and diffusion of innovations

The curve shows how the proportion of firms that introduce the new process or product innovation changes over time. The stages in the life cycle of an innovation can be described as introduction, growth, maturity and (not shown in the figure) decline (see Robertson, 1971). In certain circumstances innovations do actually diffuse in an S-shaped manner,[8] not necessarily through the 'epidemic' process described in the paragraph above. According to Stoneman (1983), for example, firms below a certain size will not be able to introduce the innovation until it becomes less expensive. So large firms adopt the innovation first, followed at a later stage (the growth stage) by smaller firms. Here cost, rather than contact, is the key factor.

Other factors in the diffusion of innovations include the nature of the innovation, the internal structures of firms, relations between firms, and legal protection for the innovator. According to Lane (1991), for example, 'in a long-term stable contractual arrangement, such as vertical integration, firms are more likely to adopt firm-specific new technologies'. Similarly, Jacobson and O'Sullivan (1994) show that demand for high quality on the part of industrial buyers can lead to the adoption of new technology by suppliers where there is a close, and/or uneven[9] contractual relationship between buyer and supplier.

Legal protection of innovators is usually in the form of patents. *Patents* are a device aimed at protecting the innovator against quick diffusion; they also constitute an indicator of innovative performance. One risk faced by the innovating firm is fast imitation before the costs of innovation have been recovered, sometimes referred to as the 'free-rider problem'. The more effectively patents can prevent free-riding, the slower will be the rate of diffusion. Thus patents have both positive effects (encouraging investment in R&D by protecting the results) and negative effects (slowing down the rate of diffusion). These are summarized in Box 11.1.

Box 11.1 The benefits and costs of patents

Hall (2003) presents in a two-by-two matrix, what she calls 'the patent system viewed by a two-handed economist'. The four cells show the costs and benefits of patents through their effects on innovation and competition. The benefits of patents for innovation are that they provide incentives for R&D and they encourage disclosure of inventions. Disclosure will not result in loss to the inventor because the patent protects her, and disclosure may be to the benefit of the inventor because it may increase the number of companies who wish to obtain a licence to use it. The negative (cost) effects of patents on innovation include that they make it more difficult for innovators to combine the protected inventions with new ideas of their own. In relation to the effects of patents on competition, the benefits are that they make it possible for new firms that do not have sufficient funds to develop their own products and processes to enter an industry, as long as they have sufficient funds to obtain licences on existing products or processes. The negative impact of patents on competition is that they create 'short-term monopolies, which may become long-term in network industries, where standards [are] important'.

Lissoni and Metcalfe (1994) show that there are different ways of studying diffusion, and that each approach emphasizes different key factors. Evolutionary theorists, for example, emphasize selection rather than imitation; the path-dependency approach focuses on increasing returns and technological 'lock-in'; and among spatial approaches are those of the industrial district analysts, who emphasize innovation and diffusion as agglomeration effects.

The different approaches to diffusion are beginning to converge, or at least to agree that diffusion is based on more than just adoption behaviour. 'A much richer pattern is emerging which distinguishes technology in terms of knowledge and skills as well as discrete arte-facts' (Lissoni and Metcalfe, 1994). Human, social and even cultural factors are increasingly being accepted as important in technology, innovation and diffusion. Tunzelman (2002) is also optimistic about more recent developments in diffusion research. He points out that older models simplistically 'explained innovation by supply factors (the science base) and diffusion by demand factors (adoption). . . . Recent theoretical developments have discarded these over-simplifying assumptions, and in doing so are very, very belatedly beginning to catch up with the real world'.

11.6 Measuring innovation in Europe

Research and development spending is usually considered to be a precondition for suc-cessful patent performance. Table 11.1 shows R&D expenditure as a percentage of GDP in the major European countries, Japan and the United States. For comparative purposes, Sweden, with one of the highest expenditures on R&D, is also included.

During the 1980s, Japan, West Germany and the United States had significantly higher R&D expenditures as a percentage of GDP than did France and the UK. Moreover, West Germany and Japan, in terms of this indicator, came from behind France and the UK in the 1960s to equal or exceed the United States by the end of the 1980s. Since its reunification, Germany has declined somewhat, owing to the relatively low level of R&D expenditure in the former East Germany. In the 1990s, Germany, Japan and the United States have remained above France and the UK but Japan is now ahead of both Germany and France. Sweden, coming from behind the other leading countries in 1991, had, by 2001, far exceeded all other OECD countries' gross domestic expenditure on R&D (GERD) as a percentage of GDP. (Israel is the only country in the world that has in recent years had consistently higher GERD as a percentage of GDP even than Sweden.) The percentage for the EU-25, including as it does the central and east european countries with very low levels of R&D, is below that of France, Germany and, especially Sweden. It is noteworthy that the UK in the most recent years is close to the EU-25 level, having declined in the 1990s from its levels of earlier decades.

The use of R&D as a percentage of GDP to measure innovativeness has limitations. In what follows, in the context of comparing Europe with Japan and the United States, and the

Table 11.1 Gross domestic expenditure on R&D as a percentage of GDP, 1991-2002[a]

	1991	1998	1999	2000	2001	2002
France	2.37	2.17	2.18	2.18	2.23	2.20
Germany	2.52	2.31	2.44	2.49	2.51	2.52
UK	2.07	1.80	1.87	1.84	1.86	1.88
Sweden	2.72	-	3.65	-	4.27	-
EU-25	-	1.73	1.77	1.80	1.83	1.83
Japan	2.94	2.95	2.96	2.99	3.07	3.12
United States	2.72	2.60	2.65	2.72	2.74	2.67

[a] Or closest year

Source: OECD, 2004b, table 2

major European countries with one another, some other ways in which R&D and innovativeness can be measured are considered.

Expenditure by governments accounts for more of R&D in some countries than in others. There has been a general decline since the 1980s, but by the end of that decade the French government still accounted for half of total R&D expenditure in that country. In the United States, the federal government's share also accounted for nearly half of all R&D but it has declined sharply since then and is now less than one-third. In both Germany and the UK, the figure was in 1991 closer to one-third, and Table 11.2 shows that it has continued to decline since then, particularly in the UK. In the EU as a whole, the figure, at 34.7, is between that of France and Germany. The Japanese government's contribution to R&D expenditure was always lower than that in other industrialized countries and has remained less than one-fifth. In other respects, however, the role of the government in Japan was, and remains, greater than in most other industrialized countries. The Swedish figure is almost as low as that in Japan; and the Swedish government is also significant in other respects (see Chapter 15).

Table 11.2   Government funding as a percentage of GERD, 1985-2002[a]

	France	Germany	UK	Sweden	EU-25	Japan	United States[b]
1985	52.9	36.7	42.7	-	-	21.0	48.3
1991	48.8	35.8	35.0	34.0	-	18.2	38.9
2002	36.9	31.5	26.9	21.0	34.7	18.2	30.2

[a] Or closest year

[b] Excluding capital expenditure

Source: OECD, 1993a and 2004b, table 14

These differences among countries in terms of government funding of R&D are attributable in part to differences in defence expenditure. According to Nelson (1993, p. 508), defence R&D 'accounts for the majority of the differences among the countries in government funding on industrial R&D, and the presence of large military programs thus explains why government industrial R&D spending in the United States, and the United Kingdom, and France is so much greater than in Japan and Germany'. Defence R&D – and defence expenditure in general – remained low in Germany and Japan as a continuing legacy from their post-Second World War demilitarization.

It is still the case in the 1990s and early 2000s that the share of defence in government budget appropriations or outlays on R&D (GBAORD) is higher in the United States, the UK and France than in most other countries (Table 11.3). At consistently over 50 per cent it is particularly high in the United States. However, overall declines in government expenditure on R&D in most countries have reduced the differences between them. Moreover, as Fransman (1999, p.182) points out, 'it is the declared intention of the Japanese government to increase its share of national R&D expenditure to a proportion more commensurate with that of' western coutries such as France, Germany and the United States. This raises the question as to the appropriateness of a high government share in the funding of research; in defence in particular, the question is whether government expenditure on R&D enhances or reduces the innovativeness of the economy. Figure 11.2 shows that despite the convergence, there remain significant differences between countries in terms of the source of financing for R&D. In Sweden and Japan, government as a source of R&D financing is particularly low.

Table 11.3 Defence budget R&D as a percentage of government budget appropriations or outlays on R&D, 1991 and 2002

	France	Germany	UK	Sweden	EU-25	Japan	United States[a]
1991	36.1	11.0	43.9	27.3	–	5.7	59.7
2002	24.2	5.5	34.1	18.2	14.9	4.1	52.1

[a] Federal government only, excluding capital expenditure

Source: OECD, 2004b, table 60

In the 1950s and 1960s, the United States and Britain had the highest R&D expenditure to GDP ratios and yet showed the lowest rates of productivity growth. As Lundvall points out, the measure 'reflects only an input effort and does not say anything about what comes out of the effort' (Lundvall, 1992, p. 6). Using R&D expenditure as a proxy of innovation intensity also implies the existence of the following linear pattern:

R&D → new idea → new product → market definition → product launch

This is associated with a smooth flow of operations from the research laboratory, to the design and then the market analysis departments. However, this linear pattern does not

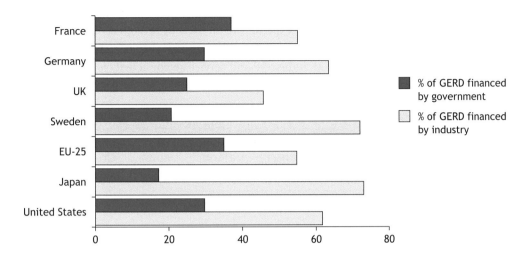

Figure 11.2 Percentage of GERD financed by government and by industry, 2002 (or nearest year)
Source: OECD, 2004b, table p.14

hold true in all cases. In many instances, innovations are born in the production department (factory floor) itself; many others are suggested by end users (customers), or by suppliers. Some innovative firms do not have research departments and, thus, apparently no R&D expenditure at all. To quote Lundvall again: 'R&D expenditure is not the only kind of relevant input to the process of innovation – learning in connection with routine activities may be more important than R&D' (Lundvall, 1992, p. 6; see also Hirsch-Kreinsen *et al.* 2003). Even in industries in which there is a research function, such as the pharmaceutical industry, there have been changes in traditionally understood patterns of development from invention to product launch.

The market is an increasingly important first element in the very identification of the need for research. Moreover, there are many ways of differentiating pharmaceutical products, including different types of delivery systems (liquids, tablets, patches), different strengths, packaging, distribution outlets, and, more fundamentally, research to alter molecular structure – which, in many cases, is influenced by national regulations. This means that the linear pattern outlined above is an oversimplification. The reality is often far more complex, with most of the stages able to influence developments in most other stages.

The fact that different elements of the technology-change process, though located within a single company, may be located in different countries, also reduces the accuracy of R&D data. The UK, for example, is an R&D base for many firms whose headquarters are elsewhere. As a result, the expected relationship between R&D expenditure and innovation may not be realized within the UK because the results of the research in the UK may be used to develop products and processes that are introduced in the countries where these firms' headquarters are located. Data on expenditure on R&D by foreign affiliates as a percentage of R&D expenditure by all enterprises are shown in Table 11.4. It is highest in Ireland, where a significant part of all industrial and service sector activity is accounted for by subsidiaries of multinational enterprises.

Table 11.4 Foreign affiliate R&D as a percentage of all enterprises R&D, 2001[a]

France	Germany	UK	Sweden	Ireland	Japan	United States
21.5	19.0	40.6	34.0	65.2	3.6	14.9

[a] Or nearest year
Source: OECD, 2004b, table 64

It is clear, then, that as an alternative to R&D expenditures, other indications of innovativeness, and of the level of technology in an economy in general, must sometimes be used. One such alternative – which can be considered an output of R&D effort – is trade in high-technology products. Over the 1980s and early 1990s, EC imports in high technology products, and particularly information technology, grew faster than exports (CEC, 1993c). In recent years, the performance of European countries has been mixed. Figure 11.3 shows that France's share of the OECD export market has declined in all of the five main high-technology sectors. Germany's share has increased in the aerospace, electronics, and office machinery and computer industries, and declined in pharmaceuticals and instruments. The UK's share has risen even more substantially than Germany's in aerospace and, like Germany, only marginally in electronics. The UK's share has declined in the other three sectors. Sweden's shares, like those of France, have fallen in all five sectors. Interestingly, the performances of Japan and the United States have also been mixed. The United States' shares have increased only in electronics and instruments; those of Japan have declined in all five.

Thus in most of these sectors, the shares of most of the leading countries have declined. This raises the question as to which countries shares have increased. In some cases, such as aerospace, the changes among the main countries balance each other out; the increases in Germany and the UK more or less offset the declines in France and the United States. The EU overall has experienced an increase in its share of the market. In other sectors, various smaller countries, especially Belgium, Hungary and Ireland in Europe, and Korea in Asia, have achieved increased export market shares. In pharmaceuticals, however, Europe overall 'has lost competitiveness vis-à-vis the United States' (McKelvey *et al.*, 2004).

In other new technology areas not addressed thus far, Europe has again had mixed fortunes. In one sector, mobile telephony, Europe has had, and continues to have, a clear lead over the United States and Japan (Tan, 2002; Edquist, 2004).[10] In another, machine tools,

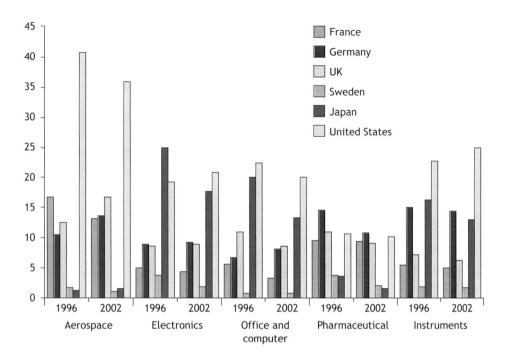

Figure 11.3 Export market shares in selected high technology sectors, 1996 and 2001
Source: OECD, 2004b, tables 72-76

although 'Europe as a whole had a negative revealed competititve advantage ... and some-what fewer patents vis-à-vis Japan and the United States measured against machine tool output ... some countries, namely Germany and Italy, performed very well in production output and productivity' (Wengel and Shapira, 2004).

Research, done in universities, national research laboratories, and to a significant extent in a limited number of large firms, is at least the foundation for innovation. It 'provides the knowledge and skills on which national systems of business R&D can build' (Patel and Pavitt, 1991, p. 42). There are significant differences between countries in terms of which of these three contexts is most important. As Fig. 11.4 shows, Sweden – as is the case in relation to its government financing of R&D – has a very low proportion of R&D performed by government laboratories.

The number of people employed in research is another way of indicating the level of tech-nology and potential for technological development of an economy.[11] This is shown in Table 11.5, in terms of research personnel per 1000 in employment. The table confirms that the main European countries lag behind the United States and Japan. Among the countries in the table, Sweden is an exception. (Finland, with a figure of 15.8, is the highest in Europe, and in the world.)

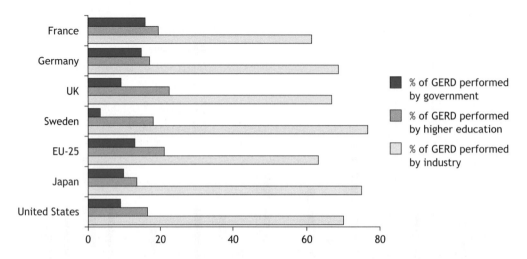

Figure 11.4 Percentage of GERD performed by government, higher education and industry, 2002
Source: OECD, 2004b, p. 14

Table 11.5 Researchers per 1000 in employment		
	1991	**2001**
France	5.7	7.2
Germany	6.3	6.8
UK	4.6	5.5
Sweden	–	10.6
Japan	9.1	10.2
United States	7.7	8.6
Source: OECD, 2004b, table 8		

R&D expenditure data and alternative indicators of levels of technological development such as high-technology trade balance and employment in R&D all show that the main EU countries in general lag behind the United States and Japan. They also show wide disparities within Europe. Both research inputs and outputs point to the same disparities.

Ideally, we should, through relating inputs to outputs, show which countries are most effective at converting R&D inputs to outputs. Patel and Pavitt (1991, p. 42) provided data 'based on the most thorough attempts made so far to compare per capita inputs and outputs of basic research' in Japan, the United States and Europe. Their output data included indices based on the CHI/NSF Science Literature Indicators Database. Their results suggested that the United States was the most productive of the three and that Japan became relatively more productive, over the 1980s. However, these results are now out of date, and no update is available.

A simple – in some ways even, simplistic – way of measuring R&D output and productivity, is to use patents. The OECD provides data on countries' shares in 'triadic' patent families, that is, patents that are filed at the European Patent Office[12] (EPO), the Japanese Patent Office (JPO) and granted by the US Patent and Trademark Office (USPTO). Table 11.6 shows how the shares (of OECD total) of selected countries have changed over the second half of the 1990s. The table shows that the main European countries shares in 'triadic' patent families have been stable or declined. Of the countries in the table, only the share of Japan has increased noticeably. If we think of Table 11.6 as measuring output, and of Table 11.1 as in some sense measuring input, then most of the changes in output are in the direction one would expect from the changes in input. For France, Germany, the UK and the United States, GERD as a percentage of GDP was stable or declining, and so, too, was share in triadic patent families. Japan's GERD as a percentage of GDP increased over the period, as did its patent share in Table 11.6. Sweden is the one country for which the two moved in opposite directions, with GERD as a percentage of GDP increasing sharply and Sweden's share in triadic patent families declining slightly. One explanation might be that it takes longer than the five- or six-year period under consideration here for the effects of the changes in R&D expenditure to be seen in patents.

Table 11.6 Share of selected countries in triadic patent families

	1994	2000
France	5.9	5.0
Germany	13.7	13.5
UK	4.6	4.2
Sweden	2.0	1.9
EU-25	34.0	32.2
Japan	25.9	27.5
United States	35.0	35.1

Source: OECD, 2004b, table 66

The reason why some kind of collective or multinational registration of patents is used, rather than patents granted within each of these countries, is because data on the latter are distorted by different national systems of registration of patents. In Japan, for example, 'patents are granted separately even when inventions behind them were closely related technologically' (Odagiri and Goto, 1993, p. 104). The main European patent system is that of the European Patent Office. 'The EPO grants patents by a centralized procedure with uniform conditions, but once granted the patents become national and subject to the divergent national laws of EPO-Member States' (Ullrich, 2002). The EPO is an independent organization, separate from the EU, and there is what Ullrich (2002) calls a 'cooperative rivalry' between the EPO and the EU over how to create a common European patent system. There are 28 member states of the EPO, including all of the EU-15 and seven of the ten new EU members of 2004.

The most important advantage of a European patent system in which patents of each member are recognized by all others, is that firms do not have the costs and the administrative effort in obtaining patent protection in each country. One European patent covers all members. This is why, though still important, the 'numbers of purely national patent applications have considerably fallen behind those of international applications' (Ullrich, 2002).

Even with a uniform international patent system, the use of patents as an indication of the output of R&D, or of innovativeness, would continue to suffer from the problem that many patents issued are not actually used in products or processes within firms. A tendency to apply for patents may be a characteristic of a particular (national or sectoral) group of firms; this does not necessarily mean that that group of firms is more innovative – in the sense of actually implementing change – than less patent-oriented groups of firms.[13]

Another way to indicate the inputs and outputs of R&D is to compare the change in GERD per capita over a period with the change in the technology balance of payments (TBP) over the same period. The TBP 'registers the commercial transactions related to international technology and know-how transfers. It consists of money paid or received for the use of patents, licences, know-how, marks, models, designs, technical services and for industrial R&D carried out abroad, etc.' (OECD, 1993a, p. 333).

There are differences in coverage from country to country, and there may also be problems arising from profit-switching transfer pricing, where firms adjust prices so as to shift profits to low tax areas. This measure is therefore also not perfect, and should be used in conjunction with others to give broad indications. Figure 11.5 shows, first, how GERD per capita has changed between 1991 and 2001. It has increased in all the countries, but particularly in Japan and the United States. Second, it provides through the TBP, an indication of change in the output of R&D. (Here receipts minus payments in 1991 are compared with receipts minus payments in 2001.) Only Germany's TBP deteriorated. France's improved marginally, and the UK's, Japan's and the United States' substantially.

It is clear, even from the partially comparable data that is available, that in terms of innovation intensity, there are significant differences among the three industrialized world regions, and among the countries of Europe itself. In terms of most indicators Europe as a whole is behind both the United States and Japan. Whether we look at inputs, such as Table 11.1 and Table 11.4, or outputs such as Table 11.6 and Fig. 11.4, Japan and/or the United States is ahead of Europe.

We have shown that among the three major countries within the EU there are significant differences. Nevertheless, in the wider European context, Germany, the UK and France are

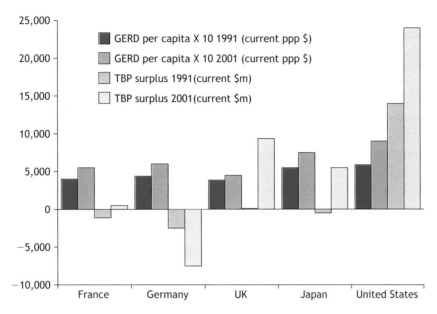

Figure 11.5 Indicators of R&D inputs and outputs: GERD per capita and technology balance of payments
Source: OECD, 2004b, tables 4 and 69-70[14]

among the most innovative; data similar to those presented in the tables above would show that, in most respects, the new accession countries are least innovative. On the basis of many of the measures introduced above, Italy and Denmark are also well below Germany, the UK and France, but, as is shown below, Italy and Denmark are, in other respects, more innovative than their major neighbours.

11.7 National systems of innovation (NSIs)

Lundvall (1992, p. 12), emphasizing the importance of learning in NSIs, differentiates between narrow and broad definitions of NSI. The narrow definition is the one underlying most of Section 11.6, including, as it does, only those organizations and institutions directly involved in 'searching and exploring – such as R&D departments, technological institutes and universities'. The broad definition, which is close to that of Nelson, 'includes all parts and aspects of the economic structure and the institutional set-up affecting learning as well as searching and exploring'.

Given that historical, social, cultural and other factors – many aspects of which are nation-specific – influence the development of institutions, it follows that any country's NSI will be unique. There may also be regional and sectoral systems of innovation, among others, but, as Lundvall (1998) insists, the national is still important. Also emphasizing the significance of national characteristics, Lundvall and Maskell (1999) attribute differences in growth rates between economies to NSIs:

Seen from the perspective of National Innovation Systems, a major role of the nation state may, actually, be to accumulate, reproduce and protect valuable social capital – some of which might originate from local pre-industrial traditions (Maskell 1998). The dissimilar form and unequal distribution of social capital across nations might thus account for at least some national differences in economic growth rates that remain unexplained by old and new growth theories.

In the context of a comparison between national and sectoral factors, there is empirical evidence that suggests that the NSI may be more important. Khanna and Singh (2002) find that 'country borders matter much more than industry affiliation in determining the innovative role of foreign subsidiaries' and they conclude that there is a need for more study of 'what drives inter-country differences in the way economic activity is organized'.[15]

In an attempt to operationalize the concept, Niosi *et al.* (1992) suggest that NSIs can be differentiated on the basis of a number of criteria. Somewhat adjusted, these are as follows:

- *Size of the country*. A large country (such as the United States) is characterized by a more diversified system than small ones (such as Austria or Finland) which have tended to focus on particular sectors.

- *Role of the country in the world*. In the UK, France and the United States, past colonialism/imperialism explains the development of R&D in military-based technology.

- *Existence and nature of natural resources*. The nuclear programme in France was developed because of the lack of fossil fuels; the success of the petrochemical industry in the United States is linked to the abundance of oil in that country.

- *Socio-cultural factors*. Culture or 'habits of thought' are specific to societies, interacting with institutions to process information. Know-how or learned routines are as important as knowledge and can be communicated to the population as a whole. This places the training and education systems at the centre of the innovation process.

- *Political factors*. These have a substantial impact on the institutional framework of a nation (role of the state, banking system, education system) and, through policy, on its economic features as well.

It can be argued that underlying these criteria are three dimensions of systems innovation. (Edquist (2001) identifies nine dimensions, but focuses on three as most important.) These are, first, that innovations arise from interactive learning between organizations; second, the nature of institutions is crucial, influencing and influenced by the behaviour of organizations and the relations between them; and third, that innovation processes are evolutionary. These are dimensions in the sense that, if they could be measured, they would distinguish real systems of innovation – for example, NSIs – from one another. It is also in this sense that they underlie Niosi *et al.*'s criteria. For example, each of organizational interaction, institutional set-up and evolutionary processes, is related in various ways to political factors. To select just one of the criteria, political factors, it is clear that policies and the success of their implementation are dependent on all three: high levels of organizational interaction, an appropriate institution set-up, and a correct understanding of the relevant evolutionary processes. While he is critical, calling for further theoretical development of the system of innovation approach,[16] Edquist (2001) considers it to constitute a major advance in the study of innovation: the 'strengths of the [systems of innovation] approach have made it absolutely central for the current understanding of innovation processes'.

These ideas inform the examination of some of the NSIs in Europe, to which attention is now turned. France and the UK are examined first, followed by a brief discussion of some of the other NSIs. Next, the international level is the focus of attention. The aim is to identify the significant aspects of the technological environments within which firms in each of these countries operate, and to consider the relative importance of the national and European scopes of those environments.

11.7.1 The national system of innovation in France

As we saw above, France has a lower R&D/GDP ratio than Germany (Table 11.1), and a higher government R&D/Total R&D ratio than either Germany or the UK (Table 11.2); its defence R&D is below that of the UK, but well above that of Germany. From these findings, a number of more detailed questions suggest themselves. Why is the state so important in R&D in France? Does this have positive or negative implications for the output of R&D? Does France's military R&D produce commercial results exploitable by French companies? Other questions are suggested by the criteria for assessing NSIs. How is France's R&D distributed? How successful is the French education system? Is there a culture of innovation within firms, and to what extent is it diffused among firms?

The significance of the state in the French economy in general, and in science and technology in particular, has roots in the Colbertism of the seventeenth century. Features were added by the *Ancien Régime* in the eighteenth century and Napoleonic governments in the nineteenth century. Apart from the education system, the actual organizations and mechanisms involved in the production and distribution of R&D have evolved since the Second World War but the broader institutional and socio-cultural aspects of innovation developed over centuries.[17]

At the centre of the NSI (narrowly defined) is the National Centre for Scientific Research (CNRS) which, while established in 1939, in its present form dates from 1945. It has had a pervasive effect on the organization of basic and long-term research in science, and on the availability of scientific and technical personnel. In particular, the CNRS directly administers laboratories and research facilities in areas not covered by universities and, in addition, it funds university research and makes its own personnel and equipment available to universities for specific projects. More broadly, the CNRS provides services to the scientific community, including documentation, training and 'assistance on patentable inventions' (Chesnais, 1993, p. 203). Unlike research agencies in some countries that have a particular sectoral or functional focus, the CNRS has 'a much broader scope of activity aiming at co-ordinating vast ensembles of research' (Coriat and Weinstein, 2004).

That an institution such as the CNRS was necessary was a consequence of the weaknesses in R&D in the tertiary education system. This system contains two separate types of institution, the professional schools (*Grandes Ecoles*), established by Napoleon, and the universities. The *Grandes Ecoles* gave priority to technical education, and French engineers were among the best in the world in the nineteenth century. French scientists, too, were very advanced, and the *Ecole Normale Supérieure* became a leading scientific institution. In terms of science graduates, however, it was too small, providing '*much too narrow a base on which to build a sound scientific edifice*' (Chesnais, 1993, p. 198; emphasis in original). The university system remained secondary to the *Grandes Ecoles*, and had a tradition of small, personal laboratories that went with the professorial chair and reflected the interests of individual professors. This situation was not corrected until the formation of the CNRS.

Despite the weakness of science in the higher education system, there is little evidence of attempts within industry to undertake scientific research. This contrasts sharply with the situation in the United States, where, at much the same time (late nineteenth and early twentieth centuries), a large number of corporate research laboratories were established.[18] Where France did excel during the first half of the twentieth century, was in areas in which the engineering skills, built up over the previous 100 years, could impinge on product and process development. French inventors and entrepreneurs were most active in 'sectors where technological development took the form of pragmatic, step-by-step innovations as in automobiles and aeronautics' (Chesnais, 1993, p. 199).

Immediately after the Second World War, France, despite its defeat, thus had a continuing tradition in engineering-based industries, based on expertise built up over the nineteenth century,[19] and, with roots as far back as the seventeenth century, the remnants of and potential for a chemical industry. One large firm still in existence today, Saint-Gobain, was established during the Napoleonic wars as a direct result of efforts by the government at the time to 'root science-based innovation in industry' (Chesnais, 1993, p. 195). The combination of the centrality of the state and selective areas of scientific and technological excellence in large firms continued into the decades after the Second World War. In the period immediately after the war, the emphasis was on the creation of state institutions. To the extent that firms derived advantages through diffusion of innovation from these state activities, it was primarily in state-owned enterprises, nationalized during this period.

In addition to the CNRS, the French government established a number of research institutions, both civil and military. Among these were the Energy Commission (CEA), which included R&D into and production of nuclear energy, a National Centre for the Study of Telecommunications (CNET) and a National Office of Aeronautical Studies and Research (ONERA). These, and a number of others in such areas as tropical agriculture, health sciences and military research, were mostly under the relevant government ministries. In the international scientific context, the most significant step was the establishment of the Saclay R&D laboratories by the CEA. In a country where no large firm, even at this late stage, had yet set up a major industrial R&D laboratory based on the US and German model,

'Saclay was France's first real step into twentieth-century fundamental and applied science' (Chesnais, 1993, p. 202).

Driven in part by a desire for technological independence from the United States, the state began to select particular firms and particular industries. 'National champions' – some publicly and some privately owned – were selected for support by the state, both directly and through state-owned financial institutions. From the 1960s onwards, this evolved into a planned restructuring of French industry in general, and a sharpening of French technological competitiveness in particular. In the late 1960s and early 1970s, four *grands programmes* were developed, covering the nuclear, aerospace, space technology and electronics industries, each of which, it should be noted, has significant military aspects.

According to Chesnais (1993), the main features of the environment for innovation in France did not vary greatly over the 1970s and 1980s.

> With respect to the overall structure and working of the French innovation system, the 1970s and 1980s have essentially brought about only shifts in emphasis in the area of overall R&D resource allocation and the location of entrepreneurial capacity, along with a clearer spelling out of features that were already contained within the system. (Chesnais, 1993, p. 204)

As we show below, however, there is some evidence that, by the end of the 1990s, the French innovation system had achieved some notable progress.

Some important aspects of the French system arise from the fundamental nature of the control and organization of French industry. First, there is the extremely important role of the state.[20] From the end of the Second World War to the end of the 1960s, both through the establishment of institutions and the implementation of policies, the state contributed an essential co-ordination role to the success of the French economy. Whereas some see this role as enhancing features of the system which would later emerge as weaknesses (de Bandt, 1987), others see it in a more positive light (Amable and Hancké, 2001).

Nelson's (1992) conclusion from studies of systems of innovation in 15 countries is that few have 'active coherent industrial policies', and government policies supporting industrial innovation are 'generally fragmented'. This concurs with de Bandt's assessment of the role of the state in the relative lack of success of French industrial innovation since the early 1970s: 'While the transfers from the state to enterprises remain very important, no attempt is now being made to define and implement a consistent industrial policy' (de Bandt, 1987, p. 49). The nationalizations by the Socialist government in 1981–82 were aimed at integrating 'some of the big firms into a consistent plan-rational approach for the redeployment and further development of the French industrial system' but they were followed by an industrial policy of 'hesitations and obfuscation' (de Bandt, 1987, p. 48). Since the early 1980s, France – along with virtually all other governments in Europe – has reduced the degree of direct intervention and progressively privatized its nationalized industries.

De Bandt is thus critical of these policies and sees the change as an expression of inconsistency. Amable and Hancké (2001) argue – perhaps with the advantage of the greater gap in time since the early 1980s – that the huge investment by the state actually enabled the major French companies to survive and compete following privatization. They point out that between 1981 and 1985, the French government 'granted, in loans and subsidies, the equivalent of $5 billion to the newly nationalized industries'. Focusing on five of the largest companies in France – General Electric, Saint-Gobain, Péchiney, Thomson and Rhône-Poulenc – they calculate that between 1982 and 1984 they 'received 10 times more capital from the government than they had received from private investors in the 7 years prior to 1981. This allowed these companies not only to accelerate investment, but also to increase R&D ... by over 20 per cent between 1982 and 1985'.

Given its importance in military-related technologies, the state's role has become associated with a need for secrecy. This is a weakness because technological information that might have contributed to commercial innovations remained within organizations developing and implementing those technologies for military purposes. Moreover, the significance of the military in directing the subsystems of innovation in France, increased during the early 1990s. The *Délégation Générale à l'Armement* (DGA) plays a key role, in most cases along with other government agencies, in innovation subsystems of nuclear power, telecommunications, defence electronics, aerospace, and aeronautics. The increasing influence of the military, 'even in telecommunications and nonmilitary space [is] a result of the ... post-Gulf war reorientation of military-strategic priorities to space observation and telecommunications systems' (Chesnais, 1993, p. 214).

As with government involvement in general, military control of R&D is not *ipso facto* negative. There might be different contributions to commercial competitiveness of military R&D, depending on whether this R&D aims at 'opening up a broad new generic technology', or whether it goes into 'highly specialized systems development'. The former is associated with greater 'spinoff', the latter with less. French and British military R&D have 'from the beginning focused largely on the latter', and 'most of the companies [from those countries] receiving R&D contracts have shown little capability to crack into non-military markets' (Nelson, 1992).

Attempts are clearly being made to broaden the access to military research findings and to extend research networks to include people external to the DGA. There is within the DGA an agency called ARES (*Animation de la Réflexion et des Etudes Stratégiques*) the primary responsibility of which is strategic studies. ARES organizes seminars and research working groups, and according to its website 'manages an annual programme of forward-looking studies ... with political, military, economic and social dimensions'. These studies are undertaken outside the Ministry of Defence 'by competitively selected contractors such as research institutes, academic teams, consulting groups, etc. They help DGA to get an external analysis on long-run questions and strategic stakes' (CHEAr, 2004).

An exception to the generalization about limited spinoff of military R&D in France, is the case of aerospace. Aerospace and pharmaceuticals (on which, see below) are the only two industry groups in the high-technology sector that have consistently had positive trade balances (see Table 11.7);[21] the trade balance in aerospace is second only to that of the United States.[22]

Table 11.7	French trade balance in high-technology sectors, 2002
	Trade balance US$m
Aerospace	9,818.9
Electronics	1,302.4
Office machinery and computers	−6,049.2
Pharmaceuticals	4,570.2
Instruments	−845.1

Source: OECD, 2004b, tables 73-76

Strong institutions, established relatively early, form the background to the success of the aerospace industry in France. The first such institution was ONERA in the immediate postwar period (see above), followed by the establishment of a Committee for Space Research in 1959, and a National Centre for Space Studies (CNES) in 1961. A key difference in aerospace was that the CNES, unlike other state institutions, involved 'public and private firms in the program from the outset by contracting out a large part of the R&D to the business sector' (Chesnais, 1993, p. 203). The main firms were Matra, Aérospatiale and Thomson-CSF. A second difference is in the scale of this industry, which is such that, from the beginning, international partners were sought. This led to the central role that France has played in Arianespace, the European competitor to the US satellite launchers.[23]

Another feature of the French NSI is its organization into vertical subsystems. Both industrial and technological policies have been implemented through programmes aimed at particular industries, and on the basis of the 'national champion' ethos, at particular large firms. While the overall economic 'plan' approach in the early postwar period also relied on large firms, this was appropriate and successful in the context of the French economy in that period. However, both the 'programme' and large-firm aspects of state intervention in the later period, resulted in an overly vertically organized set of subsystems in the 1970s and 1980s, when increasing flexibility, rapid change and globalization required a different type of state intervention. The vertical organization of industries reduced the rate of diffusion of innovation between industries.

Closely related to this is the overspecialization engendered by French industrial policy: 'firms such as Schneider or Thomson or CGE deliberately abandoned the machine tool industry, the equipment industry, and consumer electronics and invested the money provided by the state in the nuclear power industry, military electronics and telecoms' (Cohen, 1995). As a result, private industrial R&D has been weak in France, and there has been a collapse in particular of the machine tool industry. France is now well below Germany, Italy and Spain in the production of machine tools (Wengel and Shapira, 2004).

The state is not exclusively responsible for problems in the French system of innovation. Up to the late 1980s, there were a number of other aspects of French industry that impeded the diffusion of innovations. Among these were the absence of an integrated industrial infrastructure at decentralized geographical levels; the poor relations between big and small firms, particularly in the case of subcontracting; the unfavourable power relations between industry and distribution; and the weak research–business relations (de Bandt, 1987, p. 54). To these may be added characteristics of French firms and industry that reduced innovation in general: the 'more hierarchical and bureaucratic attributes of French enterprises (compared with German firms) prove particularly ill-suited to the needs of advanced technological change' (OECD, 1988, p. 79); and the influence of stock markets which (as in the UK, but unlike Germany and Japan), impose short time horizons and deter changes or investments that might reduce current profitability, but enhance future competitiveness.

Since the 1980s, according to Amable and Hancké (2001), some of the problems impeding innovation in France have been removed. They argue that over the 1980s and 1990s there was a 'profound structural change in France's production regime, initiated by the state but implemented by the large companies, the effect of which was to transform the mode of organization, the skills structure of the workforce and more generally the production methods of French industry'. They find evidence, for example, of a rise in the number and proportion of university-qualified people, of sharp increases in the proportion of SMEs (small and medium-sized enterprises) working as subcontractors, of restructuring of supply networks, and of success in export markets both where innovative design is important and where high tech is important. They conclude that:

> The state, somewhat paradoxically, used its power to give more independence and responsibility to large companies, while it was itself gradually reducing its involvement in the economy. Large companies took the opportunities that were thus offered to reorganize their production networks and internal organization in a way that favoured the upgrading of skills and product quality and wider system of industrial co-ordination. (Amable and Hancké, 2001)

The pharmaceutical industry is a high-technology industry that to some extent illustrates some of the strengths of the French system of innovation, and particularly that part of the French NSI not directly within the state's system of innovation.[24] While in some ways this industry builds on France's traditional strengths in the chemical sciences, in other ways it differs from the typical French pattern. Like other research-based industries in France, the pharmaceutical industry is dominated by large firms; Rhône-Poulenc, Sanofi and Synthélabo were the main ones. They have undergone a number of mergers and acquisitions in recent years. Rhône-Poulenc merged with the German company Hoechst in 1999 to form Aventis, and Sanofi, having merged with Synthélabo in 1999, launched a hostile bid for

Aventis in October 2004 (*The Economist*, 6 October 2004). If successful, this bid will create a single pharmaceutical giant from what, just over five years earlier, were the three largest French companies in the industry.

They have strong in-house R&D capacity, and in this are unusual (though not unique) in France. R&D has largely been self-funded by the industry and this also differentiates pharmaceuticals from most of the other innovation subsystems, including electronics, armaments and aerospace. The industry has obtained transfers of technology from its joint ventures with the public sector's Institut Pasteur – Pasteur Mérieux Sérums et Vaccins in the case of Rhône-Poulenc, and Diagnostics Pasteur in the case of Sanofi. However, in the allocation of state R&D funding at least up to the end of the 1980s 'one finds an *overwhelming bias in favor of the nuclear, aeronautics, space, telecommunications, and electronics sectors* to the detriment of the chemical, biological, and life science based sectors ... as well as to that of the machine tool and robotics industries and other small firm dominated industries' (Chesnais, 1993, n 18, pp. 207–8).

There is evidence from the pharmaceutical industry in France's positive trade balance that it is competitive. In recent years, pharmaceutical output in France has been by far the highest in Europe. However, there are aspects of the pharmaceutical industry that do not augur well for the future. First, R&D is extremely important in this industry, and Fig. 11.6 shows that among leading pharma producers in Europe this is an area where France seems to lag behind. Second, Coriat *et al.* (2004) suggest that, even where R&D is done, the nature of this R&D and the patents that result, may be less significant than in other countries. The 'more stringent the regulations are in terms of the efficacy of the therapuetic contributions

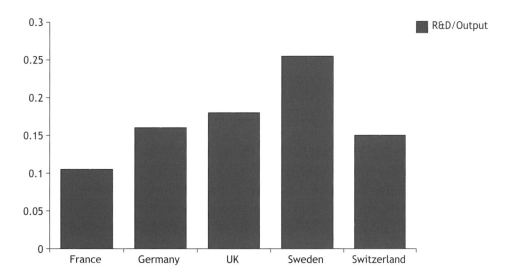

Figure 11.6 The ratio of R&D to output, pharmaceutical industry in selected European countries, 2002
Source: EFPIA, 2004, pp. 14 and 20

the more innovations will tend to be radical', they write. The French regulations have been less stringent. As a result they have favoured 'minor innovations, more directed to local markets, with few world-class products'. Third, the main growth sector within pharmaceuticals is biotechnology. Although, as in other countries, it has grown rapidly, biotech in France is in size and significance behind that sector in both Germany and the UK. There are proposals for providing significant state aid to biotech (and other research based companies) in France, but Hodson (2003) suggests that the proposed support may be resisted by the Commission as conflicting with EU competition rules.

It would appear that the origins and development of the French NSI have been dominated by state institutions and particularly the military. The pharmaceutical industry is to some extent outside this. Even more independent, though largely unresearched, is the innovative activity of small firms. A key to this is the development and transmission of skills. Amable and Hancké (2001) quote evidence of strong improvements in the number of people obtaining diplomas in technical areas. In relation to small firms, as to other aspects of the French system, they see reasons to be much more optimistic than the researchers on innovation writing in the 1980s and early 1990s.

11.7.2 The national system of innovation in the UK

The UK national system of innovation is in some respects weaker than that of France. French industry-funded R&D was below that of the UK at the beginning of the 1980s (OECD, 1993a) but by the end of the 1990s industry-funded R&D in the UK at 47 per cent was well below France's 54 per cent (Fig. 11.2). Also, whereas overall R&D expenditure as a percentage of GDP grew substantially in France from the 1960s to the 1990s, in the UK it was at best constant. By the 1990s, GERD as a percentage of GDP in the UK was well below that of France (Table 11.1). In terms of patents, too, Table 11.6 shows that the UK has been below France in the 1990s and into the 2000s (though both were, and remain, behind Germany). More significantly, in terms of number of people obtaining mechanical and engineering qualifications at the craft and technician level, the UK, well below either France or Germany in the 1970s, also grew more slowly than either over the period up to the late 1980s (Patel and Pavitt, 1991, table 3.8). In relation to researchers per 1000 people in employment, the UK was below France in 1991 and both were below Germany; by 2001 the UK was still below both France and Germany, but France had overtaken Germany (Table 11.5).

How does an examination of the British NSI contribute to our understanding of the strengths and weaknesses of R&D inputs and outputs in the UK? Does it facilitate a better understanding of technological aspects of the business environment in the UK? Does the less interventionist role of the state mean a greater rate of diffusion? Is there more commercialization of the results of military R&D in the UK? As with France, the discussion begins with the historical background, followed by a description of relevant aspects of the educational system and key R&D institutions, and concludes with some indication of the innovativeness of the UK economy.

The UK has not had the *étatist* tradition of France. While the reasons for this are complex, they are related to Britain's position as the first industrialized nation and its early and long-standing commitment to free trade. The economic role of the state in Britain between the mid-eighteenth and last quarter of the nineteenth centuries was confined to the regulation of a small number of markets, including financial and property markets, and to the advancement and protection, by military means where necessary, of foreign trade. While intervention increased over the next 100 years, it was never as coherent or determined as in France or Japan. Whether despite or because of this,[25] for much of the 200 years up to the end of the nineteenth century, the national system of innovation in Britain 'had no match, generating revolutionary changes in the techniques of energy and material transformation (the coal, iron, and steam nexus), in the organization of production (the factory system), and in transportation (railways and the steam ship)' (Walker, 1993, pp. 187–8).

Britain has not declined since then, but it has lost its leadership position.[26] There are different theories as to why this change occurred, though few attribute a significant role to the British state. Among the main explanations are the inappropriateness of culture and institutions to the conditions of the twentieth century, despite their success in the previous two centuries; a change in attitude from industrial enterprise to a rentier mentality; and the inevitable catch-up of competitor nations as industrialization spread.[27] While there is an element of truth in each of these explanations, the first fits best with the NSI framework's focus on culture and 'habits of thought'. Chandler (1984) provides a material basis to the argument by suggesting that 'Britain was the only nation to industrialize before the coming of modern transportation and communication. So its industrialists had become attuned to a slower, smaller-scale process of industrial production and distribution.'

Box 11.2 provides an explanation of why one particular leading industry in Britain declined at the end of the nineteenth century, in contrast to a similar industry that has thrived, at least until recently, in Emilia-Romagna in Italy.[28]

Box 11.2 The decline of the Lancashire cotton textile industry

In the case of the Lancashire cotton textile industry, success was based in the first instance on factors similar to those underlying British industrialization in general. British domination of world markets provided a secure and growing demand to which capitalists responded. The relatively simple and cheap technology led to ease of entry. With spinning, weaving and marketing separate but related through the market, the industry was a 'neoclassical economist's dream of a hierarchy of extremely well developed markets' (Lazonick, 1981). In Emilia-Romagna, Brusco (1982) suggests, initial success was based on the greater ability of small firms to resist the growing power of the unions, and on a growing demand for more differentiated products, produced in shorter series. In Lancashire, cotton textiles began as – and continued predominantly to be – a small-firm industry. In Emilia-Romagna, the industrial districts are small-firm

Box 11.2 (continued)

production systems achieving success in industries dominated elsewhere by large firms. In both places (Lancashire and Emilia-Romagna) and in both periods (late nineteenth century in the case of Lancashire and post-1960s in the case of Emilia-Romagna), economies of agglomeration were a significant factor in their success.

There are substantial differences between the nineteenth-century British industrial district and the modern industrial districts of Emilia-Romagna. Changing technology, adopted by large and growing firms in America, was avoided in Britain. It involved vertical integration which was contrary to the vertically specialized structure that had evolved, for example, in Lancashire. No individual firm was in any case capable of introducing the changes. The separation of distribution and production left manufacturers insecure about the nature and scale of their markets. Institutional impediments included the unions, which defended workers whose skills, developed over generations, would become redundant. There was no co-ordinated attempt to plan for change in the structure of the industry to introduce the new technologies or face the new competition from America. Firms' short-term response to market was to attempt to reduce costs. In Emilia-Romagna there is a wide range of ways in which firms collectively co-ordinate activities. These include financing, purchasing of inputs and distribution, all of which may have relevance to the short or long run. There is also co-ordinated 'real service' provision which is clearly long run, such as planning for additional factories, training and the introduction of new technologies. Economies of agglomeration in Britain were insufficient to offset the 'matrix of rigid institutional structures' that 'obstructed individualistic as well as collective efforts at economic renovation' (Elbaum and Lazonick, 1986). The industrial districts of Emilia-Romagna – and similar, more recently emerging production systems in districts in many other parts of the world (Pyke and Sengenberger, 1992) – are characterized by high levels of both competition and co-operation; those in Britain with their origins in the nineteenth century had high levels of the former, but very little of the latter.

The different paths of the Lancashire and Emilian industrial districts cannot be understood without close consideration of the institutional contexts. The presence in Emilia-Romagna (and the absence in Lancashire) of industry and municipal or commune based organizations, which have acted in the common interest of their small-firm members to co-ordinate important aspects of their activities, have been a fundamental part of the difference between the two stories.

Source: Jacobson *et al.*, 2002

Some writers have emphasized the weakness of education and training in Britain as reasons for its loss of leadership.[29] One aspect of this is that, although having a long and excellent tradition, particularly in science, the Oxford and Cambridge universities are part of an elitist system, access to which is obtained as much through wealth as through ability. The private education system, small in comparison to the total, nevertheless still provides a disproportionately large part of the country's economic and political elite. The system is, moreover, more service than production oriented. 'The French phenomenon of bright young Polytechniciens developing careers that span both government service and industrial management has no parallel in Britain'.[30] A second aspect of the weakness in education and training is that, while at the highest level (doctorate), the UK education of scientists and engineers is comparable in terms both of quality and quantity with other European countries, at the middle level (bachelor, technician and craft), it is relatively weak. At the bachelor degree level, science and engineering graduates as a percentage of the total in 2001 was higher in Germany, Sweden and France than in the UK. They were all at or near 30 per cent, and the equivalent figure in Korea was 40 per cent (OECD, 2004a, p. 23). Engineering alone, however, is in the UK much weaker, both at bachelor degree and at the technician and craft levels. Engineering graduates account for less than 10 per cent of the total in the UK, well below Germany and Sweden at or near 20 per cent, and France at over 11 per cent.

Why engineering underwent such a decline, having been a part of Britain's earlier success story, may be attributable to the onset of the rentier mentality.[31] Thus it is not just the weaknesses in the education and training systems themselves that account for the low level of engineering skills. It is also the lack of recognition of the need for a more highly skilled labour force on the part of employers. This is illustrated in the contrast between an estimated investment in training by industry of only 0.15 per cent of revenue in Britain and 2 per cent in Germany. The 'underspend' on training is at all levels. An extensive study of management training in Europe found that British firms spend less than half the amount that German firms spend per manager on training (Huber, 2004).

Intervention by the state could have imposed selective qualification prerequisites, but the state has traditionally had a *laissez-faire* attitude to the economy. This does not mean that there are no significant state institutions in the NSI, or that government policy has never impinged on innovation. Policy and institutions in the UK are almost inseparable, with the latter more or less determined by the former.[32]

As in France, policy has been inconsistent. In the 1960s, the state was more interventionist than at any other time. Industrial policy (industrial restructuring, corporation tax, capital grants), particularly under the Labour government between 1964 and 1970, aimed to reorganize industry through consolidation in particular sectors – notably steel, cars, machine tools and computers – to form national champions. At the same time, science and technology (S&T) policy (S&T education, public sector laboratories, patent laws) acting through the education system, direct support of R&D, and other measures, attempted to regain technological leadership for Britain. Generally, however, there was a lack of co-ordination, with industrial policy under the Department of Trade and Industry and S&T policy under the Department of Education and Science. In the late 1960s, an attempt was made to simplify matters by the creation of a Ministry of Technology. In the 1970s, direct intervention continued. The National Enterprise Board (NEB), set up in 1974 by the Labour government, had the role of acting as a catalyst for investments in advanced technology areas. This it attempted, for example through Inmos, a state semiconductor development company, and Celltech in the biotechnology area.

Under the Conservative governments from 1979, direct intervention was largely ruled out, and a policy of creating the right environment, or climate, for encouraging innovation was adopted. The NEB was initially instructed to act commercially, but its most public function became the bailing out of failing companies such as Rolls-Royce. Partly in consequence of this, in 1981 it merged with another state corporation[33] to become the British Technology Group (BTG), providing venture capital through equity mainly in small firms. By the mid-1980s, BTG had an investment portfolio of about £230 million in 430 companies. It was privatized in an employee and management buyout in 1992 and floated on the London Stock Exchange in 1995.[34]

Other schemes introduced in the 1980s with the aim of advancing venture capital to facilitate the introduction or development of new technologies included the Loan Guarantee Scheme and the Business Expansion Scheme. These have continued to exist in various forms, under both Conservative and Labour governments. One problem with all these schemes is that many of the firms that obtain capital through them are not actually innovative in terms of products, processes or structures.

Among the important organizations in the British system of innovation under the Conservatives were, at various times, the Advisory Council for Applied Research and Development (ACARD), the Advisory Committee on Science and Technology – both advising the Cabinet Office – and the Department of Trade and Industry. Significant programmes, such as the Alvey Programme for information technology, were launched (in 1981, becoming 'one of Britain's largest efforts to strengthen national technological capabilities' (Walker, 1993, p. 184)). It involved, for example, £350 million of public funding of collaborative research into artificial intelligence (Naylor, 2000). Defence R&D expenditure was also high – a higher proportion of government R&D than in France and much higher than in Germany. The UK topped the table of defence R&D in the early 2000s too, under the Labour government (see Table 11.2).

Despite these elements of continuity in innovation policy, during the second half of the 1980s and into the 1990s there was a substantial reduction in the state's role in the innovation system. All the major EU countries' government financing of R&D declined over the 1990s (OECD, 2004b, table 14). A number of initiatives, including many begun by the Conservative government itself during the early 1980s, were terminated. Most significant among them was the Alvey Programme, discontinued in 1989. The state has continued to have a role; the Office for Science and Technology (OST), set up by the Conservative government in 1992 has continued under Labour governments in power since 1997 to provide advice to the government on science, engineering and technology. The OST is also responsible 'for the allocation of the Science Budget (currently just under £2.4 billion per annum) into research via the Research Councils' (OST, 2004).

Awareness of problems in the British system of innovation was expressed in 1993 in the Conservative government's White Paper on science and technology. This called for a strengthening of links between academia and industry, and proposed the Technology Foresight Programme.[35] This programme resulted in the spring 1995 publication of reports on the likely technological developments in each of 15 sectors of industry. The objective of the programme was to stimulate investment by British firms in R&D so that they will be ahead of their rivals in the markets for the new products and processes. The programme was orchestrated by the OST. This, according to some commentators, confused matters because the OST dealt mainly with basic science, and Foresight is about applications and innovations for industry. The suggestion is that it should have been organized by the Department of Trade and Industry (DTI). Perhaps in response to this, the OST was moved from the Cabinet Office to the DTI with the explicit aim of improving links between government, industry and the science and engineering base. Within the OST it was believed that the move enabled it to work more closely with those responsible in the DTI for encouraging business to make more effective use of the science base.

There was also concern that the government would not fully support the implementation of Foresight. A key element in implementation was the Chamber of Commerce one-stop shops called Business Links, 'where local firms are supposed to be able to find advice about anything from new technology to staff training'. But of the planned 200 Business Links, by 1995 only 75 were operating, and many of these were underfunded. The success of Foresight depended, according to Coghlan (1995), on 'whether its message becomes embedded in the industrial culture'.

While Foresight is still in existence, it is now a much narrower programme, focusing on three or four areas at any one time. Application and innovation seem to be central to its objectives. Business Link, managed by the DTI, also still exists, providing advice on all aspects of starting and running a business, including the development and application of new ideas. Its focus has also been pared down; it is now offered through 44 local operators throughout England and one affiliated organization each in Wales, Scotland and Northern Ireland. There is, confusingly, another programme called Link, which operates across government to support collaborative R&D projects. In each project, to be eligible to obtain funding, there must be at least one firm and one research base organization (university, research centre or institute within which research is undertaken). Among the successes attributed to Link is a company called Smart Fibres, which took part in a Link project and has now taken a world lead in using optical fibres to measure stresses in composite structures ranging from yacht masts to wind turbine blades. As with other such programmes, it is difficult to prove that the company would not in any case have achieved its success without government assistance.

How important has defence R&D been to the British NSI and how much spinoff has there been? The answer to this question is similar to that for France. Most defence R&D goes on development rather than basic or applied research, and there is a sharp distinction between civil and military activities. Defence R&D may occupy an even greater proportion of Britain's technological resources than in France, and, almost certainly, defence procurement absorbs a higher proportion of high-technology *engineering* resources. There 'is broad agreement that defense spending has sapped, rather than strengthened, Britain's industrial economy' (Walker, 1993, p. 177). Among significant differences between the UK and France in relation to defence technology, is that while the UK was willing in certain areas (such as nuclear missiles) to remain dependent on the United States, France went for independence across the board, and solved the scale problem by relying to a greater extent than the UK on exports. This is changing, as 'recently a French-style policy of export maximization has been adopted that discourages product complexity' (Walker, 1993, p. 177). Figure 11.3 shows that between 1996 and 2002 the UK's export market share in aerospace grew whereas that of France declined such that France lost its leading European market share position in this industry to the UK. Among recent supports for this industry has been the Civil Aircraft and Technology Demonstration (CARAD) Programme, apparently replaced by the Aeronautics Research Programme.[36]

Among similarities between the two countries is that the two main high-technology industries are aerospace and pharmaceuticals and that, therefore, aerospace is an exception to the generalization that there is little spinoff of military R&D.[37] Britain's heavy postwar commitment to defence procurement has contributed directly to the strength of this industry. The main firms benefiting from this procurement have been British Aerospace, Rolls-Royce and Lucas Aerospace. As in France, the pharmaceutical industry is the only non-defence related high-technology industry that has performed well in international terms. Companies such as ICI, Glaxo and Beecham have been aggressive investors in R&D and have established close links with university researchers in related fields. These companies, like all major pharmaceutical companies, have undergone a number of mergers and acquisitions in recent years. ICI's pharmaceutical division became Zeneca and then merged with the Swiss firm Astra in 1999 to form AstraZeneca. Beecham merged with the American company SmithKline in 1989, Glaxo merged with Wellcome in 1995. In 2000 the two companies SmithKlineBeecham and GlaxoWellcome, both of which had in the meantime acquired a number of other companies, merged to form GlaxoSmithKline. While headquartered in the UK, this company has most of its operations in the United States. In comparison with France, British companies have far fewer new drugs under development, but the drugs they do develop have greater success in world markets. One reason for this is the British companies' strict policies of dropping products which, from the early screening process, seem unlikely to be successful.

A key difference in the pharmaceutical industries, and of the two national economies in general, is in the significance of multinational enterprises (MNEs). Subsidiaries of MNEs are far more important to the UK economy than they are either to France or Germany. There has been a long tradition, beginning in the late nineteenth and early twentieth centuries and increasing sharply after the Second World War, of American direct investment. With companies such as Ford and General Motors – and, more recently the Japanese car companies – owning manufacturing subsidiaries in the UK, it is not surprising that foreign companies account for over 40 per cent of business R&D undertaken in the UK (see Table 11.4). This is a much higher percentage than in any other major economy.

There are differences of opinion as to the implications of a significant presence of MNEs, particularly in high technology areas. Vernon's (1966) product cycle model[38] suggested that the more sophisticated parts of an MNE's production process, including R&D, would be located in the country of the firm's headquarters. Porter elaborates on this, arguing that production of sophisticated components, and core R&D, are activities, 'first and foremost, for either the multinational's home base, or nations with attributes (such as demand conditions) that make locating in them important to innovation. In addition, foreign subsidiaries do not necessarily breed managers with an orientation toward exports and international competition' (Porter, 1990, p. 679).

Vernon himself, among others,[39] now disagrees with this view: 'explanations of the behaviour of TNCs [transnational corporations] which draw on the national origins of the enterprises as a major explanatory variable are rapidly losing their value, to be replaced by an increased emphasis on the characteristics of the product markets in which the enterprises participate' (Vernon, 1992). Not that this is directly contradicted by the work of Khanna and Singh (2002), discussed earlier in this chapter.

Dunning, whose work on MNEs has been seminal, takes a position somewhere between those of Porter and Vernon. He argues that an increasing proportion of economic activity is potentially footloose in its location, though the extent to which enterprises 'are able and willing to switch locations varies according to industry, firm and country-specific differences' (Dunning, 1992).

In a related argument, Dicken (2003b) asserts that while the home-base characteristics of the MNE are dominant, MNEs are also influenced by the 'place-specific characteristics of the countries in which they operate'. Dicken's point is that, whether in terms of the influence of the home base and/or in terms of MNEs' adaptation to local circumstances, geography matters to how they 'configure their production chains' and, therefore, to their impact on the places in which they operate.

In a detailed case study of foreign-owned firms in the UK machine tool industry, Young and Dunlop (1992) point out that 'most UK production of machining centres ... is under licence from Japanese makers'. Young and Hood (1992), referring to the same study, conclude that UK competitiveness in this industry will depend on the extent of Japanese FDI, and sourcing strategies – which, in turn, may depend on EU local content rules. What emerges is a picture of an industry in which the presence of foreign, and particularly Japanese, firms may have reduced, or been a result of a decline in, the competitiveness of the indigenous machine tool industry in the UK. As the industry has advanced technologically, so has it become, in the UK, more dependent on foreign-owned firms.[40] Thus, whether as a causal or resultant factor, the high proportion of foreign-owned firms in this high-technology industry in the UK is an expression of the relative weakness of the innovativeness of the indigenous industry. A further, recent, expression of this weakness is the 25 per cent decline in production of machine tools in the UK between 1998 and 2001; by 2001 the UK ranked tenth in the world in machine tool production, having fallen from eighth position in 1998 (Wengel and Shapira, 2004). At least in this industry, location of ownership seems to be important.

Walker (1993, pp. 167–8) generalizes this finding by emphasizing the importance of distinguishing between those competitive manufacturing industries in the UK in which the strengths are indigenous – chemicals and pharmaceuticals, aerospace, and food, drink and tobacco – and those in which they derive from foreign multinationals – motor vehicles and electronics. He goes further than Young and Hood by stating that the UK's entire industrial development in the 1990s will depend on the behaviour of foreign multinationals and, in particular, on the decisions of Japanese companies.

As with foreign direct investment, so with foreign investment specifically in R&D in the UK, there is no consensus as to its effect on UK indigenous technological capabilities. Either way, it is a significant characteristic of the UK system of innovation, that the proportion of UK patents registered in the United States accounted for by foreign-owned firms in the UK, is far above the European average, and that the proportion of large UK firms' patents registered in the United States accounted for by those firms' foreign subsidiaries, is also above that average (Patel and Pavitt, 1991, table 3.6; see also above, Tables 11.4 and 11.6). These characteristics firmly underline the relatively international nature of the UK NSI. Yet, at least in the high-technology sectors, the UK has very few 'giant' manufacturing companies. At the other end of the scale, while there is a profusion of dynamic small firms in the service sector, in manufacturing 'Britain is relatively poorly endowed with small firms' (Walker, 1993, p. 167).

How these conclusions relate to the particularly British state and policy context is suggested by Grant (1995). Grant characterizes Britain as a neo-liberal 'spectator state' whose policy towards globalization has been to welcome it. Among the results of this, he argues, has been the breaking down of indigenous networks, adversely affecting, in particular, equipment suppliers.

Love and Roper (2004) also find a relative paucity of inter-firm collaboration based on mutual trust in the UK. They analyse this in terms of a 'marked contrast in the impact on innovation organisation of the social and institutional context in UK and Germany'. In Germany, they argue,

> institutional and social norms within the system of industrial relations mean that technical collaborations based on mutual trust are more feasible, . . . but the specialised skills and narrow functional orientation of management . . . make the adoption of more flexible internal systems

such as multifunctional working more difficult. In the UK, in contrast, the more adversarial nature of Anglo-Saxon capitalism makes it more difficult to establish external collaborations based on mutual trust, but easier to adopt multifunctional working and achieve internal flexibility.

The work of Lloyd and Payne (2003) updates that of Grant (1995) by examining New Labour's view of the 'knowledge society' and relates to that Love and Roper (2004) by addressing the associated policy and institutional issues. They show that the model – or system of innovation – underlying the Labour government's perspective is much closer to that of the United States than to the European social model. As they put it, New Labour's starting position is an 'acceptance of the UK's current institutional structures, something which invariably leads to an embracing of the American model said to be more in tune with British cultures and practices'. In relation to the alternative, New Labour 'considers the North European model to be too over-regulated and sclerotic to survive in the new "globalised" knowledge economy' (Lloyd and Payne, 2003). It is aspects of the UK system that are close to the American one, such as less regulated labour markets, that make possible the multifunctional working and flexibility identified by Love and Roper (2004).[41]

There are strengths and weaknesses in the UK system of innovation and both seem to have historical roots. Among the strengths is a continuing excellence in science that goes back hundreds of years. Another strength – what Love and Roper (2004) call 'multifunctional working' and 'internal flexibility' in UK manufacturing – is also built on the long-standing institutional base. There are also weaknesses in the UK's indigenous NSI. Among the key weaknesses are, first, those in the areas of technical education and training and, more broadly, general attitudes to technical skills; second, the dominance of foreign-owned companies in particular sectors; and third, those relating to the relative absence of inter-firm collaboration.[42] One must conclude that the possibility of regenerating British technological leadership is slight, notwithstanding the improvements that may be achieved by such government initiatives as the Foresight Programme. As to what the impact of European integration will be, therefore, it can only be stated that positive results will be derived more from effective institutional developments than from the further extension of market mechanisms.

11.7.3 Other European systems of innovation

Both France and the UK have strengths and weaknesses in their NSIs. In this section these will become clearer through comparisons with aspects of the NSIs of other European countries, in particular Germany and Italy.

Germany and the importance of the financial system

The control and financing of firms and, in particular, of investment in R&D and innovation varies from country to country. Moreover, different systems of control and financing (or governance) may be associated with different rates and types of innovation.

> *Management of the capitalistic firm is constrained by the propensity of the institutional investors or major individual capitalists to intervene in management decisions (they may, for example, opt for higher dividends and object to a proposed increase in R and D expenditures). The same management also faces another interventionist force, the union, which, concerned with job security of its members, may oppose management's attempt to introduce a new automation technology. (Ozaki, 1991, p. 58)*

Ozaki's argument is that Japan has had innovative success because of a hybrid form of enterprise, the 'humanistic firm', in which these problems are obviated by the fact that management and unions all act in the long-term interests of the firm. While this may be part of the explanation, others (for example, Christensen, 1992) emphasize the close relationships of Japanese firms to banks. Given the downturn and extended recession in Japan in the 1990s, with bank failures among the main features, the latter explanation is probably more relevant.

Germany's innovative success, it can be argued, has also been based on aspects of industrial relations and banking. In Germany, too, there has been a 'system of industrial relations that has limited trade union conflict within industries' and a 'banking system that enables the banks to support the restructuring of industries' (Keck, 1993).[43]

Christensen's (1992) analysis suggests that the role of finance is particularly important in Germany. The German tradition of strong banking influence in the process of industrialization goes back to the middle of the nineteenth century. As to whether there is still an important, direct influence by banks on large firms in recent years, there is some doubt. Firms like Siemens, for example, are largely internally financed. However, the banks (and, to some extent, government grants) remain important in the financing of SMEs. Moreover, the German financial system continues to have an indirect influence on large firms. In contrast to the financial systems in the UK and the United States, for example, the institutional features of the German system have made takeovers difficult. This lower frequency of takeovers mean less of the disruption in the establishment of reputations and the building of relations, both inter- and intra-firm, that arises from frequent changes in ownership.

Until recently, distinctions were drawn between financial systems based on credit and those based on the capital market. In the first, firms' financing was based mainly on bank credit, and in the second, firms raised funds mainly through the stock market. Originally, the German (and Japanese) systems were considered to be credit-based, and the UK (and US) systems equity-based. However, 'with the extension of financial deregulation all over the world during the 1980s and 1990s, this distinction became less and less relevant' (Coriat and Weinstein, 2004). The finance literature now juxtaposes 'insider' to 'outsider' models of corporate control.[44] This literature also broadly asserts that economic efficiency requires outside rather than inside ownership (Jones and Mygind, 2002). The German and continental European system is now identified as closer to the insider model, in which managers and/or employees own the company, whereas the UK and US system is closer to the outsider model, in which shareholders – who mostly do not work in the company – own it.

Each of the two systems, insider and outsider, has advantages, the former for sectors 'based on incremental innovation and long-term investments' and the latter for '"radical," breakthrough innovations' (Coriat and Weinstein, 2004). The insider model has advantages for incremental innovations because of the specialist knowledge, skills and commitment of the people in the company. Institutional innovations such as stock markets (for example, Nasdaq) specializing in venture capital funding of innovative companies, provide examples of how the outsider model is conducive to the development of radical new products and processes.

That the financial theory preference for outside ownership is not always borne out empirically, is also evident in Jones and Mygind's (2002) study of Estonia. They find that 'types of insider ownership can rank amongst the most effective forms of private ownership'. In particular, they find that manager-owned and employee-owned firms are both more productive than firms owned by domestic outsiders.[47]

Financial systems may emerge from, as well as influence, social and industrial development. There is an interrelationship between the development of a country's financial system, and its industrial and technological change. Despite a great deal of internationalization of financial markets and institutions, national financial and corporate governance systems – with all the historical, cultural, legal, linguistic and economic factors that go into differentiating them – continue to be of primary importance.[46]

German success relative to other European countries is thus based, in part, on its financial system. The technical education system is also usually mentioned as a basis of that success. To return to Love and Roper (2004), the German institutional setting is conducive to inter-firm collaboration and co-operation, but the technical education and industrial relations systems impede the introduction of internal flexibility. The consequence is that while the former is a strength, the latter is a weakness in relation to the innovativeness of German manufacturing.

With respect to nearly all the indicators of technological capability presented in the earlier part of this section, Germany has been outperformed by Japan. In relation to export market shares in particular sectors, such as aerospace and pharmaceuticals, Germany remains ahead, and in others, such as instruments, it has overtaken Japan. Japan, while still far ahead of any of the European economies in electronics, has been overtaken by the United States (see Fig. 11.3). The Japanese system is not without faults; Odagiri and Goto (1993) fear that the low share of universities in basic research in Japan may not augur well for the future of the Japanese NSI. Germany's continuing success over a much longer period than Japan, notwithstanding the increasing challenges it faces in the context of its reunification, increasing European integration and the intensification of technological competition from South East Asia, leave room for confidence about the future of its NSI.

Italy and industrial districts

Thus far, attention here has been on national, and to some extent sectoral factors in systems of innovation. There are also, however, in most EU countries, important sub-national, regional systems of innovation. In Italy, for example, in addition to an NSI which is comparable (though inferior) to those of the UK, France and Germany, there is also a second, much more successful, system of innovation, a small firms network.

> These two systems are quite different in terms of capabilities, organization, and performance. The small firms network is composed of a large population of small and medium size firms (in some cases located in industrial districts), which interact intensively at the local level. . . . Firms in the network are engaged in rapid adoption of technology generated externally and in the adaptation and continuous improvement of this technology. (Malerba, 1993, p. 230)

Within the small firms network, Malerba identifies three types of firms: first, those in industrial districts: second, the equipment manufacturers (some of which are also in industrial districts); and third, non-industrial district firms in traditional sectors.

Industrial districts were defined and discussed in some detail in Section 8.3 of Chapter 8. They are an empirical phenomenon, identified in what has become known as the Third Italy, and particularly the Emilia-Romagna region. Each industrial district contains a number of firms of different sizes, but all small or medium, all producing all or part of the same product, and all in close proximity to one another. They are closely related to Marshallian industrial districts. Emilia-Romagna has been a particular focus of attention because of its ceramic tile, textiles and clothing, metalworking and machine-making industrial districts. As can be seen from the traditional nature of some of these products, the innovativeness of the industrial districts is concentrated in their processes. There are other industrial agglomerations (or regional innovation systems), such as Silicon Valley in California, in which product innovations are more prevalent.

Metalworking and machine-making firms are examples of the large number of innovative, internationally competitive, small and medium-sized equipment manufacturers that are common in a number of different regions in the Third Italy. Among these firms, those in the machine tool industry have been particularly successful. (The biggest agglomeration of machine tool SMEs is in Lombardy.) This is illustrated by the growth in the Italian share of machine tool production – which, in contrast to UK machine tool production, is accounted for almost exclusively by indigenous firms.[47] In 1986, the Italian share of world machine tool production was 5.6 per cent; by 1990 it had grown to 8.5 per cent (*American Machinist*, various issues). By 2001, Italy had become the third largest producer of machine tools in the world, accounting for 12 per cent of world production and 11 per cent of consumption (Wengel and Shapira, 2004). The success of these firms derives partly from the high levels of skill among technicians and engineers – which transfers rapidly horizontally where the firms are part of an industrial district – and partly from the needs of sophisticated users in close vertical relationships with the suppliers. Major Italian firms such as Fiat and Olivetti, and the flexibly specialized, small-firm districts (such as the textile machinery district in Biella), interact closely with machinery designers and manufacturers. This provides 'an innovative stimulus and a continuous feedback on the use of the machinery' (Malerba, 1993, p. 239).

As we pointed out in our discussion of industrial districts in Chapter 8, the Italian industrial districts are changing, and in many cases local leader firms are emerging.[48] This is certainly so in the machine tool sector, where 'with the introduction of flexible automation, larger firms can compete more flexibly in the market place and take advantage of economies of scope as well as scale'. Larger firms have additional advantages over small ones in relation to obtaining finance and recruiting skilled workers. Most important from an innovation perspective are the large firms, emerging within industrial districts, that are contributing to the development of knowledge bases and technology. 'Such innovative leaders are able to observe and transfer within the district new production technologies, strategies and concepts that are developing elsewhere'. That the institutional context remains important is clear from the fact that in some cases the innovative leadership is taken not by any one firm, but by associations. An example of this is the association of machine tool producers, UCIMU, in Lombardy. Another recent development is in the growth, among the larger firms, of investments outside Italy. In the machine tool industry in Italy, in contrast to that in the UK, there is far more outward than inward investment.

An example of the emergence and then rapid growth of an innovative firm in a traditional sector in Italy is Benetton. In the late 1980s and early 1990s Benetton and a number of smaller examples represented a new organizational model for the Third Italian regions in which they have emerged, including Emilia-Romagna and Tuscany. This is the large, vertically integrated firm, which has been more typical of other regions. Using advanced information and communication technologies to provide remote production control, linking sales with production management, this type of firm also established 'tight relationships with fashion creation and international marketing' (Camagni, 1991, p. 156). Such firms have continued to thrive, using the most sophisticated telecommunications and/or production technologies to emulate some of the flexibility of the industrial districts.

Industrial districts are a very important part of the recent innovative success of small firms in Italy. Other examples of localized agglomerations of innovative firms in Europe that have been discussed, either as extant or potential, include those in Spain (Benton, 1992; Molina-Morales, 2002), Germany (Schmitz, 1992; Staber, 2001), Denmark (Kristensen, 1992; Hansen, 2002), Ireland (Jacobson and Mottiar, 1999) and Sweden (Melander and Nordqvist, 2002).

Two questions in particular emerge from the discussion thus far. First, are small firms, such as those in industrial districts, more innovative simply because of their size? Second, has the local focus of many of the innovative systems within Europe impeded the emergence of an integrated European system of innovation?

11.7.4 Firm size, market structure and innovation

A traditional, neoclassical view would be that competition is the major spur to innovation, and that monopoly retards it. In much recent work on technological change, culture, tradition and other elements inherent in NSIs may be key factors, rather than market structure (though market structure may itself be a factor in NSIs). But firm size and market structure continue to be of interest. If very large firms are more likely to generate innovation, then innovation will be more common in oligopolistic and monopolistic structures. If small firm size is associated with innovativeness, then competitive, or industrial district-type structures are the more likely milieu for innovations.

The debate on firm size, market structure and innovation has already been referred to, in Chapter 2 in relation to Schumpeter, and in Chapter 4 in relation to Lazonick and Best. The early Schumpeter believed that innovations were more likely to emanate from small, new firms. Later, coming to the view that high levels of investments were required for successful innovation, he concluded that large firms, possibly in collusion with others, or as monopolies, were more likely to generate innovations. Schumpeter had 'observed that the locus of innovative activities [had] shifted from the talented individual entrepreneur to the organized R&D laboratory' (Pavitt, 1994).

Whether or not Schumpeter's change of mind was a reflection of a real change in the sources of innovation, there continues to be a debate about the significance of size of firm. This debate in some ways is reflected in the work of Lazonick and Best. Lazonick's (1991) view favours large firms, whereas Best's (1990) favours small firms. Lazonick (1991, p. 198) summarizes his theory of the innovative organization as one 'in which the organizational capability of the business enterprise influences the extent to which the enterprise can transform the high fixed costs of its innovative investment strategy into high-quality products at low unit costs.' A high fixed cost innovative investment strategy is a fundamental part of this theory. High fixed costs suggest the need for firms to be large scale.[49]

Best's view of innovative (or entrepreneurial, or learning) firms is shown in the criteria he uses to distinguish them from hierarchical firms. As we showed in Chapter 4, he identifies these firms as ones that seek strategic advantage through continuous product, process and organizational innovation, maintaining organizational flexibility at all levels, including the micro production level (Best, 1990, pp. 11–14). This emphasis on organizational flexibility and relatively flat organization structures, underlines the advantages of small firms.[50]

A second difference in this context relates to market structure. Whereas Lazonick and Chandler's views favour a small number of large firms, Best's favour the industrial district concept of large numbers of firms of all sizes, competing and co-operating in a market structure undefined in neoclassical theory.

Rothwell and Dodgson (1994) summarize and compromise by suggesting that, in some cases large firms, and in other cases small firms, are more innovative: 'The innovatory advantages of large firms are in the main associated with their relatively greater financial and technological resources, i.e. they are *material* advantages; small firm advantages are those of entrepreneurial dynamism, internal flexibility and responsiveness to changing circumstances, i.e. they are *behavioural* advantages.'[51]

Empirical work on firm size, market structure and innovation faces all the same complications discussed above in relation to measurement of R&D, innovation and technological change.

◆ *Differences between countries.* Gellman Research Associates (1976) found that the percentage of innovations accounted for by firms with annual sales of less than US$50 million was as high as 57 per cent in France, as low as 20 per cent in Japan, with the United States, Germany and the UK in between. It is of course a fundamental argument of the NSI literature that there are differences between countries in terms of various aspects of innovation, including the presence and innovativeness of small firms.

◆ *Differences between regions.* SMEs tend to be more actively and extensively networked into their locality, with implications for innovative capability. Almeida and Kogut (1997), focusing on patents in the semiconductor industry in the United States, show that small-firm start-ups 'are unusually oriented toward the exploration of diversity by targeting less crowded technological fields', and that the exploration of small firms 'has a strong local character: they are more sensitive to, and contribute more to, the innovations of spatially-contiguous firms'.

◆ *Differences between cities.* Simmie (2002) shows that innovation by SMEs will tend to concentrate in particular cities. Providing evidence from a survey of innovative SMEs in the south east of England, he argues that there are two main factors that these cities have in common. First, on the supply side, they have dense sources of supply of inputs and ideas – for example, from universities – that generate knowledge spillovers among collaborating SMEs. Second, on the demand side, they facilitate international knowledge transfers through international customers, distributors and contacts. He shows that Greater London, like the other urban areas in which innovation is concentrated, has both these characteristics.

◆ *Differences between industries.* Industries such as chemicals, pharmaceuticals and electronics, in which expensive R&D laboratories are required, favour large firms; industries in which mass production, continuous process, high capital costs and/or high advertising costs are present, also favour large firms, and innovations in those industries are therefore likely to emanate from large firms;[52] in industries such as scientific instruments, specialist machinery and software, where there are relatively low entry costs or where niche markets exist (because, for example, of specific customer requirements for producer goods), small firms' share of innovation is high.

◆ *Differences over time.* There is evidence that the upward trend in the average size of firms that had been an enduring feature of economic development since the Industrial Revolution (Chandler, 1977) has slowed down or even reversed itself since the 1970s (Acs, 1996). This calls into question the view that there are increasing returns to scale – internal to firms – that drive successful firms to increase in size. Focusing on technology and innovation in particular, Acs and Preston (1997) acknowledge 'the apparent resurgence of smaller firms' and ask whether this is 'due to the emergence of a dynamic, vital innovative entrepreneurial sector' or 'to the inability of large incumbent MNEs to prevail in a technologically dynamic global environment'.[53]

- ◆ *Differences over time, within industries.* In general, small firms predominate in the early stages of a new technology, and larger firms when the technology is more mature. The new biotechnology industry, for example, came about through the inventive/innovative activities of new technology-based firms (NTBFs) – SMEs established specifically to create, exploit or develop new technologies. The production, distribution and advertising to larger markets of products of the new industry – in particular, new drugs – are handled by large, established firms in the pharmaceutical industry.[54] In some cases, the original invention/innovation occurs in large firms, and the diffusion is through NTBFs. According to Dodgson and Rothwell (1994), this is what happened in relation to semiconductor devices and computer-aided design (CAD) systems. Either way, these examples indicate that both large and small firms are involved, sometimes together, sometimes in different stages, in the evolution of a technology.[55]

- ◆ *Differences over time, within firms.* As firms grow, they may become more focused on a particular technology. They become more routinized and it becomes more difficult 'to accommodate the more creative and non-conformist types who like to immerse themselves in technical challenges' (Leavy and Jacobson, 1999). This lack of accommodation is particularly likely if the new departure being proposed is radical. The committed, creative person will tend to leave and start a new firm, as long as the barriers to entry are not too great. This intra-firm factor may explain, for example, why the biotech revolution was initiated by NTBFs rather than established pharmaceutical companies. Incremental innovations, on the basis of this argument, are more likely in large firms, and radical ones in small firms.[56] A large company like 3M, with the commandment 'Thou shalt not kill a new product idea' (Leavy and Jacobson, 1999), is an exception.

Whether innovations originate in small or large firms, both types of firms have roles in the development and diffusion of innovations. Indeed, successful innovation will often depend on the relationships between small and large firms. Close contacts between an industry and its upstream suppliers, for example, can speed innovations. An illustration is the clothing and textiles industries, in which new products have resulted from such developments in the chemical industry as rayon, nylon and polyester. There are similar examples in the printing and publishing, and wood and furniture industries.

Innovation in an industry can be dependent both on its upstream suppliers and downstream customers. In the software manual-printing industry for example, improvements in printing technology developed upstream were introduced into the relatively small software manual printing firms because of the insistence of the large software producers downstream (Jacobson and O'Sullivan, 1994).

Despite the complexity of the relationship between firm size and innovation, attempts are made to generalize. Dodgson and Rothwell (1994) conclude from available data that the relationship between firm size and innovation share is U-shaped, that is, that small and large firms have higher shares of total innovations than medium-sized firms. The value of such generalization is, however, limited because of the national, sectoral and dynamic differences already explained. It follows that, for managers trying to identify appropriate innovation strategies for their firms, there are, as Pavitt (1994) concludes, 'no easy and generalizable recipes for success'.

11.7.5 A European system of innovation?

Impediments to flows of information about innovations have been shown in this chapter to exist both within and between countries. The dual systems of innovation in Italy, and subnational regional systems of innovation elsewhere in Europe, reduce the flow of information about innovations within these countries. Military R&D and other institutional factors also impede diffusion to varying extents in each EU country. Between EU members, such impediments exist to an even greater extent, despite the increasing integration of the European economies, and sustained EU research programmes. The role of the military in the innovation system can, as has been shown, limit spillover into commercial applications, but it has also limited international diffusion (Walker, 1991, p. 367).

Nationally focused assistance for defence industries has continued despite the efforts within NATO in the 1980s of the Independent European Programme Group (IEPG), and of the Western European Union (WEU) which absorbed the functions of the IEPG. Since the Treaty on European Union entered into force on 1 November 1993, co-ordination of defence policy is undertaken by the EU itself.

The European Fighter Aircraft project, which seemed to be failing in the early 1990s, has succeeded in producing the Eurofighter, the first of which have already been delivered to the RAF in Britain. The makers of Eurofighter are Germany's DASA, Britain's BAE Systems, Italy's Alenia and Spain's CASA. France has remained autonomous, producing its own new fighter, the Rafale, which competes with Eurofighter in the world market for such aircraft. Thus while there are elements of close co-operation among high-technology defence equipment companies in different European countries, there remain important differences.

There are also a number of other, non-defence related factors, that are contributing to the generation of elements of a European system of innovation. Such factors include the development of institutions and programmes in the EU, and the improvements in information and communication technologies.

European integration and technology: the impact of EU policy

The relationship between technology and integration can be examined in two separate ways: first, in terms of attempts within the EU to 'Europeanize' (or de-nationalize) efforts to influence firms to create, produce, and introduce new technologies; second, and in the opposite direction, in terms of how new technologies have brought firms to focus on Europe (or even the world) as a terrain, both for production and distribution. The two directions of causality – from EU institutions to firms to technology, and from technology to firms to EU institutions – reinforce one another but, for the sake of presentation, this section examines the former, and the next section the latter.

During the 1970s and early 1980s, it began to be perceived that a technology gap existed, with Europe lagging behind the United States and Japan, particularly in the area of micro-electronics.[57] There were a number of unsuccessful attempts, including Unidata, to generate research co-operation within Europe. There was also success, such as the European Space Agency and the Ariane rocket but, as suggested above, though these did include technological collaboration among firms and governments of different European countries, they were more or less dominated by France. Concorde, an Anglo-French techno-logical success of the 1960s, was a commercial failure. More recently, Airbus has also been both a technological and commercial success, at least in part on the basis of a great deal of support by a number of European governments, as well as by the EU. In the midst of this very mixed record, through Commissioner Davignon's initiative, discussions were held at the beginning of the 1980s with the managing directors of the twelve leading electronics firms in Europe. Davignon's aim was to reduce the fragmentation arising from the support for national champions provided by individual member states.

Out of these discussions emerged a collaborative R&D programme, the European Strategic Programme for Research in Information Technology (Esprit). Starting as a small pilot programme, Esprit grew into a significant institutional context for co-operation between the major European firms, involving Community expenditure of ECU 750 million in 1984–88, and ECU 1.6 billion in 1988–92. More important than either the expenditure or the projects generated, was Esprit's symbolic value: first, Esprit was the first EC programme providing funds on the ('demand-led') basis of competitive bidding by groups of firms and researchers; second, subsequent programmes, such as Race (Research in Advanced Communications for Europe) and Brite (Basic Research in Industrial Technologies of Europe), were modelled on Esprit; third, it provided a context for co-operation and encour-aged converging technological expectations; and fourth, it helped generate support among large firms – accepting that for success they had to be competitive beyond their national markets – for the completion of the single market.[58]

Building on these early efforts, under the Framework Programmes, beginning in 1984 all EU R&D and science and technology (S&T) programmes have been brought together, with a 1987–91 budget of ECU 5.6 billion. The Third Framework Programme had a similar budget for the years 1990–94, its main features responding to a 1989 review of the first programme by, among other things, giving more attention to the creation or support of 'European centres of excellence'. The Fourth Framework Programme (1994–98), with a budget of over ECU 13 billion had guidelines that included, in addition to a number of specific technology-related focuses, greater co-ordination of the research being under-taken in the context of the national programmes of member countries. The Fifth Framework Programme (1998–2002) had a budget of nearly €15 billion.[59] Unlike its pred-ecessors, the FP5 had 'key actions', which were focused on mobilizing a range of disciplines to address specific problems. To maximize its impact, the FP5 focused on a smaller number of research areas than earlier programmes. The Sixth Framework Programme (2003–2006) has a budget of €17.5 billion, a 17 per cent increase over FP5, accounting for nearly 4 per cent of the total EU budget. In FP6 there is a further narrowing of focus; however, there is a broadening of projects, which are bigger, accommodating more partners, than in FP5. The aim is explicitly to promote collaboration in order to create a European Research Area.

Another programme under which funding is obtained for R&D collaboration among west European firms and institutions is the European Research Coordinating Agency (Eureka). Eureka, which includes countries outside the EU, does not fund research, but merely acts as a match-maker. The funding comes from the national governments and participating firms and institutions. There is some overlap between the EU programmes and Eureka, but the former concentrate on pre-competitive R&D and the latter on the competitive end of R&D.

There are elements of significant integration, providing at least an embryonic European system of innovation (ESI). These include outputs of the defence sector, for example Eurofighter, and of the aerospce sector, for example Airbus and Ariane. The thousands of projects in which researchers from universities and companies in different EU member states have co-operated have also contributed to this early evolution of an ESI.

Gregersen and Johnson (1997) directly address the question of whether an ESI is emerging. They construct a model to show that at least an early phase ESI has been developing through institutional learning. This happens within the EU framework, for example through the various treaties, the euro, structural funds and the various common policies. These all influence people involved at all levels in national economic and monetary policies. 'Another example is the development of Framework Programmes reflecting a process of institutional learning within the political and the administrative European organizations themselves.' However, the Framework Programmes also emerge from national discussions on science and technology and political priorities. Ultimately, the ESI and the NSIs interact in ways that change them both, in some cases enhancing the ESI and in others the NSIs. Gregersen and Johnson (1997) conclude that the ESI, to the extent that it exists, does so only in the narrow sense.

There are a number of grounds for moderating optimism (from an integrationist perspective) about the impact of EU programmes and institutions. First, as Petrella (1991, p. 15) has pointed out, many inter-firm collaborative agreements have been between European firms on the one hand, and US or Japanese on the other.[60] Second, there are vastly greater levels of public expenditure on R&D within individual countries than there are in the Framework Programmes and Eureka combined. Third, although there are projects within EU technology policy aimed at addressing the imbalance between the technological capacity of the European core and that of the periphery, such core–periphery gaps remain. Fourth, EU member states and regions continue to compete through various incentives for the mobile investment projects of US and Japanese firms. Finally, there is the unsolved problem of actual and potential national support for nationally based MNEs that continue to be seen as national champions.

Technology and European integration: the technological drive to internationalization

The development of certain technologies has greatly facilitated the emergence of firms whose terrain of activity transcends national boundaries. The most important 'enabling technologies' are transportation and communications. In relation to transportation, jet aircraft have significantly reduced the time taken to move people and goods from one part of the world to another. In communications, the application of information technology, and the convergence between computer and communication technologies into information and communication technologies (ICT), have facilitated the transmission, virtually instantaneously, of spoken and written words and data, and of images. While these technologies by themselves have not made inevitable the emergence of MNEs, the growth in scale and number of these firms would certainly not have been possible without such technologies. Related to the ways in which enabling technologies have given rise to MNEs, particularly during the second half of the twentieth century, are the developments in production processes which have required large volumes of output – and hence large firms and large markets – for competitiveness, and the continued accumulation of technologies by firms in their attempts to remain competitive (Cantwell, 1989).

Among the practical results of these forces acting on the advanced technology firms in the member states of the EU, has been the support that many of these firms have offered for the removal of trading and other barriers. To some extent this support, as shown above, was attributable to the efforts of the Commission, and to the Esprit programme, which 'created an important constituency in big business, pressing for the completion of the internal market and the abolition of all remaining internal barriers to trade, such as divergent standards and regulations' (Sharp, 1990, p. 59). At least some of this constituency, irrespective of Esprit, would have been pressing for these ends because of technological and competitive imperatives. Indeed, some authors go so far as to suggest that firms' needs resulted in such programmes as Esprit: 'Market pressure and rising R&D cost were among the main factors [in the 1980s] underlining the willingness of both managers and politicians to engage in (international) inter-firm collaboration. Shared-cost R&D programmes like ESPRIT and EUREKA are a very clear expression of this phenomenon' (Roscam et al., 1991, p. 27).

Research collaboration among European firms is important, but, following our discussion about the importance of ownership earlier in this chapter, it is of interest to identify the main trends in mergers, acquisitions and alliances (MAAs) in Europe. Alliances of various kinds were much more common, at least until the mid-1980s, between European firms on the one hand and non-European (and particularly US) firms on the other. On the basis of a study of the ICT industry in the second half of the 1980s, there were, according to Petrella (1991, table 2 and p. 17), some signs of change towards intra-European agreements, but it was not yet clear whether this was an emerging trend. The trend is clarified in a recent study of M&As among telecommunications firms between 1993 and 2000 (Warf, 2003). From Warf's data, the following facts can be extracted:

♦ Most (55 per cent) of the telecoms M&As were within the United States.

♦ Of the 87 M&As, 22 (25 per cent) involved EU firms.

♦ Unlike those involving American firms, nearly all European M&As were international.

♦ In 7 of the 22 M&As involving European firms, American firms acquired European ones. The largest of these was the acquisition in 1999 by Bellsouth of the Dutch firm Royal KPN, for US$20 billion.

♦ In two of the EU M&As, European firms acquired American firms. In both cases Deutsche Telecom was the purchaser. The largest was the acquisition of Voicestream for US$50.5 billion.

♦ Another 7 of the 22 EU M&As involved a firm from one EU country merging with or acquiring a firm from another EU country. The largest of these was the acquisition by Deutsche Telecom of Telecom Italia in 1999 for US$81.8 billion, at the time the biggest M&A in European history.

In summary, there is significant consolidation among American firms mainly intra-nationally, and among European firms mainly internationally within Europe.

This trend is not specific to ICT firms. As we showed in Chapter 10 (see Table 10.4), there has been increasing industrial integration in the EU arising both from the common currency and from the removal of cross-border barriers in general.

It may be, therefore, that the earlier pessimism of, for example, Hamill (1992) that there may be a loss of EU sovereignty arising from non-EU acquisitions of EU firms has proven to be unfounded. He also argued that intra-EU cross-border MAAs would lead to rationaliz-ation and have an adverse effect on employment and concentration. If so, then the main beneficiaries of increasing integration would 'not be European companies, consumers or workers, but rather non-EC firms which have consolidated their market positions in the EC through MAAs'. It may be that the post-New Economy recession in the early 2000s was in part due to some of this rationalization, but there is no evidence of the latter part of Hamill's argument. While there are some examples of companies (particularly American ones) obtaining strong market positions in the EU, there are also examples of the opposite, that is, of EU firms consolidating positions in the American market.

Kay's (1990b) pessimism also seems not to have been entirely borne out. He argued that it might 'be easier and cheaper to stimulate joint ventures between EC and non-EC firms than between EC firms'. This would make an EU science and technology policy of encour-aging intra-EU collaboration more difficult and expensive, notwithstanding the aims and objectives of the Framework Programmes.

11.8 Summary

In this chapter we have defined a number of concepts that are used in the study of technological change and innovation. Among the main overarching results is the significance of institutional factors in understanding the nature of national (and regional, and European) systems of innovation. Among results derived from the details of the chapter are that although all systems of innovation seem to have strengths and weaknesses, the German system of innovation remains the strongest in Europe.

Turning to the European perspective, while there is evidence of increasing integration, there remains doubt about the extent to which increasing European integration and technological development can interrelate with European firms to create a European system of innovation. This is strengthened by the organization and behaviour of most of the large, research-based companies. While many MNEs with headquarters in EU member states have supported increasing integration, there have not emerged a significant number of integrated European firms. The national base of advanced technology firms remains important. As Petrella (1991, p. 91) shows, for example, 'the country of origin remains the preponderant site of location of R&D units in Europe, USA and Japan'. Moreover, in the recent work of Khanna and Singh (2002) and Love and Roper (2004), discussed in this chapter, there is further evidence of the continuing significance of the home country base for the behaviour of firms.

What the apparently contradictory evidence suggests, is that individual European firms may support and gain from EU S&T policies in particular, and European integration in general. However, pressures arising from technological change, while they may contribute to MAAs, are, by themselves, unlikely to generate industrial integration in Europe. As a context within which R&D and innovation take place, the European system of innovation, for most research and for most firms, is far less significant than national – and in some cases subnational regional – systems of innovation.

Websites

Among the main sites for data on science, technology, R&D and patents, is that of the OECD: **www.oecd.org** (click on statistics, and then on science, technology and patents).

Whereas most statistical databases rely to some extent on patents, there is a strong argument against this. See **www.pilotproject.org** for details of a study in which innovation is considered not to be identified exclusively by patents.

Most government websites provide links to their departments or agencies responsible for science, technology and research. In the UK, among the relevant websites is that of the Office of Science and Technology (OST) at **www.ost.gov.uk/about_ost/index.htm**

On EU matters, such as the Framework Programmes, there are two main sources, the Cordis site, **www.cordis.lu**, and the Europa site, in particular the Commission's site within Europa, **http://europa.eu.int/comm/research/**

Questions

11.1 How and why do we measure innovation?

11.2 Discuss the problems with the use of patent data to measure innovation.

11.3 Explain why some writers have focused on national, and others on regional or sectoral systems of innovation.

11.4 What are the main differences between the systems of innovation of France, the UK and Germany?

11.5 How and why does size matter for firms aiming to be innovative?

11.6 Is there a European system of innovation?

11.7 How has the behaviour of firms impinged on the development of a European system of innovation?

Notes

1   And we would like to add to this innovative ways of organizing.

2   Innovation is discussed below.

3   Laibman (1981) provides one such example of an endogenous technical change model based on Marxian conceptual foundations, such as the split of the production sphere into two sectors: the capital goods and the consumer goods sectors.

4   See also the discussion on knowledge intensive industries in Chapter 13.

5   According to Freeman (1994), among economic theorists 'only Marx in the nineteenth century and Schumpeter in the twentieth could be said to place innovation at the very centre of their growth theory'.

6   See below, Section 11.7. See also Chapter 8, Section 8.6, for a discussion of systems of innovation in the context of regional systems of innovation.

7   For a critique of this model, see Freeman (1988b); for a brief but comprehensive review of approaches to diffusion, see Lissoni and Metcalfe (1994). More recent reviews are provided by Tunzelman (2002) and, in more detail, Hall (2004).

8   Investigations in agricultural technology, medicine, computers, nuclear power, energy, man-made fibres and plastics support the existence of this type of pattern.

9   By 'uneven' we mean in the sense of power derived from market structure. A monopsony can clearly impose the introduction of new technology on its suppliers; perfect competition in an industrial buyers' market will leave each of the buyers unable to influence the suppliers.

10 See also above, Chapter 10, on the role of the EU in the establishment of standards in mobile telephony.

11 It is also a non-financial input indicator.

12 For more on the EPO, see Ullrich (2002).

13 On other limitations of patents, see Lamberton (1994), and on legal issues in Europe, see Ullrich (2002).

14 For notes on the data, see Table 11.1. See also OECD original.

15 Note that Khanna and Singh (2002) explicitly see their findings as support for the NSI concept. See also below, where we discuss the importance of foreign MNEs in relation to the UK system of innovation.

16 See above, Chapter 8, Section 8.6.

17   This paragraph and much of the rest of this section are drawn from Chesnais (1993).

18   In Germany too, to a greater extent than the UK, there was growth in industrial research during the first half of the century (Mowery, 1990).

19   This engineering tradition was at the level of trained engineers. In general in France, as argued by de Bandt (1987, p. 46), even after the Second World War, 'the level of industrialization was quite low and the industrial traditions – cultural, behavioural, institutional – were rather poor'.

20   For more on the role of the state in Europe in general and in France in particular, see Nugent (1994).

21   However, see also Fig. 11.3, which shows that France's export market shares have declined in a range of high-tech industries, including aerospace and pharmaceuticals; in aerospace France was overtaken between 1996 and 2002 as the leading European exporter by the UK. Note that the UK, nevertheless, has a smaller positive trade balance in aerospace than France.

22   See also Amable and Hancké (2001, table 3). This table, providing data on trade surplus as a percentage of value added, also shows the consistent success of the aerospace and pharmaceutical sectors in France.

23   The French share in the Arianespace industrial consortium is 57.7 per cent; the second largest share-holder is Germany, with 18.43 per cent. See the Arianespace website at www.arianespace.com. It should be noted that the French leadership in Europe in relation to space research was not least a result of the Gaullist search for a leadership role for France in Europe in general.

24   It is part of the chemicals, pharmaceutical and agrochemicals complex, which, Chesnais (1993, p. 220) suggests, is a partly separate innovation subsystem. It should be noted that while the state has had significant shares in the major French pharmaceutical companies, particularly since 1982, these firms have behaved, by and large commercially.

25   It could be neither despite nor because of the role of the state from the mid-eighteenth century; the success of the British economy in the eighteenth and nineteenth centuries could be partly a result of the role of the state during the mercantilist period up to the second half of the eighteenth century.

26   Losing its leadership means, as McCloskey (1990) points out, a relative decline, though some writers fail to emphasize the fact that it is relative. See for example, Porter (1990): 'Britain declined because of growing disadvantages in each part of the "diamond"' (1990). The diamond is Porter's explanatory framework, consisting of: firm strategy; structure and rivalry; related and supporting industries; factor conditions; and demand conditions (see Chapter 8, Section 8.5).

27   See Walker (1993, pp. 158–9) for a brief elaboration of these three theories. Porter (1990, p. 506), in some ways combines each of them when he states that the most significant causes were 'weaknesses in human resources, low motivations, the lack of rivalry, and eroding demand conditions'. The main factor according to Chandler (1984) was the continuation of control by the owning families of the main corporations, long after control by salaried managers had become the norm in Germany and the United States.

28   See also n 14 in Chapter 8.

29   See, for example, Barnett (1986, Ch. 11). The discussion on the British education and training systems that follows, draws mainly on Walker (1993). See also Porter (1990, pp. 497–8).

30   This quote from Walker (1993) shows that he sees this characteristic of the French system as a strength. Chesnais (1993, p. 214) sees the same characteristic as a weakness of the French system.

31   Walker (1993), referencing Hobsbawm (1987), writes: 'resources became overextended as the Empire grew, middle class culture turned against industrial enterprise, and a rentier mentality took hold'. See also Lazonick (1990a, p. 90): 'The heads of the most successful firms, typically of middle-class origin, sought to have their sons educated at the élite public schools, and Oxford and Cambridge – institutions

that remained firmly under the control of an aristocracy of landowners and financiers who had little use for industry or technology.'

32 The discussion that follows draws on Rothwell (1987), Porter (1990, pp. 504–6) and Walker (1993).

33 The National Research Development Corporation (NRDC), set up in 1948 by the British government to commercialize publicly funded research. Among its success stories were the drug Interferon and, in engineering, the hovercraft.

34 In recent years, among its most public actions was to sue (in September 2004) Amazon.com and a number of other online bookstores for infringement of patents covering technologies related to tracking the navigational path of a user through the World Wide Web.

35 This and the next paragraph draw on Coghlan (1995). All the quotes are from this source unless otherwise stated.

36 The relevant UK government website (http://www.basictechnologies.gov.uk/Site/links/default.cfm) seems to contain a contradiction. It states in relation to CARAD: 'The Secretary of State was pleased to continue the DTI's well established partnership with the aeronautics industry by approving CARAD for another five years to 2006'. However, the link to CARAD (http://www.dti.gov.uk/aerospace/carad1.htm) brings you to 'Aeronautics Research Programme (formerly CARAD)' where, among other things, you find that 'the Aeronautics Research Programme closed on 31 March 2004'.

37 There is an interesting contrast within this similarity, though. Chesnais (1993) identifies French success in aerospace as having derived, in part, from the need for international collaboration. The result, he writes, is that, in this area 'the French subsystem of innovation has provided the overall structure and represented the backbone of Europe's involvement in space'. On the other hand, Walker (1993), using similar evidence of need for international collaboration, concludes that it has led to a diminution in the 'autonomy of the British innovation system'. We discuss this point further below.

38 See Chapter 13, Section 13.6.

39 See, for example, Reich's (1992, p. 137) argument that 'the important question – from the standpoint of national wealth – is not which nation's citizens own what, but which nation's citizens learn how to do what'.

40 We argued in 1988 that the conclusion of agreements between British and Japanese firms in the UK machine tool industry in order to give the British firms access to the newer technologies, amounted, in some respects, 'to the "peripheralisation" of Europe. The high-skill, advanced-technology parts of the production process will end up being located outside Europe – in the US and Japan' (Jacobson and Andréosso, 1988). See also Andréosso and Jacobson (1991). For a detailed discussion of the relationships between multinational corporations and national systems of innovation, see Chesnais (1992). See also Khanna and Singh (2002).

41 Love and Roper suggest a gain from 'the weakness of the industrial training system' in that it 'may have the somewhat ironic advantage of avoiding some of the barriers to adopting flexible work practices evident in German firms'. In other words 'institutional barriers to the adoption of more flexible working practices in Germany may be more constraining than the generally lower level of general skills in the UK'. They accept, of course, that there are also high costs of the inadequacy of industrial training.

42 Note that the absence of collaboration and cooperation is a feature of British manufacturing both recently, as shown by Love and Roper (2004), and historically, as seen in Box 11.2 on the decline of the Lancashire cotton textile industry.

43 Keck considers the industrial relations and banking systems to be 'other factors', outside the 'national system for technical innovation'. According to Nelson's definition of NSI quoted above, they would fall within the national system of innovation. Industrial relations in particular deserves more attention than we have space for here. See Lazonick (1990b).

44 Note that this is similar to the shareholder versus stakeholder theories discussed in Chapter 4.

45 Productivity of firms owned by foreign outsiders is somewhere between.

46 In addition to Christensen (1992), on the relationship between financial systems and innovation, see also Dosi (1990), Zysman (1990) and O'Sullivan (2000).

47 Note that there are also important large firms in the Italian machine tool industry. The biggest, Comau, which alone produces a quarter of Italian output in the industry. However, Comau is an exception; even the second biggest firm in the industry, Salvagnini Italia, has a turnover of less than 15 per cent of Comau (Wengel and Shapira, 2004).

48 The rest of this paragraph, and all quotes, are from Wengel and Shapira (2004).

49 Notwithstanding Lazonick's (1991, p. 229) insistence that 'scale economies are *economies only because of the dynamic interaction of organization and technology* that transforms high fixed costs into low unit costs'.

50 It does not preclude large firms. Microsoft, for example, is a huge organization, but purportedly remains relatively flat (non-hierarchical) in its organization structure, with electronic mail facilitating open communications among all departments and all levels. Best (2001) also allows for large firms. He emphasizes the 'open systems business model and cluster dynamics' as a means of encouraging 'entrepreneurial firm creation and proliferation'. The examples are Silicon Valley, with both small and large firms, and the Third Italy with mainly small firms.

51 Note, however, that this is a generalization. Pavitt (1994), for example, agrees that 'continuous organizational redesign to exploit emerging technological opportunities' can be a problem for large firms, but adopting an evolutionary approach he argues that successful large innovating firms can and do 'assimilate major technological discontinuities'.

52 Examples of such industries include the automotive industry (mass production), glass, steel and pharmaceuticals (continuous process), shipbuilding and aerospace (high capital costs), food, cosmetics and washing powders (high advertising costs).

53 There is some evidence that SMEs are better innovators than their larger counterparts. This is suggested, for example, by the US data associated with federal research funding which indicates that SMEs spend less on R&D than large firms, yet generate more new knowledge (Acs and Preston, 1997).

54 In some cases this has occurred through major pharmaceutical companies taking over small, innovative biotechnology firms.

55 This discussion about differences over time is similar to Best's (2001, p. 228) on differences in the ages of firms, in the context of entrepreneurial firms and open systems: 'Once the inter-firm dynamics are underway, new firm creation is built into the process. . . . Old, developmental firms provide feedstock to new firms much like fallen trees do for seedlings in the rain forest.'

56 There is some evidence that, among SMEs, larger ones are more likely to introduce radical innovations, smaller ones incremental innovations (Kalantaridis and Pheby, 1999).

57 This discussion draws heavily upon Sharp (1990, pp.57–60). See also Sharp (1991, pp.60–7).

58 In addition to the manufacturers, research institutes and small and medium firms have also gained from Esprit: 'The SMEs in particular are very positive about ESPRIT and the Commission now claim that 70 per cent of the ESPRIT budget goes to SMEs, a considerable turn-around from its early days' (Sharp, 1991, p. 67).

59 Note that the euro replaced the ECU in January 1999, at a rate of exchange of 1 to 1.

60 Over the 1990s the proportion of intra-European mergers and acquisitions among all international M&As increased. See Chapter 10; see also below.

CHAPTER 12

Performance of firms

12.1 Learning objectives

The main objectives of this chapter are:

- To review the possible criteria that can be used to define performance in general
- To discuss the link between competitiveness, as one indicator of performance, and market power
- To analyse the link between competitiveness and location, and
- To propose a brief overview of the relationship between market structure and performance

12.2 Measuring performance and the debate on market dominance versus competitive success

Performance is the firm's and the nation's ultimate concern. It refers to the degree of success in achieving stated objectives. Good performance is the result of successful, efficient conduct. The essential consideration is how efficient firms are in producing the 'right' good in the 'right' quantity at the 'right' cost.

Studying the results obtained by firms can be done at three levels:

- At the firm (or microeconomic) level

- At the industry (or mesoeconomic) level
- At the level of a country or group of countries (macroeconomic level).

12.2.1 Indicators of performance

There are several performance indicators, at the firm, industry and national levels, each of which has advantages and disadvantages. The indicators are:

- Measures of profitability
- Productivity measures
- Market shares and competitiveness
- Efficiency
- Technological advance.

For cross-country comparisons, there are several international trade-based indicators.

Estimates of performance can be undertaken as time series or cross-sectionally. A firm's profit rate, for example, can be presented on an inter-temporal basis (giving a firm's profit rate at various points in time) or on a cross-sectional basis (comparing it, at a point in time, to the profit rates of other firms).

Since Bain's seminal work was published in 1941, most analyses of the structure–performance relationship have used cross-sections of firms or industries. However, cross-sectional data often lead to like not being compared with like. They should therefore be limited to firms or industries selling almost identical (or comparable) products in distinctive geographical markets. Combining times series data with cross-sectional data enables us to determine whether the performance of a given corporation has improved or disimproved when compared with the results of rival firms.

We consider each of the above indicators in turn.

Profit rates and profitability

Since profit maximization has normally been assumed to be the single most important objective of the firm, profit rates and profitability have been treated as the primary barometers of the success of a firm. Changes in profit rates have been used, for example, as indicative of the success or otherwise of mergers.

Profit is defined by the economist as the excess of revenue over cost, including the cost represented by the income forgone from using the capital in the firm rather than in the best alternative use. A simple computation of profit rate is given by r_1, which provides an assessment of the effectiveness of the utilization of the resources used:

$$r_1 = \frac{\text{Profits (before interest payments)}}{\text{Total real capital employed}}$$

Computing this rate involves choosing between the evaluation of the firm's assets (in particular capital equipment) either in terms of their cost of acquisition or in terms of their replacement cost[1] to the firm. As demonstrated by Machlup (1952), high profit rates may be the result of undervalued assets, rather than the result of pure economic efficiency. To bypass this difficulty, economists have turned to a second profit rate r_2, which is the accounting rate of return on shareholders' equity.[2]

$$r_2 = \frac{\text{Accounting profit}[3]}{\text{Shareholders' equity}}$$

$$= \text{Rate of return on equity}$$

But this rate depends on *debt/equity* ratio variations as well as on *accounting regulations and conventions*. The debt/equity ratio is problematical because one firm might raise capital by borrowing, and a second by selling shares; the first will have a high debt/equity ratio and the second, a low one. Their performance in making and selling products may be identical, but the first firm may have a higher r_2 than the second (depending on the cost of the debt). How accounts are prepared can also cause problems when comparing the performance of firms. Different regulations in relation to tax in different countries, for example, can result in two firms with identical 'real' performance, reporting different accounting profits. Some tax rules, such as those on transfer pricing, allow large profits to be reported as small ones.

The most popular measure of profitability (and by extension, of market power)[4] in industrial economics was devised by Bain (1941, pp. 276–7): the rate of profit is 'that rate which, when used in discounting the future rents of the enterprise, equates their capital value to the cost of those assets which would be held by the firm if it produced its present output in competitive equilibrium'. This index facilitates the calculation of profits earned in excess of 'ordinary' or 'normal' returns on invested capital (that is, the returns derived in a perfectly competitive framework).

The data available on firms' balance sheets enable the accountant to write the following identity:[5]

$$\pi_a = p \cdot Q - (c \cdot Q + D)$$

where $p \cdot Q$ is total revenue; $c \cdot Q$ is the total accounting cost including wages, salaries, raw materials, rent on land, electricity and water; and D is depreciation on fixed capital.

The economist also includes the opportunity cost in the profit function. Economic profit becomes:

$$\pi_e = \pi_a - r \cdot I$$

where r is the rate of return that could have been earned, had capital been used in the best alternative, and I is the value of the investment in the firm.

From the above, *Bain's excess profit rate* is derived:

$$\pi_b = \frac{\pi_e}{I}$$

In computing this rate, it is again necessary to decide whether the firm's investment is to be evaluated at its original purchase cost or in terms of an estimate of its replacement cost.

To avoid many of the problems of profit measures, another ratio, known as *Tobin's q*, was devised in the 1960s.[6] It is defined as the ratio of market value of assets to their replacement cost:

$$q = \frac{\text{Firm's market value}}{\text{Cost of replacing total assets}}$$

where the firm's market value is determined by the value of its shares on the stock markets, and where its total assets comprise buildings, equipment, inventories and outstanding debts.

If a firm's stock is composed of 1 million shares with a market price of €50 per share in time period t_1, the firm's market value in t_1 will be €50 million. Assuming that it would cost €20 million to replace all the firm's assets, the q ratio will be equal to 2.5. This particular example illustrates the case of a firm that has managed to develop in such a manner as to be now valued more than twice as much in the marketplace than in terms of the value of its investments. Its market value is far in excess of the replacement cost of its assets. A high q ratio indicates some degree of 'extra profitability'; to have a market value higher than the value of its investments, the firm must be selling its product at prices above long-run costs, i.e. it must be earning supernormal profits.[7]

In a perfectly competitive market, the ratio will be equal to 1 for all firms operating in this market; this is the case where the market value of the firm is just equal to the value of the capital resources owned by the firm. When q is greater than 1, and entry is free, new firms will have an incentive to enter the industry, by purchasing the same capital stock as the incumbent firms, and by anticipating an increase in the market value of their investment. Also, the incumbent firms will have an incentive to expand, because of the higher return on investments. If entry barriers are low, new entry (as well as expansion) will bring the q ratio down, and the adjustment process will stop when the ratio reaches unity. If the ratio persistently assumes a value above 1, this may indicate the exercise of monopoly power characterized by the ability to bar entry. On the other hand, 'q may exceed 1 for a price-taking firm that earns economic rents because it possesses unique, efficiency-producing assets' (Martin, 1993, p. 515). This is the familiar Demsetz efficiency argument: a firm may be making supernormal profits because it is more efficient than its competitors, rather than because it has some means of holding on to market power. While Tobin's q is indicative of a firm's profitability, it does not reveal the reason for that profitability.

Economy-wide variations of the q ratio have been empirically estimated by Tobin and Brainard (1977), von Fürstenberg (1977) and Lindenberg and Ross (1981) for the US economy. Lindenberg and Ross (1981) based their analysis on a sample of 257 firms over a period of 17 years. They found the q ratio to be above 1 for most firms in the sample. It was particularly large for firms with either significant monopoly rents or with rents resulting from the use of special factors that can act as entry barriers (such as control of distribution, and patents). In a second category, with lower q ratios – but still above 1 – the authors found firms using product differentiation (cereals, cosmetics), and/or enjoying strong patent protection (photographic equipment, drugs). Low values of q were associated with declining industries, for example steel and primary metal manufacturing, as well as for regulated industries, such as electric utilities.

Lindenberg and Ross's results indicate a declining value of q over the period of their study. The average value of the ratio was 1.5; the average firm's value was approximately 50 per cent above the replacement cost of its assets. Other studies have found a cyclical pattern of change in q, but with substantial and consistent differences among them.[8]

These now classic studies laid the foundations for many more studies using Tobin's q in various ways. Among just the most recent examples are the following:

- In a study of Swedish investment, covering the period 1951–95, Assarsson *et al.* (2004) found that Tobin's q is not the only determinant of investment, and that a relative equity-price variable is found to be a good approximation of average q.

- Lee and Grewal (2004) examine the adoption by retailers of Internet access (106 firms, over nine years) and hypothesize that the strategy will affect performance, measured by Tobin's q. With various qualifications, they find evidence to support their hypothesis.

- In another industry study, Li *et al.* (2004) examine 27 airlines, from Asia Pacific, Europe and North America, over the period 1989–99. Using Tobin's q as the main measure of performance they found that the airline industry has a relatively low q, and that European airlines' q ratio is even lower than that of their counterparts in other regions.

- In a particularly interesting use of Tobin's q, Villalonga (2004) attempts to find support for elements of the resource-based view of the firm (which is similar in ways to the evolutionary theory of the firm). With Tobin's q as one measure of the firm's resource intangibility, he tests the idea that the greater the intangibility of a firm's resources, the greater the sustainability of its competitive advantage. He finds that intangibles do contribute to maintaining a firm's competitive advantage, but that they can also lock a firm into persistent underperformance.

Tobin's q ratio does not always reflect the level of competition in an industry. As we have argued, all that q shows is the relationship between the value of the firm and the replacement costs of its assets. Among the reasons why this might differ from unity are the following:

- That a rent[9] is earned on certain factors of production. These factors will lower the cost function of the firm relative to that of the marginal firm. The existence of such rents will tend to bias q upwards. In addition, these rents may not be captured in the replacement cost figure (Lindenberg and Ross, 1981).

- ◆ That the industry is a mature one, facing a permanent decline in demand. This will drive q to a value below 1.

- ◆ That there is technical change which makes the capital stock of the firm not worth replacing. The q ratio will be less than unity.

In addition, it may be difficult to calculate the ratio because of one or more of the following considerations:

- ◆ Replacement costs are difficult to estimate.

- ◆ Information on the market value of the firm is available only for publicly traded firms.

- ◆ The value of the firm (the numerator of the q ratio) is prospective, or forward looking. Since it indicates the investors' evaluation of the probable future profitability of the firm, the ratio is sensitive to errors in market valuation. Estimates may be subject to the method used for calculating depreciation expenses, or for valuing inventories (Shughart, 1990). They can also be distorted by manipulations, mistakes, and 'all the strange things that happen in Wall Street' (Shepherd, 1990, p. 115).

Another method of assessing the extent to which profits are above normal is the *Lerner index*. This index measures the excess of the firm's price over its marginal cost.[10] Because marginal cost data are not generally available, we usually use average variable costs. The Lerner index becomes:

$$L = \frac{(P - AVC)}{P}$$

Multiplying numerator and denominator by the number of units sold gives the following ratio, the data for which are readily accessible:

$$\text{Price–cost margin} = \frac{TS - (CM + PR)}{TS}$$

where TS refers to total sales (of either the plant or the firm), CM denotes costs of materials, and PR is payroll costs.

The most complete measure of profitability would be given by a comprehensive price–cost margin (PCM) index capturing, in addition to all material and payroll costs, advertising, R&D, and capital costs.

The Lerner index has been used less frequently than Tobin's q, partly because of the difficulty in obtaining such complete data for anything other than companies whose accounts are publicly accessible. Even then, to be useful in the calculation of the Lerner index, the data must be available separately for different products and this is not generally available in published accounts. Finally, data for concentration ratios are more easily obtained and concentration ratios more easily applied to the study of market structures than the Lerner index. Among recent uses of an adapted form of the Lerner index is that of Golan *et al.* (2000). They use a combination of game theory and econometrics to examine the price and advertising strategies of Coke and Pepsi. They then use the data they have generated to calculate the 'expected Lerner index, $E[(p^2 - c^2)/p^2]$' where c^2 is their estimate of firm i's marginal cost. Not surprisingly, they find different levels of profitability of the two companies depending on different assumptions and models, but Pepsi is in all cases slightly higher than Coke.

While there are pitfalls in relation to each of the measures of profitability, some of these can be overcome by using more than one measure. Results are, however, decidedly mixed. McFarland (1988), for example, finds quite high levels of correlation between q and the accounting rate of return, and finds q to be a better estimate than the accounting rate of return, but also finds errors in both to be high. According to Rob (1992), on the other hand, sales and current profits account for a much larger proportion of the variation in investment decisions than q. Some studies using these measures have arrived at conclusions that contradict the underlying theory. Chen et al. (1989), for example, using Tobin's q to investigate the relationship between barriers, concentration and profitability, obtain results at odds with the theory that greater concentration is associated with price collusion and monopoly profits. And, adding further complexity to the picture, Stevens (1990) concludes that 'positive returns to market shares ... depend on a high level of market concentration, suggesting that collusion and efficiency explanations are not clearly separated'; his results from the use of Tobin's q suggest that market power and efficiency together explain performance.

We saw in earlier chapters that there are difficulties in assuming that the maximization of profits is the primary motivation of firms. It follows from our discussions on the measures of profitability that even if a high profit rate is indicative of success from the point of view of the individual firm, it may not be so from the social standpoint (Devine et al., 1985). The less the extent to which the Demsetz efficiency argument explains profitability, and the greater the extent to which higher profits may have been achieved through the exercise of market dominance (through the eviction of other firms, and other anti-market strategies discussed in Chapters 9 and 10), arguably the more antisocial are supernormal profits. However, even this is not the whole story. Supernormal profits, which may be antisocial in the short run, may contribute to the long-run success of the firm, which in turn may have social benefits through, for example, contributions to employment, to the national system of innovation via technological development, and to other firms through buyer–supplier linkages.

Measures of performance based on profitability also have the failing – common in neoclassical economics in general – that they focus on the firm as a single, homogeneous entity. Other theories of the firm, as we saw in Chapter 4, focus on the structure of the firm. Productivity measures of performance at least recognize that different elements of the firm may have different contributions to make to performance.

Productivity measures

Productivity is normally defined as the ratio of one unit of output to one or more units of the inputs necessary for the production of the product. Partial as well as total factor productivity indices can be computed (Devine et al., 1985).

The total factor productivity (TFP) index is defined as:

$$P_T = \frac{Q}{\alpha L + \beta K}$$

with $\alpha + \beta = 1$, where α and β are weighted coefficients, and L and K are the labour and capital inputs used in the production process.

Productivity measurements lead to a host of difficulties, in particular in relation to the selection and measurement of factor inputs, and to the measurement of output. For example, the total number of employees in a firm/plant/industry may be used as a measure of labour inputs; but if two firms have the same number of employees, and the same output, and in one firm the workers work a 35-hour week, whereas in the other they work a 45-hour week, labour productivity is not the same in the two firms. In this case, total hours worked, rather than number of employees, would be a more appropriate measure of labour input.

There are similar problems in relation to measures of capital productivity – and of capital in general. Is the capital input the replacement cost of the capital stock, or its original cost? What happens to the value of machinery if more advanced machinery becomes available? How should the fact that people have become adept at using the old machinery be taken into consideration?

In relation to either capital or labour, a major problem associated with the use of productivity indicators is that they do not reflect the qualitative differences among factor inputs used. They generally assume that both labour and capital are homogeneous factors of production. An ideal labour productivity index would reflect the many different skill categories in the labour force.[11]

However they are measured, labour and capital productivity as indicators of performance suggest that the greater the output per unit of input (per person or hour of labour, per 1000 euro of value of capital), the more successful the firm.

The measurement of output is also subject to problems.[12] For example, the use of price deflators to correct for a change in the general price level only partly solves the problems associated with increasing prices. Price increases may be associated with quality upgrading and exchange rate movements (in the case of a cross-country study), as well as with domestic inflation.

Despite the many problems with productivity measures of performance, TFP has been used in different ways to examine different aspect of economic performance in a vast array of studies. Web searches for articles with 'total factor productivity' in their titles find hundreds of matches. (In comparison, similar searches for articles with 'Lerner index' in their titles find only one or two matches.) Among the common applications of the concept are in studies of the relationship between technological change and TFP. In a thorough critique both of TFP and of its application in studies of technological change, Lipsey and Carlaw (2004) argue that, 'contrary to widely held views, changes in total (or multi-) factor productivity do not measure technological change'. At best, changes in TFP 'measure only the super normal gains associated with such changes'. However, this best is rarely if ever achieved. Among the many problems that Lipsey and Carlaw (2004) point out is that increase in the use of unmeasured inputs (for example, natural resources) 'will bias measured TFP upwards'. Also, differences in interpretation and measurement frequently make cross-country comparisons inappropriate. Such comparisons are, nevertheless, frequently undertaken.

Market shares and competitiveness

Firm i's *market share* is the percentage share of total sales revenue held by firm i in a given market j. For any given product, this percentage share can be written as:

$$m_S = \frac{S_{ij}}{S_j}$$

where S_{ij} is the sales revenue of firm i on market j and S_j is the total sales revenue earned by all the firms in market j.

A firm's market shares can vary from 0 to 100 per cent. In everyday business practice, the relative success of a firm is often measured by its market share (as much as in terms of profits and stock prices).

Competitiveness is not a well-defined concept. Some see it as a broad idea, incorporating industry- or economy-wide productivity, living standards and economic growth; others focus more narrowly on success in international trade (Bailey, 1993). For the present purposes, let us define competitiveness as the ability to sustain and increase market share on both the national and the international markets. This can be applied to individual firms (microeconomic level), to industries (mesoeconomic level) and to the economy, or group of economies, as a whole (macroeconomic level). For a group of economies such as the EU, for example, we may talk of competitiveness being determined by the ability of EU firms to sustain and increase market shares in EU and international markets.

A distinction can be drawn between *price* competitiveness and *structural* competitiveness. Price competitiveness refers to all factors enabling a firm to price its products at prices below those of its competitors. Structural competitiveness refers to all the non-price elements of competitiveness, that is, all the factors that contribute to product (or process) differentiation, including quality, durability, brand and design. Normally, price competitiveness and structural competitiveness are important in different product areas:

> prices are most important in standardised and commodity-type goods which vary little in quality, and in the lower quality range of more differentiated consumer products such as clothing. [There are other] industrial products – including most capital goods, consumer durables and other branded consumer goods – in which factors such as quality, reliability, after-sales service, innovation and marketing exert a strong influence on competitive ability. (O'Malley, 1989, p. 225)

In some industries, trends since the late 1980s have shown that a new form of competitiveness has emerged in which firms must achieve both price and structural competitiveness to succeed (Andreosso, 1991).[13]

We have at various points highlighted the strategic role played by some industries in the economy of a given nation. Most important are those that form the technological core of a country's industrial structure; they are crucial to the improvement of the country's competitive edge with respect to the rest of the world. We have also emphasized the importance of the structural, as opposed to price, elements of competitiveness. This conclusion has been well stated by the European Commission's Directorate General for Economic and Financial Affairs: 'Although price remains an important element of competitiveness, non-price factors, like the ability to innovate in the presence of rapid technological progress, play a major role in determining the overall level of competitiveness' (CEC, 1993b, p. 17). It follows from this that at least one appropriate way of defining the competitiveness of an economy is on the basis of the performance of its high-technology industries. Together these arguments lead to the conclusion that one expression of improvement in the competitiveness of the EU is improvement in its trade position in high technology industries. In terms of high-technology industries, Japan was the most export oriented of OECD countries between 1970 and 1986, and the least open to foreign competition (OECD, 1992). Relying on the above definition of competitiveness, Japan was thus the most competitive of the major OECD economies. OECD (1992) also showed that the high-technology competitive position of the United States deteriorated, that Germany remained 'technology competitive', and that both the UK and Italy declined in competitiveness over the period.[14]

At the macroeconomic level, and assuming an open economy, the study of the price competitiveness of a nation leads us to the notion of *real exchange rates*. This is defined as the ratio of prices prevailing in two countries, expressed in a common currency. The real exchange rate is:

$$RER = \frac{(P_i \cdot e)}{P_j}$$

where P_i is the general price level in country i, P_j is the general price level in country j and e is the nominal exchange rate.

For country i, an increase in RER means a loss in price competitiveness with respect to country j, and a decrease in RER means that country i becomes more price competitive.[15] Exchange rates do have an impact on short-term price competitiveness, but long-term competitiveness is based on a number of other factors. Among the determinants of long-term, or structural, competitiveness are:[16]

◆ Management practices and the organization of relationships within and between firms (for example, clusters and industrial districts – see Chapter 8).

◆ The ability of firms to meet changing demand patterns, and in particular their aptitude to innovate and to move to higher-quality goods (produced by a strong system of innovation – see Chapters 8 and 11).

◆ An appropriate macroeconomic infrastructure (that is, public expenditure, tax system, optimal regulation and the correct industrial policy – see Chapter 15).

◆ The cost structures of firms and their investment levels in some cases, though note that these are related to the first point above.

Competitiveness is a complex notion; this brief discussion shows that much of this book is of relevance in explaining why some firms/industries/regions are, and others are not, competitive. As with other approaches to the performance of firms, price competitiveness should be used in conjunction with other measures to provide a comprehensive picture.

Efficiency[17]

Measuring efficiency is another way to assess performance. In common parlance, an efficient firm is one that produces its goods or services quickly, smoothly and with a minimum of waste. In economics there are a number of efficiency concepts, each defined differently. We here explore in turn productive, technical, allocative, dynamic and X-efficiency.

Productive efficiency has two main components: *technical* and *factor price* efficiency (see, for example, Devine *et al.*, 1985, p. 321). Technical efficiency entails deriving a maximum level of output from any given set of inputs, for a given state of technology. Factor price efficiency measures the ability to use the best combination of inputs, given their relative prices. The concept of productive efficiency implies producing a specific level of output at minimum cost, for any given technology. This concept is derived from the neoclassical theory of the firm, and can be shown graphically using the production function (represented by the *isoquant*) and the *isocost line*. The isoquant, or equal quantity curve, is the curve showing the different ways in which two factors of production can be combined to produce, optimally, the same quantity of output. The isocost line is the line along which the relative prices of the two factors of production are constant.

In Fig. 12.1, the curve QQ is the isoquant;[17] it indicates the minimum combinations of factor inputs X and Y that allow the firm to produce a given level of output Q, for a given state of the technology. The isocost line AB measures the relative price of the two inputs. Let us assume that the firm produces quantity Q at point F. It will use quantities OX_1 and OY_1 of X and Y respectively. The technical efficiency of the firm is given by the ratio OC/OF. Factor price efficiency is measured by the ratio OI/OC. The productive efficiency of the firm is:

$$\text{Productive efficiency} = \frac{OC}{OF} \cdot \frac{OI}{OC} = \frac{OI}{OF}$$

The closer the ratio to unity, the higher the productive efficiency of the firm. At equilibrium (point E), the ratio is equal to unity, which implies that the productive efficiency of the firm is maximum.

The theory underlying the notion of productive efficiency has been criticized by Tomlinson (1993). In this theory, he writes, production 'is conceptualized in terms of a combination of factors, where those factors are disembodied from any organization or calculative framework'. They will be optimized as a result of market forces. 'But markets

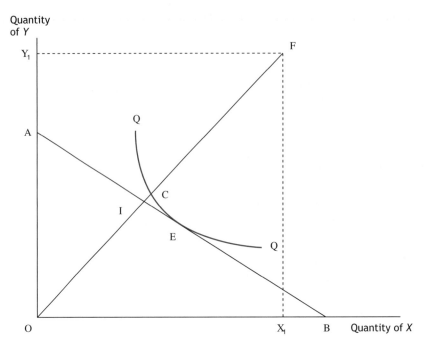

Figure 12.1 Productive efficiency of the firm

cannot be seen as compelling either organizational and calculative homogeneity or optimum efficiency. The problem with the neoclassical theory of production is that it excises crucial features of the enterprise which matter for efficiency.'

Productive efficiency, while in theory determined by factors outside the firm (market forces), refers to decisions made in relation to intra-firm operations. *Allocative efficiency* goes beyond the boundaries of the firm. The concept of allocative efficiency has been developed in the framework of general equilibrium analysis (GEA), the roots of which are found in the work of Walras. According to GEA, a competitive market system leads to an optimal allocation of resources and income distribution. In each market, each level of output is reached by equating marginal cost to price, for each consumer the marginal benefit is equal to the price, and the relative marginal benefits are the same to all consumers. This is allocative efficiency, which maximizes consumer welfare.[18] It is tempting to conclude from this that removing imperfections will improve allocative efficiency, but Lipsey and Lancaster's (1956) famous *theory of the second best* implies that, given one market imperfection, it will not necessarily improve total welfare to remove other imperfections. 'This is an awkward conclusion because it yields so little guidance on appropriate action in the real world. However, it does at least suggest that competition will not solve all individual allocative inefficiency problems' (Waterson, 1993).

The concept of X-efficiency, introduced by Leibenstein in 1966, is best explained in relation to the average cost curve. This curve shows the lowest average cost at which each different level of output can be produced. The neoclassical firm is always on its average cost curve; it is X-efficient. For all sorts of reasons, however, a firm may not be on its average cost curve. Inefficient contracts between principals (owners) and agents (managers) may result in managers being able to operate at less than the lowest costs for each level of output; for example, they may be able to give themselves perks over and above what is normally available to equivalent managers. If competition is not intense, both owners and managers may be able to relax, and instead of keeping employees, plant and equipment optimally utilized, allow some slack; the absence of competition will allow the price to be kept high enough to cover any extra costs. Hicks's (1935) famous line, 'The best of all monopoly profits is a quiet life', reflects this. In these cases there is *X-inefficiency*. In a review of the literature, Button and Weyman-Jones (1994) show that there is substantial theoretical and empirical evidence for the existence of X-inefficiency. Leibenstein himself estimated that whereas allocative inefficiency reduced GNP by 0.1 per cent, X-inefficiency reduced it by 25 per cent (Choi, 1997).

Firms that operate in industries under government protection (such as regulated monopolies) are likely to have higher levels of X-inefficiency than those in competitive industries; they will, for example, be less cost conscious. This has led to the notion that deregulation will reduce X-inefficiency. The concern over efficiency has, arguably, been a major driving force behind the regulatory reforms and privatization measures in Europe in recent decades.[19]

X-efficiency and allocative efficiency are different, but they are related. An improvement in allocative efficiency (for example, through the removal of a monopoly) drives prices down, and in turn leads to an improvement in X-efficiency. Leibenstein (1966) showed, however, that the welfare gain resulting from improvements in allocative efficiency is substantially smaller than that resulting from improvements in X-efficiency.[20]

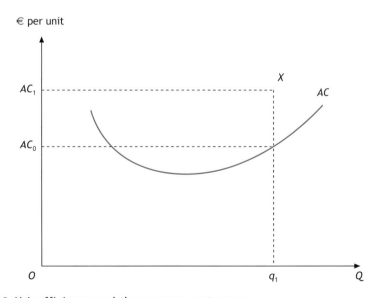

Figure 12.2 X-inefficiency and the average cost curve

The degree of X-inefficiency is measured by the extent to which actual average costs exceed the optimal average costs indicated by the average cost curve (see Fig. 12.2). The higher above the AC curve the firm's average costs are, for any given level of output q_1, the more X-inefficient the firm is.

Note that anywhere on the cost curve is efficient. The minimum point on the average cost curve is the minimum efficient scale (MES). This is the point towards which, according to neoclassical theory, perfectly competitive firms will be driven by market forces. They will even move from one short-run average cost curve to another (or from one sized plant to another) in order to achieve lower unit costs; such firms will ultimately settle at the minimum point, q_{MES}, of the long-run (envelope) average cost curve (see Fig. 12.3).[21]

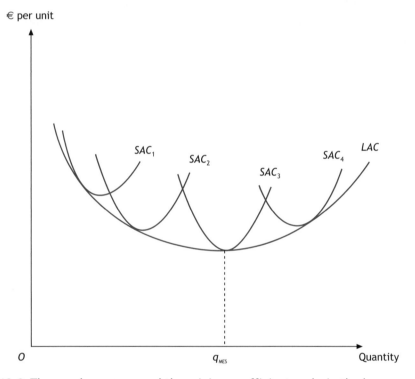

Figure 12.3 The envelope curve and the minimum efficient scale in the long run

Not only do firms often not operate along their average cost curves, they often do not operate at the level of output appropriate to minimum efficient scale. This would imply no remaining economies of scale to exploit, and the decision makers in the firm knowing that this is the case. Even if it were possible for firms temporarily to be at minimum efficient scale, constant change in prices, inputs, products, processes and technologies cause fluctuations that shift them from this ephemeral point.[22]

Another distinction in the use of the term efficiency relates to that between dynamic and static efficiency. *Static efficiency* refers to efficiency in the production and allocation of resources, given an existing technology, and therefore depends on both productive and allocative efficiency. With *dynamic efficiency* technology changes, a firm or economy is more dynamically efficient, the better it utilizes resources in improving organization systems, and introducing new and better products and processes. Static and dynamic efficiency are not always directly related. The routines that improve static efficiency can result in inertia that prevents dynamic efficiency.[23] As a result, the instruments of competition and industrial policy needed to promote static efficiency may be different from those required to promote dynamic efficiency (see Chapter 15).

One measure of efficiency is the *capacity utilization rate*. This shows the extent to which productive capacity is being realized in practice. Excess capacity is a sign of sluggish economic activity. It is, on the other hand, also a deterrent to entry since potential entrants who are aware of its existence know that if they enter the industry, the incumbent firms can immediately expand output. This is likely to impose downward pressure on prices, which the incumbent firms are more likely to survive than the new entrants.

Technological advance

As a measure of performance, what technological advance refers to is closely related to dynamic efficiency; it is the result of that efficiency. Hall (1994) provides a detailed account of various ways in which neoclassical and new growth theories can be used to measure technological advances. He praises evolutionary theories for having contributed to change in other theories, but seems to conclude that technical – diagrammatic, algebraic and statistical – economic models hold out hope for better understanding of technological advance. Much of the work on national systems of innovation (see Chapter 11) contradicts this, and some of the work on technological advance in the context of close buyer–supplier relationships also calls for a more case-based approach. For example, if factors such as trust and the level of commitment between firms – factors that cannot be measured – are key determinants of the rate at which firms introduce new products, processes and organizational systems, then a case study approach is indicated (Lorenz, 1994). Despite these comments, attempts have been made, with some success, to compare firms, industries or countries in terms of quantitative estimates of their technological intensity (see, for example, Davis, 1991; Antonelli, 1999, 2003).

Technological intensity refers to the extent to which output (exports) is accounted for by high-technology firms or industries. At the macroeconomic level, for example, technological intensity can be measured by the relative proportion of high-technology[24] industries in the industrial structure of a country or countries. Technological intensity also implies the intensive use of technologies in the production process of a country. R&D expenditures, patents, percentage shares of research personnel per industry (or per country) and percentage shares of countries in international publications in technologically advanced fields, are all common measures of technological advance. Their merits and limits have been discussed in Chapter 11. An important feature of the technology thus created is that it must be 'appropriate' to the needs of the country. There has been a long debate on this issue, starting in the nineteenth century with the claim, by the Marxist dependency school, that the developing countries of the world were in effect absorbing 'inappropriate' technologies from imperialistic nations.[25]

Trade-based indicators

The trade balance (exports minus imports, or $X - M$) is a first, and imprecise, barometer of a nation's performance on international markets. For industrial economic purposes it is more interesting to focus on the specific products or industries in relation to which an economy is successful in international competition.

According to the Ricardian model of trade specialization (as revised by Heckscher and Ohlin), a country specializes in the production of, and exports, the goods for which it has a comparative advantage. The country's comparative advantage lies, according to the theory, in being able to produce those goods relatively cheaply because it is relatively well endowed with the factor of production used most intensively in the production of those goods. More recent trade theory takes into account product differentiation and intra-industry trade.

Empirical attempts to identify in relation to which industries a country has comparative advantage have used Balassa's (1965, 1977) *revealed comparative advantage* formula:

$$RCA_i = \frac{X_i / X_{iw}}{\sum X_i / \sum X_{iw}}$$

where:
X_i = country's exports of industry i
X_{iw} = world exports of industry i
ΣX_i = country's total exports of all industries
ΣX_{iw} = world total exports of all industries.
Where $RCA_i > 1$, the country has a comparative advantage in relation to industry i.

Examples of such studies include Thornhill (1988), in which the author concludes that in relation to manufactured goods, during the 1970s Ireland's comparative advantage shifted strongly towards high-skill, capital-intensive industries, and away from low-skill, labour-intensive industries. Using revealed comparative advantage specifically to examine questions of technology transfer, Klodt (1990) shows that West Germany maintained a comparative advantage to a greater extent in those industries in which the technology was less mobile. Hibou (1993), however, calls into question the empirical use of revealed comparative advantage, and in particular the drawing of policy implications from such studies. Fertö and Hubbard (2003) similarly find limits to the usefulness of RCA. Using the EU as the comparator, they identify agricultural products in which Hungary is revealed to have a comparative advantage. They qualify this, however, with the argument that agriculture has been subject to government support.

On the basis of traditional theory, it would be expected that there would be *inter-industry specialization* in trade between countries. What this means is that one country would specialize in and export one product, while its trading partner would specialize in and export a different product. In practice, a great deal of international trade is based on *intra-industry specialization*, in which countries export and import similar goods to and from one another.

Whatever the industrial specialization of a country actually is, the normative question can be asked as to whether that structure is 'appropriate' or 'optimal', and if not, to what extent, and for what reasons, it is 'defective'. One criterion for the normative assessment of a country's industrial structure is its international competitiveness in strategic industries, where strategic industries refers to industries lying at the root of technological change. Another criterion relates to the growth of demand in international markets for its competitive industries. Declining demand for the products of a country's best industries suggests a weak industrial structure.

Another criterion for assessing a country's industrial structure is the *revealed technological comparative advantage* (RTCA). This index measures the comparative advantage of a nation in innovative activity, as opposed to its advantage in high-technology industries. For a given country i, the index is computed as follows:

$$\text{RTCA} = \frac{\text{Country i's share in world trade of high-technology products}}{\text{Country i's share in world trade of manufactured products}}$$

If, for the EU, the index is above the critical value of 1, this implies that the EU has a comparative advantage, or is relatively specialized, in high-technology goods. A country for which the index is less than 1 is specialized in traditional goods, that is, goods encompassing a low technological content. The measurement of this index suffers from limitations in the availability of statistics; high-technology products are generally defined as products of industries with high R&D content. Ideally, the RTCA should give an indication of a country's ability to sell the goods and services that are growing in importance in world markets, or that use production technologies that are growing in importance in world markets. This would indicate that country's dynamic potential to compete in markets of the future.

With all the limitations of each of the measures of performance, it is appropriate to use more than one such measure in any one study. In relation to the individual firm, the conclusion that it has, in whatever sense, performed well, raises the question as to why.

12.2.2 The debate on market dominance versus competitive success

A firm performing well in terms of profit-based measures of performance may be performing well either because of its efficiency and/or because of its own (or some regulatory authority's) ability to suppress the competition of other firms. In the first case, the firm is dominant because it is performing well compared with its competitors. In the second case, it is dominant because it is benefiting from distorted competition.

In general, a high market share held by a firm is taken as indicative of its ability to dominate the market. A firm with a low market share (10 per cent or less) has little or no market power. This situation is graphically depicted by a relatively flat demand curve facing the firm. As market share increases, control over quantities or prices increases and the demand curve facing the firm becomes less and less elastic. The higher the firm's market share, the closer it comes to being a monopoly. As a monopoly, with 100 per cent of the market, the firm's demand curve coincides with the market demand curve. We can consider a firm to be *dominant* when it has over 40 per cent of the sales of the market, no close rival, and the ability to control pricing (for example, by engaging in price discrimination).[26] Dominant firms are *near-monopolies*, in that although their control of the market is less than complete, they set the profit-maximizing decisions unilaterally, which raises the level of prices. Such firms derive supernormal profits from their ability to dominate the market.

12.3 Competitiveness as stability of leadership

When a firm does have dominance, for how long does this dominance persist? A Chicago School/efficient market approach would suggest the answer: dominance will not persist, there will usually be a rapid rate of erosion of monopoly positions.

Studying a sample of 47 firms in the UK, Shaw and Simpson (1985) found that the rate of decline of market dominance averaged 0.3 to 0.8 percentage points per year. Shepherd's (1975) estimate was around 1 percentage point per year; Geroski's (1987) study, based on 107 firms, obtained results closer to Shaw and Simpson's lower estimate. Geroski's conclusion is that if market shares and dominant positions decline, they do so only at a 'glacial pace'.[27] Looked at from the point of view of the dominant firms themselves, Chandler's (1990) work confirms that certain firms, in certain industries, have been able to maintain their leading positions over many decades. In recent years the predominance of Microsoft in the software market provides further empirical evidence.

Going beyond the sole variable of market shares, Kambhampati (2000) uses also the changes in market shares as well as the identity of market leaders to study the stability of leadership across 32 industries and over 11 years in India. He finds that only when market leaders are very stable, are market shares an adequate reflection of competitiveness. That in some industries (12 of the 32) market leadership is highly stable, is further evidence of at least some markets, in neoclassical terms, being inefficient.

The empirical results thus contradict the efficient market view of competition. For whatever reasons, firms in dominant positions are able to maintain that dominance over long periods of time. Organizational, intra-firm factors, explained for example by the evolutionary theories of the firm, are more consistent with the maintenance of dominant positions by leading firms. Jacquemin (1987b, p. 129), following an examination of the theoretical underpinnings of the process of dominance, concludes that there is a need 'to be more open to an evolutionary perspective in which the competitive process is more important than equilibrium and in which cumulative interactions among economic agents' vast strategy space and industrial structure have no chance of leading to an optimum'.

12.4 Relationship between market structure and performance[28]

The question under investigation in this section is: how and to what extent do specific elements of market structure shape performance in a given market?

12.4.1 Structure and performance

Early studies in industrial organization focused on the simple profit–concentration relationship, which is summarized by the formula:

$$P = f(S)$$

where price–cost patterns were taken as a measure of performance (P), and where concentration was taken as an indication of market structure (S). In empirical work this equation involved the use of simple regression analysis (S regressed on P). It was much easier to test than the more complete version, SCP, because data on conduct (strategies) were non-existent and in any case would have been difficult to integrate into the equation. It was expected that there would be a positive association between S and P. Firms operating in highly concentrated industries were expected to earn higher profits than firms in industries with a lower concentration ratio. The performance of firms measured by profit rates, it was thought, was determined by the market structure in which firms operated.

Early empirical work included Epstein (1931) and Summers (1932), who found evidence of an inverse relationship between firm size and profit rates – suggesting that high concentration was not necessarily related to high profit rates – and Crum (1933), whose results were that there was a positive relationship between firm size and profit rate, supporting the high concentration–high profit hypothesis.

Bain's painstaking empirical work, particularly in the 1950s, focused not just on concentration but also on entry barriers. Again not surprisingly, he found a strong, positive relationship between high concentration and high entry barriers on the one hand, and high profit rates on the other. Later work in the Bainian tradition (for example, Qualls, 1972; Weiss, 1974) in general supported this conclusion.

In the 1970s, the conclusions about the relationship between structure and performance underwent serious reconsideration, primarily on the basis that even if there was general agreement on the existence of a strong positive relationship between the two variables,[29] there was no consensus on the underlying cause of this relation.

Disagreement over cause of structure-performance relationship

We have already at various points in earlier chapters discussed this issue. It suffices here merely to reiterate that: (i) in Bain's view – and in the Harvard tradition – concentration was associated with high entry barriers. This gave the firms in the industry a degree of market power which they exerted to achieve higher prices and higher profits; (ii) in Demsetz's[30] (1973) view – and in the Chicago tradition – concentration was itself the consequence of the greater efficiency of the successful firms. It was lower costs that enabled such firms to make higher profits. A generalized form of the Chicago view was that concentration is the result of superior competitive performance, arising not just from greater efficiency in production but also, for example, from better management practices and better choice of strategies.

This disagreement shifted attention towards conduct, behaviour and strategy, all of which had been ignored by the simple structuralist perspective. This in turn generated a demand for more sophisticated techniques in the study of the structure–performance relationship. This demand was met by an increasing supply of statistical data and of the means to analyse the data: wider availability of and better access to computers.

Improvement of techniques and disagreement over results

During the 1970s, multiple regression techniques were introduced into the empirical research on the determinants of profit. The simple, two-variable models were replaced by models of the form:

$$\text{Profit rate on equity} = a + b \cdot \text{Market share of firm } i + c \cdot \text{Concentration on market } j + d \cdot \\ \text{Barriers to entry to market } j + e \cdot \text{Growth rate of } j + \ldots$$

The constant term, a, denotes the minimum competitive profit rate that a firm with no market power can attain.

There have been various ways of measuring the variables, and more and more variables have been added to improve the explanatory power of the model. Among significant empirical efforts in the 1970s were those by Shepherd (1975), who found that entry barriers had a significant 'yet secondary effect on profitability', and Scherer (1979), who added a new independent variable to the model: the proportion of each industry's sales going to final demand. As in the previous decades, most of these empirical tests involved cross-industry analyses.

In the 1980s, further sophistication was added by Bradburd and Over (1982), who found ways of incorporating into the explanation of profits such factors as capital intensity, buyer concentration and vertical integration. Smirlock et al. (1984) used Tobin's q in an attempt to distinguish between efficiency and market power: a significant positive correlation between market share and q, they assumed, reflected efficiency, and a significant positive correlation between concentration and q, market power. Disentangling the market power effect from the cost efficiency effect is also done in a study by Azzam (1997). Taking the US beef packing industry as a case study, he finds that, on average, the benefits of concentration in this industry are, in terms of cost efficiency, twice the costs of market power. By the end of the 1980s, three-equation simulation SCP models had become common (Martin, 1993, ch. 17). From the 1990s, linear and non-linear, static and dynamic, stochastic and chaotic models were being used, or proposed for use, in researching these basic questions in industrial economics (Byers and Peel, 1994). In particular, the accumulation of better data in several countries has enabled the use of time series analyses and the estimation of cointegration relationships between the variables. One such recent study is by Cable (1997) on the UK national daily newspaper industry. In this study, the analysis of several time series over the period 1975–91 shows the absence of long-run relationships between price, advertising and market shares.[31]

The increasing sophistication of empirical techniques has done little to settle the basic issues. Thus, for example, Dickson (1991), in his model of the relationship between unit cost and market concentration, finds evidence to support the efficiency hypothesis; Martin (1993, p. 498), though aware of Dickson's study, concludes that the efficiency hypothesis 'has a weak theoretical foundation and little empirical support'.

Among the reasons for this lack of consensus in relation to various SCP issues are the significant differences between industries in relation to such factors as the optimal size of firm, number of firms and rate of technological change, as well as institutional factors, both industry- and country-specific. There are also significant differences between countries, because of industry and market size differences, instititutional factors, and policy and regulatory differences. Many of these emerge in Neuberger's (1998) study of the industrial organization of banking. She shows that even between different segments of banking (for example, wholesale and retail) there are significant SCP differences. There are also regulatory changes and differences between countries. Finally, for these and other reasons, there are differences in the levels of X-inefficiency, both between segments within banking and between countries. Clearly, X-inefficiencies, supported by institutional factors, and varying as between industries and countries, will distort the results of SCP studies. Other reasons for continuing disagreement among experts are discussed below (Section 12.4.3).

12.4.2 Is growth a better performance indicator? Testing Gibrat's law

Are small firms more likely to grow than big firms, or is it more likely that industries become increasingly concentrated as large firms grow, keeping ahead of, and ultimately removing small firms? Some analysts have found no relationship between size and mean growth rate of the firm (Simon and Bonini, 1958; Hymer and Pashigian, 1962).[32] These studies have in fact reiterated the validity of Gibrat's law (also referred to as the law of proportionate effect[33]) which states that the probability of a firm growing x per cent in a given period is the same irrespective of the current size of that firm.

According to Hymer and Pashigian's study, the continuous decline of the long-run average cost curve is related to the fact that the variability of small firms' growth rates is larger than that of larger firms' growth rates. The authors explain this higher variability of growth rates among small firms by the fact that, being at a suboptimal scale of production, they have to bear high unit costs of production; consequently, many of these firms would experience negative growth rates until they are driven out of the market. Different results were obtained by Singh and Whittington (1968); in testing the law for UK firms, they showed that larger firms grew at a faster rate than smaller firms.

Other studies have investigated the link between the firm's growth rate and the growth rate of their national economies.[34] Rowthorn (1971), for example, found that the largest firms' growth rates were correlated with the national growth rates. He stressed also the fact that this link weakened with foreign trade and investment.

Caves's work (1991) assesses the closeness of association between a large firm's growth rate and the growth rate of its national market, as well as the link between the firm's and the industry's growth rates. Using data from a set of 280 manufacturing firms compiled by Fortune magazine for the years 1973–88, he finds that the growth rates of both industries and national economies have a strong influence on the growth results of firms. However, contrary to the results of Rowthorn, he concludes that the growth of industry output has more explanatory power than the growth of real GDP.

Recent studies have provided further evidence against Gibrat's law. Using an extensive data set covering all information technology (IT) firms in Sweden between 1993 and 1998, Johansson (2004) finds that the small and new firms grew extremely rapidly, accounting for all the net job creation in the industry. Larger, older firms were net job losers. With somewhat more subtlety in their results, Lotti et al. (2003) use quantile regression techniques to test Gibrat's law. With a data set of over 1500 firms over a six-year period from 1987 to 1993, they find that in five out of six industries, the law 'fails to hold during the first year following start-up – when smaller entrants grow faster than their larger counterparts – whereas it becomes acceptable once a minimum threshold in terms of size and age has been reached'. There is, in other words, an 'inverse relationship between size and growth ... during the infancy of newborn firms in some industries, but these firms display a convergence towards a Gibrat-like pattern of growth with the passage of time'. Their results, as the authors point out, corroborate those of Sutton (1997, 1998).

Sutton reviews recent work in this area and shows that a new generation of models developed from the 1980s on, have taken into account, for example, firms' and industries' intrinsic efficiency and other differences.[35] Within industries as conventionally defined, for example, there are different groups of firms and products. Some compete, others do not. 'The combination of the interdependence and the independence effects determines the patterns of post-entry growth observed in each industry' (Lotti et al., 2003).

12.4.3 Reasons for controversies

Even with improvements in data and techniques, disagreements remain. We discuss here some of the reasons for these disagreements.

Mis-specifications and omission of variables

The imperfect nature of the data used and the mis-specifications of the variables are still the most important reasons for the inconsistency of results. For example, misuse of concentration ratios can cause errors and inconsistencies.

Variables are mis-specified in the sense that they are defined in different ways. Most industry studies, for example, use three-digit industry groups, which are much broader than markets. Even in a four-digit classification, some industries must be excluded because the data do not correspond to any economic reality (Jacquemin, 1979). Only a minority of studies have used firm-level data despite the fact that, as Martin (1994, p. 212) points out: 'the advantage of using firm-level data is that one can examine the effect of changes in market share, rather than market concentration, on market performance. [O]ligopoly models ... suggest that market share will be one of the critical structural determinants of the degree of market power.'

Numerous variables have traditionally been omitted; for example, only a minority of studies have integrated trade performance data. This variable has a crucial importance for the EU as a whole and for individual European countries in particular. Intra-EU and international competition reduces the dominance of firms in national markets. Buyer concentration, vertical integration, diversification and elements of public policy have largely been ignored, and if they were, or could be included, they could have an effect on results. These factors have an impact, and their impact may vary from industry to industry; not including them in the models can result in similar studies having different results.

The intrinsic nature of different industries: consumer versus producer goods; durable versus non-durable goods

Bain's seminal work suggested that the effect of concentration on profitability in producer-good industries is less than in consumer-good industries. This may be related in some way to lower barriers to entry in producer-good industries. Product differentiation, as a major source of entry barriers, is less important for industrial purchasers than it is for individuals.

Stressing differences between industries, Brooks (1973) confirmed the fact that the strength of the relationship between concentration and performance depends upon the nature of the industry studied. Working on a sample of 417 four-digit Standard Industrial Classification manufacturing industries in 1963, Collins and Preston (1969) reached the following conclusion: the most significant impact of concentration on price–cost margins occurred in the large firms of the consumer-good industries. For small firms of the same industries, market concentration did not translate into greater margins. The fact that market concentration raises price–cost margins only where small firms are at a competitive disadvantage, suggests that product differentiation is itself an important source of competitive (dis)advantage.

In their study, Domowitz et al. (1986) reiterate the differences related to the intrinsic nature of industries: they found no significant profitability–seller concentration relationship for producer goods industries over the period 1974–81. Their distinction between producer and consumer goods industries is based upon the use of industry shipments: they assume that if more than 50 per cent of an industry's output was bought for direct use and not for further production, then this industry was a consumer goods industry.

Cowling (1976) warns that the differentiation between consumer and producer goods may be less relevant in the context of distributors' increasing power. Price–cost margins are indeed normally measured at the wholesale rather than at the retail level. The necessity to go beyond the consumer/producer distinction is reiterated by Cowling and Waterson (1976). In their study referring to UK industry, these authors split their sample into durable and non-durable goods industries. In addition, they highlight the major weakness of earlier studies (in particular, Collins and Preston's) which lies in the fact that they do not measure the price elasticity of demand on an industry-by-industry basis. Cowling and Waterson's (1976) results run counter to those of many other studies. They find a significant relationship between price–cost margins and concentration in the durable goods industries, whereas in the case of non-durable goods industries, their equations showed no explanation of changes in the price–cost margin. They conclude that 'the results are consistent with the view that durables show greater price flexibility via quality change than do non-durables' (Cowling and Waterson, 1976, p. 273).

It may well be that in some respects, each industry – or even subsector, perhaps even firm – is unique, requiring separate examination of its SCP relationships. In relation to the question of the potential for deriving efficiency gains from increasing concentration in Europe, for example, Jacquemin (1990) shows that there is such a potential for some European industries (telecommunications) but not for others (metal products).

The critical concentration level as a proof of discontinuity in the profit-concentration relationship

Bain's 1951 pioneering study clearly stated that the concentration–performance relationship held primarily for large firms. His first conclusion was that firms operating in concentrated industries were substantially more profitable than firms operating in less concentrated industries. The critical level of market concentration above which industries were concentrated – and above which concentration did explain profitability – was a CR8 of 70 per cent. Below this, concentration did not explain profitability.

Numerous empirical studies have investigated the existence of the critical level of market concentration (see in particular, Schwartzman, 1959; Mann, 1966). The studies of Meehan and Duchesneau (1973) and Dalton and Penn (1976) found evidence of discontinuity, but no significant profitability increases beyond the threshold level. Other studies disagree even with the existence of a discontinuous relationship (Collins and Preston, 1968).

The validity of studies highlighting the existence of a single critical concentration level has been questioned by Phillips (1976) and by Bradburd and Over (1982). Bradburd and Over's work brings evidence of two critical CR4 levels, K_I and K_D, and of a 'critical region of concentration' defined as $K_D < K < K_I$. K_D is referred to as the 'disintegrative' concentration ratio, and K_I as the 'integrative' concentration ratio. Their model defines two 'sticky' equilibria (a non-cooperative and a co-operative equilibrium) contained within this 'critical region'. They estimate the values of K_D and K_I at 0.46 and 0.68 respectively. Their results can be summarized as follows:

- An industry starting from a low level of concentration (below 0.46) will generate profits 'sticking' to a lower price–cost margin; its concentration level must increase to the value 0.68 before profits shift upwards to the higher value.

◆ Conversely, an industry moving from a high concentration level (above 0.68) will generate profits 'sticking' to the higher price–cost margin value; profits will not fall to their lower value until CR4 falls below 0.46.

In his 1981 article, Geroski widens Bain's 'critical concentration ratio' hypothesis. Introducing seven independent variables likely to have an impact on profitability (five-firm concentration ratio, advertising–sales ratio, capital intensity, import–sales ratio, export–sales ratio, average industry sales growth rate and an index of industry diversification), and breaking the concentration variable into seven size classes, Geroski finds the relationship between price–cost margin and industry concentration in the UK to be as follows: up to levels of concentration of about 0.35 there is weak evidence of a U-shaped relation with a local maximum at 0.35; there is also weak evidence of a second convex segment between 0.35 and about 0.75 (which is also a local maximum). At higher levels of concentration (greater than 0.75) one can observe a decline in profits followed immediately by a much sharper rise.

Geroski's major conclusions are as follows:

◆ The profit–concentration relationship is positive overall.

◆ The Bainian 'critical concentration ratio' hypothesis is only a special case of his model.

◆ His model rests on a non-linear functional form of the profit–concentration relationship.

Note, however, that even in 1994 Geroski could write: 'At the moment, we know relatively little about intra-industry market dynamics, or about the nature of the selection process that operates within industries'.

The critical concentration ratio (or ratios) hypothesis can explain some of the controversy over the relationship between concentration and performance; if they exist in practice, then not allowing for them in models can give rise to spurious results.

The relevance of business cycles in the study of the structure-performance relationship

Studies finding different relationships between concentration and performance may be doing so because the time periods on which their studies are based are at different points on the business cycle. Weiss (1974) noted that the strength of the profit–concentration relationship highlighted in earlier industry cross-section studies seemed to vary over time. The inclusion of business cycles in the study of the relationship has thus become a requirement. This is illustrated in the study by Domowitz *et al.* (1986): using a sample of 284 industries, they found that over the period 1958–81, the relationship between industry average price–cost margins and seller concentration weakened considerably. According to the same authors, cross-sectional studies drawn from relatively prosperous years (such as

1963) show a stronger link between profitability and concentration than would cross-sectional studies based on recession years (such as the mid-1970s).

Perhaps in the 1970s, weak demand combined with rising costs squeezed concentrated industry profit margins. This is consistent with the view that larger firms, having higher capital to sales ratios than smaller firms, are more vulnerable to the burden represented by fixed costs during an economic recession. During a recession, weak demand is likely to generate more intense competition; strategies based on price become more important to capture more market shares (Green and Porter, 1984).

Even incorporating the business cycle does not, however, dispel controversy. One view, as we have seen, is that during a recession, competition intensifies. This view is contested by other authors (for example, Rotemberg and Saloner, 1986) who argue that oligopolies tend to behave in a more competitive manner during boom periods.

Co-existence of several 'strategic groups of firms' in a specific industry

The co-existence of several 'strategic groups of firms' in an industry is another factor that may explain different results because it was not incorporated into the models. An industry in one country may exhibit very different SCP characteristics from those of the same industry in another country because, for example, a higher proportion of the firms are foreign-owned in one country than the other. In some situations, firms can and should be separated and classified to form different homogeneous groups of actors. Firms belonging to a distinct group, defined on the basis of certain criteria (such as nationality) will have similar patterns of behaviour.

In attempting to allow for such differences between firms that have already entered an industry, Caves and Porter (1977), for example, put the emphasis on barriers to mobility rather than on entry barriers. In the same stream of studies, Donsimoni and Kambouri (1989) isolated domestic firms from foreign firms, and assumed that their belonging to different home countries explained different behaviours. Geroski (1991a) similarly distinguished between domestic and foreign firms, though his results were that because the heights of entry barriers facing the two types of entrants were broadly similar across industries, foreign-owned firms did not appear to behave differently from domestically owned firms in the UK.

12.5 Summary

There is a marked absence of unanimity in relation to both the theory and the empirical results on SCP relationships in Europe. Among the important questions in relation to which there is still some dispute are: How and why do firms (and industries) grow? How important is size of firm? How stable are concentration levels in different industries (and regions) over time, and why? How important is clever strategy as opposed to efficient production?

One important conclusion that can be derived from the continuing controversy in so many areas, is that we require more disaggregated studies. Our own research on particular industries (Jacobson, 1991; Jacobson and O'Sullivan, 1994) has convinced us that this type of temporally and spatially aware, industry-specific work has much to commend it. Fisher (1991) has written that 'in the absence of strong guidance from theory, we need to know what happens in fact. This surely requires the detailed study of particular industries.' While we believe an entirely inductive, empirical approach is inappropriate, and epistemologically impossible, a shift in this direction is appropriate at this time in the development of industrial economics.

In addition to these methodological conclusions, there are also policy conclusions. For Europe, the implications of the empirical studies on SCP are, among others, the following:

- Because of intra-industry (and also inter-firm) differences, the struggle for growth should not be seen as something that policy should *generally* support. *EU firms should rather concentrate on other complementary strategies* in order to sustain or increase their profitability.

- Since there is no consensus on the relationship between concentration and performance, how much importance should EU competition and industrial policy attach to the prevention of concentration?

Websites

Among the most important websites for the chapter on performance, are the individual home pages of the experts working on this and related subjects. For example, John Sutton, among whose current working papers are one on 'persistence of leadership' and another on the 'determinants of market structure' has a home page at **http://personal.lse.ac.uk/sutton/** from which these papers can be downloaded. Another useful home page is that of Richard Lipsey, **http://www.sfu.ca/~rlipsey**, from which, for example, a version of Lipsey and Carlaw (2004) can be downloaded.

The RePEc website at **http://repec.org/** is an extensive source of research papers in economics. This page also contains links to a wide range of other economics-related websites.

Questions

12.1 Why is the profit rate, by itself, an inadequate measure of performance?

12.2 What is competitiveness?

12.3 Are all dominant firms competitive?

12.4 Why is there disagreement on the relationship between structure and performance?

Notes

1 'Replacement cost is the [€] outlay needed to purchase the current productive capacity of the firm at minimum cost' (Lindenberg and Ross, 1981, p. 12).

2 Equity is the 'net worth' of the firm; it is equal to: total assets – all short-term and long-term liabilities.

3 The 'accounting profit' captures all information available on a balance sheet and relating to revenue, cost and depreciation.

4 Though note that profitability could arise from efficiency – see the discussion on the Demsetz efficiency problem.

5 The following draws on Shughart (1990, p. 86).

6 See Lindenberg and Ross (1981).

7 Unless the value of the shares is based on expectation of future profit.

8 Tobin and Brainard's (1977) estimations are consistently higher, whereas von Fürstenberg's (1977) are consistently lower. Note that Tobin's q has also been used in studies of investment in Europe; see Funke et al. (1989) on Germany and the UK, and Chan-Lee and Torres (1987) on France.

9 Arising, for example, from learning effects, or from access to better quality inputs.

10 We introduced this index as a measure of concentration in Chapter 5 (Section 5.5).

11 One way to capture these differences is to incorporate data on wage differentials. For a cross-country comparison including skill differences, see Freeman, R. (1994).

12 We are referring, in general, to products. In relation to services, especially publicly provided services such as health, education and defence, the measurement of output is particularly problematical.

13 Note that most studies of competitiveness are quantitative studies, in which price (or cost) competitiveness alone is used, mainly because it is difficult to measure intangibles such as quality and design.

14 On relative technology performance, see also Chapters 11 and 13.

15 An increase in the real exchange rate can be due, among other things, to an increase in the general price level in country i, or an appreciation of the nominal exchange rate (i.e. j's currency becomes more expensive in terms of that of i).

16 Carlin et al. (2001) examine the determinants of export market performance of 14 OECD countries. They show that relative unit labour costs and embodied technology are both important, but that there are 'residual cross country trends, which appear to be correlated with longer-run features such as schooling and ownership structures'.

17 We come back to the notion of efficiency (in particular, Pareto efficiency) in Chapter 15.

18 Consumer surplus is defined as the excess of value received by consumers over what they must pay for a good. The magnitude of the consumer surplus depends in part on the elasticity of demand.

19 For an examination of this argument in the case of the UK, and in particular the electricity supply industry in the UK, see Button and Weyman-Jones (1993). An industry such as electricity supply is par-

ticularly amenable to estimation of actual and optimal average costs because of the standardized nature of the output.

20 There is also a difference between X-efficiency and technical efficiency. For a theoretical discussion and empirical evidence, see Kalirajan and Varagunasingh (1992).

21 For a critique of this view of the behaviour of the firms in relation to average cost curves, see Lazonick (1991, ch. 3).

22 Note that Leibenstein continued to work on X-inefficiency for nearly 30 years after his seminal 1966 article. Among the final papers to which he contributed was Leibenstein and Maital (1994) in which he addressed the relationship between X-inefficiency and organizational learning. He died in 1994. His work is summarized in Dean and Perlman (1998).

23 See the discussion on the evolutionary theory of the firm in Chapter 4.

24 What we are referring to here, in line with practices in both the OECD and the EU, and as discussed in Chapters 11 and 13, is high technology defined in terms of R&D as a percentage of turnover.

25 On this issue, see for example, Lall and Streeten (1977). For a recent attempt at modelling 'appropriateness', see Basu and Weil (1998).

26 We can consider competition to be effective when the four-firm concentration ratio is below 40 per cent, entry barriers and profit rates are low, and market shares fluctuate.

27 See also Pascoe and Weiss (1983) and Geroski and Jacquemin (1988). Note that rate of decline in market dominance strongly depends on antitrust legislation.

28 SCP has been examined in some detail in Chapter 2, especially Section 2.2.1.

29 Though even this was, and still is, disputed.

30 See also Brozen (1970).

31 The author uses a 'market share mobility index' instead of the conventional (and static) market share indicator.

32 Hymer and Pashigian's findings imply that the long-run average cost (LRAC) curve of the firm declines continuously. Their explanation is that small firms typically grow very rapidly because they want to avail themselves of the scale economies implied by the negatively sloped part of their LRAC curve.

33 See Gibrat (1931).

34 In the case of equi-proportionality, national economic expansion is distributed evenly among firms, and by extension, the firm's growth rate coincides with the growth rate of the national economy.

35 For more on Gibrat's Law, and for a review of models developed in the 'growth of firms' literature, see Sutton (1997) and Lotti *et al.* (2003).

CHAPTER 13

Performance of EU firms and industries

13.1 Learning objectives

The main objectives of this chapter are:

- To provide first an overview of performance at the intra-EU level

- To suggest a comparative analysis of performance with the EU's main competitors, namely the United States, Japan and, increasingly, South East Asia and China

- To examine trade-based indicators of performance so as to gauge the extent of specialization in the EU

- To give an insight into the revealed comparative advantages of EU industry

- To discuss the EU's position in high-technology industries, and

- To examine performance at the sub-national level, using the analysis in terms of clusters and systems of innovation

13.2 Performance of firms and industries at the intra-EU level

We highlight here the relative importance of manufacturing and service industries for the individual EU member states, as well as their relative performance in terms of turnover. The importance of various industries for the EU as a whole has been discussed already (see Chapter 7, Section 7.6). The analysis here highlights the differences among EU countries.

Table 13.1 The three largest companies in Europe, selected industries, 2001

Industry (NACE)	Company	Country	Indicator of relative size	
Food (16)	Nestlé	Switzerland	Sales (€bn)	52.6
	Unilever	Netherlands/UK		32.1
	Diageo	UK		19.0
Textile (17)	Coats Group	UK	Turnover (€bn)	2.6
	Gruppo Marzotto	Italy		1.6
	Chargeurs Textiles	France		1.2
Clothing (18)	Holding Partecipaz Ind.	Italy	Turnover (€bn)	3.3
	LVMH-Gruppe Clothing	France		3.2
	Zara-Ind. Dist. Text.[a]	Spain		2.6
Wood, paper (20, 21)	Stora Enso	Finland	Sales (€bn)	13.5
	UPM-Kymmene	Finland		9.9
	Svenska Cellulosa	Sweden		8.9
Chemicals (24)	BASF	Germany	Sales (€bn)	32.2 (2002)
	Bayer[b]	Germany		3.3 (2003)
	ICI	UK		8.7 (2002)
Transport equipment (34, 35)	Volkswagen	Germany	Sales (€bn)	84.0 (2003)
	PSA	France		54.2 (2003)
	Renault	France		2.4 (2003)

[a] This company is also active in the area of distribution. Its textiles activities are not included in the figure provided here.

[b] Only the sales of the chemicals division are reported here.

Source: Derived from data in Eurostat 2003c

First of all it should be noted that the ten new member countries of the EU represent only 5 per cent of the EU-25 total manufacturing turnover in value terms; this share is even smaller in the case of services, with some exceptions (such as wholesale and retail trade). The relative importance of manufacturing industries varies among member states, with Germany being one of the most industrially oriented countries of the EU, after Spain and Portugal. The four largest countries combined (Germany, France, the UK and Italy) account for more than three-quarters of total EU manufacturing turnover. The largest companies (in terms of turnover) tend also to be concentrated in these countries, although the importance of the Netherlands, Switzerland and Sweden as bases for large companies should not be underestimated. Table 13.1 shows how European countries dominate in terms of manufacturing activity at the firm level. The smaller countries appearing in Table 13.1 (Switzerland and the Netherlands) have large food companies. The large countries such as the UK, Italy, France, Germany but also Spain, tend to dominate a number of industries, whereas Ricardian-type comparative advantages explain why two relatively small countries – Finland and Sweden – also feature in this table.

Table 13.2 Top firms in selected industries in the EU-15, ranked by sales, 2003

Company	Country	Industry	Sales US$m
1 Royal Dutch Petroleum	Netherlands	Petroleum	179,431
2 Shell Transport and Trading	UK	Diversified	179,431
3 British Petroleum	UK	Petroleum	178,721
4 DaimlerChrysler	Germany	Automotive	156,838
5 Allianz	Germany	Insurance	126,804
6 TOTAL	France	Petroleum	120,602
7 Volkswagen	Germany	Automotive	102,264
8 Siemens	Germany	Electrical eng	98,815
9 ING Groep	Netherlands	Insurance	90,330
10 AXA	France	Insurance	87,890
11 Carrefour	France	Retail trade	80,836
12 Koninklijke Ahold	Netherlands	Retail trade	78,323

Source: The 2003 Global 1000 Scoreboard, *Business Week*, http://bwnt.businessweek.com/global

Crossing the two variables highlighted in Table 13.2 – geographical location and industry size – leads to the study of industrial specialization.

Industrial specialization can be defined at both the production and trade levels. The industrial specialization of a country at the production level is the extent to which its industrial structure is dominated by a few large industries; it is the extent to which output (or employment, or value added) is concentrated in the top few industries. Defined on the basis of trade results, the indicator reflects the performances of a given national industry on the world market. Normally, the trade specialization performances of a country mirror its specialization intensity at the production level.

Industrial specialization at the production level is particularly noticeable for small and open economies. Table 13.3 gives a summary of the patterns of industrial specialization in the manufacturing sector for a selected number of EU countries in 2000. These specialization indices relate, for a given country, the importance of a particular NACE industry in total manufacturing value added, to the same ratio for the EU-15 as a whole; the calculations have been performed at the three-digit level of analysis. In the manufacturing sector, Denmark tends to be specialized in fish products and optical equipment, the Republic of Ireland in basic chemicals, office machinery and computers, and Portugal in the footwear and clothing manufacturing industries. The fact that even at the three-digit level, countries are specialized in the same industry (France and the UK in aircraft and spacecraft) reflects the importance of intra-industry specialization.

Table 13.3 Industrial specialization in the EU-15 manufacturing sector, selected countries, 2000

Country[a]	NACE three-digit
Denmark	Fish; Games and toys; Optical and photographic equipment
Finland	Pulp and paper; Sawmilling and planing of wood; Telecommunications equipment
France	Aircraft and spacecraft; Processing of nuclear fuel; Steam generators
Germany	Electricity distribution; Machine tools; Motor vehicles
Spain	Cement, lime and plaster; Ceramic tiles; Stone
Italy	Ceramic tiles; Motorcycles and bicycles; Tanning and dressing of leather
Ireland	Basic chemicals; Office machinery and computers; Reproduction of recorded media
Portugal	Footwear; Knitted and Crocheted fabrics; Other wood products
UK	Aircraft and spacecraft; Pesticides and other agrochemical products; Publishing

[a] Industries are ranked in alphabetical order

Source: Derived from data in Eurostat, 2003c, p. 10

During the 1990s, production specialization, measured by the share of the three largest industries in production, increased in the UK, Sweden, Finland, Ireland, France and Germany. In particular, production specialization in Ireland, Finland and Sweden implied a greater reliance on high-technology industries and those with increasing returns to scale. With 76 per cent of its total manufacturing production represented by three industries (computers, chemicals, and electrical and optical equipment), Ireland is the most specialized of the EU countries. Finland is the second most specialized with a ratio of 55 per cent (CEC, 2003b).

In the same vein, production specialization has increased over the 1990s in all new member states from eastern Europe, with the exception of Estonia. A general idea of relative production specialization for the new EU members can be gauged from Fig. 13.1. Note that the data in this figure relate to the two-digit level of analysis, and that they include Bulgaria and Romania, two countries that have not yet joined the EU. As can be seen, the share of traditional and labour-intensive industries such as food, textiles, basic metals, and coke and refined petroleum products in the total manufacturing production of the central and east European countries (CEECs) is higher than the corresponding shares for the EU. This implies that the CEECs tend, as a whole, to be relatively specialized in traditional industries, and they tend to be relatively weak in high-technology industries such as machinery

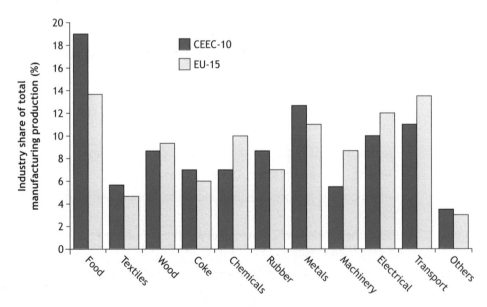

Figure 13.1 Relative importance of manufacturing industries in central and eastern Europe: comparison with the EU-15, 2000

Source: European Commission, 2003d, p. 141

Note: The above classification is as follows: Food, drinks, tobacco; Textiles, clothing and leather; Wood, pulp and paper products; Coke and refined petroleum products; Chemicals; Rubber, plastic and other non-metallic mineral products; Basic metals; Machinery and equipment; Electrical and optical equipment; Transport equipment and equipment. Obviously, a great deal of structural change has already happened in these countries since the fall of the Berlin Wall in 1989. The reorientation of trade away from the Comecon countries and towards western Europe, as well as important foreign-direct investment flows in industries such as motor vehicles, have substantially reshaped and upgraded the productive structure of these economies.

As we have seen in Chapter 7, the industrial structure of most countries of the EU has changed dramatically in the past few decades. These structural changes reflect the 'tertiarization' of the economies, or the increasing importance of services therein, in particular, of knowledge-based services. Knowledge-based services encompass communication,

Table 13.4 Specialization[a] in the EU-15 service sector, 1999

Country	NACE two-digit [NACE three-digit]
Belgium	Transport, communication (1.22) [in particular, Land transport (1.32)]; Other business services (1.1)
Denmark	Transport, communication (1.14) [in particular Post telecommunications (1.28)]; Distributive trade (1.06)
Finland	Transport, communication (1.62) [in particular Post telecommunications (1.6)]
France	Transport, communication (1.23) [in particular Post telecommunications (1.3)]; Business services (1.07); Other business services (1.06)
Germany	Distributive trade (1.06); Other business services (1.03)
Ireland	Hotels and restaurants (1.94); Distributive trade (1.06)
Italy	Transport, communication (1.06); Distributive trade (1.05)
Luxembourg	Other business services (1.08); Business services (1.06)
Netherlands	Other business services (1.31); Business services (1.21)
Portugal	Distributive trade (1.27); Hotels and restaurants (1.24)
Sweden	Transport, communication (1.33) [in particular, Land transport (1.28)]; Business services (1.12)
Spain	Hotels and restaurants (1.30); Distributive trade (1.03)
UK	Hotels and restaurants (1.17); Business services (1.09); Other business services (1.06);

[a] Specialization is defined here as the ratio between the employment share of an industry in total market service employment, and the corresponding share for the EU as a whole. A ratio greater than unity denotes specialization. Excluded from the analysis are, therefore, non-market services such as public administration, education and health, and social and personal services. Note that data on banking and finance are missing from this Eurostat analysis.

Source: Derived from data in CEC, 2002b

financial services, real estate and business services. The share of knowledge-based services in total value added for the EU-15 increased from 19.7 per cent in 1979, to 29.7 per cent in 2001. This needs to be related to a decline in the share of manufacturing activities from 27.4 per cent in 1979 to 19 per cent in 2001 (European Commission, 2003d). When taking into account market services only, specialization at the production level was in 1999 as displayed in Table 13.4.

The first remark emanating from Table 13.4 (and when analyzed in parallel with Table 7.10 in Chapter 7) is the relative insignificance of retail and wholesale trade (distributive trades) in terms of specialization. This is a large industry at EU and individual country level, representing more than 41 per cent of total market service employment in the EU as a whole. However, only a handful of countries are specialized in this area (namely Portugal, and much more loosely Denmark, Germany, Italy, Ireland and Spain). As in the case of manufacturing, Ireland tends to display an extremely specialized structure of service industries. Ireland's specialization index for hotels and restaurants, at 1.94, is the highest of all, confirming the success of the country in promoting itself as a key European destination for tourism over the 1990s. It should be noted that Ireland is not specialized at all in business services (0.63), and in other business services (0.6). In light of the country's performance in terms of relative wealth, that is, compared with other EU member states, and of high-technology manufacturing, these results appear rather puzzling. Indeed, as Table 13.4 shows, all relatively wealthy countries of the EU are either heavily (Netherlands) or loosely specialized (Luxembourg, Belgium, France, Germany, Sweden and UK) in business services and other business services. Moreover, Denmark, Finland and France are also strong in communication services. As stated above, business services and communications are all part of knowledge-based services. The explanation for Ireland lies in the fact that most business services in this country are internalized within the broad structure of the manufacturing plant, which is normally relatively large and foreign-owned. With regard to financial services, Luxembourg is heavily specialized in the area. In 2000, the value added represented by financial services in the total value added of the country was 22.8 per cent; this is more than 4 times the EU average. Other countries relatively specialized in financial services (although more loosely), are Austria, the Netherlands and Italy (European Commission, 2003d).

The importance of telecommunications services for Finland matches its manufacturing specialization in telecommunications equipment. This is referred to as *pole specialization*[1] – specialization in a small number of related products or services – in that telecommunications equipment and telecommunications services are mutually reinforcing. Land transport is relatively important for Belgium and Sweden, owing to their specific geographical features and location. Note that the Netherlands is specialized in water transport (NACE three-digit); the specialization index for water transport was 2 in 1999, mirroring the 'Rotterdam' effect.

The connections (appraised through input–output analyses) between manufacturing and services should also be highlighted. For the past 250 years, services in general have underpinned economic development. The development of nationwide postal systems, the improvements in sanitation systems and the supply of clean water and health services in some countries has been associated with the idea of 'affluent society' (the high-income economies being those with a higher share of services). In our modern economies, there has been a qualitative shift towards the *quality* of services; in particular, knowledge-based services are recognized as being the vehicles of modern growth. Official data from the European Commission show that the share of knowledge-intensive services in total intermediate demand from the manufacturing sector grew continually since the early 1970s. In the late 1990s, this share was well above 15 per cent in countries such as the UK, and above 20 per cent for the Netherlands, France and Germany.

We now turn to *change over time* in the performance of European industry, focusing in particular on investment trends, and change in productivity.

Gross fixed capital formation (GFCF) at constant prices increased by 2.7 per cent and by 2.0 per cent only in the 1980s and 1990s respectively. GFCF declined severely at the beginning of the 1990s (−5.7 for the year 1993), but recovered subsequently, in line with the investment boom recorded at the world level. In particular, investment in machinery and equipment in the EU-15 has been particularly depressed in the early 1990s (Fig. 13.2). The following period is marked by a relatively vigorous investment drive in the equipment sector. This positive performance is nevertheless overshadowed by the extremely good investment growth recorded in the United States (12.3 per cent per annum on average during 1996–2000, compared with 7.3 per cent for the EU-15). High investment rates in equipment are likely to affect performance in other industries that use the products of mechanical engineering and office and data processing equipment. The greater the output of industries such as office and data processing equipment and mechanical engineering

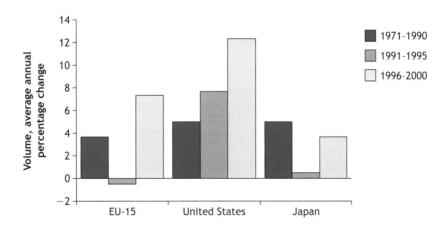

Figure 13.2 Investment in equipment, in the EU-15, United States and Japan
Source: European Commission, 2002, p. 114

and, by implication, the greater the introduction of the products of these industries into downstream industries, the greater the impact on productivity in those downstream industries. Within the EU, the cohesion countries such as Ireland, Portugal and Greece have recorded annual investment growth rates in this sector as high as those of the United States: 15.2 per cent on average for Ireland, 12.3 per cent for Greece and 11.6 per cent for Portugal, for 1996–2000).

Performance at industry level has been uneven with value added and output contracting sharply in some industries during the 1990s, such as leather and textiles (Table 13.5). Value added growth has been particularly important in electrical and optical equipment (5.4 per cent annual growth over the decade).

Table 13.5 Growth in manufacturing value added in the EU-15, at factor costs, constant prices)	
Industry	Average annual change 1991-2000 %
Food, drinks, tobacco	1.5
Textiles	−1.7
Leather and leather products	−2.3
Wood and wood products	2.4
Pulp, paper, publishing	1.8
Coke, refined petroleum products	0.4
Chemicals	2.9
Rubber and plastic products	3.1
Other non-metallic mineral products	0.8
Basic metals and fabricated metal products	1.7
Machinery and equipment	0.9
Electrical and optical equipment	5.4
Transport equipment	2.3

Source: European Commission, 2003f

Figure 13.3 shows the trends in annual labour productivity growth for a selected number of EU-15 manufacturing industries over the period 1979–2001. Labour productivity growth is defined as the growth in value added at constant prices minus the growth in hours worked. The trends conveyed by the selected industries in Fig. 13.3 mirror the picture for the manufacturing and service sectors as a whole: over the three sub-periods, there has generally been an increase in labour productivity in the EU-15. Negative productivity trends are

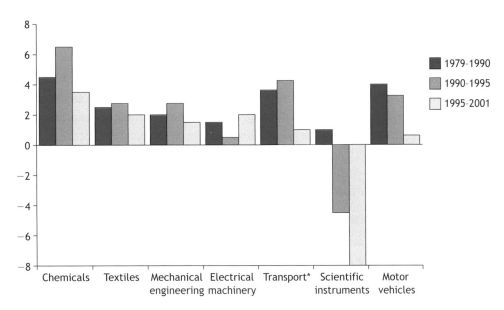

Figure 13.3 Annual labour productivity growth in selected EU-15 manufacturing industries, 1979–2001

Source: European Commission, 2003e, p. 75

* This industry relates to railroad and other transport equipment; it therefore excludes motor vehicles and aircraft

indeed an exception. These have been recorded for mineral oil refining (with a decline in annual productivity of −5.3 per cent over the 1979–1990 sub-period), and for scientific instruments since 1990. A striking observation emanating from labour productivity growth figures at industry level is the wide diversity in performance across industries. Annual labour productivity growth for office machinery (not reported in Fig. 13.3) was nearly 55 per cent over the 1995–2001 sub-period. This is in sharp contrast with scientific instruments (−7.8 per cent), and with telecommunications equipment, where productivity growth during this sub-period was negligible (at 0.3 per cent). Moreover, productivity increases have been generally much less pronounced since 1995, compared with the previous sub-periods. In motor vehicles, transport, chemicals, textiles, mechanical engineering and scientific instruments, annual labour productivity growth was substantially less vigorous since 1995 than before. This is actually a general trend, for a complete graph with all industries would show that in all industries, but a few exceptions, EU productivity growth has been sluggish since the mid-1990s. As can be seen in Fig. 13.3, electrical machinery is one such exception.

Unless accompanied by more than proportionate increases in output, labour productivity improvements are associated with declining manufacturing employment. Job contractions can also be due to restructuring, or the reorganization of firms, a widespread phenomenon in the EU in the late 1980s and 1990s.

13.3 Comparative performance: EU, United States and Japan

In this section, the position of EU industry as a whole is compared with that of Japan and the United States, the three countries forming what is conventionally known as the triad. In order to study the relative importance of the EU in the world, the most appropriate criteria are those relating to its comparative performance on the world market. The world export share and the trends in world industrial production of the EU is examined first, followed by factor productivity and specialization; next, our performance indicators will be broadened to include the trade specialization of the EU as a whole.

13.3.1 World importance of EU manufacturing and service sectors

Most of the economic growth at the world level since the 1990s has been accounted for by the dynamic economies of the Asia Pacific region, with the exception of Japan. As a result of these high growth rates in South East Asian countries and China, world industrial and international economic activity becomes more and more polarized around three main geographical areas. These are represented by the EU and its associates (mainly EFTA and non-EU east European countries), NAFTA (North American Free Trade Area, comprising the United States, Canada and Mexico) and Japan, China and East Asia.[2] Whereas Japan has been for several decades a leader in terms of economic development and economic integration in Asia, slow growth of the Japanese economy during the 1990s coupled with the dynamism of China seem to shift the epicentre of Asian economic growth towards China. However, the interest in comparing the EU to Japan, rather than to China, stems from the structural similarity existing between these countries. Many of the EU countries and Japan present indeed the same features: they are highly industrialized and, as a result, are high-income countries. As a result, and wherever possible, our analysis is based mostly on a comparison of the industrial structures and performances among the four major industrial poles of the triad:

- *Proportion of employment.* The importance of manufacturing to employment in the economies of the countries with a manufacturing tradition has been shrinking since the first oil shock (1973). This phenomenon of *de-industrialization* has been equally important in the three regions – the United States, EU and Japan – although the phenomenon has been more pronounced and has happened earlier in the United States. As a result, services account for a larger proportion of employment in the United States than in the EU or Japan. According to OECD *Quarterly Labour Force* statistics, 77.5 per cent of total employment was in services in the United States in 2003; this compares with 69.3 per cent for the EU-15 and 66.6 per cent for Japan.

- *Proportion of value added.* De-industrialization, or the rise of service activities, is confirmed by the data shown in Table 13.6. The share in the total value added (VA) of manufacturing activities has declined from 27.4 per cent to 19 per cent for the EU-15 between 1979 and 2001 (and from 23.4 per cent to 14.3 per cent for the United States).

Note that public administration activities and distributive trades have at best increased marginally their share in the total VA; these activities have in general been rather stable or even declined over the period. Most of the increase in services is therefore explained by the rise of other service activities such as real estate, business services and financial services. In 2001, these three service activities represented 27 per cent and 31.2 per cent of total VA in the EU and United States respectively; this was substantially more than the VA accounted for by manufacturing (at 19 per cent and 14.3 per cent respectively).

Table 13.6 Change in the structure of industrial activities since 1979, EU and United States

% of total value added	1979		2001	
	EU-15	United States	EU-15	United States
Agriculture, forestry, fishing	3.3	3.1	1.7	1.6
Mining and quarrying	1.9	2.8	0.9	1.3
Manufacturing	27.4	23.4	19.0	14.3
Utilities[a]	2.7	2.2	2.1	2.0
Construction	7.2	5.3	5.8	5.0
Distributive trades	12.9	16.3	14.0	15.6
Transport	4.3	4.0	4.4	3.1
Communications	2.3	2.9	2.7	2.4
Financial services	4.7	4.7	5.4	9.1
Real estate	6.7	8.7	9.9	10.5
Business services	6.0	5.2	11.7	11.6
CSPS[b]	3.3	2.3	4.4	2.8
Public administration, education, health	17.3	19.2	17.9	20.7

[a] This category encompasses electricity, gas and water supply
[b] Denotes other community, social and personal services
Source: Eurostat, 2004a

◆ *Size of firms.* Within manufacturing, size of firms is an important characteristic on the basis of which to compare the EU with its competitors. European firms are generally smaller than their American or Japanese equivalents. For example, in the late 1980s, 9.5 per cent of EU firms in the food industry were medium or large enterprises (100 employees or more), compared with 19 per cent in the United States, and 11 per cent in Japan. Small enterprises (employing 10 to 19 people) accounted for 57 per cent of employment in the clothing and footwear industry in the EU, compared with 9 per cent in the United States. Wide disparities can also be noted in the textile industry.

◆ *Growth of industrial production.* Growth of industrial production since the early 1980s has been slower in the EU than in the United States. Industrial production (excluding construction) increased by a small 1.8 and 1.9 per cent on average during the 1980s and 1990s respectively. For the same decades, industrial production grew respectively by 2 and 4 per cent for the United States, and 4 and 0.2 per cent in the case of Japan, which went through a long decade of slow growth (European Commission, 2003a).

13.3.2 International variations in productivity and efficiency

Table 13.7 and Fig. 13.4 give an indication of productivity changes since the early 1970s and until 2002. In particular, Table 13.7 compares *total, labour* and *factor productivity* changes in the United States, Japan and Europe over the period 1974–89. During this period of time, Europe has consistently ranked midway between a very productive Japanese economy and a less productive American economy in terms of changes in productivity.

Table 13.7 Annual average percentage changes in factor productivity, 1974-89						
	Total factor productivity[a]		Labour productivity[b]		Capital productivity	
	1974-79	1980-91	1974-79	1980-91	1974-79	1980-89
United States	0.2	0.5	0.5	1.0	−0.5	−0.4
Japan	2.1	1.9	3.6	2.9	−2.2	−1.4
Europe[c]	1.6	1.3	2.0	1.7	−1.1	−0.6

[a] TFP growth is the weighted average of the growth in labour and capital productivity

[b] Output per person at work

[c] This corresponds to the EU-15 plus EFTA countries

Source: OECD, 1993c

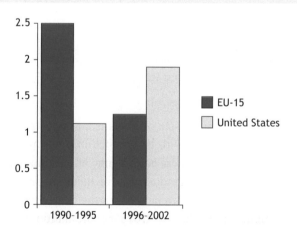

Figure 13.4 Growth in output per hour, 1990-95 and 1996-2002, EU and United States
Source: Adapted from European Commission, 2003d

Figure 13.4 shows that the trend in lower productivity gains (measured by output growth per hour) in the United States, compared with the EU, has continued over the sub-period 1990–95. Structural reforms in the EU labour markets, aimed at cost minimization through wage moderation, partly explain these favourable results (this has been particularly important in low value-added activities). However, a contrasting picture emerges for the following five years (1996–2002), with productivity being more vigorous in the United States than in the EU. After serious concerns about de-industrialization in the United States during the 1980s, the American economy has regained a competitive edge during the 1990s. The slowdown in EU productivity during the latter part of the 1990s is also confirmed by data on productivity per person employed.

In light of the discussion of Chapter 11 on the new growth theories, it is interesting at this juncture to give an indication of the proportion of the productivity increase which is explained by a substitution of capital for labour (capital deepening) and of the proportion attributable to technological change (the Solow residual). The process of capital deepening can itself be divided into new technologies and more traditional assets. The impact of the ICT (information and communication technologies) sector on productivity growth can therefore be assessed.[3]

Table 13.8 Percentage decomposition of hourly labour productivity growth, EU and United States

	1990-95		1995-2001	
	EU	United States	EU	United States
Hourly productivity growth	2.42	1.13	1.39	1.69
K/L substitution	1.89	1.03	1.18	1.28
of which:				
ICT capital	0.22	0.32	0.34	0.57
Office and computer equipment	0.09	0.15	0.18	0.25
Communication equipment	0.05	0.05	0.09	0.14
Solow residual	0.54	0.10	0.21	0.41

Source: European Commission, 2003d

As the figures in Table 13.8 suggest, much of the difference between EU and US productivity growth during the 1995–2001 period is explained by the lower growth in technological change (Solow residual) as well as by a lower contribution of ICT capital in the EU.

Obviously, aggregate figures at EU level mirror substantial intra-EU differences, with for example, relatively high productivity rates in Ireland and Greece during the second sub-period (1996–2000). Table 13.9 shows the contribution of each country to EU-15 annual labour productivity growth since the late 1970s. The contribution of each country is calculated by multiplying each country's productivity growth rate by its share in EU employment. First of all, the figures of Table 13.9 confirm the slowdown of EU productivity growth during the second half of the 1990s, after a favourable performance for the early 1990s. The economic downturn, associated with low labour productivity gains, in large countries such as Germany, France and Italy has had a large impact on the deceleration of EU productivity growth over the 1995–2001 period. It can be seen that the dynamism in smaller and/or peripheral countries such as Ireland, Spain, Portugal and Finland, was not sufficient to reverse the trend. Again, it should noted that productivity figures for Ireland should be analysed with care, given the high incidence of transfer pricing.

Table 13.9 Contributions of member states to EU-15 annual labour productivity growth, 1979-2001

	1979-90	1990-95	1995-2001
Belgium	0.08	0.09	0.03
Denmark	0.04	0.05	0.02
Germany	0.59	0.68	0.22
Greece	0.01	0.02	0.05
Spain	0.18	0.15	0.22
France	0.40	0.27	0.22
Ireland	0.02	0.04	0.10
Italy	0.27	0.36	0.18
Luxembourg	0.01	0.01	0.01
Netherlands	0.14	0.13	0.11
Austria	0.07	0.09	0.04
Portugal	0.02	0.02	0.04
Finland	0.05	−0.01	0.04
Sweden	0.06	0.03	0.06
UK	0.31	0.38	0.39
EU-15	2.26	2.31	1.72

Source: European Commission, 2003e

Finally, Table 13.10 provides a comparison of labour productivity performance between the EU and United States at industry level for the period 1979–2001. The table shows that although the EU is ahead of, or at par with, the United States in twelve industries (out of 26) in 1999–2001, it has a weak productivity performance in industries such as computers, semiconductors, telecommunications equipment, and in other technology-intensive industries such as other instruments, motor vehicles and aircrafts. In short, the EU as a whole is weak relative to the United States, in the ICT sector.

Table 13.10 Labour productivity in EU-14ª manufacturing industries relative to the United States, 1979-2001

	1979-81	1994-96	1999-2001
Food, drink and tobacco	64.5	79.7	100.6
Textiles	103.4	99.1	100.8
Wearing apparel	66.1	67.7	61.0
Leather	95.2	88.0	89.9
Wood products	63.0	86.8	101.3
Pulp and paper products	76.8	104.9	120.0
Printing and publishing	67.0	120.3	134.5
Chemicals	54.7	70.5	78.4
Rubber and plastics	180.2	145.8	127.0
Non-metallic mineral products	121.2	142.6	148.8
Basic metals	65.1	109.1	107.8
Fabricated metals	108.9	108.5	111.4
Machinery	66.5	97.4	110.8
Computers	133.3	89.8	71.9
Insulated wire	87.3	93.7	77.6
Other electrical machinery	79.7	91.3	112.1
Semiconductors	47.8	31.8	41.6
Telecommunications equipment	71.9	63.9	65.7
Radio and television receivers	44.0	62.8	63.1
Scientific instruments	114.4	106.9	103.2
Other instruments	42.8	49.2	47.3
Motor vehicles	30.0	44.9	43.7
Ships and boats	59.2	95.8	88.7
Aircraft and spacecraft	46.7	71.1	71.8
Railroad and other transport	68.8	76.4	80.4
Furniture, miscellaneous manufacturing	110.5	100.8	94.4
Total manufacturing	**84.6**	**88.0**	**80.3**

ª Luxembourg is not included in the data

Source: European Commission, 2003e

13.4 Trade-based indicators of performance

In terms of trade related indicators, the EU seems to have performed relatively well over the years, and to be relatively important in the world. In 2001, total extra-EU exports in goods exceeded €985 billion, against €400 billion in 1990[4] (Table 13.11). The EU merchandise trade represented 18.4 per cent of world trade in 2002, a decline from 20.7 per cent in 1990. However, the USA and Japan have also seen their world share decline, from 16.8 per cent to 12.1 per cent for the USA, and from 9.7 per cent to 8.2 per cent in the case of Japan (*European Economy*, 1993; CEC, 2002a). Since more than 90 per cent of EU merchandise exports are composed of manufacturing goods, these figures suggest that EU manufacturing industry is still significant worldwide.

Table 13.11 Exports, imports and merchandise trade balance of the EU

	Extra-EU exports ECU/€bn	Extra-EU imports ECU/€bn	Balance ECU/€bn
1970	54.2	61.8	−7.6
1975	118.5	132.9	−14.4
1980	216.7	282.5	−65.8
1985	378.7	406.6	−27.9
1990	419.8	462.7	−42.9
1995	573.3	545.3	+28.0
2001	985.3	1,028.0	−42.7

Sources: European Economy (1993), table 82, p. 205; Eurostat, 2003d

The EU is the world leader not only for merchandise trade, but also for commercial services. In 1990 the EU accounted for 27.1 per cent of world trade in services, compared with 16.1 per cent for the United States and 10.2 per cent for Japan. In 2001, it was still the biggest world exporter and importer of services, with nearly one-quarter of total world trade in services, against 21 per cent for the United States and 7 per cent for Japan (Eurostat, 2003b). Like the United States, but unlike Japan, the EU enjoys a trade surplus in services. Its trade surplus is particularly comfortable for the following service activities: financial services (with a trade surplus of more than €9.7 billion in 2001), and air transport (nearly €6 billion in 2001).

Given these relatively high levels of contribution of the EU to world trade, it is not surprising that the EU is economically more open than either the United States or Japan. In 1999, the share of total exports (goods and services) to GDP was 34.6 per cent for the EU-15, against roughly 12.2 per cent for the United States and 10.7 per cent for Japan (Eurostat, 2000).[5]

If we analyse EU trade over a longer period of time (1970–2001), we can see that the EU manufacturing industry has been losing ground on several fronts. First, the trade balance of the EU deteriorated gradually during the 1970s (Table 13.11). During the 1980s, the deterioration seems to have been halted, but not reversed. Following some improvement in the first half of the 1980s, it worsened again between 1985 and 1990. The trade deficit in 1990 is still important, amounting to ECU 43 billion. In line with its productivity improvements in the first half of the 1990s, the EU was able to shift its merchandise trade balance into surpluses in the mid-1990s (+€28 billion in 1995). However, adverse micro and macroeconomic circumstances (exacerbated by a strengthening of the euro against the US dollar) have led to new trade deficits since 1999.

Most of the EU deficit over several decades has been explained by the bilateral trade situation of the EU with respect to Japan (Fig. 13.5). In more recent times, the opening of China to the rest of the world through its 'open door policy', and its integration into the World Trade Organization in December 2001, have changed radically the trade patterns at world level. The EU trade deficit with China is growing inexorably, reaching €76 billion in 2001 (Eurostat *Yearbook* figures). Because some countries in the world have been growing much faster than the EU, and because the improvement of their trade balance is even more spectacular than that of the EU, the trade position of the EU since the 1970s is best characterized by loss minimization on world markets rather than by any substantial improvement.

Figure 13.5 Total exports of the triad in US$ billion, 2001
Source: OECD, 2002 and 2003

Finally, the fifth enlargement of 2004 will only, at least in the short term, increase the EU trade deficit with rest of the world, for these countries' trade balance with non EU members is generally negative (with the exception of Slovakia which has a marginally positive trade balance).

13.5 Revealed comparative advantages of EU industry

There is a great deal of diversity, involving strengths and weaknesses of particular industrial sectors, and of particular countries underlying the performance of the EU as a whole. The study of production and trade performance by type of industry enables us to look at the EU's sectoral specialization.

13.5.1 Patterns of trade specialization

Table 13.12 summarizes broad patterns of trade performance at the EU industry level. The specific weakness of the EU in electrical machinery and electronics, which we had denoted at the production level, is confirmed through trade figures. In contrast, the EU is relatively strong on world markets in a number of industries such as machinery and equipment, chemicals and transport equipment.

Table 13.12 Extra-EU trade in manufacturing, 2000

	Trade balance €m
Manufactured goods, of which:	+54,904
Electrical machinery and electronics	−64,835
Textiles, clothing, footwear	−32,098
Metals	−17,779
Other manufacturing	−6,994
Coke, refined petroleum	−1,904
Wood, paper, publishing	+2,033
Metal products	+6,994
Non-metallic mineral products	+7,490
Food, beverages and tobacco	+8,608
Transport equipment	+43,457
Chemicals	+51,825
Machinery and equipment	+58,728

Source: CEC, 2002b

Export specialization for the EU-15 as a whole, and for most of the new member states, increased during the second half of the 1990s. This was mirrored by the increasing share of six technology-intensive types of exports: pharmaceuticals, telecommunications equipment, aircraft and spacecraft, office machinery and computers, electronic components and motor vehicles. In particular, a greater export specialization in France was very much stimulated by aircraft and spacecraft, motor vehicles and pharmaceuticals. In the Netherlands, this was driven by office machinery, computers and electronic components, and in Finland by telecommunications equipment (CEC, 2003b). As a result, there seems to be a correspondence between production specialization and trade specialization. Whether the EU performance is laudable, when compared with its main competitors, and whether its trade specialization is optimal are two concomitant issues to which we now turn.

13.5.2 Is the EU's industrial specialization optimal?

From a normative point of view, optimal specialization of a given country or group of countries is one that orientates the industrial structure, to some extent, towards strong demand industries: industries with high, sustained levels of growth of demand. We can roughly categorize industries according to intensity of demand into three groups:

♦ *Strong-demand industries* are in many cases technology- and knowledge-driven industries (computers and electronics, telecommunications equipment, electrical equipment, instrument engineering).

♦ *Low-demand industries* are the declining industries (textile/clothing, steel, metal products); they are the industries where world competition is mature, or where decline has set in.

♦ *Medium-demand industries* encompass industries in which emerging new producers in the past decade have started to displace traditional EU leaders; this is the case for industrial machinery, transport equipment, motor vehicles and chemicals. In this category we also find the food industry.

Into which of these three categories do the EU's main industries fall, and are any of its strong demand industries competitive? A study done at the NACE three-digit level for the second part of the 1980s, had categorized a list of more than 100 different EU products using the demand-based indicators above as well as two other ratios (CEC, 1990):[6]

♦ Exports to imports ratio (that is, the cover rate)

♦ Exports to production ratio.

On the basis of these ratios, a set of selected EU industries was grouped into four categories. The first category encompassed industries which were highly competitive in the 1980s. These industries tended to export a high share of their production (more than 10 per cent) and the exports to imports ratio (X/M) was also high (above 3). At the end of the 1980s, there were only five such industries: textile machinery; rubber and material manufacturing machinery; iron tubes; ceramic products; and railway equipment. In a second category, there were industries performing more than moderately well, but not as competitively as the ones in the first group (machine tools; precision instruments; farming machinery; pharmaceutical products; chemical products; shipbuilding; cars and spare parts; domestic appliances; timber and wooden furniture; glass and rubber products). A third group listed a number of industries that export only a moderate part (less than 10 per cent) of their production, and for which the cover rate (X/M) is greater than 1, that is, industries that are moderately competitive on the world market. This group comprised semi-finished wooden products; non-metallic minerals; food, drink, tobacco; paper and printing; and timber and wood industries. A fourth category grouped industries that were either unable to consolidate their international position, or that had been displaced already by new international competitors. In the former subcategory, one could find electrical and electronic engineering, electronic components and, even more critically, consumer electronics and office equipment and data processing, whereas the latter subcategory comprised aerospace. A large proportion of industries in group 4 were information technology (IT) related industries, facing high demand prospects. The study concluded that the EU world competitiveness was concentrated in low-demand industries (such as iron tubes), whereas strong demand in the IT sector was met by foreign imports, mostly from Japan at the time. This suggested the conclusion that the EU industrial production structure and specialization were in some sense not optimal at that time. Has this dramatically changed?

Relying on a combination of comparable indicators, a similar exercise can be attempted using more recent figures. A first indicator measures the contribution of each industry to the manufacturing trade balance. For any industry j, its contribution to the manufacturing trade balance is measured by the following indicator:

$$CT_j = (X_j - M_j) - (X - M) \frac{(X_j - M_j)}{(X + M)}$$

A positive value of this indicator implies a structural surplus, whereas a negative value indicates a deficit. This indicator can be computed for the different categories of industries, grouped into low-, medium- and high-technology industries. This categorization also mirrors the intensity of demand, with low-demand industries (such as food products) being also low-technology industries. The evolution of the CT_j indicator between 1990 and 1999 for the EU-15 and the United States is shown in Fig. 13.6. Medium-low technology industries include coke and petroleum, rubber and plastic, other non-metallic products, basic metals, fabricated metals, and building and repair of ships and boats; medium-high technology industries include electrical machinery, motor vehicles, chemicals excluding pharmaceuticals, railroad and transport equipment, and machinery.

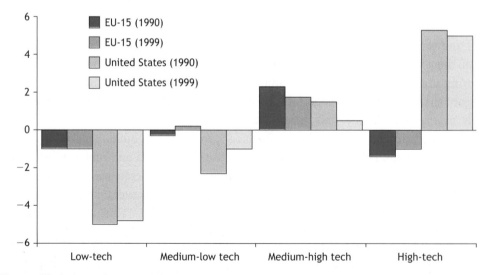

Figure 13.6 Contribution of different industries to the manufacturing trade balance, EU and United States
Source: Adapted from CEC, 2002b

The figure shows clearly that the structural trade deficit of the EU in high-technology products (particularly in computers, telecommunications equipment and instruments) is in perfect contrast with the structural surplus enjoyed by the United States over the 1990s, even though the EU performance seems to have slightly improved in 1999 compared with 1990. For the medium-high technology industries, the relative specialization of the EU in machinery, and its relatively strong position in motor vehicles explain the better performance of the EU when compared with the United States. These first results tend to suggest that, in spite of a small improvement over the 1990s, the EU has not been able to specialize fully in the most promising manufacturing areas. This is an important issue that deserves full attention. We deal more extensively with the issue of the relative strengths and weaknesses of the EU in high-technology industries in the next section.

13.6 The EU's position in high-technology industries

13.6.1 Computing the RTCA index

We can explore the EU's technological performance on foreign markets with the help of the index of revealed technological comparative advantage, RTCA.[7] For the EU as a whole, the index is computed as follows:

$$RTCA = \frac{\text{EU share in world trade of high-technology products}}{\text{EU share in world trade of manufactured products}}$$

For the EU, this index was slightly above the critical value of 1 in 1963; it declined to 0.88 in 1980 (Heertje, 1983). This implies that the EU lost ground on the world market for high-technology products. But so did the United States, for which the index declined from a value of 2 to 1.2 over the same period. These results are partly explained by the increasingly high-technology industries of Japan (office and data processing machinery, electronic equipment, telecommunications equipment). For Japan, the index went from 0.56 in 1963 to 1.41 in 1980. These trends continued into the 1980s, but during the 1990s, the performance of Japan started to deteriorate sharply. Over the period 1996–2001, Japanese high-technology export world market shares declined by 6.9 per cent on average, mirroring de-industrialization in the country (an aftermath of the revaluation of the yen in 1985 leading to relocation of Japanese plants in cost-efficient countries). High-technology export world market shares also declined for the United States during this period, albeit to a much lesser extent (1.8 per cent), whereas the market share of the EU was stable, growing only by a small 0.3 per cent per annum. In contrast, China's annual growth of the high-technology export world market share was 17.5 per cent during this period. In short, whereas the United States, the EU and Japan still hold a large portion of the world market for high-technology products (more than 41 per cent in 2001), their share declines inexorably, to the benefit of low-cost countries, such as the South East Asian countries and China (European

Commission, 2004). Based on data provided by Eurostat (2004b), our calculations of the RTCA index for 2001 are as follows: 1.11 for the EU-15; 1.35 for NAFTA countries (United States, Canada and Mexico); 0.5 for the candidate countries (that is, the ten new EU member states, Bulgaria and Romania); and 1.81 for Japan, South-Korea, Singapore and Taiwan.

As a result, the EU, United States and Japan are still relatively specialized in high-technology products (RTCA greater than 1), but other countries, such as the Philippines, Singapore, Malaysia, and Taiwan are even more so.

Coming back to the triad, the percentage of high-technology products in the total exports of each country in 2001 were as follows: 28.6 per cent for the United States, 24.7 per cent for Japan, and a small 19.8 per cent for the EU-15. Restructuring in the ten new member states enabled them to display a comfortable 9.7 per cent share.

At first sight, the technological effort of EU industry throughout the 1980s and 1990s appears remarkable. Between 1980 and 1990, extra-EU exports of high-technology products more than doubled (Table 13.13); however, extra-EU imports over the same period more than trebled. The result was an increase in the trade deficit for high technology products from ECU 5 billion (in 1980) to ECU 23 billion (in 1990). Over the following decade, exports and imports evolved in parallel, resulting in a deficit of €47 billion only. During 2001, the EU managed to halve its deficit, confirming an improvement in the EU high-technology trade performance.

Table 13.13 EU trade in high-technology products

	Extra-EU exports ECU/€bn	Extra-EU imports ECU/€bn	Balance ECU/€bn
1980	35.413	30.345	+5.068
1990	72.509	95.794	−23.285
2000	187.4	234.7	−47.3

Sources: Derived from European Economy, 1993, p. 213; figures for 2000 are from European Commission, 2004, p. 140

Although its share has declined since the 1980s, the United States was still, in 2001, the major supplier of high-technology products into the EU (35.3 per cent). The share of Japan was only 10.5 per cent, whereas newly industrializing countries (in particular from South East Asia) have accounted for an increasing proportion of EU high-technology imports.

The fifth enlargement in 2004 increases the export performance of the EU by another 7 per cent. Although the figures of Table 13.14 refer to 2001, that is, more than two years before the enlargement to include east European countries, Malta and Cyprus took place, they nevertheless give an indication of the relative contribution of the new members to high-technology trade. Of particular importance in the group of new member states are Hungary and the Czech Republic. These two countries alone represented in 2001 nearly three-quarters of the high-technology total exports of the ten new members.

Table 13.14 High-technology trade in 2001: EU-25 compared with the United States and Japan

	High-technology exports €m	High-technology imports €m	Balance €m
EU-15	195.5	218.6	−23.1
EU-25	210	244.4	−34.4
United States	233.8	243.3	−9.5
Japan	111.2	72.0	+39.2

Table 13.15a Cover rates (X/M) for four selected R&D-intensive industries

	1984				1998			
	EU	NC[a]	United States	Japan	EU	NC	United States	Japan
Aerospace	1.31	0.24	2.98	0.10	1.16	0.76	2.83	0.39
Electrical and electronic engineering	1.09	0.73	0.52	10.55	0.92[b]	1.60	0.90	2.56
Office machinery and computers	0.47	0.39	1.38	5.61	0.37	0.29	0.62	1.71
Pharmaceuticals	2.26	1.10	1.70	0.27	2.14	1.99	0.87	0.53

[a] NC: Nordic Countries (Finland, Iceland, Norway and Sweden for 1984 and Iceland and Norway for 1998)

[b] The 1998 data correspond to electronic engineering only

Source: OECD, 1995, 2000

Tables 13.15a and 13.15b suggest a brief analysis of performance at the industry level and in a comparative perspective. Table 13.15a gives an indication of trade performance at the industry level. It highlights the main feature of Japanese industrial policy (see also Chapter 15); selectivity has resulted in strong positions (pole specialization) in electronics and in office machinery, two industries where the cover rates were still impressively high, 2.56 and 1.71 respectively in 1998, in spite of de-industrialization in the economy. On the other hand, Japanese industrial policy has so far devoted only marginal consideration to the pharmaceuticals and aerospace industries. Nevertheless, the Japanese cover rates for these two industries have grown substantially during the period. Table 13.15a also shows the poor performance of the EU in electronics and in office machinery (particularly in computers).

Table 13.15.b High-technology trade by industry: EU 15, new EU members, United States and Japan, 2001

	High-tech exports in %				High-tech imports in %			
	EU-15	EU-10	Japan	United States	EU-15	EU-10	Japan	United States
Aerospace	25	3.4	1.1	20.6	17.8	2.6	5.1	11.9
Armament	0.7	1.3	0.1	1.3	0.3	0.9	0.4	0.4
Chemicals	3.3	1.7	1.0	2.1	2.2	4.8	3.8	2.0
Computers and office machinery	13.8	28.1	24.2	18.3	26.5	25.2	31.6	31.1
Electrical machinery	2.4	5.4	6.0	1.9	3.4	4.9	4.0	2.3
Electronics	30.9	47.2	48.4	35.4	32.5	43.4	37.7	37.3
Instruments	11.8	6.1	12.9	13.3	9.5	8.0	11.4	9.2
Non-electrical machinery	4.6	4.1	5.3	3.9	3.4	4.5	2.6	2.8
Pharmaceuticals	7.3	2.7	1.0	3.1	4.4	5.5	3.5	3.0
Total	100	100	100	100	100	100	100	100
Total high-technology (€bn)	195.5	14.5	111.2	233.8	218.6	25.8	72.0	243.3

Notes: EU-10 refers to the 10 members of the EU who joined the EU in May 2004. Again, figures relating to the EU-15 relate to extra-EU trade only.

Source: European Commission, 2004

Using the import penetration ratio (defined as the ratio M/C, with $C = Q - (X - M)$) as a final indicator of relative performance shows that, in the late 1990s, this ratio was highest for the computers industry (reaching over 50 per cent). For the manufacturing sector as a whole, this ratio was just above 10 per cent on average. A high import penetration ratio was also recorded for aircraft and spacecraft (at more than 45 per cent). However, the major striking difference between the two industries is that in the aircraft industry, the EU is relatively strong; its high import levels are offset by high levels of exports (cover rate above the critical value of 1).

To summarize, all indicators related to the performance of the EU high-technology sector reflect a similar pattern. The major conclusions are as follows:

◆ Cover rates for high-technology products have declined in the EU during the past decades.

◆ The EU's increasing dependence on high-technology imports is largely explained by its weakness in the office and data processing machinery sector; this is the industry that still has the highest import penetration rate.

◆ The rate of introduction of the newest processes of production has been slower in the EU than in either Japan or the United States over the past 30 years.

◆ Although the EU as a whole is still among the biggest world exporters of high-technology products, its leadership is being eroded by the rise of the Asian countries (Japan in the 1960s and 1970s, South East Asia and China since then).

13.6.2 The technology gap

All these, together with the fact that the EU's world share of inventions and innovations has decreased faster than that of the United States gave rise to concern about the *technology gap*. We introduced this topic briefly in Chapter 11. The idea is that the EU as a whole systematically lags behind the United States and developed Asian countries, in a number of 'key' or 'strategic' industries; and that the EU is less innovative[8] than its major competitors.

The theme of the technology gap is not new. The threat represented by the technology gap and/or the national challenge to overtake and surpass the world technology leaders had been made clear already in the middle of the nineteenth century by Friedrich List (1841). Obsessed by the technological superiority of Britain over Germany during the first half of that century, he was the first economist to identify the main features of what could be called a 'catching up strategy'; this strategy relied in essence on a technology policy.

A more modern version of this theme can be traced to the work of Lovasy (1941).[9] Lovasy's paper on product differentiation and international trade, highlighted the fact that a firm which introduces a *new, differentiated, product* enjoys an export monopoly situation until imitators come into the market. Product innovation highlights the importance of non-price elements. Once imitation and adoption set in, price elements become of primary importance again. Much of trade performance can thus be explained by product superiority or product uniqueness: a new high quality product emerges, making substitutes obsolete. Process innovation is equally important here. Process innovation leads to a cost squeeze. This, in turn, enhances price as a variable explaining performance in international trade.

Following this line of thought, Posner (1961) developed a technology gap theory of foreign trade. At the microeconomic level, the technology gap between one firm and another could be sustained for a period of time *depending on the imitation lag*. The longer the imitation lag, the higher the export gains. Hufbauer (1965) found empirical evidence in a clear-cut relationship between trade performance and innovative leadership, for 60 synthetic materials.

In the 1970s, the idea of the technology gap was revived and applied to the EU as a whole. It gradually gave rise to support for the promotion of technology. Its acknowledgement by EU governments gave birth to Esprit, Brite and all other similar technology programmes in the EU (see Chapter 16). By the 1980s, a plethora of studies had highlighted the existence of, or concern about, the technology gap, particularly between the EU and Japan.[10]

A number of these and other studies focused on the relationship between innovative performance and trade performance. For example, Soete (1981) regressed variations in export performance on variations in innovativeness for each of 40 industrial sectors in 22 OECD countries; he demonstrated the crucial role of the technology variable in explaining differences in export performance in most of the industries studied, but in particular in the high technology industries.[11] Freeman (1987) agreed that innovation was of fundamental importance, arguing that it explained, for example, the predominant position of the West German and US chemicals industries in the early decades of the new synthetic material era.[12] Marbach (1990) further substantiated this general view; basing his analysis on a group of French SMEs, he showed that the most successful exporters were also in the 1980s the major innovators. With the advent of the new growth theories, many studies have shown how the introduction of knowledge and technology leads to substantial productivity improvements in various economies (see, for example, Ark (2002) for an international comparison, and Ark *et al.* (2003) for the case of the EU).

Whereas much attention has been devoted to the relative inability of the EU to innovate, and to its related weak trade performances, little evidence has been gathered on whether there is a *managerial and marketing gap*. Positing something of a counter-argument to the technology gap view, Lewis (1957) suggested that:

> it is not necessary to be a pioneer in order to have a large export trade. It is sufficient to be a quick imitator. Britain would have done well enough if she merely imitated German and American innovations. Japan, Belgium and Switzerland owe more of their success as exporters of manufactures to imitation than they do to innovation.

However, because production in advanced industries is technically demanding, imitation is not as easy as it was. Imitation and innovation require equivalent levels of technical skill. It may well be, then, that imitation – and managerial and marketing ability – is particularly strong in some national systems of innovation whereas innovation is strong in others, and invention in yet others. (The ideal is to have strengths in all three.) A number of notorious past cases such as penicillin, TV, VCRs, compact discs, videotex and high-definition television, in which Europe was the inventor, often even the innovator, but rarely the market leader, may lead us to conclude that the EU has a comparative advantage in inventing, whereas Japan has a comparative advantage in fast imitation, and marketing.

The EU as a whole, in terms of growth of high-technology industries, appears to have been overtaken by other parts of the world (United States from the early part of the century, Japan since the 1960s, South East Asia since the 1990s, United States again at the turn of the millenium). However, as we noted several times, the EU is a set of heterogeneous countries, with varying technological and industrial performances.

A country by country analysis reveals strong positions held by industries in some EU countries (Table 13.16): German and Italian firms still have a leading edge in some types of machine tools; UK firms are aggressive competitors in the chemicals and biotechnology sectors; French firms still have a strong position in the transport sector; Finland has emerged as one of the world leaders in telecommunications equipment and services; Swedish firms were able to consolidate their market shares in machinery and telecommunications. A long-term perspective enables us to see how some European firms have regained a strong competitive position in the world in the past 30 or so years. The cross-border movement of goods, services and factors of production is partly responsible for this catching-up by European firms. The arguments of this paragraph suggest the need for combining industry-, country- or region-specific advantages and long-term perspectives, and to this we now turn.

International trade promotes the diffusion of innovations on a global scale. The spatial diffusion of technology led to a worldwide reorganization of production patterns. In the recent past, the spatial spillover effects have been beneficial to some countries[13] – in particular, in recent decades, Japan and South East Asia – and to some local regions – in particular *technopoles* such as Silicon Valley in the United States, Montpellier in France, Cambridge in England, Taedok in South Korea and Kansai Science City in Japan.[14] Technological developments, together with increasing international movement of goods, services and factors of production have been responsible for a *historical shift* in the competitive positions of firms, regions and countries.

Shifts in the location of the world's leading growth poles are not new.[15] Economic and industrial dominance has historically been associated with technological dominance and as the location of the latter changed, so has that of the former. In the nineteenth century, most technological innovations were pioneered by firms in Europe (mainly in the UK and, later, in Germany); but by the turn of the century, the United States had caught up (Buckley and Roberts, 1982). During the post-Second World War period, the United States consolidated its supremacy. This dominance took the form of a new pattern of production: the gradual emergence of a new international division of labour under the institutional control primarily

Table 13.16 Export specialization ratio relative to the EU, 2001[a]

	EU-15	Austria	Belgium	Denmark	Finland	France	Germany	Greece	Ireland	Italy	Luxembourg	Netherlands	Portugal	Spain	Sweden	UK
Food products, beverages and tobacco	100	72.2	120.2	313.0	25.6	116.4	60.7	253.6	111.6	75.4	70.9	195.2	87.8	139.7	37.0	75.1
Textiles and textile products	100	94.9	122.9	129.0	28.5	82.0	70.0	421.3	17.8	237.2	102.9	71.1	415.2	107.5	38.3	65.5
Leather and leather products	100	108.9	93.8	39.2	16.4	70.4	34.0	47.0	10.3	388.8	9.7	69.1	469.7	173.9	16.7	37.6
Wood and wood products	100	381.4	100.8	162.6	585.6	61.9	69.7	37.7	28.9	61.8	108.4	34.4	499.2	91.2	415.9	21.3
Pulp, paper and paper products; publishing and printing	100	168.8	80.2	65.9	610.7	70.4	87.9	48.8	50.4	64.7	72.2	78.0	141.0	95.5	331.9	74.6
Coke, refined petroleum products	100	23.9	162.1	73.4	131.0	78.6	36.7	524.6	11.3	80.7	2.7	289.4	55.2	111.6	137.6	116.2
Chemicals, chemical products and man-made fibres	100	58.7	161.9	90.6	40.2	101.6	83.2	66.3	264.3	63.5	43.2	113.7	36.4	77.5	78.5	112.0
Rubber and plastic products	100	116.2	110.6	116.1	60.6	92.5	112.9	109.3	31.0	122.1	264.2	72.9	92.3	128.8	86.8	80.0
Other non-metallic mineral products	100	138.4	104.6	86.8	66.5	86.1	79.5	218.1	25.0	204.7	161.3	46.8	207.4	215.6	52.8	63.7
Basic metals and fabricated metal products	100	152.0	115.7	71.7	110.6	86.0	109.9	203.9	15.0	102.8	289.6	87.6	67.1	102.1	130.2	90.0
Machinery and equipment n.e.c.[b]	100	123.2	61.8	112.8	99.9	72.2	136.8	37.8	18.2	176.2	58.7	50.9	47.1	65.9	116.7	84.3
Electrical and optical equipment	100	90.1	51.0	98.3	143.2	83.6	94.5	38.6	224.0	53.2	159.5	159.7	73.3	52.6	101.0	146.2
Transport equipment	100	88.9	89.5	26.3	43.7	157.4	134.9	14.7	6.0	59.9	39.1	33.9	94.4	150.2	83.0	95.5

[a] The ratio measures the share of exports for each CPA subsection in manufacturing exports for each country and compares this ratio to the same ratio for the sum of the EU member states, expressing the results as a percentage. Values over 100 show that a country exports relatively more of those products than the EU average.

[b] Not elsewhere classified

of MNEs. While the first half of the twentieth century was characterized by the internationalization of exchange, the period since then has been characterized by the internationalization of production. International trade between independent firms (inter-firm trade) has been supplanted by international trade between subsidiaries of the same MNE (intra-firm trade).

The technological superiority, and more rapid internationalization of American firms left European firms with a new challenge: they had to narrow the technological and managerial gaps with their large American counterparts. According to Cantwell (1989), from the mid-1950s there was a resurgence of some industries in Europe. The growth rate of manufactured exports of the six founding members of the EC between 1955 and 1975 was twice as high as that of the United States. Firms in the aircraft, coal and petroleum products, tobacco products and pharmaceuticals industries in Europe experienced the fastest growth rates relative to their equivalents in the United States (see Table A13.1 in Appendix 13.2). However, two factors militate against an optimistic assessment of Europe's performance in this period. First, the performance of firms in the office machinery industry in the EC-6 was very poor; and, as a 'generic' or 'pervasive' industry, office machinery was particularly important. Second, American MNEs' subsidiaries that had been set up in Europe during the period were partly responsible for the improvement in the trade performance of Europe. Cantwell (1989) estimated that over half of the increase in Europe's share of total European and US manufacturing exports, over the period 1957–75, was due to an increase in the exports of US-owned affiliates in Europe. The contribution of US affiliates is marked in all industries, with the exception of transportation equipment (see Table A13.2 in Appendix 13.2). Only in this industry did the share of US affiliates fall; this is the one industry in which an indigenous revival did occur. Cantwell goes on to analyse the variation in the competitive response to the 'American Challenge'[16] among European firms and nations:

- In West Germany, indigenous firms performed well in food products, motor vehicles, mechanical engineering and chemicals.
- In France, improvements were discernible in electrical equipment, and non-metallic mineral products.
- In Italy, the performances of indigenous firms improved in motor vehicles and electrical equipment.
- In the UK, good results were achieved in food products, chemicals, and electrical equipment.

The revival of indigenous firms in response to the American challenge was strongest among the firms of the big four EC countries. There was, however, also some success in the Netherlands, where firms achieved quite satisfactory results in electrical equipment (radio and television receivers), and coal and petroleum products (Royal Dutch Shell), and in Belgium and Luxembourg, where firms in the non-metallic mineral products and professional instruments sectors were also quite active.

Cantwell (1989, p. 86) summarizes the pattern as follows: 'While in the case of the larger industrialised countries the presence of US affiliates tended to act as a spur to the technological capacity of indigenous firms, in the smaller countries indigenous competition has been inhibited.'

13.6.2 Theoretical explanations

In the 1950s, a number of theories of international trade and investment, enriched by the introduction of technical change as a crucial and new explanatory variable, followed a more dynamic approach than the traditional theories. Among these were theories that also provided frameworks for analysing the existence and behaviour of MNEs.

The eclectic model

The eclectic model provides a good framework for explaining the existence of American MNEs in Europe and reasons for their presence there.[17] It does this by focusing on country- or region-specific advantages in Europe, the ownership advantages that gave American MNEs the competitive edge in the first place, and the advantages of internalization that explain why they set up subsidiaries rather than licensing European firms to produce for them.

Product life cycle model (PLCM)

Another influential theory was the product life cycle model (PLCM) developed by Vernon (1966); it was the best known of the so-called new technology theories of international trade emerging in the 1960s.[18] According to the PLCM, a new product will originate in a high-income country (the United States), where there is a demand for it (with a high-income elasticity) and superior skills to produce the good. In the early stages, the manufacture of the new product will take place in the country of origin because any adjustments that need to be made at this – the prototype product, and not yet standardized process – stage will need to be made quickly, in response to the home market. Production will be at relatively high unit costs but costs are less significant in the early stages of marketing because the demand for innovations is price inelastic. In the next stage of the cycle, production of the product becomes standardized. The market widens as demand for the new product develops in other relatively high income countries. This is at first met by exports (from the United States). A wider market will give rise to economies of scale, and hence to a falling price. This will widen the market still further, making possible the sale of the product in lower-income countries. A combination of increasingly international distribution of the product, and the relatively lower unit costs of production outside the United States, will result, in the next stage of the cycle, in relocation of the standardized (vertically integrated) production to a country where factor – and mainly labour – costs are lowest.

The PLCM was useful in explaining the pattern of postwar US foreign direct investment (FDI) in Europe and South East Asia. It also helped explain international trade in the 1950s and 1960s, in that more sophisticated, innovative products and products of innovative processes tended to be exported from advanced countries, but some manufactured goods were produced by and exported from less developed countries. There were also other applications, Buckley and Roberts (1982), for example, finding the model useful in explaining the case of European FDI in US manufacturing industry before 1914.[19]

The PLCM has, however, been criticized, not least by Vernon himself.

- It focuses on a discontinuity created by the emergence of an entirely new product. However, technological innovation can also be viewed as a continuous, gradual and cumulative process.

- The PLCM leaves unanswered the question of why the international relocation of production is done through FDI rather than, say, through licensing.

- The PLCM does not take into consideration oligopolistic market structures in determining the location strategies of MNEs.

- While the PLCM may have had some explanatory power for the 1950s to the 1970s, increasingly rapid changes in technology, and the multiplicity of new locations (in particular Japan and the newly industrializing countries) from which competitive firms have originated since then, have made the model less and less applicable.[20]

Vernon posited an alternative explanation, based on the oligopolistic behaviour of MNEs, though he believed that strong traces of his original product life cycle sequence would remain.[21] In the alternative he suggested that there were three phases in the development of MNEs:

- *Innovation-based oligopolies*, when production will tend to be in the home market.

- *Mature oligopolies*, when pricing, investment and locational decisions are made in response to expectations about the behaviour of competitors; for example, a follow-the-leader strategy might result in a firm setting up in a location simply because a competitor set up there.

- *Senescent oligopolies*, when differences in costs determine the location of production.

This, Vernon's second PLCM, does 'describe today's oligopolistic global MNEs. It is surprising that the second version of the model still receives less attention than the first' (Eden, 1991).

Structural changes in the 1980s

Another reaction to the inadequacies of the first PLCM was that of Strange (1991), who argued that, over the 1980s, there were radical and irreversible changes in global structures, in particular the *production structure* and the *financial structure*. In relation to the first, she theorized that the increasingly rapid changes in technology meant that local, national markets were insufficient to recoup in profits the R&D costs of creating or installing new products or processes. If this is so, then internationalization is essential. The financial structure changed through 'the integration of capital markets into one, worldwide market for savings and credit'. Albeit partial and incomplete, this integration gave MNEs 'far greater possibilities than smaller local concerns of raising money wherever they operate' (Eden, 1991). These two structural changes reinforce one another, and make likely increasing significance of MNEs' global economic activity.

The theory of technological accumulation

The last of the reactions to the first PLCM that we will deal with is the theory of technological accumulation. The notion of technological accumulation is based on the idea that the development of technology within a firm is a continuous and cumulative process. In Cantwell's (1989, p. 16) words:

> the industrial composition of innovative activity in a given location or amongst a given national group of firms reflects past technological accumulation. This suggests that international patterns of technological advantage, having been established, will remain relatively stable over time. The sectors in which each group of firms is technologically strongest change only gradually.

In order to assess the 'stability over time of technological advantage', Cantwell (1989, p. 19) uses the following methodology. First, he constructs an index of revealed technological advantage as follows:[22]

$$RTA_{ij} = \frac{\dfrac{P_{ij}}{\sum_j P_{ij}}}{\dfrac{\sum_i P_{ij}}{\sum_i \sum_j P_{ij}}}$$

where P_{ij} is the number of US patents in industry i granted to residents of country j.

The United States is taken as a country of reference because it grants a higher number of patents to non-residents than any other country. If i is the chemicals industry, and j is Germany then the RTA is calculated as the share of US patents taken out by German firms in this industry, divided by the total share of US patents due to non-US residents. Cantwell calculated an index of 1.68 and 1.18 for the time periods 1890–1912 and 1963–83 respectively. This means that, in spite of a decrease of the index over time, Germany still holds an innovative advantage in this particular industry.

Second, Cantwell measures the stability of the sectoral distribution of the RTA index over time. The more stable this is, the better will be the correlation of RTA indices calculated for a national group of firms at two different points in time.[23] The correlation between the sectoral distribution of the RTA index at time t and at the earlier time $t - 1$ is estimated through a linear equation of the form:

$$RTA_{it} = \alpha + \beta RTA_{it-1} + \varepsilon_{it}$$

where i refers to a specific industry, t to a particular time, α and β are coefficients and ε is the error.

Cantwell found a positive and significant correlation between the two RTA distributions ($\beta > 0$) for 15 out of 16 countries; Pavitt (1987), in a similar study, found a positive and significant correlation for 9 out of 10 countries.[24]

Cantwell's conclusion is that past success in an area strongly determines future innovation and growth in that or adjacent areas.[25] In his view, the gradual change in the nature of technology 'disturbed only slightly the pattern of technological advantage held by the firms of the major industrialised countries in the 20 years between the early 1960s and the early 1980s' (Cantwell, 1989, p. 45).

There are criticisms of Cantwell's work. First, he himself acknowledges that the statistical link becomes 'tenuous over longer periods'.[26] Second, and more fundamentally, he calculates innovative output solely on the basis of patents. The limits of patents as an indicator of innovative output was discussed in Chapter 11. Ironically, his results may not be indicative of the type of gradual accumulation of technology and skill that, for example, underlies the success of industrial districts. We have included this statistical analysis based on patents, despite our reservations, because it constitutes a large part of the literature in this area.

With these reservations, we agree that there is evidence for a degree of stability in the global distribution of production of innovations, at least over the short to medium term. For example, the ability of European firms in some industries to catch up with their American counterparts depended on the accumulation of technological experience over years and decades. To take another example, this time looking into the future rather than the past, it may be that, based on cumulated technological experience in the chemical and pharmaceutical industries, Europe will have a greater potential to exploit discoveries in the new biotechnology field than will other regions of the world.

13.7 Clusters, regions, cities and performance (including European systems of innovation)

From previous chapters, and in particular Chapters 2 and 8, it is clear that, under certain circumstances, the relationships between firms are enhanced by spatial proximity. Moreover, this combination of relationships and proximity improves the performance of the firms involved. This is where there are economies of agglomeration (as explained in Chapter 8). Where there is frequent exchange of information between firms, as in the early stages of the development of products and their components, or where there is a particular configuration of value, volume and weight of components, then component production will take place in close proximity to the production or assembly of the final product.

In what can now be considered to be a classic example of this cumulative contribution of information exchange and proximity to performance, Silicon Valley in California became the centre of much of innovation and production in the global microcomputer industry. There are also, as we have shown above, a number of European cities and regions that have high-technology agglomerations. It should be emphasized, however, that not all examples of successful industrial performance are also examples of performance enhanced by proximity, that is by economies of agglomeration. In a detailed study of the computer industry in Ireland and Scotland, for example, Egeraat and Jacobson (2004) show that a very high proportion of the personal computers sold in Europe in the 1990s were assembled in Ireland and Scotland. Very few of the inputs into the assembly process were manufactured in either location, however. They explain this in terms of lower costs of production in the Far East and South East Asia. These cost differentials can offset the tendencies for logistics and technical information exchange to bring component production into close proximity with production or assembly of the final product.

The personal computer industry in Ireland and Scotland seems to have peaked in the 1990s. With the Asian crisis in 1997/98, and changes in exchange rates that reduced the euro and dollar costs of importing from that region, followed by declines in demand in the recession of 2001/02, there have been a number of closures and mergers that have reduced output and employment in the industry. In other examples of successful industries, clustering and economies of agglomeration seem to provide some 'recession-proofing' that enables them to survive over the longer term. Examples include the industrial districts of the Third Italy, and some of the high-technology clusters such as those in Cambridge in England, Montpellier in France and Baden Wurtemberg in Germany. Scott (1998, pp. 146–7) describes these and many other European examples of economic development encouraged by local authorities. In relation to Italy, for example, he writes of 'the strong local governments created by the reforms of the 1970s [that] promote technological innovation, labor training, market research, export activity, information sharing, and so on'.

This Italian example suggests a strong element of localized innovation in the success of the industry. Where firms in the same or closely related industries are co-located and there are economies of agglomeration, and in addition there are high levels of interaction both among the firms and between the firms and research institutions, then these are successful systems of innovation. They may be local or regional, or, if they extend throughout an economy, national systems of innovation (as discussed in Chapter 8). What others have called 'technopoles' are often successful high-technology agglomerations resulting from highly developed systems of innovation.

The successful performance of a group of firms, even over an extended period, is not necessarily the result of those firms being high-technology firms. It should be emphasized that the generally accepted definition of high technology is in terms of R&D. Thus according to OECD definitions, high-technology industries are those that spend more than 5 per cent of their turnover on R&D. However, many firms, and indeed industries, may be innovative without any explicit expenditure on R&D. Broadly, 'innovation' includes the adoption of product, process or organisational technologies that are new to the firm, industry or region, not necessarily new to the world. Where there are groups of firms that are innovative in these ways, they are generally very successful, even though they may be in so-called low-technology industries. The furniture, clothing and textile industrial districts of Italy are illustrative examples. This again shows why we are reluctant to use patent data as the sole measure of innovation. In addition, if we stretch R&D to include design, then the couture subsector of the clothing industry may become consistent with the OECD definition of high technology.

13.8 Summary

We have at various points highlighted the strategic role played by some industries in the economy of a given nation. Most important are those that form the technological core of a country's industrial structure; they are crucial to the improvement of the country's competitive edge with respect to the rest of the world. We have also emphasized the importance of the structural, as opposed to price, elements of competitiveness.

This conclusion has been well stated by the Commission's Directorate-General for Economic and Financial Affairs: 'Although price remains an important element of competitiveness, non-price factors, like the ability to innovate in the presence of rapid technological progress, play a major role in determining the overall level of competitiveness' (CEC, 1993b, p. 17). It follows from this that at least one appropriate way of defining the competitiveness of an economy is on the basis of the performance of its high-technology industries. Together these arguments lead to the conclusion that one expression of improvement in the competitiveness of the EU is improvement in its trade position in high-technology industries.

In terms of high-technology industries, Japan was the most export oriented of OECD countries between 1970 and 1986, and the least open to foreign competition (OECD, 1992). Relying on the above definition of competitiveness, Japan was thus the most competitive of the major OECD economies. OECD (1992) also showed that the high technology competitive position of the United States deteriorated, that Germany remained 'technology competitive', and that both the UK and Italy declined in competitiveness over the period.

The 1990s witnessed the growth of knowledge-based manufacturing and service activities in the world. A statistical analysis reveals that the United States (and US firms) have been able to capitalize much better than the EU (and EU firms) on these new challenges. Investment in equipment (particularly in high-technology equipment) has been more vigorous in the United States than in the EU during the 1990s; most figures on productivity growth suggest that the contribution of ICT capital to growth has been much stronger in the United States than in the EU over the sub-period 1996–2000; the United States enjoys a comfortable trade surplus in high-technology products, whereas the EU has been unable, during and since the 1990s, to lessen significantly its structural trade deficit in this sensitive group of products.

> At a more global level, the emergence of the dynamic Asian economies (DAEs) leaves a smaller proportion of world exports to the traditional exporters of manufactured goods: the EU, but also the United States and Japan. What is of major concern is the inability of the EU as a whole to respond adequately to changing demand patterns in international markets, and in particular to focus satisfactorily on high technology industries.

Websites

Cordis (Community Research and Development Information Service): **http://www.cordis.lu**

Enterprise DG's printed publications: **http://europa.eu.int/comm/enterprise/library/**

Questions

13.1 What are the advantages and disadvantages of using RTCA ratios?

13.2 Compared with US industry, EU industry has lost ground in the second half of the 1990s. Explain how this is related to an unsatisfactory performance in the high-technology (and knowledge-intensive) manufacturing and service activities.

13.3 What does the persistence over time of a low cover rate for high-technology products imply?

13.4 In which industries are the most internationally competitive European firms to be found, and why?

13.5 Is the EU's industrial specialization optimal?

Notes

1 See Turpin (1989).

2 For our purpose, East Asia or the Asian Pacific countries will encompass the six 'dynamic Asian economies', to borrow an expression used by the OECD. These are: South Korea, Taiwan, Hong Kong, Singapore, Thailand and Malaysia.

3 For more on the explanation of the divergence between EU and US productivity rates over the years, see Ark et al. (2003).

4 Since the pace of economic integration has increased substantially in the EU, it is more accurate for the purpose of international comparisons to refer to extra-EU trade rather than intra-EU trade. Intra-EU exports are exports originating from one EU country and the destination of which is another EU partner country. Extra-EU exports are all EU exports directed towards the rest of the world.

5 It should be noted, however, that the degree of openness varies according to the changes in the relative prices, and according to exchange rate movements.

6 Even this classification may be too aggregated. For example, the agricultural machinery industry (NACE

code 321) is composed of many different types of sub-products or segments. All results should thus be interpreted with great caution, since an apparently weak industry for the EU as a whole can conceal many very competitive positions in specific segments of this particular industry as well as in specific countries.

7   See also the high-technology balance of trade and Table 13.13.

8   In the sense of conversion of inventions into marketable products.

9   Recently rediscovered (see McGovern, 1994).

10   See for example Richonnier (1984), Woolcock (1984), Woods (1987), and Sharp and Shearman (1987).

11   Exceptions were found for food, petroleum and stone, clay and glass, where natural resource endowments play a significant role, and also for mature industries such as textiles and clothing.

12   See also Walker's (1979) study for the OECD area, and Mayes, Buxton and Murfin (1990) for the UK.

13   Assisted by appropriate industrial policies.

14   For a detailed discussion of the *Technopoles of the World*, see Castells and Hall (1994); see also Scott (1988).

15   On this theme, see for example the work of Fernand Braudel in France and of Immanuel Wallerstein in the United States.

16   To borrow an expression from Servan-Schreiber (1967).

17   See, for example, Jacobson and Andreosso (1990), for an application of the eclectic framework to the analysis of US MNEs in Ireland.

18   The PLCM has been credited to Vernon, but see also Hirsch (1967) and Hufbauer (1965); for an application of the PLCM to early American investment in Europe (that of Ford in Ireland in 1917), see Jacobson (1977).

19   Among the original aims of the PLCM was to explain the famous Leontief paradox.

20   Walker (1979) in relation to the reaction of Japanese firms to US FDI in the car industry, and Baba (1987) on the response of Japanese firms to US penetration of the Japanese TV market, both provide evidence for this point.

21   For a summary of Vernon's work in this area, from 1966 to the end of the 1970s, see Dicken (1992, pp. 139–42); for a more detailed discussion of Vernon's work, up to 1990, see Eden (1991).

22   This index was first used by Soete (1981).

23   The statistical methodology used in the Galtonian regression model (see Cantwell, 1989, p. 25).

24   Pavitt regressed the RTA index in 1975–80 on the equivalent RTA index in 1963–68, whereas in Cantwell's study, the two RTA distributions relate to the periods 1977–83 and 1963–69.

25   He has developed this idea further in an article entitled 'The international agglomeration of R&D' (1991).

26   What exactly is meant by 'longer periods' is very unclear in Cantwell's study.

27   For more on innovation in low-tech industries, see www.pilotproject.org

Appendix 13.1

High-technology industries as defined by Eurostat, *Statistics in Focus,* *Theme 4, Industry, Trade and Services* **(2003)**

1 Aircraft and spacecraft

2 Office machinery and computers

3 Electrical machinery and apparatus

4 Telecommunications equipment, TV, radio

5 Pharmaceuticals

6 Medical, precision and optical instruments

This list is based on SITC (Standard International Trade Classification). This classification is in essence based upon the R&D intensity of each industry defined as the ratio of R&D expenditure to turnover or output.

Highly R&D-intensive industries as defined by the OECD, *Main Science* *and Technology Indicators,* **no. 1 (2004)**

1 Aerospace

2 Electronics

3 Office machinery and computers

4 Pharmaceuticals

5 Medical, precision and optical instruments

This list is based upon R&D expenditures in various industries.

Appendix 13.2

Product	Export growth EEC-6/US export growth[a]
Aircraft	8.45
Coal and petroleum products	8.06
Tobacco products	5.29
Pharmaceuticals	4.24
Motor vehicles	3.24
Rubber products	3.17
Food and drink	2.45
Mechanical engineering	2.35
Electrical equipment	1.96
Chemicals	1.93
Professional instruments	0.60
Office machinery	0.18
Total manufacturing	2.00

[a] The figure for aircraft, for example, shows that the rate of growth of EC-6 exports over the period was 8.45 times that of US exports in this industry.

Source: Calculated from data in UN, *Commodity Trade Statistics*, various years

Table A13.2 Contribution of US affiliates in Europe to total European and US exports of selected manufactured products, 1957 and 1975

	1957 %	1975 %
Food products	0.6	2.0
Chemicals and allied	3.1	14.2
Primary and fabricated metals	1.8	3.5
Mechanical engineering	2.7	11.4
Electrical equipment	3.4	6.5
Transportation equipment	16.3	12.1
Rubber products	7.4	16.6
Paper and allied products	0.5	6.3
All products	3.8	8.8

Source: Calculated from data in UN, *Commodity Trade Statistics*

CHAPTER 14

Multinational enterprises and globalization

14.1 Learning objectives

The main objectives of this chapter are:

◆ To use the historical background to define and explain globalization in an industrial economic context

◆ To define and explain multinational enterprises in an industrial economic context

◆ To show some recent evidence of the nature of flows of direct investments across borders

◆ To explain the relationships between the global and the local, and how these are mediated by the state, and

◆ To discuss aspects of how multinational enterprises and the EU impact on each other

14.2 Introduction

Many of the key themes of this chapter have already been alluded to at various points in the book, through mention of multinational enterprises (MNEs) and globalization. In this chapter, we elaborate on these themes and consolidate the references in order to provide a reasonably complete discussion of this topic in the context of industrial economics. We should immediately make clear that we do not attempt a thorough review of either of these topics, nor even of the intersection of the two sets of literature covering MNEs and globalization. Any such attempt would take far more space than we have available. Where relevant we will incorporate ideas from disciplines other than economics; both topics, and the intersection between them, have been addressed in great detail by a wide range of disciplines including sociology, international relations, political science and organizational behaviour. However, our main focus will be on the theories and applications already discussed in this book. Thus, issues such as the use of specific theories of the firm (Chapter 4) to attempt to explain MNEs, the application of ideas from economic geography (Chapter 8) to MNEs and their spatial reach, and the importance of technological change and innovation (Chapters 11 and 13) to the globalization of firms are our focus. Issues addressed in other disciplines, such as the power of MNEs relative to that of states, are also important, and in particular in preparation for our discussion of industrial policy in Chapter 15, but they are not central.

14.3 Definitions and history

In this section we explain and discuss a number of concepts. Many of these concepts are defined in different ways by different scholars so some clarity is required from the beginning.

- *Foreign direct investment* (FDI)[1] is where a firm from one country sets up, or takes over another firm's, production facility in another country.[2] Greenfield FDI is the former; FDI by merger or acquisition is the latter. This is direct, as opposed to indirect, investment in that there are physical assets in the host country, in relation to which the firm in the home country has an element of control and ownership. The FDI flow, measured per time period, is from the firm in the home country to the host country. The total value of all foreign-owned assets is the stock of FDI. We can also distinguish between vertical FDI, where the foreign facility is upstream or downstream from the main activity of the firm in its home country, and horizontal FDI where the firm's foreign activity is similar to that in its home country. The difference between FDI and foreign indirect investment, is that with indirect investment the firm or individual in the home country acquires stocks or bonds (that is, paper assets) that are part of a portfolio of investments in a foreign country. Foreign indirect investment is therefore also known as foreign portfolio investment.

- The *multinational enterprise* is a firm that has physical assets in more than one country. An MNE in a manufacturing sector has production facilities in more than one country; a service sector company becomes an MNE if it provides its service or related services in more than one country. What this means is that if a pharmaceutical company manufactures medicines in one country and distributes them in another, it is not usually considered to be an MNE. However, a pharmaceutical distribution company that has distribution networks in two countries is considered to be an MNE.

- *Globalization* is the process whereby countries integrate, reducing the degree of control that states have over actions of economic and other actors that are resident in their territories. As Kogut and Gittelman (2002) put it 'Globalization has come to signify integration among countries, occurring at deep levels of social, political and economic organization'. Stiglitz (2000) agrees that globalization is 'the closer integration of the countries and people of the world' and, in elaborating his definition asserts that 'globalization is powerfully driven by international corporations, which move not only capital and goods across borders but also technology'.

These definitions set the scene for a discussion about the relationship between MNEs and globalization. There are reasonable arguments that both globalization and MNEs have deep historical roots.

14.3.1 Globalization in the past

Rodrik (1997), among others, argues that, 'by many measures, the world economy was possibly even more integrated at the height of the gold standard in the late 19th century than it is now'. He goes on to summarize those measures: international trade, expressed as the ratio of exports to GDP; convergence in commodity prices; international labour migration; capital mobility, measured in terms of 'the share of net capital outflows in GNP'. He shows that each of these was higher, in at least some parts of the world in the late nineteenth century, than today. His argument, drawing on Williamson (1996), is that the current wave of globalization is not necessarily irreversible. If the globalization wave of the nineteenth century ended, at least in part because of the high levels of inequality that that globalization created, then so too can the current wave be reversed.

Two questions arise from Rodrik's view of globalization. First, is the globalization being experienced in recent decades a new phenomenon or have most of its important characteristics already been experienced in previous centuries? And second, is it possible that, either because of its own internal contradictions or because of the conscious decisions of national and international leaders, the globalization trends will be reversed? In answer to the first of these questions, an obvious element differentiating modern globalization from that of the nineteenth century is the MNE. We address the history of MNEs in the next section. Following that we address the extent to which modern globalization is historically unique, based on the presence of MNEs. MNEs also lie at the heart of the answer to the second question; we address this question towards the end of the chapter.

14.3.2 MNEs in the past

Under mercantilism, in the seventeenth and eighteenth centuries, a number of companies were established, given monopoly rights to trade by their respective governments. Among these were the Dutch East India Company, the Dutch West India Company, the British East India Company as well as French, Danish and Swedish East India Companies. Many aspects of the operation of these companies are reminiscent of modern MNEs. They were powerful, accumulated huge amounts of wealth, were in some respects instruments of national policy but in other respects often operated independently of their home states. They issued shares and had shareholders, who were usually rich and powerful businessmen. A fundamental difference between these companies and modern MNEs is that they had national monopoly rights to trade in particular areas of the world. There was competition, which often led to war, between, say, the British and the Dutch companies trading in the same area, but no other British company had the right to trade where the British East India Company traded. By the early nineteenth century, the doctrine of *laissez-faire* was beginning to spread and most of those companies that were still in business lost their monopoly trading rights. Some continued to exist, but more as instruments of government political and military policy than as private companies.

With the end of the international mercantilist trading companies came the rise of what Chandler (1990, p.4) calls the 'modern industrial enterprise'. This was a key element in 'a new form of capitalism' that emerged in the second half of the nineteenth century; what was new was a 'separation of ownership from management'. A combination of new technology (especially in transport and communications), mass marketing and mass production led to these enterprises having to 'recruit teams of salaried managers'. Managers, who were not owners, became the decision makers.

While the international mercantilist trading companies were international from the start, and on the basis of monopoly trading rights, the modern industrial enterprise became international on the basis of national growth and competition. As Chandler (1990, p. 8) puts it:

> Rivalry for market share and profits honed the enterprise's functional and strategic capabilities. These organizational capabilities, in turn, provided an internal dynamic for the continuing growth of the enterprise. In particular, they stimulated its owners and managers to expand into more distant markets in their own country and then to become multinational by moving abroad.

Among the first such firms to set up production facilities abroad was the German firm Siemens. With their headquarters in Berlin, Werner Siemens and his brothers had, by the end of the 1860s, set up factories in St Petersburg in Russia and Woolwich in England. In 1879 the firm opened a factory in Vienna, Austria (Chandler, 1990, p. 464). Another early example is the American company, Singer Sewing Machines, which, having set up in New Jersey in the 1870s, and having achieved full interchangeability of parts by 1883, built 'a factory of comparable size and capacity in Scotland to produce for markets in Europe and the Eastern Hemisphere' (Chandler, 1990, p. 66).

14.3.3 Globalization and MNEs

It is clear that MNEs existed in the second half of the nineteenth century; together with the very high levels of international trade, and capital and labour there was, therefore, also FDI. Does anything differentiate modern globalization from the process of internationalization of capitalism that took place in the nineteenth century? Let us begin with the scale of FDI. Chandler (1990, tables 14 and 15) shows how the numbers of manufacturing operations set up in Britain by American companies grew over the twentieth century. The number grew from an average of just over one per year in the first decades of the century to over five per year in the period 1930 to 1948. In the following 20 years the average went up to nearly 25 per year. Similar growth was experienced in relation to manufacturing operations set up by American companies in Germany over the same period. These numbers reflected the main flows of FDI in that period, with global FDI dominated by flows from the United States to Europe, starting slowly during the late nineteenth century and then growing much more rapidly in the period after the Second World War.

In the period since the 1970s, FDI has grown much more rapidly still. Dicken (2003a, fig. 3.12) shows that, apart from a dip during the recession of the early 1990s, FDI has grown continuously since the beginning of the 1980s. Moreover, it has outpaced the growth in international trade. As Hill (2001) puts it: 'between 1984 and 1998, the total flow of FDI from all countries increased by over 900 percent, while world trade grew by 121 percent, and world output by 34 percent'. Further emphasizing the importance of MNEs is the fact that a significant proportion of international trade is intra-firm; it is around one-third of all trade. Dicken (2003a) estimates that there are now 60,000 parent MNEs controlling 700,000 foreign affiliates.

The vast amount of cross-national economic activity is closely related to technological change in the twentieth century, just as the emergence of the modern industrial enterprise was related to technological change in the nineteenth century. Among the technologies of relevance today are: the transport technologies that have reduced the time and cost of moving goods and people around the world; the information and communication technologies (ICTs) that have brought the means of monitoring business activities in real time, at great distances; computer-based production technologies that have increased speed, control, quality and scale; and new ways of organizing production, including such techniques as just-in-time (JIT), total quality management (TQM) and world class manufacturing (WCM). These have all in various ways driven the process of growth in number and size of MNEs.

The quantitative difference, in terms of the number and significance of MNEs, between the late nineteenth century and the current period is indicative of a qualitative difference. Dicken (2003a) calls the economic integration of the earlier period 'shallow integration' in which the trade was primarily between independent companies in different countries, and in which international capital flows were mainly for foreign portfolio investment. In contrast, 'deep integration', involving international production networks of 'transnational corporations', is becoming more pervasive.[3] Globalization is therefore, as we defined it above, a process; in terms of the extent to which globalization is characterized by MNEs, it is the process of transnational production networks becoming more pervasive. They are not, nor will they ever be, the only way in which production is organized. Thus, although we may agree that there is something historically unique about the globalization we are currently experiencing, we may well conclude that the world economy will never be completely globalized.

Another way of distinguishing qualitatively the period since the middle of the twentieth century is to describe it as characterized by the internationalization of production, in contrast to the previous century's internationalization of exchange.[4] However, there have been different trends in this process of internationalization of production. As we showed in Chapter 13, the American economic predominance in the period after the Second World War was expressed in the emergence of a new international division of labour under the institutional control primarily of MNEs. Kogut and Gittelman (2002) write of American MNEs' extraordinary dominance in global FDI in the decades immediately after the war. However, they also describe the later changes in flows of FDI, such that at the end of the 1980s Japan replaced the United States as the top source country for FDI; in 1999 the UK overtook the United States which, as a result, slipped to third.

Recent trends in global FDI flows are reported in *World Investment Report 2004*, published by the United Nations Conference on Trade and Development (UNCTAD). The trend in these flows was significantly upward in the late 1990s, peaking in 2000. There has been decline since then, though there is some evidence, according to the report, that FDI flows 'bottomed out' in 2003. In relation to the UK, the data show continuing year-on-year declines, with 2002's inward FDI 61 per cent below that of 2001; the equivalent outward FDI decline was 44 per cent. However, this came after very sharp rises in the three years 1998, 1999 and 2000. FDI inflows went from an annual average of around £10 billion in the early 1990s to £79 billion in 2000. The rise in outward flows of FDI from the UK was even steeper, from an average of £20 billion in the early 1990s to a peak of £154 billion in 2000. These trends are shown in Fig. 14.1.

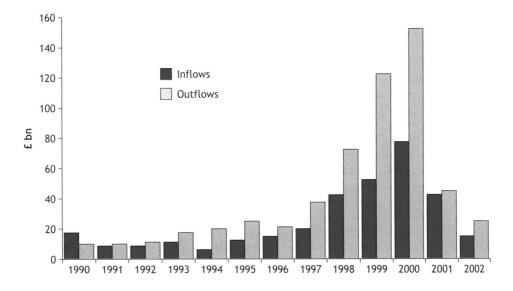

Figure 14.1 UK FDI flows, 1990-2002
Source: UNCTAD, 2004, table 3a

Other trends in global FDI flows are also reflected in the UK data. There is an overall shift towards services, for example. In the UK services as a percentage of total FDI flows have been high throughout the 1990s, averaging over 50 per cent both for inflows and outflows. However, this percentage peaked for both in 2000, when services accounted for 82 per cent of inflows and 87 per cent of outflows. The largest sector within services FDI has been finance, but recently the transport, storage and communications sector (mainly telecommunications) overtook finance in outward FDI from the UK.

We suggested in Chapter 10 (Section 10.5.1) that increasing integration in the EU was a factor in the increase in intra-EU mergers in the late 1990s. Among the interesting conclusions from the FDI data in this context is that the EU has replaced the United States as the main source and target of the UK's FDI flows since 1999. What this suggests is that there are factors other than the common currency encouraging the shift in focus of MNEs. The UK has, so far, opted out of the euro, and is one of three countries (with Denmark and Sweden), which, although they were at the time (1999) full members of the EU, decided to keep their own currencies.

The increasing significance of services in the UK's FDI is a reflection of a much wider trend. For both developing and developed countries, the UNCTAD report (2004) points out that the increase in service-sector FDI can be particularly problematical. Services, it points out, 'are deeply embedded in the social, cultural and political fabric of host societies'. As a result, FDI in services could be even more far-reaching than industrial FDI. Financial services are the most obvious, but services that have traditionally been provided by public utilities, such as transport, telecommunications, water and energy, and even hospitals and education, could, in a completely deregulated context, become susceptible to takeover by MNEs. 'Therefore', UNCTAD concludes, 'national policies matter – not only to attract FDI in services, but also to maximize its benefits and minimize its potential negative impacts'.

This conclusion is consistent with a more general conclusion that Chang (2003) arrives at, concerning policy towards FDI. He emphasizes a number of well-known, but sometimes forgotten facts, to support his case. Among these are that 'the bulk of FDI occurs among the developed countries'; of the small proportion of FDI going to developing countries, the majority goes to the ten biggest; most MNEs continue to have a strong home base;[5] MNEs undertake R&D in their home bases (or close by);[6] among the most successful newly industrializing countries (NICs), some have had very restrictive policies towards inward FDI, and other developing countries that have had pro-MNE policies have not been successful. Chang's conclusions are, first, that globalization remains extremely uneven, and second, that developing countries are not necessarily dependent on MNEs: with the right strategic policies, even if selective and assertive in relation to MNEs, they can achieve successful economic development.

Dicken (2003b) illustrates some other unexpected facts about MNEs. We show some of his data in Table 14.1. He describes a *transnationality index* (TNI) developed by UNCTAD. It is a composite index, made up of the weighted average of three indicators: foreign as a percentage of total sales; foreign as a percentage of total assets; and foreign as a percentage of total employment. The TNI for the 100 firms with the highest scores has been stable over the 1990s. In other words, the world's most global companies have not become more global. The companies with the highest TNIs tend to be from smaller countries.[7] The average TNI for the top 100 companies is just over 50, implying that even these highly transnational companies have nearly half their activities in their home countries. He concludes that there is a great deal of organizational diversity, related to 'the place-specific context in which firms evolve'. The 'country of ownership continues to matter a lot for the behaviour of TNCs'; and '"global" corporations are, indeed, a myth'.

Table 14.1 The top five MNEs ranked by transnationality index and by foreign assets

Rank FA[a]	Company	Country	Rank TNI	Rank TNI	Company	Country	Rank FA
1	General Electric	United States	75	1	Thomson	Canada	57
2	ExxonMobil	United States	22	2	Nestlé	Switzerland	11
3	Shell	UK	43	3	ABB	Switzerland	21
4	General Motors	United States	83	4	Electrolux	Sweden	80
5	Ford	United States	77	5	Holcim	Switzerland	59

[a] Foreign assets

Source: Dicken, 2003b, table 2.1

14.4 MNEs and theories of the firm

The spatial unevenness in the flows of FDI has been there since the beginning. Early attempts at providing explanations came from critics such as Hobson and Marxists such as Lenin.[8] In general, they agreed that once large industrial and financial enterprises had come to dominate in their home markets, then they began to move abroad, sometimes in collusion with other such enterprises. (What Lenin called capitalist associations we might today refer to as strategic alliances.[9]) It follows that the most developed countries are the sources of FDI. The gaining of control over colonies was also part of their focus. They considered this to be the political pillar of the process. It should follow that MNEs' main activities would be in the colonies, but, apart from primary product companies, the bulk of MNEs' activity has always been in other relatively developed countries. This stream of critical analysis of MNEs has continued in the work of scholars such as Sweezy (whose writings began in the 1930s) and Mandel (whose work appeared from the 1960s).[10] Mandel (1975), for example, emphasized technological change, which increased the minimum efficient scale of production to a level of output well beyond that of the home market;[11] high levels of R&D expenditure which required larger output and sales in order to cover the costs; significant international differences in costs of inputs and labour; and protectionism, which reinforced the tendency for firms to set up abroad (to escape tariffs) rather than to simply export their products.[12] Some aspects of the explanations of the radical political economists found their way into more orthodox writings, but their mostly critical perspectives set up barriers to acceptance.

There were many other attempts to explain the rise in MNEs. The direction of the initial surge of FDI gave rise to what became known as the American challenge (Servan-Schreiber, 1967). As a result, explanations concentrated on US firms, and, to varying extents, on cost differences between home and host countries, in other words factors exogenous to the firm. The pioneering work on endogenous aspects of the economics of MNEs has been attributed to Hymer (1976),[13] and among the most influential theories of internationalization was Vernon's product life cycle model (Vernon, 1966).[14] Dunning (1988), building on the work of others, incorporated the earlier theories of internationalization to develop an 'eclectic' framework for explaining why production is sometimes organized internationally.

14.4.1 Hymer and international production

Hymer's was the first explanation of the MNE based on an industrial organization foundation.[15] He showed how barriers to entry like product differentiation and economies of scale, derived from the Bain SCP model,[16] 'allowed firms to enjoy monopolistic advantages which could be profitably exploited in overseas markets' (Kogut and Gittelman, 2002). He focused on explaining why FDI would take place, rather than other types of international operation like equity ownership, licensing, formal cartels or tacit collusion. The crucial difference between FDI and these other types of international operations, as he saw it, was control. There were two reasons for control, the first relating to the exploitation of advantages that the firm had over other firms, and the second to removal of conflict between firms. Having an advantage over other firms – such as technology or 'know-how' – was not sufficient to explain why a firm would undertake FDI; it could, for example, license another firm in the foreign location to manufacture its product. The problem was that if there was not a competitive market for the advantage, its value would not be clear. The market was likely to be monopolistic, or at least oligopolistic, and, under such circumstances the firm possessing the advantage would be likely to value it much more highly than the potential licensee. In such circumstances it would invest directly itself, and expect to extract higher profits than if it agreed a lower value with the licensee. In addition, there was likely to be a general reluctance to licence because of a fear of losing the advantage; any fault in the contractual arrangement would make this a possibility. As Yamin (2000) points out, this part of Hymer's theory rests on the assumption that the potential MNE has a tradeable advantage. (Whereas a patented technology, for example, is tradeable, 'know-how' may not be.) It also confuses, Yamin argues, between an advantage the firm owns, and an advantage it derives from its location. The latter is in this sense similar to an untradeable advantage. If the advantage is not tradeable, then there is no way of distinguishing between the gains from licensing and the gains from FDI.

The second reason for control related to the removal of conflict between firms. What this boils down to is the avoidance of competition in order to increase profits. This is impossible in the context of competitive markets, but where there are imperfect markets – a small number of firms – then collusion, or, preferably, mergers or acquisitions bringing all or most of the production in the industry under one decision maker is possible. This again will only generate supernormal profits where there are barriers to entry (see Chapter 5). As Yamin (2000) points out, what is significant about this explanation for FDI is that it does not rest on any firm-specific advantage. He goes on to point out that, albeit in a modified form, the 'removal of conflict' part of Hymer's theory, although generally ignored, may be more relevant in the current context of international alliances and networks. This, indeed, fits in well with Dicken's (2003a, p. 17) definition of the transnational corporation as a 'firm that has the power to coordinate and control operations in more than one country, even if it does not own them. In fact, TNCs generally do own such assets but they are also... typically involved in a spider's web of collaborative relationships with other legally independent firms across the globe'.

14.4.2 The eclectic paradigm

Building on the work of Hymer and others, Dunning (1977, 1988) developed what he called the 'eclectic framework' or 'eclectic paradigm' for explaining the internationalization of a firm.[17] It is also called the OLI framework because it pulls together three preconditions for a firm to become an MNE: ownership (or firm) specific advantages (O), location (or country) specific advantages (L) and internalization (I).[18] O explains why the firm in question, and not some other firm, produces the good. This includes all the reasons why the firm is better at serving the market – domestic and international – for that good than its competitors. There are two types of ownership-specific advantages. First, there are those which arise from 'the privileged possession of income generating assets', including patents, the capacity to innovate, superior production technique, exclusive access to raw material and markets, and the systems for buying, producing and marketing. Ownership-specific advantages of the second type are those that arise from a firm's superior ability 'to take advantage of the economies of common governance of separate but related activities which might otherwise have been coordinated through external markets'. These include economies of scale and scope, and diminution of the political and financial risks associated with concentration in a single country.

L explains why the firm wishes to produce the good in the host country. L advantages arise from natural differences between countries including differences in endowments of natural resources, differences in input, production and transport costs, and cultural differences between markets requiring adaptation of the product for specific markets. L advantages also arise from artificial differences, particularly those related to government policies on, for example, trade barriers, technical specifications and other second-order barriers.

I explains why the production of a firm's product abroad is done by setting up a subsidiary rather than, for example, licensing some other firm in the host country to produce the good. Here, even more explicitly than in relation to O, Dunning draws on transaction cost analysis. MNEs emerge, he argues, where the 'net production and transaction costs are lower' when the international production and transactions are 'undertaken within internal hierarchies' rather than through the external market.[19] Of the variables which are likely to cause firms to internalize markets, the likelihood and costs of a contractual default and the inability of a contractor to capture the external economies of any transaction are perhaps the two most important (Dunning, 1993, p. 136). The three together (O, L and I) provide a framework for explaining the proliferation and location of subsidiaries of MNEs.

The eclectic framework, as Cantwell (2000) indicates, was 'not in itself another theory. It was instead intended to provide an overall analytical framework for empirical investigations which would draw the attention of the analyst to the most important theories for the problem at hand.' As a framework, it incorporates a number of theories. Dunning is explicit on the extent to which he rests on transaction cost theory. He uses it mainly in the manner of Coase,[20] considering the alternative institutions of market and hierarchy. Internalization occurs, as in Coase, where the transaction costs are thereby minimized. The only difference is that the transaction in the case of the eclectic framework is international. This is, of course, a big difference, and it is in the idea of internalization that Dunning finds the explanation for why a firm will set up a subsidiary rather than contract a firm in the foreign location to produce for it under licence.

For Hymer, rather than transaction cost and internalization, problems in valuing the firm's advantages and the risk of losing these advantages, are reasons for controlling production abroad and avoiding licensing. In his main work, Hymer's theory does not refer to transaction costs. It rests, rather, on market power. 'In his work, Hymer was concerned with the relationship between the efficiency with which production is organised within the firm and the extent of market power and collusion' (Cantwell, 2000).

The eclectic framework incorporates the market power argument. If its market power in a foreign market is a factor in why a firm becomes an MNE, then, from an eclectic framework perspective, it is a result of a combination of O and L advantages. The O advantages are what differentiate the firm or its product. If there are no (or few) other producers of the product in a foreign market then that, all other things being equal, constitutes an advantage that location has over other locations in which there is more competition.

The Hymer market power, and Coasian transaction cost theories are not the only ones that are in some sense present in the eclectic paradigm. Internalization variables, Dunning (2000) states, 'all relate to the production and transaction costs and benefits of different modalities of coordinating multiple economic activities'. These modalities, in particular, are the firm or the market. Explaining where these ideas come from, he continues:

> Here, we draw upon Coasian, Williamsonian, and Penrosian theories of the firm (or the growth of the firm), and, like these scholars, we argue that the higher the net production and transaction

costs (or the lower the net benefits) of using the cross-border markets, relative to those of internal administrative fiat as a mechanism for coordinating resource usage, the greater will be the incentive for firms to engage in international production.

The 'Penrosian' influence and an element of evolutionary theory in Dunning's work are clear from how he treats the firm. Its organizational capabilities, and how they relate to the firm's business environent, are all part of the firm's O advantages. It is not surprising that in Kay's (2000) formulation of a 'resource-based approach to multinational enterprise', at the heart of which is the Penrosian view of the firm and its growth, he draws much of his empirical evidence from Dunning's work.

Additional connections can be made to Penrose: in reflecting on the origins of the eclectic paradigm, Dunning (2000) refers approvingly to Caves' introduction of 'surplus entrepreneurial capacity as a potential ownership advantage of a foreign investor, that clearly was only translated into an actual advantage if and when the foreign investment was made'. The idea that, through familiarization with existing systems, executives both gain knowledge and have their capacity (or capability) less fully utilized, is a fundamental idea in Penrose (1995).[21] It is also the basis of the notion that Dunning attributes to Caves, of surplus entrepreneurial capacity.

As we pointed out in Chapter 4, Penrose (1995) does not accept the transaction cost contrast between firm and market as an adequate foundation for the analysis of economic organization. She emphasizes aspects of the behaviour of firms that are neither market based nor within the firm but within networks of competitors, buyers and suppliers, some with 'special relationships'. A great deal of the work on these types of networks has emphasized their geographical propinquity, as we showed in Chapter 8. In her introduction to the 1995 edition of her book, Penrose twice suggests that real-world developments have required responses in theory to explain them. First, she refers to the MNE as a 'form of organization requiring a different analysis of the nature of the firm and the relation between the firm and the market'. Next, she writes of the development and spread of business networks, which 'may call for a new "theory of the firm" in economics and changed views about the behaviour of markets and the effects of "free market" competition'. We turn in the next section to a consideration of the relationships between these two phenomena: MNEs and local networks.

14.5 Global and local

In Chapter 8, in our discussion of clusters, we raised the question of the role of MNEs. Porter considers local and national factors as key to clusters and therefore originally excluded foreign-owned companies from clusters. We described various criticisms of Porter for this exclusion and Dunning's (1992) suggestion that a new variable be added to Porter's diamond to include MNEs. In this section we consider the questions of the relationship between MNEs and local areas and, more generally, the relationship between the global and the local.

Globalization, as we defined it, is a process of increasing integration. The global economy is not globalized but globalizing. Localization, as explained in Chapter 8, is the tendency for firms to agglomerate. These two processes can and do occur simultaneously. MNEs, for example, can become part of more widely dispersed production networks, parts of which are elements in local agglomerations. Defining globalization differently would give a different result. In a perfectly competitive neoclassical world, without government intervention of any kind, economic activity would be evenly distributed spatially. Leaving aside the contradictions in perfect competition that we pointed out in Chapter 5, it is the market failures, such as externalities, that result in agglomeration. Other departures from perfect competition, like increasing returns to scale and product differentiation, also contribute to an understanding of agglomeration. They are elements of a process whereby, even in the absence of state intervention of any kind, production of a good can become concentrated in a particular place. Let us assume that Firm A defeats all other firms in the market for X because it has lower costs, perhaps because it has higher output and economies of scale. Due to the existence of transportation costs[22] all upstream and downstream production, distribution and other services associated with the production of X are now more likely to be located near to Firm A. Other products using similar inputs – or downstream services – to those of X may now also have an incentive to locate near to Firm A. The result is a concentration of economic activity in that place. And location of ownership of Firm A, it should be emphasized, has no impact on this conclusion. Whether or not Firm A – or the other firms that now have an incentive to locate near to Firm A – is a subsidiary of an MNE makes no difference to the argument.

What Held *et al.* (1999) have called the 'hyperglobalizers' see the world in terms similar to those of the global perfectly competitive model. Thus, for Ohmae (1995): 'today's global economy is genuinely borderless. Information, capital, and innovation flow all over the world at top speed, enabled by technology and fueled by consumers' desires for access to the best and least expensive products'.[23] This suggests that globalization is in some sense complete, that there are no barriers to flows of goods and services, nor to the entry of firms to markets, wherever they happen to be. This is a world in which countries, regions and localities have been homogenized by, for example, global communication and media networks. While not going so far, there are a number of scholars who have argued that, to varying extents, there has been a decline in the power of the state and an increase particularly in the power of MNEs. The neoliberal writers, such as Ohmae, with these kinds of views on globalization, see all this as a positive set of developments; critical writers with similar conceptions of recent developments, such as Gray (1998) and Strange (1996), view it all with trepidation and call for political governance changes to limit the freedom, for example, of capital markets.

We would concur rather with Dicken's (2003a, p. 14) view of a reality that 'is far more complex and messy than many of the grander themes and explanations would have us believe'. Globalization processes, he points out, (ibid., pp. 13–14), *do not occur everywhere in the same way and at the same rate; they are intrinsically geographically uneven, both in their operations and in their outcomes. The particular character of individual countries and of individual localities interacts with the larger-scale processes of change to produce quite specific outcomes.*

Localization and globalization can and do co-exist. Though not attracting mainstream interest in economics, these forces have, as we have seen at various points in this book, not been ignored. However, serious examination of the relationships between them is rare.

In a recent paper, Malmberg (2003) examines 'local milieus and global connections'. He places emphasis on local learning and innovation processes, and shows that despite a great deal of theoretical argument about the importance of these processes in encouraging spatial clustering, the empirical evidence is at best mixed. He goes on to argue that the problem is 'the expectation at the outset that there should be a high magnitude of local inter-firm relations for a cluster to be said to exist – and indeed for a cluster to be dynamic and prosper'. He suggests that industrial clusters may not be confined to local milieus and he proposes dropping the normative assumption that 'the more localized the interaction, the better'. The tendency is for researchers on industrial districts and clusters to feel 'unease' about the role of MNEs; at the same time, researchers on MNEs tend to focus on these firms' operations at a global scale. Too great a gap exists, Malmberg suggests, between these two bodies of work. In the next section we present a case study of the evolution of local relationships between MNEs in the software industry and the local economy in Ireland.

Case study   Software MNEs and the Irish supply base

This case is an evolving one, covering the period from 1985 to 2000. It begins with a brief discussion of Irish industrial policy[24] as a key initiator of the process. It continues with the outline of a success in that policy, namely the establishment in Ireland of a number of subsidiaries of software MNEs. We then discuss the question of the 'embeddedness' of those MNEs in the Irish economy, and, again, policy aimed at encouraging this embeddedness. We then turn to the local firms and consider their relationships to the MNEs. A series of product life cycles then enter the picture, and we show how, in general, the local firms are displaced by subsidiaries of other MNEs as a convergence in complementary and substituting technology changes occurs. We then conclude with a discussion about the ways in which the case illustrates various aspects of the relationship between the global and the local.[25]

It is well known that Irish industrial policy has been based, since the end of the 1950s, on encouraging inward FDI. This policy has in general been argued to be successful, and virtually no professional Irish economists have seriously considered alternatives to this policy in over two decades. There is little doubt, for example, that the rapid inflow of FDI in the second half of the 1990s contributed significantly to the 'Celtic Tiger' phenomenon, an historically unprecedented increase in growth rates and employment.

Case Study (continued)

First phase

Among the successes of the policy of encouraging inward FDI was the establishment in Ireland in the mid-1980s of a number of subsidiaries of software MNEs. These are shown in Table 14.2.

Table 14.2 Software MNEs in Ireland, 1992

Company	World ranking	World revenues $m	Revenue from international sales %
Microsoft	1	3252	55
Lotus	2	900	50
Borland	5	463	62
Symantec	8	218	33
Quarterdeck	17	52	19
Wordstar	26	34	47
Claris	n/a	155	43

Source: Jacobson and O'Sullivan, 1994

These firms were among the industry leaders in the world at the time. Since then a number of them have ceased to exist and the extent to which Microsoft dominates has increased substantially. Other changes since then include the merging of IBM and Lotus, the disappearance or acquisition of a number of the smaller companies such as Wordstar and Quarterdeck, and new arrivals such as Digital and Oracle.

Having arrived in Ireland, these software companies had an important supply decision to make, namely whether to outsource their software manuals or print them themselves. If they decided to outsource them, there was another decision to be made, namely whether to obtain them from existing manual-printing companies in Britain or Belgium, or to try to source them locally. The problem in relation to local sourcing was that there were no appropriate high-quality manual printers in Ireland.

For reasons relating to their own perceptions of their core organizational capabilities, the software companies decided to outsource manual printing. It should be pointed out that in Ireland at the time, the incentives offered by the state focused on manufacturing companies;[26] software development was not seen as manufacturing. In order to obtain these incentives the software MNEs duplicated the discs in their Dublin 'factories'. Any 'manufacturing' was undesirable, as far as the software MNEs were concerned, but

Case Study (continued)

given the Irish policy environment it was undertaken as a 'necessary evil'. Choosing disc duplicating rather than manual printing – which would also have satisfied the manufacturing requirement – revealed their preference for disc duplicating. It was in some sense closer to their core capability than printing.

The focus on manufacturing was, from the point of view of the state, employment based. Although the policy changed within a few years, in the mid-1980s inadequate attention was paid to labour market issues. Computer science, software engineering and electronics were all available as courses in the Irish universities, but only to relatively small numbers of students. Rapid expansion of these and other programmes began in all Irish universities in the late 1980s. Thus the software MNEs were undertaking operations that, for most of their employees, were relatively low-skilled. Other than grants and low tax rates, an English-speaking population and, at the time, relatively low wage levels, there were no obvious long-run factors in the attractions of Ireland as a location. English is spoken in other places, and wages were susceptible to rises (and did); the only location-specific advantages, therefore, were artificial ones that could be changed with a change in state policy. In other words, these software MNEs do not, at first sight, appear to have been particularly deeply embedded in the Irish economy.

For agglomerative reasons, the software MNEs decided to outsource the manuals locally. Most of the need for proximity at the time related to control: companies needed to be able to monitor manual production closely. They also needed high security of supply, which, it was believed, could better be achieved through local suppliers.

Another factor in the decision to source locally was an Irish government policy innovation. While from the late 1950s until the mid-1980s the focus was almost exclusively on the encouragement of inward FDI, the failure of the policy to significantly reduce unemployment resulted in a slight change of focus. A National Linkage Programme (NLP) was introduced in 1985. In this the agency responsible for encouraging inward FDI, the Industrial Development Authority (IDA) attempted to encourage MNEs to buy some of their inputs from local suppliers. It was hoped that this would help to embed the subsidiaries of the MNEs more firmly into the Irish economy.

Within two or three years, nine companies had set up software manual-printing operations, mainly in Dublin, to supply the software MNEs. Some of these were new start-ups, others were additional operations set up by existing printing companies. One, Donnelley, was a subsidiary of a large American printing company; all the rest were indigenous companies. None of the manual printers, during this early phase and up to about 1990, had other than arm's-length relationships with any of the software MNEs. Total revenues from software manual sales in Ireland grew from under IR£4 million in 1984 to over IR£45 million in 1990.

Case Study (continued)

Second phase

During the second phase in the evolution of these two groups of firms and the relationships between them, there were two sets of technological changes and two sets of consequences. The first set was technological changes that were 'hard'; these included the introduction of the most advanced printing machinery, sophisticated (and expensive) optical character readers (OCRs) to ensure that all the manuals were fault-free, and telecommunications innovations such as electronic data interchange (EDI) that would enable customers (software MNEs) to download manuals for printing.

Second, and closely related to the hard changes, were organizational innovations such as just-in-time (JIT) and total quality management (TQM). The introduction of both the hard technological changes and the organizational innovations were demanded by the software MNEs. These changes became conditions which, if not fulfilled, would result in the discontinuation of orders.

Among the results was a cementing of relations between particular software MNEs and particular manual printers. Microsoft, for example, gave 'preferred supplier' status to four of the smaller manual printers in the industry. Preferred suppliers were the only manual printers that a software MNE dealt with; they eventually obtained 'ship-to-stock' status, meaning that there was no monitoring by the software MNE of the manual printer's output. The specific EDI links, and the JIT relationship, all intensified the relationship. The printer, it is important to emphasize, had no other market. In a reflection of very high asset specificity, the equipment that the manual printers bought could be used for nothing other than manuals. The second result is thus that many of the manual printers became trapped in a monopsonistic relationship with their customer company. This happened to some of Microsoft's suppliers, for example Mount Salus Press.

The two sets of organizational innovations are also interrelated. The preferred suppliers of Microsoft, for example, were forced to provide output on a JIT basis. This could mean anything from twice daily to once weekly deliveries. It was impossible for these small firms (average employment in the Microsoft four was just over 100) to impose JIT delivery on their own suppliers, who were mostly local wholesalers of imported paper and other raw materials, so in practice they produced for stock and stored manuals until they were needed. JIT meant just-in-time delivery for the MNE, but for the manual printer it meant a shift in warehousing and inventory costs from the customer to the supplier.

During this second phase, too, some of the manual printers began to diversify, either internally or through alliances with other companies. They saw a dependence on

Case Study (continued)

printing as too risky and began to move into disc duplication, packaging and logistics. However, this was impossible for those with narrow, printing-specific skills, and an absence of entrepreneurial management.

Third phase

During 1995 there was a sea change in the market facing the manual printers. With the introduction of Microsoft's Windows 95, software and software manuals began to be supplied on CD-ROMs. The preferred supplier relationship guaranteed three months of orders; this was basically a three-month notice period of discontinuation of custom. There was a rapid decline in the market for software manuals, and a rapid rise in the market for CD-ROMs.

In this third phase, too, it was no longer necessary for the software MNEs to undertake any manufacturing operations. They were at last able to retract into their core competences. By this time there had been a sharp increase in the number of graduates in areas related to the interests of the software companies, including software and technical language translation. Later in this third phase, by around 2001, there was a tightening in this labour market and the relatively low wage levels increased.

Retraction into their core competences meant, for companies such as Microsoft, developing relationships with 'turnkey' companies. These are 'first-tier' suppliers that undertake to organize all the other suppliers along the supply chain so that Microsoft need deal only with one company. Turnkey companies are often also logistics companies that may, in addition, undertake some manufacturing operations in the final stages, for example packaging or shrink-wrapping all the parts provided by the other suppliers (CD-ROM, plastic case, booklet and so forth).

Partly through the IDA and partly through existing strategic alliances between MNEs, five CD-ROM pressing companies set up subsidiaries in Ireland in the mid-1990s (Table 14.3).

Table 14.3 CD-ROM pressing companies, home country and set-up year in Ireland

Company	Home country	Set-up year in Ireland
Sonopress	Germany	1994
Kao	Japan	1993
MPO	France	1996
Maxell	Japan	1996
Saturn	Canada	1995

Case Study (continued)

The output of these CD-ROM companies, as had that of the manual printing companies less than ten years earlier, grew rapidly. Also similar to the manual printers, they developed strategic relationships – in some cases international – with particular software companies. Figure 14.2 provides an illustration, for Microsoft, of the type of tiered supply network through which the production and distribution of software was organised in Ireland during the second half of the 1990s.

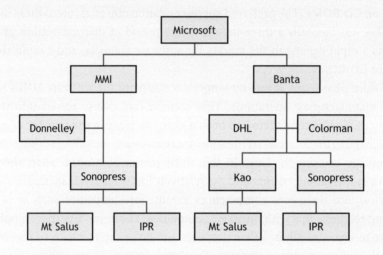

Figure 14.2 Microsoft's network of software production and distribution, Ireland, 1995–2000

Figure 14.2 shows that the two first-tier, turnkey companies were MMI (Modus Media International) and Banta. Each organized CD-ROM pressing, leaflet printing, packaging and distribution with slightly different companies, though with substantial overlaps. Particular note should be taken of Mount Salus Press. The management of this company, on realizing that the old software manual market was disappearing, in 1995 downsized to less than half its original size, moved to a cheaper premises outside Dublin, and switched its printing machinery to high-speed, multi-colour, small-size printing so as to be able to print the leaflets that are inserted into the CD-ROM's plastic case. Staying within its own core competences, the firm managed to hold on to its changing market. Its final customer was the same, but it no longer dealt with Microsoft as it was organized in supply networks by MMI and Banta.

In more recent developments, MMI expanded in Ireland in 2001, and an American company, Zomax, acquired Kao in Europe. More seriously for the CD-ROM pressing industry in Ireland, there was an internationalization of sourcing so that, for example, MPO in France began to supply the French market removing one of Ireland's export

Case Study (continued)

markets. Ultimately, the most serious implication for the CD-ROM industry is its displacement by the next phase in the evolution of this subsector: the supply of software and software manuals by internet. In mid-2001, Hitachi–Maxell announced the closure of its Dublin CD-ROM plant.

The two waves or product life cycles are shown in Fig. 14.3.

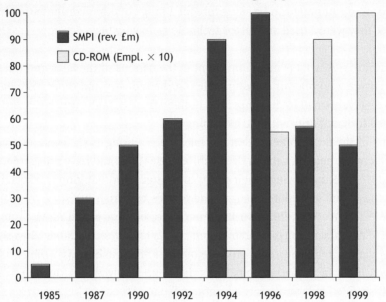

Figure 14.3 The life cycles of the software manual-printing industry and CD-ROM pressing, Ireland, 1985-99
Source: Forfas Ireland database

The software manual-printing industry has declined sharply since its peak in 1995. CD-ROM pressing has also peaked – though it is not shown in the diagram – and is now declining. The next method for distributing software – downloading from the web – is not located in Ireland, mainly because of inadequacy of telecommunications infrastructure.

Discussion

The supply system for the software MNEs in Ireland evolved from a simple open market of a small number of small, indigenous manual printers supplying manuals locally to a similar number of MNE subsidiaries, to a number of complex, organized groupings of CD-ROM pressing MNEs, indigenous printers, logistics companies and turnkey companies. Within these organized groupings there were also subsets of strategic alliances. The small indigenous firms were shifted outward in terms of their

Case Study (continued)

relationships to the final MNE customer, but some of them, for example Mount Salus Press, managed to hold on to their changing market.

How did the shift from indigenous suppliers to MNE suppliers take place so rapidly? As suggested above, there was a convergence in complementary and substitute technologies. CD-ROMs are both a substitute and a complement. They are both a complement to computers and a substitute for a range of other computer media. At the same time they were a tried and tested technology, having been developed in the music industry.

For our purposes what is most important in the context of the local and the global is that there were a number of existing MNEs in the industry and there were barriers to entry for relatively small Irish companies, both because of high entry costs and because of the need for familiarity with the technology.

In terms of the developments that did take place among Irish firms, it is clear that some of them learned from their relationships with MNEs and have prospered, in some cases like Mount Salus through their ability to change with changing markets, in others through the ability to initiate change. There were two Irish logistics companies, for example, Walsh Western and Irish Express Cargo, both of which moved into various elements of manufacturing while remaining mainly logistics companies. In a sense they leveraged their warehousing space to develop their relationships with their customers.

However, many of the indigenous firms that were involved in supplying to the software MNEs gained only temporary advantage. Some of them no longer exist and others have returned to their traditional markets in the printing industry. Ultimately, it is clear that opportunities for collaborative horizontal development among Irish firms have not been taken. For example, when the manual printers moved into TQM, and had to buy OCRs in order to do so, the capacity of the OCRs was beyond what any one of the firms needed. It was clearly in their interest to set up some kind of joint venture to own the OCRs and provide the quality control services that the machines provided to all of them. Asked in interview why they had not done this, they replied that the main reason was that there was a strong tendency for them to 'keep their cards close to their chests'. In other words the norms of Irish business behaviour seemed to preclude trust and co-operation, even where this was in the firms' collective interest. We can call these 'institutional barriers to local development'.

Many of the MNEs have also come and gone. The inconsistent developments of technology and organizations – and the messy lack of general pattern alluded to by Dicken – have resulted in some of the MNEs, such as Microsoft, maintaining and even deepening their presence in Ireland. Others, such as Maxell and Kodak (which had a brief collaboration with Matsushita in a CD-ROM plant) came and went. Irish state policy

Case Study (continued)

remains of deep significance to these decisions of MNEs, but the industry and product life cycles are just as important.

To return to Malmberg (2003), we have examined more or less simultaneously the behaviour of MNEs and of local networks. We have shown that they can and do work together, but in terms of delimited time scales and in terms of very specific technologies. While the Irish base has been a 'sticky place' for 20 years for some of the software MNEs, in this sector there is little evidence of the local supply base constituting a serious means of embedding these firms into the Irish economy. In the end, if the artificial location-specific advantages are removed – for example through EU agreements on harmonized tax rates – then the 'slippery space' of globalization may facilitate a move for these firms away from Ireland.[27]

Among the explanations for this may be the core–periphery tendencies alluded to in Chapter 8. These are the tendencies for skilled labour and capital to locate in central locations, usually large markets, by so doing denuding peripheral locations of their resources.[28]

14.6 MNEs and European integration

The predominance of American – and, in some industries, Japanese – MNEs was related to the technology gap argument (discussed in Chapters 11 and 13). In relation to the machine tool industry, for example, we showed in Chapter 11 that as a result of acquisitions by Japanese MNEs, the industry in the UK became more or less foreign owned. We pointed out Walker's (1993) prediction that the future of the industry in the UK would depend on the behaviour of Japanese MNEs. In fact the period since then has brought significant changes in overall trends, and the emergence of a number of major European MNEs of global significance. Among these, we have given examples of companies in the chemical and pharmaceutical industries (such as GlaxoSmithKline) and in telecommunications (Deutsche Telecom). Kogut and Gittelman (2002) point out that technology-intensive, oligopolistic industries in the United States are those in which foreign-owned MNEs are particularly strong; 'in the US chemical/pharmaceutical industry, affiliates of foreign-owned companies account for about one-third of total US sales and assets and 40 per cent of industry employment'. Most of this is accounted for by EU MNEs in an interesting reversal of a situation that, as we explained in Chapter 13, was seen in Europe in the 1960s and 1970s as the 'American challenge'.

From a European point of view, globalization and its impact on the nature of the triad and the performance of Europe within that triad, give mixed results. On the one hand there is the increasing integration within Europe that we identified in Chapter 10. This seems to be enhanced by intra-EU consolidation by European MNEs. A combination of EU regulation and the activities of firms such as Deutsche Telecom have made this particularly evident in the telecommunications sector. On the other hand, in other high-technology sectors, Chapters 11 and 13 provide evidence of a continuing lag in European high-technology performance behind that of Japan and the United States. The importance of this lag may be tempered somewhat by our critique (in Chapter 11) of the ways in which technology is measured. There are, as we argued, unmeasured (and probably unmeasurable) innovations in many non high-technology industries. (Figure 13.6 shows that the EU has continued in recent decades to outperform the United States in medium-high technology industries such as electrical machinery, motor vehicles, chemicals excluding pharmaceuticals, and railroad and transport equipment.)

Dunning has for many years had an interest in European integration and in the use of the eclectic framework for examining the position of MNEs in Europe. The increasing significance of MNEs in Europe, particularly since the early 1960s, raised the possibility of an interrelationship with European economic integration (what Dunning called 'regional integration'). Somewhat confusingly, in the light of such integration concepts at the corporate level as vertical and horizontal integration, Dunning referred to 'corporate integration' as 'the causes and effects of cross-border activities by and within multinational enterprises' (Dunning, 1988). Dunning's regional integration is the integration of the economies of different countries, arising from formal agreements to remove trade and other barriers – those defined above as barriers of the second order. Although this type of integration involves increasing the extent to which the group of economies together constitute a region, in general it is referred to in the literature as *international (or European) economic integration*. The cross-border activities of MNEs, either internally or with other firms, may both result from and have an impact on the process of removing barriers between economies. This type of integration is not corporate in the sense that it occurs only within a firm, and is more appropriately called *international industrial integration*.[29]

Dunning pointed out that there had 'been few attempts systematically to analyze the interaction between the two kinds of integration', and proceeded to provide a first pass at just such an analysis (Dunning, 1988, ch. 11).[30] In doing so he distinguished between EC and non-EC firms and concluded that, in general, industrial integration by EC firms *does* aid European integration, where such firms are 'prompted to overcome structural market distortions and transactional markets failure'. However, industrial integration by non-EC firms may or may not enhance European integration. There is a danger, for example, 'of Europe moving down a path towards a decreasing technological capability and a worsening international competitive position' as a result of the shift of high-value parts of the production process from Europe to the United States (Dunning, 1988, p. 300) or Japan (Jacobson and Andréosso, 1988). The study by Hamill (1992) shows that of the total value of acquisitions in the EC in 1989 and 1990, US firms accounted for the highest proportion (19 per cent). He concluded with the warning that 'the main beneficiaries of the Single European Market may not be European companies, consumers or workers, but rather non-EC firms which have consolidated their position in the EC through MAAs [mergers, acquisitions and strategic alliances]'.

In other work, Dunning (1993) has contributed further to the systematic analysis of the relationship between the two types of integration. Focusing in different chapters on Japanese, European and US MNEs, and multinational investment in general in the EU, he identifies different effects over time as the EU has developed.[31] He shows that in the early years of integration in Europe, the competitiveness of US MNEs improved to a greater extent than did that of European MNEs, and was exploited by the US firms through FDI in Europe. Over time, the competitive stimulus of the US presence in Europe, together with European integration, 'led to an improvement of ownership advantages of European companies which, by the late 1970s, were increasingly penetrating the US market through direct investment'. The preparations for, and implementation of, Europe 1992 have had two main consequences for non-EU direct investment. First, there has been an intensification of the fear of 'Fortress Europe' – the fear that the EU will become increasingly protectionist, favouring production within the Union; and second, there has been a recognition of the increasing opportunities arising from the completion of the internal market. From the perspective of non-EU MNEs, these underlie 'the astonishingly rapid growth of Europe's L advantages as a production base, for manufacturing and service industry' (Dunning, 1993, p. 159). Together these have resulted in a growth of FDI from both the United States and Japan. FDI into the EU from both the United States and Japan has grown more rapidly than exports from either country.

A concern that the growth of non-EU FDI into Europe might in some way weaken the European economy is offset by the fact that European FDI into the United States has grown even more rapidly than that from the United States into the EU. By 1990, the 'ratio of the US capital stake in the EC to that of the EC stake in the US had fallen to 0.75' (Dunning, 1993, p. 186). This does not, however, remove the need for concern and analysis of the strategic implications of FDI. We would agree with Dunning that it is difficult to generalize. The policy implications will differ, depending on such factors as 'the type of inward direct investment, the extent of the existing foreign investment stake, the sectors in which it is made, the conditions under which it is made, and the home and host countries involved' (Dunning, 1993, p. 382).

More recent data show that there has been more intense integration through intra-EU cross-border mergers and acquisitions (M&As) and FDI. This has even included FDI from the UK to the EU and from the EU to the UK, despite the UK not being in the eurozone. Moreover, the United States, so dominant in FDI flows in the decades immediately after the Second World War, has in various years since 1990 been overtaken by Japan and the UK.

The prognosis for the interrelationship between European economic and industrial integration depends on developments at two levels: first, the policies and capabilities of European firms relative to those of other countries; and second, the nature of the collaborative programmes, and competition, merger, tax, technology, trade and investment policies introduced by the EU, at the EU level (Dunning, 1988, p. 303; see also Dunning, 1992, 1993; Yannopoulos, 1992).

The study of globalization and European integration has recently been deepened by Weber (2001) and his colleagues. What they show is that in various ways the EU is an example of globalization, both internally and externally. Internally it provides some sense of what results from intense levels of the integration processes that we have defined as the kernel of globalization. Externally the EU is now in itself an actor in the global context. As such, no study of globalization can omit the EU. We have, in fact, discussed many aspects of the integration of the EU internally in different parts of this book. We discuss the EU as a global actor with separate policies, in the context of a discussion of industrial policies in general, in the next chapter.

14.7 Summary

In this chapter we have explained some key aspects of globalization and MNEs. We have avoided many of the polemical conclusions about either the advantages of globalization that its supporters claim, or the failings that its detractors emphasize. Rather we have tried to maintain an academic distance, presenting data and summarizing the arguments of others. We have argued that MNEs do in fact characterize the modern period of globalization and distinguish it, through their volume and scale, from previous periods. However, we have also agreed with Dicken and Chang, among others, that the 'global-ness' – to use Dickens' phrase – of so-called global companies is limited. These companies are, in general, not global but national.

The global and the MNEs do not exist on a plane separate from the real world of localities. Using a case study from Ireland we have shown how MNEs interact with the local, attempting to identify simultaneously how the local and the global affect each other. The global – in this context the software MNEs – set up in Ireland in response primarily to artificial location-specific advantages. They have interacted with many local firms, some of which have learned from the experience, in a process more or less determined by the life cycle of the producer goods that are in their supply chains.

Finally, we have examined the relationship between MNEs and European integration. There is no such set relationship. It varies over time and by industry. What we have emphasized is the need to have an agreed set of terms for describing the various processes that interact when intra-national, intra-EU, and EU–US and EU–Japanese economic transactions take place. The EU, as Weber (2001) suggests, can constitute a model, albeit an extreme one, for studying globalization.

Websites

The most important website for data on FDI and other aspects of globalization and MNEs, is that of UNCTAD at **http://www.unctad.org**

There are many polemical sites on globalization. While many of them are enjoyable and interesting, they are mostly not relevant in the context of the study of industrial economics. Nevertheless, we suggest the following:

Globalisation Guide: **http://www.globalisationguide.org/**. This is mostly critical but it provides links to many other relevant websites.

International Monetary Fund: **http://www.imf.org**

World Bank **http://www.worldbank.org**

World Trade Organization: **http://www.wto.org**

A number of academics provide their articles online at their own websites. For example, Dani Rodrick, who has written many articles and books of relevance for this chapter, has some of them downloadable at **http://ksghome.harvard.edu/~drodrik/**

For other examples of websites providing serious academic research on globalization, MNEs and policy, see the following:

University of California, Los Angeles Center for Globalization and Policy Research: **http://www.sppsr.ucla.edu/cgpr**

University of California, Santa Cruz Center for Global, International and Regional Studies: **http://repositories.cdlib.org/cgirs/**

London School of Economics Centre for the Study of Global Governance: **http://www.lse.ac.uk/Depts/global/** (see also **http://www.lse.ac.uk/collections/global DimensionsLibrary/**)

Leverhume Centre for Globalisation and Economic Policy at the University of Nottingham: **http://www.nottingham.ac.uk/economics/leverhulme/research_papers/**

Questions

14.1 In what senses can it be argued that the current processes of globalization are similar to, and in what senses different from, the period of trade growth in the late nineteenth century?

14.2 What are MNEs and how do they differ from the great mercantilist trading companies? How do they differ from the MNEs of the late nineteenth and early twentieth centuries?

14.3 Discuss the interaction of the global and the local, using an example of your own to illustrate.

14.4 In the Irish case study, what were the key factors encouraging, and discouraging, cooperation between the local firms and the MNEs?

14.5 How has the impact of MNEs on the EU changed over time?

Notes

1 This paragraph draws on Shenkar and Luo (2004, ch. 3). See also Hill (2001, ch. 5).

2 Note that this definition refers to manufacturing FDI. There is also FDI in the service sector, where, for example, an international bank sets up its own – or takes over another firm's – branch bank in another country.

3 Kogut and Gittelman (2002) express it more directly: 'what sets the recent phase of internationalization apart from past waves is that it is primarily being driven by foreign direct investment (FDI) rather than by arm's-length trade'.

4 See Chapter 13, Section 13.6.

5 According to Dicken (2003b), the world's leading MNEs 'still retain more than 50 per cent of their activities in their home country'.

6 US firms do some of their R&D in Canada, and EU firms do nearly all their R&D in the EU, but not necessarily in their national home base.

7 This is not surprising. If there are increasing returns to scale then in order for a firm to derive the benefits, it must grow; for a large company in a small country this means having to have a higher proportion of its activities abroad than would an equivalent company in a large country.

8 Lenin's famous *Imperialism, the Highest Stage of Capitalism* is available on the web at http://www.marxists.org/archive/lenin/by-title.htm

9 It should be emphasized that the collusion that Lenin and others identified in the late nineteenth and early twentieth centuries would today be illegal.

10 A brief discussion of 'radical political economy', with appropriate links, can be found at http://cepa.newschool.edu/het/schools/neomarx.htm

11 Note that by itself this could result in expansion in the home country and growth of exports. Together with the other factors, however, it is likely to result in FDI.

12 Mandel (1975, p.320) points out that US and British companies 'established numerous branches within the EEC in order to protect their share of the market from the effects of the common EEC tariff on exports from third countries'.

13 Hymer (1976) is a reprint of his influential 1960 dissertation.

14 Vernon's product life cycle model is explained in Chapter 13, Section 13.6.

15 In addition to Hymer (1976), we are using three sources for our summary of Hymer's work: Kogut and Gittelman (2002), Kumar (2002) and Yamin (2000).

16 See Chapter 2, Section 2.2.1.

17 Dunning (2000) himself suggests that the ownership and location components arose from his own work. He mentions a paper by J.C. McManus as his first source of the internalization idea, but adds that he was also influenced by conversations with Buckley and Casson at Reading University, and Lundgren at Uppsala in Sweden, in formulating the eclectic paradigm.

18 Our description of Dunning's framework is based on Dunning (1993).

19 Note the difference between the O advantages arising from the superior ability to take advantage of the economies of common governance and the I advantages which are those economies of common governance themselves.

20 See Chapter 4, Section 4.5.

21 For more on Penrose, see Chapter 4, Sections 4.5 and 4.6.

22 Or other economies of agglomeration.

23 Quoted in Dicken (2003a, p. 11).

24 Which is elaborated in Chapter 15.

25 The early part of the story can be found in Jacobson and O'Sullivan (1994) and Jacobson and Mottiar (1999).

26 This is no longer the case; under EU rules the corporate profit tax rate (12.5 per cent), for example, is now the same for all companies, manufacturing and service sectors, MNEs and indigenous firms.

27 The allusion here is to the article 'Sticky places in slippery space' by Markusen (1996).

28 Most famous for this view is Myrdal (1957), who saw, rather than a neoclassical equilibrium, a process of cumulative causation in which prosperous parts of the world become richer, and those that are less economically successful become poorer.

29 For a related discussion on the double process of spatial and industrial integration, see Andréosso and Jacobson (1991).

30 There has been, as Dunning acknowledged, some work in this area. For some reason, he omitted Dunning and Robson (1987). See also, Jacobson and Andréosso (1990), and Andréosso and Jacobson (1991).

31 This paragraph draws on Dunning (1993), especially chs 6 and 7.

CHAPTER 15

Aspects of industrial policy

15.1 Learning objectives

The main objectives of this chapter are:

- To explain the rationale for government intervention in industrial affairs

- To discuss the various types of industrial policy

- To venture into the debate of public versus private firms, and depict the trends in terms of privatization, and

- To review briefly industrial policy in other countries, including the United States, Japan and a number of newly industrialized Asian countries

15.2 Why do governments intervene?

State intervention in economic activity can be traced as far back as the time of the Egyptian pharaohs. The nature of intervention has of course changed over time. Industrial policy, in particular, is a much more recent phenomenon. By industrial policy we mean something close to Johnson's definition (1984, p. 8): 'Industrial policy means the initiation and coordination of governmental activities to leverage upward the productivity and competitiveness of the whole economy and of particular industries in it.' Industrial policy can refer to all activities of public authorities that affect, directly or indirectly, the performance (for example, productivity, profitability, international competitiveness) of the manufacturing and service sectors.[1]

The expressions 'industrial strategy', launched in the early 1970s in Canada (Grant, 1989), and *Strukturpolitik*, officially used in the German language, are euphemisms aimed at subduing objection to the interventionist element. That there is a range of views on how interventionist industrial policy might be is clear from Harrop's (1989, p. 86) definition: 'Industrial policy creates the condition in which industry can flourish and its main concern has been to create a competitive and efficient industrial structure.' Johnson's definition allows for much more active intervention than Harrop's; Johnson's suggests, for example, policies aimed at particular industries, whereas Harrop's implies only a general policy environment.

These are just two out of a whole range of views. One reason for the diversity of views is that the notion of industrial policy is a confusion of three types of policies, as described by Cohen (1995):[2]

- 'Policies designed to shape the environment in which the company operates'. This is part of industrial policy because, as we already mentioned in relation to Johnson's definition, macroeconomic and macro-social policies affect industrial activity.

- 'Sectoral policies (structuring, promotion of high tech industries, aid to lame ducks)'.

- 'The strategy of the shareholding state'.

We expand on this point, providing a taxonomy of industrial policy types, but first, let us raise the question as to why governments might intervene at all.

The explanations for state intervention can be discussed under four main headings: *market failure, paternalist intervention, transaction cost,* and *new growth theories*. The prominence taken by the latter in economic thinking since the mid-1980s (see Chapter 11, Section 11.4) reinforces the justification for state intervention. Although this can be related to the traditional market failure argument – many firms are too small to engage in costly research programmes, for example – we treat this element on its own.

In neoclassical theory, only perfect competition, and only at long-run equilibrium, provides a situation in which the economic welfare of all the main interests in society are optimized. In all other situations (and, if our critique of perfect competition is correct, this means in all situations) at least one of the parties in the economy is at a less than optimal level of welfare. Most of the economics literature on state intervention is concerned with this failure of the market mechanism to achieve Pareto optimality.[3] There are other theories of state intervention, and, in addition to the market failure theory, we also discuss the paternalist and transaction cost theories of state intervention. In this chapter, we are concerned directly with a general perspective on state intervention as a backdrop to industrial policy in particular.

15.2.1 Market failure

The possibility of market failure provides the major justification for government intervention in neoclassical economics. Market failure refers to situations where the market fails to achieve the allocative efficiency standard and where it leads to *misallocation* of resources. Market failure is therefore likely to occur in markets that are non Pareto efficient. This is the case for imperfect markets, public goods and incomplete markets. The emphasis here is on imperfect markets.[4] Imperfect markets are therefore markets other than those in which the conditions of perfect competition apply. According to de Bandt (1995), the multiplicity of exceptions to the smooth functioning of markets justifies government intervention in industry. Imperfect markets are characterized by varying degrees of oligopolistic and monopolistic conditions. Examples of market failure include:

◆ The existence of externalities

◆ Prohibitively large sums of capital needed to start production or to engage in R&D (sunk costs)

◆ The existence of increasing returns to scale

◆ Information imperfections.

Externalities

In its narrowest sense, the concept of external economies (and diseconomies) refers to the effect the production of a good or service has on the production or consumption of another good or service. More broadly, externalities arise when the benefits and costs of a given economic activity at the level of the individual differ from those at the level of society. Externalities can be external economies (also called *benefit externalities*) or external diseconomies (also called *cost externalities*). For example, a firm investing in R&D may derive direct benefits from this investment; if the R&D results in a better way of producing its product, it will have reduced its costs. Now other firms, close to the first one – geographically and/or sectorally – learn about the improvements.[5] Without having spent any money on the R&D, the other firms derive some of the benefits; these are benefit externalities. This example provides one of the explanations for the success of industrial districts, discussed in Chapter 8: the community is so integrated that there are external economies to all improvements any of the firms introduce.

What have externalities to do with state intervention? If a private economic activity can have implications – positive or negative – for a wider community, and if it is difficult or impossible for markets to cost these implications, then state intervention may be appropriate. The state can, for example, ensure that the actions inducing cost externalities are reduced, by charging for them. For instance, let us take the case of pollution, the most common example of cost externalities. Before government intervention, the polluter does not pay to remove these negative consequences of production. In this case, there may be zero costs to the individual polluter (if, for example, he or she does not live in the area where the factory is), but substantial costs to society. Government can remedy this market failure by imposing a tax on polluting activities ('polluter pays' principle). Ideas can also, in a sense, pollute. Let us take, for instance, a clothing industrial district, in which one firm introduces a new design for a shirt, convinced that it is going to be the latest fashion. Many other firms hear about, and copy, the new design. If it succeeds, there will have been benefit externalities; if it fails, however, and no consumers buy the product, then there will have been cost externalities.

However, because so many goods have externalities, both negative (as in the case of pollution) and positive (for example, where an apiary is located adjacent to an apple orchard), it is difficult to be precise about what the state can do to bring private and social costs into line with one another. On the one hand this argument can be used to oppose all state intervention to offset externalities (Friedman, 1962); on the other, 'once we begin to accept the pervasiveness of externalities, it seems questionable whether we are justified in having market transactions at all' (Chang, 1994, p. 11).

It is important to emphasize that just because there are externalities does not mean there is a case for state intervention. The case of the new shirt design in an industrial district emphasizes the complexity of the issue: it may not be clear until after the event whether the externalities are positive or negative. Intervention by an authority to ensure that the other firms pay the first firm for the new design – and so reduce the extent of the copying – may reduce losses if the new design fails. But such intervention may reduce the gains if the new design succeeds. Arguably, reducing the general gains does not matter, as long as the creator of the new design is rewarded. However, if, as in industrial districts, individual success is dependent on general success then by reducing general gains the intervention will also reduce individual gains. Even at the risk of failure of the entire district, this type of intervention would not be appropriate.[6]

Large sunk costs

Sunk costs explain why a firm may be reluctant to enter an industry. The point is that if there is some sense in which this industry is socially necessary, but is not (or not sufficiently) profitable to justify the entry into the industry of a profit-maximizing firm, then the state must intervene. The state can, in a sense, create a contestable market by providing the sunk capital; the airline industry could, after all, become a contestable market if the state provided the airports, runways, air traffic control and so on. More realistically, in rail transport, privately owned firms could offer the service, if the government invests in electrification, stations and tracks.

Increasing returns to scale

If the technology for producing a particular good or service is such that even at levels of output that would capture substantial shares of the market, the firm is still experiencing increasing returns to scale (that is, it has not yet reached the minimum point on the long-run average cost curve), then this is a *natural monopoly* (see Chapter 5). The nature of the technology – indivisibilities – prevents more than one firm from entering and competing in the industry without substantially increasing costs. Following this line of thinking, Forte (1967) argued that in the case of an indivisible or very large scale project, public sector production is the best choice. Alternatively, the state could intervene by regulating a private, natural monopoly firm.

Large sunk costs and increasing returns to scale are the well-known features of imperfect markets such as oligopolies and monopolies. Collusive behaviour on the part of a group of firms, and/or the existence of economies of scale, will result in firms having an element of *market power*, such as in a monopoly or oligopoly situation, where each firm faces a downward-sloping demand curve; price will be greater than marginal cost, and output will be less than it would be under perfect competition. Some of the consumers' welfare is transferred to the firm in the form of supernormal profit. Social welfare would be improved if more resources were used to expand output up to the equilibrium point in perfect competition. As discussed above, there are various means at governments' disposal to correct this second market failure, including taxes, price controls and regulation to provide competition (or deregulation that removes legislation preventing competition). Collusive behaviour of a group of firms is opposed in nearly all countries by antitrust legislation, prices commissions, monopoly and merger commissions and such like.

The traditional neoclassical view is that government regulation against monopoly and excessive concentration in general will raise consumer welfare. There are a number of arguments against this view. First, as Shughart (1990, p. 169) puts it, it is possible 'that certain industries have become concentrated by virtue of the superior economic efficiency of the established firms'. Public policy to prevent this would be against the interests of consumers. Second, there is the *theory of the second best*, according to which a gain from intervention to 'correct' a non-competitive market can only be guaranteed if all other markets are perfectly competitive. This can be used to justify both widespread intervention and no intervention. In any case, the theory does not state that there will definitely be no gain, only that gain cannot be guaranteed. Third, Friedman (1962) among others has argued that state intervention is itself a frequent cause of monopoly. Complete absence of intervention is, in this view, the best option. Regulation may indeed be responsible for monopolies in some cases, but, as Chang (1994, p. 10) points out, forces other than collusion and state intervention – including business cycles, structural change and luck – have been far more important in transforming competitive markets into non-competitive ones.

Information imperfection

Where a market could exist, but it is not known – and not reasonably knowable – to potential investors that this is the case, then there is an argument for intervention by the state to provide the information. In the absence of a stock market, for example, information about the nature and price of potential investments would be difficult to obtain. This is an argument for the public provision – though not necessarily operation by the state – of a stock market. Following the same line of reasoning, *asymmetric information* between two parties involved in a given transaction can also lead to market failure. For example, where one group of consumers of a product are unable to obtain the information (or where the cost of obtaining the information is greater than the potential savings) that there are alternative, lower-price suppliers of the product, then a variety of prices, and a degree of monopoly power for sellers, will exist. In a more life-threatening example, someone requiring a doctor for the first time, would, in the absence of occupational licensing, not know which doctor to go to. In both these examples, state intervention is justified, in the first by providing or enforcing the provision of information, and in the second by imposing the need for those wishing to practise as doctors to obtain the appropriate qualifications. Note that *public goods* provide another type of market failure, but it can be considered as a special case of asymmetric information. Public goods are goods whose consumption (or use) by people who have not paid for this use cannot be prevented – unpaid consumption is non-excludable. Examples include public roads, public lighting and public parks (with no gates). A public good leads to market failure because there will tend to be an underestimation of the value (utility) of the good to the consumer when it comes to paying for it, followed by an overutilization by consumers once the good has been provided. The usual solution is for the government to tax people and provide the public good with the revenue. This type of market failure is a special case of asymmetric information in the sense that a good is public because it is impossible for the provider of the good to know who is consuming and how much they are consuming. This leads to the suggestion of improved means of providing that information as a way of correcting the market failure (Peacock, 1979), but this may not always be possible.

15.2.2 Paternalist intervention

A second broad set of reasons for government intervention in industry stems from sociopolitical and ethical considerations. Since the competitive process results in a misallocation of resources, with high levels of unemployment, a shortage of particular skills and regional disparities, it was increasingly accepted in the 1970s that it was up to governments to ensure that the distribution of welfare emerging from the economic process was in accord with the concepts of equity.[7] A major problem was (and is) how to define equity.

Political concern, sometimes about unemployment, sometimes about the strategic need to prevent a firm from becoming foreign-owned, was a key motivation in the rescuing of ailing companies by the state. Such state rescues were carried out by both Labour and Conservative governments in the UK, particularly in the 1970s. Several companies were taken wholly or partly into public ownership: Rolls-Royce (aero-engines), British-Leyland (motor cars), Ferranti (electronics), Alfred Herbert (machine tools) and ICL (computers) (George, 1991).

Another political reason for takeovers by the state was prevalent in France after the Second World War. The state in France transferred some firms into public ownership because these firms had collaborated with the enemy during the war. The 'nationalizations-sanctions' affected Renault, and the builder of aircraft engines Gnome et Rhône, which became SNECMA. The same kind of political argument applies, though *ex post*, where the private production of a good or service may give private individuals access to political influence or power beyond their constitutional rights. This has particular relevance in the case of the defence sector and its related armaments industry.

There are two main cases of paternalist intervention. The first relates to the existence of what Musgrave (1959) called 'merit and demerit wants'. *Merit and demerit goods* are particular goods for which the state makes the (normative) judgement that they are 'beneficial' (merit goods) or 'detrimental' (demerit goods) to the individual. This will lead to public spending on merit goods, such as education and basic research, and taxes on demerit goods, such as alcohol and tobacco. If, indeed, education is seen as a merit good, then the possibility that people will consume too little of it is 'an argument for state intervention to ensure that provision is at an optimal level' (Ferguson and Ferguson, 1994, p. 195). In the second case there is a belief that it is not morally acceptable for certain goods or services to be bought and sold. Examples include human organs for transplants, and police services. There is a normative argument that the 'state, as the social guardian, should remove such activities from the domain of the market and conduct them itself' (Chang, 1994, p. 12).

Ferguson and Ferguson (1994, pp. 195–6) point out that these types of arguments for state intervention ignore the possibility of *government failure*. They go on to exclude further discussion on the grounds that the argument 'largely turns on paternalistic and normative judgements beyond the scope of economic analysis'. Chang (1994, pp. 13–15) outlines the more detailed, contractarian criticism of paternalist intervention, according to which there should be no interference in the decisions of the individual. He then provides a critique of this argument, based on the idea that an economic theory resting on individualism is no more scientific, and no less moralistic, than one resting on collectivism (ibid., pp. 15–18). Chang would disagree with Ferguson and Ferguson on the question of whether paternalistic and moral judgements are beyond the scope of economic analysis, but he would agree with them that there has been inadequate attention by economists to the possibility of government failure.

15.2.3 A transaction cost theory of state intervention

Chang (1994) introduced a transaction cost theory of state intervention. It was already clear, long before Chang, that transaction costs – or the costs associated with any market transaction – which are generated by imperfect information call for state ownership. For example, rather than allowing firms to struggle over the establishing of rules of conduct in a particular market, by intervening to establish the rules of the trading game the state may actually improve the functioning of the market. This type of transaction cost argument belongs to the same category as information asymmetry, imperfect market explanations for intervention. Chang's theory goes further, arguing that markets are just one allocative mechanism, the state is another. Markets are imperfect, leading to a degree of allocative inefficiency; state intervention, with costs measured in terms of transaction costs, can reduce this allocative inefficiency. This provides a framework for questioning where and whether state intervention is justified: if the net improvement through transaction cost reduction resulting from state intervention is greater than if left to the market, then such intervention should be made.

From a neoclassical perspective, there is either an efficient or an inefficient allocation of resources. The costs of achieving either of these allocations is generally ignored. If we reinterpret the costs of state intervention as transaction costs (see, Chapter 4, Section 4.5) then 'the real question is whether the state can achieve the same allocative efficiency at a lower cost than the market, . . . and not whether state intervention is costly *per se*' (Chang, 1994, p. 48). This approach emphasizes a fundamental role of the state in the economy, namely the lowering of general transaction costs. There are three main ways in which the state, in preference to any other actor in the economy, can reduce transaction costs: (i) by establishing and enforcing property rights; (ii) by reducing macroeconomic instability; and (iii) by intervening in cases of co-ordination failure.

Property rights

A clear and stable set of generally accepted property rights reduces transaction costs because, without it, individuals would have to expend far more time, effort and money to establish their rights in each transaction.

Douglass C. North (a 1993 Nobel Prize winner for economics) provides a clear historical example of institutions of the state in Britain reducing transaction costs through the establishment of property rights. In the early seventeenth century, the Stuart kings responded to repeated fiscal crises by practices such as selling various monopoly rights, confiscating property, and forcing the wealthy to make loans to them, 'that rendered property rights less secure'. What followed was a struggle between Parliament and Crown, and civil war, with stability not being re-established until much later in the century, when 'parliamentary supremacy, central (parliamentary) control in financial matters, curtailment of royal prerogative powers, independence of the judiciary (at least from the Crown) and the supremacy of the common law courts were established'. An immediate consequence of the increased security of property rights was the rapid development of the public and private capital market. These were instrumental factors in England's rise to economic and political dominance (North, 1990, p. 139).

For the systematic reduction of transaction costs by the establishment and enforcing of property rights, it is not essential that the state intervene. However, as the most central institution, with the most pervasive power, it is far more likely that this role would be adopted by the state than by a firm.

Macroeconomic instability

To the extent that the actions of governments reduce macroeconomic instability (and it is debatable whether they do), this contributes to the reduction of transaction costs. For example, where long-term contracts are concluded in order to achieve the security of known prices or interest rates, the costs of agreeing, monitoring and enforcing such contracts would be avoided if prices and interest rates were stable.

Co-ordination failure

The co-ordination problem arises where some people prefer one outcome, and others prefer another. If the same number of people prefer each of the two outcomes, and there is no objective way of distinguishing between them, then there is a co-ordination problem if only one outcome is possible. To illustrate, let us assume a society in which there is no rule as to which side of the road people must drive. To avoid accidents, a rule must be made, but half the drivers wish to drive on the left, the other half on the right. In such situations, 'superseding private attempts at coordination with state intervention may greatly reduce transaction costs in the economy' (Chang, 1994, p. 52).

Chang (1994, p. 51) provides a game-theoretic example of the co-ordination problem (Fig. 15.1). The video recorder industry requires a national product standard because of network externalities. Firm A would prefer VHS whereas Firm B would prefer Betamax, but whatever the outcome, each would prefer to use the same, rather than different standards. State imposition of a standard may be a way of arriving at a solution that minimizes transaction costs because the alternative, private solution, would involve a great deal of negotiation and bargaining.

		Firm B	
		VHS	Betamax
Firm A	VHS	(2, 1)	(0, 0)
	Betamax	(0, 0)	(1, 2)

Figure 15.1 A co-ordination problem

A more generalized example is provided by the exit game (Fig. 15.2). Here there is an industry which, because of the contraction of the market, has been reduced to two firms.[8] Further contraction is necessary because only if there is one firm can that firm operate profitably. However, neither firm exits.

		Firm B	
		Exit	Remain
Firm A	Exit	(E, E)	(E, S)
	Remain	(S, E)	(R, R)

Figure 15.2 The exit game

There will be a barrier to exit where $S > R > E$. Even if S is the only positive outcome, a maximum strategy will result in both firms remaining. Firm A, deciding whether to exit or remain will consider its options: if Firm B exits, it will be best for Firm A to remain, because $S > E$; if Firm B remains, it will be best for Firm A to remain, because $R > E$. Firm

B, by identical reasoning, will also remain. As with the previous example, intervention by the state in choosing which firm is to remain, will minimize the transaction costs involved in negotiation and bargaining (and other acts of attrition) between the firms.

In order to reduce transaction costs, the state need not replace market transactions completely. First, it can change institutional configurations, for example encouraging the creation of representative organizations of employers and trade unions, so as to reduce the amount of bargaining. Second, it can attempt to generate, through education and the media, a more homogeneous ideology. The conclusion of 'contracts between agents sharing the same ideology will reduce the bargaining, monitoring and enforcement and other transaction costs required' (Chang, 1994). Third, the state can provide a focal point around which decisions can be co-ordinated, thus saving transaction costs. French and Japanese planning exercises are examples of such provision of focal points, 'where the state provides a "vision" for the future economy and induces private agents to work toward the same goal' (ibid., p. 52).

Chang's transaction cost theory of state intervention, drawing on the work of economists such as Coase and North, provides a framework for comparing the costs and benefits of intervention. This theory shows that intervention may or may not be justifiable, and provides a means of assessing the extent to which intervention might improve the situation. Such a general framework is necessary, because without it it is difficult to identify where regulation is, and where it is not, appropriate. For example, arguments about the necessity of regulating against entry where there is thought to be a natural monopoly will confront arguments about the need in all cases to encourage competition.

15.2.4 New growth theories

As we have seen in Chapter 11, investments in R&D and the degree of appropriability of knowledge are the major determinants of long-term economic growth. Consequently, it is up to the governments to provide incentives for R&D (eventually to engage in large R&D-based investment projects), and to improve the appropriability of innovations. These innovation-based policies are prerequisites for long-term economic growth in a region such as the EU, and as we will see below, many of the EU governments have embarked upon an 'innovation strategy' since the 1990s.

15.3 Results of industrial policy

A quick glance at the record of postwar economic development suggests that the best performing countries in terms of growth and international trade shares were the countries which implemented an industrial policy: Japan and other East Asian countries, Germany, France and Italy. The United States maintained its leadership only in areas where it did have an industrial policy, or at least a significant amount of state intervention and support (aerospace, armament, nuclear energy, and related electronic fields). In contrast, British Conservative governments were sceptical about the merits of an industrial policy and the British economy was among the worst performers in Europe and the OECD.

This cursory view suggests that industrial policy may improve an economy's performance. Two important issues should be mentioned here. First, what would have happened anyway, had no government intervention taken place (this is known as the 'deadweight' problem). Second, through an evaluation of industrial policy, can we conclude that industrial policy in these high-performing countries was desirable? That is, was the marginal private and social cost of government intervention more than compensated for by the marginal private and social benefit? In practice, nearly all economies have some degree of intervention that impacts on industry. The dilemma is not between implementing an industrial policy or not having an industrial policy at all, but rather it involves choosing among the various degrees of industrial policy, at appropriate times.

15.4 Types of industrial policy

Table 15.1 shows the main features of the five types of industrial policy to be described in this section. These types of policies are not necessarily mutually exclusive; the broad range of policies adopted in any one country at any one time could – and usually does – include more than one type of industrial policy.

Table 15.1 Various degrees of government intervention in industry

Degree of intervention	Policy objectives
1 Passive and negative	Control, restriction, penalization of dominant positions, regulation of monopolies (competition policy)
2 Passive but positive	Creation of a favourable economic environment (degree 1 + fiscal, financial, legal measures; deregulation). Also monetary policy culminating with monetary union
3 Active but negative	Sectoral policies and trade policies (defensive) (with rising barriers) to curb threats from new emerging economies
4 Active and positive	Co-ordination of national economic policies. The state as a supplier of capital. Picking the winner policy
5 Active, positive and directly involved	The state as an entrepreneur and innovator

15.4.1 A minimalist approach

The least interventionist industrial policy seeks to improve industrial performance through the creation of a favourable macroeconomic environment. This encompasses an appropriate fiscal policy, the attainment of adequate technological and educational standards, and a good infrastructure. We can call this, the first degree of industrial policy, a minimalist approach to industrial policy. Under this approach, monopolies are condemned because they result in a misallocation of resources; they restrict output to below the competitive level, and set prices above the competitive level. Nothing ensures that, in the long run, the monopolist will move towards its minimum efficient scale. A minimalist approach to industrial policy thus usually includes competition policy, for example to monitor mergers and acquisitions and prevent the formation of monopolies.

Although it appears that this policy is active in, for example, implementing competition policy, we consider it more appropriate to identify the policy as passive. It does not initiate any industrial activity, it merely waits for firms to act. If the actions of the firms bring them into the net of competition policy, they will be examined; if not, they are left alone. It is negative in that it prevents some actions, penalizes others; competition policy does not involve any positive encouragement.

Note that even a minimalist approach, even if it includes nothing other than competition policy to prevent the emergence of monopolies, has international implications, all the more so in the absence of trade and other barriers between countries. At the European level, the adoption of a competition policy by one country, for example, will have serious negative implications for that country. A simple prisoner's dilemma game illustrates how the co-ordination of monopoly policies by various governments, or indeed a common monopoly regulation, leads to the best payoff for all concerned.[9]

Beginning with the top, right-hand cell in Fig. 15.3, if the home country regulates monopolies and the trading partner country does not, then monopolies in the partner country will be able to make more profits and, ultimately, out-compete the home country monopolies. There will be a high positive payoff to the partner, and a negative payoff to the home country. The home country will not choose the monopoly regulation strategy for fear that the partner country will choose the no regulation strategy. The same considerations will face the partner country. In the absence of discussion and binding agreement

| | | Partner country | |
		Monopoly regulation	No monopoly regulation
Home country	Monopoly regulation	(10, 10)	(−10, 20)
	No monopoly regulation	(20, −10)	(0, 0)

Figure 15.3 Effects of monopoly regulation: an international prisoner's dilemma

to opt for monopoly regulation, the countries will settle in the bottom, right-hand cell. This is the non Pareto optimal equilibrium point. With such discussion and agreement, they will settle in the top, left-hand cell, which is Pareto optimal.

15.4.2 The favourable economic environment approach

In this approach there may be, in addition to competition policy, fiscal and other policies that encourage certain actions. Usually these policies are very broad, rather than focused. For example, a fiscal policy relieving all new firms of tax liability in the first two years of operation is positive in that it encourages or generates certain actions (the starting up of new firms); it is general in that it applies to all firms, rather than being focused on firms in a particular industry. It is passive in that once the environment – fiscal policy – has been set, it is up to the firms to respond. This type of policy is closest to that implemented by governments apparently ideologically opposed to industrial policy but faced with problems such as industrial decline and unemployment that are seen to require intervention. In the late 1990s, a number of EU countries have adopted a single European currency. The way in which economic and monetary union (EMU) interacts with industrial policy is given more consideration later (see Chapter 16, Section 16.6).

15.4.3 The active, negative sectoral policy approach

The rise of the Japanese and East Asian economies in the 1950s and 1960s, and the structural adjustments of the early 1970s, gave birth to a new form of industrial policy in western Europe. The newly industrialized countries (NICs) were gradually encroaching on the established markets of the traditional world manufacturers (the United States, and northern Europe). Some industries in Europe began to be referred to as 'traditional' or as 'declining' industries. These developments were in line with Rostow's (1960a, b) stages approach to economic development, expanded later by Balassa (1977) in what became known as 'the stages approach to comparative advantages'.[10] Industrial restructuring in Europe, or the phasing out of non-viable sectors, was hampered by social considerations, and the EC industrial policy at the time took the form of a defensive policy. Vertical or sectoral policies were implemented and were combined with restrictive trade policies. For example, in order to protect North America and Europe against cheap imports from Japan and some less developed countries, a long-term arrangement regarding international trade in cotton textiles was concluded in 1962. This arrangement introduced the philosophy embodied in what later became the Multi-Fibre Agreements (MFAs).

This type of industrial policy, usually including such trade policies as MFAs and voluntary restraint agreements (VRAs), is activist in the sense that it allows for a more determined involvement of the state in specific activities, but negative because it is aimed at restricting the degree of competition worldwide. It does not directly encourage domestic producers, but changes their competitive environment by reducing the impact of foreign competition.

15.4.4 The active co-ordinator approach

An active and positive industrial policy has a number of aspects. Broadly speaking, the state remains outside the industrial framework itself. It does not directly own or control production, but it does influence it, sometimes directly. As co-ordinator, the state ensures consistency between policies (for example, industrial and educational) and actively focuses such policies on achieving industrial outcomes (for example, by encouraging research in universities to be applied to the needs of industry). This encouragement may be by providing funds through an appropriate channelling of credit, or by directly covering (usually only partially) the cost of a project. The state also acts as counsellor and information provider to firms. In order to act in all these ways, the state is required to actively select the sectors, or subsectors, to support. The notion of the state 'picking winners' usually refers to state support for individual firms. This is not quite what occurs here, but it is close to it. To provide special support for a particular subsector, for example, the state must have, or have access to, expert knowledge on the activities and potential of this subsector. It must know about the industry worldwide, as well as about the strengths or potential strengths of the domestic firms in the industry.

15.4.5 Direct involvement in production

The most intense degree of industrial policy involves the building up of public enterprises.[11] Following Parris et al. (1987, p. 23), public enterprises can be grouped into three distinct categories:

- Enterprises 'directly managed by a government department or semi-public authority'. This is the case of, for example, the railway and postal systems in Italy, and of telecommunications in the Netherlands, where such undertakings are called 'state enterprises'.

- Enterprises 'with a special legal status, subject to a public authority but possessing also a measure of managerial autonomy'. This is the case for most public enterprises in Ireland where they are also called 'state-sponsored bodies'; those involved in production of goods and services other than public services are called 'commercial state-sponsored bodies'. In the UK these are known as quangos (quasi-autonomous non-governmental organizations).

- Companies 'with the same legal status as those in the private sector and enjoying a substantial degree of managerial autonomy, whose shares are owned (wholly or partly) by the state'. These include British Leyland (private today), Air France, the French SNCF; they are referred to as 'mixed-societies' or 'state-owned enterprises'.

Totally or partially owned and controlled by the state, the public enterprise may pursue other goals besides the economic goal of producing a good or service efficiently and selling it at prices compatible with cost and demand conditions. The typical public firm also serves a social purpose. It is as concerned about the availability of the good or service as about profitability. A state-owned bus company, for example, will provide a service throughout the day. If it were profit maximizing, it would have no, or fewer, buses running outside peak hours. The public pays for the use of the good or service on a payment-for-use basis and/or by means of subsidies which are raised through taxation.

15.5 Public versus private firms

An endless debate about the type and extent of public enterprise a nation should have – and about the role of the state in an economy in general – has been the feature not only of modern economics, with the privatization era starting in the 1980s, but of politics and political economy since the time of Plato and Aristotle.[12]

Even those in the classical and neoclassical traditions have accepted economic and non-economic arguments in favour of public enterprise as a second best. In his *Wealth of Nations*, Adam Smith (1776) himself advocated government intervention in four types of economic activity: defence, justice, certain public works, and education. It was up to the government, he argued, to create and maintain defence, justice and educational institutions and to engage in some public works that are not economically profitable but which may be socially desirable and advantageous.

Up to 1939, public enterprises in Europe were rare and were usually in the first category of public enterprises-directly managed by public or semi-public authorities. They included postal services, armaments and arsenals, and financial institutions, often created during the nineteenth century. In addition, public firms were created in France in 1919, the role of which was to exploit the German assets taken over as war payments (for example, potash in Alsace). After the Second World War, the public sector was extended to cover many more areas: utilities (supply of water, gas, electricity, rail and air transport);[13] defence; finance and insurance; social services (transport, health, education); telecommunications; and nuclear energy.[14]

In the late 1940s and 1950s, public enterprises in France and Italy were formed in order to serve the major concern which was the rebuilding of the devastated economies. The public sector played a major role in the reconstruction and modernization of French industry during that time. French and Italian state capitalism served as a model for British Labour Party policy makers (Hager, 1982).

One way this was expressed in Britain was in successive waves of nationalizations and privatizations.[15] In some cases, usually relating to whether there were Labour or Conservative governments, firms were transferred back and forth between private and public ownership in just a few years; British Steel, for example, was nationalized in 1949, de-nationalized in the mid-1950s, nationalized again in 1967, and re-privatized in the 1980s (George, 1991).

During the 1960s, trade performance and technological independence (with respect to the United States, and the increasingly challenging Japan) came to the fore as new objectives of industrial Policy.[16] The formation of national champions was favoured as one means of achieving these objectives. National champions have been described by Hager (1982, p. 241) as 'large firms favored by national procurement policies, capital sources, etc., and able to negotiate with American companies on the terms under which US technology was utilized'.

In the 1970s, the economic crisis reinforced the role of the public sector. The aim of narrowing the technology gap led to support for the creation of large *European champions* – Airbus, for example (see below) – that would open up to the world market and respond to the challenge of the American and Japanese competitors. At the purely national level in Europe, various nationalization programmes increased the number of state-owned multinationals. In the second half of the 1970s, British Leyland was nationalized, the shipyards and steelworks in Sweden were nationalized (despite the advent to power of a Conservative government), and there was a wave of nationalizations in Portugal (this time ideologically based, following as it did the revolution of 1974).

European public enterprises in general grew – in size and in number – over the 1960s, 1970s and 1980s. In 1965, only 19 of the 200 largest companies in the world outside the United States were publicly owned; in 1975 and 1985, there were respectively 29 and 38 such companies (Anastassopoulos *et al.*, 1987). The number of state-owned firms among the world's top enterprises outside the United States thus doubled over the two decades; the number of all state-owned multinationals increased six-fold in the same period. Economic internationalization and political nationalization combined to put state-owned multinational enterprises at the forefront of European industrial development.

The biggest public multinationals at the time were to be found in the traditionally interventionist countries, namely France and Italy. Austria has also traditionally been a country with a strong public sector. The countries the least represented are Germany, the UK and the Netherlands, countries where the *laissez-faire* attitude has been more pervasive. It should be noted that if the 1970s and the 1980s saw ideologically inspired waves of nationalizations and privatizations in countries such as the UK, France and Portugal, the attitude of politicians in Germany and the Netherlands was probably more balanced. In these latter countries, 'it is as though [the public firms] had been accepted as belonging to the industrial landscape' (Anastassopoulos *et al.*, 1987, p. 59). As pointed out by the same authors, the managements of these firms require that they be as efficient as if they were private companies.

However, political ideology opposing state intervention probably reached its apogee in the 1980s, resulting in a radical break with the past in most European countries. The case against state enterprises led to massive privatization programmes, starting in Thatcherite Britain and spreading over Europe.[17] During the 1990s and early 2000s, the wave of privatizations continued in the EU, albeit at a much slower pace than before. In contrast with the previous period, this was motivated less by political ideology than by deeper European integration. The restrictive budgetary policies brought about by the preparation for economic and monetary union (EMU), as detailed in the 1992 Treaty of Maastricht, as well as the ensuing EU directives in relation to liberalization in the public utilities sector in the late 1990s, have provided additional stimuli to privatizations in countries with a long-estab-lished state tradition in economic affairs (namely Italy and France). Among the questions addressed in relation to privatization, are: How important is the social service provided by the postal system? Should the likes of tennis courts and universities (used only by a minority of the public), be subsidized by all taxpayers? Is it socially desirable to continue to subsidize the steel industry?

15.6 The wave of privatization

UK

A non-exhaustive list of companies that have been sold off wholly or in part in the late 1980s is given in Appendix 15.1. As one would expect, the number of public companies de-nation-alized or privatized is quite high in the UK. British privatized companies include: British Airways, British Aerospace, British Telecom (the biggest sale), British Petroleum, Cable & Wireless, Ferranti, International Computers, Jaguar Cars (previously part of British Leyland, now part of Ford), Rolls-Royce, Amersham International and British Gas. Following the pri-vatization of the public utilities (water, gas and telecommunications), the UK government set up new regulatory bodies to control prices and to limit diversification. In the telecom-munications sector, together with the privatization of BT, the government also facilitated the establishment of another company, Mercury. During the 1990s, a duopoly existed in many segments of the British telecommunications sector, until the entry of a myriad of firms who made the industry more competitive at the turn of the millennium. It should be noted that it is not privatization per se, but rather the entry of many firms, that has rendered the British telecommunications industry more efficient. In other areas, such as rail trans-port, the experience of privatization in the UK has been far less positive. Privatization of rail transport in the 1990s meant the breaking down of the once integrated UK railway system into more than 100 distinct businesses, such as track maintenance companies and rolling stock leasing companies, most of them being short-term contractors. The collapse of pro-fessionalism in the industry, augmented with inefficiencies, with the duplication of effort and the lack of safety, have resulted in several major collisions since the late 1990s as well as thousands of train cancellations and delays. These below pre-privatization standards have inevitably led to major changes in the industry. In 2002, a non-profit and non-government entity, Network Rail, took over from Railtrack, the private entity formed in 1993. Contracts with profit-making companies have since been curtailed, transferring thereby thousands of workers out of the private sector.

France

In France, a list of companies said to be '*privatisables*' was determined by the law of 31 July 1986. A list of French companies privatized between 1986 and 1988 can be found in Appendix 15.1. In 1993 alone, 22 companies were sold. In January 1994, the share of manufacturing employment in state firms had dropped to 7 per cent (*Le Monde*, 13 January 1994) from 16 per cent in 1984, that is, shortly after the wave of nationalizations. More companies were being privatized in 1994, of which Compagnie des Machines Bull, Banque Nationale de Paris, Crédit Agricole and Renault were most important. Ironically, while in the latter part of 1993 the Minister for Trade and Industry was confirming these future privatizations, he was also corroborating the fact that the French state was going to increase its capital participation in SNECMA and Aérospatiale. In spite of the different privatization waves, France is still regarded as the major EU country in terms of its public sector employment share. Public firms, such as La Poste (302,000 employees in 2002), SNCF (216,000) are among the largest employers in the country. The selling of shares (opening of the capital) of the electricity and gas producer EDF-GDF is still the theme of an extremely animated debate in France.[18]

Germany

The reunification of the two Germanies prompted intense efforts to privatize the 13,400 previously state-owned firms of the eastern Länder. The *Treuhandanstalt* (privatization agency) played a major role in this process. During the first six months of 1991, the Treuhand Agency managed to sell some 2600 companies. The assets sold by the agency between 1991 and 1994 have been valued at DM 45 billion (€22.5 billion), that is, DM 275 million short of the expected figure, leaving an equivalent deficit to the German taxpayer. Of the 4 million people originally employed in these firms, the privatized firms planned to keep roughly 1.5 million jobs (*Le Monde*, 25 January 1994). The agency temporarily held minority shares in the de-nationalized firms; for example, it held 40 per cent of the shares in EKO, a steel company, 60 per cent of which had been sold to the Italian firm Riva. The mission of the Treuhand Agency came to an end in 1994, when it was taken over by the German authorities. Although costly in the short term, the agency achieved a great deal in a short period. When it was dissolved, it had sold 17,000 firms or parts of firms, mostly to German firms; only 700 passed into foreign ownership.

In France, where right-wing and left-wing governments have alternated in the 1980s and 1990s, in Thatcherite UK, and in East Germany, the privatization wave was intense. Elsewhere, European governments have privatized more cautiously, selling only part of their assets and retaining a substantial share of public interest. In Spain, and to a certain extent Italy, de-nationalization has been seen as a means to reduce the public deficit in order to comply with the convergence criteria for participation, first, in the European Monetary System, and, more recently, in moves towards economic and monetary union.

Italy

In Italy, the massive losses of the IRI (Istituto per la Ricostruzione Industriale), amounting to FF35 billion (€5.3 billion) in the early 1990s (*Le Monde*, 1 February 1994), and the exigencies of the Maastricht Treaty have prompted the sale of its companies to private interests (such as Alitalia, Aeritalia, Sirti telecommunications, Enel, Agip, Ina). Born in 1933 with the aim of bailing out the industrial and banking system in a crisis-hit Italy, the IRI finally dissolved in June 2000 (Amatori and Colli, 1999). In the early part of 1994, the government announced the sale of the main Italian industrial bank, the Banca Commerciale Italiana (known as Comit).This is not to say that public firms have disappeared in a country such as Italy. In the area of defence, aerospace, automation and transportation, the Italian public sector has expanded substantially in the early 2000s. Through Italy's second largest industrial group Finmeccanica, the Italian public sector has acquired a few private companies such as Marconi Mobile, Fiat Avio and Telespazio.

Austria

Austria is another country with a traditionally large public sector. In 1987, of the nine largest enterprises, five were totally state owned, one was under majority state ownership, two others were state controlled through large nationalized banks, and only one was privately owned. Following the crisis of Voest-Alpine (steel and engineering group) in the 1980s, the Austrian government announced that it would introduce private funding in the companies owned by the state. As a result, proceeds acquired through privatization programmes increased from US$ 80 million in 1990/91 to a peak of US$ 3.9 billion in 1996/97 (Belke and Schneider, 2004). Among the latest privatizations in Austria are: Austrian Tobacco (in 2001) and Postal Bank (in 2000). However, the Austrian government still has substantial capital shares in the partly privatized firms (such as Airport Vienna AG).

The Netherlands

Unlike other countries in Europe, Dutch governments never implemented large programmes of nationalization. This explains why the public sector in this country has always been relatively small, and why privatization has only been very slight. In the 1980s, the Dutch state reduced its stake in the airline KLM to 55 per cent, and two-thirds of the chemical firm DSM was sold to the public.

Spain

The Spanish government's majority stake in the car manufacturer Seat was sold to Volkswagen in 1986. SKF Española (tyre manufacturer) was de-nationalized, and 39 per cent of ENCE was sold on the stock exchange. Negotiations for the sale of a minority stake in Enasa (motor car) and MTM (railway equipment) started in the late 1980s. The Spanish government did not follow a systematic strategy of de-nationalization of public enterprises, but rather followed a 'process of clarification of their objectives that necessitated the denationalization of some of them' (Garcia Delgado *et al.*, 1989, p. 496). Public utilities such as electricity generation, electricity distribution and gas transmission are partly privatized in this country.

Belgium

In Belgium, the sale of 50 per cent of the stock of the country's second largest state bank, Société Nationale de Crédit à l'Industrie (SNCI), began in December 1993. Since that year, the Belgian government privatized nearly €7 billion worth of public sector assets, with Sabena and Belgacom being the last two firms on the list. It should be noted that Belgacom is one of the rare EU telecommunications companies that still has majority state ownership in 2004.

Denmark

In Denmark, one enterprise, Statsangstalten for Livsforsikring (State Life Insurance Company) was sold to a private firm, and in 1993, the Danish government sold 25 per cent of the shares in Kobenhavns Lufthavnsvaesen (KLV), 25 per cent of Postgiro, and 49 per cent of the shares in TeleDanmark. As the economy was characterized by a small public sector, apart from the traditional areas such as public utilities and telecommunications, there were

Table 15.2 Employment, value added (VA) and gross fixed capital formation (GFCF) in European public enterprises in the 1990s

	Share of total employment[a] %	VA as a % of total (at current prices)[a]	Share in total GFCF[a] %	Average index of the three criteria %		
	1998			1991	1995	1998
Austria	9.1	13.0	14.0	na	21.5	12.0
Belgium	10.4	13.5	10.9	11.0	11.6	10.9
Denmark	6.1	7.5	9.9	11.5	9.7	7.9
Finland	10.9	10.5	11.4	na	17.6	10.9
France	10.3	11.5	13.5	17.6	14.7	11.8
Germany	9.0	9.9	14.0	11.1	10.7	10.9
Greece	12.3	13.5	17.0	20.2	15.4	14.2
Ireland	8.0	9.4	12.9	12.3	11.8	10.1
Italy	7.7	10.0	11.0	18.9	14.2	9.6
Luxembourg	5.3	5.3	6.4	6.4	6.4	5.7
Netherlands	2.5	5.8	5.5	7.5	6.8	4.6
Portugal	5.3	8.4	12.0	20.7	12.3	8.5
Spain	3.9	3.3	5.0	9.0	8.0	4.1
Sweden	11.6	13.7	14.0	na	12.9	13.1
UK	2.5	1.9	2.5	4.4	2.7	2.3
EU-15	7.1	8.5	11.0	11.8	10.4	9.0

[a] Figures refer to the non-agricultural sector only

Source: CEEP, 2000

only 12 privatizations of state companies, and these had only a small impact in terms of GDP.

The impact of the privatization and de-nationalization programmes is shown in Table 15.2. It is clear that the most spectacular decline in the impact of state-owned enterprises in the past decade or so took place in the UK. The average index measuring the impact of public enterprises on the British manufacturing and service economy (average index of the three criteria) declined from 15 per cent in 1979 (not shown in the table) to 2.3 per cent in 1998. There were also substantial declines in Portugal (from 20.7 to 8.5), Italy (from 18.9 per cent to 9.6 per cent), and France (from 17.6 per cent in 1991 to 11.8 per cent in 1998). In other countries (such as in Denmark), the public sector declined to a lesser extent, or else remained almost stable over the period (as in Belgium, Germany, Luxembourg and Sweden). Note that even where firms remain in state ownership, EU rules prevent the state from intervening in the operation or financing of these firms in any way that might improve their competitive position.

15.6.1 Public private partnerships

The late 1990s have been witness to the development and multiplication of public private partnerships (PPPs). These are defined as a form of collaboration between public bodies such as local communities and central government, and private companies for the provision of asset-based services. Born in the UK in the early 1990s, PPPs were viewed as a means to revive the public sector. Although many PPPs have been developed in the area of infrastructure, they also affect other areas such as health, education, safety, waste management and water distribution. The aim of the EU Green Paper *Public Private Partnerships* is, through a wide ranging debate, to ascertain the role of the Community in this domain, given its well known principles in terms of legal certainty and effective competition (CEC, 2004).

15.7 Industrial policies in other countries: the experience of the United States, Japan and East Asian NICs

15.7.1 US industrial policy

The English trade policies of the seventeenth and eighteenth centuries were perceived to favour England at the expense of its overseas colonies (Miller, 1943). The newly independent federal state lived its first decade 'under the Articles of Confederation, which denied the central government both the power to tax and the ability to regulate trade' (Diebold, 1982, p. 159). These historical developments partly explain why US industrial policy is weak and non-interventionist by tradition.[19] According to Grant (1989, pp. 115–16), 'The dominant values of US society are at odds with any interventionist industrial policy. . . . The episode of the New Deal . . . cannot be said to have created a legitimate interventionist tradition in the USA.'[20]

Notwithstanding, Alexander Hamilton's Report on Manufactures of 1791 is a first proposal for an American industrial policy. It advocated the use of tariffs, and the selection of industries that best suited the country at the time. Although Hamilton's report had no lasting impact on the conception of industrial policy in the United States (Hudson, 1985), it did provide a basis for industrial development in the newly independent federal state. A decade after its publication, the report returned to the forefront of discussions on American industrial policy. The 1816 tariff protected new (or infant) industries, and trade protection gave American industry the ability to produce a wide range of products and to focus on the domestic market (Diebold, 1982).

In the latter part of the nineteenth century, antitrust laws formed the fundamental pillar of US industrial policy. A new type of industrial policy emerged with the Interstate Commerce Act 1887, and antitrust policy was created with the Sherman Act 1890. It was designed to reduce monopoly and dominant positions in the economy. In 1914, both the Clayton Act and the Federal Trade Commission Act emerged from the dissatisfaction generated by judicial interpretations and enforcement of the Clayton Act (Shughart, 1990). The Clayton Act (amended partially in 1936 by the Robinson Patman Act) prohibits all discriminatory practices that reduce competition substantially. In short, antitrust policies are aimed at punishing price fixers and at preventing anti-competitive practices.[21] These laws still play an important part in contemporaneous US economic policy. Postwar US industrial policy has many features: a secular devotion to antitrust laws, an increased commitment to tariff reduction, and a more interventionist policy, the driving force of which has been the defence industry and its space-related programmes.

Since the Second World War, defence spending has been massive. In the 1960s, government financial assistance was extended with the introduction of the space programmes. At the peak of this phenomenon, more than 50 per cent of all US engineers and scientists were directly involved in government supported R&D programmes. This effort has generated many civilian spinoffs in the fields of advanced materials, high-technology computer languages and semiconductors. Other aspects of postwar American interventionist industrial policy include: quotas on foreign oil aimed at import substitution, and subsidies for the shipping and shipbuilding industries.[22] The watch industry was protected on the grounds that only the watchmakers had the appropriate skills for the manufacture of bomb sights (Diebold, 1982).

The energy crisis, the monetary disorder, and the emergence of NICs (newly industrializing countries) in the 1970s introduced the themes of 'American industrial decline', and 'loss of US technological leadership'.[23] In the 1970s, the terms 'industrial policy' and 'industrial strategy' re-emerged in the official language (Diebold, 1982). In the 1980s, these expressions were overshadowed by the notion of 'competitiveness'. The new Reagan administration focused on macroeconomic issues, such as tax cuts and the reduction of government expenditure. Although these measures were aimed at expanding industrial production and productivity, 'they were not thought of as "industrial policy", a term abjured by many in the new administration' (Diebold, 1982, p. 181). With the recovery of the US economy in the 1990s, policy has focused on R&D tax credits and other fiscal incentives to promote the knowledge-intensive industries.

In spite of its negative attitude towards the concept of industrial policy, subsequent federal administrations continued to intervene in the defence-related industries.[24] In some ways it is as if the US government had proceeded all along with an industrial policy without it having been either deliberate or acknowledged.

15.7.2 MITI (Ministry of International Trade and Industry) and the Japanese model of industrial policy[25]

Industrial policy in Japan can be traced back to the late nineteenth century when the country opened to the outside world. Today's large companies such as Toshiba were founded with Meiji government support in 1875.[26] In postwar Japan, industrial policy (*Sangyo Seisaku*) has been anchored on a societal consensus and on a network of extended economic and business relationships. Hosomi and Okumura (1982) view industrial policy in Japan as 'constructive', and as a well-approved and purposeful tool for the advancement of the national economy. Undeniably, the prolonged economic recession of the 1990s (referred to as 'the lost decade') and the Asian crisis in 1997, have both changed the production fabric as well as policy making in Japan, without nevertheless jeopardizing the fundamental pillars of Japanese industrial policy. The Japanese production model is still based on a co-operative form of capitalism; industrial planning in Japan still incorporates a long-term view; the government still plays an important role in industrial and economic affairs, although it may be argued that this has been somewhat diminishing. The privatization of public enterprises has also affected Japan since the 1980s, but high levels of public spending have been regarded as an adequate response to the economic recession of the 1990s and early 2000s.[27]

Industrial policy should be viewed as one of the many internal and external factors that aided the economic 'miracle' in postwar Japan, giving rise to a specific business model in the country. Other internal elements explaining the rapid economic development of the Japanese economy after the Second World War are anchored on the traditional virtues of patience, work and savings. In particular, savings (and low consumption) nurtured the accumulation of capital. The two pillars of the Japanese business model are social consensus and a network structure of business relations. Social consensus entails that the relations between labour and management are harmonious, and that all the employees of a corporation, not only the senior managers, are involved in the determination of the long-term objectives of the firm. The Japanese business network (*keiretsu*) is best represented as a series of concentric circles (Imai, 1989). The core is a bank or an insurance company, surrounded by large firms, controlling other firms of equal dimension or smaller. Each firm is then connected to a myriad of suppliers. In turn, the suppliers develop strong relations with the trading houses (*sogo shosha*).[28] The Japanese banking institutions are strongly involved in industrial policy offering cheap long-term capital through modest interest rates. There are many business networks of this kind or industrial conglomerates, one competing with another.

The Japanese model of industrial policy is based on government-business synergies. The Japanese state is neither dominant/coercive nor submissive to private firms. In Kitschelt's words (1991, p. 478), 'the Japanese state contributed more intelligence than funding to economic development, backed up by sanctions if industries failed to comply with market-conforming government programs, primarily those of the revered Ministry of International Trade and Industry (MITI)'. Market-conforming government programmes entail the specification of long-term objectives of industrial policy by MITI. Firms belonging to competing networks try to meet these objectives.

Japanese industrial policy is best represented by its three major components: general measures, sectoral measures, and organizational measures (Hosomi and Okumura, 1982). The general measures, such as quality standardization, are designed to promote industry as a whole. Sectoral measures aim to improve the productivity and the employment opportunities of specific sectors (modernization and rationalization of the steel and textile industries; import restrictions on computers, and so forth). Institutional measures ensure the non-disruption and the smooth functioning of competition (antitrust laws). These measures also encompass taxation and financial actions to promote SMEs.

One of the major roles of the Japanese state is to *create comparative advantages* for Japanese industry. This role is best summarized by a statement of the Japanese minister, Ojimi, more than 30 years ago (OECD, 1972, p. 149):

> The MITI decided to establish in Japan industries which require intensive employment of capital and technology, industries that in consideration of comparative cost of production should be the most inappropriate for Japan, industries such as steel, oil-refining, petro-chemicals, automobiles, aircraft, industrial machinery of all sorts, and electronics, including electronic computers. From a short-run, static viewpoint, encouragement of such industries would seem to conflict with economic rationalism. But, from a long-range viewpoint, these are precisely the industries where income elasticity of demand is high, technological progress is rapid, and labor productivity rises fast.

The launching by MITI of the Very Large Scale Integration (VLSI) Initiative in the 1970s which brought together the major electronics manufacturers, proved very successful. It supported the entry of Japanese firms into volume commodity chip manufacture with the 64K-RAM chip. The fifth generation computer program was launched in October 1981. It was backed by US$200–300 million of government financial investment. However, not all industrial planning has been successful in Japan, as the attempt to rationalize the automotive industry in the 1950s – through the mergers of SMEs such as Honda and Mazda with giant firms such as Toyota – failed (Jansen, 2000). Nevertheless, many Japanese high-technology industries have flourished on international markets, and in spite of the long economic recession of the 1990s, the Japanese economy was still, at the turn of the new millennium, second only to that of the United States.

15.7.2 The East Asian NICs

In all East Asian newly industrializing economies (Hong Kong, South Korea, Singapore, Taiwan, Malaysia, Philippines, Thailand), with the exception of the *laissez-faire* Hong Kong, active industrial policies with selective industrial targeting have been set in place; they were aimed at promoting specific industrial activities at different times (Chowdhury and Islam, 1993). For example, finding partly his inspiration in the experience of Japan, South Korean President Park Chung Hee's (1961–79) policy of 'rapid industrialization through invitation', stirred what is known as the Korean economic miracle. This miracle referred to the period following the year 1965, when growth rates jumped to 8.9 per cent in 1967, culminating at 16.9 per cent in 1973 (Hakwon Sunoo, 1994). From that time, South Korea became a fast-growing, export-oriented economy.

There are important differences, but also common features in the industrial policies of these countries.

Selection by the government of industrial growth sectors, target industrial areas or priority industries

In the mid-1960s, the 'strategic' industries of South Korea were identified as textiles and consumer electronics. This policy of selecting priority industrial activities was repeated again in the early part of the 1970s. Capital-intensive activities, such as steel, non-ferrous metals, chemicals, machinery, shipbuilding and subsequently, electronic industrial equipment, became the priority. Thanks to significant government support, Korean semiconductor manufacturers had become, by 1990, major players in the IT field (Steers, 1999). The Taiwanese government played an important role in promoting capital and technology-intensive industries in the 1970s. In Singapore, the Economic Development Board (EDB) 'lays down its priorities for industrial activities in anticipation of changes in Singapore's comparative advantage' (Chowdhury and Islam, 1993, p. 96).

Flexibility in the industrial policy philosophy

Flexibility in industrial policy philosophy has materialized at three levels:

◆ A change from import substitution towards export-led growth. In 1964, South Korea underwent this change which involved selecting new target industries such as textiles and consumer electronics (Hakwon Sunoo, 1994). The Taiwanese economy experienced the same transformation in the mid-1960s. In addition, to facilitate exports, the exchange rate systems were reformed.

◆ A change from labour-intensive to capital-intensive and to R&D (or high skills) intensive industries. This was expressed in the shift from textiles, to steel, shipbuilding, petrochemicals, and finally to electronics, biotechnologies, new material sciences. In Taiwan, the government promoted the expansion of capital-intensive industries in the 1970s, whereas the 1980s have witnessed an expansion of high-technology and skill-intensive activities (IT, electronics, machinery and biotechnology). The 1973 industrial restructuring programme launched by the Korean government put the emphasis on the development of new priority sectors: steel and non-ferrous metals, chemicals and petrochemicals, machinery, shipbuilding and electronic industrial equipment. In Singapore, the 1979 industrial restructuring programme was aimed at discouraging labour-intensive activities. High wages, a payroll tax and a Skill Development Fund levy on the employers of unskilled labour were all measures intended to shift industrial activities towards skill- and technology-intensive activities.

- A change from sectoral objectives to horizontal measures, such as R&D support, promotion of SMEs, introduction of new technologies (automated manufacturing systems). But, as noted by the OECD (1991c, p. 66), 'the R&D and technology support measures often have a marked sectoral bias, with the focus on electronics, IT and biotechnologies'.

Policy instruments

- *Financial instruments.* The regulation of the financial sector, taking the form of investment funds channelled in favour of the target industries, has been documented by Wade (1988, 1990). Through tight control over the financial sector at the end of the 1960s, the Korean government was able to administer preferential credit to the industries it had identified as being strategic. In Singapore, the EDB allocated selective grants and loan schemes to the target industries.

- *Training.* In Korea, through active R&D and human resource development (HRD) programmes in the 1970s, the government played a crucial role in expanding engineering education. In Taiwan, R&D activities were promoted by the establishment of publicly funded industrial and technological parks. During the early 1990s, the erosion of the competitiveness of the East Asian economies on international markets and the gradual liberalization of their domestic markets called for a renewed interest in R&D programmes.

- *The state as an investor.* Government enterprises are non-existent in Hong Kong, and are of minor importance in South Korea. In Taiwan, government enterprises were present in heavy industry (steel and petrochemicals) and in advanced sectors (components, silicon smelting) (OECD, 1991c). In Singapore, the state has heavily invested in construction, iron and steel, and ship repair industries.

It has often been alleged that, in Hong Kong, economic growth has been achieved with minimal state intervention. The role of the state has been mainly confined to creating an appropriate economic environment, with low (ideally zero) price distortions. But even in this *laissez-faire* colony, the government did have an input in the shaping of the industrial structure through, for example, a sectoral policy to promote the electronics industry (OECD, 1991c, p. 65).

Since the 1980s, industrial policies of the Asian countries have changed with the introduction of privatization programmes. These programmes were implemented in the 1980s in Singapore; they began in March 1989 in Taiwan. What is interesting to note is that the privatization of state enterprises in the East Asian countries has responded less to a general ideological and fashionable trend, which was very pronounced during these years, than to a logical requirement. State involvement in the early stages of industrial development is seen as a prerequisite for growth. Once the industry has become viable, private entrepreneurs are encouraged to take over. This is why in Singapore, for example, the privatization programmes affecting some industrial sectors, such as the firms associated with the defence industry, and the rubber association, are totally compatible with the creation or development of public enterprises in other new sectors – the leading edge industries.

The 1997 Asian crisis, seen by many as 'the end of the Asian economic miracle', did lead to a new reconfiguration of the productive structure in many of these countries. The conglomerates, which had been at the heart of the 'Asian miracle', had to undergo sweeping reforms in these countries. In South Korea, the *chaebol* were highly indebted and were starting to collapse before the crisis. This was essentially due to the lack of a sound financial policy, a phenomenon aggravated by the liberalization of the Korean capital markets in 1996 (Milelli and Grou, 2001).

Websites

On Japanese industrial policy, see **www.meti.go.jp/** and on the Korean industrial policy, see **www.kiep.go.kr/**

Questions

15.1 Can economics adequately explain why states intervene in the economy?

15.2 Are there particular reasons why states have intervened in the economies of the EU?

15.3 Are there important differences between the industrial policies of European countries on one hand and those of NICs on the other? If yes, what are they, and why do they exist?

15.4 Could there be an active, positive European industrial policy? What would be its main features?

15.5 Should the rules, taxes and grants offered to non-EU multinationals be harmonized? If yes, describe the policies that would/should emerge from this harmonization.

Notes

1   Note that among policies that can impact on the performance of firms and industries are fiscal, monetary and other aspects of macroeconomic policy in general. While we must, in examining industrial policy, be aware of these impacts, macroeconomic policy is not the primary concern. We are more concerned with policy designed to influence industry directly.

2   Cohen was referring specifically to French industrial policy, but it seems to us that his point is valid for all industrial policy.

3   A link with the first theorem of welfare economics can be established at this juncture. This theorem stipulates that every competitive economy is Pareto efficient.

4   For more on incomplete markets, see Stiglitz (2000) Chapter 4.

5   This might, for example, be through an employee from the first firm leaving and joining another firm.

6   Another type of intervention may be appropriate, such as improved information and skills for all firms so as to reduce the likelihood of a bad design.

7   Though see the theory of the second best.

8   On exit games see, for example, Geroski and Jacquemin (1985).

9   This example is from Nielsen *et al.* (1991, ch. 5).

10 According to this approach, a country's comparative advantage evolves in stages: first, a typical developing country will have comparative advantages in labour-intensive industries (e.g. clothing and textiles); with rising living standards and wages, these labour-intensive activities will be phased out, and the country will develop capital and subsequently technology and skill-intensive activities.

11 There is no common legal definition of a public enterprise in the EU. However, a 1980 Directive (OJCE, 29 July 1980) stipulates that a public undertaking is one 'over which the public authorities may exercise directly or indirectly a dominant influence by virtue of their ownership of it, their financial participation therein, or the rules that govern it'. Public authorities are the state: government, central, regional or

local authorities.

12   For Plato, the state and the individual are both subservient to the attainment of the objective good. The tasks of the ideal state, as defined by Plato, are: to maintain the equality between individuals (excluding slaves), divided into social classes, to supervise the production and distribution of commodities – for example, to fix the conditions if agricultural production takes place – and to authorize exports and imports. Despite his strong advocacy of private property, Aristotle asserted even more strongly than Plato the existence of the state as a spiritual reality.

13   In France, Air France and the SNCF (Société Nationale des Chemins de Fer Français) are mixed societies that were created in the 1930s.

14   The Commissariat à l'Energie Atomique was founded in 1945.

15   Nationalization is the taking into state ownership of private firms; in privatization ownership is transferred back into private hands; de-nationalization refers to that type of deregulation that removes the barriers preventing private firms from entering a nationalized industry; it allows for some private ownership, whereas privatization implies no state ownership.

16   The publication in 1967 of Servan-Schreiber's book *Le défi américain* partly explains the formulation of this new objective; it culminates in the resurgence of the theme of the 'technological gap'. For more on the significance of Servan-Schreiber's book, see Hayward (1995).

17   Note that the wave of privatization started in Pinochet's Chile in the mid-1970s.

18   See, for example, *Le Monde* of 19 May 2004.

19   For a contrary view, see Solo (1982).

20   On the New Deal experience, see also Hawley (1966) and Diebold (1982).

21   For more on the origins and specifications of US antitrust policies, see Shepherd (1990, ch. 19) and Shughart (1990, pp. 199–202).

22   There are only a few cases of bailing out by the federal government; one is the Lockheed Company (see Diebold, 1982, p. 172).

23   It is not possible to refer to the plethora of studies related to these themes. However, the reader can refer, for example, to Prestowitz (1988) and Nelson (1993).

24   The Pentagon's long-lasting commitment to technology is reflected through various programmes, among which are the Strategic Defence Initiative (see Colijn, 1987) and the Navy's programme called the Rapid Acquisition of Manufacturing Parts (RAMPs).

25   Note that MITI is today known as the Ministry of Economy, Trade and Industry (METI).

26   For more on a concise historical snapshot of Toshiba, see Rothacher (2004).

27   For more on Japanese industrial policy, see Okuno (1988). On historical developments of Japanese industrial policy, see Hosomi and Okumura (1982), and Jansen (2000).

28   The *sogo shosha* have at their disposal a very dense and developed network of information. They can respond quickly to changes in the foreign demand and they help Japanese MNEs in their location decisions (see, for example, Kojima, 1978; Peyrard, 1990).

Appendix 15.1

Sales of public assets in European countries

In the following table, partial sales of public assets correspond to de-nationalizations whereas full sales are privatizations.

Country	Utilities	Manufacturing and others
Austria	Graz-Koflacher Kisenbahn[p]	Bayou Steel Co.
	Bergau GmbH[p]	Fepla Hirsch GmbH[p]
	ÖMV (oil products)[p]	Futurit Werk AG[p]
Denmark	Statsangstalten	Kryolitselskabet
	Livsforsikring	Kobenhavns Lufthavn
		Postgiro
		TeleDanmark
France	TF 1	Elf-Aquitaine
		CGCT
		St Gobain-Pont-à-Mousson
		Compagnie Générale d'Electricité
		Matra
		Crédit Commercial de France
		Société Générale
		Caisse Nationale de Crédit Agricole
		Sogénal
		BBTP
		BIMP
		Paribas
		Indosuez
		Dassault
		Mutuelle Générale Française
		Agence Havas
		BNP
		Rhône-Poulenc
		UAP
		AGF[p]
		Bulle Framatome[p]
		Renault[p]

Country	Utilities	Manufacturing and others
Germany	IVG	VEBA (totally private)
		VIAG (totally private)
		Volkswagen (totally private)
		Deutsche Pfandbriefantstalt
		Deutsche Siedlungs and Landesrentenbank
		Deutsche Industrieanlagen
		Salzgitter (totally private)
		Lufthansa
		Schenker & Co.[P]
		Deutsche Verkehrskreditbank[P]
		Treuarbeit
Italy		Alitalia[P]
		Aeritalia
		Sirti
		Selenia
		Alfa Romeo
		Banco Nazionale del Lavoro[P]
		Credito Italiao
		Istituto Immobiliare
		Comit[P]
The Netherlands	KLM	Stoovaart Maatschappij Zeeland
		NMB Postbank
		NV Gerofabriek
		Hongovens
		DSM II
		NIB
		Vredestein
		DSM I
Spain	MIPSA	IGFISA (food)
	FOVISA	Frigsa (food)
		Olcesa (food)
		Gypsa (food)
		Seat (motor car)
		Secoinsa (electronics)
		SKF Española

Country	Utilities	Manufacturing and others
		Industrias Semimetalicas (aluminium)
		Remetal, Aluflet (aluminium)
		Textil Tarazona (textiles)
		Hilaturas Gossypium (textiles)
		Pamesa (paper)
		Entursa (hotels)
		Viajes Marsans (tourism)
UK	Associated British Ports	BP (Petrol)
	British Gas	Cable & Wireless
	British Telecom	Britoil
	Sea Link	Enterprise Oil
	National Bus Company	British Aerospace
	British Airways	Jaguar
	British Airports Authority	Inmos
	British Steel	International Aeradio
	Water (England and Wales)	British Shipbuilders Electricity
	North of Scotland Hydro-Electric Board[p]	(England and Wales)[p]
		British Sugar Corp.
	South of Scotland Electricity Board[p]	Fairey Engineering
		Ferranti
	Forestry Commission	ICL
	Scottish Bus Group	Wytch Farm
		Scott Lithgow
		Vosper Thorneycroft
		Vickers Shipbuilding
		Yarrow Shipbuilders
		Leyland Bus Company
		BA Helicopters
		Swan Hunter
		British Rail Hotels
		Unipart[p]
		Shorts[p]
		Rolls-Royce
		Royal Ordnance
		North Sea Oil Licence
		Amersham International

Country	Utilities	Manufacturing and others
		Council House
		Girobank[p]
		Istel
		Rover Group
		National Freight Company
		Plant Building Institute
		National Enterprise Board
		General Practice Finance

[p] Prospective sales

Source: OECD (1990a) and national sources

CHAPTER 16

Industrial policy in the European Union

16.1 Learning objectives

The main objectives of this chapter are:

◆ To delve into a concise history of industrial policy in a selected number of EU economies

◆ To briefly review the economic transition in the new EU member states from central and eastern Europe

◆ To present the EU Competition Policy, define and discuss what we mean by a positive industrial policy, and

◆ To conclude with a debate on industrial policy in the EU

16.2 History of industrial policy in Europe

There was a near consensus on industrial policy in Europe and, in general, on the role of the state in economic affairs during the period of the Renaissance. A divergence of views developed during the Industrial Revolution, and marked differences have persisted since. In the twentieth century, even with the spread of widely influential schools of thought, there is no unanimity on what constitutes appropriate intervention. First, Keynes's thinking influenced the national policies of virtually all west European and North American countries after the war, providing support for anti-cyclical budgetary policies. Since the early 1980s, the neoliberal, anti-interventionist, 'new classical economists' have convinced the governments of Europe (and elsewhere) of the merits of deregulation. The significance of Robert Lucas's contribution to this school of thought, through his theory of 'rational expectations', was recognized in his being awarded the 1995 Nobel Prize for Economics.

Modern economic thought about intervention has emerged from a number of earlier schools of thought. Mercantilism, prevalent up to the eighteenth century, held that a country's wealth was represented by the wealth of the state – controlled by the sovereign. This was an interventionist, protectionist doctrine, owing much to (among others) Machiavelli.[1] The state had power and used it to determine which individuals or groups obtained trading and other commercial rights. This led to the enrichment of a mercantile bourgeoisie and possibly to an increase in general welfare. In the seventeenth and early eighteenth centuries, many merchants, bankers and industrialists were in favour of a strong state because they felt that the commercial prosperity of a nation was strictly linked to the political power of the monarch and to the success of its military conquests abroad.

The physiocrats in France in the eighteenth century and the classical political economists in Britain in the eighteenth and nineteenth centuries vigorously opposed state intervention. Their views are expressed in the famous saying, *laissez-faire, laissez-passer*, strongly advocating free trade, the freedom of the individual and the freedom of enterprise. This was a philosophy and ideology consistent with what was required for the Industrial Revolution. By the late eighteenth and early nineteenth centuries, the emerging commercial and industrial bourgeoisie saw itself as inhibited by various economic and social regulations of the state. Different paces of industrialization in Europe, as well as different degrees of penetration of the ideas of the classical economists, resulted in the twentieth century in Keynesian policies being applied to differing extents in different countries. Together these explain the differences in national industrial policies. Such differences have persisted, and underlie the difficulties in designing an industrial policy for the EU.

16.2.1 Major historical trends in national industrial policies

Germany

After the Second World War, Germany became one of the major proponents of a free market economy in Europe. In official language, *Strukturpolitik* is the word used to refer to industrial policy in Germany. But in the 100 years or so before the war, Germany had had an intensely interventionist, centralist state. State intervention, and constraints on competition, started in Bismarckian Germany and culminated in the 1930s. The *Zollverein*, established in 1834 under Prussian leadership, began the process, also providing the opportunity to build a strong industrial economy.

The central philosophy embodied in the Erfurt Programme, adopted in 1891, was to develop public enterprises as a means to bring about production on a large scale and also as a means to improve general social welfare (Russell, 1965). The Erfurt Programme remained in force until 1921; it was then replaced by the Goerlitz Programme which endorsed the principle of public ownership. In the late-nineteenth century cartels, *Syndikate*, *Konzerne* and monopolies were formed in heavy industries.[2] The *Syndikat* is a superior form of cartel, in which the total production of a firm, of an industrial sector and of a stage of production is transferred and sold to a common point of sale (Maschke, 1914). In the late nineteenth century, *Syndikate* were formed in the coke and coal industries (called *Kokssyndikat* and *Kohlensyndikat*) (Hallgarten and Radkau, 1974). By the end of the century, German coal production was the second largest in the world. List's ideas, and in particular his criticism of the 'dwarf economy', had a definite influence on the constitution of large groups in German industry at that time.[3] The *Kartellgesetz* of July 1933 increased state intervention in the economy, which further intensified under Hitler.

Breaking radically with this interventionist, authoritarian system, postwar Germany dedicated itself to the building of a free domestic economy within the Common Market. The necessity to reconstruct a devastated economy explains the continued and concentrated aid to some industrial sectors (coal, shipbuilding and steel). The year 1957 is crucial for German industry as it marks, through the Treaty of Rome, the launching of unprecedented opportunities for German industrial goods, and the determined dismantling of large groups and conglomerates. The 1957 *Kartellgesetz* – prohibiting anti-competitive behaviour – was subsequently amended and passed by the Bundestag in 1964 (Hallgarten and Radkau, 1974). An anti-merger bill was passed in the early 1970s.

The first wave of privatizations began in 1958, and was revived in 1982 with the coming into power of a right-wing coalition. For example, the oil company VEBA was privatized in 1983. From the 1960s onwards, the German *Strukturpolitik* gave the government only a supporting role. Even after the late 1960s, with the advent of the SDP (*Sozial Demokratische Partei*) as the dominant partner in a coalition with the Free Democrats, the public sector did not increase. Over all these years, the preferred form of support was tax relief, the major aims were to increase productivity and to promote innovation and technological development. This was made possible by the existence of three circumstances:

+ The federal structure of the country which gives the various Länder a large margin of manoeuvre. The federal structure of the country allows a *Strukturpolitik* to be carried out at the state level coupled with actions at the level of the Länder. The German Constitution gives the Länder the responsibility for education and vocational training.

+ The apparent absence, *in the past*, of acute regional problems. Before the reunification of the two Germanies in 1990, industrial activity was more or less evenly distributed. In 1978, one-third of the German population lived in assisted areas, which covered more than 60 per cent of the German territory (regional aid represented 40 per cent of total federal and Länder aid). However, since reunification, the regional problem has become severe. The politicians of the new Länder have sought for more decentralization, increased economic activity, and a more active and positive industrial policy aimed at rescuing the remaining public companies.[4] Already in 1992, per capita investment was higher in the new Länder compared with western Germany (Hochberg, 1998).

◆ The co-operation between different partners involved in the design and implementation of the policy, namely government, industry, research institutes, universities, trade unions and large banks. In particular, the role of the banking system is crucial to industrial development in Germany. Since the middle of the nineteenth century, large banks have exercised a 'weeding-out' function. In Hager's words (1982, p. 240):

> The ability of the big German banks to have detailed knowledge of all major firms in the key sectors of the economy (through their representatives on the boards of directors) and their willingness to go for long-term capital gains rather than short-term high dividends are examples of the many fortunate historically derived arrangements that lessen the need for active industrial policies in that country.

The efficiency of the banking system meant financial support could be extended to many more industrial sectors, including nuclear power, aircraft, computer and ocean-related industries, than was the case in most other countries. Although, today, many large companies (for example, Siemens) are internally financed, banks remain important in financing SMEs (as does the government, within EU constraints).

One area where the state's contribution was important was in education and training. Even here, however, success was due, at least in part, to close relationships between education and training on the one hand and industry on the other. One result was the predominance of German firms in technology-oriented industries.[5] As pointed out by Freeman (1982, p. 100) 'by the late nineteenth century, Germany had developed a "national system of innovation" which proved superior to the British in terms of the education and training system, as well as the organisation of in-house R&D in the new chemical and electrical industries'.

The absence of intervention in Germany should not be overemphasized. An important *social market economy* co-exists with the market economy. In the social market economy competition is limited – through state regulation and direct intervention – in the interests of political or social goals. 'These types of politically regulated enterprises can be found in the services sector (transport, postal services, telecommunications, energy supply, banking, and insurance) . . .' (Esser, 1995). However, even in the regulated industries there is now a mix of private and public enterprise.

Another, more centralized, example of state intervention in Germany is in research and technology. Through the Federal Ministry for Education and Research (*Bundes Ministerium für Bildung und Forschung*, BMBF), and its precursor, the Federal Ministry for Research and Technology, the research and technology policies have been the major ingredients of the German *Strukturpolitik* since the 1950s. The leading technological position of Germany is credited to its technological and educational policies. In 1988, German industry spent around DM 35 billion (€17.5 billion) on R&D programmes, of which two-thirds were government funds (Schuster, 1990), whereas in 1999, R&D expenditure by businesses exceeded DM 60 billion. The ratio of gross domestic expenditure on R&D to GDP was therefore 2.4

per cent in 1999, one of the highest in the EU. The BMBF co-ordinates all federal expenditures on R&D, and can be seen, to some extent, as actively and positively interventionist, because the allocation of funds is based (not entirely, but preferentially) on the government's calculated guesses about winners of the future.

The German *Strukturpolitik* has been primarily of the first and second types of industrial policy, but also with minor elements of the third, fourth and fifth types. It has, in general, been a more *laissez-faire* than interventionist approach; where there have been government subsidies, they have been limited in scope and have attempted to leave most decisions to market forces, with the exception of the social market areas.

The UK

There has long been a commitment to free trade in the UK, and a widespread scepticism as to the ability of the state to intervene beneficially in economic matters has always been widespread.[6] This is normally seen as the legacy of Adam Smith (1776), and he was no doubt influential. However, it is not coincidental that the UK was the most powerful trading country in the world and the one most strongly in favour of free trade. The intense intervention of the mercantilist era provided the foundation on which private entrepreneurs and individuals could build the first industrialized nation. The Victorian values spread through the nineteenth century dominated the government–industry relationship (Grant, 1989). The result, as Walker (1993) writes, was that the role of the state in Britain 'was confined to some regulatory functions (financial markets, property law, etc.) and to the advancement and military protection of foreign trade'. In more recent times, the British commitment to as little government intervention as possible is exemplified by the 1965 anti-merger legislation, and by the Industry Act passed in 1972.

In the 1960s, the National Economic Development Council, the Industrial Reorganization Corporation and other bodies were set up to help companies to catch up with their European and international counterparts (Hager, 1982). This suggests an active, positive policy, but in the view of many commentators, government intervention in Britain (be it under the leadership of the Labour Party or of the Conservative Party) has often occurred as a policy of last resort. In Grant's words (1989, p. 87), 'the main motive for intervention has been the collapse of an enterprise . . ., or at least the fact that it is in such a poor state that it would be unable to continue without government aid'.

There are exceptions to this such as the steel industry which was built up as part of a national industrial strategy under Labour immediately after the war. From then on, Grant may be correct even for the steel industry. The 1951 Conservative government de-nationalized the industry. When the 1964 Labour government re-nationalized it, at least part of the reason, unlike the earlier nationalization, was the need to support the industry because it had been technologically backward and generally uncompetitive. Under the Thatcher government, restructuring and radical rationalization were required to bring British Steel Corporation towards profitability. This prepared it for re-privatization in 1988 (Grant, 1995). In relation to steel, and to the other industries in which nationalizations had taken place, the extraction of the state in the 1980s was thorough. Of the major countries of Europe, 'Britain is the one in which the transition from the old conception of a "national champion" to that of the international firm has gone furthest' (Grant, 1995).

Where policy was active and positive, as for example in the nuclear and aircraft industries, large amounts of resources were inappropriately committed by the state. In Hager's (1982, p. 238) view, this aspect of industrial policy was an outstanding failure, since 'it drained the rest of the economy of scarce engineering talent'.

Over the past decades, the retrenchment of the state from a number of industrial sectors went in parallel with a shift from sectoral to horizontal measures. Current industrial policy in the UK embraces three major components: (i) it emphasizes the promotion of science and technology; (ii) it assists small firms; and (iii) it has a clear regional focus. This shift has occurred to such an extent that British industrial policy today can be seen merely as a subset of an overall competitiveness policy (Wren, 2001).

In general, British industrial policy, like Germany's, has been more about attempting to get the environment right for industrial success, than about intervening actively or positively. Where intervention has been active and positive, unlike in Germany it has generally failed in Britain.

France

It has been customary to view industrial policy in France as an extension of the seventeenth-century mercantilist 'Colbertist policy'. It should be remembered, however, that Colbert, minister of Louis XIV, applied the same protectionist policy as his predecessors (Sully, for example). The originality of Colbert's approach lay in the fact that manufacturers were, in his time, the key sector to be developed. In order to protect and promote the domestic manufacturers, high and prohibitive tariffs were imposed on imported manufactured goods. This trade policy was supplemented by a meticulous industrial policy aimed in particular at raising the quality of products.[7] The consolidation of the state led to unprecedented wars and to distress and famine in the countryside. An anti-Colbertist movement arose, which nourished the emerging physiocratic doctrine. Turgot, the minister of Louis XVI, demonstrated an indisputable efficiency in restoring free trade and in deregulating manufactures.

Among Napoleon's legacies to France was an educational system – the *Grandes Ecoles* – which was to constitute an indirect means of intervention by the state; in these colleges was to be created a new elite: the civil servants who were to administer industrial (and other) policies. The schools remain today a most important training ground for senior administrators of the state apparatus in France.

After the Second World War, France isolated itself from the international community. It experienced enormous difficulties in breaking with the protectionist era inherited from Méline,[8] but this isolationist policy did enable France to consolidate trade links with its colonies and to strengthen the role of the state (Eck, 1990). State intervention became embodied in the French planning system. It may seem ironic that the *Commissariat au Plan*, created in 1946, had as its first director the businessman Jean Monnet, one of the founding fathers of the European Union.[9] However, this illustrates the fact that planning in France involved a social compromise (Cohen, 1995).

The French planning system is best characterized by its three closely associated epithets: it is flexible, indicative and concerted, as it involves the co-operation of different economic partners. The plan involves non-binding quantitative targets for global, sectoral and regional production, investment and employment. These targets normally cover a period of five years.[10]

An objective of the first French plan was to modernize some industrial sectors and industrial infrastructure (railway, electricity, coal and steel). Among major objectives in subsequent plans, was to create industries capable of withstanding international competition through the supply of capital to industries that needed to replace old capital stock, through incentives to merge, and through the provision of technological know-how. In the 1950s, France imitated Britain by laying the ground for the active development of the nuclear and aerospace industries. This latter was militarily motivated.

During the 1960s, the 'German miracle' and the 'American challenge' led the French government to focus on the building up of technologically advanced national champions able to reap the full benefits arising from the associated economies of scale. Among the candidates for national champion status were CGE (electrical), PUK (aluminium and chemicals), Saint-Gobain (glass), Rhône-Poulenc (chemicals), SNIAS, Dassault and Bréguet (Messerlin, 1987).

Although one of the objectives of French planning was to build up strong national groups, and although the French state has been a major actor in the shaping of industrial policy and industrial structures in postwar France, the state gradually changed its philosophy. It was more *dirigiste* than other European governments throughout the period after the war, but it was less so later than earlier. According to Eck (1990), from France's participation in the EEC in 1958 onwards, the French state became more respectful of the principles and mechanisms of the market.

The French government's answers to the oil crisis were many, and sometimes contradictory policies. Under the presidency of Giscard d'Estaing (1974–81), a policy of specialization in selected sectors was favoured (the so-called *politique de créneaux*). Public funds were poured into the mechanical equipment industry. For military and strategic reasons, the French industrial policy of the 1970s was also geared towards the objective of import substitution. The Electronic Components Plan was drawn up for that purpose. Large sums of public funds were also allocated to rescue the ailing textile companies (*Plan Textile*). Most of these policies, though in practice aspects of industrial policy, were 'largely outside the remit of the ministry supposedly in charge of industry' (Cohen, 1995). Radically opposed to Giscard d'Estaing's conception of industrial policy, the socialist governments in the early 1980s favoured a policy of *filières*.

Other contradictions arising in the conduct of industrial policy in the 1980s centred on the role of the state as entrepreneur. For the first socialist governments of the early

1980s, public firms were seen as an essential instrument in boosting economic growth. Through its 1981–82 policy of nationalizations, the government gained control, wholly or partially, of 12 large industrial groups, two financial groups and 36 banks.[11] Although this new wave of nationalizations had economic objectives, it was overshadowed by political ideology. In 1986, the short-lived conservative government de-nationalized all the above, with the exception of Sacilor and Usinor. Its privatization programme was very comprehensive since it was extended to cover companies and banks that had been under state control since the 1940s (Agence Havas, Banque Nationale de Paris, Crédit Lyonnais). A new form of pragmatism emerged, however, in the latter part of the 1980s as the new socialist governments also partly privatized some state companies. Since the late 1980s, French industrial policy has been characterized by a lesser amount of restriction and by increased openness to foreign investors. This has been in line with the various governments' dedication to the building of a more economically integrated Europe.[12]

The role of the French state in economic development in general, and in industrial development in particular, has often been overemphasized. The French planning system is not coercive, but indicative, and based on consensus. But though not focused, the power of the state in France is pervasive. On the basis of the index of impact of public enterprises calculated in Table 15.2 (see Chapter 15), France is not far below Sweden, and well above the UK. Industrial policy in France is mixed. It has varied over time, to some extent dependent on which government was in power, except since the late 1980s. There have also been a number of different instruments of policy at any one time. So, as in the UK, there are elements of all five types of industrial policy in France. Also as in the UK, industrial policy is not concentrated in the fourth and fifth types, but rather the first, second and third. However, French industrial policy has been more interventionist than Britain's; greater weight has been put on the fourth and fifth types than in the UK.

Italy

Italy is another country with a relatively long tradition of state intervention in the economy. The depression of the early 1930s, with a generalized downward movement of shares on the stock exchanges explains the creation in 1932 of the *Istituto per la Ricostruzione Industriale* (IRI) which soon controlled part of the banking system in Italy (Corbino, 1962). The first mission of the IRI was to integrate the large, newly constituted public firms who had a participation in its capital, and eventually to control them totally. The IRI gained control, albeit indirectly, of the shipbuilding industry (Fincantieri), of the maritime transport industry (Finmare) and of the steel industry (Ilva) (Corbino, 1962).

The IRI, in a sense a legacy of fascism in Italy, in more recent times, developed interests in the automotive and civil aviation industries (by controlling Alfa Romeo and Alitalia) and in the food industry (SME). It also helped to establish a modern heavy and light engineering industry, as well as technologically advanced sectors such as computing, electronics and telecommunications (STET). It developed extensive interests in the banking sector, becoming the majority shareholder of the Credito Italiano, Il Banco di Roma, and of La Banca Commerciale.

In the 1950s, as the Italian economy was starting to register unprecedented growth rates, massive state intervention was developed in order to solve two of the major domestic problems at the time: the transformation of the economy from an agricultural-based economy to an industrialized economy, and the increasing *Mezzogiorno*[13] issue. The law of October 1950, known as the *legge stralcio*, facilitated the expropriation, improvement and redistribution of land to farmers. Public concern about the less developed regions of Italy, and in particular about the *Mezzogiorno*, led to the creation of the *Cassa per il Mezzogiorno* and to the involvement of the state holding company, IRI, in the industrialization of the south (Ranci, 1987). The objective of the *Cassa* was to develop infrastructure and industry in the south of the country. This *Cassa* dissolved at the turn of the millennium. The IRI represented a driving force in southern industrialization until the early 1970s. It supported the development of heavy industries (chemicals, steel, aluminium, oil and gas) mainly in the south. A study by Del Monte (1977) estimated that between 1953 and 1971, regional investment incentives generated between 79,000 and 124,000 manufacturing jobs in the *Mezzogiorno*.

Until the early 1970s, industrial policy in Italy was intimately conducted in relation to regional policy. After 1973, a radical change was implemented: industrial policy became defensive. As an aftermath of the economic recession, the state sought to avoid too many bankruptcies by simply taking over large private firms.

Government intervention in Italian industry is best represented as a network of multi-focal relationships. The IRI has certainly been a mainstay in industrial development in Italy. For example, SGC, a subsidiary of IRI, became in 1983 the twentieth largest producer in the area of semiconductors (Anastassopoulos *et al.*, 1987).

In the second and last phase of its existence (between the 1980s and 2000), the IRI was unable to face the level of intense political influence. Corruption[14] helped to create massive losses and debts, which represented 5 per cent of Italian GDP in January 1994. The large size of the public deficit, the inefficiency of public administrations, and a faster pace of European integration, radically changed the nature of industrial policy in the 1980s. Italian industrial policy has become more market oriented (Ranci, 1987), and new policy instruments have been introduced (Balcet, 1997). In particular, technological innovation becomes an important tool of the Italian industrial policy.

Since the mid-1980s, the combination of the completion of the single market and the general intensification of global competition has forced restructuring on Italian industries. It was just in these years, however, that 'the internal crisis of the Italian political system exploded and made the development of national strategies for international economic growth extremely difficult to carry out' (Bianchi, 1995). There is something of a vacuum, with all awaiting the outcome of the political struggles.

Though not necessarily coherent, Italian intervention has traditionally been intense, greater than in any other major European country. The data in Table 15.2 (Chapter 15) show that the impact of public enterprise in Italy has been greater than in other major European countries, although it receded forcefully in the late 1990s. This puts Italy more into industrial policy types four and five than its European partners, at least until recent decades.

Spain

State intervention in the Spanish economy has been a creation of twentieth-century economics. Before the civil war, the state had only a marginal impact on Spanish economic life. Its activities were limited to justice, defence, police, and to infrastructural works which were not profitable enough to be carried out by private initiatives. According to Garcia Delgado *et al.* (1989), the optimal state during that time was seen as one that exercised the lowest possible level of interference with private initiatives, and that could protect the domestic market against foreign competition.[15]

State intervention intensified as a result of the Great Depression of the early 1930s and of the diffusion of Keynes's ideas. The action of the state took three forms:

◆ Protection against foreign competition through trade barriers, such as import quotas, which became even more popular later under Franco's rule.

◆ Stimulation of national production, through fiscal and financial aid to domestic enterprises.

◆ Regulation of production and commercialization through corporatism.

State regulation and state intervention increased sharply under the Franco dictatorship; it reached its peak during the 1940s and 1950s. The creation of an intrepreneurial public sector – an expression borrowed from the *Instituto Nacional de Industria* (INI) – is the very peculiar characteristic of Francoism (Garcia Delgado *et al.*, 1989). The INI was set up in 1941. In the 1950s there was a gradual liberalization of the Spanish economy, culminating in the 1959 *Plan de Estabilización y Liberalización* (Garcia Delgado *et al.*, 1989). This plan initiated the deregulation of both production on the domestic market and international economic transactions. Quantitative restrictions on imports and custom duties were reduced, imports of financial capital and of technology were facilitated.

This liberalization trend was short-lived, since the subsequent decade brought with it a new wave of protectionism and regulation, to such an extent that in the mid-1970s, the Spanish economy was still characterized by many institutional rigidities and by many administrative controls. In particular, its public sector was totally inefficient.

A new era opened for Spain with the advent of a democracy, and with the prospect of joining the EC. There was a definite opportunity to deregulate and liberalize the economy.[16] Spain joined the then EC, together with Portugal, in 1986.

Public enterprises in Spain have been an integral part of the industrial policy. Born in the period 1941–61, they were organized around holding companies, as is the case in Italy, Germany and Austria. For several decades, there has been three holding companies: INI, *Instituto Nacional de Hidrocarburos* (INH) and the *Dirección General del Patrimonio del Estado*

(DGPE) (Garcia Delgado *et al.*, 1989). These holding companies controlled roughly two-thirds of the value added of state-owned enterprises, which were assigned clear and determined objectives, such as: being export-driven, maintaining a high level of employment, combating the regional inequalities, improving the balance of technological trade, re-industrializing the country, and providing an example of the 'work ethos' (Garcia Delgado *et al.*, 1989). As in other EU countries, the INI's huge losses invited the central government to initiate a restructuring programme, culminating with its partial privatization in the mid-1980s. Another major tenet of this restructuring strategy was a major drive into research and development. In 1995–96, further restructuring of the public sector entailed the closure of the INH.

Ireland

There have been five main periods (and types) of industrial policy in Ireland since independence. From the beginning of fiscal autonomy in 1923 to 1932 the policy was one of agriculture-led growth, with little or no industrial intervention and a very low tariff regime. With the changes in the world economy following the depression in 1929, Irish policy, like most others in Europe, changed.

The second policy period was from 1932 to 1958, during which import-substituting industrialization (ISI) was implemented. Industrialization, based on indigenous firms, was to be achieved through protectionism. A set of Control of Manufactures Acts (1932 and 1934) aimed – with limited success – to keep ownership of the protected industries in Irish hands. This was also a period during which a number of public enterprises were established.

When all the employment that could be created through ISI had been created, the combination of outflows of people from the land, and high natural population growth still left Ireland in the 1950s with very high unemployment rates and high net emigration (Ireland's population decreased by around 1 per cent every year between 1951 and 1961). At the same time, developments in Europe expressed a general movement towards more liberal trade policies. This combination of factors resulted in a sharp change in Irish industrial policy.

The third policy period, 1958 to 1990, was one of export-led industrialization. Through a semi-autonomous government agency, the Industrial Development Authority, foreign direct investment was encouraged. There were high, though varying, rates of inflow of foreign capital, and the United States replaced the UK as the main origin of foreign economic interest in Ireland. The task of encouraging FDI was assisted by Ireland – along with the UK and Denmark – joining the EC in 1973. Today, subsidiaries of US companies account for more than half of all employment in foreign-owned firms in Ireland; foreign-owned firms account for over 40 per cent of all manufacturing employment and for over 70 per cent of all manufactured exports.

Since the early 1990s, a fourth policy period has been evident. The roots of the change were in the questioning of the concentration in industrial policy on encouraging FDI. Already in the early 1980s a report commissioned by the National Economic and Social

Council (and carried out by the American consultancy group, Telesis) had recommended a shift in favour of the development of internationally trading indigenous firms. A number of steps were taken in this direction, and over the 1980s the proportion of capital grants going to foreign firms declined from over 90 per cent to around 50 per cent, with the other 50 per cent going to indigenous firms. The change gathered pace in the early 1990s, culminating in reorganization of the industrial development agencies in 1994/95. A separate agency was established to encourage the development of indigenous firms, and both this new agency – Forbairt – and the Irish Development Agency, came under the control of an industrial policy and planning agency, Forfas.

With the advent of the third millennium, the emphasis shifted towards the promotion of a knowledge driven industrial structure. The fifth and most recent industrial policy report published on the Irish economy (the National Development Plan 2000–2006), proposes to devote more spending on human capital (such as training and development) than on grants as before. Also, following the partition of the Irish economy into two regions, there is today more emphasis on balanced regional development.

Recent decades have also seen Irish governments following European privatization trends. Sales of shares of previously state-owned enterprises have occurred in insurance and in sugar production, for example.

Denmark

Danish industrial policy integrates some elements found in the German *Strukturpolitik*. Traditionally liberal, it aimed at creating a favourable economic and industrial environment for firms, through fiscal and monetary instruments. During the Second World War, the state had a massive involvement in technological matters; it designed a 'science policy' which became subsequently a 'research policy', and in more recent years a 'knowledge strategy'. Postwar Danish industrial policy concentrated on technology promotion schemes.

In the 1980s, Danish industrial policy changed from a more *laissez-faire*, to a more interventionist, approach. The new policy had three main elements:

* A general model using the market mechanism
* A selective strategy (a large part of public spending for industrial policy benefits only a small part of manufacturing industry)
* A social-need oriented strategy.

As summarized by Braendgaard (1986, p. 181), 'the public sector has, directly or indirectly, helped create many of the strong competitive positions of Danish industry in international markets'.

The major state-owned enterprises were traditionally found in the postal, telecommunications, transportation and energy sectors. As stated above, their combined annual turnover used to be quite small in European terms, since it amounted only to 5 to 6 per cent of GDP in the early 1990s, that is, before the privatization move in this country (OECD, 1993b). At the beginning of the 1990s, the government started to transform the legal status of public enterprises. Tele Sonderjylland (Telecom Southern Jutland), Kobenhavns Lufthavnsvaesen (Copenhagen Airport), Statens Teletjeneste (Telecom, covering wireless communication) and Postgiro have all become limited liability companies. The Danish Competition Act 1990 has replaced the Monopolies Act 1955 and the Prices and Profits Acts 1974. Its aim is to promote competition and to strengthen the efficiency of production and distribution. Collusive tendering and resale price maintenance (that is, binding resale) agreements are prohibited.

Denmark has followed very closely the European leaders (namely the other Scandinavian countries such as Finland and Sweden) in the area of research and technology policies, and in emphasizing the knowledge component of industrial development. The creation in November 2001 of the Ministry for Science, Technology and Innovation is testimony of this new trend. With a ratio of business R&D expenditure to GDP still below 2 per cent (see Chapter 11) but growing steadily, Denmark aspires to close the gap with its neighbours. This is the broad mission carried out by the new Danish ministry, and this is all clearly spelled out in the Danish government's knowledge strategy (Danish Government, 2003). In particular, the Ministry provides support for technological innovation in all sectors and industries (including tourism and social services), and promotes spillovers, in the form of technology, education and management.

The Netherlands

Although the Netherlands is one of the most *laissez-faire* oriented European countries in terms of industrial policy and economic policy in general, it also provides an example of planning. Integrated projection planning is used. This is a set of conditioned, mutually compatible sectoral forecasts ascertained econometrically (Franzmeyer, 1979). The projections are only decisional aids. This country tries to overcome its regional problems by encouraging investment in the less-developed regions with the help of the Investment Grant Scheme (IPR).

16.2.2 The case of central and eastern Europe[17]

After the fall of the Berlin Wall in 1989, Poland, Hungary, the Czech Republic, Slovakia, Bulgaria, Romania and the ex-USSR (all former CMEA – Council for Mutual Economic Assistance – countries) initiated programmes of structural reform that were to culminate in the emergence of a market-led economy, and minimal intervention by the state in economic and industrial affairs. This is known as the period of 'transition', from a command economy with state and social ownership of the means of production, to a market economy with predominantly private ownership. The issue of privatization and restructuring in the new member states of the EU, and more specifically in central and east European countries (CEECs), deserves indeed a treatment of its own, for these countries were for many decades command economies. This means that their production and distribution systems were *for the most part* disconnected from market mechanisms, and that their means of production were *mostly* under state control. Manufacturing and service activities were normally carried out in state-owned enterprises (SOEs). These SOEs were generally characterized by low levels of technology (except in some strategic sectors such as defence), by low productivity levels, and by a highly vertically integrated structure, from input providers to final consumers. It should be noted that there were substantial differences and degrees of state control, productivity and so forth within the ex-communist countries of Europe. For example, under Tito's rule, the former Socialist Federative Republic of Yugoslavia (of which Slovenia used to be an integral part before it gained independence in 1991), was one of the most open countries of the group, allowing a certain degree of private ownership, with the 1988 New Enterprise Law consolidating private ownership in this country. Hungary was another country that had, in the course of its postwar economic history, allowed its economic system to evolve into a dual system that combined elements of a Soviet type command economy with aspects of free market, enterprise autonomy and private enterprise. Under this new economic policy launched by Kadar in 1968, and known as the New Economic Mechanism (NEM), profit, rather than plan fulfilment became the enterprises' main goal.

The transition towards a market economy has been carried out simultaneously with the process of their *rapprochement* and accession to the EU. This process started in December 1991 with the signing of the so-called Europe Agreements. Signed on a bilateral basis between the EU and most of the new member states, the Europe Agreements were *de facto* a first step towards the integration of the central and east European countries into a wider EU. These agreements allowed for a gradual tariff reduction and elimination of all quantitative restrictions for the CEEC signatories' exports. However, trade liberalization with the EU has been slower for certain 'sensitive products' (textile, clothing, iron, steel and agricultural products). The Europe Agreements were followed by the CEECs' application for membership to the EU during the 1990s. These countries could only become members on the condition that they fulfilled three broad criteria (known as the Copenhagen criteria), which included the ability to put in place a market economy and to cope with competitive pressures and market forces within the Union. Privatization has therefore been an extremely important ingredient of the CEECs' preparation to join the EU.

From a purely economic point of view, privatization in these countries has been carried out successfully, judging by the evolving composition of GDP over the 1990s (Table 16.1). In only a few years, the structure of production (measured for example by the share of the private sector in GDP) has changed dramatically. This economic change is particularly perceptible in a country such as the Czech Republic, as well as in Slovakia, where more than 75 per cent of GDP is accounted for by the private sector. Much of this restructuring has been stimulated by foreign inward investment. Indeed, there have been only a limited number of domestic investors in the privatization of the Hungarian state companies' assets (Blahó and Halpern, 1995); the Czech Republic and Romania have tried to make their privatization programmes more popular by, for example, distributing some company shares among the population.

Table 16.1 Private sector value added as a percentage of total GDP (selected CEEC countries, 1990, 1995 and 1999

	1990	1995	1999
Bulgaria	10	45	60
Czech Republic	5	70	80
Hungary	20	60	80
Poland	25	60	65
Romania	15	40	60
Slovakia	5	60	75
Slovenia	10	45	55

Source: Ministry of Finance of the Republic of Slovenia, 2000

Although the pace of economic reform has been very unequal in the former centrally planned economies, with for example Bulgaria and Romania not having yet been able to put in place an economic system able to cope with competitive pressures and market forces within the EU, there were some common features: the major instruments put forward to enable the industrial and economic transition were privatization, attraction of FDI, reform of the legal system, measures to support SMEs, and fiscal and monetary reforms with the creation of a competitive capital market. Again, the signing of Europe Agreements[18] with the EU in the early 1990s, and the formal application of these countries as well as their preparation for EU membership in subsequent years have greatly helped in shaping these reforms.

The prospects for these countries were not helped, however, by the bleak macroeconomic results achieved in the early 1990s, with soaring levels of inflation, large declines in national output and rising unemployment in countries once characterized by a theoretical full employment. The reasons for such results were predominantly the many distortions inherited from the inefficient centrally planned economic system prevailing in the past. At the core of the economic systems of these countries was central planning – embracing the most extreme *dirigiste* industrial policy – the importance of which varied from country to country. The characteristics of industrial policy in these countries were the quasi-absence of private enterprise, administratively set prices, production which generated negative value-added (the so-called Value Subtractor), labour hoarding, and centrally managed international trade. Since between one-half and three-quarters of all Hungarian, Bulgarian, Czechoslovakian and Polish trade was conducted within the sphere of the former CMEA before the fall of the Berlin Wall, a distorted industrial structure emerged in these countries. Intra-CMEA trade was concentrated essentially on the more industrially advanced products and resulted in the predominance – or 'overrepresentation' – of industries such as mechanical engineering and heavy chemicals. Trade with western Europe was limited and was concerned only with primary products (minerals), and with labour-intensive, low-value-added products (such as clothing and footwear). Little room was accorded to production and trade in industries such as computers, instrument engineering and food processing.

It has been widely acknowledged that the leaders in the reform process were the Visegrad four, namely Hungary, Poland, Slovakia and the Czech Republic. While the majority of countries opted for 'shock therapy' reforms, characterized by large privatization pro-grammes, others were more gradual in their approach. As seen above, the transition from a centrally planned to a market economy started 30 years ago in Hungary. Although Hungary has today been outpaced by some other countries in its progress towards economic reforms, it is seen as the most successful country in having set up a relatively sophisticated banking and financial system, an attractive element for would-be foreign investors. Already in the early 1990s, trade patterns between Hungary and the EU-12 showed that motor vehicles, office machinery and optical instruments were among the fastest growing Hungarian exports.

According to Eurostat data, inflation has been brought down to acceptable levels in the new member and applicant countries, in particular in Lithuania (where the rate was as low as 1.3 per cent in 2001), and in Latvia (2.5 per cent). However, the inflation rate was still as high as 34.5 per cent in Romania during the same year, although this represented a decline from 154.9 per cent in 1997.[19] All countries – with the exception of Bulgaria – have experienced positive growth rates in real GDP from the mid-1990s. Some economic recovery has been on the way, albeit this has not yet fully translated in job creation. The unemployment rates for some of these countries are still very high; in 2001, unemployment affected more than 18.5 per cent of the Slovak, Bulgarian and Polish labour forces. In Lithuania, Latvia and Estonia, the unemployment rate was still well above 11 per cent during the same year.

Hungary and the Czech Republic have shown a clear commitment to becoming the east European leaders in the high-technology industries. The emergence of high-technology industries in Hungary is partly explained by the superiority of its system of innovation when compared with other central and east European countries. 'Hungary took an early interest in the development of technology, and a National Committee for Technological Development (OMFB) was set up as far back as 1964' (OECD, 1994, p. 295). In the late 1990s, some 19 per cent of all Hungarian exports were classified as high-technology exports; this figure compares with 21.6 per cent for Sweden, 20 per cent for Denmark and 13 per cent for Austria. In 2002, the percentage of the labour force employed in medium- and high-technology manufacturing industries was as follows: 9.2. per cent for the Czech Republic, 8.8 per cent for Hungary, 8.7 per cent for Slovenia, 7.9 per cent for Sweden, 7.2 per cent for Finland and 7 per cent for Denmark.[20]

Reducing the technology and quality gaps through the intensification of trade and invest-ment with the EU-15 implies designing a coherent industrial structure at the pan-European level. Whereas EU policy has to some extent taken cognisance of the CEECs' problems and needs, through the allocation of structural funding, some of the CEECs' governments have initiated industrial policies centred on targeting inward investment for high-technology projects. For example, in June 1998, the new Czech government defined and implemented a first real R&D policy by placing R&D and innovation among its main priorities.

16.2.3 Summary

In general, there appears to be a trend in the development of industrial policies in different (west European) countries: government intervention reaches a peak in the early 1950s – this period of intervention being explained by the need for postwar reconstruction – and in the mid-1970s, following the oil crisis. During the 1960s, the major objective of industrial policy in Europe was to catch up with the more technologically developed United States, and the increasingly threatening Japan. Since the 1980s, there has been a general withdrawal of the state, represented by deregulation and privatization.

Have industrial policies in Europe converged during the period since the Second World War? According to Hager (1982), if there is a trend, it is not to be found in the amount of intervention as such, but rather in the fact that the increasing importance of the international environment provides incentives for developing industrial policy.

In *Germany*, the view is that the role of the government is to provide an adequate framework or climate conducive to innovation and investment by firms. The government is to provide a research base, but not direct research towards a particular industry; positive financial assistance (state subsidies), and a 'picking the winner' strategy is to be the exception rather than the rule. Protection of infant industries will not be allowed.

The *British* view is close to the German one in that it advocates total freedom to be given to firms. The UK government has become heavily involved in supporting research directed at developing technology. However, the British attitude is the least European oriented of all since it stresses that in sectors where Europe has fallen behind its competitors, the only way to catch up is to welcome direct investment from the United States or Japan. Also, some officials in the UK have traditionally been sceptical with regard to the development of further European R&D and technological initiatives.

In some ways, the *French* attitude has been radically opposed to that of Germany and the UK. With its tradition in government interventionism, and in planning, France would have been in favour of transferring the national tools of industrial policy to the European level. It calls for further European industrial integration, and for more public investment in research-based and strategic sectors.

In the new member countries (the CEECs), much of structural change, production and trade reorientation facilitated by the privatization programmes, can be explained by: (i) the importance of FDI; (ii) the Europe Agreements, the preparation to EU membership and, the expectation ultimately of (iii) a combination of both (that is, intensive trade flows between the two Europes facilitated by west European direct investment). In these countries, the transition from centrally planned systems to market economies shaped by the wave of *laissez-faire* that swept across Europe in the late twentieth century, corresponds, from an industrial policy standpoint, to the passage from too much state intervention to too little organization of industrial affairs. The drive for a new type of industrial policy anchored on selective tools such as R&D and high-technology inward investment has been a distinctive feature of some of these countries in the late 1990s.

The clear differences in industrial policy prospects even among the three major European countries suggests difficulties in the building of a positive European industrial policy.

16.3 Competition policy in the EU

During the first 15 years of its existence, the then EC did not have an industrial policy in the sense of drafting the course of and stimulating industrial development.[21] This was not necessary because the favourable macroeconomic conditions of the 1960s (low inflation and unemployment rates, stable currencies, catching-up of European firms with their US counterparts) created a healthy competitive environment that would have kept prices down and have assured the efficient use of factors of production. To the extent that there was a European investment policy, it was confined to competition policy (first type of industrial policy in Table 15.1, see Chapter 15), and to commercial policy.

Horizontal measures, that is, measures with a wide and universal application throughout the Common Market, such as the harmonization of company laws, were almost non-existent. Vertical measures, that is, measures implying a selective Community intervention in depth in particular sectors or industries, were kept to a minimum. For security and strategic reasons, the atomic energy sector, the coal and steel industries and the agricultural sector were given special treatment.[22] It was not until the 1970s that it began to be seen that an adequate response at the European level to structural changes required more than provided for by the Competition Policy.

Nine articles in the Treaty (81 to 89; formerly 85 to 94 in the Treaty of Rome) are devoted to the designing of the EU Competition Policy.[23] The philosophy of the Community Competition Policy is based on the *laissez-faire* approach: the free interplay of supply and demand in all EU markets[24] is expected to provide the major ingredient for economic efficiency. Any firm willing to engage in some arrangement with another firm in the EU must notify the Commission, through the relevant national body. The Commission stipulates the incompatibility of such arrangements with the essence of the Common Market. *Article 85* specifies that 'the Commission shall investigate cases of suspected infringement of these principles' [of competition], and 'shall propose appropriate measures to bring [them] to an end'. It provides for action to be taken in cases where strategies followed by EU firms violate the principles of competition in the Common Market, and for exemptions in some specific circumstances. The Community Competition Law has precedence over national legislation, although it does not annul it.[25]

Articles 81 and 82 (see Appendix 16.1) prohibit every agreement (or strategy) that appreciably distorts open competition or that creates unfair competition in the member states. In particular, Article 81 deals with collusive behaviour. All practices that affect trade (price fixing, market sharing, control of production markets and investment, joint selling and joint purchasing agreements, and so on) are 'incompatible with the common market' in the sense that 'they affect trade between Member States' and limit the degree of competition. Article 81 clearly aims at controlling cartels; for example, it was found that in 1986 the EU market for polypropylene, a key product used in the manufacture of a wide range of plastics, was controlled by four EU-based firms: Royal Dutch Shell, Imperial Chemicals International, Montedipe and Hoechst. The Commission sought to prove that these four firms were operating a cartel with a view to fixing prices. However, price agreements have been more difficult to prove; some price movements may only be coincidental. In the case of a tight oligopoly, the price takers will often react instantaneously to the signals of the price leader.

Minor exceptions were envisaged under paragraph 3 of the same Article: some restrictive agreements, of minor importance, and/or encouraging co-operation between SMEs, such as R&D agreements, were permissible. To qualify for exemption from the prohibitions of Article 81/1 a co-operative research agreement must satisfy certain conditions (for example, the co-operation should have a specific objective). Finally, a 1968 Notice on Co-operation Between Enterprises states that co-operative agreements relating exclusively to basic research and development do not fall under Article 81.

Article 82 deals with the *abuse of a dominant position*. This refers to concentration or monopoly power that enables any firm, as a buyer or seller, to influence the outcome of the market. The essence of this article has to be found in the early days of the ECSC when France feared any renewed concentration of the German coal and steel industries. No precise definition of the level of concentration is given. There is, for example, no mention of the market share that a firm must have before it can be called a dominant firm. Such a general definition would be impossible, because a market share required for a firm to be dominant in one industry will be different from that required in another; it varies from product to product, industry to industry, market to market. In any case, it is not the existence of dominance that is prohibited, but the abuse of the dominant position. This view enables the Commission to intervene after a firm has acquired dominance and has sought to abuse it; it does not enable the Commission to prevent the emergence of that dominance in the first place.

Dominant firm abuse is illustrated, for example, by the case of Hoffman La Roche, a Swiss firm dominating the market for vitamins, that abused that position by charging different prices in different markets (price discrimination), and by the case of Commercial Solvents which controlled materials and refused to supply them freely to other firms. However, this view has been challenged in the *Continental Can* case in 1973 and in the *Philip Morris–Rothmans* case in 1987. In the *Continental Can* case,[26] the Commission argued that a dominant firm necessarily abused its position by seeking a merger with another firm (and that a merger between a dominant firm and another was in itself an abuse of dominance). In this particular case, the judgment of the European Court of Justice (ECJ) made it clear that proof of dominance required a definition of the market, and that the determination of the relevant market was essential (see discussion in Chapter 5).

The verdicts issued under these two cases opened the possibility for the use of Article 82 (and also 81) for *ex ante* EU control in some specific cases.

In 2003, the Council of Ministers adopted a new regulation that represented the most comprehensive Competition Policy reform ever.[27] Partly motivated by the looming enlargement to the CEECs, and partly explained by more than 40 years of practice and experience of handling Competition Policy tools, the reform replaces the 40-year-old procedural rules embodied in Articles 81 and 82, without altering the substantive content of these two articles (Box 16.1).

Box 16.1 The new rules of the EC Competition Policy

Regulation EC No. 1/2003 fundamentally modifies and simplifies the way in which the Treaty's antitrust rules are enforced throughout the EU.

The first substantial modification is that companies no longer need notify their agreements to the Commission in order to obtain antitrust approval. It is now up to the companies themselves to assess whether their agreements restrict competition, and if so, whether the restriction qualifies for an exemption under Article 81(3). Obviously, guidance from the Commission can be sought in cases of uncertainty.

The second major thrust of the reform is that the task of policing anti-competitive behaviour and handling complaints is no longer of the exclusive competence of the Commission. This task is now shared with the European Competition Authorities existing at national level. This implies that all competition authorities involved will co-operate closely in applying the antitrust rules.

This reform also extends to the case of mergers. These new rules have been in force since 1 May 2004, the day marking the fifth enlargement.

Article 86-2 (formerly 90-2) allows certain firms providing services of 'general economic interest' to exempt themselves from the general competition rules and to conduct purely national policies.

The EU position with regard to the competition rules has become somewhat ambiguous and unclear. Firms appreciably distorting or impeding the smooth functioning of a competitive environment are penalized, and yet it is recognized that large firms are necessary in some sectors to compete technologically and efficiently with US and Japanese firms. Large firms are more able to benefit from economies of scale and scope, and are more able to spend on R&D. The 1985 White Paper *Completing the Internal Market* endorsed the view that the EU needs companies of a sufficient size to compete with the large international corporations. This makes unequivocal opposition to all restriction of competition more and more difficult.

Free and undistorted competition in the Community requires strict monitoring and surveillance of state aids. *Article 87* (formerly 92; see Appendix 16.1) forbids any government aid to EU enterprises. In that regard, a very cautious approach was at first adopted by the Commission. The philosophy of the Commission was to try to limit subsidization and to try to incorporate it into the context of restructuring. Exemptions were allowed for particular economically weak industries and regions of the Community. National governments have to notify the Commission about any intention to allocate or alter existing aid schemes to particular industries, and the Commission decides on the compatibility of these aids with the provisions of the Treaty of Rome. If incompatibility arises, the member state is asked to amend or to abolish the aid. For example, in 1986 the EU Commission asked 'the West German government for an explanation of its alleged subsidy to Daimler Benz to build a new plant in Baden Würtemberg, an area not eligible for special regional assistance. The local authorities replied that it was merely a general aid to improve the region's industrial infrastructure' (Harrop, 1989, p. 112). Bianchi (1995, table 4.9) shows that of 15 disputes between Italy and the EC over subsidies to industry, in four cases (clothing and textiles, leather and footwear, man-made fibres and paper production) the national subsidies were forbidden. In four other cases various restrictions were imposed.

During the 1970s, on the onset of the recession, it was perceived that much state aid (in the steel industry in particular), was in fact 'sustaining lame ducks'. In subsequent years, the Commission looked for a tougher stance: state aids should be carefully monitored and controlled; they should decrease in size and importance. In its first comprehensive report on state aids published in 1989, the Commission described the structure of state aids to firms in the EU.[28] According to this first report, total public aid amounted to an average of 3.0 per cent of EU-10 GDP during 1981 to 1986. Eight other surveys have been undertaken and published by the Commission since. The Council's ambition of making the EU the most competitive and dynamic knowledge-based economy in the world by 2010, as expressed by the Lisbon Council in March 2000, implied additional efforts to scale down the general level of state aids in EU countries. To that end, a specific indicator and target date concerning the reduction of aid were introduced.

State aids have trended down, from 3 per cent of EU-10 GDP during 1981 to 1986, to less than 1 per cent of EU-15 GDP in 2001. As revealed in the *Ninth Report on State Aids* (CEC, 2001b), the level of overall state aid declined from an annual average of €102 billion during 1995–97 to €90 billion during 1997–99. Table 16.2 shows that differences among member states are still important. The countries with the highest shares in terms of GDP are Finland (1.74 per cent), Portugal (1.56) and Belgium (1.41), because of the predominance of regional aids. Note that the level of state aid has decreased in all member states in the late 1990s with the exception of Denmark, Ireland, Luxembourg and the Netherlands. In the case of Denmark, this is explained by substantial increases in aid to combat unemployment and support training, whereas in the case of Ireland, this is due to the inclusion of corporation tax figures since 1998 (corporation tax figures that are well below average are considered as an aid to industry).[29]

Table 16.2 State aid in EU members states (constant prices, annual averages), 1997-99		
	In % of GDP	In € per person employed
Austria	1.16	550
Belgium	1.41	830
Denmark	1.08	622
Germany	1.39	712
Greece	1.21	338
Spain	1.17	416
Finland	1.74	914
France	1.38	772
Ireland	1.36	706
Italy	1.28	607
Luxemburg	1.31	912
The Netherlands	0.90	406
Portugal	1.56	326
Sweden	0.84	436
UK	0.60	280
EU	1.18	563

Source: CEC, 2001b

Aids to the manufacturing sector have also tended to decrease, albeit more than proportionately. This decline is very much due to important reductions in state aids to manufacturing in large countries such as Germany and Italy.

16.3.1 Merger and takeover policy

The economic rationale for controlling mergers and takeovers is again that these practices could endanger competition, which is ultimately the unique means to achieve economic efficiency and increased economic welfare.

The Commission at first had to direct power to control mergers *ex ante*. This is understandable in the light of the long history of cartelization in the steel industry. The first proposals for EC anti-merger legislation were initiated in 1973. During that year, the Commission introduced a draft regulation on the control of concentrations between undertakings.[30] This draft was vehemently criticized by both industry and the member states. However, the Commission remained determined to have an agreement reached at some stage. Proper European merger legislation was becoming a prerequisite for the efficient functioning of a single market free of internal frontiers. Increased cross-border merger and acquisition activity of European firms in the second half of the 1980s made European legislation an urgent matter. In the absence of European legislation, the cross-border deals would be subject to the jurisdiction of more than one country, which would make control increasingly complex.

The Commission had to wait until 1989 to see the Council of Ministers finally move in favour of merger legislation. At that stage, only the UK, Ireland, France and Germany had legislation on this type of activity. Many of the other EU countries seldom took action in this regard. Greece and Portugal still did not exercise any merger control; the Belgian and Danish competition laws were much more permissive, since merger controls were exercised only over banking (Belgium) and under some specific circumstances (Denmark). Spain had very recently drafted a law on mergers. The Commission's Merger Regulation (Regulation No. 4064/89) was adopted in December 1989, and came into force in September 1990.[31]

Under Article 1 of the Regulation, all mergers having a 'community dimension' are covered. A 'community dimension' is defined as where:

(i)   *the aggregate world-wide turnover of all the undertakings concerned is more than ECU 5 billion, and*

(ii) *the aggregate Community-wide turnover of each of at least two of the undertakings concerned is more than ECU 250 million,*

unless each of the undertakings concerned achieves more than two-thirds of its aggregate Community-wide turnover within one and the same Member State. (OJ L 395/3)

The Regulation also applies to concentrations resulting from undertakings which do not have their principal field of activity in the Community, but are likely to have an effect within the Community. Between 1990 and August 2004, some 2559 merger cases have been notified to the Commission.

The definition of the Community dimension helps member states decide which legislation – national or Community – should be used. Member states shall not apply their national legislation on competition to concentrations which have a Community dimension, as defined in Article 1. Mergers which fall outside the scope of application of the Regulation can be dealt with by member states. The EU Merger Regulation reflects a preference for more competition and acknowledges the fact that large size is no guarantee of international competitiveness. A strong German influence can be detected in the drafting of this Regulation. The EU merger legislation still leaves a lot of room for decisions by national authorities; as in other respects, the EU regulatory legal framework here co-exists with strong national regulation.

EU policy on acquisitions is covered by the 13th Council Directive on Company Law, concerning takeovers and public bids (see OJ C 64, 14 March 1989, and its amendments in COM (90) final). This piece of legislation aims at creating a more liberal takeover market in the EU; it tries to establish certain minimum standards for the conduct of takeover bids, with the objective of ensuring equality of treatment for shareholders.

The 1989 Merger Regulation has been amended on two occasions: first by Council Regulation No. 1310/97 of 30 June 1997, and more recently by Council Regulation No. 139/2004 of 20 January 2004.[32] The 1997 piece of legislation introduces new thresholds, in addition to those above, for the definition of a concentration with a Community dimension, depending on the number of member states involved. The latest amendments to the 1989 Merger Regulation are written in the spirit of the new EC Competition Policy, for example with a shared responsibility between EU and national competition authorities. However, and in contrast to agreements, mergers still need prior clearance either by the Commission or the national authorities.

16.4 Towards a positive industrial policy

The EU industrial policy (EIP) has graduated from having mainly a supervisory function in the 1960s, to adopting a defensive stance in the 1970s, and to becoming more positive in the 1980s, and research driven in the 1990s and early 2000s. For example, although the need for Community initiatives in the area of R&D as a vital facet of the process of economic integration was appreciated by the original founders of the EU,[33] the Treaty of Rome did not give the Commission and the Council of Ministers explicit powers to promote research, and indeed, industry. In this section, we will study how the European industrial policy, as a simple competition policy in its early days (type 1), evolved from being a vague regulatory framework aimed at shaping the right market environment, to becoming a more positive industrial and technological policy.

16.4.1 The Colonna Report (1970): a first attempt at designing an EIP

By the mid-1960s, 'the EC Commission had begun working out a coherent industrial policy concept for the Community' (Franzmeyer, 1979, p. 116). In 1967, the Commission established the General Directorate for Industrial Affairs, which, among other objectives, sought to encourage cross-border industrial co-operation. During the same year, the first Council of Science Ministers met; it commissioned studies in six broad areas of technological development (of which data processing and telecommunications were two), and its initiatives led to the establishment of COST (European Co-operation in the field of Science and Technical Research).

The first working documents on industrial policy appeared. In particular, the second programme for medium-term economic policy (OJ L 129, 30 May 1969) laid down the cornerstone for the memorandum on 'the industrial policy of the Community' known as the 1970 Colonna Report (CEC, 1970). This constitutes the first attempt by the commission to define and to implement a Community industrial policy. This very ambitious report emphasizes six broad needs:

◆ To create a single market based on the elimination of intra-Community barriers to trade.

♦ To harmonize company laws, banking laws and taxation if the free movement of capital is to become a reality.

♦ To promote trans-EC mergers in order to enable European firms to adapt to the needs of the Common Market and to international competition.

♦ To have the Community play a role in the promotion of new technology.

♦ To integrate social and regional policies.

♦ To develop the Community's commercial policy with third countries.

After the 1972 Paris Summit, a Communiqué explicitly called for a common policy in the sphere of science and technology. This gave birth to a Commission memorandum (the Spinelli Memorandum) which set out the parameters of a Community Policy. The 1973 Spinelli *Memorandum on the Technological and Industrial Policy Programme* (CEC, 1973) put the emphasis on some elements of the Colonna Report, but the essence of the document was the promotion of a free-market-oriented common industrial policy based on:

♦ The elimination of technical obstacles to trade and the harmonization of national regulations

♦ The opening up of national markets for purchasing by public sectors

♦ The harmonization of company laws and the liberalization of capital markets

♦ The encouragement of trans-EC enterprises

♦ The encouragement of co-operation and mergers between Community firms through the diffusion of information.

In December 1973, a programme was adopted by the Council of Ministers along these lines, which partially reconciled the French *dirigism* with the German views influenced by the virtues of the *laissez-faire* approach. In spite of its adoption by the Council, its implications were kept to a minimum, since no real consensus on the necessity for or on the form of a common industrial policy existed at the time (Hitiris, 1994). The oil crisis and its concomitant economic recession caused it to fall short of its declared objectives. Both national governments and the Community were forced to divert attention, energy and investment from the 'sunrise' technologies, to the 'sunset' industries which were being seriously hit by the recession. However, one concrete proposal that emerged was the creation of the European Economic Interest Group (EEIG), which was finalized (that is, adopted by the Council of EU Ministers) in 1985, and which came into effect in July 1989. The EEIG is the first harmonized legal framework facilitating co-operation of EU firms. It enables EU companies, and more particularly SMEs, to merge part of their economic activities in a structure with full legal standing, while retaining their independence.

There had long been a need for such a framework. When the theme of the technological gap emerged, European governments initiated the promotion, via mergers and subsidies, of a series of national champions, as well as of cross-national groupings in key technological sectors. One of these early collaborative ventures was the Eurodata consortium which comprised Philips, AEG-Telefunken, ICL, CII, Olivetti and Saab. Its aim was to gain a contract in order to provide for the computer needs of the newly established European Space Research Organization.[34] Among the early collaborative attempts in the field of technology and industry, many, like the Eurodata Consortium, did not meet with much success, but the aerospace sector became a notable exception (see discussion on technological collaboration in Section 16.4.3, below).

16.4.2 The 1970s: a 'defensive' EIP

The American challenge, as well as the gradual shift of comparative advantages, gave birth to a defensive industrial policy, centred mostly on vertical actions. However, timid and unfruitful attempts were made to instigate and consolidate mergers in the EU. The Dunlop–Pirelli merger of 1971 dissolved in 1981 (Harrop, 1989). In 1973, Bull, Siemens and Philips tried to form the first computer group in Europe, Unidata. Its aim was to challenge the American IBM, but the group sank very quickly.

Limited traditionally to the coal and steel sector, more sectoral policies were introduced with the advent of the economic recession. Vertical actions were implemented to remedy the problems of the 'crisis industries' such as:

♦ The shipbuilding industry from 1969

♦ The textile and clothing industry, with the Multi-Fibre Agreements (MFAs) signed in 1974

♦ The automotive and machine tools industries, where quotas and VERs (voluntary export restraints) limit the annual imports of Asian products into each individual EU country.

According to Balassa's 'stages approach to comparative advantage' and to economic development (Balassa, 1977), these industries were since that time all declining industries. Since they were bound to contract in a given period of time, was it worth promoting them? Some economists have criticized the many bail-out actions in these industries, and have equated them to measures sustaining 'lame ducks'. British Steel, British Coal, Sacilor, Usinor, ENI Quimica in Italy and RUMASA in Spain are all well-known examples of firms where a poor strategy and a poor management have led to nationalizations as the only solution for their survival.

In the *shipbuilding* industry, Japan overtook western Europe as a major world producer in the 1960s. The shift in comparative advantage, which moved in favour of Asian countries (first Japan, and then South Korea and China) and, in the early 1990s, of east European countries (Poland), produced the first alarming signs for the European shipyards. The 1973 economic recession accentuated them. The growing difficulties of the industry in the 1970s are best summarized by Edwards (1982, p. 85):

> *Demand in the shipbuilding industry has traditionally been cyclical. Rarely, however, has the collapse of the market been as severe as in the mid-1970s. . . . The expansion in merchant ship-*

building during the 1960s and early 1970s was rapid. ... With the 1973–74 oil crisis ... demand for new shipping collapsed. While orders derived from the earlier optimistic forecasts of continued expansion cushioned the immediate impact, by 1978 the world order book was at its lowest in 13 years.

In 1992, the EU world market share, computed on the basis of order book, was close to its 1976 level, at slightly over 22 per cent. Over the same period of time, Japan's market share stabilized at roughly 28.6 per cent, whereas Korea's and China's shares were multiplied by 2.5 and 5 respectively. Employment in the construction of new vessels in the EU plummeted from roughly 209,000 in 1975 to 77,000 in 1992 (CEC, 1993b).

Overcapacity, losses and redundancies nurtured a host of generous government subsidies in both the European countries and the rest of the world. The influx of state capital into the industry went totally against the initial objective of the Commission which was to liberalize the market by 1975, through the phasing out of state aids. These state aids or 'crisis aid' were to be temporary, since they were to enable the restructuring of the industry in the long term.[35] In the late 1980s, talks with Japan and Korea were initiated for the purpose of stabilizing the international market.

In the *steel* industry, one of the most important industries for the Community in the past, a similar scenario existed. Soon after the creation of the ECSC in 1952, demand expanded considerably until the oil recession.

Table 16.3 Loss per ton (£) in the European steel industry, 1977-78

Company	Loss per ton £
Sacilor	42
Usinor	29
BSC (Italsider)	25
Cockerill	24
Kockner	21
Ensidesa	16
Estel	13
Arbed	11
Salzgitter	11

Source: British Steel Corporation Annual Press Conference, 4 July 1978, as reported in Woolcock (1982)

In the 1970s, falling demand, technological change, increased competition from composite materials and other substitutes, and increased global competition all led to overcapacity (up to 30 per cent for certain products), losses (Table 16.3), contraction in the workforce (by 50 per cent between 1974 and 1986), and a slump in prices.

The Commission attempted to regulate the market by introducing indicative targets for the major sub-products by country in 1975. Three years later, the Davignon Plan was introduced establishing minimum prices for some sub-products, increased guidance prices, import quotas, as well as anti-dumping duties on steel imports.[36] Bilateral agreements were concluded with EFTA, east European and developing countries. These various measures kept imports at their traditional level and increased prices successfully (Woolcock, 1982).

During the early 1990s, the signing of the Europe Agreements with east European countries initiated new turbulences in the market, with prices in the EU-12 decreasing by 30 per cent. Imports from central and eastern Europe rose by 40 per cent in 1992. However, negotiations with east European producers (Czech Republic, Slovakia, Poland, Russia, Ukraine and Kazakhstan) focusing on the 'smooth reorganization' of their exports into the EU enabled the Commission to implement safeguard measures and stabilized imports from these countries.[37] The Braun Report of November 1992[38] estimated over-capacity of crude steel at 30 million tonnes, and of rolled products at between 19 and 26 million tonnes (*Le Monde*, 11 February 1993). For all steel products combined, the capacity utilization rate was down to two-thirds. The Report called for a drastic reduction of numbers employed (by 50,000 in three years), for a reduction of overcapacity through plant closures, and for the reorientation of the market, as various means to rescue the European industry. Market orientation involved recommendations made by the Commission on the level of production required and was to be aimed at redressing prices. The Braun Report, and its subsequent Council meeting of February 1993, led to the reorganization of the market. For example, between February 1993 and April 1994, the production of hot-rolled products went down by 11 million tonnes. This resulted from the partial closures and privatizations of Freital, EKO-Stahl, ILVA, Sidenor, CSI and Siderurgia Nacional. (CEC, 1994a) If in the 1970s and in the early part of the 1980s, the political support of declining industries was explained mostly by protectionist motives (Hillman, 1982), the late 1980s and 1990s have introduced a more pragmatic approach, making structural adjustment a requirement. This is reflected in the new type of industrial policy pursued since that time.

16.4.3 Technological and research collaboration since the 1980s

Whereas, in the 1970s, EIP was fundamentally negative, as it was endeavouring to apply short-term remedies to the 'problem industries',[39] in the 1980s the approach was more constructive. A wide range of new technological programmes were set up. Some degree of technological collaboration and co-ordination has been achieved in the EU, through the launching of, *inter alia*, Esprit, Race, Brite–Euram and Comett.[40]

The technological gap discussed earlier, and the sluggish improvement in competitiveness of European industry generally – and of the information technology (IT) sector in particular – led to a complete rethinking of the appropriate strategies for EU industry. In particular, it was thought that the lack of European collaboration widened substantially the technological and competitive gaps (Mytelka and Delapierre, 1987). By the early 1980s, 12 major European IT companies had begun to collaborate under the instigation and with the assistance of the then Commissioner for Industrial Affairs, Etienne Davignon.[41] The group produced the first set of technological programmes, which ran from 1984 to 1987 (OJ L 208, 25 July 1983). Esprit was the IT component in this programme. Esprit was in fact the first technological programme ever implemented in the EU (see Box 16.2).

Box 16.2 The Esprit programme

Launched in 1984 with a financial base of ECU 750 million, the programme is based upon the idea of pre-competitive and collaborative research. This is compatible with EU Competition Policy, for Articles 81 and 82 of the Treaty prohibit collaboration for the purpose of competitive research (that is, at the later development stage), whereas collaboration at the pre-competitive stage may be granted a block exemption. The purpose of Esprit was ultimately to enable European firms to collaborate and through that, to catch up in the field of IT and information processing. Pre-competitive research refers to research conducted at a sufficient distance from the market so as not to infringe antitrust laws or competition policy; such research is aimed at a specific problem whose results may not lead directly to commercial products. This notion is distinct from the one of basic research, and of scientific research whose application leads to commercially useful results. Building on the German experience, the implementation of Esprit involved the co-operation of firms, research centres, governments and trade unions.

  Esprit-I was followed by a number of other Esprit programmes; the last one (Esprit-IV) covered the period 1994–98.

Esprit was a 'source of inspiration' for other programmes such as Race in the field of telecommunications, Brite on the introduction of new technologies in traditional industries, BAP (Biotechnology Action Programme, 1985–89), Bridge (1990–93), Biotech (1992–96), Flair (Food Linked Agroindustrial Research for Innovation, Development and Growth in Europe, 1989–93), Eclair (European Collaboration Linkage of Agriculture and Industry through Research) and Media 2 in the audiovisual field.[42]

The idea of inserting an explicit commitment to research and technology into European legislation originated from a Memorandum that the Commission presented at the Milan Summit in 1985.[43] Subsequently endorsed by the Council of Ministers, it became one of the basic documents which provided for the foundations of the Single European Act (SEA). The ratification by all member states of the SEA in 1987 rendered the proliferation of technological programmes easier. The SEA explicitly legitimated the scientific and technological dimension of the EU; this first revision of the Treaty of Rome introduced an item on 'research and technological development'.[44] Article 13 of the revision of the Treaty made clear the objective of 'strengthening the scientific and technological bases of Community industry and encouraging it to become more competitive at international level'. A means of achieving this aim is through the common technology programmes, grouped from 1987 onwards under the umbrella of the so-called Framework Programme (Article 130I).

In the course of the following two decades, attempts at evaluating the relative success of the EU technological programmes have been made. In particular, the Esprit Review Board, composed of an independent panel, was given the task of evaluating the impact of the programme. In its first mid-term review (1986), the Board concluded that Esprit was on its way to meeting its objectives, and that it led to a significant increase in R&D activity in the EU (through spillover linkages between EU companies outside the programme). Many criticisms have, notwithstanding, been addressed to this programme. As pointed out by Amin *et al.* (1992), among others, large firms in the core IT-based regions have received more money than firms situated in Spain, Greece, Portugal and Italy. In their review of EU technological policy, Grahl and Teague (1990) argue similarly that Davignon's policy has privileged the largest and most powerful companies.

Not surprisingly, Esprit-II and III were subsequently designed to amend and improve Esprit-I. Esprit-II (1988–92) focused on the necessity to lessen regional disparities.[45] ECU 1.6 billion were allocated to this second phase of the programme, which involved the participation of nearly 1500 organizations, two-thirds of which were SMEs. Finally, Esprit-III (1990–94) placed more emphasis on the application of research and on the improvement of the 'manufacturing capability of the European integrated circuit industry' (OJ C 30, p. 17, 1991). The last call for proposals under the Esprit programme (Esprit-IV) was launched in 1994 with a deadline and completion date of 1998. The last tranche of funding under Esprit-IV (amounting to ECU 205 million) allowed the selection of more than 200 proposals in the area of high-performance computing and networking, multimedia systems and so forth.

Since the late 1990s, the technology priorities of the EU Commission, grouped for example under the well known 'thematic priorities' of the Sixth Framework Programme (2002–06), have emphasized biotechnology, research on genomics, nanotechnologies and nanoscience, as well as aerospace technology as the main research areas for pan-EU collaboration.

We should note that intra-European R&D co-operation in sectors characterized by new technologies, and actively promoted by the programmes launched and implemented by the Commission, has not been restricted to the EU. These programmes have had an EEA (European Economic Area) dimension since firms such as Volvo, Nestlé and Asea, Brown Boveri have all been involved (prior to the inclusion of Sweden in the EU).

European technological collaboration also took the form of the building up of government-supported multinationals created by countries who came together to form an economic association and who developed a project of common interest.[46] Well-known examples are Airbus in the field of aeronautics, Arianespace which was developed to design and market a space-launcher, and Eurodif, a European consortium that has produced a uranium enrichment process (see Box 16.3).

Box 16.3 Airbus Industrie - a success story of European collaboration?

Resenting US domination in the aerospace area, the 1960s President of France, Charles de Gaulle, was keen to build either a French or a European aircraft that could compete with US companies, in particular with Boeing. Although he was eager to develop the Concorde supersonic jet, he became convinced nevertheless of the necessity to initiate and develop a product filling a market niche, that of short- to medium-range and high-capacity aircrafts. The agreement reached in 1970s between the French Aérospatiale and the German Deutsche Aerospace, created Airbus Industrie, a European consortium working under French law governing multinational collaborative programmes that relied partly on government funds. The consortium was joined shortly after its creation by Construcciones Aeronauticas SA (CASA) of Spain, and in 1979 by British Aerospace (now BAe Systems). In 2000, the consortium reconfigured itself as a private company (as the European Aeronautic Defence and Space Company, EADS), and today Airbus is jointly owned by EADS and BAe Systems (see Thornton, 1995). This was prompted partly by the planned development of the new A380, the world's largest commercial passenger aircraft (555 seats), which will be in service in 2006.

The success of Airbus can be judged by the fact that it has achieved substantial market shares. Starting from an extremely low and slow base (38 orders only between 1972 and 1977), Airbus soon established itself as one of the main players in the market. After the sale of 69 aircraft in 1978, the new company saw a continuous increase in its market share. The market share of Airbus Industrie increased to nearly 50 per cent in 1998, reaching 55 per cent the subsequent year (compared with a low 7 per cent in 1980). In 2003, sales by Boeing were outstripped by Airbus. Having sold more than 2000 aircraft, Airbus Industrie employs 40,000 people in Toulouse (France), Hamburg (Germany) and other plants across the EU.

Government subsidies (estimated at US$13.5 billion by 1990) have been an important industrial policy tool that contributes to explain such success. The various governments involved financed nearly three-quarters of the development budget for the various aircraft in the early decades. Increasing employment in Airbus Industrie plants has been paralleled with decreasing employment in the US civil aircraft manufacturing industry. This has obviously nurtured allegations of unfair competition voiced by the US authorities on several occasions (McGuire, 1997).

16.4.4 EU industrial policy since 1990

In a 1990 document submitted to the Council and to the European Parliament on the theme of industrial policy, the EU Commission defined the broad orientations of an EIP compatible with a global competitive environment.[47] In this document, the Commission endeavoured to develop and give precision to the concept of a common industrial policy in three distinct steps.

First, it stressed that an industrial policy should be built around the essential task which is that of 'maintaining a favourable business environment'. The merits of the common competition policy (Articles 81, 82 and 87) were reiterated, but in addition the need to 'promote economic and social cohesion', that is, the necessity to introduce and to deal with the problem of regional disparities, was acknowledged. Also, the objective of achieving a high level of economic growth in parallel with a high level of protection for the environment was clearly voiced. Second, it saw the process of completion of the internal market as a 'catalyst for adjustment'. Third, it referred to a 'positive approach' to industrial adjustment; this implied the implementation of policies that help accelerate the process (such as technology policies, a dynamic policy towards SMEs).

Aimed at securing a stimulating economic environment, the approach of the Commission was again in essence inspired by the virtues of the free market economy. In placing the emphasis on the creation of a sound economic environment, the Commission reiterates a view inherited from the traditional and highly criticized S–C–P paradigm. This approach was 'new' at the time, in that the Commission's document asserted for the first time the necessity of conducting a more positive EIP, in the sense of attempting to bring about a convergence of views between member states that had until then often followed rather different industrial policy approaches. It was new also because it stressed the necessity to move towards a horizontal approach, by providing framework conditions in which industry can flourish, instead of relying on vertical initiatives. Another new feature of the document was the fact that it incorporated both a regional and an environmental dimension.[48] It should be remembered that these two dimensions had emerged at an early stage of the process of European construction. The Community Environmental Policy began in 1973. It was agreed that the 'polluter pays' principle should be used as much as possible. The concern of 'economic and social cohesion' preceded the Commission's 1990 document and finds its roots in the regional policy of the EU set up in 1975. Apart from these three elements, the Commission's document on industrial policy lacked originality, and according to Bance (1992), the Commission's proposals did not break with its previous strategy in the area of industry.

Several documents (Council Decisions, Council Resolutions, Exchange of Letters) have since been published, that have in the main consolidated the major thrust of the 1990 Commission Document. In the latter part of the 1990s and early 2000s, greater emphasis was being placed on three major dimensions: (i) globalization; (ii) the increasing importance of the knowledge economy; and (iii) sustainable development. With regard to globalization, several documents refer to the international dimension of research, by encouraging co-operation with the United States, Japan, Australia, Canada and EFTA countries, in areas such as intelligent manufacturing systems.[49] The necessity to upgrade the research capability of the EU has led to EU programmes designed at improving the socio-economic knowledge base in the EU.[50] In the same vein, the Council Resolution of 15 June 2000 provides a first attempt at defining and establishing a European area of research and innovation.[51] The growing concerns of the European citizens in terms of sustainable development and health safety are clearly spelled out in a Commission document *Industrial Policy in an Enlarged Europe* (CEC, 2002c). This is the latest major document published by an EU institution (the Commission in this instance), and it reasserts the broad lines of the 1990 document. Finally, the importance of sustaining innovation in SMEs, of stimulating entrepreneurship and of conducting an industrial policy in tandem with the EU's other policies, are also important elements enshrined in this contemporary view of EIP.

In spite of a timid involvement in industrial affairs, the EU governments have, through EU technological collaboration, witnessed a certain improvement. To illustrate this, the case of the EU electronics industry is quite instructive. During the late 1980s, EU firms underwent a major restructuring through mergers, acquisitions, and other partnership deals. This led to the emergence of pan-EU electronics firms. This restructuring process has undoubtedly been facilitated by the various technology programmes. In the area of semiconductors and consumer electronics, the industry is now less fragmented than it was in the early 1980s, with national champions giving way to European champions, supported by the EU, rather than by national governments. For example, in commodity chip technology, the EU Megaproject (with a financial envelope of US$930 million) enabled Siemens and Philips to develop and market advanced chips. In these segments of the industry, restructuring and EU funding allowed EU firms to catch up with their US (and also Japanese) counterparts. However, despite restructuring and EU funding (under the various Framework Programmes), EU firms are still smaller, on average, than their US and Japanese counterparts.

16.5 The debate over industrial policy

Among EU scholars and politicians, there has been and still is an endless debate between those who want as little industrial policy as possible and those who wish to give it a more positive, constructive and indeed interventionist role.[52] The first group is predominant in Germany, in the Netherlands and in the UK; the second group would be found in France and in other Mediterranean countries. The first group is in favour of developing a range of substitutes for an EIP, such as a trade and competition policy, and/or economic and monetary union (EMU). The second group calls for increased financial means – for fiscal federalism, for example – and for a greater political consensus and commitment. The view of the Commission is an attempted compromise, but it is in fact closer to the liberal German philosophy than to the French 'Colbertist' approach.

Since we have discussed the EU Competition Policy earlier, we will here briefly explore whether budgetary and monetary integration can be seen as a substitute for a more positive EIP. In subsequent paragraphs of this section, we will venture into the many facets of a more positive EIP: European *filières* and districts, the optimal mix between private and public firms, the financial constraints, and the implications for third countries.

16.6 Is economic and monetary union a substitute for a more positive EIP?

For the EU, EMU has been the culminating point of 20 years of monetary integration.[53] The primary aim of economic and monetary union is to create a favourable economic environment. This is theoretically achievable if:

◆ Budget deficits are contained within 'reasonable' limits

◆ Price stability is achieved throughout the Union, and inflation rates are minimal

◆ Interest rates are kept low.

All these positive conditions would boost business confidence, would increase growth and per capita income, and would obviate the need for a more positive EIP. On the other hand, the irrevocable fixing of exchange rates eliminates the possibility of compensating losses in industrial competitiveness by a decline in the exchange rate. Since the strategy of competitive devaluation[54] is not a viable option for EMU countries any more, economic adjustments will increasingly have to take place at the structural or industrial levels. Accordingly, monetary integration – in cases of recession – clearly calls for a more positive EIP.

As can be seen, EMU brings radically antagonistic results, depending on whether the euro area economy goes through a cycle of economic growth and stability or of recession. Are EMU and a more positive EIP incompatible, or can they be mutually reinforcing policies? In some ways, EMU can absent itself from a more positive EIP in cases of macroeconomic stability, or in the absence of macroeconomic asymmetric shocks. An example of a macroeconomic asymmetric shock is the fall of the Berlin wall and the detrimental impact it had on the Finish economy in the early 1990s, which was once economically dependent on the USSR. Luckily, since 1999, the year when exchange rates became fixed, the EMU countries have not been exposed to any major macroeconomic asymmetric shocks. However, in the absence of stability, some means other than exchange rate adjustments are necessary to respond to macroeconomic asymmetric shocks. Adjustments through the labour markets are hampered by a lack of geographical mobility in the EU. It may be in the end that industrial adjustments and thus a more positive EIP are necessary in case of a major instability.

16.7 An active, positive European industrial policy

The EU has developed in the past a strong competition policy, but what is lacking today is the same legal basis for the development of a strong industrial policy. Is it possible that support will be generated for the development of such a policy? 'If, in future, a more interventionist-minded Commissioner were to be appointed to DGIV [Competition Policy], this could tip the balance in favour of a more industrial-policy-based EC' (Woolcock and Wallace, 1995). A more constructive and positive EIP should not be confused with systematic government intervention and with protectionism. In addition to a stronger technological policy, such a policy could entail:

◆ The completion of a 'favourable European business environment'
◆ The building up of European *filières*, clusters and industrial districts
◆ The building-up of 'Euro-champions'
◆ The allocation of greater levels of finance, in order, *inter alia*, to develop a European system of innovation
◆ A concerted policy with respect to third countries.

16.7.1 A favourable business environment

In spite of all progress made in trying to build a more integrated EU – a European Financial Area, EMU and a certain degree of fiscal harmonization – problems remain which prevent the attainment of even a minimalist EIP. These problems relate to the many different regulations with respect to the functioning of stock exchanges, to conflicting labour laws, to institutional factors, and also to continued absence of full fiscal harmonization. For example, tax dumping (referring to extremely low corporation tax rates in some countries, such as Ireland and in the CEECs), affects the movement of capital in the EU. These different rates and tax systems have an important impact on firms' investment decisions and create thereby distortions to the smooth functioning of a competitive market. During the 1990s, the increasing opening of markets to foreign investors – even in countries such as France, which was notorious for its hostility towards foreign investors – has led to a downward pressure on the level of corporation tax rates in the EU. In addition to globalization, two elements have aided and accentuated this downward pressure: further economic integration in the early 1990s, and more recently, the prospects of enlargement to the CEECs (see Chapter 7). Although allegations of tax dumping proffered by the German and French governments have been rejected by the EC Commission, the Brussels institutions do nevertheless acknowledge the fact that the strengthening of tax policy co-ordination is a prerequisite for a successful EMU, and that further economic integration in Europe will require greater co-operation in fiscal matters (CEC, 2000). However, the legal requirement of unanimity with regard to progress towards tax harmonization at the EU level leaves the debate entirely open.

16.7.2 European *filières*, clusters and industrial districts: the role of European MNEs

A more constructive EIP must integrate spatial parameters. The concept of *filière* was defined earlier (Chapter 8). We have stressed the limited validity of the concept at the national level and its relevance at the European level. In an early study (Andréosso and Jacobson, 1991) we explore the way a peripheral country such as Ireland could become more integrated in the EU at both the spatial and corporate/industrial levels. Our argument rests on the examples of two 'strategic' industries: the computer/office equipment industry and the machine tools/robotics industry. The point we make is that spatial and corporate integration could eventually lead to the constitution of a European *filière*. It is thus essential that all types of alliances between European firms be fostered in order to build a series of European *filières*.

As we saw above, subcontracting is one of the lowest degrees of firms' interdependence; it could thus represent a first step in the constitution of European *filières*. Where the relationship between firms spreads beyond that of buyer–supplier, the potential exists for the formation of clusters which, as we saw in Chapter 8, incorporates horizontal as well as vertical relationships. The consequence of this type of cross-border activity is ultimately the formation of European MNEs, as European, rather than as German, British or French firms with a presence elsewhere in Europe. Where small, local firms exist on the basis of traditional crafts, the potential exists under a positive EIP to incorporate a regional element and find ways of encouraging the development of competitive industrial districts among such firms.

16.7.3 Picking winners and Euro-champions

The instruments of a policy favouring Euro-champions includes public aid, tax incentives, and public (EU) procurements. Dierickx *et al.* (1991) show that the design of an appropriate policy based on the selection of potential winners is a very complex task. In their simple duopoly model with a single homogeneous commodity, the appropriate intervention in a declining industry depends upon the interplay of cost differences, the amount of production of the low variable cost firm, the discount rate, and the rate and pattern of demand decline. Their work highlights the fact that 'simple rules for picking survivors based on current unit cost, profitability, or productive efficiency simply do not provide sound guidance for policy' (Dierickx *et al.* 1991). The technical complexity of the task is only one of the many difficulties that such a policy encounters. Other obstacles are of a political and institutional nature. Such obstacles should not, however, prevent the continuing efforts to develop such a policy.

It is increasingly felt in the EU that without a strong supranational co-ordination (in other words, some kind of European Political Union (EPU)) it is impossible to design a more positive industrial policy. EPU is a prerequisite for a stronger European Technological Collaboration. For instance, Tsoukalis (1991) is sceptical as to the development of Euro-champions in present circumstances. Since the EU is characterized by a weak state, it can only have a weak industrial policy, so that it does not have at its disposal many instruments to promote such an active policy. Bance (1992) underlines this with a description of the minimalist role of the EU Competition Policy as a 'chasse aux gros' (Bance, 1992, p. 7). The EU Competition Policy does not contribute greatly to the possibility of agreement on other issues in industrial policy.

16.7.4 The financial constraint

Related to the fact that the EU has a weak state, the weak EU budget and its minuscule share devoted to industry, energy and research, hamper the development of a more positive EIP.

The adjustments in the agricultural sector stemming from the reform of the Common Agricultural Policy since the early 1990s have enabled the redistribution of European resources towards other programmes (of a technological and regional nature). However, the commitment to accommodate the new member states (characterized by vast budgetary requirements) with an unchanged ceiling of own (budgetary) resources as a percentage of EU GDP, does not augur well. Also, costly R&D in the aircraft industry, nuclear energy, armament and biotechnology sectors needs more than a redistribution of funds.

Many economists and politicians are hostile to increased financial resources being provided, either via the EU budget or via national budgets, because of the financial burden on the taxpayer implied by such a policy. Indeed, 'picking winners' and/or promoting Euro-champions may lead to a high level of public spending incompatible with the Stability Pact (and with the EMU convergence criteria for the new member states), and may also lead to a familiar harmful consequence known as the 'crowding-out' effect.[55] To avoid this recessionist effect, private funding can be increasingly sought, leading to the development of private public partnerships. This is particularly plausible in the case of public works that have a high rate of return. The most famous example in the EU is certainly the FF90 billion (€13.5 billion) Eurotunnel project, in which more than 200 banks in the world have participated (Le Monde, 25 May 1993). Large sums of money are available on the international capital markets for other projects of this nature.

Through the stimulation of venture capital, the EU has responded to the need of addressing the financial constraint. Although venture capital has grown immensely in Europe during the 1990s, American venture capital has grown even faster, making the gap between the two wider (Bottazzi and Da Rin, 2002). There are still in the EU constraints inhibiting the development of this type of financing, compared with the United States; one barrier is the fact that the personal tax laws of most member states penalize the stock option schemes.

16.7.5 Policy with respect to third countries

Economic relations with third countries range from pure trade relations to direct investment. The trade relations of the EU countries are organized within the framework of the Common Commercial Policy (CCP) of the EU, and are influenced by the broader international framework under the aegis of the World Trade Organization (WTO). Article 131 (formerly 110) of the Treaty stipulates that 'by establishing a customs union ... Member States aim to contribute to the harmonious development of world trade, the progressive abolition of restrictions on international trade and the lowering of customs barriers'. The CCP ensures that the Customs Union and EMU are compatible with free trade at a global level. One of the major instruments of the CCP is the Common External Tariff (CET), established for each category of manufacturing product as an arithmetic average of the tariffs applied by the different member states (Article 19/1 of the Treaty of Rome). In the past, the successive GATT rounds have progressively diminished the incidence of the CET. The Dillon

Round (1960–62) and the Kennedy Round which started in 1963 cut the tariffs on manufacturing goods by about half. The Tokyo Round of the mid-1970s led to a further cut of 30 per cent. The last GATT agreement, known as the Uruguay Round (1986–94), led to tariff cuts by more than one-third. Since the setting up of the EEC in 1958, the average level of CET on manufacturing products has decreased from 40 per cent to less than 5 per cent today. In the same period, the dispersion has narrowed considerably; only a few (sensitive) products are today subject to the so-called peak tariffs, that is, those between 10 and 20 per cent. These tariffs are today the exception rather than the rule. For example, pharmaceutical products, paper and printing, and books enter the EU freely, whereas tariffs are very low for steel products (2 to 3 per cent) and mechanical appliances (2 to 4 per cent). Only a few products such as clothing and footwear products, some electrical machinery products (such as video monitors and television equipment) and some types of motor vehicles are still protected through relatively high tariffs.[56] It can thus easily be ascertained that since its inception, the CCP has worked towards freer trade on a global scale in the manufacturing sector. There is some foundation for the criticism aimed at the EU for its protectionist stance (Fortress Europe) only if a minority of products – the sensitive manufactured goods, services (for example broadcasting) and agricultural products – are referred to. Progress was made during the Uruguay Round and further announced at the November 2001 Doha Ministerial Conference to decrease the level of tariffs in these sectors as well.

However, it should be borne in mind that tariff cuts do not equate simplistically with trade liberalization. Many other non-tariff barriers (NTBs) have been increasingly used by all nations in general and by the EU in particular to protect the vulnerable industries. In Lindert's (1991, p. 152) words: 'By the time the Kennedy Round of tariffs cuts was consummated in 1967, non tariff barriers had emerged as the main roadblocks in the way of trade. Since the early 1970s, non-tariff barriers have been getting even more formidable.' NTBs can be expressed as tariff equivalents (see Whalley, 1985; Deardorff and Stern, 1983; Balassa and Balassa, 1984).[57] The oldest and most popular form of NTBs used by the EU are (import) quotas, but in the 1970s and 1980s, the EU operated also voluntary export restraints (VERs) and orderly marketing arrangements (OMAs), which were negotiated on a bilateral basis, and which existed outside the WTO framework. Today, anti-dumping measures on products originating from China, such as metals, chemicals, non-electrical machinery and electrical equipment, have taken prominence.

Export promotion, through the use of export credits, and the implementation of a minimum EU content can also be viewed as non-tariff obstacles to trade. The minimum content clause specifies that for a product to be considered as European, a certain percentage at least of its final value must originate from the EU; such a product can thus escape the realm of the CET. This rule is aimed at restricting the practice of 'screwdriver' plants or low-skilled assembly operations set up by Japanese and American multinationals in the EU. Today, local (EU) content requirements affect, in particular, the audio-visual sector.

It has been widely acknowledged that the existence of the CET has provided an additional reason for the location of American and Japanese plants in the EU (Jacobson and Andréosso, 1990). Foreign direct investment (FDI) is one of the many strategies offered to MNEs facing high trade barriers. The study of FDI trends in the EU is a complex task explained by the ambiguity of the concept. Nicolaides (1993) notes that official statistics relate only to investment registered in the balance of payments. Concentrating solely on externally financed greenfield investment, they omit all financing performed through the international capital markets. Léonard (1990) proposes two definitions of FDI: a 'narrow' or more traditional definition, and an 'enlarged' definition. The narrow definition of FDI refers to the MNEs' participation in the capital of a firm, the benefits reinvested in the host country, as well as the loans granted by the headquarters of the MNE. The enlarged definition encompasses all types of contracts such as joint venture agreements (where foreign participation does not exceed 50 per cent), licence agreements, franchising and other agreements, as well as international subcontracting practices (Léonard, 1990). Since all data relating to FDI are based on the traditional, or restricted, definition, official statistics underestimate the true extent of FDI. Since even a biased measurement of the phenomenon is preferable to no measurement at all, we can rely on the traditional definition and state that during the second half of the 1980s, Japanese and American direct investment in the EU has doubled from the 1980–84 period to the 1985–89 period (UNCTC, 1991). The world total of extra EU FDI stock more than doubled between 1995 and 1999, reaching nearly €1200 billion in 1999. This is larger than the FDI stock held by US firms abroad in that year (CEC, 2001b).

An appropriate tool of EIP would be to design a *concerted and appropriate FDI policy*. FDI brings both positive and negative effects to the economy of the recipient country. On the positive side, benefits include job creation, positive net foreign exchange earnings, technological flows, possibilities of sourcing materials and inputs locally (linkages), development of an adequate educational base, and taxes on rents or profits earned by foreign enterprises (MacDougall, 1960; Dicken, 2003a). Some of these positive effects should, however, be carefully assessed. In many instances, MNEs have not met the objectives of the national governments. Many jobs created have been low-skilled jobs ('screwdriver plant syndrome'), and linkages have been unsatisfactory.[58] On the purely negative side, FDI may result in negative balance of payment earnings,[59] and may destroy jobs. It certainly weakens the domestic industrial structure and leads eventually to a loss of national industrial identity. This loss reduces in turn the breadth of the national industrial policy. To take Ireland as an example again, the Irish government can use fiscal incentives to attract MNEs and can improve the domestic educational base; it *cannot*, however, build up strong indigenous firms on a basis comparable to that of France and Denmark.[60]

A concerted and appropriate FDI policy must not be equated with a protectionist policy. Too often, the EU has taken protectionist stances, as a result of its inability to devise a sound, positive EIP. A positive and active EIP gives priority to policy instruments that are exercised upstream,[61] for example: increased technological collaboration; lending facilities on capital markets in the EU (through a greater synergy between banks and firms similar to German or Japanese models); and fiscal allowances. These instruments are aimed at making the strategic industries more competitive. In particular, the technological policy of the EU should be reviewed. We have seen that Esprit-III has initiated a move, but a much greater emphasis should be placed on the applied and scientific research as opposed to 'pre-competitive' research.

In the same way, too often the development of common (industrial) policies has been perceived by non-EU countries as the building of 'Fortress Europe' (Curzon Price, 1991). Co-operation with third countries should be encouraged provided this co-operation maximizes the benefits of the Union. It is in this direction that perhaps the EU external relations have evolved since the early 1990s. More aware of the necessity to develop its policies with reference to the outside world, the EU has embarked upon a myriad of bilateral agreements (covering economic and political issues) with nearly all countries of Asia and South America, (in addition to the western countries such as the United States, Japan and Australia). In particular, its 1994 New Asia Strategy, is aimed at strengthening its economic presence in Asia, the most dynamic region in the world (CEC, 1994b). It is in the background of poor EU FDI involvement in China, the most promising market in the world, that such policies have been designed and that such agreements have been signed.

The crux of a positive and constructive EIP rests on technology and finance. Extended financial means in the EU would facilitate more coherent technological programmes, and the design of a strong European technological system. Referring to the case of the UK only, Geroski (1991b) is of the opinion that an appropriate industrial policy aimed at stimulating the diffusion of existing technology would prove more effective than a policy designed to foster the generation of new knowledge. However, in the case of the EU, stimulation of the creation as well as the diffusion of new knowledge, is required.

Success (and failure) depends 'not only on a match between the properties of technology in individual sectors and the national institutional capabilities but also on the ability to translate these properties and capabilities into efficient sectoral governance structures' (Kitschelt, 1991, p. 490).

16.8 Summary

A fully fledged industrial policy has been a project attempted at different stages of the history of EU-building. The pooling of the productive capacity of the coal and steel industries through the European Coal and Steel Community (ECSC) in 1952, was followed by many attempts such as the Colonna Report in 1970 and the Eureka project in the early 1980s. However, most of these attempts have failed, and this is explained by the great diversity of views pertaining to the degree of state intervention espoused by the different countries in the EU. In nearly half a century, the EU industrial policy (EIP) has graduated from being of a vertical type and defensive (sectoral policies), to favouring a horizontal approach in the 1990s, with a specific focus on creating the right business environment conditions. Today, technological collaboration remains the mainstay of what we have called a positive EIP. It has been argued that co-operation in science and technology in the EU has nevertheless been driven more by negative elements than by positive ones. Williams (1989) writes that in many instances, fear of the United States, Japan, and latterly of the NICs, exorbitant costs attached to the development of some projects, and risk aversion have explained the European orientation of firms. Indeed, the problem of the technology lag (or 'innovation deficit') discussed in previous chapters did lead the Commission to initiate a number of corrective initiatives. In particular, the launch of the first Esprit programme in the early 1980s, and the following Framework Programmes, have been aimed at addressing the problems of critical size, duplication of research efforts and capital constraints in the EU. In spite of these efforts, the EU has not been able to close the gap with the United States, in terms of industrial specialization, R&D and research output such as innovation and patents. One major explanation for this lies in the restricted financial resources devoted to the EU technology and innovation policy. Representing only a small percentage of total civilian private and public spending in Europe, EU financing of research programmes is still extremely modest and insufficient.

Websites

On the German research policy and infrastructure, consult: **http://www.bmbf.de/pub/facts_and_figures_research_2002.pdf**

On merger legislation in the EU: **http://europa.eu.int/comm/competition/mergers/legislation/regulation/#implementing**

On the structure of tariffs in the EU: **http://europa.eu.int/eur-lex/en/archive/2003/l_28120031030en.html**

Questions

16.1 What is the difference between competition policy and industrial policy?

16.2 Compare and contrast the industrial policies of any two European countries.

16.3 Discuss the argument that with EMU a European industrial policy is no longer necessary.

16.4 Has the EU innovation policy paid off?

Notes

1   Niccolò Machiavelli (1520) saw in the co-existence of a rich state and of poor citizens the condition for an increasingly vast and powerful empire (see *Discorsi sopra la prima deca di Tito Livio*, Book II, Chapter 19).

2   For a history of the emergence of cartels and syndicates in Germany see, for example, Chandler (1990).

3   See List (1842).

4   It is not necessarily contradictory to want more decentralization – more power for the *Länder* – and a more active, positive industrial policy which includes financial flows from the centre.

5   For an influential early view on the importance of technology, see List (1841).

6   An exception being the period of the 1930s, when free trade was abandoned to leave way for the Import Duties Act (see Gribbin, 1991).

7   Colbert's economic policy was subsequently jeopardized by the religious policy of Louis XIV. The revocation of the Edict de Nantes in 1685 led to a massive emigration of the industrially oriented Huguenot elite, to the benefit of the neighbouring countries (England, Holland, Prussia and Switzerland).

8   Having signed the Havana Charter in 1948, France kept on imposing substantial customs barriers. Although France was a member of the European Payment Union from 1950, it did not implement the 1955 monetary agreement. The French franc remained non-convertible, unlike the Deutschmark and sterling.

9   Jean Monnet was in fact an influential businessman and politician who played a leading role in keeping sound relations with the United States at the time.

10   During the 1950s, indicative planning was adopted, with many variations, by Italy, the UK, Ireland and Belgium. These planning systems did not however reach the same sophisticated degree as in the French system (Franzmeyer, 1979).

11   Among which were: Usinor and Sacilor (steel); CGE, Thomson, PUK; Paribas, Indosuez; CII-Honeywell Bull.

12   President François Mitterand (1981–95) was adamant to be perceived as a major architect of European economic integration through, for example, the launching of the euro. For more on an overview of French economic and industrial policy during the 1980s and 1990s, see Andreosso-O'Callaghan (2004).

13   The *Mezzogiorno* is the poorer, more agricultural, southern part of Italy.

14   With the *lottizzazzione* (i.e. attribution) of posts on the basis of political affiliation.

15   Authors' translation of. 'El mejor Estado era et que menos interfería la iniciativa privata; ni siquiera para proteger et mercato interior de la competencia extranjera' (García Delgado *et al.*, 1989, p. 435).

16   Article 149 of the 1978 Constitution specifies the restricted role of the state.

17   This section draws partly on Andreosso-O'Callaghan and Noonan (1996).

18   Above and beyond the Europe Agreements, the financial assistance of the EU takes the form of the

Phare programme (Pologne Hongrie: Assistance à la Reconstruction Economique) and the Tacis programme (Technical Assistance to the Commonwealth of Independent States). (See: *Revue du Marché Commun*, 1993; OECD, 1991c.)

19 The source of these data is European Commission (2003b). Note that the inflation rate reported here is the harmonized index of consumer prices (HICP) used by the EU Commission; this index has been adopted by all new member states in 2004, and therefore these figures are directly comparable with figures available for old member states.

20 These two sets of figures are from the World Bank (2001), *World Development Indicators*, and from the European Commission (2003b) Innovation and Technology and Transfer, p. 11, 'Enlargement and Innovation', respectively.

21 The Treaty of Rome does not provide for a European industrial policy (EIP), if we conceive an EIP as a complete set of horizontal and vertical measures. Horizontal measures are measures with a wide and universal application throughout the Common Market, such as the harmonization of company laws. Vertical measures require a selective Community intervention in depth in particular industries.

22 The pooling of the European coal and steel industries gave birth to the ECSC (European Coal and Steel Community) in 1952. The ECSC was supranational – it was empowered to intervene directly in the industries of member states. Integration in the EC agricultural markets took the form of the Common Agricultural Policy (CAP).

23 We discuss only the main articles here.

24 These articles do not apply to the coal and steel, and nuclear energy industries, which are subject to the rules laid down in the ECSC (European Coal and Steel Community) and Euratom Treaties.

25 Article 234 of the Treaty stipulates that the implementation and enforcement of EU law is left to the national courts, whereas the European Court of Justice plays a residual and guiding role.

26 Continental Can, a large American manufacturer, took over a German firm that had a dominant position in the market for preserved meat and fish (and for metal caps for preservative jars). This was followed by another takeover on the Dutch market, and resulted in a dominant position held by Continental Can on both markets.

27 Regulation EC No. 1/2003; see OJ L1, 4 January 2003, Council Regulation on the Implementation of the Rules on Competition laid down in Articles 81 and 82 of the Treaty.

28 See CEC (1989).

29 A difficulty that arose in the past with regard to the computation of state aids was that in the case of nationalized firms, it was difficult to distinguish between pure investments (legitimate) and state aids (illegitimate). In spite of the privatization movement, this problem has not disappeared.

30 See the Council Regulation COM/73/1210 Final.

31 See OJ L 395, 30 December 1989.

32 See OJ L 180, 9 July 1997 and OJ L 24, 29 January 2004 respectively.

33 As illustrated by the fact that R&D formed an important part of Jean Monnet's Action Committee for a United States of Europe.

34 Formed in 1969, the Consortium subsequently fell apart partly because of the pressure from the German government as Siemens had been left out.

35 Several directives have provided the legal framework for the attribution of state aids to the shipbuilding industry in the 1980s and early 1990s. In particular, the Seventh Directive on aid to shipbuilding creates special arrangements for the former GDR in order to allow it to restructure.

36 Anti-dumping duties on imports are permitted under GATT (General Agreement on Tariffs and Trade), provided that it can be shown that imports are entering at a price below cost.

37 The safeguard clause, enabling any party to curb temporarily its imports of steel and coal products originating from the associated area, has been integrated *ab initio* in the Europe Agreements signed subsequently with Bulgaria and Romania (Andréosso, 1993a).

38 For more details, see 'Towards greater competitiveness in the steel industry: the need for further restructuring' (SEC (92) 2160).

39 A notable exception is the establishment in 1978 of the JET (Joint European Torus), an experimental nuclear fusion tokomak at Culham, England.

40 Esprit: European Strategic Programme for Research in Information Technology; Race: Research and Development in Advanced Communications Technology for Europe; Brite–Euram; Basic Research for Industrial Technology in Europe and European Research on Advanced Materials; Comett: Community Programme in Education and Training in Technology.

41 The 'Big Twelve' comprised the heads of Bull, Thomson, and CGE from France; AEG, Nixdorf, and Siemens from Germany; ICL, Plessey, and GEC from Britain; Olivetti and STET from Italy; and Philips from The Netherlands.

42 For a more comprehensive approach, see Sharp and Pavitt (1993).

43 See CEC (1985b).

44 The second revision of the Rome Treaty gave birth to the Maastricht Treaty signed in February 1992.

45 Although the substance of Esprit-I remained unchanged, Esprit-II aimed at upgrading the IT programme. New areas were covered (microelectronics and peripheral technologies), EFTA participation was fully acknowledged.

46 The creation of consortia is not limited to the EU. Other integrated areas have experienced the same. The ASEAN countries (Singapore, Indonesia, the Philippines, Malaysia, Thailand and Brunei) have set up a network of industrial enterprises in priority sectors (copper, chemicals). (Anastassopoulos *et al.*, 1987).

47 CEC (1990).

48 It should be noted that from the awareness of 'economic and social cohesion' emerged the STRIDE programme. With a fund of ECUs 400 million over the years 1990–93 (extended to the year 1994 since), it is aimed at increasing the research, technological and innovatory capacity of less developed regions in the Union. (See OJ C 196, 4 August 1990.)

49 See, for example, OJ L 161, 18 June 1997.

50 OJ L 064, 12 March 1999.

51 OJ C 205, 19 July 2000.

52 For recent debates on industrial policy in Europe, see Cowling (1999), and for proposals to address the problem of the lag with the United States, see Cohen and Lorenzi (2000).

53 Monetary integration in Europe started in March 1979 with the European Monetary System, the aim of which was to create a zone of monetary stability in Europe. It culminated with the irrevocable locking of exchange rates in January 1999, and with the advent of a single European currency (the euro) in January 2002. Note that not all EU countries have adopted the euro. For example, Denmark, Sweden and the UK still use their national currency. The new member states can join the euro under the same conditions as the others, i.e. they need to meet the so-called Maastricht criteria.

54 The cascade 'competitive devaluations' of sterling, the Irish punt, lira, escudo, peseta, Swedish krone, during the fourth quarter 1992 and the first quarter 1993, with the exit from the Exchange Rate Mechanism of sterling and the lira, had to be seen as an attempt to regain structural/industrial competitiveness by means of currency devaluation. See the limits of such a policy in the case of Ireland in Andréosso (1993b).

55 When the government sells bonds to the public to finance its industrial programme, this can result in higher interest rates which may in turn reduce private sector investment. Note that in the case of the reunification of the two Germanies, the 'crowding out' effect has not occurred at all in spite of an unprecedented budgetary deficit.

56 Tariffs for these 'sensitive' products are as follows: 12 per cent for most clothing products; 17 per cent for footwear products; 14 per cent for video monitors and television projection equipment; 15 per cent for bicycles; and 22 per cent for certain large vehicles. The full tariff structure is given in OJ EU L 281 of the 30 October 2003, Commission Regulation (EC) No. 1789/2003 on the tariff and statistical nomenclature and on the CET.

57 The results of these studies are summarized in Molle (1990, p. 445).

58 O'Malley (1989) highlights the paucity of linkages in the case of Ireland in the early decades of its outward looking policy, whereas Görg and Ruane (2000) note the increase of linkages in Ireland over the 1990s.

59 The net foreign exchange earnings of FDI encompass capital inflow and export earnings on the one hand, balanced against foreign royalty payments and profit outflows (due to profit repatriation) on the other. It is clear that if profit outflows are nil, and if all production is for export, these effects are positive and are at their maximum. Conversely, if profit outflows are high, and all the production is absorbed by the domestic market, the balance of payments effects will be negative.

60 With reference to the case of Japanese investors, de Bernis (1990) refers to the 'destructuring effect of foreign investment'.

61 Policy instruments that are exercised downstream attempt at minimizing the losses of the 'problem industries'. Such instruments refer to any kind of protective measure, and such a policy is what we have termed an 'activist but negative' policy (Table 15.1 in Chapter 15).

Appendix 16.1

The Competition Policy in the EU

Article 81

1 The following shall be prohibited as incompatible with the common market: all agreements between undertakings, decisions by associations of undertakings and concerted practices which may affect trade between Member States and which have as their object or effect the prevention, restriction or distortion of competition within the common market, and in particular those which:

   (a) directly or indirectly fix purchase or selling prices or any other trading conditions;

   (b) limit or control production, markets, technical development, or investment;

   (c) share markets or sources of supply;

   (d) apply similar conditions to equivalent transactions with other trading parties, thereby placing them at a competitive disadvantage;

   (e) make the conclusion of contracts subject to acceptance by the other parties of supplementary obligations which, by their nature or according to commercial usage, have no connection with the subject of such contracts.

2 Any agreements or decisions prohibited pursuant to this Article shall be automatically void.

3 The provisions of paragraph 1 may, however, be declared inapplicable in the case of:

   ◆ any agreement or category of agreements between undertakings;

   ◆ any decision or category of decisions by associations of undertakings;

   ◆ any concerted practice or category of concerted practices which contributes to improving the production or distribution of goods or to promoting technical and economic progress, while allowing consumers a fair share of the resulting benefit, and which does not:

   (a) impose on the undertakings concerned restrictions which are not indispensable to the attainment of these objectives;

   (b) afford such undertakings the possibility of eliminating competition in respect of a substantial part of the products in question.

Article 82

Any abuse by one or more undertakings of a dominant position within the common market or in a substantial part of it shall be prohibited as incompatible with the common market in so far as it may affect trade between Member States.

Such abuse may, in particular, consist in:

(a) directly or indirectly imposing unfair purchase or selling prices or other unfair trading conditions;

(b) limiting production, markets or technical development to the prejudice of consumers;

(c) applying dissimilar conditions to equivalent transactions with other trading parties, thereby placing them at a competitive disadvantage;

(d) making the conclusion of contracts subject to acceptance by the other parties of supplementary obligations, which, by their nature or according to commercial usage, have no connection with the subject of such contracts.

Article 87

1 Save as otherwise provided in this Treaty, any aid granted by a Member State or through State resources in any form whatsoever which distorts or threatens to distort competition by favouring certain undertakings or the production of certain goods shall, in so far as it affects trade between Member States, be incompatible with the common market.

2 The following shall be compatible with the common market:

(a) aid having a social character, granted to individual consumers, provided that such aid is granted without discrimination related to the origin of the products concerned;

(b) aid to make good the damage caused by natural disasters or other exceptional occurrences;

(c) aid granted to the economy of certain areas of the Federal Republic of Germany affected by the division of Germany in so far as such aid is required in order to compensate for the economic disadvantages caused by that division.

3 The following may be considered to be compatible with the common market:

(a) aid to promote the economic development of areas where the standard of living is abnormally low or where there is serious under-employment;

(b) aid to promote the execution of an important project of common European interest or to remedy a serious disturbance in the economy of a Member State;

(c) aid to facilitate the development of certain economic activities or of certain economic areas, where such aid does not adversely affect trading conditions to an extent contrary to the common interest. However, the aids granted to shipbuilding as of 1 January 1957 shall, in so far as they serve only to compensate for the absence of customs protection, be progressively reduced under the same conditions as apply to the elimination of customs duties, subject to the provisions of this Treaty concerning common commercial policy towards third countries;

(d) such other categories of aid as may be specified by decision of the Council acting by a qualified majority on a proposal from the Commission.

References

Aaker, D. (2003) 'The power of the branded differentiator'. *Sloan Management Review*, vol. 45, no. 1, pp. 83–8.

Abegglen, J. C. and G. Stalk Jr (1985) *Kaisha: The Japanese Corporation*. Basic Books, New York.

Abramovitz, M. (1956) 'Resource and output trends in the United States since 1870'. *The American Economic Review*, vol. 46, no. 2, pp. 5–23.

ACEA (2004) *EU-15 Economic Report*. Association des Constructeurs Européens d'Automobiles, Bruxelles.

Acs, Z. (ed.) (1996) *Small Firms and Economic Growth*, 2 vols. Edward Elgar, Cheltenham.

Acs, Z. and L. Preston (1997) 'Small and medium-sized enterprises, technology, and globalization'. *Small Business Economics*, vol. 9, no. 1, pp. 1–6.

Aiginger, K. (1991) 'Concentration et profitabilité: leçons de l'expérience autrichienne'. *Revue du Marché Commun et de l'Union Européenne*, no. 350, September, pp. 639–45.

Aiginger, K. and M. Pfaffermayr (2004) 'The single market and geographic concentration in Europe'. *Review of International Economics*, vol. 12, no. 1, pp. 1–11.

Aitken, N. D. (1973) 'The effects of the EC and EFTA on European trade: a temporal crosssection analysis'. *American Economic Review*, vol. 63, pp. 881–92.

Alchian, A. A. (1950) 'Uncertainty, evolution and economic theory'. *Journal of Political Economy*, vol. 58, June, pp. 211–21.

Alchian, A. (1984) 'Specificity, specialization, and coalitions'. *Zeitschrift für die gesamte Staatswissenschaft (JITE)*, vol. 140, no. 1, pp. 34–49.

Alchian, A. A. and H. Demsetz (1972) 'Production, information costs and economic organization'. *American Economic Review*, vol. 62, no. 5, pp. 777–95.

Alchian, A. A. and S. L. Woodward (1988) 'The firm is dead; long live the firm: a review of Oliver E. Williamson's *The Economic Institutions of Capitalism*'. *Journal of Economic Literature*, vol. 26, no. 1, pp. 65–79.

Almazan, A., J. Suarez and S. Titman (2003) 'Stakeholder, transparency and capital structure'. NBER Working Paper no. W10101. Available at http://papers.ssrn.com

Almeida, P. and B. Kogut (1997) 'The exploration of technological diversity and the geographic localization of innovation'. *Small Business Economics*, vol. 9, no. 1, pp. 21–31.

Amable, B. and B. Hancké (2001) 'Innovation and industrial renewal in France in comparative perspective', *Industry and Innovation*, vol. 8, no. 2, pp. 113–33.

Amatori, F. and A. Colli (1999) *Impresa e industria in Italia dall'Unità a oggi*. Marsilio Editori, Venice.

Amin, A. and M. Dietrich (1991) 'From hierarchy to "Hierarchy": the dynamics of contemporary corporate restructuring in Europe'. In A. Amin and M. Dietrich (eds), *Towards a New Europe?* Edward Elgar, Aldershot.

Amin, A. and K. Robins (1990) 'Industrial districts and regional development: limits and possibilities'. In F. Pyke *et al.* (eds), *Industrial Districts and Inter-firm Co-operation in Italy.* International Institute for Labour Studies, Geneva.

Amin, A. and N. Thrift (1992) 'The local in the global'. Paper presented at the Fourth Annual Conference of the European Association for Evolutionary Political Economy, Paris, November.

Amin, A., D. R. Charles and J. Howells (1992) 'Corporate restructuring and cohesion in the new Europe'. *Regional Studies*, vol. 26 no. 4, pp. 319–31.

Amiti, M. (1998) 'New trade theories and industrial location in the EU: a survey of evidence'. *Oxford Review of Economic Policy*, vol. 14, no. 2.

Anastassopolous, J. P., G. Blanc and P. Dussauge (1987) *State-owned Multinationals.* Wiley, New York.

Andersen, C. (1993) *Getting European Community Help for Your Company: A Guide for Small and Medium-sized Businesses.* Kogan Page, London.

Anderson, E. and A. T. Coughlan (1987) 'International market entry and expansion via independent or integrated channels of distribution'. *Journal of Marketing*, vol. 51, January, pp. 71–82.

Andréosso, B. (1986) 'Une structure industrielle européenne optimale: concepts et application à la Machine outil/robotique'. Unpublished PhD dissertation, University of Lille, France.

Andréosso, B. (1991) *The Clothing Industry and the Single European Market.* Special Report no. 2081, Economist Intelligence Unit, London, and Fitzpatrick and Associates, Dublin.

Andréosso, B. (1993a) 'Aperçu sur les relations CE–Bulgarie'. *Revue du Marché Commun et de l'Union Européenne*, no. 369, June, pp. 516–19.

Andréosso, B. (1993b) 'Dévaluation: l'Irlande est-elle un "cas spécial"?' *Revue Banque*, no. 539, July, pp. 62–4.

Andréosso, B. and D. Jacobson (1991) 'Le double processus d'intégration spatiale et industrielle à la lumière du cas Irlandais'. *Revue du Marché Commun et de l'Union Européenne*, no. 350, September, pp. 648–58.

Andreosso-O'Callaghan, B. (2004) 'The French economy in the throes of increased openness'. In F. Royall (ed.), *Contemporary French Cultures and Societies*, pp. 71–90. Peter Lang AG, Oxford.

Andreosso-O'Callaghan, B., and J.P. Bassino (2001) 'Explaining the EU–ASEAN intra industry trade through Japanese foreign direct investment – the case of high-tech industries'. *Journal of the Asia Pacific Economy*, vol. 6, no. 2, pp. 179–93.

Andreosso-O'Callaghan, B. and C. Noonan (1996) 'European intra-industry trade: emerging industrial specialization in central and eastern Europe'. *Journal of World Trade*, vol. 30, no. 6, pp. 139–68.

Antonelli, C. (1998) 'Localized technological change and the evolution of standards as economic institutions'. In A. D. Chandler, Jr *et al.* (eds), *The Dynamic Firm: The Role of Technology, Strategy, Organization, and Regions.* Oxford University Press, Oxford.

Antonelli, C. (1999) *The Microdynamics of Technological Change.* Routledge, London.

Antonelli, C. (2003) *The Economics of Innovation, New Technologies and Structural Change*. Routledge, London.

Antonelli, C., P. Petit and G. Tahar (1992) *The Economics of Industrial Modernization*. Academic Press, London.

Aoki, M. (1984) *The Co-operative Game Theory of the Firm*. Clarendon Press, Oxford.

Aoki, M. (1988) *Information, Incentives, and Bargaining in the Japanese Economy*. Cambridge University Press, Cambridge.

Aoki, M. (1990) 'Toward an economic model of the Japanese firm'. *Journal of Economic Literature*, vol. 28, no. 1, pp. 1–27.

Aoki, M., B. Gustafsson and O. E. Williamson (1990) *The Firm as a Nexus of Contracts*. Sage, London.

Appleyard, M. M. (2001) 'Cooperative knowledge creation: the case of buyer–supplier co-development in the semiconductor industry'. Available at http://emlab.berkeley.edu/users/bhhall/appleyard901.pdf

Areeda, P. and D. F. Turner (1975) 'Predatory pricing and related practices under section 2 of the Sherman Act'. *Harvard Law Review*, vol. 88, February, pp. 697–733.

Ark, B. van (2002) 'Measuring the new economy: an international perspective'. *Review of Income and Wealth*, vol. 48, no. 1, pp. 1–14.

Ark, B. van, J. Melka, N. Mulder, M. Timmer and G. Ypma (2003) 'ICT investments and growth accounts for the European Union 1980–2000', Research Memorandum GD-56, University of Gröningen, Gröningen Growth and Development Centre.

Armstrong, M. and J. Vickers (1993) 'Price discrimination, competition and regulation', *Journal of Industrial Economics*, vol. 41, no. 4, pp. 335–59.

Arrow, K. J. (1962) 'The economic implications of learning by doing'. *Review of Economic Studies*, vol. 29, June, pp. 155–73.

Arrow, K. J. and G. Debreu (1954) 'Existence of an equilibrium for a competitive economy'. *Econometrica*, vol. 22, pp. 265–90.

Asanuma, B. and T. Kikutani (1992) 'Risk absorption in Japanese subcontracting: a microeconometric study of the automobile industry', *Journal of the Japanese and International Economies*, vol. 6, no. 1, pp. 1–29.

Assarsson, B., C. Berg and P. Jansson (2004) 'Investment in Swedish manufacturing: Analysis and forecasts'. *Empirical Economics*, vol. 29, no. 2, pp. 261–81.

Aubry, P. (2000) 'The "Television Without Frontiers" directive, cornerstone of the European broadcasting policy'. European Audiovisual Observatory. Available at http://www.obs.coe.int

Auerbach, P. (1989) *Competition: The Economics of Industrial Change*. Basil Blackwell, Oxford.

Axelrod, R. (1984) *The Evolution of Cooperation*. Basic Books, New York.

Azzam, A. M. (1997) 'Measuring market power and cost-efficiency effects of industrial concentration'. *Journal of Industrial Economics*, vol. 45, no. 4, pp. 377–86.

Baba, Y. (1987) 'Internationalisation and technical change in Japanese electronics firms, or why the product cycle does not work'. Paper presented at EIASM meeting on Internationalisation and Competition, Brussels, June.

Babbage, C. (1832) *On the Economy of Machinery and Manufacturers*. Knight, London. Reprinted (1993) Routledge, London.

Bagwell, K. and G. Ramey (1994) 'Coordination economies, advertising and search behaviour in retail markets'. *American Economic Review*, vol. 84, no. 3, pp. 498–517.

Bailey, E. E. (1981) 'Contestability and the design of regulatory and antitrust policy'. *American Economic Review*, vol. 71, no. 2, pp. 179–83.

Bailey, E. E. and J. C. Panzer (1981) 'The contestability of airline markets during the transition to deregulation'. *Law and Contemporary Problems*, vol. 44, no. 1, pp. 125–45.

Bailey, M. N. (1993) 'Review of international productivity and competitiveness'. *Journal of Economic Literature*, vol. 31, no. 3, pp. 1483–4.

Bain and Company (1989) French industry in the global marketplace. Strategies for the future. France 300 Research Programme carried out on behalf of the French Ministry of Industry, Paris, September.

Bain, J. S. (1941) 'The profit rate as a measure of monopoly power'. *Quarterly Journal of Economics*, vol. 55, February, pp. 271–93.

Bain, J. S. (1951) 'Relation of profit rate to industry concentration: American manufacturing 1936–40'. *Quarterly Journal of Economics*, vol. 65, August, pp. 293–323.

Bain, J. S. (1956) *Barriers to New Competition*. Harvard University Press, Cambridge, MA.

Bain, J. S. (1958) *Industrial Organization*. Wiley, New York.

Bain, J. S. (1968) *Industrial Organization*, 2nd edition. Wiley, New York.

Balassa, B. (1965) 'Trade liberalisation and "revealed" comparative advantage'. *The Manchester School Economic and Social Studies*, vol. 33, pp. 99–124.

Balassa, B. (1967) 'Trade creation and trade diversion in the European Common Market'. *Economic Journal*, vol. 77, pp. 1–21.

Balassa, B. (1975) 'Trade creation and trade diversion in the European Common Market: an appraisal of the evidence'. In Balassa (ed.), *European Economic Integration*. North-Holland, Amsterdam.

Balassa, B. (1977) 'A stages approach to comparative advantage'. *World Bank Staff Working Papers*, no. 256.

Balassa, B. and C. Balassa (1984) 'Industrial protection in the developed countries'. *World Economy*, vol. 7, no. 2, pp. 179–96.

Balcet, G. (1997) *L'economia italiana: Evoluzione, problemi e paradossi*. Feltrinelli, Milano.

Balcombe, R. J., J. M. Hopkins and K. Penet (1988) *Bus Deregulation in Great Britain*. Research Report no. 161.

Bance, P. (1992) 'Europe industrielle: la politique communautaire en question'. *Problèmes Economiques*, no. 2261, February, pp. 1–9.

Banerjee, B. and S. Bandyopadhyay (2003) 'Research note: Advertising competition under consumer inertia'. *Marketing Science*, vol. 22, no. 1, pp. 131–44.

Barnett, C. (1986) *The Audit of War*. Macmillan, London.

Basu, S., and David N. Weil (1998) 'Appropriate Technology and Growth'. *The Quarterly Journal of Economics*, vol. 113, no. 4, pp. 1025–54.

Baumol, W. J. (1967) *Business Behavior, Value and Growth*. Harcourt Brace Jovanovich, New York.

Baumol, W. J. (1979) 'Quasi-permanence of price reductions: a policy for prevention of predatory pricing'. *Yale Law Journal*, vol. 89, no. 1, pp. 1–26.

Baumol, W. J. (1984) 'Towards a theory of public enterprise'. *Atlantic Economic Journal*, vol. 12, no. 1, pp. 13–19.

Baumol, W. J. and R. D. Willig (1986) 'Contestability: developments since the book'. *Oxford Economic Papers*, vol. 38, November, supplement, pp. 9–36.

Baumol, W. J., J. C. Panzar and R. D. Willig (1982) *Contestable Markets and the Theory of Industrial Structure*. Harcourt Brace Jovanovich, New York.

Becattini, G. (1990) 'The Marshallian industrial district as a socio-economic notion'. In F. Pyke et al. (eds), *Industrial Districts and Inter-firm Co-operation in Italy*. International Institute for Labour Studies, Geneva.

Becuwe, S. and C. Mathieu (1998) 'Globalisation, commerce intra-branche et échanges intra-groupe: L'Europe avant le grand large'. Working Paper, CNRS.

Beggs, J. (1982) 'Long run trends in patenting'. Working Paper no. 952, National Bureau of Economic Research, Washington, DC.

Beije, P. R., J. Groenewegan, I. Kostoulas, J. Paelinck and C. van Paridon (eds) (1987) *A Competitive Future for Europe? Towards a New European Industrial Policy*. Croom Helm, New York.

Belke, A. and Schneider, F. (2004) 'Privatization in Austria: some theoretical reasons and performance measures'. Economics working paper no. 2004–04, Department of Economics, Johannes Kepler University, Linz.

Belleflamme, P. and E. Toulemonde (2003) 'Product differentiation in successive vertical oligopolies'. *Canadian Journal of Economics*, vol. 36, no. 3, pp. 523–46.

Benton, L. (1992) 'The emergence of industrial districts in Spain: industrial restructuring and diverging regional responses'. In F. Pyke and W. Sengenberger (eds), *Industrial Districts and Local Economic Regeneration*. International Institute for Labour Studies, Geneva.

Benzing, C. (1990) 'The determinants of aggregate merger activity: before and after-Celler-Kefauver'. *Review of Industrial Organization*, vol. 6, no. 1.

Berle, A. A. and G. C. Means (1932) *The Modern Corporation and Private Property*. Macmillan, New York.

Bernard, J. and A. Torre (1991) 'L'énigme du chainon manquant, ou l'absence des strategies dans les verifications empiriques du paradigme SCP'. *Revue d'Économie Industrielle*, no. 57, 3rd quarter, pp. 93–105.

Bernhardt, I. and K. D. Mackenzie (1968) 'Measuring seller unconcentration, segmentation, and product differentiation'. *Western Economic Journal*, vol. 6, December, pp. 395–403.

Bernhofen, D.M. (2001) 'Product differentiation, competition, and international trade'. *Canadian Journal of Economics*, vol. 34, no. 4, pp. 1010–23.

Bernstein, J. and M. Nadiri (1989) 'Research and development and intra-industry spillovers: an empirical application of duality theory'. *Review of Economic Studies*, vol. 56, pp. 249–69.

Bertrand, J. (1883) 'Théorie mathématique de la richesse sociale'. *Journal des Savants*, September, pp. 499–508.

Besanko, D. and M. K. Perry (1994) 'Exclusive dealing in a spatial model of retail competition'. *International Journal of Industrial Organization*, vol. 12, no. 3, pp. 297–329.

Best, M. H. (1990) *The New Competition*. Polity Press, Cambridge.

Best, M. H. (2001) *The New Competitive Advantage: The Renewal of American Industry*. Oxford University Press, Oxford.

Bianchi, P. (1995) 'Italy: crisis of an introvert state'. In J. Hayward (ed.), *Industrial Enterprise and European Integration*. Oxford University Press, Oxford.

Bianchi, P. and L. Forlai (1993) 'The domestic applicance industry 1945–1991'. In H. W. de Jong (ed.), *The Structure of European Industry*. Kluwer, Dordrecht.

Bigarelli, D. and P. Crestanello (1994) 'An analysis of the changes in the knitwear/clothing district of Carpi during the 1980s'. *Entrepreneurship and Regional Development*, vol. 6, no. 2, pp. 117–44.

Bingham, T. (1985) *Banking and Monetary Policy*. OECD, Paris.

Blahó, A. and L. Halpern (1995) 'Stabilisation, crisis and structural change in Hungary'. In Landesmann and Székely (eds), *Industrial Restructuring and Trade Reorientation in Eastern Europe*. Cambridge University Press, Cambridge.

Blair, M. M. (1995) *Ownership and Control: Rethinking Corporate Governance of the Twenty-First Century*. Brookings Institution, Washington, DC.

Blair, R. D. and D. L. Kaserman (1978) 'Uncertainty and the incentive for vertical integration'. *Southern Economic Journal*, vol. 45, July, pp. 266–72.

Blair, R. D. and D. L. Kaserman (1985) *Antitrust Economics*. Irwin, Homewood, IL.

Bley, J. and J. Madura (2003) 'Intra-industry and inter-country effects of European mergers'. *Journal of Economics and Finance*, vol. 27, no. 3, pp. 373–95.

Böckem, S. (1994) 'A generalized model of horizontal product differentiation'. *Journal of Industrial Economics*, vol. 42, no. 3, pp. 287–98.

Bolton, P. and D. S. Scharfstein (1998) 'Corporate finance, the theory of the firm and organizations'. *Journal of Economic Perspectives*, vol. 12, no. 4, pp. 95–114.

Bottazzi, L. and M. Da Rin (2002) 'Venture capital in Europe and the financing of innovative companies'. *Economic Policy*, vol. 17, no. 34, pp. 229–70.

Bradburd, R. M. and A. M. Over (1982) 'Organizational costs, "sticky" equilibria and critical levels of concentration'. *Review of Economics and Statistics*, vol. 64, February, pp. 50–8.

Braendgaard, A. (1986) 'Danish industrial policy: liberalism revised or revisited'. In G. Hall (ed.), *European Industrial Policy*. Croom Helm, London.

Brimelow, P. (1994) 'Taxation without representation'. *Forbes*, vol. 153, no. 2, pp. 74–5.

Brittan, S. (1990) 'Conditions of progress: determinants of industrial success'. *Financial Times*, 24 June.

Brooks, D. G. (1973) 'Buyer concentration: a forgotten element in market structure models'. *Industrial Organization Review*, vol. 1, no. 3, pp. 151–63.

Brown, R. (2000) 'Clusters, supply chains and local embeddedness in Fyrstad,' *European Urban and Regional Studies*, vol. 7. no. 4, pp. 291–305.

Brozen, Y. (1970) 'The antitrust task force deconcentration recommendation'. *Journal of Law and Economics*, vol. 13, October, pp. 279–92.

Brülhart, M. and R. Hine (1998) (eds) *Intra-Industry Trade and Adjustment: the European Experience*. Macmillan, Basingstoke.

Brülhart, M. and D. McAleese (1993) 'Intra-industry trade, adjustment and the EC Single Market: the Irish experience'. Unpublished, Trinity College Dublin, December.

Brusco, S. (1982) 'The Emilian model: productive decentralisation and social integration'. *Cambridge Journal of Economics*, vol. 6, pp. 167–84.

Buckley, P. J. and B. R. Roberts (1982) *European Direct Investment in the USA Before World War 1*. Macmillan, London.

Bugbee, B. W. (1967) *Genesis of American Patent and Copyright Law*. Public Affairs Press, Washington, DC.

Bullock, C. J. (1901) 'Trust literature: a survey and criticism'. *Quarterly Journal of Economics*, vol. 15, February, pp. 167–217.

Butler, R. (2002) 'Simon, Herbert Alexander (1916–2001)'. In W. Lazonick (ed.), *The IEBM Handbook of Economics*. Thomson, London.

Button, K. J. and T. G. Weyman-Jones (1993) 'X-inefficiency and regulatory regime shift in the UK'. *Journal of Evolutionary Economics*, vol. 3, no. 4, pp. 269–84.

Button, K. J. and T. G. Weyman-Jones (1994) 'X-efficiency and technical efficiency'. *Public Choice*, vol. 89, nos 1–2, pp. 83–104.

Byers, J. D. and D. A. Peel (1994) 'Linear and non-linear models of economic time series: an introduction with applications to industrial economics'. In J. Cable (ed.), *Current Issues in Industrial Economics*. Macmillan, London.

Caballero, S. F. and M. Catinat (1992) 'European technology policy and cohesion: a reconciliation in practice'. *Revue d'Economie Industrielle*, no. 59, 1st quarter, pp. 192–203.

Cable, J. (1994) 'Introduction and overview: recent developments in industrial economics'. In J. Cable (ed.), *Current Issues in Industrial Economics*. Macmillan, London.

Cable, J., A. Carruth and A. Dixit (1994) 'Oligopoly and welfare'. In J. Cable (ed.), *Current Issues in Industrial Economics*. Macmillan, London.

Cable, J. R. (1997) 'Market share behavior and mobility: an analysis and time-series application'. *Review of Economics and Statistics*, vol. 79, no. 1, pp. 136–41.

Cabral, Luis M.B. (ed.) (2000) *Readings in Industrial Organization*. Blackwell, Oxford.

Camagni, R. P. (1991) 'Regional deindustrialization and revitalization processes in Italy'. In L. Rodwin and H. Sazanami (eds), *Industrial Change and Regional Economic Transformation: The Experience of Western Europe*. HarperCollins, London.

Campbell, D. (ed.) (1983) *Legal Aspects of Doing Business in Western Europe*. Kluwer, Dordrecht.

Cantillo Simon, M. (1998) 'The rise and fall of bank control in the United States: 1890–1939'. *American Economic Review*, vol. 88, no. 5, pp. 1077–93.

Cantwell, J. (1989) *Technological Innovation and Multinational Corporations*. Basil Blackwell, Oxford.

Cantwell, J. (ed.) (1992) *Multinational Investment in Modern Europe: Strategic Interaction in the Integrated Community*. Edward Elgar, Aldershot.

Cantwell, J. (2000) 'A survey of theories of international production'. In C. N. Pitelis and R. Sugden (eds), *The Nature of the Transnational Firm*. Routledge, London.

Cantwell, J. A. (1991) 'The international agglomeration of R&D'. In M. Casson (ed.), *Global Research Strategy and International Competitiveness*. Basil Blackwell, Oxford.

Carbonara, N. (2002) 'New models of inter-firm networks within industrial districts'. *Entrepreneurship and Regional Development*, vol. 14, pp. 229–46.

Carlin, W., A. Glynn and J. Van Reenen (2001) 'Export market performance of OECD countries: an empirical examination of the role of cost competitiveness'. *Economic Journal*, vol. 111, no. 468, pp. 128–62.

Carlton, D. W. (1979) 'Vertical integration in competitive markets under uncertainty'. *Journal of Industrial Economics*, vol. 27, March, pp. 189–209.

Carpenter, G. S., R. Glazer and K. Nakamoto (1994) 'Meaningful brands from meaningless differentiation – the dependence on irrelevant attributes'. *Journal of Marketing Research*, vol. 31, no. 3, pp. 339–50.

Castells, M. and P. Hall (1994) *Technopoles of the World: The Making of 21st Century Industrial Complexes*. Routledge, London.

Castle, E.N. (2003) 'The social capital paradigm: bridging across disciplines – an overview'. *American Journal of Agricultural Economics*, vol. 85, no. 5, pp. 1208–10.

Catinat, M. (1989) Les conditions de réussite du grand marché intérieur. Concrétiser les opportunités. *Economie et Statistique*, nos 217–218, January–February, pp. 97–115.

Caves, R. E. (1971) 'International corporations: the industrial economics of foreign investment'. *Economica*, vol. 38, February, pp. 1–27.

Caves, R. E. (1991) 'Growth of large enterprises and their market environments'. In P. de Wolf (ed.), *Competition in Europe: Essays in Honour of H. W. de Jong*. Kluwer Academic, Dordrecht.

Caves, R.E. and D. P. Greene (1996) 'Brands' quality levels, prices, and advertising outlays: empirical evidence on signals and information costs'. *International Journal of Industrial Organization*, vol. 14, pp. 29–52.

Caves, R. E. and M. E. Porter (1977) 'From entry barriers to mobile barriers: conjectural decisions and continued deterrence to new competition'. *Quarterly Journal of Economics*, vol. 91, pp. 241–61.

Caves, R. E. and M. E. Porter (1978) 'Market structure, oligopoly and stability of market shares'. *Journal of Industrial Economics*, vol. 26, no. 4, pp. 289–313.

CEC (1965) *Mémorandum sur le problème de la concentration dans le marché commun*. CEC, Brussels.

CEC (1970) *Industrial Policy in the Community: Memorandum from the Commission to the Council* (Colonna Report). CEC, Brussels.

CEC (1973) *Memorandum on the Technological and Industrial Policy Programme* (Spinelli Memorandum). CEC, Brussels.

CEC (1977) *VIth Report on Competition Policy*. CEC, Brussels.

CEC (1983) *XIIth Report on Competition Policy*. CEC, Brussels.

CEC (1984) *XIIIth Report on Competition Policy*. CEC, Brussels.

CEC (1985a) *Completing the Internal Market*. COM (85) 310 final. CEC, Brussels.

CEC (1985b) *Towards a Technology Policy*. COM (85) 530, final. CEC, Brussels.

CEC (1988) *The Cost of Non-Europe in Public Sector Procurement*, vol. 5, Part A. CEC, Brussels.

CEC (1989) *First Survey on State Aids in the European Community*. Luxembourg.

CEC (1990) *Industrial Policy in an Open Competitive Environment. Guidelines for a Community Approach*. COM (90) 556 final. CEC, Brussels.

CEC (1991) *XXIst Report on Competition Policy*. CEC, Brussels.

CEC (1992) *Third Survey on State Aids in the EC in the Manufacturing and Certain Other Sectors*. Luxembourg.

CEC (1993a) *The Opening-up of Public Procurement*. DG Internal Market and Industrial Affairs, Luxembourg. CEC, Brussels.

CEC (1993b) *Report from the Commission on the State of the Shipbuilding Industry in the Community – Situation in 1992*. COM (93) 562 final, 16 November 1993. CEC, Brussels.

CEC (1993c) 'The European Community as a world trade partner'. European Economy, no. 52. CEC, Brussels.

CEC (1993d) *XXIIIrd Report on Competition Policy*. CEC, Brussels.

CEC (1993e) *European Economy, Social Europe*. CEC, Brussels.

CEC (1993f) *Bulletin of the European Communities*, vol. 26, no. 6, pp. 12–13.

CEC (1994a) *Intermediate Report on the Restructuring of the Steel Industry*. COM (94), 125 final. CEC, Brussels.

CEC (1994b) *Towards a New Asia Strategy*. COM (314) final. CEC, Brussels.

CEC (2000) *Tax Policy in the European Union*. CEC, Luxembourg.

CEC (2001a) *XXXth Report on Competition Policy*. Office for Official Publications of the European Communities, Luxembourg.

CEC (2001b) *Ninth Survey on State Aids in the European Union*. COM (2001) 403 final. Brussels.

CEC (2001c) *European Union FDI Yearbook, Data 1992–2000*. Eurostat, Brussels.

CEC (2002a) *XXXIst Report on Competition Policy*. Office for Official Publications of the European Communities, Luxembourg.

CEC (2002b) *Statistical Elements in Support of the Communication on Industrial Policy in an enlarged Europe*, Commission Staff Working Document; SEC (2002) 1340, Brussels, December.

CEC (2002c) *Industrial Policy in an Enlarged Europe*. COM (2002) 714 final, 11 December. Brussels.

CEC (2003a) *XXXIInd Report on Competition Policy*. Office for Official Publications of the European Communities, Luxembourg.

CEC (2003b) *European Competitiveness Report 2003*. CEC, Brussels.

CEC (2003c) *XXXIIIrd Report on Competition Policy*, Office for Official Publications of the European Communities, Luxembourg.

CEC (2004) *Public Private Partnerships. Green Paper*. COM (2004) 327 final. CEC, Brussels.

CEC (various years) *Panorama of EC Industries*. CEC, Brussels.

Cecchini, P. (1988) 1992: The European Challenge: The Benefits of a Single Market, Gower, Aldershot.

CEEP (2000) CEEP Statistical Review: The Development of Enterprises of Public Participation and of General Economic Interest in Europe since 1996. CEEP, Brussels.

Cellini, R., L. Lambertini and G. I. P. Ottaviano (2004) 'Welfare in a differentiated oligopoly with free entry: a cautionary note'. Research in Economics, vol. 58, no. 2, pp. 125–34.

Chamberlin, E. H. (1933) The Theory of Monopolistic Competition. Harvard University Press, Cambridge, MA.

Chamberlin, E. H. (1962) The Theory of Monopolistic Competition, 8th edn. Harvard University Press, Cambridge, MA.

Chandler, A. D. (1977) The Visible Hand: The Managerial Revolution in American Business. Harvard University Press, Cambridge, MA.

Chandler, A. D. (1992a) 'What is a firm?' European Economic Review, vol. 36, nos 2/3, pp. 483–92. (This is a paper presented at the Sixth Annual Congress of the European Economics Association, Aug./Sept. 1991, and is an earlier version of Chandler, 1992b.)

Chandler, A. D. (1992b) 'Organizational capabilities and the economic history of the industrial enterprise'. Journal of Economic Perspectives, vol. 6, no. 3, pp. 79–100.

Chandler, A. D., Jr (1984) 'The emergence of managerial capitalism'. Business History Review, vol. 58, no. 4, pp. 473–503.

Chandler, A. D., Jr (1990) Scale and Scope: The Dynamics of Industrial Capitalism. Belknap/Harvard University Press, Cambridge, MA.

Chandler, A. D. Jr, P. Hagström and Ö. Sölvell (eds.) (1998) The Dynamic Firm: The Role of Technology, Strategy, Organization, and Regions. Oxford University Press, Oxford.

Chang, H-J. (1994) The Political Economy of Industrial Policy. Macmillan, London.

Chang, H-J. (2003) Globalisation, Economic Development and the Role of the State. Zed Books, London, and Third World Network, Penang.

Chan-Lee, J. and R. Torres (1987) 'q de Tobin et taux d'accumulation en France'. Annales d'Economie et de Statistique, no. 5, Jan./March, pp. 37–48.

Charbit, C., J. Ravix, and P. M. Romani, (1991) 'Sous-traitance et intégration industrielle européenne'. Revue d'Economie Industrielle, no. 55, 1st quarter, special issue, pp. 178–89.

CHEAr (2004) 'Strategic studies: ARES'. Available on the Centre des Hautes Etudes de l'Armement website at http://www.chear.defense.gouv.fr/fr/etudes_strategiques/ contenuuk.html

Chen, K. C., G. L. Hite and D. C. Cheng (1989) 'Barriers to entry, concentration, and Tobin's q ratio'. Quarterly Journal of Business and Economics, vol. 28, no. 2, pp. 32–49.

Chesnais, F. (1992) 'National systems of innovation, foreign direct investment and the operations of multinational enterprises'. In B-Å. Lundvall (ed.), National Systems of Innovation. Pinter, London.

Chesnais, F. (1993) 'The French national system of innovation'. In R. R. Nelson (ed.) National Innovation Systems. Oxford University Press, Oxford.

Choi, Y. B. (1997) 'Professor Choi's response' [to a review of his book, *Paradigms, Conventions and the Entrepreneur*]. *American Journal of Economics and Sociology*, vol. 56, no. 1, pp. 59–69.

Chowdhury, A. and Y. Islam (1993) *The Newly Industrialising Economies of East Asia*. Routledge, London.

Christensen, J. L. (1992) 'The role of finance in national systems of innovation'. In B-Å. Lundvall (ed.), *National Systems of Innovation*. Pinter, London.

Church, C. H. and D. Phinnemore (1994) *European Union and European Community*. Harvester-Wheatsheaf, Hemel Hempstead.

Ciccone, A. (2002) 'Agglomeration effects in Europe'. *European Economic Review*, vol. 46, no. 2, pp. 213–27.

Clark, J. M. (1940) 'Towards a concept of workable competition'. *American Economic Review*, vol. 30, pp. 241–56.

Clark, N. and C. Juma (1987) *Long Run Economics: An Evolutionary Approach to Economic Growth*. Pinter, London.

Coase, R. H. (1937) 'The nature of the firm'. *Economica*, vol. 4, November, pp. 386–405. Reprinted in Coase, R. H. (1988) *The Firm, the Market and the Law*. University of Chicago Press, Chicago, chapter 2.

Coase, R. H. (1992) 'The institutional structure of production'. *American Economic Review*, vol. 82, no. 4, pp. 713–19.

Coghlan, A. (1995) 'A very British tragedy?' *New Scientist*, no. 1973, 15 April, pp. 12–13.

Cohen, E. (1995) 'France: national champions in search of a mission'. In J. Hayward (ed.), *Industrial Enterprise and European Integration*. Oxford University Press, Oxford.

Cohen, Elie and Jean-Hervé Lorenzi (2000) *Politiques industrielles pour l'Europe*. Conseil d'Analyse Economique du Premier Ministre, Paris.

Cohendet, P., P. Llerena and A. Sorge (1992) 'Technological diversity and coherence in Europe: an analytical overview'. *Revue d'Economie Industrielle*, no. 59, 1st quarter, pp. 9–26.

Colijn, G. J. (1987) 'Non-strategic aspects of SDI'. Working Paper no. 45, Department of Politics, University of Warwick.

Collins, G. (2003) 'The economic case for mergers: old, new, borrowed, and blue'. *Journal of Economic Issues*, vol. 37, no. 4, pp. 987–98.

Collins, N. R. and L. E. Preston (1968) *Concentration and Price–Cost Margins in Manufacturing Industries*. University of California Press, Berkeley.

Collins, N. R. and L. E. Preston (1969) 'Price–cost margins and industry structure'. *Review of Economics and Statistics*, vol. 51, August, pp. 271–86.

Comanor, W. S. and T. A. Wilson (1967) 'Advertising, market structure and performance'. *Review of Economics and Statistics*, vol. 49, pp. 423–40.

Comanor, W. S. and T. A. Wilson (1979) 'The effect of advertising on competition: a survey'. *Journal of Economic Literature*, vol. 17, pp. 453–76.

Cooke, P. (1992) 'Regional innovation systems: competitive regulation in the new Europe', *Geoforum*, vol. 23, pp. 365–82.

Cooke, P. (2001) 'Regional Innovation Systems, Clusters, and the Knowledge Economy', *Industrial and Corporate Change*, vol. 10, no. 4, pp. 945–74.

Cooke, P. and K. Morgan (1990) *Learning through networking: regional innovation and the lessons of Baden-Wurttemberg*. Regional Industrial Research, Cardiff, report no. 5, May.

Corbino, E. (1962) *L'Economia Italiana dal 1860 al 1960*. Zanichelli Editore, Bologna.

Corden, W. (1972) 'Economies of scale and customs union theory'. *Journal of Political Economy*, vol. 80, pp. 465–75.

Coriat, B. and P. Petit (1991) 'Deindustrialization and tertiarization: towards a new economic regime?' In A. Amin and M. Dietrich (eds), *Towards a New Europe?* Edward Elgar, Aldershot.

Coriat, B. and O. Weinstein (2004) 'National institutional frameworks, institutional complementarities and sectoral systems of innovation'. In F. Malerba (ed.), *Sectoral Systems of Innovation: Concepts, Issues and Analyses of Six Major Sectors in Europe*. Cambridge University Press, Cambridge.

Coriat, B., F. Malerba and F. Montobbio (2004) 'The international performance of European sectoral systems'. In F. Malerba (ed.) *Sectoral Systems of Innovation: Concepts, Issues and Analyses of Six Major Sectors in Europe*. Cambridge University Press, Cambridge.

Cournot, A. (1980) *Recherches sur les Principes Mathématiques de la Théories des Richesses*. Librairie Philosophique J. Vrin, Paris. First published in 1838.

Cowling, K. (1976) 'On the theoretical specification of industrial structure–performance relationship'. *European Economic Review*, vol. 8, July, pp. 1–14.

Cowling, K. (1999) (ed.) *Industrial Policy in Europe: Theoretical Perspectives and Practical Proposals*. Routledge, London.

Cowling, K. and R. Sugden (1998) 'The essence of the modern corporation: markets, strategic decision-making and the theory of the firm'. *The Manchester School*, vol. 66, no. 1, pp. 59–86.

Cowling, K. and M. Waterson (1976) 'Price-cost margins and market structure'. *Economica*, vol. 43, August, pp. 267–74.

Cowling, K., P. Stoneman, J. Cubbin, J. Cable, G. Hall, S. Domberger and P. Dutton (1980) *Mergers and Economic Performance*. Cambridge University Press, Cambridge.

Cox, A. and G. Watson (1995) 'The European Community and the restructuring of Europe's national champions'. In J. Hayward (ed.), *Industrial Enterprise and European Integration: From National to International Champions in Western Europe*. Oxford University Press, Oxford.

Crum, W. L. (1933) *Corporate Size and Earning Power*. Harvard University Press, Cambridge, MA.

Cubbin, J. (1981) 'Advertising and the theory of entry barriers'. *Economica*, vol. 48, August, pp. 289–98.

Curzon Price, V. (1991) 'The threat of "Fortress Europe" from the development of social and industrial policies at a European level'. *Außenwirtschaft*, St Gallen, vol. 46, no. 2, July, pp. 119–38.

Cyert, R. and J. G. March (1963) *The Behavioural Theory of the Firm*. Prentice Hall, Englewood Cliffs, NJ.

D'Asprement, C., J. J. Gabszewicz and J. F. Thisse (1979) 'On Hotelling's "Stability in Competition"'. *Econometrica*, vol. 47, pp. 1145–50.

Dalton, J. A. and D. W. Penn (1976) 'The concentration–profitability relationship: is there a critical concentration ratio?' *Journal of Industrial Economics*, vol. 25, December.

Danish Government (2003) *The Danish Government's Knowledge Strategy – Knowledge in Growth*, 13 May, Copenhagen.

Dankbaar, B., J. Groenewegen and H. Schenk (eds) (1990) *Perspectives in Industrial Organization: Studies in Industrial Organization*, vol. 13. Kluwer Academic, Dordrecht.

Datta-Chaudhuri, M. (1990) 'Market failure and government failure'. *Journal of Economic Perspectives*, vol. 4, no. 3.

Davies, S. and B. Lyons (1988) 'Introduction'. In S. Davies *et al.* (eds), *Economics of Industrial Organisation*. Longman, London.

Davies, S., P. Geroski and A. Vlassopoulos (1991) 'La concentration au Royaume-Uni'. *Revue du Marché Commun et de l'Union Européenne*, no. 350, September, pp. 646–7.

Davis, D.R. and D.E. Weinstein (1999) 'Economic geography and regional production structure: an empirical investigation'. *European Economic Review*, vol. 43.

Davis, L. A. (1991) 'Technology intensity of US, Canadian and Japanese manufacturers output and exports'. In J. Niosi (ed.), *Technology and National Competitiveness: Oligopoly, Technological Innovation and International Competition*. McGill-Queen's University Press, Buffalo.

de Bandt, J. (1983) 'A propos de la reconquête du marché intérieur'. *Les Cahiers français*, no. 212, pp. 62–73.

de Bandt, J. (1987) 'French industrial policies: successes and failures'. In P. R. Beije *et al.* (eds), *A Competitive Future for Europe?* Croom Helm, New York.

de Bandt, J. (1995) 'Quelles conceptions des entreprises, des systèmes et des processus productifs inspirent quelles politiques industrielles'. *Revue d'Economie Industrielle*, no 71, 1st quarter.

de Bernis, G. (1990) 'Investissement extérieur direct et systèmes productifs en France et au Japon'. In A. Androuais (ed.), *L'Investissement extérieur direct*. University Press, Grenoble.

de Jong, H. W. (1990) 'The takeover market in Europe: control structures and the performance of large companies compared'. *Review of Industrial Organization*, vol. 6, no. 1.

de Jong, H. W. (ed.) (1993) *The Structure of European Industry*. Kluwer Academic, Dordrecht.

de Wolf, P. (ed.) (1991) *Competition in Europe: Essays in Honour of Henk W. de Jong*. Kluwer Academic, Dordrecht.

de Wolf, P. (1993) 'The pharmaceutical industry: towards one single market?' In H. W. de Jong (ed.), *The Structure of European Industry*. Kluwer Academic, Dordrecht.

Dean, J. W. and M. Perlman (1998) 'Harvey Leibenstein as a pioneer of our time'. *Economic Journal*, vol. 108, no. 446, pp. 132–53.

Deardorff, A. and R. Stern (1983) 'Economic effects of the Tokyo Round'. *Southern Economic Journal*, vol. 49, no. 3, pp. 605–24.

Del Monte, A. (1977) *Politica Regionale e Sviluppo Economico*, F. Angeli, Italy.

Demsetz, H. (1973) 'Industry structure, market rivalry and public policy', *Journal of Law and Economics*, vol. 16.

Demsetz, H. (1974) 'Two systems of belief about monopoly'. In H. Goldschmid, H. M. Mann and J. F. Weston (eds), *Industrial Concentration: The New Learning*. Little, Brown, Boston.

Demsetz, H. (1988) 'The theory of the firm revisited'. *Journal of Law, Economics and Organization*, vol. 4, no. 1, pp. 141–61.

Denison, E. F. (1985) *Trends in American Economic Growth, 1929–1982*. Brookings Institute, Washington, DC.

Dertouzas, M. L., R. K. Lester and R. M. Solow (1989) *Made in America: Regaining the Productive Edge*. MIT Press, Cambridge, MA.

Devine, P. J., N. Lee, R. M. Jones and W. J. Tyson (1985) *An Introduction to Industrial Economics*. Allen & Unwin, London.

Dicken, P. (1992) *Global Shift*. Macmillan, London.

Dicken, P. (2003a) *Global Shift: Reshaping the Global Economic Map in the 21st Century*. Sage, London.

Dicken, P. (2003b) ' "Placing" firms: grounding the debate on the "global" corporation'. In J. Peck and H. W. Yeung (eds), *Remaking the Global Economy*. Sage, London.

Dicken, P. and P. E. Lloyd (1990) *Location in Space: Theoretical Perspectives in Economic Geography*. Harper & Row, New York.

Dickson, V. A. (1991) 'The relationship between concentration and prices and concentration and costs'. *Applied Economics*, vol. 23, no. 1A, pp. 101–6.

Diebold, W. (1982) 'Past and future industrial policy in the United States'. In J. Pinder (ed.), *National Industrial Strategies and the World Economy*. Croom Helm, London.

Dienel, H-L., K. G. Hammerlund and M. Peterson (2002) 'The historical context of the evolution of national research systems and international RTD collaboration'. *Innovation*, vol. 15, no. 4, pp. 265–78.

Dierickx, I., C. Matutes and D. Neven (1991) 'Cost differences and survival in declining industries: a case for "picking winners"?' *European Economic Review*, vol. 35, pp. 1507–28.

Dixit, A. (1979) 'A model of duopoly suggesting a theory of entry barriers'. *Bell Journal of Economics*, vol. 10, Spring, pp. 20–32.

Dixit, A. and V. Norman (1978) 'Advertising and welfare'. *Bell Journal of Economics*, vol. 9, Spring, pp. 1–17.

Dodgson, J. S., Y. Katsoulacos and R. W. S. Pryke (1990) *Predatory Behaviour in Aviation*. Report for the Commission of the European Communities.

Dodgson, M. and R. Rothwell (eds) (1994) *Handbook of Industrial Innovation*. Edward Elgar, Aldershot.

Doeringer, P. and M. Piore (1971) *Internal Labour Markets and Manpower Analysis*. D. C. Heath, Boston, MA.

Domowitz, I., R. G. Hubbard and B. C. Petersen (1986) 'Business cycles and the relationship between concentration and price–cost margins'. *Rand Journal of Economics*, vol. 17, Spring, pp. 1–17.

Donaldson, G. and J. W. Lorsch (1983) *Decision Making at the Top*. Basic Books, New York.

Donsimoni, M. P. and M. Kambouri (1989) 'The SCP paradigm revisited'. Working Paper no. 8506, University Catholique de Louvain.

Dorfman, R. and P. O. Steiner (1954) 'Optimal advertising and optimal quality'. *American Economic Review*, vol. 44, December, pp. 826–36.

Dosi, G. (1990) 'Finance, innovation and industrial change'. *Journal of Economic Behavior and Organization*, vol. 13, no. 3, pp. 299–313.

Dosi, G. and L. Orsenigo (1988) 'Structure industrielle et evolution technologique'. In A. Heertje (ed.), *Innovation, Technologie et Finance*. Basil Blackwell, Oxford.

Dosi, G., C. Freeman, R. R. Nelson, G. Silverberg and L. L. G. Soete (eds) (1988) *Technical Change and Economic Theory*. Pinter, London.

Douma, S. and H. Schreuder (1992) *Economic Approaches to Organizations*. Prentice Hall, Hemel Hempstead.

Downie, J. (1958) *The Competitive Process*. Duckworth, London.

Duchêne, F. and G. Shepherd (eds) (1987) *Managing Industrial Change in Western Europe*. Pinter, London.

Dunford, M. and R. Hudson (1996) *Successful European Regions. Northern Ireland Learning from Others*. Northern Ireland Economic Council, Belfast.

Dunning, J. H. (1977) 'Trade, location of economic activity, and the MNE: A search for an eclectic approach'. In B. Ohlin, P-O. Hesselborn and P.M. Wijkman (eds), *The International Allocation of Economic Activity*. Macmillan, London.

Dunning, J. H. (1988) *Explaining International Production*. HarperCollins, London.

Dunning, J. H. (1992) 'The global economy, domestic governance strategies and transnational corporations: interactions and policy implications'. *Transnational Corporations*, vol. 1, no. 3, pp. 7–45.

Dunning, J. H. (1993) *The Globalization of Business*. Routledge, London.

Dunning, J. H. (2000) 'The eclectic paradigm of international production: a personal perspective'. In C. N. Pitelis and R. Sugden (eds), *The Nature of the Transnational Firm*. Routledge, London.

Dunning, J. H. and P. Robson (1987) 'Multinational corporate integration and regional economic integration'. *Journal of Common Market Studies*, vol. 26, no. 2.

Earl-Slater, A. (1993) 'Pharmaceuticals'. In P. Johnson (ed.), *European Industries*. Edward Elgar, Aldershot.

Eatwell, J., M. Milgate and P. Newman (eds) (1987) *The New Palgrave*. Macmillan, London.

Eck, J. F. (1990) 'Forces et faiblesses de l'industrie'. In *Histoire de l'Economie Française depuis 1945*, pp. 82–110. Cursus, Paris.

Eden, L. (1991) 'Bringing the firm back in: multinationals in international political economy'. *Millennium: Journal of International Studies*, vol. 20, no. 2, pp. 197–224.

Edquist, C. (2001) 'The systems of innovation approach and innovation policy: an account of the state of the art'. Paper presented at the DRUID Conference, Aalborg, 12–15 June 2001, under theme F: 'National Systems of Innovation, Institutions and Public Policies'. Available at http://www.druid.dk/conferences/nw/conf-papers.html

Edquist, C. (2004) 'The fixed Internet and mobile telecommunications sectoral system of innovation: equipment production, access provision and content provision'. In F. Malerba (ed.),

Sectoral Systems of Innovation: Concepts, Issues and Analyses of Six Major Sectors in Europe. Cambridge University Press, Cambridge.

Edquist, C. and B-Å. Lundvall (1993) 'Comparing small Nordic systems of innovation'. In Nelson (ed.), *National Systems of Innovation.* Oxford University Press, Oxford.

Edwards, C. D. (1955) 'Conglomerate bigness as a source of power'. In *Business Concentration and Price Policy.* National Bureau of Economic Research conference report, Princeton University Press, Princeton, NJ.

Edwards, G. (1982) 'Four sectors: textiles, man-made fibres, shipbuilding, aircraft'. In J. Pinder (ed.), *National Industrial Strategies and the World Economy.* Croom Helm, London.

EFPIA (European Federation of Pharmaceutical Industries and Associations) (2004) *The Pharmaceutical Industry in Figures.* Available at http://www.efpia.org/6_publ/default.htm

Egeraat, C. Van and D. Jacobson (2004) 'The rise and demise of the Irish and Scottish computer hardware industry'. *European Planning Studies,* vol. 12, no. 6, pp. 809–34.

Elbaum, B. and W. Lazonick (eds.) (1986) *The Decline of the British Economy.* Clarendon Press, Oxford.

Elliott, C. (2004) 'Vertical product differentiation and advertising'. *International Journal of the Economics of Business,* vol. 11, no. 1, pp. 37–53.

Ellis, W. (1826) 'Effect of the employment of machinery upon the happiness of the working classes'. *Westminster Review,* vol. 5, January, article IV. (Cited in B. L. Anderson (ed.) (1974) *Capital Accumulation in the Industrial Revolution,* J. M. Dent, London.)

Emerson, M., M. Aujean, M. Catinat, P. Goybet and A. Jacquemin (1988) *The Economics of 1992. The EC Commission's Assessment of the Economic Effects of Completing the Internal Market.* Oxford University Press, Oxford.

Enright, M. (1998) 'Regional clusters and firm strategy'. In A. D. Chandler, Jr *et al.* (eds), *The Dynamic Firm: The Role of Technology, Strategy, Organization, and Regions.* Oxford University Press, Oxford.

Epstein, Ralph C. (1931) 'Profits and size of firms in the automobile industry, 1919–27'. *American Economic Review,* vol. 21, December, pp. 636–47.

Erickson, G. M. (1997) 'Note: Dynamic conjectural variations in a Lanchester oligopoly'. *Management Science,* vol. 43, no. 11, pp. 1603–9.

Esser, J. (1995) 'Germany: challenges to the old policy style'. In J. Hayward (ed.), *Industrial Enterprise and European Integration.* Oxford University Press, Oxford.

Estall, R. C. and R. O. Buchanan (1973) *Industrial Activity and Economic Geography.* Hutchinson, London.

European Commission (2001) *Proposal for a Directive of the European Parliament and the Council on Market Access to Port Services.* Brussels, 13 February.

European Commission (2002) *European Economy.* Special Report, no. 2, DG for Economic and Financial Affairs, Brussels.

European Commission (2003a) *The Internal Market: 10 Years Without Frontiers,* DG Internal Market, Brussels.

European Commission (2003b) *European Business: Facts and Figures*. European Commission, Luxembourg.

European Commission (2003c) 'The EU economy: 2003 review', *European Economy*, no. 6, Brussels.

European Commission (2003d) *European Competitiveness Report 2003*. European Commission, Brussels.

European Commission (2003e) *EU Productivity and Competitiveness: An Industry Perspective*. DG III, Luxembourg.

European Commission (2003f) *Business in Europe: Data 1995–2002, Theme 4, Industry, Trade and Services*. European Commission, Brussels.

European Commission (2003g) *Statistical Yearbook on Candidate Countries: Data 1997–2001, Theme 1, General Statistics*. European Commission, Luxembourg.

European Commission (2004) *Statistics on Science and Technology in Europe: Data 1991–2002*. European Commission, Brussels.

European Parliament (2003) *Working Paper on Taxation in Europe: Recent Developments*, DG for Research, Brussels.

Eurostat (1989) *Statistical Analysis of Extra-EC Trade in High-tech Products*. Eurostat, Luxembourg.

Eurostat (1992) *Enterprises in Europe, 2nd Report*. Eurostat, Luxembourg.

Eurostat (2000) *Statistics in Focus: Theme 4–23, Industry Trade and Services*. Eurostat, Luxembourg.

Eurostat (2003a) *European Business 2003: A Statistical Portrait of Industrial and Service Activities in the EU*, No. 136/2003, 26 November 2003.

Eurostat (2003b) *Statistics in Focus: Theme 2. Economy and Finance*. Eurostat, Luxembourg.

Eurostat (2003c) *European Business 2003: Facts and Figures*. Eurostat, Luxembourg.

Eurostat (2003d) *Yearbook 2003: The Statistical Guide to Europe*. Eurostat, Luxembourg.

Eurostat (2003e) *Statistics in Focus: Theme 4, Industry, Trade and Services*. Eurostat, Luxembourg.

Eurostat (2004a) *Statistics in Focus: Theme 4, Industry, Trade and Services*. Eurostat, Luxembourg.

Eurostat (2004b) *Statistics in Focus: Theme 9*. Eurostat, Luxembourg.

Fabricant, S. (1954) *Economic Progress and Economic Change*. 34th Annual Report of the National Bureau of Economic Research, New York.

Fama, E. and M. C. Jensen (1983) 'The separation of ownership and control'. *Journal of Law and Economics*, vol. 26, no. 2, pp. 301–325.

Fama, E. F. (1980) 'Agency problems and the theory of the firm', *Journal of Political Economy*, vol. 88, April, pp. 288–307.

Farrands, C. and P. Totterdill (1993) 'A rationale for an appropriate level of regulation in the European Community'. In R. Sugden (ed.), *Industrial Economic Regulation*. Routledge, London.

Ferguson, P. R. and G. J. Ferguson (1994) *Industrial Economics: Issues and Perspectives*. Macmillan, London.

Fertö, I. And L. J. Hubbard (2003) 'Revealed comparative advantage and competitiveness in Hungarian agri–food sectors'. *World Economy*, vol. 26, no. 2, pp. 247–60.

Fischer, M. M. (2001) 'Innovation, knowledge creation and systems of innovation', *Annals of Regional Science*, vol. 35, pp. 199–216.

Fisher, F. M. (1991) 'Organizing industrial organization: reflections on *The Handbook of Industrial Organization*'. *Brookings Papers on Economic Activity: Microeconomics*, pp. 201–25.

Fisher, F. M. and J. J. McGowan (1983) 'On the misuse of accounting rates of return to infer monopoly profits'. *American Economic Review*, vol. 73, no. 1, pp. 82–97.

Fisher, F. M., J. W. McKie and R. B. Mancke (1983) *IBM and the US Data Processing Industry: An Economic History*. Praeger, New York.

Fishwick, F. (1986) *Definition of the Relevant Market in Community Competition Policy*. European Commission, Brussels.

Fishwick, F. (1993) 'The definition of the relevant market in the competition policy of the European Economic Community'. *Revue d'Economie Industrielle*, no. 63, 1st trimester, pp. 174–92.

Fjell, K. and J. S. Heywood (2002) 'Public Stackelberg Leadership in a Mixed Oligopoly with Foreign Firms'. *Australian Economic Papers*, Vol. 41, No. 3, pp. 267–283.

Focsaneanu, L. (1975) 'La jurisprudence de la Cour de Justice des C.E. en matière de concurrence: Marché des produits en consideration'. *Revue de Marché Commun*, no. 191, December.

Forges, F. and J-F. Thisse (1992) 'Game theory and industrial economics: an introduction'. In G. Norman and M. La Manna (eds), *The New Industrial Economics*. Edward Elgar, Aldershot.

Forte, F. (1967) 'Should public goods be public?' *Papers on Non-Market Decision Making*, vol. 8, pp. 39–46.

Foss, N. J. (1993) 'Theories of the firm: contractual and competence perspectives'. *Journal of Evolutionary Economics*, vol. 3, no. 2, pp. 127–44.

Fox, E. M. (1983) 'Abuse of a dominant position under the Treaty of Rome – a comparison with US Law'. *Annual Proceedings of the Fordham Corporate Law Institute*, pp. 367–421.

Franko, L. G. (1976) *The European Multinationals: A Renewed Challenge to American and British Big Business*. Harper & Row, New York.

Fransman, M. (1999) *Visions of Innovation: The Firm and Japan*. Oxford University Press, Oxford.

Franzmeyer, F. (1979) *Industrielle Strukturprobleme und sektorale Strukturpolitik in der Europäischen Gemeinschaft*. Duncker & Humbolt, Berlin.

Fraser, C. D. (1994) 'Conjectural variations'. In J. Cable (ed.), *Current Issues in Industrial Economics*. Macmillan, London.

Freeman, C. (1982) *The Economics of Industrial Innovation*. Pinter, London.

Freeman, C. (1987) *Technology Policy and Economic Performance: Lessons from Japan*. Pinter, London.

Freeman, C. (1988a) 'Japan: a new national system of innovation?' In G. Dosi *et al.* (eds), *Technical Change and Economic Theory*. Pinter, London.

Freeman, C. (1988b) 'Diffusion: la propagation des nouvelles technologies dans les entreprises, les différents secteurs et états'. In A. Heertje (ed.), *Innovation, Technologie et Finance*. Basil Blackwell, Oxford.

Freeman, C. (1994) 'Innovation and growth'. In M. Dodgson and R. Rothwell (eds), *Handbook of Industrial Innovation*. Edward Elgar, Aldershot.

Freeman, C. (1995) 'The economist as mythmaker Stigler's kinky transformation'. *Journal of Economic Issues*, vol. 29, no. 1, pp. 175–210.

Freeman, C. and L. Soete (1997) *The Economics of Industrial Innovation*, 3rd edition. MIT Press, Cambridge, MA.

Freeman, C., M. Sharp and W. Walker (eds) (1991) *Technology and the Future of Europe: Global Competition and the Environment in the 1990s*. Pinter, London.

Freeman, R. B. (ed.) (1994) *Working Under Different Rules*. Russell Sage Foundation, New York.

Freeman, R. E. and R. Phillips (1999) 'Stakeholder theory: a libertarian defense'. Paper presented at the Annual Meeting of the Society for Business Ethics, Chicago. Later version available at http://papers.ssrn.com

Friedman, J. W. and C. Mezzetti (2002) 'Bounded rationality, dynamic oligopoly, and conjectural variations'. *Journal of Economic Behavior and Organization*, vol. 49, no. 3, pp. 287–307.

Friedman, M. (1962) *Capitalism and Freedom*. University of Chicago Press, Chicago.

Frigo, M.L. (2004) 'Focusing strategy on fulfilling customer needs'. *Strategic Finance*, vol. 85, no. 7, pp. 9–10.

Funke, M., S. Wadewitz and D. Willenbockel (1989) 'Tobin's Q and sectoral investment in West Germany and Great Britain: a pooled cross-section and time series study'. *Zeitschrift für Wirtschafts and Sozialwissenschaften*, vol. 109, no. 3, pp. 399–420.

Galbraith, J. K. (2003) *What is the American Model Really About?*. Levy Economics Institute, Public Policy Brief 72.

Garcia Delgado, J. L. (1989) *España-Economia*. Espasa-Calpe, Madrid.

Gardner, R. (1995) *Games for Business and Economics*. Wiley, New York.

Gatignon, H., E. Anderson and K. Helson (1989) 'Competitive reactions to market entry: explaining interfirm differences', *Journal of Marketing Research*, vol. 86, no. 1, pp. 44–55.

Geithman, F. E., H. P. Marvel and L. W. Weiss (1981) 'Concentration, price, and critical concentration ratios'. *Review of Economics and Statistics*, vol. 63, August, pp. 346–53.

Gellman Research Associates (1976) *Indicators of International Trends in Technological Innovation*. NSF, Washington.

George, K. (1991) 'Public ownership versus privatisation'. In P. de Wolf (ed.), *Competition in Europe: Essays in Honour of Henk W. de Jong*. Kluwer, Dordrecht.

George, K. D., C. Joll and E. L. Link (1992) *Industrial Organisation: Competition, Growth and Structural Change*. Routledge, London.

Geroski, P. A. (1981) Specification and testing the profits–concentration relationship: some experiments for the UK. *Economica*, vol. 48, August 1981, pp. 279–88.

Geroski, P. A. (1987) 'Do dominant firms decline?' In J. S. Hay and D. A. Vickers (eds), *The Economics of Market Dominance*, Basil Blackwell, Oxford.

Geroski, P. A. (1991a) 'Domestic and foreign entry in the UK: 1983–1984'. In P. A. Geroski, and J. Schwalbach (eds), *Entry and Market Contestability: An International Comparison*. Blackwell, Oxford.

Geroski, P. A. (1991b) 'Innovation and the sectoral sources of UK productivity growth'. *Economic Journal*, vol. 101, November, pp. 1438–51.

Geroski, P. A. (1994) 'Entry and market share mobility'. In J. Cable (ed.), *Current Issues in Industrial Economics*. Macmillan, London.

Geroski, P. A. and A. Jacquemin (1985) 'Industrial change, barriers to mobility, and European industrial policy'. *Economic Policy*, vol. 1, November, pp. 169–218.

Geroski, P. A. and A. Jacquemin (1988) 'The persistence of profits: a European comparison'. *Economic Journal*, vol. 98, June, pp. 375–89.

Geroski, P. A. and J. Schwalbach (eds) (1991) *Entry and Market Contestability: An International Comparison*. Blackwell, Oxford.

Gibrat, R. (1931) *Les Inegalités Economiques*. Receuil Sirey, Paris.

Gilpin, R. (2000) 'The retreat of the state?' In T. C. Lawton *et al*. (eds), *Strange Power: Shaping the Parameters of International Relations and International Political Economy*. Ashgate, Aldershot, pp. 197–213.

Glas, M., and M. Drnovsek (1999) 'Small business in Slovenia: expectations and accomplishments'. Faculty of Economics, Ljubljana.

Globerman, S. and J. W. Dean (1990) 'Recent trends in intra-industry trade and their implications for future trade liberalization'. *Weltwirtschaftliches Archiv*, vol. 126, no. 1, pp. 25–49.

Golan, A., L. S. Karp and J. M. Perloff (2000) 'Estimating Coke and Pepsi's price and advertising strategies'. *Journal of Business and Economic Statistics*, vol. 18, no. 4, pp. 398–409.

Goldberg, P. K. and F. Verboven (2001) 'The evolution of price dispersion in the European car market'. *Review of Economic Studies*, vol. 68, no. 4, pp. 811–48.

Görg, H. and F. Ruane (2000) 'An analysis of backward linkages in the Irish electronics sector'. *Economic and Social Review*, vol. 31, no. 3, pp. 215–35.

Gowland, D. H. (1991) 'Financial policy after 1992'. In D. H. Gowland and S. James (eds), *Economic Policy after 1992*. Brookfield, Aldershot/Dartmouth, USA.

Grahl, J. and P. Teague (1990) *1992: The Big Market*. Lawrence & Wishart, London.

Grant, W. (1989) *Government and Industry: A Comparative Analysis of the US, Canada and the UK*. Edward Elgar, Aldershot.

Grant, W. (1995) 'Britain: the spectator state'. In J. Hayward (ed.), *Industrial Enterprise and European Integration*. Oxford University Press, Oxford.

Gray, J. (1998) *False Dawn*. Granta, London.

Green, A. and D. Mayes (1991) 'Technical inefficiency in manufacturing industries'. *The Economic Journal*, vol. 101, May, pp. 523–38.

Green, E. J. and R. H. Porter (1984) 'Non-cooperative collusion under imperfect price information'. *Econometrica*, vol. 52.

Gregersen, B. and B. Johnson (1997) 'Learning economies, innovation systems and European integration'. *Regional Studies*, vol. 31, no. 5, pp. 479–90.

Grether, E. T. (1970) 'Industrial organization: past history and future problems'. *American Economic Review*, vol. 60, p. 83.

Gribbin, D. (1991) 'The contribution of economists to the origins of UK competition policy'. In P. de Wolf (ed.), *Competition in Europe: Essays in Honour of Henk W. de Jong*. Kluwer, Dordrecht.

Griliches, Z. (1957) 'Hybrid corn: an exploration in the economics of technical change'. In Z. Griliches (1988) *Technology, Education and Productivity: Early Papers with Notes to Subsequent Literature*. Blackwell, Oxford.

Groeneweyen, J. and Beije, P. R. (1989) 'The French communication industry defined and analyzed through the social fabric matrix, the *filière* approach, and network analysis'. *Journal of Economic Issues*, vol. 23, no. 4, pp. 1059–75.

Groot Bruinderink, R., D. Deneffe and F. Hoyos (2003) 'Cooperative game theory: splitting the gains without the pain'. *Prism*, no. 2. Available at http://www.adl.com/insights/prism/

Grubel, H. G. and P. J. Lloyd (1975) *Intra-industry Trade: The Theory and Measurement of International Trade in Differentiated Products*. Macmillan, London.

Grünsteidl, W. (1990) 'An industrial policy for Europe'. *European Affairs*, Autumn.

Gual J. and D. Neven (1992) 'Deregulation of the European banking industry (1980–1991)'. CEPR Discussion Paper no. 703, August.

Guelle, F. (2001) 'The links between Japanese Investment in Asia and de-industrialization in Japan'. In B. Andreosso-O'Callaghan, J.P. Bassino, and J. Jaussaud (eds), *The Changing Economic Environment in Asia*. Palgrave, Basingstoke.

Hagedoorn, J. and J. Schakenraad (1990) 'Strategic partnering and technological co-operation'. In B. Dankbaar, J. Groenewegen and H. Schenk (eds), *Perspectives in Industrial Organization*. Kluwer, Dordrecht.

Hager, W. (1982) 'Industrial policy, trade policy, and European social democracy'. In J. Pinder (ed.), *National Industrial Strategies and the World Economy*. Croom Helm, London.

Haines, W. W. (1970) 'The profitability of large-size firms'. *Rivista Internazionale di Scienze Economiche e Commerciali*, vol. 17, no. 4, pp. 321–51.

Hakwon Sunoo, H. (1994) *Twentieth Century Korea*. NANAM Publishing House, Seoul.

Hall, B.A. (2003) 'Business method patents, innovation, and policy'. Available at http://emlab.berkeley.edu/users/bhhall/bhpapers.html

Hall, B.A. (2004) 'Innovation and Diffusion'. In J. Fagerberg, D. C. Mowery and R.R. Nelson (eds), *The Oxford Handbook of Innovation*. Oxford University Press, Oxford.

Hall, M. and L. W. Weiss (1967) 'Firm size and profitability'. *Review of Economics and Statistics*, vol. 49, August, pp. 319–31.

Hall, P. (1994) *Innovation, Economics and Evolution: Theoretical Perspectives on Changing Technology in Economic Systems*. Harvester-Wheatsheaf, London.

Hall, R. L. and C. J. Hitch (1939) 'Price theory and business behaviour'. *Oxford Economic Papers*, vol. 2, May, pp. 12–45.

Hallgarten, G. W. F. and J. Radkau (1974) *Deutsche Industrie and Politik von Bismarck bis heute*. Europäische Verlagsanstalt, Frankfurt.

Hamill, J. (1992) 'Cross-border mergers, acquisitions and alliances in Europe'. In S. Young and J. Hamill (eds), *Europe and the Multinationals*. Edward Elgar, Aldershot.

Hannah, L. (1983) *The Rise of the Corporate Economy*, 2nd edition. Methuen, London.

Hansen, L.G. (2002) 'Transportation and coordination in clusters: networks, capabilities, and the role of transportation'. *International Studies of Management and Organization*, vol. 31, no. 4, 2001/02, pp. 73–88.

Hansen, N. (1991) 'Factories in Danish fields: how high-wage, flexible production has succeeded in peripheral Jutland'. *International Regional Science Review*, vol. 14, no. 2, pp. 109–132.

Harbor, B. (1990) 'Defence electronics before and after 1992'. In G. Locksley (ed.), *The Single European Market*. Belhaven, London.

Harrison, B. (1992) 'Industrial districts: old wine in new bottles?' *Regional Studies*, vol. 26, no. 5, pp. 469–83.

Harrop, J. (1989) *The Political Economy of Integration in the European Community*. Edward Elgar, Aldershot.

Hart, P. and R. Clarke (1979) 'Profit-margins, wages and oligopoly: a survey of the evidence for the UK'. Working Paper, University of Reading.

Hart, P. E. and E. Morgan (1977) 'Market structure and economic performance in the UK'. *Journal of Industrial Economics*, vol. 25, no. 3, pp. 177–193.

Haskel, J. and C. Martin (1994) 'Capacity and competition: empirical evidence on UK panel data'. *Journal of Industrial Economics*, vol. 42, no. 1, pp. 23–42.

Hawley, E. W. (1966) *The New Deal and the Problem of Monopoly*. Princeton University Press, Princeton, NJ.

Hay, D. A. and D. J. Morris (1991) *Industrial Economics and Organization: Theory and Evidence*. Oxford University Press, Oxford.

Hayek, F. A. (1949) *Individualism and Economic Order*. Routledge & Kegan Paul, London.

Hayward, J. (1995) 'Introduction: Europe's endangered industrial champions'. In J. Hayward (ed.), *Industrial Enterprise and European Integration. From National to International Champions in Europe*. Oxford University Press, Oxford.

Heanue, K. and D. Jacobson (2002) 'Organizational proximity and institutional learning: the evolution of a spatially dispersed network in the Irish furniture industry'. *International Studies of Management and Organization: Special Issue on Clustering, Capabilities and Coordination*, vol. 31, no. 4.

Heertje, A. (1973) *Economics and Technical Change*. Weidenfeld & Nicolson, London. (First published in Dutch; English translation in 1977).

Heertje, A. (1977) *Economics and Technical Change*. Weidenfeld & Nicolson, London. First published in Dutch in 1973 by H. E. Stenfert Kroese BV.

Heertje, A. (ed.) (1983) *Investing in Europe's Future*. Blackwell, Oxford.

Heertje, A. (ed.) (1988) *Innovation, Technologie et Finance*. Published (in French) for the European Investment Bank by Basil Blackwell, Oxford.

Heertje, A. (1996) 'On Stackelberg's oligopoly theory'. *Journal of Economic Studies*, vol. 23, no. 5/6, pp. 48–58.

Heertje, A. and M. Perlman (eds) (1990) *Evolving Technology and Market Structure: Studies in Schumpeterian Economics*. University of Michigan Press, Ann Arbor.

Heffernan, S. A. (1993) 'Competition in British retail banking'. *Journal of Financial Services Research*, vol. 7, no. 4, pp. 309–32.

Held, D., A. G. McGrew, D. Goldblatt and J. Perraton (1999) *Global Transformations: Politics, Economics and Culture.* Polity Press, Cambridge.

Henderson, J. V. (1974) 'The sizes and types of cities'. *American Economic Review*, vol. 64, no. 4, pp. 640–56.

Hertzendorf, M. N. (1993) 'I'm not a high-quality firm – but I play like one on TV'. *Rand Journal of Economics*, vol. 24, no. 2, pp. 236–47.

Hertzendorf, M. N. and P. B. Overgaard (2001) 'Price competition and advertising signals: signaling by competing senders'. *Journal of Economics and Management Strategy*, vol. 10, no. 4, pp. 621–62.

Hibou, B. (1993) 'Indicateurs d'avantages comparatifs et contrainte extérieure'. *Economies et Sociétés*, vol. 27, no. 9, pp. 41–68.

Hicks, J. R. (1932) *Theory of Wages.* Macmillan, London.

Hicks, J. R. (1935) 'Annual survey of economic theory: the theory of monopoly'. *Econometrica*, vol. 3, no. 1, pp. 1–20.

Hill, C. W. L. (2001) *International Business: Competing in the Global Market Place.* McGraw-Hill, New York.

Hilliard, R. M. and D. Jacobson (2003) 'Dynamic capability, the pharmaceutical industry and technical change'. Paper given at the DRUID Summer Conference, Copenhagen, June. Available at http://www.druid.dk/conferences

Hillman, A. (1982) Declining industries and political support for protectionist motives. *American Economic Review*, vol. 72, no. 5, pp. 1180–7.

Hirsch, S. (1967) *Location of Industry and International Competitiveness.* Oxford University Press, Oxford.

Hirschey, M. and J. L. Pappas (1993) *Instructor's Manual to Accompany Managerial Economics.* Dryden Press, Fort Worth, TX.

Hirsch-Kreinsen, H., D. Jacobson, S. Laestadius and K. Smith (2003) 'Low-tech industries and the knowledge economy: state of the art and research challenges'. Paper for the EU Fifth Framework Programme project, PILOT – Policy and Innovation in Low-Tech. Available at http://www.pilotproject.org/publications/publications.html

Hitchens, D. M., K. Wagner and J. E. Birnie (1992) 'Measuring the contribution of product quality to competitiveness: a note on theory and policy'. *Economic and Social Review*, vol. 23, no. 4, pp. 455–63.

Hitiris, T. (1994) *European Community Economics.* Harvester-Wheatsheaf, Hemel Hempstead.

Hobsbawm, E. J. (1987) *The Age of Empire 1875–1914.* Weidenfeld & Nicolson, London.

Hochberg, A. (1998) 'Transition without metamorphosis – East Germany's regional policy reconsidered'. 38th European Congress of the European Regional Science Association, Vienna, 28 August – 1 September.

Hodgson, G. (1998a) 'Evolutionary and competence-based theories of the firm', *Journal of Economic Studies*, vol. 25, no. 1, pp. 25–56.

Hodgson, G. (1998b) 'The approach of institutional economics', *Journal of Economic Literature*, vol. 36, no. 1, pp. 166–92.

Hodgson, G. (2002) 'Evolutionary theories of the firm'. In W. Lazonick (ed.), *The IEBM Handbook of Economics*. Thomson, London.

Hodgson, G. (2004) 'Opportunism is not the only reason why firms exist: why an explanatory emphasis on opportunism may mislead management strategy'. *Industrial and Corporate Change*, vol. 13, no. 1, pp. 403–20.

Hodson, J. (2003) 'Ambitious French biotech plan faces EU hurdle'. *Nature Biotechnology*, vol. 21, no. 2, pp. 113–14. Available at www.nature.com/nbt

Hoernig, S. H. (2003) 'Existence of equilibrium and comparative statics in differentiated goods Cournot oligopolies'. *International Journal of Industrial Organization*, vol. 21, no. 7, pp. 989–1020.

Hofstede, G. (1983) 'The cultural relativity of organizational practices and theories'. *Journal of International Business Studies*, vol. 14, no. 2, pp. 75–89.

Holmstrom, B. R. and J. Tirole (1989) 'The theory of the firm'. In R. Schmalensee and A. Willig (eds), *Handbook of Industrial Organization*. North-Holland, Amsterdam.

Hosomi, T. and A. Okumura (1982) 'Japanese industrial policy'. In J. Pinder (ed.), *National Industrial Strategies and the World Economy*. Croom Helm, London.

Hotelling, H. (1929) 'Stability in competition'. *Economic Journal*, vol. 39, pp. 41–57.

Huber, N. (2004) 'UK comes bottom of the league in Europe on IT career development'. *Computer Weekly*, 6 August, p. 24.

Huck, S., H-T. Norman and J. Oechssler (2004) 'Two are few and four are many: number effects in experimental oligopolies'. *Journal of Economic Behavior and Organization*, vol. 53, no. 4, pp. 435–47.

Hudson, W. E. (1985) 'The feasibility of a comprehensive US industrial policy', *Political Science Quarterly*, no. 100, pp. 461–78.

Hufbauer, G. C. (1965) *Synthetic Materials and the Theory of International Trade*. Duckworth, London.

Hunt, E. K. and H. J. Sherman (1990) *Economics: An Introduction to Traditional and Radical Views*. Harper & Row, New York.

Hurdle, G. J., R. L. Johnson, A. S. Joskow, G. J. Werden and M. A. Williams (1989) 'Concentration, potential entry, and performance in the airline industry'. *Journal of Industrial Economics*, vol. 38, no. 2, pp. 119–39.

Hyman, D. (1992) *Economics*. Irwin, Homewood, IL.

Hymer, S. (1976) *The International Operations of National Firms: A Study of Foreign Direct Investment*. MIT Press, Cambridge, MA.

Hymer, S. (1976) *The International Operations of National Firms: A Study of Direct Foreign Investment*. MIT Press, Cambridge, MA. (Reprint of 1960 dissertation.)

Hymer, S. and P. Pashigian (1962) 'Firm size and rate of growth'. *Journal of Political Economy*, vol. 70, December, pp. 556–69.

Ijiri, Y. and H. A. Simon (1977) *Skew Distributions and the Sizes of Business Firms*. North-Holland, Amsterdam.

Imai, K-I. (1989) 'Evolution of Japan's corporate and industrial networks. In B. Carlsson (ed.), *Industrial Dynamics: Technological, Organizational and Structural Changes in Industries and Firms.* Kluwer, Dordrecht.

Imai, K-I. (2000) 'Platforms and real options in industrial organization'. *Japanese Economic Review,* vol. 51, no. 3, pp. 308–34.

Insead (1990) *Removing the Barriers in Manufacturing.* Report on the 1990 Manufacturing Futures Survey, Fontainebleau.

IRDAC (1992) *Skill Shortages in Europe.* Industrial Research and Development Advisory Committee of the CEC, Special Report to the EC Commission, Brussels.

Ireland, N. J. (1992) 'Product differentiation and quality'. In G. Norman and M. La Manna (eds), *The New Industrial Economics.* Edward Elgar, Aldershot.

Isaksen, A. and Hauge, E. (2002) *Regional Clusters in Europe,* no. 3. Observatory of European SMEs, Brussels.

Itoh, M., K. Kiyono, M. Okuno-Fujiwara and K. Suzumura (1991) *Economic Analysis of Industrial Policy.* Harcourt Brace Jovanovich, San Diego, CA.

Iwanek, M. (1992) 'Some issues in the transformation of ownership institutions in Poland'. *Journal of Institutional and Theoretical Economics,* vol. 148, no. 1, pp. 52–65.

Jacobs, D. and M. W. de Jong (1991) 'Industrial clusters and the competitiveness of the Netherlands'. TNO Policy Research, 90/NR/064, May.

Jacobson, D. (1991) *Europe's Pharmaceutical Industry: Tackling the Single Market.* Special Report no. 2085, Economist Intelligence Unit, London.

Jacobson, D. (1994) 'The technological and infrastructural environment'. In N. Nugent and R. O'Donnell (eds), *The European Business Environment.* Macmillan, London.

Jacobson, D. and B. Andréosso (1988) 'Investment and industrial integration in western Europe'. *Administration,* vol. 36, no. 2, pp. 165–85.

Jacobson, D. and B. Andréosso (1990) 'Ireland as a location for multinational investment'. In A. Foley and M. Mulreany (eds), *The Single European Market and the Irish Economy.* Institute of Public Administration, Dublin.

Jacobson, D. and D. O'Sullivan (1994) 'Analysing an industry in change: the Irish software manual printing industry'. *New Technology, Work and Employment,* vol. 9, no. 2, pp. 103–14.

Jacobson, D. and H. McGrath (2004) *Developing Sustainable Industrial Clusters in North Dublin,* NorDubCo. Available at http://www.nordubco.ie/publications.html

Jacobson, D. and R. Mack (1994) 'Core–periphery analysis: a tale of two nations'. Paper presented to the Regional Science Association International Conference, Dublin, October.

Jacobson, D. and T. McDonough, (1999) 'International trade and European integration'. In Eamon O'Shea and Michael Keane (eds), *Core Issues in European Integration.* Oak Tree Press, Dublin.

Jacobson, D. and Z. Mottiar (1999) 'Globalisation and modes of interaction in two sub-sectors in Ireland', *European Planning Studies,* vol. 7, no. 4, pp. 229–45.

Jacobson, D., K. Heanue and Z. Mottiar (2001) 'Industrial districts and networks: different modes of development of the furniture industry in Ireland?' In D. Felsenstein *et al.* (eds), *Public Investment and Regional Economic Development*. Edward Elgar, Aldershot.

Jacobson, D., K. Heanue and C. van Egeraat (2002) 'Industrial agglomeration'. In W. Lazonick (ed.), *IEBM Handbook of Economics*. Thomson International, London.

Jacobson, D. S. (1977) 'The political economy of industrial location: the Ford Motor Company at Cork 1912–1926'. *Irish Economic and Social History*, vol. 4, pp. 36–55.

Jacquemin, A. (1979) *Economie industrielle européenne: structures de marché et stratégies d'entreprises*, 2nd edition. Dunod, Paris.

Jacquemin, A. (1987a) 'Comportements collusifs et accords en recherche-développement'. *Revue d'Economie Politique*, vol. 97, no. 1, pp. 1–23.

Jacquemin, A. (1987b) *The New Industrial Organization: Market Forces and Strategic Behavior*. MIT Press, Cambridge, MA.

Jacquemin, A. (1990) 'Mergers and European policy'. In P. H. Admiraal (ed.), *Merger and Competition Policy in the European Community*, Basil Blackwell, Oxford.

Jacquemin, A. and H. W. de Jong (1976) *Markets, Corporate Behaviour and the State*. Martinus Nijhoff, The Hague.

Jacquemin, A. and A. Sapir (1987) 'Intra-EC trade: a sectoral analysis'. CEPS Working Paper no. 24, January.

Jacquemin, A. and D. Wright (1993) 'Corporate strategies and European challenges post-1992'. *Journal of Common Market Studies*, vol. 31, no. 1, pp. 525–73.

Jacquemin, A. and L. Philips (1974) 'Concentration, size and performance of European firms'. Working Paper no. 7409, Institut des Sciences Economiques, Louvain.

Jansen, Marius, B. (2000) *The Making of Modern Japan*. Harvard University Press, Cambridge, MA.

Jenny, F. and A. P. Weber (1974) 'Taux de profit et variables structurelles dans l'industrie manufacturiere française'. *Revue Economique*, November, Paris.

Johansson, D. (2004) 'Is small beautiful? The case of the Swedish IT industry'. *Entrepreneurship & Regional Development*, vol. 16, no. 4, pp. 271–88.

Johnson, C. (1984) 'The idea of industrial policy'. In C. Johnson (ed.), *The Industrial Policy Debate*. Institute for Contemporary Studies, San Francisco.

Johnson, P. (ed.) (1993) *European Industries: Structure, Conduct and Performance*. Edward Elgar, Aldershot.

Jones, A. and J. R. Clark (2003) 'From *filière* to *territoire*: changing rural policy in the Languedoc'. *Modern and Contemporary France*, vol. 11, no. 3, pp. 335–47.

Jones, D. C. and N. Mygind (2002) 'Ownership and productive efficiency: evidence from Estonia'. *Review of Development Economics*, vol. 6, no. 2, pp. 284–301.

Jones, T. M. (1995) 'Instrumental stakeholder theory: a synthesis of ethics and economics'. *Academy of Management Review*, vol. 20, no. 2, pp. 404–42.

Joskow, P. L. and A. K. Klevorick (1979) 'A framework for analyzing predatory pricing policy'. *Yale Law Journal*, vol. 89, no. 2, December, pp. 213–70.

Kalantaridis, C. and J. Pheby (1999) 'Processes of innovation among manufacturing SMEs: the experience of Bedfordshire'. *Entrepreneurship and Regional Development*, vol. 11, pp. 57–78.

Kaldor, N. (1934) 'The equilibrium of the firm'. *Economic Journal*, vol. 44, March, pp. 60–76.

Kaldor, N. (1950) 'The economic aspects of advertising'. *Review of Economic Studies*, vol. 18, pp. 1–27.

Kalirajan, K. P. and T. V. Varagunasingh (1992) 'In pursuit of identifying technical efficiency and X-efficiency'. *Journal of Economic Development*, vol. 17, no. 2, pp. 81–92.

Kambhampati, U. S. (2000) 'Industry competitiveness: leadership identity and market shares'. *Applied Economics Letters*, vol. 7, no. 9, pp. 569–74.

Kay, J. (2002) 'Business economics'. In W. Lazonick (ed.), *The IEBM Handbook of Economics*. Thomson, London.

Kay, J. A. (1990a) 'Identifying the strategic market'. *Business Strategy Review*, Spring, pp. 2–24.

Kay, N. (1990b) 'Industrial collaboration and the Single European Market'. In G. Locksley (ed.), *The Single European Market*. Belhaven, London.

Kay, N. (2000) 'The resource-based approach to multinational enterprise'. In C.N. Pitelis and R. Sugden (eds), *The Nature of the Transnational Firm*. Routledge, London.

Keck, O. (1993) 'The national system for technical innovation in Germany'. In R. R. Nelson (ed.), *National Innovation Systems*. Oxford University Press, Oxford.

Khalilzadeh-Shirazi (1974) 'Market structure and price–cost margins in UK manufacturing industries'. *Review of Economics and Statistics*, vol. 56, no. 1, pp. 67–76.

Khanna, T. and J. Singh (2002) 'What drives innovation by foreign multinationals?' Harvard Business School Strategy Working Paper Series. Available at http://ssrn.com/abstract_id=329101

Khün, T. S. (1962) *The Structure of Scientific Revolutions*. University of Chicago Press, Chicago.

Kim, E. H. and V. Singal (1993) 'Mergers and market power: evidence from the airline industry'. *American Economic Review*, vol. 83, no. 3, pp. 549–69.

Kim, Y-C. and R. McElreath (2001) 'Managing operating exposure: a case study of the automobile industry'. *Multinational Business Review*, vol. 9, no. 1, pp. 21–7.

Kimball, G. E. (1957) 'Some industrial applications of military operations research methods'. *Operations Research*, vol. 5, pp. 201–4.

Kirman, A. and N. Schueller (1990) 'Price leadership and discrimination in the European car market'. *Journal of Industrial Economics*, vol. 39, no. 1, pp. 69–91.

Kitschelt, H. (1991) 'Industrial governance structures, innovation strategies, and the case of Japan: sectoral or cross-national comparative analysis?' *International Organization*, vol. 45, no. 4, pp. 453–93.

Klein, B., R. G. Crawford and A. Alchian (1978) 'Vertical integration, appropriable rents and the competitive contracting process'. *Journal of Law and Economics*, vol. 21, no. 2, pp. 297–326.

Klodt, H. (1990) 'Technologietransfer und internationale wettbewerbsfähigkeit'. *Aussenwirtschaft*, vol. 45, no. 1, pp. 57–79.

Koch, J. V. (1980) *Industrial Organization and Prices*. Prentice-Hall, Englewood Cliffs, NJ.

Kogut, B. and M. Gittelman (2002) 'Globalization'. In W. Lazonick (ed.), *The IEBM Handbook of Economics*. Thomson, London.

Kojima, K. (1978) *Direct Foreign Investment, a Japanese Model of Multinational Business Operations*. Croom Helm, London.

Kotowitz, Y. and F. Mathewson (1979) 'Advertising, consumer information, and product quality'. *Bell Journal of Economics*, vol. 10, no. 2, pp. 566–88.

Koutsoyiannis, A. (1979) *Modern Microeconomics*. Macmillan, London.

Kreps, D. M. and R. Wilson (1982) 'Reputation and imperfect information'. *Journal of Economic Theory*, vol. 27, August, pp. 253–79.

Kristensen, P. H. (1992) 'Industrial districts in West Jutland, Denmark'. In F. Pyke and W. Sengenberger (eds), *Industrial Districts and Local Economic Regeneration*. International Institute for Labour Studies, Geneva.

Krugman, P. (1980) 'Scale economies, product differentiation and the pattern of trade'. *American Economic Review*, vol. 70, no. 5, pp. 950–9.

Krugman, P. (1983) 'New theories of trade among industrial countries'. *American Economic Review*, vol. 73, no. 2, pp. 343–7.

Krugman, P. (1987a) 'Is free trade passé?' *Journal of Economic Perspectives*, vol. 1, no. 2, pp. 131–44.

Krugman, P. (1987b) 'Economic integration in Europe: some conceptual issues'. In T. Padoa-Schioppa (ed.), *Efficiency, Stability, and Equity: A Strategy for the Evolution of the Economic System of the European Community*. Oxford University Press, Oxford.

Krugman, P. (1989) 'Industrial organization and international trade'. In R. C. Schmalensee and R. D. Willig (eds), *Handbook of Industrial Organization*, vol. 2. North-Holland, Amsterdam.

Krugman, P. (1991) 'Increasing returns and economic geography'. *Journal of Political Economy*, vol. 99, pp. 183–99.

Krugman, P. (1993) *Geography and Trade*. Leuven University Press, Leuven/MIT Press, Cambridge, MA.

Krugman, P. (1998) 'What's new about the new economic geography?' *Oxford Review of Economic Policy*, vol. 14, no. 2, pp. 7–18.

Krugman, P. and M. Obstfeld (1991) *International Economics: Theory and Policy*. HarperCollins, New York.

Kumar, N. (2002) 'Multinational corporations'. In W. Lazonick (ed.), *The IEBM Handbook of Economics*. Thomson, London.

Kumps, A. M. (1974) *Le Conglomérat*. La Renaissance du Livre, Bruxelles.

Kumps, A. M. (1975) *Conglomerate Mergers: The Case of Great Britain*. Working Paper, CRIDE, no. 751.

Kuznets, S. (1930) *Secular Movements in Production and Prices*. Houghton Mifflin, Boston and New York.

Lafay, G. and C. Herzog (1989) 'Vingt ans d'échanges internationaux. L'Europe sur la defensive'. *Economie et Statistique*, nos 217–18, January–February, pp. 29–36.

Laibman, David (1981) 'Two-sector growth with endogenous technical change: a Marxian simulation model'. *Quarterly Journal of Economics*, vol. 96, no. 1, pp. 47–75.

Lall, S., and P. Streeten (1977) *Foreign Investment, Transnationals and Developing Countries*. Macmillan, London.

Lamberton, D. (1994) 'Innovation and intellectual property'. In M. Dodgson and R. Rothwell, (eds), *Handbook of Industrial Innovation*. Edward Elgar, Aldershot.

Lambin, J. J. (1976) *Advertising, Competition and Market Conduct in Oligopoly Over Time*. North-Holland, Amsterdam.

Lancaster, K. (1979) *Variety, Equity and Efficiency*. Blackwell, Oxford.

Lane, S. J. (1991) 'The determinants of investment in new technology'. *American Economic Review*, May, pp. 262–5.

Lanzillotti, R. F. (1957) 'Competitive price leadership: a critique of price leadership models'. *Review of Economics and Statistics*, vol. 39, February, pp. 56–64.

Lanzillotti, R. F. (1959) 'Pricing objectives in big companies', *American Economic Review*, vol. 48, December, pp. 921–40.

Lassudrie-Duchêne, B. (1971) 'La demande de difference et l'êchange international'. Cahiers de l'ISEA, *Economies et Sociétés*, June.

Lawrence, R. Z. and D. E. Weinstein (1999) 'The role of trade in East Asian productivity growth: the case of Japan'. In J. Stiglitz. (ed), *Rethinking the East Asia Miracle*. World Bank, Washington, DC.

Layson, S. K. (1994) 'Market opening under third-degree price discrimination'. *Journal of Industrial Economics*, vol. 42, no. 3, pp. 335–40.

Lazerson, M. and G. Lorenzoni (1999) 'The firms that feed industrial districts: a return to the Italian source'. *Industrial and Corporate Change*, vol. 8, no. 2, pp. 235–66.

Lazonick, W. (1981) 'Competition, specialization, and industrial decline'. *Journal of Economic History*, vol. 41, no. 1, pp. 31–8.

Lazonick, W. (1990a) 'Organizational integration in three industrial revolutions'. In A. Heertje and M. Perlman (eds), *Evolving Technology and Market Structure*. University of Michigan Press, Ann Arbor.

Lazonick, W. (1990b) *Value Creation on the Shop Floor. Organization and Technology in Capitalist Development*. Harvard University Press, Cambridge, MA.

Lazonick, W. (1991) *Business Organization and the Myth of the Market Economy*. Cambridge University Press, Cambridge.

Lazonick, W. (1993) 'Industry clusters versus global webs: organizational capabilities in the American economy'. *Industrial and Corporate Change*, vol. 2, no. 1, pp. 1–24.

Lazonick, W. (2002) 'Innovative enterprise, theory of'. In W. Lazonick (ed.), *The IEBM Handbook of Economics*. Thomson International, London.

Leavy, B. and D. Jacobson (1999) 'Innovation – the case for multi-level research'. *IBAR-Irish Business Administration Research*, vol. 19/20, no. 1, pp. 16–35.

Lee, R. P. and R. Grewal (2004) 'Strategic responses to new technologies and their impact on firm performance'. *Journal of Marketing*, vol. 68, no. 4, pp. 157–72.

Leibenstein, H. (1966) 'Allocative efficiency vs "X-efficiency"', *American Economic Review*, vol. 56, pp. 392–415.

Leibenstein, H. and S. Maital (1994) 'Organizational foundations of X-inefficiency'. *Journal of Economic Behavior and Organization*, vol. 23, no. 3, pp. 251–69.

Léonard, J. (1990) Mutations de l'investissement direct international et processus d'endettement du Tiers-Monde: des ambiguïtés théoriques aux difficultés de la mesure. In A. Androuais (ed.), *L'Investissement extérieur direct*. University Press, Grenoble.

Leonard, R. J. (1995) 'From parlour games to social science: von Neumann, Morgenstern, and the creation of game theory 1928–1944'. *Journal of Economic Literature*, vol. 33, no. 2, pp. 730–61.

Lerner, A. (1934) 'The concept of monopoly and the measurement of monopoly power'. *Review of Economic Studies*, vol. 1, June, pp. 157–75.

Levin, R. C. (1988) 'Appropriability, R&D spending and technological performance'. *American Economic Review*, vol. 78, no. 2, pp. 424–8.

Lewis, W. A. (1957) 'International competition in manufacturers'. *American Economic Review (Papers and Proceedings)*, vol. 47, May.

Li, M. Z. F., T. H. Oum and Y. Zhang (2004) 'Tobin's q and airline performances'. *Public Works Management and Policy*, vol. 9, no. 1, pp. 51–65.

Linda, R. (1988) 'The food and drinks industry: large firm strategies'. In H. W. de Jong (ed.), *The Structure of European Industry*. Kluwer, Dordrecht.

Linda, R. (1991) 'Industrial and market concentration in Europe'. In P. de Wolf (ed.), *Competition in Europe. Essays in Honour of Henk W. de Jong*. Kluwer, Dordrecht.

Lindenberg, E. and S. Ross (1981) 'Tobin's q ratio and industrial organization'. *Journal of Business*, vol. 54, January, pp. 1–32.

Linder, S. (1961) *An Essay on Trade and Transformation*. Wiley, New York.

Lindert, P. H. (1991) *International Economics*, 9th edition. Irwin, Boston.

Lipsey, R. and K. Lancaster (1956) 'The general theory of the second best'. *Review of Economic Studies*, vol. 56, pp. 11–32.

Lipsey, R. G. and K. I. Carlaw (2004) 'Total factor productivity and the measurement of technological change'. *Canadian Journal of Economics*, vol. 37, no. 4, pp. 1118–51. Version available at Lipsey's home page, http://www.sfu.ca/~rlipsey

Lissoni, F. and J. S. Metcalfe (1994) 'Diffusion of innovation ancient and modern: a review of the main themes'. In M. Dodgson and R. Rothwell (eds), *Handbook of Industrial Innovation*. Edward Elgar, Aldershot.

List, F. (1841) *Das nationale System der politischen Ökonomie*. Published in English (1909) by Dent, London.

List, F. (1842) 'Die Ackerverfassung, die Zwergwirtschaft, and die Auswanderung'. *Deutsche Vierteljahrschrif*, vol. 4, pp. 106–91.

Lloyd, C. and J. Payne (2003) 'What is the 'high skills society'? Some reflections on current academic and policy debates in the UK'. *Policy Studies*, vol. 24, nos. 2/3, pp. 115–33.

Loasby, B. J. (1990) 'Problem-solving institutions'. *Scottish Journal of Political Economy*, vol. 37, May, pp. 197–202.

Locksley, G. (ed.) (1990) *The Single European Market and the Information and Communication Technologies*. Belhaven, London.

Lorenz, E. H. (1994) 'Review of "Prices, Quality and Trust: Inter-firm Relations in Britain and Japan", by M. Sako. Cambridge University Press, Cambridge'. *Journal of Economic Literature*, vol. 32, no. 4, pp. 1918–20.

Losch, A. (1954) *The Economics of Location*, Yale University Press, New Haven, CT. First published in German in 1940.

Lotti, F., E. Santarelli and M. Vivarelli (2003) 'Does Gibrat's Law hold among young, small firms?' *Journal of Evolutionary Economics*, vol. 13, no. 3, pp. 213–36.

Lovasy, G. (1941) 'International trade under imperfect competition'. *Quarterly Journal of Economics*, vol. 55, August, pp. 567–83.

Love, J.H. and S. Roper (2004) 'The organisation of innovation: collaboration, cooperation and multifunctional groups in UK and German manufacturing'. *Cambridge Journal of Economics*, vol. 28, no. 3, pp. 379–95.

Lucas, R. E. (1988) 'On the mechanics of economic development', *Journal of Monetary Economics*, vol. 22, pp. 3–42.

Lundvall, B-Å (1992) 'Introduction'. In B-Å Lundvall (ed.) *National Systems of Innovation: Towards a Theory of Innovation and Interactive Learning*. Pinter, London.

Lundvall, B-Å. (1998) 'Why study national systems and national styles of innovation?', *Technology Analysis and Strategic Management*, vol. 10, no. 4, pp. 407–21.

Lundvall, B-Ä. and P. Maskell (1999) 'Nation states and economic development – from national systems of production to national systems of knowledge creation and learning'. In G. L. Clark, M. P. Feldmann and M. S. Gertler (eds), *Oxford Handbook of Economic Geography*. Oxford University Press, Oxford.

Lynch, R. (1990) *European Business Strategies: An Analysis of Europe's Top Companies*. Kogan Page, London.

Lyons, B. R. (1984) 'The pattern of international trade in differentiated products: an incentive for the existence of multi-national firms'. In H. Kierzkowski (ed.), *Monopolistic Competition and International Trade*. Clarendon Press, Oxford.

MacDougall, G. D. A. (1960) 'The benefits and costs of private investment from abroad: a theoretical approach'. *Economic Record*, vol. 36, pp. 13–35.

Machiavelli, N. (1520) *Discorsi sopra la prima deca di Tito Livio*, Book II, G. C. Santoni Editore, Firenze (1966 edition).

Machlup, F. (1946) 'Marginal analysis and empirical research'. *American Economic Review*, vol. 36, September, pp. 519–54.

Machlup, F. (1952) *The Political Economy of Monopoly*. Johns Hopkins University Press, Baltimore, MD.

Machlup, F. (1967) 'Theories of the firm: marginalist, behavioral, managerial'. *American Economic*

Review, vol. 57, March, pp. 1–33.

Malerba, F. (1993) 'The national innovation system: Italy'. In R. R. Nelson (ed.), *National Innovation Systems*. Oxford University Press, Oxford.

Malmberg, A. (2003) 'Beyond the cluster – local milieus and global connections'. In J. Peck and H.W. Cheung (eds), *Remaking the Global Economy*. Sage, London.

Malone, T. A. (1998) 'Evolving Oligopolies'. *Physician Executive*, vol. 24, no. 2, pp. 30–3.

Maltby, J. and R. Wilkinson (1998) 'Can UK learn art of stakeholding?' *Guardian*, 7 February.

Mandel, E. (1975) *Late Capitalism*. New Left Books, London.

Mann, H. M. (1966) 'Seller concentration, barriers to entry, and rates of return in 30 industries, 1950–1960'. *Review of Economics and Statistics*, vol. 43, August, pp. 296–307.

Mannering, F. (1991) 'Brand loyalty and the decline of American automobile firms'. *Brookings Papers on Economic Activity*, no. 1, pp. 67–114.

Manser, W. A. P. (1994) *Control from Brussels*. Addison-Wesley/Economist Intelligence Unit, Wokingham, Berkshire.

Mansfield, E. (1961) 'Technical change and the rate of imitation'. *Econometrica*, vol. 29, no. 4, pp. 741–66.

Mansfield, E. (1968) *The Economics of Technical Change*. W. W. Norton, New York.

Mansfield, E. (1971) *Research and Innovation in the Modern Corporation*. W. W. Norton, New York.

Mansfield, E. (1986) 'Patents and innovation: an empirical study'. *Management Science*, vol. 32, February.

Mansfield, E. (1993) *Managerial Economics: Theory, Applications, and Cases*. W. W. Norton, New York.

Mansfield, E., J. Rapoport, A. Romeo, S. Wagner and G. Beardsley (1977) 'Social and private rates of return from industrial innovations'. *Quarterly Journal of Economics*, vol. 10, pp. 221–40.

Marbach, C. (1990) 'L'industrie de l'après-1990'. *Politique Industrielle*, no. 21, pp. 71–88.

March, J. G. and H. A. Simon (1958) *Organization*. Wiley, New York.

Marcus, M. (1969) 'Profitability and the size of the firm'. *Review of Economics and Statistics*, vol. 51, pp. 104–7. Reprinted in B. Yamey (1973) *Economics of Industrial Structure*. Penguin, Harmondsworth.

Marfels, C. (1988) *Recent Trends in Concentration in Selected Industries of the European Community, Japan and the United States*. European Commission, Luxembourg.

Markham, J. W. (1951) 'The nature and significance of price leadership'. *American Economic Review*, vol. 41, December, pp. 891–905.

Markusen, A. (1996) 'Sticky places in slippery space: a typology of industrial districts'. *Economic Geography*, Vol. 72, pp. 293–313.

Marris, R. (1963) 'A model of the "managerial" enterprise'. *Quarterly Journal of Economics*, no. 77, May, pp. 185–209.

Marris, R. (1966) *The Economic Theory of Managerial Capitalism*. Macmillan, London.

Marshall, A. (1898) *Principles of Economics*, Macmillan, London.

Marshall, A. (1899) *The Economics of Industry*, 3rd edition. Macmillan, London.

Marshall, A. (1961) *Principles of Economics*, 8th edition. Macmillan, London.

Martin, R. (1999) 'The new "geographical turn" in economics: some critical reflections'. *Cambridge Journal of Economics*, vol. 23, pp. 65–91.

Martin, S. (1988) *Industrial Economics*. Macmillan, London.

Martin, S. (1993) *Advanced Industrial Economics*. Blackwell, Cambridge, MA.

Martin, S. (1994) *Industrial Economics: Economic Analysis and Public Policy*. Macmillan, New York.

Marx, K. (1972) *Capital*. J. M. Dent, London. First published in German in 1867.

Maschke, E. (1914) *Grundzüge der deutschen Kartellgeschichte bis 1914*. Dortmund.

Maskell, P. (1998) 'Learning in the village economy of Denmark: the role of institutions and policy in sustaining competitiveness'. In H. J. Braczyk, P. Cooke and M. Heidenreich (eds), *Regional Innovation Systems: The Role of Governance in a Globalized World*. UCL Press, London.

Maskin, E. and J. Tirole (1992) 'The principal–agent relationship with an informed principal, II: common values'. *Econometrica*, vol. 60, no. 1, pp. 1–42.

Mason, E. S. (1939) 'Price and production policies of large scale enterprise'. *American Economic Review*, suppl. 29, pp. 61–74.

Mason, E. S. (1949) 'The current state of the monopoly problem in the United States'. *Harvard Law Review*, vol. 62, pp. 1265–85.

Matsumuro, T. (2003) 'Stackelberg mixed duopoly with a foreign competitor'. *Bulletin of Economic Research*, vol. 55, no. 3, pp. 275–88.

Mayer, T.F. and Y. Varoufakis (1993/94) 'Game theory: an exchange'. *Science and Society*, vol. 57, no. 4, pp. 446–60.

Mayes, D. G., T. Buxton and A. Murfin (1990) 'R&D, innovation and trade performance'. In B. Dankbaar, J. Groenewegen and H. Schenk (eds), *Perspectives in Industrial Organization*. Kluwer, Dordrecht.

Mazzeo, M. J. (2002) Competitive outcomes in product-differentiated oligopoly'. *Review of Economics and Statistics*, vol. 84, no. 4, pp. 716–29.

McCloskey, D. N. (1990) *If You're So Smart*. University of Chicago Press, Chicago.

McFarland, H. (1988) 'Evaluating q as an alternative to the rate of return in measuring profitability'. *Review of Economics and Statistics*, vol. 70, no. 4, pp. 614–22.

McGovern, S. (1994) 'A Lakatosian approach to changes in international trade theory'. *History of Political Economy*, vol. 26, no. 3, pp. 351–68.

McGrath, B. (1995) 'HB still freezing out ice cream competition'. *Irish Times*, 11 March.

McGuire, J. W., J. S. Y. Chiu and A. O. Elbing (1962) 'Executive incomes, sales and profits'. *American Economic Review*, no. 52, September, pp. 753–61.

McGuire, S. (1997) *Airbus Industrie: Conflict and Cooperation in US EC Trade Relations*, St Martin's Press, New York.

McKelvey, M., L. Orsenigo and F. Pammolli (2004) 'Pharmaceuticals analyzed through the lens of a sectoral innovation system'. In F. Malerba (ed.), *Sectoral Systems of Innovation: Concepts, Issues and Analyses of Six Major Sectors in Europe*. Cambridge University Press, Cambridge.

Meehan, J. W. and T. D. Duchesneau (1973) 'The critical level of concentration: an empirical analysis'. *Journal of Industrial Economics*, vol. 22, September, pp. 21–30.

Melander, A. and M. Nordqvist (2002) 'Investing in social capital: networks, trust, and beliefs in the Swedish furniture industry'. *International Studies of Management and Organization*, vol. 31, no. 4, pp. 89–108.

Menon, J. (1996) 'The dynamics of intra-industry trade in ASEAN'. *Asian Economic Journal*, vol. 10, no. 11, pp. 105–15.

Messerlin, P. (1987) 'France: the ambitious state'. In F. Duchêne and G. Shepherd (eds), *Managing Industrial Change in Western Europe*. Pinter, London.

Mikic, M. (1998) *International Trade*. Macmillan, London.

Milelli, C. and P. Grou (2001) 'The Asian conglomerates at a crossroads'. In B. Andreosso-O'Callaghan, J.P. Bassino and J. Jaussaud (eds) *The Changing Economic Environment in Asia*. Palgrave, Basingstoke.

Milgrom, P. and J. Roberts (1982) 'Limit pricing and entry under incomplete information: an equilibrium analysis'. *Econometrica*, vol. 50, pp. 443–59.

Milgrom, P. and J. Roberts (1992) *Economics, Organization and Management*. Prentice-Hall, Englewood Cliffs, NJ.

Miller, J. G. (1943) *Origins of the American Revolution*. Little, Brown, Boston.

Ministry of Finance of the Republic of Slovenia (2000) *Annual Report*. MoF, Lubljana.

Mirrlees, J. (1976) 'The optimum structure of incentives and authority within an organization'. *Bell Journal of Economics*, vol. 7, pp. 105–31.

Mizuno, M. and H. Odagiri (1990) 'Does advertising mislead consumers to buy low-quality products'. *International Journal of Industrial Organization*, vol. 8, no. 4, pp. 545–58.

Moerland, P. (1991) 'Efficacy and freedom of mergers and acquisitions'. In P. de Wolf (ed.), *Competition in Europe*. Kluwer Academic, Dordrecht.

Molina-Morales, F.X. (2002) 'Industrial districts and innovation: the case of the Spanish ceramic tiles industry'. *Entrepreneurship & Regional Development*, vol. 14, no. 4, pp. 317–36.

Molle, W. (1990) *The Economics of European Integration: Theory, Practice, Policy*. Brookfield, Aldershot/Dartmouth, USA.

Moner-Colonques, R., J.J. Sempere-Monerris and A. Urbano (2004). 'The manufacturers' choice of distribution policy under successive duopoly', *Southern Economic Journal*, vol. 70, no. 3, pp. 532–48.

Montfort, J. (1983) 'A la recherche des filières de production'. *Economie et Statistique*, no. 151, January, pp. 3–12.

Monti, M. (2000) 'Foreword by Professor Mario Monti, member of the Commission with special responsibility for competition policy'. In European Commission, *XXIXth Report on Competition Policy 1999*, Office For Official Publications of the European Communities, Luxembourg.

Monti, M. (2003) 'Contribution of competition policy to competitiveness of the European economy'. Paper given at a conference at the Institute of European Affairs, Dublin, 26 May. Available at www.tca.ie/speeches/monti_may03.pdf

Moschandreas, M. (2000) *Business Economics*. Thomson Learning, London.

Mowery, D. C. (1990) 'The development of industrial research in US manufacturing'. *American Economic Review*, vol. 80, no. 2, pp. 345–54.

Mowery, D. C. and N. Rosenberg (1993) 'The US National Innovation System'. In R. Nelson (ed.), *National Innovation Systems*. Oxford University Press, Oxford.

Müller, J. and N. Owen (1985) 'The effect of trade on plant size'. In J. Schwalbach (ed.), *Industry Structure and Performance*. Sigma, Berlin.

Murphy, K. J. (1985) 'Corporate performance and managerial remuneration'. *Journal of Accounting and Economics*, vol. 7, April, pp. 11–42.

Musgrave, R. A. (1959) *The Theory of Public Finance*. McGraw-Hill, New York.

Myrdal, G. (1957) *Economic Theory and Underdeveloped Regions*. Duckworth, London.

Mytelka, Z. and K. M. Delapierre (1987) 'The alliance strategies of European firms in the information and technology industry and the role of ESPRIT'. *Journal of Common Market Studies*, vol. 26, no. 2, pp. 231–53.

Nagler, M. G. (1993) 'Rather bait than switch: deceptive advertising with bounded consumer rationality'. *Journal of Public Economics*, vol. 51, no. 3, pp. 359–78.

Nalebuff, B. and A. Brandenburger (1997) *Co-Opetition*. Profile Business, London.

Nash, J. F. (1951) 'Non-cooperative games'. *Annals of Mathematics*, vol. 54, no. 2, pp. 286–95.

Naylor, C. (2000) 'Personal view – e for empty?' *Strategy Magazine*, January. Available at http://www.sps.org.uk/d19.htm

Nelson, P. (1974) 'Advertising as information'. *Journal of Political Economy*, vol. 82, July/August, pp. 729–54.

Nelson, R. R. (1984) *High Technology Policies: A Five Nation Comparison*. American Enterprise Institute, Washington, DC.

Nelson, R. R. (1992) 'National innovation systems: a retrospective on a study'. *Industrial and Corporate Change*, vol. 1, no. 2, pp. 347–73.

Nelson, R. R. (ed.) (1993) *National Innovation Systems: A Comparative Analysis*. Oxford University Press, Oxford.

Nelson, R. R. (1995) 'Recent evolutionary theorizing about economic change'. *Journal of Economic Literature*, vol. 33, no. 1, pp. 48–90.

Nelson, R. R. and S. G. Winter (1982) *An Evolutionary Theory of Economic Change*. Harvard University Press, Cambridge, MA.

Neuberger, D. (1998) 'Industrial organization of banking: a review'. *International Journal of the Economics of Business*, vol. 5, no. 1, pp. 97–118.

Neumann, M., I. Böbel and A. Haid (1979) 'Profitability, risk and market structure in West German industries'. *Journal of Industrial Economics*, vol. 27, March, pp. 227–42.

Nicolaides, P. (ed.) (1993) *Industrial Policy in the European Community: A Necessary Response to Economic Integration?* Martinus Nijhoff, Dordrecht.

Nielsen, J., H. Heinrich and J. Hansen (1991) *An Economic Analysis of the EC*. McGraw-Hill, Maidenhead, Berkshire.

Niosi, J., B. Bellon, P. Saviotti and M. Crow (1992) 'Les systèmes nationaux d'innovation: à la recherche d'un concept utilisable'. *Revue d'Economie Française*, vol. 7, no. 1, pp. 215–50.

Norman, G. and M. La Manna (eds) (1992) *The New Industrial Economics*. Edward Elgar, Aldershot.

North, D. C. (1990) *Institutions, Institutional Change and Economic Performance*. Cambridge University Press, Cambridge.

Notteboom, T. E. (2002) 'Consolidation and contestability in the European container handling industry'. *Maritime Policy Management*, vol. 29, no. 3, pp. 257–69.

Nugent, N. (1994) 'The political environment'. In N. Nugent and R. O'Donnell (eds), *The European Business Environment*. Macmillan, London.

Nugent, N. and R. O'Donnell (eds) (1994) *The European Business Environment*. Macmillan, London.

O'Donnell, R. (1994) 'The economic environment'. In N. Nugent and R. O'Donnell (eds), *The European Business Environment*. Macmillan, London.

O'Donnellan, N. (1994) 'The presence of Porter's clustering in Irish manufacturing'. *Economic and Social Review*, vol. 25, no. 3, pp. 221–32.

O'Malley, E. (1989) *Industry and Economic Development; the Challenge of the Latecomer*. Gill and Macmillan, Dublin.

O'Malley, L. (1982) *Business Law*, Sweet & Maxwell, London.

O'Sullivan, M. (2000) *Contests for Corporate Control: Corporate Governance and Economic Performance in the United States and Germany*. Oxford University Press, Oxford.

Odagiri, H. and A. Goto (1993) 'The Japanese system of innovation: past, present and future'. In R. Nelson (ed.), *National Innovation Systems*. Oxford University Press, Oxford.

OECD (1972) *The Industrial Policy in Japan*. OECD, Paris.

OECD (1985) *The Semi-Conductor Industry, Trade and Related Issues*. OECD, Paris.

OECD (1986) *Science and Technology Indicators II: R&D, Invention and Competitiveness*. OECD, Paris, pp. 58–61.

OECD (1988) *New Technologies in the 1990s: A Socio-economic Strategy*. OECD, Paris.

OECD (1989) *Predatory Pricing*. OECD, Paris.

OECD (1990) *Competition Policy and the Deregulation of Road Transport*. OECD, Paris.

OECD (1990a) *The Public Sector: Issues for the 1990s*, Department of Economics and Statistics, Working Paper no. 90. OECD, Paris.

OECD (1991a) *Trade, Investment and Technology in the 1990s*. OECD, Paris.

OECD (1991b) *Science and Technology Indicators Report*. OECD, Paris.

OECD (1991c) *Industrial Policy in OECD Countries. Annual Review*. OECD, Paris.

OECD (1992) *Science and Technology Policy – Review and Outlook*. OECD, Paris.

OECD (1993a) *Basic Science and Technology Statistics*. OECD, Paris.

OECD (1993b) *OECD Economic Surveys: Denmark*. OECD, Paris.

OECD (1993c) *Economic Outlook*, no. 54, December. OECD, Paris.

OECD (1994) *Science and Technology Policy – Review and Outlook*. OECD, Paris.

OECD (1995) *Main Science and Technology Indicators*. OECD, Paris.

OECD (2000) *Main Science and Technology Indicators*, no. 2. OECD, Paris.

OECD (2002) *International Trade by Commodity Statistics*. OECD, Paris.

OECD (2003) *International Trade by Commodity Statistics*. OECD, Paris.

OECD (2004a) *Science and Technology Statistical Compendium*. OECD, Paris.

OECD (2004b) *Main Science and Technology Indicators*, no. 1. OECD, Paris.

Ohmae, K. (1995) *The End of the Nation State*. Free Press, New York.

Okuno, M. (ed.) (1988) *Industrial Policy of Japan*. California Academic Press, San Diego.

Ordonez de Haro, J. M. (1993) 'Effectos de la publicidad estrategica en una industria con producto diferenciados'. *Investigaciones Economicas*, vol. 17, no. 3, pp. 527–49.

Ornstein, S. I. (1977) *Industrial Concentration and Advertising Intensity*. American Enterprise Institute, Washington, DC.

Orzach, R., P. B. Overgaard and Y. Tauman (2002) 'Modest advertising signals strength'. *Rand Journal of Economics*, vol. 33, summer, pp. 340–58.

OST (2004) 'About OST'. Office of Science and Technology. Available at http://www.ost.gov.uk/about_ost/index.htm

Østerdal, L. P. (2003) 'A note on the stability of collusion in differentiated oligopolies'. *Research in Economics*, vol. 57, no. 1, pp. 53–65.

Ozaki, R. (1991) *Human Capitalism: The Japanese Enterprise System as World Model*. Kodansha International, Tokyo.

Pagoulatos, E. and R. Sorenson (1976) 'Foreign trade, concentration and profitability in open economies'. *European Economic Review*, vol. 8, pp. 255–67.

Pal, D. and J. Sarkar (2001) 'A Stackelberg oligopoly with nonidentical firms'. *Bulletin of Economic Research*, vol. 53, no. 2, pp. 127–35.

Pareto, V. (1911) 'Economie mathématique'. *Encyclopedie des Sciences Mathematiques*, Book 1, vol. 4. Paris.

Parris, H., P. Pestieau and P. Saynor (1987) *Public Enterprise in Western Europe*. Croom Helm, London.

Parrott, N., N. Wilson and J. Murdoch (2002). 'Spatializing quality: regional protection and the alternative geography of food', *European Urban and Regional Studies*, vol. 9, no. 3, pp. 241–61.

Pascoe, G. and L. W. Weiss (1983) 'The extent and permanence of market dominance'. Federal Trade Commission, Washington, DC.

Pashigian, B. P. (1968) 'Limit price and the market share of the leading firm'. *Journal of Industrial Economics*, vol. 16, July, pp. 165–77.

Patel, P. and K. Pavitt (1991) 'Europe's technological performance'. In C. Freeman, M. Sharp and W. Walker (eds), *Technology and the Future of Europe*. Pinter, London.

Pavitt, K. (1982) 'R&D, patenting and innovative activities: a statistical exploration'. *Research Policy*, vol. 11, no. 1.

Pavitt, K. (1985) 'Patent statistics as indicators of innovative activities: possibilities and problems'. *Scientometrics*, vol. 7, nos 1–2, January.

Pavitt, K. (1987) 'International patterns of technological accumulation'. In N. Hood and J. E. Vahne (eds), *Strategies in Global Competition*. Croom Helm, London.

Pavitt, K. (1994) 'Key characteristics of large innovating firms'. In M. Dodgson and R. Rothwell (eds), *Handbook of Industrial Innovation*. Edward Elgar, Aldershot.

Pavitt, K. and M. Sharp (1992) 'Key technologies and new industrial policies'. Paper presented at Conference, Europe and Global Economic Interdependence, Bruges, January.

Peacock, A. (1979) 'The limitations of public goods theory: the lighthouse revisited'. In A. Peacock (ed.), *The Economic Analysis of Government*. Martin Robertson, Oxford.

Pearson, E. S. (1994) *Law for European Business Studies*. Pitman, London.

Pelkmans, J. (1984) *Market Integration in the European Community*. Martinus Nijhoff, The Hague.

Peng, S-K. (2004) 'Spatial monopoly with product differentiation'. *Southern Economic Journal*, vol. 70, no. 3, pp. 646–60.

Penrose, E. T. (1959) *The Theory of Growth of the Firm*. Blackwell, Oxford.

Penrose, E. (1995) 'Foreword to the Third Edition'. In E. Penrose, *The Theory of the Growth of the Firm*. Oxford University Press, Oxford.

Pepall, L. and G. Norman (2001) 'Product differentiation and upstream–downstream relations'. *Journal of Economics and Management Strategy*, vol. 10, no. 2, pp. 201–33.

Petrella, R. (1991) *Four Analyses of Globalisation of Technology and Economy*. FAST, Commission of the EC, Brussels.

Petrochilos, G. A. (2004) *Managerial Economics: A European Text*. Palgrave Macmillan, Basingstoke.

Peyrard, J. (1990) 'Les théories des investissements directs à l'étranger dans les pays industrialisés depuis 1950'. In A. Androuais (ed.), *L'Investissement extérieur direct*. University Press, Grenoble.

Peyrefitte, J. and P.A. Golden (2004) 'Vertical Integration and Performance in the United States Computer Hardware Industry'. *International Journal of Management*, vol. 21, no. 2, pp. 246–51.

Phelps, Edmund, S. (1966) 'Models of technical progress and the golden rule of research'. *Review of Economic Studies*, vol. 33, April, pp. 133–45.

Phillipps, A. (1976) 'A critique of empirical studies of relations between market structure and profitability'. *Journal of Industrial Economics*, vol. 24, June, pp. 241–9.

Phlips, L. (1971) *Effects of Industrial Concentration: A Cross Section Analysis for the Common Market*. North-Holland, Amsterdam.

Phlips, L. (1983) *The Economics of Price Discrimination*. Cambridge University Press, Cambridge.

Phu, N.V., F. Laisney and U. Kaiser (2004) 'The performance of German firms in the business-related service sector: a dynamic analysis'. *Journal of Business and Economic Statistics*, vol. 22, no. 3, pp. 274–96.

Pigou, A. C. (1932) *The Economics of Welfare*. Macmillan, London.

Pinder, J. (ed.) (1982) *National Industrial Strategies and the World Economy*. Allanheld, Osmun Publishers/Croom Helm, London.

Piore, M. and C. F. Sabel (1984) *The Second Industrial Divide: Possibilities for Prosperity*. Basic Books, New York.

Piore, M. J. (1990) 'Work, labour and action: work experience in a system of flexible production'. In F. Pyke *et al.* (eds), *Industrial Districts and Inter-firm Co-operation in Italy*. International Institute for Labour Studies, Geneva.

Piore, M.J. (2001) 'The emergent role of social intermediaries in the new economy,' *Annals of Public and Cooperative Economics*, vol. 72, no. 3, pp. 339–50.

Pitelis, C. (2002) 'Transaction cost economics'. In W. Lazonick (ed.), *The IEBM Handbook of Economics*. Thomson, London.

Poirier, D. (1976) *The Econometrics of Structural Change*. North-Holland, Amsterdam.

Porter, M. E. (1974) Consumer behavior, retailer power and market performance in consumer goods industries'. *Review of Economics and Statistics*, vol. 56, no. 4, pp. 419–36.

Porter, M. E. (1990) *The Competitive Advantage of Nations*. Macmillan, London.

Porter, M. E. (1991) 'Towards a dynamic theory of strategy'. *Strategic Management Journal*, vol. 12, Winter, pp. 95–117.

Porter, M.E. (1998a) *The Competitive Advantage of Nations*, rev. edn. London: Macmillan.

Porter, M.E. (1998b) 'Clusters and the new economics of competition'. *Harvard Business Review*, vol. 76, no. 6, pp. 77–91.

Porter, M.E. (2000), 'Location, competition, and economic development: local clusters in a global economy'. *Economic Development Quarterly*, vol. 14, no. 1, pp. 15–20.

Porter, R. H. (1991) 'A review essay on *Handbook of Industrial Organization*'. *Journal of Economic Literature*, vol. 29, no. 2, pp. 553–72.

Posner, M. V. (1961) 'International trade and technical change'. *Oxford Economic Papers*, vol. 13, October, pp. 323–41.

Posner, R. A. (1969) 'Natural monopoly and its regulation'. *Stanford Law Review*, vol. 21, February, pp. 548–643.

Powell, W.W. (2001) 'The capitalist firm in the twenty-first century: emerging patterns in western enterprise'. In P. DiMaggio (ed.), *The Twenty-first-century Firm: Changing Economic Organization in International Perspective*. Princeton University Press, Princeton, NJ.

Prakke, F. (1988) 'Le financement de l'innovation technologique'. In A. Heertje (ed.), *Innovation, Technologie et Finance*. Basil Blackwell, Oxford.

Pratten, C. (1987) *A Survey of Economies of Scale*. Report prepared for the EC Commission, Brussels.

Prestowitz, C. V. (1988) *Trading Places: How We Allowed Japan to Take the Lead*. Basic Books, New York.

Pyke, F. and W. Sengenberger (eds) (1992) *Industrial Districts and Local Economic Regeneration*. International Institute for Labour Studies, Geneva.

Pyke, F., G. Becattini and W. Sengenberger (eds) (1990) *Industrial Districts and Inter-firm Cooperation in Italy*. International Institute for Labour Studies, Geneva.

Qualls, P. D. (1972) 'Concentration, barriers to entry and long run economic profit margins'. *Journal of Industrial Economics*, vol. 20, April, pp. 146–58.

Radner, R. (1992) 'Hierarchy: the economics of managing'. *Journal of Economic Literature*, vol. 30, no. 3, pp. 1382–415.

Raikes, P., M. F. Jensen and S. Ponte (2000) 'Global commodity chain analysis and the French filière approach: comparison and critique'. *Economy and Society*, vol. 29, no. 3, pp. 390–418.

Ramstad, G. O. (1997) 'A model for structural analysis of the media market'. *Journal of Media Economics*, vol. 10, no. 3, pp. 45–51.

Ranci, P. (1987) 'Italy: the weak state'. In F. Duchêne and G. Shepherd (eds), *Managing Industrial Change in Western Europe*. Pinter, London.

Ranci, P. and R. Helg (1987) *Economies of Scale and the Integration of the European Economy: the Case of Italy*. Report prepared for the EC Commission, Brussels.

Ray, G. F. (1984) *The Diffusion of Mature Technologies*. Cambridge University Press, Cambridge.

Reekie, W. D. and J. N. Crook (1995) *Managerial Economics*. Prentice Hall, Hemel Hempstead.

Reich, R. (1992) *The Work of Nations*. Vintage Books, New York.

Renner, M. (2000) 'Corporate mergers skyrocket'. Global Policy Forum. Available at www.globalpolicy.org

Rhys, G. (1993) 'Motor vehicles'. In P. Johnson (ed.), *European Industries. Structure, Conduct and Performance*. Edward Elgar, Aldershot.

Ricardo, D. (1817) *On the Principles of Political Economy and Taxation*. (Reprinted in P. Sraffa, and M. Dobb (eds) (1953) *The Works and Correspondence of David Ricardo*, vol. I. Cambridge: Cambridge University Press.)

Ricci, L.A. (1999) 'Economic geography and comparative advantage: agglomeration versus specialisation'. *European Economic Review*, vol. 43.

Richardson, G. B. (1972) 'The organization of industry'. *Economic Journal*, vol. 82.

Richonnier, M. (1984) 'Europe's decline is not irreversible'. *Journal of Common Market Studies*, vol. 22, no. 3.

Rob, R. (1992) 'Sales, uncertainty and the determinants of investment'. University of Pennsylvania CARESS Working Paper, 92–03.

Robertson, P. L. and R. N. Langlois (1994) 'Institutions, inertia and changing industrial leadership'. *Industrial and Corporate Change*, vol. 3, no. 2, pp. 359–78.

Robertson, P. L. and R. N. Langlois (1995) 'Innovation, networks, and vertical integration'. *Research Policy*, vol. 24, no. 4, pp. 543–62.

Robertson, T. S. (1971) *Innovative Behavior and Communication*. Holt, Rinehart & Winston, New York.

Robinson, E. A. G. (1958) *The Structure of Competitive Industry*. University of Chicago Press, Chicago.

Robinson, J. (1933) *The Economics of Imperfect Competition*. Macmillan, London.

Robinson, J. (1956) *The Accumulation of Capital*. Macmillan, London.

Rodrik, D. (1997) *Has Globalization Gone Too Far?* Institute for International Economics, Washington, DC.

Romer, P. M. (1986) 'Increasing returns and long-run growth'. *Journal of Political Economy*, vol. 94, no. 5, pp. 1002–37.

Root, F. R. (1990) *International Trade and Investment*. South-Western, Cincinnati, Ohio.

Roscam, A., M. Schakenraad and J. Schakenraad (1991) *Intended and Unintended Effects of Participation in ESPRIT and EUREKA for Small Countries' Industrial Policies*. MERIT, Maastricht.

Rosenberg, N. (1963) 'Technological change in the machine tool industry'. *Journal of Economic History*, vol. 23.

Ross, S. A. (1973) 'The economic theory of agency: the principal's problem'. *American Economic Review*, vol. 63, no. 2, pp. 134–9.

Rossi, S. and P. F. Volpin (2003) 'Cross-country determinants of mergers and acquisitions'. CEPR Discussion Paper no. 3889. Available at http://ssrn.com/abstract=418721

Rostow, W. W. (1960a) *The Process of Economic Growth*. Clarendon Press, Oxford.

Rostow, W. W. (1960b) *The Stages of Economic Growth*. Cambridge University Press, Cambridge.

Rotemberg, J. J. and G. Saloner (1986) 'A supergame-theoretic model of price wars during booms'. *American Economic Review*, vol. 76, pp. 390–407.

Rothacher, A. (2004) Book review of 'Toshiba', by R. L. Cutts, *Asia Europe Journal*, vol. 2, no. 2, pp. 307–11.

Rothwell, R. (1987) 'Technology policy in Britain'. In P. R. Beije *et al.* (eds), *A Competitive Future for Europe?* Croom Helm, New York.

Rothwell, R. and M. Dodgson (1994) 'Innovation and size of firm'. In M. Dodgson and R. Rothwell (eds) *The Handbook of Industrial Innovation*. Edward Elgar, Hemel Hempstead.

Rowthorn, R. (1971) 'International big business 1957–1967: a study of comparative growth'. Occasional Paper no. 24, University of Cambridge.

Russell, B. (1965) *German Social Democracy*. Allen & Unwin, London.

Ryan, M. J. (2000) 'Economies of scale and scope, contestability, windfall profits and regulatory risk'. *Manchester School*, vol. 68, no. 6, pp. 701–22.

Sabel, C. F. (1989) 'Flexible specialisation and the re-emergence of regional economies'. In P. Hirst and J. Zeitlin (eds), *Reversing Industrial Decline? Industrial Structure and Policy in Britain and Her Competitors*. Berg, Oxford.

Saloner, G. (1991) 'Modeling, game theory and strategic management'. *Strategic Management Journal*, vol. 12, Winter, pp. 119–36.

Samuels, J. M. and Smyth, D. J. (1968) 'Profits, variability of profits and firm size'. *Economica*, vol. 35, pp. 127–39.

Sapir, A. (1993) 'Regionalism and the new theory of international trade: do the bells toll for GATT? A European outlook'. *World Development*, vol. 16, no. 4, pp. 423–38.

Say, J-B. (1803) *Traité d'économie politique ou simple exposition de la manière dont se forment, se distribuent et se consomment les richesses*. Paris.

Scassellati, A. (1991) 'European integration in the context of international capital'. *Socialism and Democracy*, no. 13, May, pp. 159–65.

Schelling, T. C. (1960) *The Strategy of Conflict*. Harvard University Press, Cambridge, MA.

Scherer, F. M. (1965) 'Firm size, market structure, opportunity, and the output of patented inventions'. *American Economic Review*, pp. 1097–126.

Scherer, F. M. (1970) *Industrial Market Structure and Economic Performance*. Rand McNally, Chicago.

Scherer, F. M. (1979) 'The causes and consequences of rising industrial concentration'. *Journal of Law and Economics*, vol. 22, April, pp. 191–211.

Scherer, F. M. (1992) *International High-technology Competition*. Harvard University Press, Cambridge, MA.

Scherer, F. M. (1996) 'An accidental Schumpetarian'. *American Economist*, vol. 40, no. 1, pp. 5–14.

Scherer, F. M. and D. Ross (1990) *Industrial Market Structure and Economic Performance*. Houghton Mifflin, Boston.

Schmalensee, R. (1973) 'A note on the theory of vertical integration'. *Journal of Political Economy*, no. 81, March/April, pp. 442–9.

Schmalensee, R. (1974) 'Brand Loyalty and Barriers to Entry'. *Southern Economic Journal*, vol. 40, no. 4, pp. 579–89.

Schmalensee, R. (1978a) 'Entry-deterrence in the ready-to-eat breakfast cereal industry'. *Bell Journal of Economics*, vol. 9, Autumn, pp. 305–27.

Schmalensee, R. (1978b) 'A model of advertising and product quality'. *Journal of Political Economy*, vol. 86, pp. 485–504.

Schmalensee, R. (1981) 'Output and welfare implications of monopolistic third-degree discrimination'. *American Economic Review*, vol. 71, pp. 242–7.

Schmalensee, R. (1982) 'The new industrial organization and the economic analysis of modern markets'. In W. Hildebrand (ed.), *Advances in Economic Theory*. Cambridge University Press, Cambridge.

Schmalensee, R. (1987) 'Industrial organization'. In J. Eatwell *et al.* (eds), *The New Palgrave Dictionary of Economics*. Macmillan, London.

Schmalensee, R. and R. D. Willig (eds) (1989) *Handbook of Industrial Organization*, vol. 1. North-Holland, Amsterdam.

Schmitz, H. (1992) 'Industrial districts: model and reality in Baden-Württemberg, Germany'. In F. Pyke and W. Sengenberger (eds), *Industrial Districts and Local Economic Regeneration*. International Institute for Labour Studies, Geneva.

Schmitz, H. and B. Musyck (1994) 'Industrial districts in Europe: policy lessons for developing countries?' *World Development*, vol. 22, no. 6, pp. 889–910.

Schumpeter, J. A. (1912) *Theorie der Wirtschaftlichen Entwicklung*. Duncker & Humboldt, Leipzig.

Schumpeter, J. A. (1934) *The Theory of Economic Development*. Harvard University Press, Cambridge, MA.

Schumpeter, J. A. (1939) *Business Cycles*. McGraw-Hill, New York.

Schumpeter, J. A. (1943) *Capitalism, Socialism and Democracy*. Allen & Unwin, London.

Schumpeter, J. A. (1983) *The Theory of Economic Development*. Transaction Publishers, New Brunswick, NJ.

Schuster, G. (1990) 'Technology policy'. In C. C. Schweitzer and D. Karsten (eds), *FRG and EC Membership Evaluated*. Pinter, London.

Schwalbach, J. (1988) 'Economies of scale and intra-community trade'. In *Research on the 'Costs of non-Europe'*. CEC, vol. 2, ch. 3.

Schwartz, D. (1973) 'Zum Stand der Wirtschaftskonzentration im Gemeinsamen Markt'. *Der Burger im Staat*, vol. 4.

Schwartzman, D. (1959) 'Effect of monopoly on price'. *Journal of Political Economy*, vol. 67, August, pp. 352–62.

Scitovsky, T. (1943/44) 'A note on profit-maximization and its implications'. *Review of Economic Studies*, no. 11, pp. 57–60.

Scott, A. J. (1988) *New Industrial Spaces: Flexible Production Organization and Regional Development in North America and Western Europe*. Pion, London.

Scott, A.C. (1998) *Regions and the World Economy: The Coming Shape of Global Production, Competiton, and Political Order*. Oxford University Press, Oxford.

Selten, R. (1978) 'The chain store paradox'. *Theory and Decision*, vol. 9, pp. 127–59.

Semlinger, K. (1991) 'New developments in subcontracting: mixing markets and hierarchy'. In A. Amin and M. Dietrich (eds), *Towards a New Europe?* Edward Elgar, Aldershot.

Servan-Schreiber, J-J. (1967) *Le défi américain*. Denoël, Paris.

Shaffer, S. (1991) 'Consistent conjectures in a value-maximising duopoly'. *Southern Economic Journal*, vol. 57, no. 4, pp. 993–1009.

Shaked, A. and J. Sutton (1987) 'Product differentiation and industrial structure'. *Journal of Industrial Economics*, vol. 36, no. 2, pp. 131–46.

Shapiro, C. (1980) 'Advertising and welfare: comment'. *Bell Journal of Economics*, vol. 11, no. 2, pp. 749–52.

Sharp, M. (1990) 'Technology and the dynamics of integration'. In W. Walker (ed.), *The Dynamics of European Integration*. Pinter/RIIA, London.

Sharp, M. and C. Shearman (1987) *European Technological Collaboration*. Routledge & Kegan Paul, London.

Sharp, M. and K. Pavitt (1993) 'Technology policy in the 1990s: old trends and new realities'. *Journal of Common Market Studies*, vol. 31, no. 2, pp. 129–51.

Sharp, M. L. (1991) 'Pharmaceuticals and biotechnology: perspectives for European industry'. In C. Freeman, M. Sharp and W. Walker (eds), *Technology and the Future of Europe*. Pinter, London.

Shaw, R. (1982) 'Product proliferation in characteristics space: the UK fertilizer industry'. *Journal of Industrial Economics*, vol. 31, nos 1–2, pp. 69–92.

Shaw, R. and P. Simpson (1985) 'The Monopolies Commission and the persistence of monopolies'. *Journal of Industrial Economics*, vol. 34, pp. 355–72.

Shenkar, O. and Y. Luo (2004) *International Business*. Wiley, Hoboken, NJ.

Shepherd, W. G. (1972a) 'The elements of market structure'. *Review of Economics and Statistics*, vol. 54, no. 1, pp. 25–37.

Shepherd, W. G. (1972b) 'Structure and behaviour in British industry'. *Journal of Industrial Economics*, vol. 21, pp. 35–54.

Shepherd, W. G. (1975) *The Treatment of Market Power*. Columbia University Press, New York.

Shepherd, W. G. (1990) *The Economics of Industrial Organization*. Prentice-Hall, Englewood Cliffs, NJ.

Shetty, Y. K. and V. M. Buehler (eds) (1983) *Quality and Productivity Improvements: US and Foreign Company Experiences*. Manufacturing Productivity Center, Chicago.

Shughart, W. F. (1990) *The Organization of Industry*. Irwin, Boston.

Simmie, J. (2002) 'Knowledge Spillovers and Reasons for the Concentration of Innovative SMEs'. *Urban Studies*, vol. 39, nos 5–6, pp. 885–902.

Simon, H. (1959) 'Theories of decision-making in economics and behavioral science'. *American Economic Review*, vol. 49, June, pp. 253–83.

Simon, H. A. (1960) *The New Science of Management Decision*. Harper & Row, New York.

Simon, H. A. and C. P. Bonini (1958) 'The size distribution of business firms'. *American Economic Review*, vol. 48, September, pp. 607–17.

Singh, A. (1972) *Takeovers: Their Relevance to the Stock Market and the Theory of the Firm*. Cambridge University Press, London.

Singh, A. and G. Whittington (1968) *Growth, Profitability and Valuation*. Cambridge University Press, Cambridge.

Singh, A. and G. Whittington (1975) 'The size and growth of firms'. *Review of Economic Studies*, vol. 42, no. 1, pp. 15–26.

Slade, M. (1987) 'Interfirm rivalry in a repeated game: an empirical test of tacit collusion'. *Journal of Industrial Economics*, vol. 35, no. 4, pp. 499–516.

Sleuwaegen, L. and H. Yamawaki (1988) 'The formation of the European Common Market and changes in market structure and performance'. *International Journal of Industrial Organization*, vol. 32, no. 7, pp. 1451–75.

Smirlock, M., Th. Gilligan and W. Marshall (1984) 'Tobin's q and the structure–performance relationship'. *American Economic Review*, vol. 74, December, pp. 1051–60.

Smith, A. (1776) *An Inquiry into the Nature and Causes of the Wealth of Nations*. Reprinted 1976 by University of Chicago Press, Chicago.

Smith, K. (2002) 'Innovation'. In W. Lazonick (ed.) *The IEBM Handbook of Economics*. Thomson, London.

Soberman, D.A. (2003) 'The role of differentiation in markets driven by advertising'. *California Management Review*, vol. 45, no. 3, pp. 130–46.

Soete, L. (1979) 'Firm size and inventive activity: the evidence reconsidered'. *European Economic Review*, pp. 312–90.

Soete, L. L. G. (1981) 'A general test of technological trade theory'. *Weltwirtschaftliches Archiv.*, vol. 117, no. 4, pp. 638–66.

Solo, R. A. (1982) *The Positive State*. South-Western Publishing, Cincinatti.

Solow, R. M. (1957) 'Technical change and the aggregate production function'. *Review of Economics and Statistics*, vol. 39, pp. 312–20.

Sorenson, O. (2003) 'Interdependence and adaptability: organizational learning and the long-term effect of integration'. *Management Science*, vol. 49, no. 4, pp. 446–63.

Spence, A. M. (1977) 'Entry, capacity, investment and oligopolistic pricing'. *Bell Journal of Economics*, vol. 8, pp. 534–44.

Sraffa, P. (1926) 'The laws of returns under competitive conditions'. *Economic Journal*, vol. 26, pp. 535–50.

Staber, U. (2001) 'Spatial proximity and firm survival in a declining industrial district: the case of knitwear firms in Baden-Württemberg'. *Regional Studies*, vol. 35, no. 4, pp. 329–42.

Steedman, H., G. Mason and K. Wagner (1991) 'Intermediate skills in the workplace: deployment, standards and supply in Britain, France and Germany'. *National Institute Economic Review*, May, pp. 60–73.

Steers, R. M. (1999) *Made in Korea. Chung Ju Yung and the Rise of Hyundai*. Routledge, New York.

Steiner, R. L. (1973) 'Does advertising lower consumer prices?' *Journal of marketing*, vol. 37, October, pp. 19–26.

Stephen, F. H., J. H. Love, D. D. Gillanders and A. A. Paterson (1993) 'Deregulation and price discrimination in the conveyencing market'. *Managerial and Decision Economics*, vol. 14, no. 4, pp. 365–75.

Steuart, S. (1767) *An Inquiry into the Principles of Political Economy: Being an Essay on the Science of Domestic Policy in Free Nations*. London.

Stevens, J. L. (1990) 'Tobin's q and the structure–performance relationship: comment'. *American Economic Review*, vol. 80, no. 3, pp. 618–21.

Stewart, J. C. (1989) 'Transfer pricing: some empirical evidence from Ireland'. *Journal of Economic Issues*, vol. 16, no. 3.

Stigler, G. J. (1947) 'The kinky oligopoly demand curve and rigid prices'. *Journal of Political Economy*, vol. 55, October, pp. 444–6.

Stigler, G. J. (1961) 'The economics of information'. *Journal of Political Economy*, vol. 69, June, pp. 213–25.

Stigler, G. J. (1963) *Capital and Rates of Return in Manufacturing Industries*. Princeton University Press, Princeton, NJ.

Stigler, G. J. (1966) *The Theory of Price*, 3rd edition. Macmillan, London.

Stigler, G. J. (1968) *The Organization of Industry*. Irwin, Homewood, IL.

Stigler, G. J. (1971) 'The economic theory of regulation'. *Bell Journal of Economics*, vol. 2, no. 1, pp. 3–21.

Stiglitz, J. (1974) 'Incentives and risk sharing in sharecropping'. *Review of Economic Studies*, vol. 64, pp. 219–56.

Stiglitz, J. (1991) 'Symposium on organizations and economics'. *Journal of Economic Perspectives*, vol. 5, no. 2, pp. 15–24.

Stiglitz, J. (2000) *Economics of the Public Sector*, 3rd edition. W. W. Norton, New York.

Stiglitz, J. (2002) *Globalization and its Discontent*. Allen Lane/Penguin, London.

Stiglitz, J. E. and G. F. Mathewson (eds) (1986) *New Developments in the Analysis of Market Structure*. Macmillan, London.

Stiving, M. (2000) 'Price-endings when prices signal quality'. *Management Science*, vol. 46, December, pp. 1617–30.

Stoffaes, C. (1980) 'Politique industrielle et filières'. *Revue d'Economie Industrielle*, no. 13, 3rd quarter.

Stolper, W. F. (1994) *Schumpeter*. Princeton University Press, Princeton, NJ.

Stoneman, P. (1983) *The Economic Analysis of Technological Change*. Oxford University Press, Oxford.

Storper, M. and R. Walker (1989) *The Capitalist Imperative: Territory, Technology and Industrial Growth*. Blackwell, Oxford.

Strange, S. (1991) 'Big business and the state'. *Millennium: Journal of International Studies*, vol. 20, no. 2, pp. 245–50.

Strange, S. (1996) *The Retreat of the State: The Diffusion of Power in the World Economy*. Cambridge University Press, Cambridge.

Sugden, R. (ed.) (1993) *Industrial Economic Regulation: A Framework and Exploration*. Routledge, London.

Summers, H. B. (1932) 'A comparison of the rates of large-scale and small-scale industries'. *Quarterly Journal of Economics*, vol. 46, May, pp. 465–79.

Sutton, J. (1997) 'Gibrat's legacy'. *Journal of Economic Literature*, vol. 35, no. 1, pp. 40–9.

Sutton, J. (1998) *Technology and Market Structure: Theory and History*. MIT Press, Cambridge, MA.

Sweezy, P. (1939) 'Demand under conditions of oligopoly'. *Journal of Political Economy*, vol. 47, no. 4, pp. 568–73.

Sylos-Labini, P. (1962) *Oligopoly and Technical Progress*. Harvard University Press, Cambridge, MA.

Tan, Z. (2002) 'Testing theory of bandwagons: global standardization competition in mobile communications'. *International Journal of Information Technology and Decision Making*, vol. 1, no. 4, pp. 605–19.

Teece, D. J. (1982) 'Towards an economic theory of the multiproduct firm'. *Journal of Economic Behavior and Organization*, vol. 3, pp. 39–63.

Teece, D. J. (ed.) (1987) *The Competitive Challenge*. Ballinger, Cambridge, MA.

Telser, L. G. (1987) *A Theory of Efficient Cooperation and Competition*. Cambridge University Press, Cambridge.

Thomsen, S. and S. Woolcock (1993) *Direct Investment and European Integration: Competition among Firms and Governments*. RIIA/Pinter, London.

Thornhill, D. J. (1988) 'The revealed comparative advantage of Irish exports of manufactures 1969–1982'. *Journal of the Social and Statistical Enquiry Society of Ireland*, vol. 25, no. 5, pp. 91–146.

Thornton, D. W. (1995) *Airbus Industrie: The Politics of an International Industrial Collaboration*. St Martin's Press, New York.

Tobin, J. (1969) 'A general equilibrium approach to monetary theory'. *Journal of Money, Credit and Banking*, vol. 1, February, pp. 15–29.

Tobin, J. and W. Brainard (1977) 'Asset markets and the cost of capital'. In B. Ballassa and R. Nelson (eds), *Economic Progress, Private Values and Public Policies: Essays in Honour of William Fellner*. North-Holland, Amsterdam.

Tomlinson, J. (1993) 'Is successful regulation possible? Some theoretical issues'. In R. Sugden (ed.), *Industrial Economic Regulation*. Routledge, London.

Trigilia, C. (1990) 'Work and politics in the Third Italy's industrial districts'. In F. Pyke, G. Becattini and W. Sengenberger (eds), *Industrial Districts and Inter-firm Co-operation in Italy*. International Institute for Labour Studies, Geneva.

Truel, J. L. (1983) 'Structuration en filière et politique industrielle dans l'electronique: un comparaison internationale'. *Revue d'Economie Industrielle*, no. 23, 1st trimester, pp. 293–303.

Tsoukalis, L. (1991) *The New European Economy: The Politics and Economics of Integration*. Oxford University Press, Oxford.

Tu, A. H. and S-Y. Chen (2000) 'Bank market structure and performance in Taiwan before and after the 1991 liberalization'. *Review of Pacific Basin Financial Markets and Policies*, vol. 3, no. 4, pp. 475–91.

Tunzelman, N. von (2002) 'Development and diffusion of technology'. In W. Lazonick (ed.), *The IEBM Handbook of Economics*. Thomson International, London.

Turpin, E. (1989) 'Le commerce extérieur français: une spécialisation industrielle fragile'. *Economie et Statistique*, nos 217/18, January/February, pp. 51–61.

Ullrich, H. (2002) 'Patent Protection in Europe: Integrating Europe into the Community or the Community into Europe?' *European Law Journal*, vol. 8, no. 4, pp. 433–91.

UNCTAD (2004) *World Investment Report 2004: The Shift Towards Services*. UNCTAD, Geneva.

UNCTC (1991) *Foreign Direct Investment in the Triad*. United Nations, New York.

UNICE (Union of Industrial and Employers' Confederations of Europe) (1994) *Making Europe More Competitive: Towards World Class Performance*. UNICE, Brussels.

US Congress (1982) *Technology, Innovation, and Regional Economic Development*. Office of Technology Assessment, 9 September.

Utton, M. (1971) 'The effects of mergers on concentration. UK manufacturing industry, 1954–1965'. *Journal of Industrial Economics*, vol. 20, no. 1, pp. 42–58.

Utton, M. (1974) 'On measuring the effects of industrial mergers'. *Scottish Journal of Political Economy*, vol. 21, no. 1, pp. 13–27.

Uzawa, H. (1965) 'Optimum technical change in an aggregative model of economic growth'. *International Economic Review*, vol. 6, January, pp. 18–31.

Vernon, J. M. and D. A. Graham (1971) 'Profitability of monopolization by vertical integration'. *Journal of Political Economy*, vol. 79, no. 4, pp. 924–5.

Vernon, R. (1966) 'International investment and international trade in the product cycle'. *Quarterly Journal of Economics*, vol. 80, May, pp. 190–207.

Vernon, R. (1992) 'Transnational corporations: where are they coming from, where are they headed?' *Transnational Corporations*, vol. 1, no. 2, pp. 7–36.

Villalonga, B. (2004) 'Intangible resources, Tobin's q, and sustainability of performance differences'. *Journal of Economic Behavior and Organization*, vol. 54, no. 2, pp. 205–31.

Viner, J. (1950) *The Customs Union Issue*. Stevens, New York.

Vipond, P. A. (1994) 'The financial environment'. In N. Nugent and R. O'Donnell (eds), *The European Business Environment*. Macmillan, London.

Vives, X. (1991) 'Banking competition and European integration'. In A. Giovannini and C. P. Mayer (eds), *European Financial Integration*. Cambridge University Press, Cambridge.

von Fürstenburg, G. M. (1977) 'Corporate investment: does market valuation matter in the aggregate?' *Brookings Papers on Economic Activity*, vol. 2, pp. 347–97.

von Neuman, J. and O. Morgenstern (1944) *Theory of Games and Economic Behavior*. Princeton University Press, Princeton, NJ.

von Stackelberg, H. (1934) *Marktform und Gleichgewicht*. Julius Springer, Vienna.

Von Thunen, J. (1826) *The Isolated State*.

Wade, R. (1988) 'The role of government in overcoming market failure: Taiwan, Republic of Korea and Japan'. In H. Hughes (ed.), *Achieving Industrialization in Asia*. Cambridge University Press, Cambridge.

Wade, R. (1990) *Governing the Market: Economic Theory and the Role of Government in East Asian Industrialization*. Princeton University Press, Princeton, NJ.

Waelbroeck, J. (1962) 'La demande extérieure et l'évolution des exportations belges'. *Cahiers Européens*, Bruxelles, no. 15, July.

Walker, W. (1979) *Industrial Innovation and International Trading Performance*. JAI Press, Greenwich, Conn.

Walker, W. (1991) 'Defence'. In C. Freeman, M. Sharp and W. Walker (eds), *Technology and the Future of Europe*. Pinter, London.

Walker, W. (1993) 'National innovation systems: Britain'. In R. R. Nelson (ed.), *National Innovation Systems: A Comparative Analysis*. Oxford University Press, Oxford.

Walras, L. (1874) *Eléments d'Economie Politique Pure ou Théorie de la Richesse Sociale*. Librairie Générale de Droit et de Jurisprudence, Paris. Reprinted in 1952.

Warf, B. (2003) 'Mergers and acquisitions in the telecommunications industry'. *Growth and Change*, vol. 34, no. 3, pp. 321–44.

Warner, M. (1994) 'Innovation and training'. In M. Dodgson and R. Rothwell (eds), *The Handbook of Industrial Innovation*. Edward Elgar, Aldershot.

Waterson, M. (1982) 'Vertical integration, variable proportions and oligopoly'. *Economic Journal*, vol. 92, March, pp. 129–44.

Waterson, M. (1992) 'International advertising expenditure statistics'. *International Journal of Advertising*, vol. 11, no. 1, pp. 14–68.

Waterson, M. (1993) 'Allocative inefficiency and monopoly as a basis for regulation'. In R. Sugden (ed.), *Industrial Economic Regulation*. Routledge, London.

Weber, A. (1909) *Über den Standort der Industrien*. English translation, *Theory of the Location of Industries*, published in 1929 by University of Chicago Press, Chicago.

Weber, S. (ed.) (2001) *Globalization and the European Political Economy*. Columbia University Press, New York.

Weiss, L. W. (1974) 'The concentration–profits relationship and anti-trust'. In H. Goldschmid *et al.* (eds), *Industrial Concentration: The New Learning*. Little, Brown, Boston.

Welford, R. and K. Prescott (1994) *European Business: An Issue-based Approach*. Pitman, London.

Wengel, J. and P. Shapira (2004) 'Machine tools: the remaking of a traditional sectoral innovation system'. In F. Malerba (ed.), *Sectoral Systems of Innovation: Concepts, Issues and Analyses of Six Major Sectors in Europe*. Cambridge University Press, Cambridge.

Werlauff, E. (1992) 'The development of Community company law'. *European Law Review*, vol. 17, no. 3, pp. 207–31.

Weston, J. F. (1973) 'The nature and significance of conglomerate firms'. *St John's Law Review*, vol. 44. Reprinted in B. Yamey (1973), *Economics of Industrial Structure*. Penguin, Harmondsworth.

Whalley, J. (1985) *Trade Liberalization among Major World Trading Areas*. MIT Press, Cambridge, Mass.

Whitaker, J. K. (2002) 'Marshall, Alfred (1842–1924)'. In W. Lazonick (ed.), *The IEBM Handbook of Economics*. Thomson, London.

Whittam, G. and M. Danson (2001) 'Power and the spirit of clustering'. *European Planning Studies*, vol. 9, no. 8, pp. 949–64.

Williams, R. (1989) 'The EC's technological policy as an engine for integration'. *Government and Opposition*, vol. 24, no. 2, pp. 158–76.

Williamson, J. (1996) 'Globalization and inequality then and now: the late 19th and late 20th centuries compared'. NBER Working Paper no. 5491.

Williamson, O. E. (1967) 'Hierarchical control and optimum firm size'. *Journal of Political Economy*, vol. 75, pp. 123–38. Reprinted in B. Yamey (1973) *Economics of Industrial Structure*. Penguin, Harmondsworth.

Williamson, O. E. (1977) 'Predatory pricing: a strategic and welfare analysis. *Yale Law Journal*, vol. 87, no. 2, December, pp. 284–340.

Williamson, O. E. (1979) 'Transaction-cost economics: the governance of contractual relations'. *Journal of Law and Economics*, vol. 22, October, pp. 233–61.

Williamson, O. E. (1985) *The Economic Institutions of Capitalism*. Free Press, New York.

Williamson, O. E. (1992) 'Some issues in the transformation of ownership institutions in Poland: comment'. *Journal of Institutional and Theoretical Economics*, vol. 148, no. 1, pp. 69–71.

Wilson, F. (1992) 'Modern workshop industry in Mexico: on its way to collective efficiency?' IDS *Bulletin*, vol. 23 no. 3. pp. 57–63.

Wood, J. C. (2002) 'Schumpeter, Joseph (1883–1950)'. In W. Lazonick (ed.), *The IEBM Handbook of Economics*. Thomson International, London.

Woods, S. (1987) *Western Europe: Technology and the Future*. Paper no. 63. The Atlantic Institute for International Affairs/Croom Helm, London.

Woolcock, S. (1982) 'The international politics of trade and production in the steel industry'. In J. Pinder (ed.), *National Industrial Strategies and the World Economy*. Croom Helm, London.

Woolcock, S. (1984) 'Information technology: the challenge to Europe'. *Journal of Common Market Studies*, vol. 22, no. 4.

Woolcock, S. and H. Wallace (1995) 'European Community regulation and national enterprise'. In J. Hayward (ed.), *Industrial Enterprise and European Integration*. Oxford University Press, Oxford.

World Competitiveness Report (1993) IMD International, Lausanne.

Wren, C. (2001) 'The Industrial Policy of Competitiveness: A Review of Recent Developments in the UK'. *Regional Studies*, vol. 35, no. 9, pp. 847–60.

Yamin, M. (2000) 'A critical re-evaluation of Hymer's contribution to "The Theory of International Operations"'. In C. Pitelis and R. Sugden (eds.) *The Nature of the Transnational Firm*. Routledge, New York.

Yannopoulos, G. N. (1992) 'Multinational corporations and the Single European Market'. In J. Cantwell (ed.), *Multinational Investment in Modern Europe*. Edward Elgar, Aldershot.

Young, S. and S. Dunlop (1992) 'Competitive dynamics in the world machine tool industry: battleground UK'. In S. Young and J. Hamill (eds), *Europe and the Multinationals*. Edward Elgar, Aldershot.

Young, S. and J. Hamill (eds) (1992) *Europe and the Multinationals: Issues and Responses for the 1990s*. Edward Elgar, Aldershot.

Young, S. and N. Hood (1992) 'Transnational corporations and policy dilemmas: the problems of the machine-tool industry in the United Kingdom'. *Transnational Corporations*, vol. 1, no. 3.

Zaphirious, G. A. (1970) *European Business Law*. Sweet & Maxwell, London.

Zhao, H. (2000) 'Raising awareness and signaling quality to uninformed consumers: a price–advertising model'. *Marketing Science*, vol. 19, no. 4, pp. 390–96.

Zineldin, M. (2002) 'Managing in the @ age: banking service quality and strategic positioning'. *Measuring Business Excellence*, vol. 6, no. 4, pp. 38–44.

Zollo, M. and G. Winter (2001) 'Deliberate learning and the evolution of dynamic capabilities.' Paper presented at the DRUID Nelson and Winter Conference, Aalborg, 12–15 June 2001. Available at http://www.druid.dk/conferences

Zysman, J. (1990) 'Trade, technology and national competition'. Paper presented at the OECD Conference, Paris, June.

Index